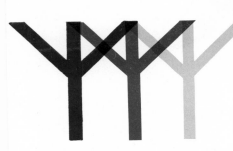

THE WISLEY

BOOK OF
GARDENING

THE WISLEY BOOK OF GARDENING

A Guide for Enthusiasts

Foreword by Lord Aberconway

Editor: Robert Pearson

Consultant Editor: Elspeth Napier, B.Sc. (Hort.); Editor,
The Royal Horticultural Society's Publications.

With contributions by C. D. Brickell, B.Sc. (Hort.),
V.M.H., Director of Wisley Garden, key members of
his staff and other distinguished horticulturists

Line drawings by Charles Stitt

W·W·NORTON & COMPANY
New York   London

Editor's Note

There are so many people, in addition to the distinguished team of authors, whom I must thank for their invaluable help in bringing this major book to fruition. First, The Royal Horticultural Society for making it possible, and the Society's President, Lord Aberconway, for writing the Foreword. Then Mr. C.D. Brickell, Director of Wisley Garden, and Miss Elspeth Napier, Editor of R.H.S. Publications, who have given me so much support during the book's gestation period.

Of the contributors, I find it difficult to express my thanks in adequate words, for it has been such a pleasure to work with them – experts in so many horticultural disciplines. Likewise, my thanks to Charles Stitt for contributing the exquisite line drawings and Margaret Saunders for designing the book overall. My thanks, too, to Mrs. D. Frame for compiling the index and the photographers who have allowed their colour pictures to be used. The latter are acknowledged on p.352.

Contents

ENTHUSIASTS' PLANTS

THE KITCHEN GARDEN

PROTECTED CULTIVATION

PRACTICALITIES

Colour Illustrations

Foreword

The Lord Aberconway, V.M.H.
President of the
Royal Horticultural Society

Robert Pearson is a gardening man for all seasons, for all genera of plants, fruit and vegetables, and for all writers on gardening subjects. When he suggested that he would like to organise such a book as we knew would reflect his wide knowledge of plants, of propagation and of cultivation, and asked whether the Royal Horticultural Society would be prepared to sponsor and help the work, and to encourage contributions from specialist authors, mostly closely associated with the Society, we, at the R.H.S. had little need to hesitate. Who could bring to bear a wider-ranging expertise than Robert Pearson? Who indeed could himself write with greater clarity and a more pleasing style, and so ensure a high standard of writing by contributors? So we gladly offered him our support, and our readiness to vouch for the excellence of the proposed work.

And excellent indeed the outcome is. Those wise enough to possess the book will derive from it equal pleasure, whether they are window box plant lovers, or whether they are practical do-it-yourself gardeners. It is however aimed at the true enthusiast, to lead him to even better gardening.

Better gardening is the theme of many contributors to this book who take into account the up-to-date results of research, and expound many modern, promising, ideas.

But even so is there indeed, with the recent flow of excellent gardening books, room for yet another? We thought there was, given the range and the depth of the practical approach which we knew this book would show.

Robert Pearson would be the first, with his typical generosity, to acknowledge the help given in this project by many, writers or otherwise, at the R.H.S. or closely connected with the R.H.S. But basically it is his, as the Editor: his in conception, in planning, in scope. He and his contributors have been helped by his talented floral draughtsman, Charles Stitt, the clarity and simplicity of whose work tends to belie its underlying skill and accuracy: his illustrations vividly supplement and embellish the text.

The Society is proud to sponsor *The Wisley Book of Gardening*. It needs for its success no good wishes from me. Robert Pearson, its father-figure, deserves our congratulations and thanks, as do all those who have written for it on their specialised subjects.

1.

Nomenclature and the Gardener

"What's in a name? That which we call a rose
By any other name would smell as sweet."
Romeo and Juliet (Act II,ii, 43–4)

Shakespeare's approach to plant naming in *Romeo and Juliet* is one that may well appeal to a gardener who is annoyed and perhaps bewildered by Latin plant names, the complications of distinguishing nomenclaturally between wild and cultivated plants and above all by botanists who, apparently at random, change the names of familiar plants. This reaction is very natural as the main interest of most gardeners is in growing plants and not in ensuring they are correctly named.

COMMON NAMES "Why can't we just use common names" is a plea often heard. The answer is that you can, but for many garden plants there are no common names and although certain common names may be well-known in one country they will be incomprehensible elsewhere. Even in Britain common names are not necessarily generally accepted and are often imprecisely applied. The common name bachelors buttons, for example, has been used for double-flowered forms of *Ranunculus acris*, the buttercup, *Bellis perennis*, the daisy, and *Centaurea cyanus*, the cornflower, and no doubt for several other plants. Similarly, many plants have a number of common names applied to them in different countries or regions of a country.

Most of us would recognise the genus *Sempervivum* by the common name houseleek but it is also known in Britain as St. Patrick's cabbage and "Welcome-home-husband-however-drunk-you-be", names of fascinating derivation but scarcely likely to be universally accepted or understood and not even applied constantly to any one species of *Sempervivum*.

INTERNATIONAL CODES OF NOMENCLATURE World-wide usage of plants for scientific, commercial and other purposes demands that a precise, international system of naming should be available. It is essential that the name used for a particular plant should be readily understood by people of any nationality. Latin, or more accurately botanical Latin, which is in effect a biological language that diverges considerably from classical Latin and is heavily spiced with words of Greek derivation, has been developed during the last 250 years as the internationally recognised language for naming plants of wild origin and is understood and used by botanists throughout the world. Codes of Nomenclature have been devised in various forms for over 100 years but only recently have they been generally accepted. Gradually order and stability is being established in dealing with plant names but it must be remembered that, with an estimated $\frac{1}{4}$ million or more species of flowering plants in the world and an uncounted multitude of mainly undocumented hybrids and man-made selections, the task of rationalising their naming is neither simple nor easy.

Inevitably there are areas of disagreement but happily botanists are now committed to apply the rules laid down in the *International Code of Botanical Nomenclature* (1978) and there is widespread acceptance by horticulturists of the rules and recommendations provided by the *International Code of Nomenclature for Cultivated Plants* (1980) which, in effect, is a supplement to the

Botanical Code dealing with cultivated plants. The aim of both documents is to promote uniformity, accuracy and precision in the naming of plants so that a high degree of stability is eventually achieved. Understandably, when one considers that man has been applying names to plants from before the time of Theophrastus, over 2,000 years ago, these aims have not yet been realised but, during the last 50 years, enormous strides have been made in rationalising plant naming and providing procedures for us to use in the future.

A formidable array of national and international organisations is involved in the formation of these Codes and the servicing processes that result from their application, so it is pleasantly surprising to find that bureaucracy is kept to a minimum. The chart below* shows, in abridged form, the connections between them and, as gardeners, we are mainly concerned with those organisations marked in bold on the chart.

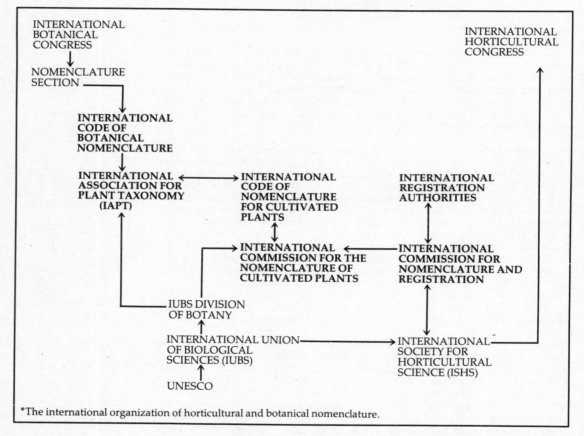

*The international organization of horticultural and botanical nomenclature.

The International Association for Plant Taxonomy (IAPT), an organisation of representatives of plant science institutions and scientists, is responsible for the production of the Botanical Code and this governs the formation and application of botanical names in Latin form for both wild and cultivated plants (excluding graft-chimaeras).

It is also responsible for publishing the International Code of Nomenclature for Cultivated Plants, for convenience called the Cultivated Code, although strictly speaking a code cannot be cultivated! It is formulated and adopted by the International Commission for the Nomenclature of Cultivated Plants (ICNCP) which, with the IAPT, comes under the aegis of the International Union of Biological Sciences (IUBS). This code originated from suggestions submitted to and agreed by both the International Horticultural Congress and the International Botanical Congress in 1952 and controls the naming of horticultural, agricultural and silvicultural cultivars, in horticultural terms what we know as "garden varieties". The Cultivated Code was first published by the Royal Horticultural Society in 1953 and has since been amended and up-dated at intervals. In the 1958 Code, published under the auspices of IAPT, it was decided that, to be legitimate, cultivar names given on or after January 1, 1959 must be validly published according to certain Articles of the Code. Cultivar names published prior to that date are also subject to certain Articles of the Code in order to be legitimate. These organisations, IAPT and ICNCP, are not involved directly with implementing the Cultivated Code so the International Society for Horticultural Science (ISHA), an offshoot of IUBS, which is responsible for a number of International Commissions covering various aspects of horticulture, formed in ISHS Commission for Nomenclature and Registration to organise and encourage the implementation of the rules.

INTERNATIONAL REGISTRATION AUTHORITIES The stabilisation of names for cultivated plants is by no means an easy task on a world scale as since man has cultivated and used plants he has applied names to them but the documentation and identification of most cultivated plants has been hazy and inexact. Through the Nomenclature and Registration Commission the ISHS has appointed International Registration Authorities for particular genera or groups of plants. Their purpose is to maintain registers of cultivar names, register new and acceptable cultivar names and thus to stabilise the naming of cultivars within the genus or group for which they have undertaken responsibility.

At present over 60 genera or groups are covered by International Registration procedures; as examples, the Royal Horticultural Society is responsible for eight of these genera or groups, including rhododendrons, orchids, lilies and daffodils, while the Arnold Arboretum has accepted responsibility for 12, mainly woody, genera.

The major purpose of international registration of cultivar names is to obtain stability so that duplication of names within the genus or group concerned is avoided and confusion between names and plants is prevented or minimised; in the words of the Cultivated Code "to promote uniformity, accuracy and fixity in the naming of cultivars".

It is important to realise that the rules of the Code are formulated to apply to a very wide spectrum of horticultural, agricultural and silvicultural plants. The misapplication or misuse of cultivar names may have repercussions in horticultural research, farming, forestry and medicine as well as in our gardens. Specialists in particular genera sometimes find it difficult to understand why some of the rules have been made since they do not seem to apply directly to the particular genus in which they are interested. It must be realised that there is no desire to apply these rules arbitrarily or to apply them through any wish to restrict the enthusiast's pleasure in his or her plants. The rules have been formulated after very careful thought by horticulturists and botanists of wide experience and periodically are reviewed and amended. Most of the rules included in the Code are based on knowledge of past confusion and are designed to minimise this in the future.

It is equally important, therefore, for anyone raising and wishing to name a new plant to make certain first that the proposed name has not been used previously; secondly that it is in accordance with the rules; and thirdly to ensure that it is properly registered with the appropriate authority. No registration authority exists for some genera, in which case the person naming the plant should check as far as possible that the name proposed has not previously been used in the genus and should then publish a short description of the plant, preferably with an illustration, giving details of its origin and distinctive characters. Establishing a reference point in an International Register or in a widely distributed publication helps greatly to avoid the possibility of the name being used for another plant of the same genus and provides characters by which it may be distinguished should confusion over the correct application of the name occur in the future.

This process may appear troublesome and unnecessary to many people

but the principle behind accurate naming of garden plants is the same as for
any other product – ease of recognition – so that you obtain the article which
bears the name under which it is offered. If you go into a supermarket and
buy a tin labelled baked beans which, when it is opened, produces carrots
you will be justifiably annoyed.

However, if you were to go to a nursery and purchase *Rhododendron* 'Polar
Bear' you might be offered either a low-growing evergreen azalea which will
grow 3ft(1m) in height or a large-leaved rhododendron that will eventually
reach 20 to 30ft(6 to 9m). Both have white flowers and both are botanically
rhododendrons but unfortunately the cultivar name 'Polar Bear' has been
used for two quite distinct plants within the same genus, once correctly and
once invalidly. This dual usage of cultivar names is not permitted under the
rules of the Cultivated Code because of the obvious confusion that can and
does result but unfortunately the rules are not enforcible legally. Had the
raiser of the second plant now called 'Polar Bear' used the registration
procedure this duplication and consequent confusion could have been
avoided.

It is to the advantage of all involved with gardening, therefore, whether
amateurs, nurserymen, scientists or journalists, to support the aims of
International Registration and to try to maintain the rules of the Cultivated
Code so that name duplication, in particular, is avoided.

THE BOTANICAL AND CULTIVATED CODES   It is not my purpose here to
attempt to describe in any detail the various provisions of the two Codes or
their applications, but some guidance on aspects of classification and
nomenclature as applicable to the plants we grow in gardens may be
helpful.

Any attempt to place the plant kingdom into neat (if sometimes imprecisely defined) boxes or units of classification involves using a number of
terms which may be unfamiliar to, or hazily understood by, gardeners. The
units of the classification system may be referred to botanically as "taxa"
(singular, taxon), that is taxonomic groupings or categories such as genus,
species or cultivar.

All gardeners recognise fairly readily what is meant by a "genus", like
Rosa or *Calluna*, and perhaps, with slightly less certainty, a "species", such
as *Rosa canina*, the dog rose, or *Calluna vulgaris*, the heather or ling. Below
these ranks, however, there is often a blurring of the distinctions between
categories. The following table shows in simplified form, omitting any
reference to hybrids, the botanical and horticultural categories used in
naming plants below the rank of genus:

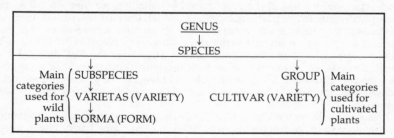

In this table only the categories Group and Cultivar are governed by the
Cultivated Code, the remaining categories being subject to the rules of the
Botanical Code whether cultivated or in the wild. The main category of
importance to gardeners (apart from genus and species) is the cultivar.

Variety   We all think we know what is meant when we use the word
"variety" in a horticultural or botanical context, but unfortunately the term
is used in three different ways.

Inevitably confusion has arisen as use of the word "variety" on its own
does not indicate the exact meaning. If we say "This is an excellent variety
of delphinium" what we are talking about is a "garden variety" whereas if

we say "This is a very variable species and there are several distinct varieties" it is usually a reference to botanical varieties that occur naturally in the wild. The third usage is when "variety" is loosely applied to any "different kind" of plant, even to a genus or species. This latter usage should be firmly discouraged and technically the word "variety" would best be applied only to the botanical variety or *varietas* of which it is the English equivalent.

Varietas – wild or botanical varieties   Any plant species may show degrees of variation as more than morphological variation is involved in different areas of its natural range. Sometimes these variations are considered sufficient to be recognised taxonomically within the species and the variety or *varietas* is one of the ranks below that of species which has been used to cover such geographical and morphological variants.

As an example, the common mountain ash, *Sorbus aucuparia*, which is widespread in temperate Europe and Asia, has in southern, central and southeast Europe, in limestone areas, more persistently hairy undersides to the leaflets and inflorescences than in the typical state. This variant has been recognised as *S. aucuparia* var. *lanuginosa*, differing slightly from most elements of the species but not sufficiently to be considered a species in its own right. A botanical variety is essentially different from a garden variety or cultivar in its origin and as with any botanical taxon the nomenclature is subject to the rules of the Botanical Code.

Variants with more marked differences may be given the higher rank of *subspecies* (abbreviated to ssp.) while minor variants such as albinos may be given the rank of *forma* (abbreviated to f.). Thus *Galanthus nivalis* ssp. *reginae-olgae*, an autumn-flowering variant of the common early spring-flowering snowdrop, is given the rank of subspecies because of its distinct geographical distribution and time of flowering. *Calluna vulgaris* f. *alba*, however, is used for white-flowered individuals in populations which occur quite frequently as minor variants throughout its range.

Cultivar   As gardeners we are mainly concerned with "garden varieties", plants selected or hybridised and maintained in cultivation by man. The naming of these "garden varieties" by both botanists and horticulturists was a haphazard affair for a very long period, some being given names in Latin form as were wild plants while others were given "fancy names" in the language of the country concerned. The confusion between "garden varieties", now called *cultivars*, and true "botanical varieties", *varietas*, was, and still is, enormous and the lack of any distinction between them has caused many nomenclatural problems. Since the Botanical Congress of 1867 ideas have been put forward for distinguishing between the two categories, but not until 1953 did they come to fruition when the first edition of the *International Code of Nomenclature for Cultivated Plants* was published and the category of *cultivar* for "garden varieties" was formally established.

The term *cultivar* is derived from the words "cultivated variety" and may be defined as a group of cultivated plants clearly distinguished by particular characters and which, when reproduced vegetatively (asexually) or from seed (normally sexually), retains its distinctive characters. Rose 'Peace', apple 'Cox's Orange Pippin' and *Chamaecyparis lawsoniana* 'Green Hedger' are all cultivars that are vegetatively propagated; *Nicotiana* 'Lime Green', *Salvia splendens* 'Red Hussar' and onion 'Ailsa Craig' are examples of seed-raised cultivars which, by consistent selection, retain their original distinctive characteristics.

Individual plants selected from wild populations, brought into cultivation, propagated and named may also be designated as cultivars. As an example 'Gurkha' is a named cultivar of *Daphne bholua*, selected from seedlings brought into cultivation from Nepal in 1962.

There are several different types of cultivar but only two of these are of importance to most gardeners. The first of these is the *clone* which is usually defined as a group of individuals that are genetically uniform and are produced from a single ancestor by vegetative propagation, that is by cuttings, division or grafting. All the plants of rose 'Queen Elizabeth' have been derived by vegetative propagation from the original, selected seedling given this name. All those individuals together constitute the clone, rose 'Queen Elizabeth'.

Occasionally "sports" or mutations occur in a named clone which through genetic change produces a plant or part of a plant differing in some character, such as flower colour, from the original clone. As an example, the pink-flowered rose 'Queen Elizabeth' produced a growth bearing red blooms and this sporting branch was propagated to produce the new clone 'Red Queen Elizabeth'.

The second type of cultivar of concern to the gardener is that normally raised from seed like most vegetables and annuals. If left to their own devices, plants raised from seed will themselves produce seed and further plants in due course but the new generation is likely to vary greatly in characters such as flower colour, height and vigour due to the natural variation of the species concerned. Over the years seedsmen, by constantly selecting for particular characteristics, have produced what are known as "breeding lines" of vegetables and annuals that give a high degree of consistency in their offspring so that they breed true or nearly so. By repeated selection and controlled crosses the populations of these plants become sufficiently uniform to be acceptable as cultivars. Examples include tomato 'Moneymaker', lettuce 'Webb's Wonderful' and petunia 'White Cascade'.

The Cultivated Code gives clear regulations on the way cultivar names should be written and what names are admissible. The most important is that cultivar names should not be in Latin form but should be in a modern language using the so-called Roman alphabet which immediately distinguishes them from wild varieties which *must* be written in Latin form. As from January 1, 1959 the use of Latin for cultivar names was prohibited under the rules of the Cultivated Code but the accumulation of hundreds of existing Latinised cultivar names such as 'Aurea', 'Nana', 'Prostrata' and 'Variegatus' remains. This has been dealt with by the typographical devices of using Roman type, an initial capital letter and *either* preceding the cultivar name by the abbreviation cv. *or* enclosing it in single quotes. This immediately distinguishes a cultivar name in print from the name of a botanical *varietas* which is printed in italics, is written with a small initial letter and is not enclosed in quotation marks. The following examples illustrate certain aspects of the correct and incorrect formation of cultivar names. They cover only a limited number of the recommendations and rules governing the formation of cultivar names and for fuller information it is important to consult the latest edition of the International Code of Nomenclature for Cultivated Plants.

1.   A cultivar name published on or after January 1, 1959 must be a "fancy name", that is, not a botanical name in Latin form.
Examples: *Chamaecyparis lawsoniana* 'Silver Queen' but *not* 'Argentea Regina'; *Aconitum* 'George Arends' *not* 'Arendsii'.
A cultivar name published in Latin form prior to January 1, 1959 should, however, be retained and not replaced by a fancy name.
Examples: *Chamaecyparis lawsoniana* 'Erecta Viridis' *not* 'Upright Green'; *Chamaecyparis obtusa* 'Pygmaea' *not* 'Pigmy'.
2.   Cultivar names published on or after January 1, 1959 should not include the words variety (or var.), form, cross, crosses, hybrid or hybrids.
Examples: *Polygonum affine* 'Donald Lowndes' *not* 'Lowndes Variety' or 'Lowndes Var.'; *Iris chrysographes* 'Inshriach' but *not* 'Inshriach Form'; *Lilium* 'George Soper' but *not* 'Soper's Hybrid'.
Cultivar names including these words that were published prior to January 1, 1959 should, however, be retained.
Examples: *Campanula lactiflora* 'Prichards Variety' should not be altered to 'Prichard'; or *Anthemis tinctoria* 'Perrys Variety' to 'Perry'; or *Linum* 'Gemmell's Hybrid' to 'Gemmell'.
3.   Cultivar names which were published on or after January 1, 1959 should preferably consist of one or two words and must not consist of more than three words.

HYBRIDS Horticulturally the term hybrid is generally used for crosses between different genera or different species of the same genus. A rather wider definition as "the offspring of the sexual union of plants belonging to different taxa" is sometimes given, in which case the progeny of two (or more) subspecies or *varietas* of the same species could be considered to be hybrids.

Under the Codes, hybrids produced by sexual crossing may be indicated by using the multiplication sign (×). All hybrids derived from crossing *Camellia japonica* and *C. saluenensis*, for instance, may be designated by the collective name in Latin form, *Camellia × williamsii*. Such latinised names must be correctly published under the rules of the Botanical Code to be valid. This will cover all the progeny raised from any cross between these two species. If a particular cultivar of this hybrid is selected and named then it may be cited as *Camellia × williamsii* 'Donation' or simply as *Camellia* 'Donation'. It is incorrect to use the multiplication sign directly in front of a cultivar name to indicate its hybrid origin and, although names like *Campanula* × Norman Grove or *Saxifraga* × Peter Pan are frequently to be seen written in this way in books and catalogues, they are clearly cultivar names and not hybrid groups and should be cited as *Campanula* 'Norman Grove' and *Saxifraga* 'Peter Pan'. The multiplication sign should be restricted for use with collective names of hybrids.

Similarly, an intergeneric cross may be designated by a collective name in Latin form such as × *Cupressocyparis* which covers all the progeny derived from crossing any *Cupressus* with any *Chamaecyparis*. With intergeneric crosses the multiplication sign is placed in front of the "generic" collective name.

All the derivatives from a particular combination of species in an intergeneric cross, however, have the same collective epithet. So all the offspring of *Cupressus macrocarpa* × *Chamaecyparis nootkatensis* are given the collective name × *Cupressocyparis leylandii* while those from *Cupressus glabra* × *Chamaecyparis nootkatensis* are grouped as × *Cupressocyparis notabilis*.

NAME CHANGES Gardeners are frequently annoyed to find that "some botanist" has changed the name of a well-known garden plant. Such changes are also a source of frustration to many scientists in related disciplines (including numerous botanists not involved with taxonomy) although they are not, as some may suspect, merely malicious devices of "the botanists" to keep gardeners on their toes! There are, in fact, good reasons in most cases for these changes.

There are three distinct causes of name changes: misidentifications; nomenclatural errors; and taxonomic revisions.

Sometimes a plant may be introduced into our gardens and become well-known under a name which is later found to be incorrect due to misidentification. As an example, the small South African shrub *Euryops acraeus* brought into cultivation in 1946 was initially identified as *E. evansii*, a related but distinct species. It was later realised that the plant in cultivation was not *E. evansii* so the error was corrected, necessitating the change of a name that had become, through an error in identification, well-established in nursery catalogues and gardens.

Less easy to understand are name changes for nomenclatural reasons when a name is not in accordance with the rules of the Botanical Code. Usually they are based on the principle of priority in this Code which states that the earliest validly published name given in 1753 (the date of Linnaeus's *Species Plantarum*) or after for a particular taxon is the correct one to use. This means that an earlier validly published name that has been overlooked must take precedence over the name currently in use. Other causes of nomenclatural changes are due to the misapplication of names by botanists and the use of names in the past that, under the present Code, are contrary to certain of the rules.

Perhaps the best known example of a nomenclatural change is that of *Viburnum fragrans*, given this name in 1833. In 1966 it was pointed out that this same name had been published in 1824 for a different species of

Viburnum. Under the priority law the 1833 use of the name had to be rejected and the "new name", *V. farreri*, provided for the plant known to thousands as *V. fragrans*.

Similar problems in connection with generic names are covered by a provision in the Code for the conservation of well-known later names and the rejection of strictly correct but unfamiliar earlier published names after a well-argued case has been put and accepted. Logically it would seem reasonable to create a similar system for specific epithets but in spite of attempts at Botanical Congresses to introduce such a scheme the proposals have always been rejected.

The third cause of name changes is a re-assessment of the taxonomic status of a plant. Usually this occurs during the taxonomic revision of a genus in the light of research and additional knowledge on the relationships of the plant concerned.

Similar research and re-assessments occur all the time in horticultural practice and gardeners will argue vehemently, for example, about the correct compost or cultural conditions to use for a particular plant. As new knowledge and techniques come along gardeners quickly bring them into use so it is, perhaps, not unreasonable to allow botanists the same latitude in taxonomic matters.

In a short chapter it is not possible to cover fully the many aspects of plant nomenclature as it affects gardeners but it is important that, in order to stabilise the names of plants in our gardens, we should attempt to apply the Codes of Nomenclature properly. In particular, we should take care to name our cultivars correctly – and, if possible, sparingly – in view of the apparently uncontrolled rash of cultivar names that appear in increasing numbers, often undocumented and imprecisely applied, in garden literature each year.

Part I

PLANNING AND PLANTING

2.

Elements of Garden Design

It is probably correct to say that many successful garden lay-outs started to take shape on a drawing board. At the beginning – although it will be known what sort of garden is envisaged and some of the features to be included – it is not necessary to formulate any definite ideas on design but better to concentrate first on measuring and recording all the existing features so that an accurate bird's-eye view of the garden can be drawn to scale. There is no other way of seeing the area as a whole and the position of the house satisfactorily. It is from this stage that ideas for the design of the garden and planting plans can be formulated.

THE EARLY PLANNING STAGE It is unusual for a plot of land to be exactly rectangular and the sides are often unequal in length. The essential aids at this early stage are a measuring tape, at least 60ft(18m) in length; a metal spike to secure the end, and a large writing pad. Even without the aid of a surveyor's more elaborate apparatus, a fairly accurate survey can be made to determine the direction of the boundaries and the position of the house relative to these, by taking the measurement from a corner of the house or building in line with the wall to the boundary (Fig.1). If the same process is repeated on the same side from another corner it will show if the boundary is at an angle or parallel to the building. A further check can be made by

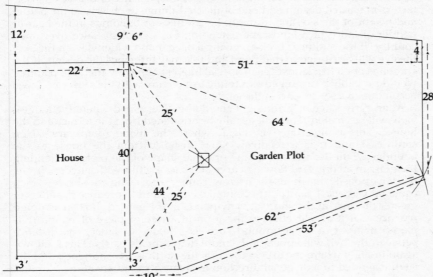

1. *The direction of the boundaries and the position of the house relative to these can easily be determined by taking the sides of the latter as datum lines.*

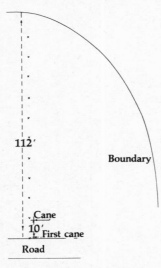

112'

Boundary

Cane
10'
First cane

Road

2. *Marking out a sight line with canes.*

3. *Marking out a proposed plan on the ground (see text, right)*

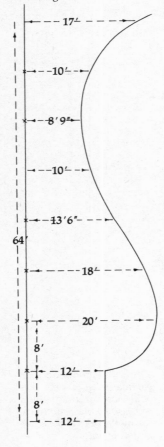

17ᴸ

10ᴸ

8'9"

10ᴸ

13'6"

64'

18ᴸ

20'

8'

12ᴸ

8'

12ᴸ

fixing the tape in one of the far corners of the site and proceeding along the bottom boundary until the wall of the building – which would be seen at right angles – disappears from view. If this measurement is compared with the others made earlier the points on the boundary should touch at the three places.

If it is necessary to mark a sight line across a piece of land from one point to another, it is useful to have available 10 or more 6ft(2m) bamboo canes (see Fig.2). The canes are then spaced, perhaps 8 or 10ft(2.5 or 3m) or more apart, over a given distance, and when five or six canes are in position the line is made exactly straight by adjusting the intermediate canes between the two end ones. When a sighting is made from the furthest end, only the nearest cane will then be visible. The position of a tree or other permanent features can be recorded by measuring from the object in question to two points which are separated by a known distance; this could be two corners of the house. The measurements are then transcribed to paper with the use of a compass and the place marked where the arcs cross.

Having noted as many details as possible that are likely to be useful, a plan of the area can be drawn to scale. It can usually be assumed that if the design appears to be right on paper it will probably be right on the site. The need to see the garden first in plan form applies particularly if the beds and contours follow a curved outline. To ensure that the shapes are the same on the ground the method of marking out consists of dividing a boundary line or similar datum into measured divisions 6 to 10ft(2 to 3m) apart and from these points measure at right angles to the outline of the proposed bed or path and mark the shape with pegs and string (see Fig.3).

To digress briefly, it is appropriate to mention here, in the context of design, that when a new lawn is sown on a light soil a considerable time elapses before the roots of the grass have consolidated sufficiently for an edge to be cut without the soil crumbling away. This can be avoided by laying a single line of good-quality turf to follow the shape of the beds. It will then be possible to cut a firm edge and will at the same time give an immediate outline to the lawn.

A small, empty plot less than 50ft(15m) long by 20ft(6m) wide and fenced in on three sides may not seem to offer the best prospects for garden making, but size has little to do with what can be achieved. Indeed, it is sometimes easier to make a garden on a piece of land which might be described as "featureless", for then the designer has full scope to impose his or her personality on the layout and a completely free hand in the choice of plants which are grown.

LINE, BALANCE AND SCALE Continuity of line, balance and scale are basic factors in garden design and one of the first things to observe is the nature and height of the sky-line. It might be tall trees or buildings in the near or middle distance or a landscape extending for a great distance over open country. If the outline is broken, giving a deeper and wider view of the sky, the eye will be carried to that point and this may influence the design. If the garden is open to a landscape of special interest or beauty then the planting would probably be arranged as a frame to a picture with the view (or views) becoming, in a sense, part of the garden.

At an early stage of planning it should be determined where the longest view will be created. This will usually be orientated from the terrace and the house. This is illustrated in Fig.4, where the living rooms are facing south-east and it is a relatively short distance from the house to the boundary. Full use is made of the unusual shape of the plot by extending the grass in an outward flowing curve and backing this with a hedge. In the border opposite the house a narrow conifer and fastigiate shrub, which could be *Mahonia* 'Charity', are planted well forward to produce the effect of greater distance at the shortest view-points in the garden. It is an accepted practice that if an elevation in the form of a tree or piece of sculpture is placed in front of a background such as a hedge or fence, the distance between the two will appear to be more than actually exists. This is shown again in Fig.5 where the aspect towards the north is foreshortened and the lawn extended in a diagonal direction to create a paved area for tables and

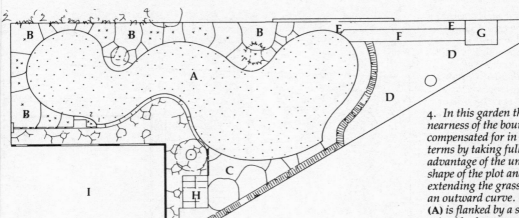

4. In this garden the
nearness of the boundary is
compensated for in visual
terms by taking full
advantage of the unusual
shape of the plot and
extending the grass area in
an outward curve. The lawn
(A) is flanked by a sweep of
mixed herbaceous perennial
plants, shrubs and
ornamental conifers (B) and
by more perennial plants
(C). Soft fruits and
vegetables are
accommodated in the area
marked (D) and cordon fruit
trees against the boundary
(E) and flanking the path (F)
which leads to the garden
shed (G). A greenhouse (H)
is located near the house (I).

chairs in the sunny part of the garden, away from the shaded side of the
house.

It is possible to create a long view in the smallest of gardens, as in Fig.6
overleaf. Again, the grass area is extended towards the corner, and the
sundial gives the illusion of distance and makes a point of focal interest. If
an acceptable garden feature does not readily come to mind – much of the
neo-classical sculpture available is a poor imitation of the original – it would
perhaps be better to have something that is functional (if it is to be modern),
such as a plant urn that would provide an accent of colour or a bird bath. It
might also be thought there is little reason to find space for a replica sundial,
with the exception of one device that has been copied from ancient times.
This takes the form of an equatorial sundial of interesting design. It consists
of three metal rings set at right angles to each other with a shaft passing
through them which casts a shadow on the graduated ring. It is seen to best
advantage mounted on a stone plinth 3 to 5ft(1 to 1.5m) from the ground.

Another important elevation in this garden is a greenhouse of hexagonal
shape. Instead of partially screening it as might be desirable in the case of a

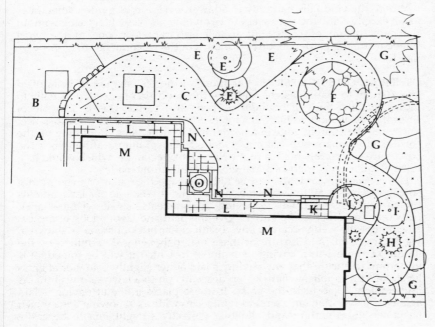

5. A long view is created by
extending the lawn and
siting a paved area (F) in the
sunny part of the garden.
There is an area for
vegetables (A), a play area
(B) with paving stones level
with the grass area (C) in
which is set a sand pit (D).
The planting area (E)
includes Prunus × hillieri
'Spire', Escallonia ×
edinensis and a
wedge-shaped planting of
perennials to the right. To
the right of the paved area
(F) is a mixed planting of
shrubs and perennials (G), a
conifer, Chamaecyparis
lawsoniana 'Columnaris'
(H) set in the lawn as well
as a fruit tree (I). Low
conifers and shrubs (J) link
this feature to a paved area
(K), and steps lead to
another paved area (L)
around the house (M). This
is flanked by a retaining
wall (N) and a raised bed
(O).

6. *A long view is created in this garden by extending the grass area towards the corner and using a sundial (A) as a focal point of interest. Plantings around the lawn (B) include three specimens of* Polygonum bistorta 'Superbum' (C); *a specimen of* Jasminum nudiflorum *against the wall* (D); Pyracantha × watereri (E), *with* Elaeagnus pungens 'Maculata' (F) *to one side and* Hydrangea villosa (G) *to the other. Behind the hydrangea the climbing rose* 'Golden Showers' (H) *clothes the wall. Further round,* Cupressus macrocarpa 'Goldcrest' (I) *is flanked by* Ceanothus impressus (J) *(against the wall) with the cluster-flowered rose* 'Iceberg' (K) *in front of it. On its other side is the hybrid musk rose 'Buff Beauty'* (L), Euonymus fortunei 'Silver Queen' (M) *and* Cistus 'Silver Pink' (N). *Two other wall shrubs are* Cotoneaster lacteus (O) *and* Garrya elliptica (P), *this last providing winter colour, as does* Viburnum tinus (Q). *Planted in the border* (R) *are* Daphne mezereum, *various* Hemerocallis, Agapanthus *Headbourne Hybrids, hardy fuchsias and* Liriope muscari. *A specimen of* Vitis vinifera 'Purpurea' *is situated at the edge of the paved area* (S). *A raised bed* (T) *for low-growing plants, a vegetable plot* (U) *and a hexagonal greenhouse* (V) *complete the garden.*

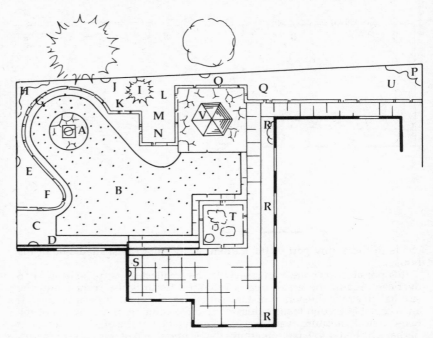

more conventionally shaped house, the hexagonal greenhouse is an attractive architectural feature, balancing the sundial and standing on an area of paving with crevices for flat-growing plants to soften the texture of the stone.

A raised scree bed retained with stone walls 15in(38cm) high seems more appropriate than a rock garden which can look out of place in a small flat area unless it is kept low. It can be a satisfactory alternative that provides a place for rock plants; indeed, some of the smaller alpines are seen to better advantage grown in this way than in the relatively rugged terrain of a rock garden. (See also Chapter 13, "Ways with Alpines", p. 138.)

Where the land falls naturally to a lower level, a rock garden sometimes looks exactly right and may seem to be an obvious way of terracing without the construction of walls, but it will also represent one of the most time-consuming garden features, for most of the weeding has to be done by hand.

OTHER ASPECTS OF DESIGN Variations of the "S" shape can be applied successfully to many designs and give the effect that is needed visually to reduce parallel lines of boundaries, beds and paths. This is a theme of several plans illustrated in this chapter. It is a satisfactory way, for instance, to change the straight edge of a border into a curved line. Rounding off the corners of a square only slightly usually lacks definition, although, if the curves are sufficiently bold, a rounded end to a rectangle, which would be a full half-circle, or corners of a triangle, can be usefully made.

Lawns, like flower beds, can be kidney-shaped, circular or ovoid, but it sometimes makes an uneasy relationship if the curved line of a lawn adjoins the straight edge of a path or paving. It also creates small, wedge-shaped beds that are difficult to plant. To give the path and lawn a look of mutual attachment the wedges can be paved with either brick or stone as shown in Fig.7, the colour and texture of these materials being determined by the nature of the existing paving or material to which it will be joined. It is important to ensure that any paving is laid either slightly below or at grass level, and this applies where a step descends on to a lawn or a wall that is immediately adjacent to the grass. In these places a line of paving is laid against the elevation 6in(15cm) to 12in(30cm) wide as a mowing edge which facilitates grass cutting and allows a perfectly straight line to be easily maintained, by thrusting a sharp half-moon turf cutter between stone and grass. This is even quicker to carry out than cutting a grass edge with shears.

It is not only an advantage to have a flat line of stone where levels are different but also between the lawn and a bed, particularly an herbaceous border where plants near the edge, such as *Oenothera missouriensis*, *Nepeta × faassenii* and *Geranium* cultivars, can sprawl unrestricted. In a mixed border, too, where flat or cushion-like shrubs such as *Cistus*, *Halimium*, *Genista* and *Hebe* can be planted they will be given a different dimension than when restrained to keep within the bounds of the grass edge.

SITING PATHS If a path is needed for getting from one part of the garden to another, along the boundary of the lawn might be a good place for it to be sited; it would be both functional and aesthetic. But unless a path is actually needed there is little reason for its existence, taking up space and reducing the garden area. If it is necessary, however, and the above suggestion is not suitable, another advantageous position for it is at the back of a border so that it is between this feature and a hedge or fence. The reason for this is fourfold. First, it does not divide the garden and so direct the eye to a place where there is perhaps no view-point. Secondly, if a wall or fence forms the boundary this feature can be used to train fruit trees or ornamental shrubs and climbers. A space 18in(45cm) wide is usually enough to leave between the path and the boundary, but even if it is not intended to do any planting against the wall, the edge of the paving should be at least 9in(23cm) away to allow shoulder room, otherwise it is only possible to walk on the outer side of the path. Thirdly, if the boundary is formed by a hedge it is easier to pick up the trimmings from a path. Fourthly, another good reason for so siting a path is that the ground within a yard or two (1 to 2m) from the hedge is probably the least fertile. Roots from the hedge compete with plants or shrubs in the border and there is sometimes a problem of perennial weed roots encroaching from outside the boundary. This invasion can be controlled by digging a narrow trench close to the fence or hedge to a depth of 18in(45cm) to 2ft(60cm) and burying, in a vertical position, with the tops just below soil level, sheets of old roofing material such as are usually available from a builder or demolition firm. All weeds can then be eradicated from the bed and there will be no further spread, unless, for instance, if ground elder or couch grass has entered into clumps of perennial plants, such as paeonia and asters. The most effective way then to ensure that no trace of such roots remain is to dig up the plants in the winter, wash out all the soil and pick out the weed roots before replanting the perennials in a nursery bed for

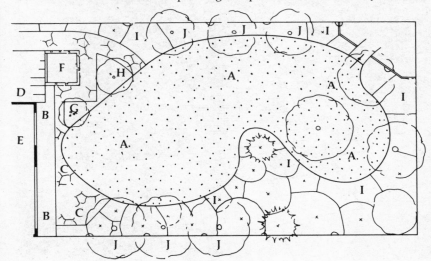

7. *The curved outline of the grass* (**A**) *is integrated with the straight path* (**B**) *by a paved area* (**C**), *which successfully links the two features. A greenhouse* (**D**) *adjoins the house* (**E**) *with a raised herb bed* (**F**) *set in the paved area* (**C**) *where a planting of* Dianthus 'Mrs Sinkins' (**G**) *and another of* Hamamelis mollis *and* Juniperus communis 'Repanda' (**H**) *provide interest. Shrubs and herbaceous perennial plants* (**I**) *as well as selected roses are planted to provide colour around the year. Fruit trees* (**J**) *are both decorative and productive.*

return to the border after it has been cleared the following year. If this is not done, feeding the perennials with fertiliser only further encourages hedge and weed roots.

COVERING HIGH BANKS, CLIFFS AND TERRACING The use of climbing plants as a cover for banks is generally neglected even though in some more difficult situations it is an easy and attractive way of overcoming the weed problem. The plants are not provided with any support so that they make a thick layer of growth which will cover a wide area of the bank. Plants for such purposes that come immediately to mind are *Hedera* (ivy), *Lonicera* (honeysuckle) and various rambler roses, but other vigorous climbing plants can be pressed into service. Specimens of *Lonicera japonica halliana*, a semi-evergreen honeysuckle, planted at 4ft(1.25m) apart towards the top of a bank will spread downwards for 15 to 20ft(4.5 to 6m) and make a thicket of twining shoots producing scented biscuit-coloured flowers from May to October. Another strong-growing *Lonicera*, grown almost entirely for its foliage, is *L. japonica* 'Aureoreticulata', with small, oval, golden-dappled leaves which give colour and contrast without being garish.

A lesson can be taken from nature in the shape of the mounds of brambles which can be seen in the countryside and through which practically no other plants can penetrate. This effect can be simulated in the garden by planting such rambler roses as 'Alberic Barbier', 'Albertine' and 'Sander's White'; these forming thick, rounded hummocks up to 12ft(3.75m) across and 5 to 6ft(1.5 to 2m) high. Cultivars of ivy will thrive under trees in dry or damp shade, the large variegated leaves of *Hedera colchica* 'Dentata Variegata' making lively patterns of colour where other plants will not grow.

It is sometimes desirable to clothe a very steep slope or cliff face but the gradient makes it impossible to plant in the face itself. A variation of this situation posing similar problems could be planting against a high retaining

8. A detail from the garden plan opposite (Fig.9) which shows an alternative to separating two different levels with one high wall or a series of parallel terraces. Three retained sections flank the steps, two of which are planted with shrubs of low stature while the third take the form of a small formal pool.

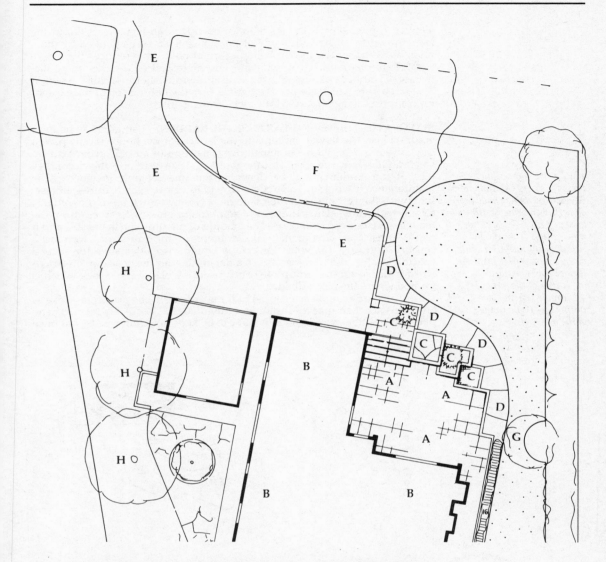

wall. Here, if it is necessary to suppress weeds, thicker-growing climbers are planted at the top to grow downwards, perhaps 12ft(3.75m) or more. To cover or partially hide a high wall or a cliff, such as in an old quarry, some of the *Clematis* species can be used. Any of the cultivars of *Clematis montana* and the exquisitely scented *C. flammula* would be ideal for the purpose.

Parthenocissus quinquefolia is spectacular in the autumn, the leaves, like fingers of orange and scarlet, trailing downwards against brown or lichen-covered stone. *Vitis amurensis* is also a magnificent sight cascading over in a similar way. *Muehlenbeckia complexa* drops like a curtain down cliffs facing the sea of our south and west coasts, its small, bright green leaves set against wiry stems. It is equally effective against a wall of concrete.

To use a contradiction in terms, it could be said that some climbing plants are seen to better advantage growing downwards than upwards – for example, winter-flowering jasmine, *Jasminum nudiflorum*. The basement flat of a terraced town house often faces towards a retaining wall of concrete or brick – an ideal position for this jasmine would be on the level above where, if a suitable planting position were available, it could hang over the edge and delight in winter.

In certain places a variation in the construction of retaining walls can be

9. *A feature of this garden is its differences in level. The paved area (A) near the house (B) is bordered on the other side by the retained sections (C). Behind is a border planted with shrubs and perennials (D) with two small planting pockets being left for annuals. There is a drive (E), a mature horse chestnut (F) and* Catalpa bignonioides *'Aurea' (G). Mature cherry trees (H) have been integrated into the design.*

allowed for, as shown in Figs.8 and 9 on pp. 22 and 23. Access from the slope down from the south side of the house is by steps flanked by three retained sections, the lowest being a formal pool. This reduces the steepness of the bank and avoids having one high wall or a series of parallel terraces. The beds can be planted with numerous choice shrubs – even, if wished, plants which are not compatible with the natural soil of the garden, for compost can be imported into such growing areas.

INTEGRATING DIFFERENT PARTS OF THE GARDEN   A situation sometimes occurs where the flower garden and the lawn near the house is only part of the garden *in toto*, with the remainder consisting of an old orchard copse, small paddock or the like. To integrate such a feature into the decorative part of the garden might be desirable but unacceptable in view of the maintenance it would involve. One way to integrate such features successfully with the rest of the garden is to have closely mown paths 4 to 6ft(1.25 to 2m) wide intersecting the area of semi-rough grass with access from the main lawn (see Figs.10 and 11). The amount of planting can be flexible and it might consist of having naturalized bulbs in the grass and forming a conservation area for wild flowers. It would also offer sites for several specimen trees, the number and size depending on the space involved. To add further interest a group of shrubs could be planted in a fork which is formed where the paths divide.

Shrub groups could each consist of three or five shrubs planted as close as 2ft(60cm) apart so that a substantial individual unit is quickly formed. The planting positions would initially have to be kept free from weeds, but once

10. *In this garden the flower borders (A) and lawn (B) near the house have been cleverly integrated with the area of fruit trees (C) and semi-rough grass (D) by intersecting the latter with closely mown paths (E). A formal pool is situated in the far corner of the garden (G). Two apple (H) and two plum trees (I) lie to the side of the house (J).*

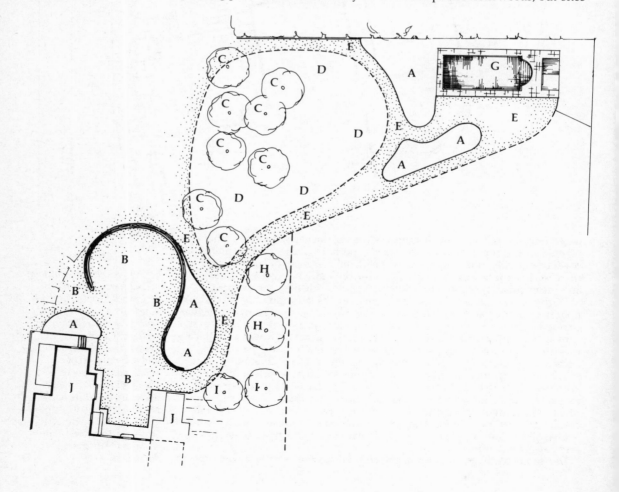

11. *Mown paths through
semi-rough grass can be
extremely pleasing to the
eye. A detail relating to
Fig.10 (opposite).*

the shrubs had established themselves the thickness of the growth would make continuous cultivation unnecessary. The ultimate spread of such shrubs, if, for example, some viburnums, variegated dogwood and cotoneaster were planted, should be considerable; and they could be sited so that their branches will not spread over the paths within a few years. Alternatively, the position of the mown paths can be altered to pass around the established groups.

The concept of linking a naturalized area and the garden proper can be adapted to other conditions. There are new houses in Surrey, Hampshire and elsewhere, with fenced-in plots of Scots pine, birch and heather which had previously been part of indigenous heathland, and it might be better, instead of considering total clearance of the site, to relate the natural flora to the garden with grass walks or trodden paths of peat or, perhaps, sand. On heathland, much of the heather can remain *in situ* with paths being cut through it and with plantings made of specimen trees and shrubs that are at their happiest growing in acid soil. The shrubs would include cultivars of *Erica* and *Calluna*. Similarly, gardens on heavier soils or perhaps the sites of coppiced ash and hazel would provide conditions suitable for quite different plants – primroses, cowslips, hardy ferns and the like. The concept of having intersecting paths in a natural but controlled area would, however, be the same.

Planting trees of different habit close together is not usually recommended for overcrowding is a common fault. On the other hand, not every tree has to be an isolated specimen. It is appropriate to mention the work of that great landscape gardener, Capability Brown, who could visualise the effect of his plantings on landscape many years hence. Plantings of groups of trees of one species, such as lime or beech, three or five trees to a group, are today features in the landscapes of country estates. These result from planting about 18ft(5.5m) apart so that, as the trees increase in size, their heads grow together, to present one uniform outline (Fig.12) supported

12. *A group planting of
trees of the same kind
quickly forms an integrated
canopy which has visual
impact. This kind of feature
is only suitable for large
planting schemes.*

by several stems. Group planting of this kind can be adopted to the very much smaller scale of modestly sized gardens. *Malus, Crataegus* or *Sorbus*, for instance, planted close together (in groups of a single kind, not mixed), will quickly form an integrated canopy, and in a large planting scheme have more impact than a single tree, or several trees planted widely apart.

The kitchen garden is often considered essential and should be fitted into a part of the garden where good crops are likely to be produced. The vegetable and soft fruit section is sometimes placed right across the lower part of the garden, this forming a good work area that can be divided into plots of the desired size. For the serious grower it is the most convenient way of growing vegetables and fruits, but inevitably it foreshortens the garden. Again, it is possible to modify the practice used in gardens a century or more ago when the walled kitchen garden was intersected at right angles by gravel paths edged with box, behind which there were sometimes borders of herbaceous perennial plants. Under present-day conditions, maintenance considerations alone prevent the adoption of such lay-outs, but a modification of the theme is to make a gap 4 to 6ft(1.25 to 2m) wide, giving access to a grass walk flanked on each side by lavender and pillar roses trained against posts 10 to 12ft(3 to 3.75m) apart; or shrub roses, such as hybrid musks, terminating in an architectural feature or small tree. This gives a longer, more attractive view of the garden without the loss of too much space for growing vegetables or fruits. As an alternative to lavender and roses, cordon or espalier fruit trees could be planted about 2ft(60cm) from the edge of the grass. These have the attraction of being both decorative and productive.

As to providing a screen between the kitchen garden and the rest of the garden, a hedge, if planted, needs maintaining, it casts shade and wastes space. Panels of square pattern lattice, painted brown with a wood preservative, provide a useful means of division, and although not a total screen such panels do form an effective visual barrier. They also provide a support for trained fruit or ornamental climbing plants.

COPING WITH DIFFICULT SITUATIONS   It is relatively easy to grow plants in ideal or near-ideal conditions, but the position often arises where a part of the garden or an individual plant bed offers very little encouragement for cultivation. Maybe the garden is very wet in winter and sometimes floods, while in summer the water table drops and the soil is relatively dry. It is obvious that plants which thrive when given good drainage are not likely to be successful where the roots lie in wet ground for several months of the year. There are, however, certain shrubs and plants of other types that will tolerate these physical extremes. They include, among shrubs, *Viburnum opulus, V.o.* 'Sterile', *Cornus alba* 'Elegantissima', *Cornus alba* 'Sibirica' and *Arundinaria* (all cultivars); among trees, *Taxodium distichum, Metasequoia glyptostroboides* and *Salix*, all cultivars, provided the ground is not water-logged at the time of planting; and, among perennial plants, *Astilbe*, most cultivars; *Filipendula*, most cultivars; *Zantedeschia aethiopica*; *Lysimachia punctata*; *Lysimachia nummularia*; *Polygonum amplexicaule*, all cultivars; *Iris sibirica* and its cultivars and *Trollius × cultorum* cultivars.

Another problem site is the disused concrete pond, which, for various reasons, it might not be practical to break up and remove. A disused pool in the garden is not too difficult to cope with for if there is adequate drainage the depression can be filled in with soil and planted or grassed over. Such a pool might, however, be part of a paved formal garden with raised sides and low retaining walls. This could be structurally difficult to demolish. A suggestion of the presence of water can be created by filling the pool site to within a few inches of the top with a good soil mixture and then covering this with several inches of 2 to 3in(5 to 8cm) pebbles. In this, plants can be grown, choosing those with good leaf shapes which are often seen near water; for example, *Hemerocallis, Bergenia, Astilbe, Iris sibirica* and *Hosta*. When they are in position the stones are drawn up close around the crowns of the plants and a few largish water-worn rocks can also be partly buried to give the effect of a pool or stream bed.

Another difficult position is at the back of a bed where the soil receives virtually no rain because the eaves of the building or a projecting bay window overhang the area. To cover the ground, very flat shrubs can be planted just outside the dry area where the soil is moist and the prostrate growth should spread out in all directions. Suitable shrubs for this purpose include *Cotoneaster dammeri* and *Rubus calycinoides*, interplanted with larger subjects such as Dutch lavender (*Lavandula angustifolia* 'Vera') and *Hebe*. These are clothed to the ground and would also spread towards the wall.

In places where an area of paving on a terrace or patio might seem disproportionately large, something more decisive and bolder than rock plants is necessary to soften the texture. This can be achieved by removing a stone at appropriate places and planting a conifer such as *Juniperus communis* 'Repanda', less than 12in(30cm) high and up to 12ft(3.75m) across which, if planted in a group, almost give a lawn-like appearance. Another rug-like conifer is *Juniperus procumbens* 'Nana' up to 9ft(2.75m) across; also the wide-spreading and contour-following *Juniperus communis* 'Horni-brookii' can be pressed into service. There are few shrubs to equal the qualities of the cotoneaster – so very undemanding in its requirements and thriving in sun or shade. Here again, *Cotoneaster dammeri* will trail over the stone and the mat of small, deep green leaves and red berries only 2 to 3in(5 to 8cm) high show up attractively against the colour of the paving. *Polygonum vacciniifolium* is an ideal plant to grow over a flat surface, the long, trailing, reddish-brown leaf sprays tipped with 6in(15cm) spikes of pink flowers in autumn.

It sometimes happens that with certain conifers the spread of the lower branches exceeds the allotted space with the result that a view is hidden or access is obstructed. In some circumstances such conifers can be saved from destruction by removing the lateral branches up to 6 to 8ft (2 to 2.5m) from the ground to leave a clean stem (Fig.13) and give the tree the shape of a standard. If there are two or three main stems the side branches can be cut in the same way making a tree with twin or triple stems. Shrubs that eventually attain small-tree-like proportions can be pruned in a similar way; by removing all the lower growth from several ascending stems which form the plant's main structure (Fig.14). The shrubby magnolias are usually low-branched in the earlier years but eventually attain a height of up to 25ft(7.5m); the bay (*Laurus nobilis*) and *Genista aetnensis* are other examples.

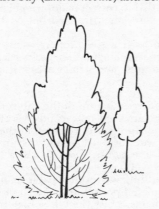

13 *and* 14. *Conifers and tall shrubs which eventually achieve the proportions of small trees can have their lower laterals removed if, for instance, they are obstructing a path. Fig.13 (top left) shows two conifers so treated, Fig.14 (below right) shows a large shrub from which the lower branches could be removed as depicted by the lighter outline.*

3.

Lawn-Making and
After-Care

The lawn is a basic feature of many gardens, whether purely ornamental or as a play area for children. When planning a new lawn the shape and size will be influenced by various factors but the shape should always be simple, with a minimum of sharp angles so that mowing is facilitated. Ideally, the site should be in full sun. Grass in deeper shade is difficult to maintain satisfactorily. In such situations it may be better to plant shade-tolerant shrubs or ground cover plants.

LAWN MAKING

Begin site preparation at least two to three months before sowing or turfing is to take place, allowing extra time if the site has to be drained or graded.

Clear away any rubble or debris and remove stumps or broken roots. If the site is heavily infested with perennial weeds use appropriate weed-killers; annual weeds can be controlled by alternating cultivations and fallowing.

If the site has been disturbed or the top-soil removed establish the depth of top-soil by trial excavations. Ideally, there should be at least 9in(23cm) of top-soil; if less than 6in(15cm) are present purchase sufficient top-soil to bring it up to this minimum depth.

A turfed area with minor undulations can be attractive and quite acceptable but grading may be needed to correct major irregularities. When grading, the top-soil is removed, levelling is carried out on the sub-soil, then the top-soil is returned.

Few people take the trouble to level a site properly with spirit level, straight edge and pegs, but for fine ornamental lawns, particularly small areas with formal surrounding features, and games areas, it is worth the effort involved.

DRAINAGE Thorough digging and breaking up of the sub-soil where this is compacted, a problem often encountered on recently vacated building sites, should ensure that excess moisture is not retained at the surface. If, however, the site is known to be wet, level it first and then install clay or plastic drains – a single diagonal line across a wet patch, a herringbone system where the whole site is very wet.

The next step is to dig the site, adding well-rotted stable manure, garden compost, leafmould or moist granulated peat at up to 14lb per square yard (6.3kg per m^2). On heavier soils coarse, gritty, lime-free materials can also be incorporated to improve drainage and aeration.

Few lawn sites need lime. The ideal pH level for most lawn grasses is between 5.5 and 6.0, a moderately acid reaction. They can grow outside these levels but with increasing acidity or alkalinity growth problems occur. Heathland sites may be too acidic for lawn grasses. Test, and if the reading is below pH 5.0 apply a moderate dressing of lime (see Chapter 34, Manures and Fertilisers, p.297). On strongly alkaline soils the incorporation of acidic peat will help the early growth of young grasses, but will not appreciably reduce soil alkalinity. If lime is needed apply after digging, as a surface dressing. The final preparation of the site is done when the soil is fairly dry and a few weeks before sowing or turfing. Break down the clods using a metal rake or garden fork, then firm or consolidate the soil. A roller can be used on large areas but a more satisfactory approach is by "treading" – taking very short or overlapping steps with the body weight mainly on the heels. Tread, then rake, then tread again until satisfied that the surface is perfectly level and uniformly firm.

If a site has recently been heavily manured and fertilised the application of a fertiliser is not essential, but if in any doubt apply and rake in the following fertiliser, preferably a few days before sowing seeds or laying turf: ½oz(14g) sulphate of ammonia, 1oz(28g) superphosphate and ¼oz(7g) sulphate of potash per square yard (m²).

LAWN GRASSES The grass family is large but only a few kinds are suitable for lawn purposes. Important requirements are a tolerance of close mowing and of drought. They should be naturally low-growing, hard-wearing and be resistant to disease. A further important requirement is cold resistance and foliage retention throughout the year under the climatic conditions experienced in northern Europe.

As yet no single grass appears to possess all these desirable qualities plus the ability to thrive in the widely varying soil conditions existing where lawns are to be created. New strains of grasses are constantly being developed, however, and the recently introduced cultivar 'Hunter', a fine-leaved strain of rye grass, is a promising but as yet not fully assessed step in this direction. Although seeds of single strains or kinds of grasses can be obtained from seedsmen specialising in grass seeds, most grass seeds are supplied as mixtures of two or more kinds of grass, usually a mixture of tufted and creeping types which blend to give a satisfactory turf on most kinds of soils and in most situations.

The most widely used cold-climate turf grasses are:

1. Chewings fescue (*Festuca rubra* ssp. *commutata*): densely tufted, tolerant of close mowing and poor soils.
2. Browntop bent (*Agrostis tenuis*): dwarf, tufted, tolerant of close mowing and dry acid soils.
3. Creeping red fescue (*Festuca rubra* ssp. *rubra*): creeping, hard-wearing, tolerant of wet, dry and cold conditions.
4. Smooth-stalked meadow grass (*Poa pratensis*): tufted with creeping rhizomes, dislikes wet, heavy conditions and acid soils.
5. Perennial rye grass (*Lolium perenne*): loose tufted habit, hard-wearing, suitable for all soils, particularly those of a heavy nature. Do not close-mow.

15. *Breaking down the clods and firming the soil during the final site preparation for sowing or turfing.*

The following are basic mixtures which are normally successful in a very wide range of conditions:

1. *High-quality ornamental turf*: 80 per cent Chewings fescue and 20 per cent Browntop bent (sowing rate 1oz per square yard [25g per m²]).
2. *General purpose ornamental turf*: 30 per cent Chewings fescue, 25 per cent Creeping red fescue, 10 per cent Browntop bent and 35 per cent Smooth-stalked meadow-grass (sowing rate ¾oz per square yard [21g per m²]).
3. *Utility or hard-wearing turf*: 20 per cent Chewings fescue, 20 per cent Creeping red fescue, 10 per cent Browntop bent, 20 per cent Smooth-stalked meadow-grass and 30 per cent perennial rye grass (sowing rate ½oz per square yard [14g per m²]).

All grasses grow reasonably well in light shade, if growing conditions are satisfactory, but in shade areas note the extent of less satisfactory growth of seedling grasses, leaving the grass considerably longer over this area when mowing. Where there is recurring poor growth replace with shade-tolerant ground-cover plants.

SEED OR TURF? In the United Kingdom the usual methods of establishing lawns are to sow seeds or to lay turf: planting of rhizomes is seldom attempted.

Turf laying creates an immediate visual effect, can be used sooner than

16. *When sowing grass seed by hand sow half the seed by traversing the plot lengthways, the other half crossways, in yard-wide strips, as shown.*

seeded turf and the work of turf laying is done in the autumn or winter when there are few other pressing tasks. Turfing is, however, more expensive than seeding. Laying to a good standard is more difficult and time-consuming than the sowing of seeds and good quality turf is often difficult to acquire.

A lawn from seed is more dependent on good weather conditions for successful establishment; it takes longer to establish, and there is more risk of weed problems and disturbance by cats, birds and moles. The gardener can, however, choose a mixture of seeds to suit his needs with confidence in the eventual quality of the turf.

A LAWN FROM SEED   The two most suitable periods for sowing grass seeds are early autumn and spring. In early September (late August in colder parts of the United Kingdom) the soil is usually still warm but moister autumn weather has replaced dry summer conditions. Under these conditions germination is rapid (seven to 10 days). Sowing later may result in poor germination and seedling establishment with risk of substantial winter-kill in a severe winter.

In spring, sow in April when soil temperatures are rising and there is a full growing season ahead. Drawbacks to spring sowing are slower germination and a greater risk of dry conditions with the need to have artificial irrigation available.

Sow during a period of calm, dry weather. The surface of the seed bed should be dry so that soil does not adhere to the boots or to seed-drill wheels, but there should be moisture just below the surface. If a drill is hired to sow grass seed make sure that it is calibrated to sow seed at the required rate. Divide the seeds into two halves, then, starting along the least accessible side, sow half the seeds lengthways and the other half crossways, using the wheel marks from the previous run as a guide. Newspaper or a strip of hessian laid along the edges will permit overrun without seed wastage.

If sowing by hand, divide the seeds into two halves, sowing half the seeds by traversing the plot lengthways, the other half crossways. This approach gives more accurate distribution. Sow larger areas in yard-wide strips, using marker canes and two lengths of line. Smaller areas can be marked out in yard squares.

After sowing rake the seed bed, to lightly cover most of the seeds; if buried too deeply they may not germinate. Do not roll after sowing. If there is no rain within two or three days of sowing irrigate gently but thoroughly with a garden sprinkler.

If the soil is slightly lifted at germination, when the grass is 2 to 3in(5 to 8cm) high lightly roll. This can be done with the rear roller of a mower, the cutting blades being held well clear. Two or three days later cut lightly with a sharp-bladed mower (with the front roller removed) to reduce the height of the grass by about a third. With autumn sowing there may be no further need to mow until spring. With spring-sown grass continue mowing as growth dictates, gradually reducing the height of the cut to the normal height for an established lawn ½in(1cm).

Fungal diseases can kill both grass seeds in the soil and young grasses. If young seedling grasses turn yellow and collapse or brown, shrivelled patches occur water immediately with Cheshunt Compound at ½oz in 1gal of water per square yard (14g in 4.5l of water per m²). Captan seed dressings will give useful protection if sowing when the weather conditions do not allow quick germination.

During the first season of growth use the new lawn as little as possible. Begin the process of gradually eliminating any minor surface irregularities by lightly top-dressing at intervals after the first spring cut. Feed autumn-sown turf in spring as growth becomes vigorous and carry out supplementary summer feeding of both autumn and spring sown turf.

WEED CONTROL IN NEW LAWNS   To avoid the risk of damage to the grass do not use selective lawn weedkillers on newly laid turf until it is well established and growing strongly. Do not use them on newly seeded lawns during the first three months, and preferably not during the first six months. Strong-growing annual weeds can smother young seedling grasses. Guard against this by hand-weeding, removing any seedlings of coarser grasses at the same time. Where annual weeds are numerous spray with the contact weedkiller ioxynil, but not until the seedling grasses have developed at least two leaves.

A LAWN FROM TURF Turfing is best done during the winter months from October to the end of February, avoiding periods when the soil is frozen or heavy with recent rain. During this period there is little risk of hot sunshine or drying winds which, at other periods, may subject the turf to considerable stress and interfere with inter-rooting between turves. If turves are laid in the summer they may need frequent irrigation. This can seriously affect levels and firmness of the underlying soil-bed leaving the lawn with an uneven surface.

Before buying turves check the quality carefully. The grass should be free of coarser grasses and weeds. Weedy turf indicates poor management. It may break up easily when handled and provides an immediate problem of weed control. It should be suitably mown. Tangled, unmown turf may hide defects, and may have been lifted for some time with consequent risk of deterioration. The turf should handle satisfactorily without breaking up. It should be well-rooted, with the soil a good loamy texture.

Most turf is machine cut to a thickness of 1 to 1½in(2.5 to 4cm). The thickness should be uniform or there will be extra work involved in trimming to an even thickness. Thinner turf is acceptable if well rooted but will need extra care in laying and subsequent irrigation until well established. The size may be 1ft(30cm) square or 3ft(1m) by 1ft(30cm), the smaller size being the easiest to handle.

Check on delivery and reject sub-standard turves. Lay as quickly as possible. If work cannot begin immediately turves can be stacked, rolled or folded three or four deep for two or three days. If there is to be longer delay lay them flat in a shaded situation and keep them well watered.

Begin laying by marking out the area to be turfed. If possible, allow a 1 to 2in(2.5 to 5cm) overlap, which can be trimmed back on completion to give a perfect neat accurate edge. Use a tautly stretched line as a guide when laying the first line of turves. Work forwards from the most accessible side of the site, facing the unturfed area, always standing on broad planks placed over the newly laid turves. Do not walk on the prepared bed or the new turf.

Place each turf in as close contact with its neighbour as possible, bonding by staggering successive lines of turf and using half turves at the end of each alternate row. Have a rake handy for keeping the bed level. Also a bucket of ordinary soil for packing under any thinner turves. Never force turves into position by hitting them with a spade; always adjust the soil level under the turf.

17. *Use half turves at the end of each alternate row so that the adjacent lines of turves are staggered and so correctly bonded.*

When laying is finished firm lightly with a small garden roller or with a turfing board made by attaching a wooden handle to the centre of a 9in(23cm) by 15in(38cm) piece of board. Then apply a light overall dressing of sandy loam soil working this well into the crevices between the turves with the back of a rake. This will also help to correct minor differences in levels.

When the grass resumes growth in spring lightly top at the first mowing, then adopt the routine treatment for established lawns but, if possible, leave until early summer, when the turves should be well rooted in, before subjecting it to regular use.

LAWN MAINTENANCE

FEEDING   Regular feeding is an important aspect of lawn maintenance. It encourages vigour and density in the turf, giving more resistance to disease, drought, hard wear and invasive weeds and moss.

Spring   A single dressing in early spring of a compound fertiliser containing nitrogen, phosphate and potash will supply most of a lawn's seasonal nutrient requirements. Apply in mild, showery settled weather as the grass is beginning to grow freely – in southern Britain usually towards the end of March; in northerly regions early to mid-April. If weather conditions are unsuitable delay application for two or three weeks.

The simplest approach to feeding is to use a proprietary turf fertiliser formulated for spring and summer use. The analytical content of different brands may vary considerably. An analysis of 5 to 7 per cent nitrogen, 10 to 15 per cent phosphoric acid and 2 to 4 per cent potash provides a good and economical balance of nutrients.

Alternatively a simple, quick-acting spring lawn feed can be made up from: 35 parts by weight sulphate of ammonia, 60 parts by weight superphosphate and 5 parts by weight sulphate of potash, applied at 2oz. per square yard (55g per m^2). Although such mixtures will usually provide sufficient phosphate and potash to meet the season's requirements, vigour will decline as the season advances and nitrogen becomes depleted. To counteract apply sulphate of ammonia two or three times during the season, as necessary, at the rate of ¼ to ½oz per square yard (7 to 14g per m^2). It is safer to mix this with 3 to 4oz (85 to 110g) per square yard of sandy soil before application to ensure more even distribution and to guard against the risk of scorch. Apply in cool, moist conditions, not during hot, dry periods.

Alternatively, add slow-acting nitrogenous fertilisers to the spring lawn dressing to extend the period of nitrogen release, e.g.: 15 parts by weight sulphate of ammonia, 15 parts by weight dried blood, 40 parts by weight fine bone meal, 25 parts by weight superphosphate and 5 parts by weight sulphate of potash, applied at 2oz per square yard (55g per m^2).

Poor colour in turf can often be strengthened by adding calcined sulphate of iron to the spring dressing at the rate of ⅒oz per square yard (5g per m^2). Use in moderation; excessive amounts can cause deterioration of the turf.

AUTUMN   If a lawn has suffered from summer drought or heavy compaction, an autumn fertiliser dressing will aid recovery. It should contain a good level of potash and phosphate to encourage healthy roots but should be low in nitrogen, e.g.: 25 parts by weight superphosphate, 50 parts by weight fine bonemeal, 15 parts by weight sulphate of potash and 10 parts by weight sandy soil, and should be mixed well and applied at 2oz per square yard (55g per m^2), in September. Apply lawn fertilisers by hand to measured strips, at half the recommended rate, working lengthways, then repeat the application working crossways. If using a fertiliser or linear distributor apply in parallel strips using the wheel tracks of the previous run as a guide line. Be careful to avoid overlapping, particularly if it is necessary to turn on the turf.

18. *The use of a wheeled distributor will ensure even distribution of fertiliser.*

Scarifying   Scarifying is the term used to describe the removal of "thatch" from turf by the vigorous use of a spring-tine rake (illustrated on p. 33) or specially designed scarifying tool.

All established lawns have an intermediate layer between roots and leaves; a build-up or accumulation of both living and dead material, including grass stems, stolons and uncollected decaying mowings – thatch, as we call it. It gives the turf a springy resilience and a moderate accumulation of up to ½in (1cm) can be beneficial, acting as a moisture-conserving mulch in hot weather and giving a degree of protection against compaction and hard wear.

Too great a depth of thatch can, however, impede both moisture and nutrient penetration, and in wet conditions surface drainage and aeration can be impeded, favouring the establishing and spreading of disease.

If thatch is present deal with it as the first step in the autumn programme of renovation, followed by aerating, autumn feeding, top-dressing and reseeding, as necessary. Begin de-thatching in early September. Use a spring-tine rake or ordinary garden rake. If thatch is dense use one of the scarifying tools with especially designed teeth, or, for large areas, hire a mechanised scarifyer.

Thatch is most usually troublesome on the more strongly acid soils or where drainage is poor, conditions in which there is reduced bacterial activity and a slow rate of decay of organic materials. If the site is wet install a drainage system. If the soil is only moderately acid, top-dressing regularly in autumn with good-quality loam should encourage more rapid thatch decomposition.

If the lawn is below pH 5 apply a light dressing of calcium carbonate (ground chalk or ground limestone) during the winter months to raise the pH reaction slightly and increase the rate of decay. On light sandy soils apply at no more than 2oz per square yard (55g per m²); on heavier soils at not more than 4oz per square yard (110g per m²).

Scarify (rake) lightly at intervals in the autumn to remove accumulating leaves and debris.

Aerating Aeration is the process of spiking or deeply piercing the lawn surface to reduce soil compaction and to improve air circulation within the soil. Compaction is a squeezing together of soil particles, caused by heavy usage. It may be localized as, for example, where a short-cut is taken across the lawn, or it may be more general due to the frequent passage of a heavy mower.

The compressing of the soil particles impedes the passage of air and encourages a build-up of carbon-dioxide in the soil, interfering with and restricting root up-take of moisture and nutrients. In hot weather the roots may not be able to absorb sufficient moisture to compensate for transpiration loss, even though there is moisture in the soil. This can give rise to

19. *Too great a depth of living and dead material in lawns (thatch, as it is called) can impede moisture and nutrient penetration as well as surface drainage and aeration. Begin raking this out in early September.*

20. *Aerate the lawn surface with an ordinary garden fork or a wheeled spiking tool.*

progressive deterioration and perhaps eventual death of the turf in heavily compacted areas.

Compression can also prevent excess water draining away freely, giving a misleading impression of adequacy when irrigating, or, in wet weather, encouraging the build-up of thatch and the spread of moss.

Various tools are available for aerating. Wheeled models which penetrate to an inch or two (2.5 to 5cm or so) may be useful for relieving light overall surface compaction or capping, to improve penetration of rain or sprinkler irrigation, but where there is deeper and more general compaction choose tools which will penetrate to at least 3in (8cm), and preferable 4 to 6in(10 to 15cm). An ordinary garden fork is quite suitable for the purpose.

On heavier clayey soils use a hollow-tine fork. Each tine removes a core or plug of soil, expelling it onto the surface at the next penetration. This allows the soil to expand. After sweeping up the cores top-dress with a sandy soil mixture, working this into the holes with a besom or brush. This leaves the turf pierced with permanent cores of free-draining, aerated, sandy soil into which new roots rapidly develop. This technique has little value on sandy soils but can be practised with benefit on heavier soils every three or four years.

Deeper and more general aerating should be done in September, when the soil is moist. Localized areas of compaction can be relieved at any time during the spring or summer, irrigating thoroughly afterwards. Repeat at four- or five-week intervals where there is continuous heavy usage.

Top-Dressing Top-dressing is the name given to a mixture of loam, sand and well-decomposed organic matter applied in moderate amounts to the surface of a lawn. It is also the term used for the operation itself. Top-dressing helps achieve and maintain a true even surface by eliminating minor irregularities; on poor or difficult soils the surface layer is improved so that there is better rooting in of grass runners and stolons giving a denser, healthier turf.

Sand or peat alone can be used but too frequent use of peat can build up a spongy surface which holds excessive moisture at the surface in wet conditions and is difficult to re-moisten following dry periods. Heavy dressings of sand can build up into an unstable surface layer.

A simple and basic formula for a top-dressing mixture is 3 parts (by weight) loam, 6 parts sand and 1 part granulated peat. Finely sieved leafmould or well-decomposed garden compost can be substituted for the peat content: sand should be lime-free with a particle size of 0.2 to 0.5mm. Apply by broadcasting with a shovel at the rate of about 4lb per square yard (1.8kg per m^2), increasing up to 6 to 7lb per square yard (2.7 to 3.2kg per m^2) where there are considerable irregularities. Work well into the base of the grass using a "lute" or the back of a wooden rake. On a level surface distribution will be even; on an irregular surface bumps will be left clear with proportionately more deposited in hollows. Do not apply too heavily, or finer grasses will be smothered.

Top-dress in early autumn as part of the autumn programme, but delay for a time if the grass is still growing strongly. Mow the lawn before applying the top-dressing in settled, dry conditions. It may take two or three years to obtain a true even surface; once achieved there is no need for further top-dressing except on difficult soils.

MOWING The height of cut and frequency of mowing are important factors in lawn maintenance. Too close mowing weakens the turf and leaves it susceptible to moss and low-growing weeds. Coarser grasses become more dominant where it is allowed to grow too long and is mown infrequently.

Frequency of mowing must be related to differing seasonal growth rates. During late spring to early autumn when growth is vigorous mow the finest ornamental lawns every two to three days; average lawns every three to five days; other general-purpose and utility areas every seven days. As vigour declines in the autumn reduce the frequency. From October until March there will be little need for the mower, except in very mild winters or in

sheltered coastal areas where an occasional light topping may be necessary.

The height of cut is determined by the time of year and the kind of turf being mown. During the period of vigorous growth mow the finest ornamental lawns to between ¼ to ½in (0.5 to 1cm), average lawns to ½in(1cm) and general-purpose or utility turf to about 1in(2.5cm).

Turf is weakened if regularly mown to below ¾₆in(0.46cm) and coarser grasses begin to dominate finer grasses where it is not kept to 1½in(4cm) or less.

From autumn to early spring when growth is slow, raise the height of cut by ¼in(0.5cm). Also raise slightly during periods of drought when irrigation is not available.

MOWINGS Most gardeners remove the mowings from ornamental lawns as there are usually few periods when they will rapidly shrivel and disappear from the surface. If not collected, they are likely to remain to spoil the appearance of the lawn as they slowly decay. Often the mowings will contain viable weed seeds, such as annual meadow grass, or the severed stems of white clover or speedwell which, if scattered, will take root in moist conditions. Mowing is certainly less arduous without the weight of a filling grassbox and the necessity for frequent trips to the compost heap. Also, nutrients are returned to the soil if mowings are allowed to "fly" and they act as a mulch in periods of drought. Obviously, therefore, there are occasions when it is advantageous to leave the mowings uncollected, but in most instances it is more advantageous to remove them.

MOWERS When buying a mower ensure that it is of a suitable type and size to deal easily and satisfactorily with the turf to be cut. All lawn mowers are based on one of two cutting principles. Cylinder mowers have several moving blades arranged in a cylinder and cut by trapping the grass between a fixed blade and each successive moving blade. Rotary mowers have a cutting device suspended and rotating beneath a protective canopy, cutting the grass by the high-speed impact of a sharp-edged bar or with blades attached to a rapidly revolving disc.

Modern rotary mowers give a neat finish and will cut grass of any height but the scissors-action of the cylinder mower will give the finest finish to a lawn. Width of cut is important as the wider the cut the less time it will take to mow a given area. Usually a machine giving a 12 to 14in (30 to 35cm) cut will be satisfactory for smaller lawns. If the lawn is of larger size, measure the area and consult a mower specialist regarding the most suitable size of machine.

Important points to observe when mowing: Mow only when the grass is dry/Always plan mowing to minimize compaction and wear from overlapping and reversing/Always mow at right angles to the line of the previous

21. When top-dressing the lawn with a mixture of loam, sand and well-decomposed organic matter in early autumn, work this well into the base of the grass with a "lute" or the back of a wooden rake.

cut as this helps to control creeping weeds and bents/Always scatter worm casts before mowing/Never leave the mower standing on the lawn. Fuel drips leave disfiguring brown patches.

IRRIGATION During dry periods water should be given as soon as the first signs of drought are recognised; namely a dullness in leaf colour and loss of resilience. These signs may be encountered when there has been no rainfall for seven to 10 days, excluding light showers. If ignored the leaves progressively turn yellow then brown, the crowns shrivel, the roots become dessicated and the grass dies.

WEED CONTROL No lawn remains free of weeds indefinitely. Weed seeds are blown in by the wind, deposited by birds or by muddy footwear from where weeds have seeded on nearby paths. Small, quick-rooting sections of creeping weeds are spread by the mower or by nesting birds, e.g. speedwell.

Hand-weeding is practical where there are only scattered large weeds such as plantain, but where weeds are numerous or varied the most effective approach is to use a selective lawn weedkiller spray (see Table 4, Chapter 34, Herbicides for Lawns, p.339).

A product containing two ingredients will usually control a wider range of weed species than one with a single active ingredient.

For maximum effect apply in spring or summer in warm, damp weather conditions when grass and weeds are growing vigorously. Apply fertiliser seven to 10 days before spring weedkilling which will stimulate weed growth, increase the effectiveness of the kill and encourage rapid grass recolonization of bare patches left as the weeds shrivel and die.

Some weeds will be killed by a single carefully applied treatment but at least two applications at five- to six-week intervals may be needed to kill others.

Do not apply lawn weedkillers in cold or windy conditions, or immediately before or after mowing.

MOSS CONTROL Moss colonizes lawns whenever grass growth is weak. It can be temporarily controlled by using moss killers but will return unless the reasons for infestation are established, then corrected. These may be poor soil fertility and lack of feeding, lack of aeration, faulty drainage, excessive shade, too close mowing or disease or pest attack. Occasionally the soil may be too acid and will benefit from a dressing of lime, but various mosses may be encountered as troublesome lawn weeds on all types of soil. Permanent control lies in the identification and correction of the cultural factors causing poor turf growth.

22. *A dribble bar fitted to a watering can allows accurate placement of selective lawn weedkiller spray, especially if the area is marked out in yard-wide (1m. wide) strips with a garden line and canes.*

For temporary control apply moss-killers. Lawn sands containing sulphate of ammonia and sulphate of iron will give good contact kill. A suitable formula is 3 parts sulphate of ammonia and 1 part calcined sulphate of iron mixed with 10 parts medium grade lime-free sand. Apply at 4oz per square yard(110g per m²) during fine weather, ideally on a moist, dewy morning with fine weather ahead. Subsequently irrigate the lawn if, after 48 hours, there has been no rain.

Dichlorophen is an effective chemical moss-killer and is the active ingredient in some proprietary lawn moss-killers. It is applied as a spray to wet the moss thoroughly. When the moss is dead rake it out, then attend to whatever cultural factor initiated the infestation.

LAWN PESTS   Among the most troublesome are:

1. Leatherjackets (*Tipula* spp.). These are the larvae of the crane fly, hatching from eggs laid in late summer to feed on grass roots during autumn and winter. Damage shows the following summer as patches of yellow turf. Check for larvae by lifting a piece of turf and forking underneath, or soak a patch of lawn and cover overnight with sacking to bring grubs to the surface. To control, water with HCH in late September-October or in mild, humid conditions late March-April.
2. Chafer grubs (*Phyllopertha horticola*). These have creamy-white curved bodies, brown heads and three pairs of legs. They feed on grass roots, emerging in late May or June as large brown beetles to lay eggs and continue the cycle. To control, dust with HCH in late May or June.
3. Earthworms (*Allolobothora* spp.). These eat only decaying organic matter, not grass roots, but their surface casts are unsightly and encourage weeds if flattened by the mower. Scatter casts as they are drying, when they crumble readily. They are most troublesome in the autumn and early spring and are encouraged by liming and by leaving mowings uncollected. If troublesome, they can be controlled by watering the turf with chlordane as worms are becoming active. They are killed underground, the treatment being effective for about a year.

LAWN DISEASES   The two most troublesome diseases are fusarium patch disease and corticium disease or red thread.

1. Fusarium patch disease (*Micronectriella nivalis*, syn. *Fusarium nivalis*). This disease is also called snow mould and usually occurs in spring or autumn during mild, damp weather, showing as small, irregular, yellow patches which eventually turn brown and die but often grow larger and coalesce before doing so. In damp weather snow-like white or pinkish fungus forms around the patches. Attacks are more likely where turf is compacted or has received nitrogen-rich dressings in late summer.

To control mild attacks and check more serious attacks water with a solution of ¼oz sulphate of iron in ½gallon of water per square yard (7g in 2.5l of water, per m²). To control heavy attacks apply fungicides containing quintozene, benomyl, thiobendazole or thiophanate-methyl, according to manufacturer's instructions.
2. Corticium disease or red thread (*Corticium fusiforme*). This is most usually troublesome in late summer-autumn but can be encountered at any time of the year. It shows as pinkish patches of grass, the colour being due to pink, horn-like, branching fungus growths growing among the grass blades, often binding them together. They may later turn white and dry out, then being easily scattered by the mower to spread the disease. The grass is weakened by these attacks but rarely killed. Red thread usually occurs where turf is poor, under-nourished and needing aeration. Control is as for fusarium patch plus spring-summer feeding with sulphate of ammonia and attention to aeration and removal of thatch.
3. Fairy rings. These are caused by fungi which live in the soil in the form of densely matted threads among the grass roots; in summer and autumn they produce circles of whitish toadstools or puff-balls; for the remainder of the year they show as irregular circles of lush, dark green grass. *Marasmius*

oreades is the most troublesome species, showing as a strip of brown dead turf or bare soil between two rings of lush grass, the central dead strip having been killed by the dense mat of fungal threads through which moisture cannot penetrate to reach the grass roots.

Single rings, and multiple rings at a very early stage, may be controlled by thoroughly watering then applying iron sulphate solution (1lb in 1½ gal of water [450g in 6.75l of water]) at ½ gal per square yard (2.5l per m²). Once established, *Marasmius oreades* is very difficult to eradicate and specialist advice should be sought.

BASIC LAWN-CARE PROGRAMME

January Remove dead leaves; check and improve drainage if necessary; over-haul mower and other lawn tools.

February Check for worm activity or unhealthy turf; complete all turfing; moss-kill if necessary at end of month.

March Scatter worm casts, remove debris, roll if lifted by frost, then lightly mow.

April Increase frequency of mowing; feed early to mid-month, then weed-kill; re-seed sparse patches; check newly-turfed areas and top-dress if necessary.

May Adjust mower to summer cutting height; weed-kill again; apply nitrogenous fertiliser mid-late May.

June Mow frequently; spike local areas of compaction; weed-kill or irrigate as needed.

July Mow regularly; feed lightly early in the month.

August In mid-late August give final summer feed, if needed, followed by final weed-kill for year.

September Modify cutting height towards end of month; scarify to remove thatch; aerate; top-dress; apply moss-killer where necessary; sow grass seeds.

October Set mower to winter height, brushing to remove dew, and dry out turf before mowing; aerate and top-dress if unable to do so in September; remove leaves regularly; if worms troublesome apply worm-killer; begin turfing work.

November A final mow may be needed, but do not mow in frosty conditions; continue leaf removal and turfing.

December If *very* acid apply lime this month.

4.

Trees for Gardens

Never before has there been a period when so much real interest in tree planting has been supported by such a wealth of planting material being available, as well as good advice about the best use to make of it. This chapter is concerned with tree selection (see pp. 45 to 52) for gardens of up to about ½ acre (.205 hectare) in size, tree planting and tree care.

Generally, a knowledge of your soil and climate is essential. Is the soil acid or alkaline, heavy or light in texture? These are questions to which answers must be provided. The average rainfall will have a bearing on the choice of the trees to be planted, for there will be differences in growth on the East Coast with its low rainfall to that on the western seaboard. Trees which make luxurious growth given a high rainfall will make more restricted growth in harsher, dry conditions. Always it is a question of "The right tree in the right place".

In addition to such cultural matters there is the need to appreciate other factors which influence tree planting, such as being conversant with local bye-laws – tree preservation orders, for instance, the proximity of overhead wires and the location of underground cables and drains. Also, there is the need to consider the effect of planting trees too close to buildings, especially on certain soils and the nuisance that can result from branches intruding into (or coming from) a neighbouring property. In its widest aspects, tree planting can involve seeking advice from lawyers, surveyors and arboriculturists.

TREES IN EXISTING GARDENS If you have moved house recently make a survey of the trees growing in your new garden. If you have had your present garden for a long time, still, occasionally, look at your trees with a fresh eye. All trees should be correctly identified, for this influences the treatment they are given. In extreme cases, when trees are overgrown and may even be dangerous, their complete removal may be the only solution. In other cases skilful pruning may suffice and this may justify engaging the services of a specialist tree surgeon. In any case, trees should not be removed in a restricted space by the inexperienced, nor should sizeable branches be severed using unsuitable equipment, even by those with specialist knowledge. Any suspicion of serious damage being caused by pests or diseases should be referred to a qualified entomologist or plant pathologist for diagnosis and remedial advice. There is no such thing as a cure-all spray.

TREES FOR NEW GARDENS When creating a new garden the aim should be to achieve a balanced effect. Foliage, tree trunks and branches have to be looked at over much longer periods than flowers. Imagine the joy of looking out of a window on a winter's day and seeing the low sun lighting up a shining tree trunk, and the cheerfulness provided by evergreens which have been especially selected for their effect. To get a complete picture of the planting material available, you should read this chapter in conjunction with Chapter 5 on conifers (pp. 53 to 64). Also, when considering flowering trees, fruit trees should not be overlooked, for it is worth bearing in mind that the apple 'Arthur Turner' gained an Award of Garden Merit from the Royal Horticultural Society for its flowers.

Experience has shown that tree planting schemes for new gardens tend to fall into two groups, mainly dependent on the age of the owners. First, there are those at the end of their working life who have acquired a new house or bungalow. For them the first priority is to plant trees which will grow quickly, and perhaps provide shade under which to rest. They will naturally not be unduly concerned about selecting trees which will eventually outgrow the positions they occupy. "These will do for my time" sums up their attitude and who can really blame them.

Secondly, there are the young married couples who are selecting trees which will grow up with them. If they are keenly interested they will study tree catalogues, specialist books and journals, visit public parks and botanic gardens, look around garden centres and gardens open to the public, attend lectures and generally take a pride in developing their home and garden as a linked unit. They are to be envied.

Ideally, if, as does happen sometimes, several adjacent gardens are being developed simultaneously, as on a new housing estate, neighbours could discuss together their tree planting plans. This could result in the achievement of effective open views, or screens being formed which will not be a future cause of embarrassment through branches overhanging other gardens and, perhaps, creating a shut-in feeling. Also, planting can be so arranged that homes are not overlooked.

A word of warning may be appropriate here about what is called "sentimental planting" – bringing home a seedling Scots pine, or a "conker" from a chestnut tree under which one played as a child, and planting this in a small garden. This can only end, sadly, in the removal of the tree one day, when it has outgrown its space, whereas a rowan or silver birch in the same position could be left to give pleasure.

Planting and Maintenance

The planting of a tree is only the beginning of the programme of work which must be carried out. Now that garden centres offer container-grown trees of many kinds planting can safely be undertaken during most months of the year. It is better, however, to avoid doing this in the height of summer because so much regular care is then required in respect of watering and spraying, just when absence on holiday may prevent this being done.

Aim to reduce to the minimum the period between acquiring and actually planting the trees. It is not usually possible to transport container-grown trees by car and delivery by suitable transport has to be arranged. If the trees are delivered during a spell of frosty weather place those in containers close together in a sheltered position and cover both the containers and base of the stems with sacking, straw or bracken. If the trees have been removed from the open ground and arrive in skilfully packed bundles of packing material they should be placed in an outbuilding or be stood upright in a sheltered corner outdoors until planting can be carried out. Deciduous trees so packed can be left for up to six weeks without harm, but after, say, two weeks it is beneficial to loosen the tops of the bundles to admit air to the branches. The root ends should not be disturbed. The transport of trees with bare roots unprotected from the elements is something to be avoided.

Planting should not be done in frozen soil, but a thin frosty crust can be scraped away from the surface to allow planting to proceed in the open soil beneath.

Have everything ready for planting, so far as this is possible, before the trees arrive. You will have taken care to ensure that the right tree occupies the right position. It is a good idea to attach labels with the names of the trees you intend to plant to canes and to move these around freely until you are satisfied you have found them the best positions, and bear in mind that the shape of trees is as important as beauty of flower and foliage.

There will be occasions when it is best to prepare a planting scheme by setting this out to scale in a plan. Never be placed in the position of having to rearrange trees because insufficient foresight was exercised.

Preparing planting holes on established lawns involves marking out

1. *The lily-flowered tulips with their underplanting of forget-me-nots* (Myosotis) *and the formality of the hedges and topiary specimens give this scene, at Court Farm, Broadway, Worcestershire, enormous charm. It is elegance personified, the perfect example of the marrying of sympathetic shapes and soft colours to create a desired effect.*

2. *The mixed border at Great Dixter, near Northiam in Sussex where in late summer the eye is led past perennial plants like Monarda 'Cambridge Scarlet' in the foreground and the scarlet rose to the billowing "cloud" of rich yellow which issues from the Mount Etna broom,* Genista aetnensis.

3. *The Laboratory at Wisley viewed from the west side beyond the formal pool.
This attractive building – completed in 1915 and the ''heart'' of the garden –
provides homes in its wall beds for a host of climbers and other plants which
benefit from the sheltered conditions.*

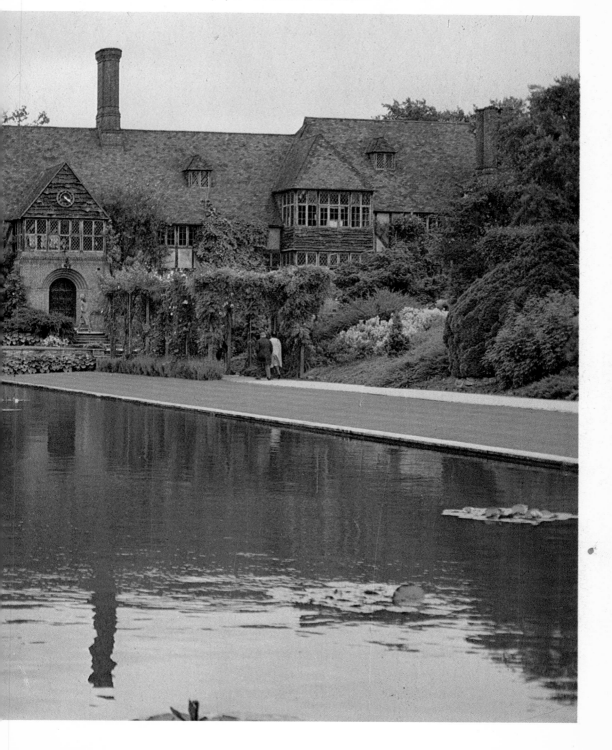

4.   *Annuals at the Northern Horticultural Society's garden, Harlow Car,*
Harrogate, Yorkshire, where these flowers are always superbly displayed. The
clary named Salvia horminum *'Blue Bird' (left) acts as a fulcrum for a*
diversity of other annuals from tagetes to annual dianthus, salpiglossis and the
Carnival selection of Phlox drummondii *(see pp. 120 to 128).*

circles usually 4ft(1.25m) in diameter. Drive a peg into the ground where the tree will be planted and loop a strong piece of string 2ft(60cm) in length around this. Then attach the free end of this string to a strong pointed cane so that you can scratch a distinct circle on the grass. Follow this by cutting through the marked-out circle with a sharp edging iron to the depth of about 2in(5cm). It is most helpful to spread out a suitably sized square of sacking or strong polythene sheeting adjacent to the hole, on which the turf and excavated soil can be placed, keeping the turf, top-soil and sub-soil in separate heaps. The top-soil can be up to 1ft(30cm) deep, and the division between one and the other is usually obvious as the top-soil is invariably darker in colour than the sub-soil. Excavate a planting hole 2ft(60cm) deep, fork over the soil at the bottom of the hole and prod the smooth sides to make root access easier. The finished planting hole should never resemble a sunken, smooth container.

Next place the broken-up turf upside down at the bottom of the hole and then refill with soil up to the correct planting depth. The soil used can be a mixture of top-soil with some sub-soil added, provided the latter has an open, friable texture. The correct planting depth is determined by the soil mark at the base of the tree stem, which denotes the depth at which the tree had been growing in the nursery lines or in its container. Before planting, a tree stake of adequate length and of durable quality should be driven into the undisturbed soil at the bottom of the hole, placing it just off centre. Round stakes are best, as the sharp edges of square stakes injure the tree stems. Pointed, round tree stakes which have been pressure-treated with a safe wood preservative are freely available. For the normal standard trees which are more often planted in gardens than other kinds, tree stakes 8ft(2.5m) in length are required, this allowing for 5½ft(1.65m) of the stake to protrude above the level of the refilled hole. The top of the stake should be so arranged that it does not reach above the lowest branches of the trees. It is helpful to round-off the sharp top edge of the stake nearest to the tree. Half-standard trees, of course, need shorter stakes.

Much could be said on the various methods of tree staking and useful leaflets can be obtained from the British Standards Institution. One form of staking involves using two stakes, neither of which comes in direct contact with the tree stem; these stakes are linked with a suitable cross support. For the home gardener, however, the most popular support is a single, round stake with tree ties providing a protecting buffer between this and the tree stem. The tree ties can be adjusted as the tree stem increases in diameter, and regular inspections should be made to avoid harmful constriction.

When planting arrange the tree roots at the right depth. Almost invari-ably a tree will have a natural front and back which allows the stem to fit snugly against and in front of the tree stake. The roots should be spread out and then about half a pailful of fine peat, to which has been added a small handful of bonemeal or proprietary tree fertiliser, should be worked in among the roots. This feed results in the quick production of new roots and should suffice until a new root system is established. Ideally, tree planting is a job for two people. The tree should be gently shaken up and down in its planting hole so that the granules of peat find their way in among the roots. Make sure that the soil added displaces air pockets and that with planting completed it is not piled up above the original soil mark on the stem. If the planting is being done by one person the tree should be loosely tied to the stake while the soil is replaced. Firm the soil as planting proceeds by treading with the feet.

If the soil is rather dry, then water the tree but with soil of average moistness this will not be necessary. If the planting site is normally wet plant the tree slightly above the surrounding soil level; if it is dry plant slightly below normal soil level, leaving a shallow saucer-like depression in which rainwater will collect.

PLANTING EVERGREENS   Apart from conifers (see Chapter 5, pp. 53 to 64), hollies are the most-planted evergreens, and only a limited number of these develop into trees. With the exception of a few cotoneasters, few evergreens are available as standard or half-standard trees, and in severe winter weather even these tend to become defoliated.

The planting time for evergreens is more restricted than for deciduous trees, but the old idea that early autumn and late spring are the only suitable times should be less rigidly adhered to. It is better to plant during a mild spell, in suitable soil conditions, in late autumn or early winter than during a period of dry, searing winds in spring. The application of a plastic spray, e.g. S 600, to the leaves and branches of evergreens immediately after planting has proved to be a considerable help in achieving successful establishment. Spraying overhead with clean water, applied through a fine-nozzle spray during sunless periods, is also very helpful, much more so than pouring unwanted water around the inactive roots.

The erection of temporary screens made of hessian or other suitable material on the windward side of newly planted evergreens is worthwhile. Staking, even of small evergreens, should not be neglected, and the support of these can be improved by placing the stakes at a suitable angle against the prevailing winds.

After-care

It is vital that the initial planting of trees should be followed up by adequate after-care. So much depends on this, but it tends to be neglected.

Mulching This means the spreading on the surface of cultivated ground, above the tree roots, of a 2in(5cm) layer of matter such as peat, leafmould, spent hops, chopped up bracken or straw, decomposed compost, well-rotted farmyard manure or processed pine bark. The last-mentioned is becoming more popular as it is sterile and helps to reduce weeding, besides being readily available.

The objective is to conserve moisture and to insulate the soil against fluctuations in temperature. Avoid spreading fresh lawn mowings unless this is done very thinly, and never use any after the recent application of herbicides to lawns. The most effective time to mulch is generally considered to be at the very end of winter and in early spring, just as active growth recommences. It will be found that an occasional topping-up of the material used becomes necessary. Birds searching for food will scatter some of the mulch, and strong, drying winds will also lessen the covering.

Weeding The surface of the ground should be kept cultivated and weed free. The mulch which has been applied will assist in keeping down the weeds, and although weeds can be killed by applying herbicides the dead vegetation remains to form unsightly circular patches which are irritating to see in a well-kept garden.

No precise time scale can be given when grass may be allowed to grow up to the base of tree stems, so much depends on local conditions; but maintaining a clean mulched surface for, say, three years undoubtedly helps in the establishment of healthy, free-growing specimens. Great care should be taken to avoid damaging the stems of trees with a lawnmower; it is better to use shears to finish off the grass cutting. Untidy, jagged wounds provide inlets for disease.

Feeding Good preparation of the planting sites will keep young trees in a thriving condition for at least three years. Over-feeding, particularly of deciduous flowering trees, can result in the production of soft, leafy growth at the expense of shorter-jointed flowering wood.

As trees grow older and the new roots penetrate into what are usually less good soil conditions outside the perimeter of the planting holes, it may be noticed that growth slows up and leaves and flowers tend to be not as good as they were. In such cases a proprietary tree fertiliser can be applied, strictly in accordance with the manufacturer's instructions. Very good results will follow the use of foliar feeds, and many tired-looking plants so treated will regain their former vigour.

The occasional feeding of older specimen trees in gardens is an established practice which brings rewards. The usual procedure is to note the position of the perimeter of the canopy of branches, then to mark out roughly on the surface of the ground under these an area extending to 5ft(1.5m) beyond the spread of the branches and 5ft(1.5m) back from the limit of spread towards the tree trunk. This then forms a continuous belt around the tree 10ft(3m) wide. This is the area where most of the feeding roots are active. Next, take a soil auger or a crowbar and make holes about 1½ to 2in (4 to 5cm) in diameter within this area, and about 18in(45cm) apart some 15 to 24in(38 to 60cm) deep and fill the cylinders thus formed with a slow-release tree fertiliser. A good time to do this work is from mid-February to early April. This treatment is described in the British Standards publication B.S. 3998, "Recommendations for Tree Work".

Protection of Trees Tree guards such as are used in public parks and gardens are seldom, if ever, required in private gardens, but it is reassuring to know that effective proprietary makes are available. Serious damage can be caused by rabbits, even in small gardens, particularly during spells of hard weather. It is curious that rabbits will often damage newly planted trees and ignore established specimens. They will gnaw the stems from ground level upwards as far as they can reach. To combat these attacks the stems can be wrapped around with spiral-shaped plastic tree guards. These can be seen used in quantity on young trees planted on the banks of the motorways. Grey squirrels have become a serious pest, and advice about dealing with these can be obtained from the Forestry Commission's Leaflet No. 56., "Grey Squirrel Control", by Judith Rowe, published by Her Majesty's Stationery Office.

Snow Damage The lodging of heavy, wet snow on trees with horizontal branches can cause breakages. It pays to dislodge this from garden specimens, and a stout forked stick is a suitable tool with which to gently shake the branches. Snow lodging among the close, upright fastigiate growths of such trees as *Prunus* 'Amanogawa' will force open the branches, and these do not always return to their original positions after a thaw. Pay particular attention to such trees, even to the extent of tying in those branches – especially of cypresses – which, if distorted out of shape, would spoil the appearance of the trees.

Suckers In the Royal Horticultural Society's *Dictionary of Gardening* a sucker is described as a "shoot of underground origin". Such suckers often form an unsightly mass of vigorous shoots forming a ring around the base of a tree. A typical example is the growth of the common white-flowered hawthorn on which has been budded the double red cultivar. It is useless cutting these off at ground level for this only encourages numerous new growths to develop. The suckers should be severed at the point where they join the roots. If each individual sucker can be given a sharp tug back against the direction of growth this will sometimes suffice to remove it, but very often it can only be done with the help of a sharp-edged tool. Moving the soil to expose the base of the suckers and then getting to work on them with a sharp pointed trowel or small, sharp spade will prove effective.

TREE SELECTION

The selection of trees for your garden should be an enjoyable exercise. To settle on a final choice from the great number now available can involve browsing through books (preferably well illustrated); looking through nurserymen's catalogues which, it is pleasant to note, are nowadays much more than just price lists; visiting well-known arboreta – gardens renowned for their tree collections; and attending talks and walks organised by recognised authorities on the subject. Always, there are professionals ready to give sound guidance when problems arise.

In the following lists (pp. 45 to 52) the trees are grouped under various headings. These should not be considered rigid classifications, as they allow for overlapping. Certain basic terms should be understood, but the amateur gardener need not concern himself with the jargon so freely used among professionals. It should, however, be appreciated that a standard tree for garden planting usually means one having a clean stem measuring at least 5½ft(1.65m) from ground level to the first branch, while a half-standard has a stem of about 4½ft(1.45m). These are the two sizes generally planted, and, for such practical reasons as the need to have the lowermost branches at a height which will not impede lawn-mowing, more standards are planted than any other kind.

In a garden a full ½ acre (.205 hectare) in extent, space may be found for planting some trees in groups of, say, three specimens. There is no reason why three different flowering cherries of similar habit of growth should not form such a group, but it is not advisable to plant, say, one hawthorn, one maple and one crab apple together. (See also Chapter 2, p. 25, for more on this subject.)

Planting distances cannot be standardised, but sensible spacing between individual standard trees in a group should not be less than 18ft(5.5m). Individual specimens should be so placed that room becomes available as they age and increase in size. They can, for example, be given a surround of shrubs which can later be removed.

Instead of trying to estimate the dimensions which the trees in the lists which follow will attain, these have been classified as large, medium or small, hence the abbreviations L, M or S after each name. However, to give some indication of the sizes these categories represent, a larger tree would be one which eventually grows to 40ft(12m) or more in height; a medium-sized one 25 to 40ft(7.5 to 12m) and a small tree one up to 25ft(7.5m) in height. Those falling in the "L" category will also be suitable, of course, for planting in gardens larger than the half-acre limit in mind. Groups of those classified as "M" will not be out of place in larger settings. Under "S" will be found some trees small enough for gardens occupying no more than a few hundreds of square yards. Attention is drawn particularly to those of formal outline, e.g. *Prunus* 'Amanogawa' which makes a narrow column.

23. *A selection of tree shapes represented, left to right, by* Catalpa bignonioides *(round-headed);* Carpinus betulus *'Columnaris' (conical);* Prunus *'Amanogawa' (fastigiate);* Betula pendula *'Youngii' (weeping); and* Pyrus calleryana *'Chanticleer' (pyramidal). All are described in the pages which follow (pp. 45 to 52).*

RECOMMENDED TREES

To make reference easier, the first mention of any genus is denoted by the use of italic capitals.

Deciduous Flowering Trees

AESCULUS × *CARNEA* 'BRIOTII' (L). The best form of red horse chestnut. May.

A. indica (L). Pinkish flowers in June, early July. 'Sydney Pearce' is a very attractive cultivar.

AMELANCHIER LAMARCKII (S). The tree often cultivated as *A. canadensis*. Racemes of white flowers in April. Brilliant autumn colour.

CATALPA BIGNONIOIDES (L). An imposing large-leaved tree with spectacular white flowers with yellow and purple markings in July and August.

CERCIS SILIQUASTRUM (M), Judas tree. Rose-purple, pea-shaped flowers in April and May.

CORNUS KOUSA (S). White petal-like bracts freely borne in June, followed by strawberry-like fruits and bronzy-crimson autumn colouring. The variety *chinensis* has rounder "flowers".

C. mas (S). Small yellow flowers on the leafless branches in February. Bright red, edible, cherry-like fruits in autumn.

C. nuttallii (M). More tree-like than those listed above. Large white bracts in May, sometimes suffused pink.

CRATAEGUS MONOGYNA (M), hawthorn. The species planted to form quickthorn hedges. A wonderful spectacle in our countryside as hedgerow trees. For garden purposes the coloured forms of *Crataegus oxyacantha* are usually planted, such as 'Paul's Scarlet' (double, red), 'Plena' (double, white), 'Punicea' (single, scarlet), 'Rosea' (single, pink), 'Rosea Flore Pleno' (double, pink).

DAVIDIA INVOLUCRATA (L), handkerchief tree. An unusual tree with large white pendulous bracts in May.

FRAXINUS ORNUS (L), Manna ash. Masses of whitish flowers in May.

GENISTA AETNENSIS (S). Graceful drooping branches with yellow pea-shaped flowers in July. Usually seen with more than one trunk from ground level.

KOELREUTERIA PANICULATA (M). A slow-growing tree with yellow flowers in July and August, followed by bladder-like fruits. Attractive pinnate leaves turning bright yellow in autumn.

+*LABURNOCYTISUS ADAMII* (M). A graft hybrid of great interest, bearing in May typical yellow laburnum flowers, purple broom flowers and others intermediate between these two.

LABURNUM × *WATERERI* 'VOSSII' (M). The most attractive laburnum with the longest pendulous racemes of yellow flowers in May and June.

MAGNOLIA DENUDATA (M) (still often known as *M. conspicua*), the Yulan. Pure white, cup-shaped, fragrant flowers in late February and March.

M. kobus (M). Masses of white flowers on the leafless branches in April.

M. × *loebneri* 'Leonard Messel' (S). Lilac-pink flowers with white centres in April and early May. 'Merrill' has larger white fragrant flowers in April.

M. salicifolia (M). An elegant conical shaped tree with fragrant white flowers on the leafless branches in April.

M. × *soulangiana* (M). This is the magnolia which is seen most often, usually with more than one trunk. Large tulip-shaped flowers, white on the inside and purplish on the outside starting in April.

M. × *veitchii* (L). This hybrid succeeds in gardens where the exotic Himalayan and Chinese species do not thrive. Masses of white, flushed purplish-pink flowers in April.

MALUS (M). The decision to select 10 different *Malus* (see below) from a total of about 80 is deliberate. Those listed are all tried favourites, but others are equally meritorious. The wisdom, therefore, of inspecting collections and making personal notes cannot be over-emphasised.

M. coronaria 'Charlottae'. Rather unusual in having semi-double, shell-pink, fragrant flowers in late May and richly coloured leaves in autumn.

M. floribunda. Cultivated for over 100 years and still very popular. Countless

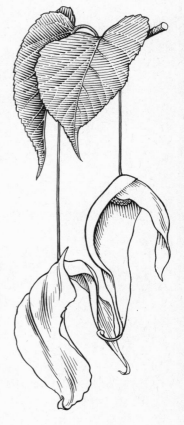

24. Davidia involucrata

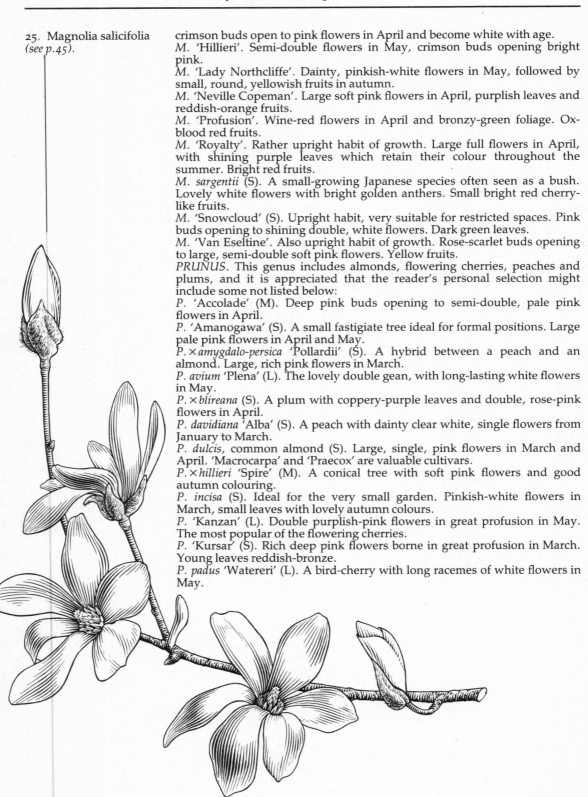

25. Magnolia salicifolia
(see p.45).

crimson buds open to pink flowers in April and become white with age.

M. 'Hillieri'. Semi-double flowers in May, crimson buds opening bright pink.

M. 'Lady Northcliffe'. Dainty, pinkish-white flowers in May, followed by small, round, yellowish fruits in autumn.

M. 'Neville Copeman'. Large soft pink flowers in April, purplish leaves and reddish-orange fruits.

M. 'Profusion'. Wine-red flowers in April and bronzy-green foliage. Ox-blood red fruits.

M. 'Royalty'. Rather upright habit of growth. Large full flowers in April, with shining purple leaves which retain their colour throughout the summer. Bright red fruits.

M. *sargentii* (S). A small-growing Japanese species often seen as a bush. Lovely white flowers with bright golden anthers. Small bright red cherry-like fruits.

M. 'Snowcloud' (S). Upright habit, very suitable for restricted spaces. Pink buds opening to shining double, white flowers. Dark green leaves.

M. 'Van Eseltine'. Also upright habit of growth. Rose-scarlet buds opening to large, semi-double soft pink flowers. Yellow fruits.

PRUNUS. This genus includes almonds, flowering cherries, peaches and plums, and it is appreciated that the reader's personal selection might include some not listed below:

P. 'Accolade' (M). Deep pink buds opening to semi-double, pale pink flowers in April.

P. 'Amanogawa' (S). A small fastigiate tree ideal for formal positions. Large pale pink flowers in April and May.

P. × *amygdalo-persica* 'Pollardii' (S). A hybrid between a peach and an almond. Large, rich pink flowers in March.

P. *avium* 'Plena' (L). The lovely double gean, with long-lasting white flowers in May.

P. × *blireana* (S). A plum with coppery-purple leaves and double, rose-pink flowers in April.

P. *davidiana* 'Alba' (S). A peach with dainty clear white, single flowers from January to March.

P. *dulcis*, common almond (S). Large, single, pink flowers in March and April. 'Macrocarpa' and 'Praecox' are valuable cultivars.

P. × *hillieri* 'Spire' (M). A conical tree with soft pink flowers and good autumn colouring.

P. *incisa* (S). Ideal for the very small garden. Pinkish-white flowers in March, small leaves with lovely autumn colours.

P. 'Kanzan' (L). Double purplish-pink flowers in great profusion in May. The most popular of the flowering cherries.

P. 'Kursar' (S). Rich deep pink flowers borne in great profusion in March. Young leaves reddish-bronze.

P. *padus* 'Watereri' (L). A bird-cherry with long racemes of white flowers in May.

P. 'Pandora' (M). Upright habit of growth with masses of large, pale pink flowers in late March and April. Young leaves bronze-red, good autumn colouring.

P. persica 'Aurora' (S). A double-flowered peach with rose-pink, frilled flowers in April. 'Iceberg' has semi-double, pure white flowers, and 'Klara Mayer' double, peach-pink flowers in April.

P. 'Pink Perfection' (M). Upright habit of growth. Pale pink flowers in May, more suitable for restricted spaces than 'Kanzan'.

P. sargentii (M). Single pink flowers in March and April, very fine autumn colouring.

P. 'Shimidsu Sakura' (S) (syn. *P. longipes*, 'Shogetsu'). Very suitable for small gardens. Double white flowers with wavy-edged petals and long, hanging flower stalks. Late flowering, in May.

P. 'Shirofugen' (L). A wide-spreading tree with coppery-coloured young leaves, double, purplish pink buds changing to white flowers, changing again to purplish-pink. Late flowering, in May.

P. subhirtella 'Autumnalis' (S). Semi-double white flowers from November to March. 'Autumnalis Rosea', semi-double, blush pink and *P. subhirtella* 'Fukubana', with semi-double, rose-madder flowers in spring are also very attractive.

P. 'Tai Haku' (L). Very large single white flowers in April, coppery young leaves. A spreading tree.

P. 'Ukon' (M). Semi-double, pale yellow flowers, tinged green and flushed pink in April. Bronze young leaves.

ROBINIA × HILLIERI (M). A graceful tree with slightly fragrant lilac-pink pea-shaped flowers in June.

SALIX AEGYPTIACA (S). A small willow tree with bright yellow male catkins in February and March.

STUARTIA (STEWARTIA) PSEUDOCAMELLIA (S). Large, single, white flowers with bright yellow anthers in July. Good autumn colour.

STYRAX JAPONICA (S). Dainty downward-pointing white flowers with golden anthers freely borne on fan-like branches in June.

Deciduous Trees with Coloured Foliage in Spring and Summer

ACER CAPPADOCICUM 'AUREUM' (L). Young leaves reddish at first, turning to golden-yellow. Cultivar 'Rubrum' has bright red young foliage.

A. negundo 'Auratum' (M). Golden-yellow. 'Variegatum', white-margined leaves.

A. palmatum 'Atropurpureum (S). Bronzy-crimson throughout the spring and summer.

A. palmatum 'Aureum' (S). Soft yellow becoming golden-yellow with age.

A. platanoides 'Crimson King' (L). Deep crimson-purple.

A. platanoides 'Drummondii' (M). White margins to leaves.

A. pseudoplatanus 'Brilliantissimum' (S). A small-growing sycamore changing from shrimp-pink to pale yellowish-green and finally green.

ALNUS INCANA 'AUREA' (S). Yellow leaves and young shoots.

BETULA PENDULA 'PURPUREA' (S). A birch of restricted growth with purple leaves.

CATALPA BIGNONIOIDES 'AUREA' (L). Large, spectacular, soft-yellow leaves.

CRATAEGUS LACINIATA (C. ORIENTALIS) (S). Deeply cut silver-grey leaves.

GLEDITSIA TRIACANTHOS 'SUNBURST' (M). Golden yellow, fern-like leaves changing to green.

HIPPOPHAE RHAMNOIDES (S). A small tree with silver leaves.

POPULUS CANDICANS 'AURORA' (L). Large, creamy-white, pink-tinged, variegated leaves.

PRUNUS × BLIREANA (S). See p. 46.

P. cerasifera 'Pissardii' (M). The popular purple-leaved plum. The cultivar 'Nigra' has darker leaves.

P. spinosa 'Purpurea' (S). The elegant purple-leaved sloe which forms an ideal tree for very small gardens.

26. Acer griseum

P. virginiana 'Shubert' (S). Upright growth with leaves turning light purple throughout the spring and summer.
PYRUS SALICIFOLIA 'PENDULA' (S). The weeping willow-leaved pear with silver-grey leaves.
ROBINIA PSEUDOACACIA 'FRISIA' (M). Bright yellow pinnate leaves from spring to autumn.
SALIX ALBA f. *ARGENTEA* (syn. S.A. 'SERICEA') (M). An elegant willow with silver-grey leaves.
SORBUS ARIA 'LUTESCENS' (M). Upright growth, silver-grey leaves covered in the early stages with a creamy-yellow down.
S. aucuparia 'Dirkenii' (S). Young leaves yellow becoming yellowish-green.

Deciduous Trees for Autumn Colour

This list includes trees for both colour of foliage and fruit.
ACER CAMPESTRE (M), the field or common maple. Predominantly yellow autumn leaves, sometimes reddish.
A. cappadocicum (L). Butter-yellow leaves.
A. ginnala (S). Orange to crimson three lobed leaves.
A. griseum (M). Red and scarlet leaves.
A. grosseri var. *hersii* (M). Rich red leaves.
A. japonicum 'Aconitifolium' (S) and 'Vitifolium' (S). Rich ruby-crimson leaves.
A. nikoense (M). Orange to flame leaves.
A. palmatum (M). A variable species with autumn leaf colours ranging from yellow through orange to red and crimson.
A. pensylvanicum (M). Large three lobed leaves, bright clear yellow.
AMELANCHIER LAMARCKII (S). See p. 45.
CERCIDIPHYLLUM JAPONICUM (M). Heart-shaped leaves with a mixture of pink, red and yellow autumn colours.
CRATAEGUS CRUS-GALLI (S). Scarlet leaves and red fruits which persist into winter.
C. × lavallei (M). Upright growth, orange leaves remain until December and orange berries until February.
C. phaenopyrum (M). Orange to scarlet leaves and small dark crimson fruits.
C. prunifolia (S). Rich crimson, glossy leaves and large red fruits which fall early.
LIQUIDAMBAR STYRACIFLUA (L). A large tree with maple-like leaves, bright crimson and gold.
MALUS 'GOLDEN HORNET' (M). Bright yellow crab apples which persist into December.
M. 'John Downie' (M). Bright orange-scarlet fruits – a favourite for making crab-apple jelly.
M. 'Red Sentinel' (M). Brilliant red fruits retained until early March.
M. × robusta (M). Fruits resembling large red cherries persisting until February.
M. tschonoskii (M). Upright growth, superb autumn foliage, showing yellow, orange, crimson, scarlet and purple at the same time.
NYSSA SYLVATICA (M). Slow growing, rich scarlet, orange and yellow leaves in late October.
OXYDENDRUM ARBOREUM (M). For lime-free soils only. Racemes of white flowers in summer followed by crimson-yellow autumn colouring.
PARROTIA PERSICA (M). Spreading habit, often with more than one main trunk. Unusual small red tufts of flowers in February and March. Spectacular red, orange and gold leaves in autumn.
PRUNUS SARGENTII (M). See p. 47.
SORBUS AUCUPARIA (M), mountain ash, rowan. Few garden trees can surpass this well-known native tree for autumn colour. Both the red berries and golden-yellow leaves are a great feature in early autumn. The varieties 'Aspleniifolia' with fern-like leaves and 'Xanthocarpa' with amber-yellow fruits are of great merit.
S. cashmiriana (S). A small tree with soft pink flowers in May and persistent white marble-like fruits in autumn.

27. Malus *'John Downie'*

S. commixta (M). Upright growth, copper-tinted young leaves, crimson in autumn, and bright red fruits.

S. 'Embley' (M). Often confused with, and grown as, *S. discolor.* Upright growth, red leaves and orange-red fruits.

S. hupehensis (M). Compact growth, bluish-green leaves, changing to red, pinkish-white persistent fruits.

S. 'Joseph Rock' (M). Upright growth, red, orange, copper and purplish autumn leaves and amber-yellow fruits.

S. sargentiana (M). Spectacular, brilliant, large vermilion-coloured leaves, scarlet fruits and conspicuous shining sticky winter buds.

S. vilmorinii (S). Fern-like leaves changing to purple and red. Fruits change from rose-red to pink and almost white.

Trees with Attractively Coloured Stems

ACER CAPILLIPES (m). "Snake-bark" maple, with red young branches.

A. griseum (M). Slow-growing, with old bark flaking off to reveal a rich orange coloured trunk. See p. 48.

A. grosseri (M). Striated green and silver trunk. The variety *hersii* is equally attractive. See p. 48.

A. palmatum 'Senkaki' (S). Ideal for the smallest garden, coral red trunk and branches.

A. pensylvanicum (M). Scattered white stripes on a green trunk. See p. 48.

ALNUS INCANA 'AUREA' (S). Yellow young shoots.

ARBUTUS × ANDRACHNOIDES (M). Cinnamon-red trunk and branches. See p. 50.

A. menziesii (M). Cinnamon-red. See p. 50.

A. unedo (S). Peeling deep brown bark. See p. 50.

BETULA species. All birches have very attractive trunks and the best selection would include: *B. albo-sinensis* (L), *B. ermanii* (L), *B. jacquemontii* (M), *B. papyrifera* (L), *B. pendula* 'Dalecarlica' (L), *B. pendula* 'Tristis' (M), *B. pendula* 'Youngii' (S) and *B. utilis* (L).

FRAXINUS EXCELSIOR 'JASPIDEA' (L). The golden ash, yellow wood.

PRUNUS MAACKII (M). Golden-brown.

P. × schmittii (M). Shining brown.

P. serrula (M). Shining mahogany.

SALIX ALBA 'CHERMESINA' (L). Orange-scarlet.

S. alba 'Vitellina' (L). Yellow.

S. 'Chrysocoma' (L). The very popular weeping willow with golden-yellow branches. Also known by other names, including *babylonica*.

S. daphnoides (S). The violet willow with purple-violet stems having a powdery white bloom.

S. matsudana 'Tortuosa' (M). Spiralling, corkscrew-like stems.

SORBUS AUCUPARIA 'BEISSNERI' (M). Pinkish-red.

Weeping Trees

ALNUS INCANA 'PENDULA' (S). Grey-green leaves.

BETULA PENDULA 'YOUNGII' (S). A spreading, dome-shaped head of weeping branches.

CARAGANA ARBORESCENS 'PENDULA' (S). Ideal for very small gardens; yellow, pea-shaped flowers.

COTONEASTER 'HYBRIDUS PENDULUS' (S). Has to be trained to form a small tree. Brilliant red fruits carried into the winter.

FAGUS SYLVATICA 'PURPUREA PENDULA' (S). A small-growing purple beech.

FRAXINUS EXCELSIOR 'PENDULA' (L). The weeping ash.

ILEX AQUIFOLIUM f. *PENDULA* (S). A berry-bearing weeping holly.

Ilex aquifolium 'Argentea Pendula' (S). A lovely berry-bearing, weeping, silver-variegated holly.

LABURNUM ANAGYROIDES 'PENDULUM' (S). The weeping laburnum.

MALUS 'EXCELLENZ THIEL' (S). A weeping crab-apple with semi-double white flowers.

PRUNUS 'CHEAL'S WEEPING' (S). Long pendulous branches with double, pink flowers.

P. subhirtella 'Pendula Rosea' (S). Umbrella-shaped, blush pink flowers in March and April. 'Pendula Rubra' (S) has deep rose-pink flowers.

PYRUS SALICIFOLIA 'PENDULA' (S). See p. 48.

SALIX CAPREA 'PENDULA' (S). A small-growing weeping willow with pussy-willow catkins.

S. 'Chrysocoma' (L). See p. 49.

S. purpurea 'Pendula' (S). A small tree with long, slender, purple branches.

SOPHORA JAPONICA 'PENDULA' (S). An unusual tree with stiff-growing drooping branches and attractive pinnate leaves.

Deciduous, Fastigiate, Pyramidal, Columnar and Conical-Shaped Trees

These are grouped together as the shapes cannot be separated with any precision.

ACER × LOBELII (M). A compact pyramidal to columnar grower, with yellow autumn colouring.

A. platanoides 'Columnare' (L). A columnar Norway maple.

BETULA PENDULA 'FASTIGIATA' (L). An upright birch.

CARPINUS BETULUS 'COLUMNARIS' (M) and 'Fastigiata' (M). Two very useful formal-shaped hornbeams.

CRATAEGUS MONOGYNA 'STRICTA' (M). A narrow, upright-growing hawthorn.

FAGUS SYLVATICA 'DAWYCK' (L). The tall, columnar, green-leafed beech. 'Dawyck Purple' has purple leaves.

GLEDITSIA TRIACANTHOS 'ELEGANTISSIMA' (S). A small tree with fern-like foliage.

LIRIODENDRON TULIPIFERA 'FASTIGIATUM' (L). A tall, narrow-growing form of the tulip tree.

MALUS TSCHONOSKII (M). See p. 48.

PRUNUS 'AMANOGAWA' (S). See p. 46.

P. × hillieri 'Spire' (M). See p. 46.

PYRUS CALLERYANA 'CHANTICLEER' (M). A pyramidal-shaped pear with white flowers in April and leaves which persist into December.

QUERCUS ROBUR 'FASTIGIATA' (L). A columnar form of the common oak.

SORBUS AUCUPARIA 'FASTIGIATA' (M). The narrow-growing, upright mountain ash.

S. scopulina of gardens (S) (syn. *S. americana nana*). A slow-growing, narrow, upright tree of uncertain origin with dark green leaves and large sealing-wax red fruits.

S. × thuringiaca 'Fastigiata' (S). Closely arranged upright branches, lobed leaves and scarlet fruits.

Evergreen Trees

ARBUTUS × ANDRACHNOIDES (M). Whitish, pitcher-shaped flowers in autumn and winter. See p. 49.

A. menziesii (M). Large, glossy green leaves with panicles of whitish-green flowers followed by orange-red fruits. See p. 49.

A. unedo (S), the strawberry tree. Pinkish-white to red flowers borne at the same time in late autumn and winter as the red, strawberry-like fruits. See p. 49.

AZARA MICROPHYLLA (S). Dainty small dark green leaves with yellow vanilla-scented tiny flowers in early spring.

BUXUS SEMPERVIRENS (S). The common box.

COTONEASTER 'CORNUBIA' (S). Can be trained to form a single-stemmed small tree. Masses of bright red fruits.

C. × watereri 'John Waterer' (S). A similar small tree to the above. Both may become partially defoliated in a severe winter.

EUCALYPTUS GUNNII (L). The hardiest member of the genus. Silvery-blue leaves. Others which have given good results are *E. niphophila* (S), *E. parvifolia* (M), *E. pauciflora* (S) and *E. urnigera* (M).

EUCRYPHIA × NYMANSENSIS 'NYMANSAY' (M). Masses of large white flowers in August.

GRISELINIA LITTORALIS (M). This New Zealander is seen as a tree where the climate is not severe, and is worth experimenting with for hardiness.

ILEX AQUIFOLIUM (Holly) (L). The common holly is a first-class evergreen growing up to over 50ft(15m) high. There are numerous cultivars suitable for small gardens, and the mature collection at the Royal Botanic Gardens, Kew and the newly planted one at Wisley should be studied.

The Award of Garden Merit has been given by the Royal Horticultural Society to: *Ilex × altaclarensis* 'Golden King' (S), *I. aquifolium* 'Argentea Marginata' (S), *I. aquifolium* 'Golden Queen' (S), *I. aquifolium* 'Handsworth New Silver' (S), *I. aquifolium* 'Madame Briot' (S), and *I. aquifolium* 'Pyramidalis (S). The last-mentioned is a free-berrying variety even when planted alone.

LIGUSTRUM LUCIDUM (S). A fine evergreen privet with dark, shining leaves and large panicles of white flowers in August and September.

PHILLYREA LATIFOLIA (S). Resembles the olive tree. Dull white flowers in spring. Good specimens up to 20ft(6m) high grow in the cold climate of East Anglia.

PITTOSPORUM TENUIFOLIUM (M). Pale green, wavy edged leaves, much in demand as cut branches by florists.

PRUNUS LUSITANICA (M). The Portugal laurel. Usually grown as a bush but makes a fine small tree with masses of white, scented flowers in June.

STRANVAESIA DAVIDIANA (S). Can be trained into a most attractive small tree. Some leaves turn bright red in the autumn. Bunches of bright red fruits.

28. Eucryphia ×
nymanensis 'Nymansay'

Trees for Alkaline Soils

Sometimes one comes across trees unexpectedly thriving in alkaline soils. An example is the large *Arbutus × andrachnoides* at Highdown in Sussex. The following are known to flourish (but most will also grow in other soils): *Acer campestre, Acer cappadocicum, Acer griseum, Acer grosseri, Acer × lobelii, Acer negundo, Acer platanoides, Acer pseudoplatanus* 'Brilliantissimum', *Aesculus × carnea* 'Briotii', *Aesculus indica, Alnus incana* 'Aurea', *Amelanchier lamarckii, Arbutus × andrachnoides, Arbutus unedo, Azara microphylla, Betula pendula* (L), *Buxus sempervirens, Carpinus betulus* 'Columnaris' and *C.b.* 'Fastigiata', *Catalpa bignonioides, Cercis siliquastrum, Cornus mas, Cotoneaster* 'Cornubia' and *C. × watereri* 'John Waterer', *Crataegus* (all), *Davidia involucrata, Eucalyptus gunnii, Eucryphia × nymansensis* 'Nymansay', *Fagus sylvatica* 'Purpurea Pendula', *Fraxinus* (all), *Gleditsia triacanthos* 'Sunburst', *Griselinia littoralis, Hippophae rhamnoides, Ilex* (all), *Koelreuteria paniculata, Laburnum* (all), *Ligustrum lucidum, Liriodendron tulipifera, Magnolia kobus, Magnolia × loebneri, Malus* (all), *Parrotia persica, Pittosporum tenuifolium, Prunus* (all), *Pyrus calleryana* 'Chanticleer', *Pyrus salicifolia* 'Pendula', *Robinia × hillieri, Salix* (all), *Sophora japonica* 'Pendula', and *Sorbus aria* 'Lutescens'.

Trees for Seaside Gardens

Arbutus unedo, Cotoneaster 'Cornubia' and *C. × watereri* 'John Waterer', *Eucalyptus gunnii, Fraxinus ornus, Griselinia littoralis, Ilex × altaclarensis* and cvs., *Ilex aquifolium* and cvs., *Phillyrea latifolia, Quercus ilex* (L), evergreen oak, *Salix aegyptiaca, Salix alba* f. *argentea* (syn. *S.a.* 'Sericea'), *Salix daphnoides, Sorbus aria* 'Lutescens' and *Sorbus aucuparia*.

Trees for Gardens in Industrial Areas

Acer platanoides, Aesculus × carnea 'Briotii', *Amelanchier lamarckii, Betula pendula* (L), *Carpinus betulus* 'Columnaris' and *C.b.* 'Fastigiata', *Catalpa bignonioides, Crataegus × lavallei, Crataegus oxyacantha* and cvs., *Fraxinus ornus, Laburnum* (all), *Magnolia kobus, Magnolia × loebneri, Magnolia × soulangiana*,

Malus (all), *Prunus × amygdalo-persica* 'Pollardii', *Prunus avium* 'Plena', *Prunus cerasifera* and cvs., *Prunus dulcis, Prunus* (Japanese cherries), *Prunus padus* 'Watereri', *Sorbus aria* and cvs., and *Sorbus aucuparia* and cvs.

Trees for Individual Lawn Specimens

Acer griseum, Acer grosseri var. *hersii, Acer negundo* 'Auratum', *Acer platanoides* 'Crimson King', *Aesculus indica* and *A. indica* 'Sydney Pearce', *Alnus incana* 'Aurea', *Arbutus unedo, Betula pendula* 'Dalecarlica', *Betula pendula* 'Youngii', *Cercidiphyllum japonicum, Fraxinus excelsior* 'Jaspidea', *Ilex aquifolium* 'Argentea Marginata', *Liriodendron tulipifera* 'Fastigiatum', *Prunus avium* 'Plena', *Prunus* 'Pink Perfection', *Prunus serrula, Prunus* 'Shimidsu Sakura', *Pyrus salicifolia* 'Pendula', *Robinia pseudoacacia* 'Frisia', *Sophora japonica* 'Pendula', *Sorbus aria* 'Lutescens', *Sorbus aucuparia* 'Aspleniifolia', *Sorbus sargentiana*, and *Sorbus vilmorinii*.

5.

Conifers for Gardens

Conifers, unfortunately, are poorly represented among our native plants. We have, in fact, just three species, the Scots pine, *Pinus sylvestris*, the common juniper, *Juniperus communis*, and the common yew, *Taxus baccata*, although several other species are today very obviously part of the British landscape, due mainly to the efforts of the forester. Even with these additions we have a very mean share of this remarkable group of woody plants which, in the main, hail from the temperate regions of the world and, in particular, the Northern Temperate regions.

If we lack a variety of conifers in our landscape, native or otherwise, we are not lacking in introduced species which are well represented in our gardens, pineta and parks. The great plant collectors have been responsible for the introduction of a wealth of species beginning with those from the eastern American seaboard, circa 1600; the cedar of Lebanon, *Cedrus libani*, and numerous European species following rapidly. The flow continued with many exciting and very special species being introduced from Asia and Western America, two of the richest areas of the world for conifers suitable for the British Isles. In our own lifetime the fossil-age dawn redwood, *Metasequoia glyptostroboides*, has appeared, having been rediscovered in China in 1941.

While the wild species are of the greatest importance it is from the numerous cultivars (selections made by man in the main in a horticultural and arboricultural environment) that we draw the greatest wealth of conifers for gardens, parks and ornamental plantings. For these we owe much to observant nurserymen and gardeners, both amateur and professional, whose keen eyes have noted, selected, assessed and grown the seedling mutations and sports. From this source have come the great range of dwarf and slow-growing forms, the variegated gold and silver selections, those with fine blue foliage and, perhaps the most important group of all, the cultivars with narrow, upright or weeping habits.

Considering the evergreen trees and shrubs which are available for use in our gardens, conifers rank well to the fore. While, in the main, they lack showy flowers their great variety of colour, form and adaptability provides ample compensation. When used in our gardens or, for that matter, in a landscape on a grander scale, one of the main contributions made by conifers is the addition of "strength" to the planting. This is particularly noticeable when they are associated with deciduous trees and shrubs, either intermixed or used as a background.

As with any permanent planting the greatest care should be taken when choosing a conifer or group of conifers for a given site. Consideration concerning the speed of growth and ultimate height and spread are of prime importance for it is a sad and all-too-frequent occurrence that the heartbreaking decision has to be made whether or not to remove a tree which has out-grown its allotted position. It is all the more difficult to make such a decision when the tree in question is a stately, well-grown conifer. In view of the slow development of many conifers, and of the fact that they rely so much on having a near-perfect, uncluttered outline, an alternative plan may be adopted. This again needs very careful thought. Having placed the permanent, long-term specimens, short-term additions can be made which will add further enjoyment for a number of years and, of course, act as nurses for the choicer subjects, much as is practised in forestry. In this case, a wide range of ornamental conifers could be used, possibly of lesser value than the main planting. It is imperative that the plan should be adhered to. This plan could also apply to groups of dwarf and slow-growing conifers or stately forest species. Mixtures of deciduous trees and shrubs and conifers could also be used in this manner. It is proposed now to consider the various uses of conifers with particular emphasis on the smaller garden (up to ½ an acre [.205 hectare] in extent), for very few of today's garden owners have space to plant extensive arboreta or pineta.

Conifers are predominately informal in appearance and very few lend themselves to a formal setting. Notable exceptions are the column-forming cultivars. The Irish yew, *Taxus baccata* 'Fastigiata', is a good example of this category, and here also must be included conifers which have been clipped into formal hedge form. Great care should be taken to keep natural plantings of conifers well away from areas of the garden devoted to formal bedding schemes, hybrid roses (wild roses associate extremely well), dahlias and similar plantings.

Dwarf and Slow-growing Conifers

At a time when nurserymen's catalogues are being drastically reduced in content, the gardener will still find a great wealth of dwarf and slow-growing conifers available. This is a popular and exciting group of conifers which are ideally suited to smaller gardens.

The numbers of really dwarf conifers which are available, however – forms attaining a maximum of 2ft(60cm) or so after many years – are very few. It is intended to include those conifers which can be described as slow-growing (ultimate height 6ft[2m]) to the list, thus providing a really wide choice for use in our gardens. It is important to remember that a species or cultivar may well have taken as much as 50 years to attain 6ft(2m) – a very long time, even in gardening where patience and foresight is all-important.

Most dwarf conifers are the results of selection by observant enthusiasts, either as seedling mutations or from sports of species or existing cultivars. Others are true species or variations from mountainous areas which have adapted naturally to an alpine environment. Many dwarf conifer enthusiasts practise a little careful pruning. This is quite admissible, and, in many cases, necessary, provided that skill and great care is taken in carrying it out. The aim is to remove rank growth which appears occasionally – in a few cultivars far too frequently – and maintain the dwarf character for many more years. The operation should consist of stopping and pinching out odd growths and definitely not be an overall shearing.

The uses of dwarf and slow-growing conifers are numerous. First and foremost they have, quite rightly, a great appeal to the alpine gardener. Planted in limited numbers as feature shrubs in the rock garden they add interest at all seasons. Here, as with the planting of all conifers, very careful consideration must be given to the ultimate height and spread, for scale is all-important in the rock garden. Ultimate development must be limited to the size of area. Luckily, the numbers of dwarf conifers available with an ultimate height of 6in(15cm) to 6ft(2m) are legion. While reliable dwarfs should be chosen for the main area of the rock garden, conifers with an ultimate height of 4 to 6ft(1.25 to 2m) can provide a first-rate backcloth. Among the truly dwarf conifers are a range of diminutive bun-shaped cultivars which are best grown in an alpine house; outdoors, the very tight growth is often disfigured by frost and winter wet.

A "mini pinetum", a collection of dwarf and slow-growing conifers selected for their diverse form and colour would provide a very fine, and labour-saving, feature for the garden. Again care should be taken to plant conifers of appropriate size for the allotted space. While a natural, informal planting is desirable such a collection of conifers could well be presented in the more formal setting of a large bed or border. In both cases dwarf shrubs and sun-loving ground-cover could be used in association with the conifers to good effect.

There are no more suitable associates for heathers than dwarf and slow-growing forms of conifers. Heathers are essentially plants for full exposure and most conifers also provide their best form and colour in similar conditions. Conifer species and cultivars of irregular shape are more suitable for the heather garden than those with a formal outline.

There is always much interest in plants suitable for ground-cover and here again there are a good range of conifers which are suitable. The robust, spreading junipers (see pp.60 and 61, and Chapter 12, "Ground-Cover Plants", pp.129 to 137) are good examples of those conifers which provide dense and attractive ground-cover. This type of conifer is more than capable of choking weed growth and covering effectively unsightly banks, drain covers and the like.

The Taller Conifers

Still on the theme of conifers for the smaller garden, only those attaining a reasonably narrow form and ultimate height of 50ft(15m) will be considered. Again, the uses are numerous with the taller conifers of quality making superb specimens for important positions; companion evergreen trees for mixed plantings; and effective screens and hedges, for which last purpose there is no better choice of planting material.

Apropos the ultimate size of the chosen conifer. It is very important to be most careful in this matter – or is it? Do remember that your perfect lawn specimen of 30ft(9m), while it may fit the scene perfectly at that height (because it is a comparatively small tree when fully grown) will take a life-time to attain that height. In view of this, a conifer may be chosen for the position just described which is faster growing and will provide the desired effect in perhaps half the waiting period. It is possible that the faster-growing specimen will have to be removed eventually, but far more pleasure for a far longer period will have been obtained. Clearly, a careful choice has to be made; no one would recommend a giant redwood, *Sequoia sempervirens*, for growing in a limited space, and we have all seen those Victorian monkey puzzles, *Araucaria araucana*, growing a few feet from a house!

Choosing and Planting Conifers

Great care should be taken when choosing conifers from nurseries and garden centres. Stock should be of a good healthy colour, well furnished (clothed with branches to ground level) and, where appropriate, have a strong, vigorous leader. Most stock is container-grown; make sure that the container is sufficiently large to accommodate a good root system. If open-ground plants are available, always insist that the chosen specimen is lifted with a large root ball. Many owners of new gardens are impatient and plant large specimens in the hope that an immediate effect will be gained; but caution is necessary for time and money can be wasted if the larger trees are old and tired and they fail to grow satisfactorily. The ideal planting sizes are in the region of 15 to 18in(38 to 45cm) and 18in to 2ft(45 to 60cm). For planting suggestions see the "Conifer Guide" (pp.56 to 64).

Methods of propagation have a bearing upon the price of conifers; seed-raised species are less costly than those raised from cuttings and, obviously, those propagated by grafting, which is a highly skilled and time-consuming operation, are considerably more expensive. Another factor affecting costs is speed of growth; a large, well-grown specimen of a really slow-growing dwarf conifer will command a very high price.

Remember when planting to give your new conifer the very best start in its new home, for it will provide a considerable return for many years. Prepare a 3ft(1m) hole, two spits deep, and mix a generous quantity of well-rotted manure, compost and peat, or leafmould with the soil which will be used to refill the hole. The soil should be well-firmed around the plant's roots, and the plant should be staked if this is necessary. The area around the tree should be kept weed free and be mulched for at least three years.

Notable Collections of Conifers

It is a good plan, before making a final decision on what to plant, to pay a visit to a pinetum, arboretum or garden of note to assess the garden value of conifers. Perhaps the most notable and useful such establishment to visit in Britain is the National Pinetum at Bedgebury, near Hawkhurst, Kent. Bedgebury clearly does not enjoy the favourable climate of the western seaboard; in fact, the conditions are decidedly hard and the results are of particular interest to those who garden in areas which are not favoured by the Gulf Stream. The National Pinetum, as would be expected, contains an exceptionally fine range of conifers of all sizes, both species and cultivars.

Many conifers, both large and small, are grown at the Royal Botanic Gardens, Kew and, for an even finer collection, Kew's country home, Wakehurst Place, near Haywards Heath, Sussex, should be visited. Other great gardens in the Sussex Weald with important plantings of conifers are Borde Hill, also near Haywards Heath; Leonardslee, near Horsham; Nymans, Handcross, and Sheffield Park, near Uckfield (particularly fine).

Reference has been made to our favourable western seaboard, and, as would be expected, Devon and Cornwall both have their share of gardens with excellent conifer collections. Scotland too has much to offer the conifer enthusiast, both in the milder west and further inland where the mountain ranges produce a high rainfall, conditions which many conifers enjoy. The Royal Horticultural Society's garden at Wisley also has a great deal to offer in this respect – a pinetum of note, dwarf conifers in several areas of the garden and a display of conifer hedges. The Savill and Valley Gardens in Windsor Great Park are not far from Wisley and are also very much on the conifer map. If travelling from a distance by car, both could be visited on the same day. Like Wisley, these gardens are on dry soil with a comparatively low rainfall. The Valley Gardens contain the greatest number of conifers in a large, well-stocked pinetum and throughout the gardens generally. A recent development is the establishment in the Valley Garden of a dwarf and slow-growing conifer collection. This collection adjoins the large heather garden which also contains a number of good conifers, and will eventually absorb an area of 10 acres(4.05 hectares). There are obviously many more fine plantings in Britain which should be visited. Many nurseries have good plantings of conifers.

CONIFER GUIDE

ABIES (silver fir) The silver firs, *Abies* species and their forms, are among the finest and grandest of conifers. Unfortunately they are, in the main, far too large for the smaller garden. All of the species are broadly pyramidal with a near-perfect outline when young, often becoming irregular in outline with age. Their foliage, almost without exception, is handsome, with intense silver on the reverse. The cones, when produced, are quite outstanding and are held upright on the flattened branches.

There are a number of cultivars of the European silver fir, *Abies alba*, but very few are of real garden value and they are rarely offered by nurserymen. Two forms of *A. balsamea*, the North American balsam fir, are among the most popular dwarf conifers. *A. balsamea* 'Hudsonia' and *A.b.* 'Nana' both grow into mounds of dark green and are totally reliable.

Abies cephalonica 'Meyer's Dwarf' a variety of the Grecian fir, is eventually flat-topped and spreading to an ultimate height of 3 to 5ft(1 to 1.5m). It is well worth placing in an important focal position in any garden, large or small. *A. concolor* 'Glauca Compacta' is probably the only dwarf form of the Colorado fir likely to be found in the nursery trade, and then only in specialist catalogues.

One species, *A. koreana*, hails from the mountainous areas of Korea and is, therefore, a good example of a natural, slower-growing conifer. It is extremely variable and in some forms can attain 30ft(9m) or so; others will remain really dwarf. This species is well furnished with very pretty foliage and as a bonus produces cones when quite small, often when 2 to 3ft(60cm to 1m) high. There are several dwarf cultivars, all of which are well worth hunting for in the nursery trade.

5. *Foliage effects can often be of greater garden value than rather fleeting floral beauty. In this detail in a mixed border the grey-leaved lamb's ear,* Stachys byzantina *(syn.* S. lanata*), complements perfectly the spreading* Viburnum davidii *with its deeply veined leaves, while dominating all is* Acer negundo *'Auratum' with its creamy-yellow leaf variegation. Background colour in this early-summer scene is provided by* Nepeta *(catmint), the lovely* Geranium psilostemon *and tall bearded irises.*

6. *Junipers like* Juniperus x media 'Pfitzerana' *and* J. x media 'Pfitzerana Aurea' *(middle distance and foreground) make superb ground cover in reasonably spacious surrounds (see pp.61 and 135).*

7. *What could be more beautiful than this mid-winter scene in which the eye is carried beyond the flowers of* Hamamelis mollis 'Pallida' *(see p.67) to the sweep of winter-flowering cultivars of* Erica herbacea *(syn.* E. carnea) *in the Heather Garden at Wisley.*

8. Cotoneaster *'Rothschildianus', one of the finest of the yellow-fruited cultivars provided by this genus (see p.75).*

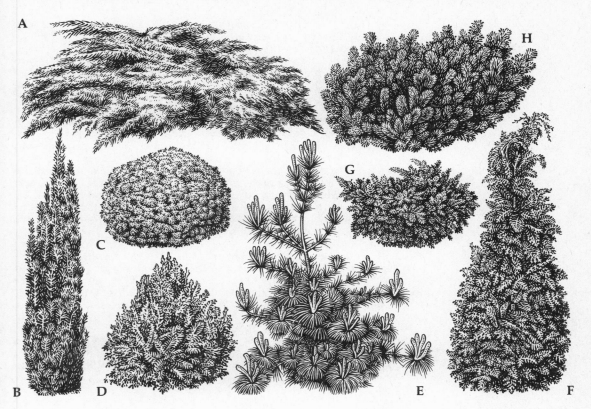

Two more conifers from high mountains are *A. lasiocarpa*, the Rocky Mountains fir, and its variety *arizonica*. Both will grow slowly to a height of 60 to 70ft(18 to 21m) but, in spite of their eventual height, they have distinct possibilities for smaller planting areas in view of their extremely slim, pyramidal outline. Again there are, as is inevitable with montane species, several dwarf selections.

Golden foliage is scarce among the cultivars of the silver firs. *A. nordmanniana* 'Golden Spreader' is most attractive and one to be searched for. The habit is low-spreading, and it appears to be completely reliable as a dwarf.

CEDRUS (cedar) If we think of cedars we almost certainly picture a great specimen of *Cedrus libani*, the cedar of Lebanon – growing in parkland or in a similar position – or the slightly smaller, but still substantial, *C. atlantica* f. *glauca*, displaying its fine blue foliage to advantage. All too often the last-named is to be found in far too confined conditions.

Of the four species of *Cedrus*, only *C. brevifolia* is suitable for the half-acre (.205 hectare) garden. It is another mountain species (from Cyprus) and is variable when raised from seed. If the secateurs are used sparingly and carefully, a very desirable, slow-growing specimen can be produced. A little judicious pruning can help produce yet another attractive cedar, *Cedrus deodara* 'Pendula'. This should be a large, graceful tree; it is invariably encountered as a tumbling mound, and with the timely removal of the few ascending branches this form can be maintained.

The cedar of Lebanon has at least one good dwarf offspring. This is *C. libani* 'Comte de Dijon' which, in the course of time, grows into a stocky shrub with a height of 9ft(3m) or so and a 6ft(2m) spread.

CHAMAECYPARIS (false cypress) The genus *Chamaecyparis* must provide the greatest number of suitable conifers for the smaller garden. If this is true of

29. *Shapes in conifers:* Juniperus × media *'Pfitzerana'* (A)*;* Taxus baccata *'Fastigiata'* (B)*;* Chamaecyparis pisifera *'Nana'* (C)*;* Chamaecyparis lawsoniana *'Pygmaea Argentea'* (D)*;* Pinus parviflora (E)*;* Chamaecyparis lawsoniana *'Stewartii'* (F)*;* Juniperus squamata *'Blue Star'* (G)*; and* Pinus mugo (H)*.*

the genus as a whole, then *C. lawsoniana* certainly ranks as the most prolific of any coniferous species and, for that matter, any hardy tree or shrub. The numerous cultivars have originated as seedling mutations and to a lesser extent as branch sports. The results are extremely variable; dwarfs of 12 to 15in(30 to 38cm) are known and great trees of 75ft(22.5m) or so and, of course, every height in between. While many of these are very good there are legions of stereotyped, rather ordinary forms, and a degree of discretion is needed when deciding which to grow.

Let us consider first the tall cultivars of *C. lawsoniana* – those with an ultimate height of at least 6ft(2m) and a maximum of 40 to 50ft(12 to 15m) after many years. Golden foliage is, quite rightly, much in demand, and there are numerous cultivars with such colouring to choose from. The following are among the finest: 'Golden Wonder'; 'Hillieri', slower-growing than some; 'Lanei', a very pretty and reliable small tree; 'Lutea'; 'Naberi', a most attractive form with a mixture of sulphur-yellow and blue foliage; 'Smithii'; 'Stewartii', totally reliable; and the more recently introduced 'Winston Churchill'. A cultivar with a different form, 'Westermanii', is a densely branched golden type with pendent branchlets. The overall effect is very pretty and distinct.

There are also a number of cultivars with splashed variegation which are sometimes available in the nursery trade. Their use in the garden is a matter of taste. The clear golden forms are considered by many to be more desirable. If there are a large number of golden forms it is not surprising that there are even more with blue foliage, as the species usually has a blue-green appearance overall. A short list of those which are readily available should include 'Allumii', which is possibly inferior to some new introductions; 'Columnaris' and the very similar 'Grayswood Pillar', two excellent narrow "blue flames"; f. *glauca* (many good seedlings have been named with this prefix); 'Triompf van Boskoop', when well-grown, quite lovely, looser and more graceful than most; and 'Wisselii', which must be considered one of the best of the "Lawsons". The branches of 'Wisselii' are held radially in cocks-comb form, and for an added bonus the crowds of red male flowers contrast wonderfully with steely-blue foliage. 'Triompf van Boskoop' also produces red male flowers with similar effect.

In common with several other coniferous genera a number of juvenile-foliaged forms of *C. lawsoniana* have occurred, the foliage being awl-shaped and open and distinct from the normal flattened, scale-like leaves. The widely grown 'Ellwoodii' is such a form, again blue in colour and darkening in winter to steely-blue. Beware, for it is frequently offered as a dwarf, although it will quickly attain 20ft(6m) in height, plus. It is inevitable with a plant which has been propagated in such numbers that several good sports should have occurred. 'Chilworth Silver' has paler foliage and possibly a more dwarf habit, and 'Ellwood's Gold' is a very worthy addition to the range. Equally popular is 'Fletcheri', again juvenile but stronger growing than the previously described cultivars. It will rapidly attain 40ft(12m). Again, there are several named sports of this popular "blue".

The upright green selections of *C. lawsoniana* are valuable architectural forms which are completely hardy in comparison with the Italian cypress, *Cupressus sempervirens*, which is far from reliable in our climate. Once again a warning; cultivars of *C. lawsoniana* like 'Erecta Viridis' and 'Pottenii' have numerous ascending branches which are liable to become bare at the base very early in life. If this happens, the bare areas, sadly, never refurnish themselves; the branches also tend to fall open following a gale or heavy snowfall. Two post-war introductions, 'Green Pillar' and 'Green Spire', are completely reliable and should be chosen in preference to these forms. 'Kilmacurragh' is an even finer cultivar with a single main stem and short side growths which are not harmed by snow or wind. The foliage is dark, rich green and the ultimate height is 30ft(9m).

The weeping forms offer a complete contrast to the formal columns previously described, and none is more graceful than 'Filiformis', a "whipcord" type with a weeping habit. A heavier, more normally foliaged specimen, 'Intertexta', grows with age into a fine, noble tree. Several forms will be found in nurseries and garden centres labelled 'Pendula', and most

30. Chamaecyparis lawsoniana *'Wisselii'*.

of these are worth a place in the garden.

Chamaecyparis lawsoniana is much used for formal hedges, responding well to annual shearing. If seed-raised stock is used – and it is far less costly than named cultivars – a hedge showing considerable variation of colour, and possibly form, is usually produced which may be acceptable to some gardeners. If a formal hedge of one colour is preferred, one of the suitable cultivars should be chosen. Here again, the gardener should heed the warning made previously concerning the tendency for some cultivars to become bare at the base. This would be particularly undesirable in a hedge. The dark green cultivar 'Green Hedger' is a superb selection and far superior to any other for this purpose.

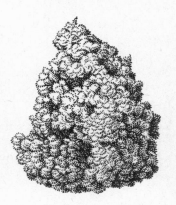

31. Chamaecyparis obtusa *'Nana Gracilis'*.

To digress for a moment, let us consider other conifers which may rival the Lawson's cypress for hedging. The common yew, *Taxus baccata*, is by far the best choice for a truly formal hedge. It is more tolerant of shearing than any other conifer and can be "stopped" at a height of 4ft(1.25m). A height of 6ft(2m) is more usual for other hedging conifers. Two thujas, *Thuja occidentalis* and *T. plicata*, show very little variation in colour and are strong contenders for use as a formal hedge. Both have a number of forms which are also suitable for this purpose.

To return to the Lawson's cypress, and in particular the dwarf and slower-growing forms (ultimate height 6ft[2m]), tiny forms are uncommon, but two, 'Gnome' and 'Green Globe', are recent arrivals which eventually grow into small bun form. It is difficult to accept that this great species as seen in the wild can produce such tiny forms. Of green or blue-green selections, 'Gimbornii', 'Minima', 'Minima Glauca', 'Nana' and 'Nana Glauca' are all reliable, first-class, slow-growing conifers which will eventually reach a height of 3 to 4ft(1 to 1.25m) and be broadly pyramidal in outline. Of similar colour and size, but very different in form, are 'Caudata' and 'Forsteckensis'; both are irregular in outline.

Gold- and silver-foliaged cultivars also feature here, and the following are excellent coloured variants of the green pyramidal forms described above: 'Aurea Densa', 'Lutea Nana' and 'Nana Aurea', all fine golds, and 'Pygmaea Argentea', with pretty silver variegation.

There is also an extremely useful group of cultivars with wide-spreading branches and a height of 3 to 4ft(1 to 1.25m) or so. All are blue-green and all are superb "architectural" shrubs. In addition, they are useful for ground-cover purposes. Those to search for are 'Dow's Gem', 'Knowefieldensis' and 'Tamariscifolia'.

The Nootka cypress, *Chamaecyparis nootkatensis*, although a very fine species with a few excellent forms, is best suited to gardens and arboreta of larger size.

The remarks concerning the above species certainly do not apply to the Japanese species, *Chamaecyparis obtusa*. This has produced a wealth of first-class offspring which are the favourites of dwarf and slow-growing conifer enthusiasts throughout the world. The species is seldom available today but a wide range of its numerous cultivars are much to the fore in nurserymen's catalogues, particularly specialist lists. Beginning with the taller cultivars, 'Crippsii' is a first-rate golden form, indeed, probably the best golden chamaecyparis for the smaller garden. Typical of the species, it eventually grows to a height of 30ft(9m) or so. For something different – and many of the *obtusa* cultivars are different – 'Filicoides', when well grown, is distinctive and quite beautiful. The branches are presented in fern-frond style, the foliage is deep green and the ultimate height is 15ft(4.5)m. Although the name suggests "dwarf", 'Nana Gracilis' will eventually attain 10ft(3m) in height. This outstanding form with dark green foliage held in neat shell-like sprays should, without doubt, be represented in every garden and conifer collection. Turning again to golden foliage, 'Tetragona Aurea' is an exciting form of great merit. The branchlets have a close, mossy appearance and are borne on a large shrub of up to 20ft(6m) in height in a most attractive manner.

The really true dwarf forms of *C. obtusa* are numerous and many are collector's pieces. Most are best suited to alpine house conditions, winter wet playing havoc with the close, tight, mossy foliage. Of those suitable for the garden 'Kosteri' is a distinctive deep green form; 'Nana' is superb, but be sure to obtain the true form and not the much faster growing 'Nana Gracilis'; 'Pygmaea' takes on an attractive winter mantle of bronze, and 'Repens' is a particularly well-named, spreading form.

Again, a range of coloured forms of *C. obtusa* are in commerce. 'Mariesii' is heavily variegated with white and a very pretty, slow-growing shrub; 'Nana Aurea' is a superb golden dwarf; 'Nana Lutea' a paler clear gold; 'Pygmaea Aurescens' bronze-gold, darker in winter and a most interesting recent arrival from New Zealand; and 'Fernspray Gold' – also from New Zealand – is well named.

A large number of forms of *Chamaecyparis pisifera* have been named. This is yet another species from Japan and again it is extremely variable. Neither this nor its cultivars are as important as those previously described but one dwarf domed-shaped cultivar of real value is *C. pisifera* 'Nana' (illustrated on p. 57).

CRYPTOMERIA JAPONICA (Japanese cedar)   *Cryptomeria japonica* is too large for the smaller garden, and again there are many forms both large and small. The named tall forms are as unsuitable as the species for growing in a limited space, with the possible exception of the juvenile-foliaged 'Elegans', which is always attractive. The red-bronze winter colouring provides a fine addition to the winter scene.

Many of the slow-growing forms also take on attractive winter colouring, particularly if they are planted in full exposure. The following are usually available: 'Bandai-Sugi' (syn. 'Nana'), an excellent 4ft(1.25m) shrub with distinctive contorted growth, eventually growing into a specimen of great character; 'Globosa Nana', a greener dome of attractively presented branchlets, and making a shrub of 4 by 4ft(1.25 by 1.25m) when fully grown; 'Jindai-Sugi' a dense, small, tight, slow-growing specimen of 4 to 5ft(1.25 to 1.5m); 'Spiralis', a dome of twisted branchlets; and the much dwarfer 'Vilmoriniana', eventually 2 by 2ft(60 by 60cm) and extremely well coloured in winter.

× **CUPRESSOCYPARIS LEYLANDII (Leyland cypress)**   Probably the fastest growing and most satisfactory conifer for use as a screening evergreen is the intergeneric hybrid × *Cupressocyparis leylandii*. Thousands of reasonably priced plants are used annually and there is no doubt that this conifer has no rival where a quick return is required and when the need arises for a good dense screen. Eventually far too large for the smaller garden, plans should be made to use the Leyland cypress as a "nurse" for a more suitable long-term, slower-growing screen. It grows rapidly into a fine broad column, eventually up to 75ft(22.5m) tall. As to the choice of nursery stock, choose containerised plants of 1½ to 2ft(45 to 60cm) or 2 to 3ft(60cm to 1m) in height; larger stock can be more difficult to establish and smaller plants will rapidly overtake recently planted tall plants.

CUPRESSUS (cypress)   The true cypresses have among their ranks a number of highly desirable species and cultivars of medium growth. *Cupressus glabra* 'Pyramidalis', a grey blue cone of 30ft(9m) makes an excellent specimen when well established. *Cupressus macrocarpa* was once used extensively as a cheap hedging plant; it is now rarely offered for such purposes, it being recognised as useless, mainly because of its intense dislike of the shears. The species has produced a number of very good golden forms, some having attractive juvenile foliage; 'Donard Gold' and 'Goldcrest' are the ones most usually available. If you live in a mild area or your garden is particularly well sheltered, the Italian cypress, *Cupressus sempervirens*, can be used with confidence. This is the characteristic slim, dark green column which is such a part of the Mediterranean landscape. If this species is unsuitable, as it is throughout much of Britain, for climatic reasons, then turn to Lawson's cypress of similar habit (see p.58) which will be equally useful and totally reliable.

JUNIPERUS (juniper)   The large genus *Juniperus* has much to offer the gardener. Junipers are usually tough, hardy inhabitants of poor soil and hard conditions. A good example is, of course, *Juniperus communis*, one of the three British native conifers.

Juniperus chinensis and its cultivars are typically small, narrow, conical trees, many with very prickly juvenile leaves. Grey-green to blue is the general colouring. Most of the forms which are available are well worth a place in the garden, particularly if small sentinel specimens are required.

Almost certainly the conifer with the greatest distribution range is the wild *J. communis*, which is to be found throughout the major part of the Northern Temperate regions. The many named forms are usually ground-hugging or low prostrate and are ideally suited for ground-covering purposes. Happy in any soil, the following are among the best low forms which are to be found in the nursery trade: 'Depressa Aurea', very pretty, particularly in its winter colour; 'Hornibrookii' and the very similar 'Prostrata', both truly contour following; and the slightly taller 'Repanda'. There are several forms of *J. communis* which are upright rather formal columns, 'Compressa' for instance, being the diminutive Noah's Ark juniper. A good choice for a rock or sink garden, it will eventually attain 2ft(60cm) in height. The Irish juniper, *J. communis* 'Hibernica', will grow to an eventual height of 10ft(3m) and is obviously much faster growing than 'Compressa'. There are several other intermediates.

For the very best ground-hugging weed suppressors there are no more suitable contenders then the numerous cultivars of the North American *J. horizontalis*. The foliage colours range from grey-green to excellent blues, and many take on an attractive winter mantle of bronze. No attempt will be made to suggest which are the best cultivars; hunt through the nursery catalogues and garden centres and select the living carpet which has the greatest appeal. Most will cover a square yard(m^2) or more in a matter of three or four years.

Perhaps the most popular and useful junipers are to be found in the hybrid group *J. × media*. The range of strong cultivars which grow to a height of 4 to 6ft(1.25 to 2m) with spreading branches extending from 6 to 20ft(2 to 6m) have many uses. They are obviously of great value architecturally, capable of covering a large unsightly area, or of clothing a difficult bank and they will certainly choke strong weed growth. The grey-blue *J. × media* 'Pfitzerana' is the best example; if smaller editions are required, and it must be made clear that 'Pfitzerana' will very rapidly attain the maximum measurements, then a choice should be made from the following: 'Armstrongii' with pale green foliage; 'Gold Coast', 'Old Gold' and 'Pfitzerana Aurea' which are all golden and all comparatively slow-growing; and 'Pfitzerana Compacta', a 3 by 6ft(1 by 2m) version of 'Pfitzerana'.

Two taller junipers are the graceful *J. recurva coxii*, the Chinese coffin tree, which will slowly attain 25ft(7.5m) in Britain, and is well worth planting in a reasonably sheltered position, and *J. rigida*, which is a native of Japan, Korea and north China; this will eventually grow into a most attractive small, open-branched tree. *J. rigida* would make an ideal specimen for a lawn where something "different" is required. *Juniperus sabina* and its cultivars are again predominately low, spreading shrubs, perhaps best described as mini versions of 'Pfitzerana'. *J. sabina* 'Tamariscifolia' is by far the best and quickly grows into an excellent 9 to 12in(23 to 30cm) high grey-green carpet. This cultivar is the best choice to cover an unsightly drain and it has, of course, many other uses. *J. scopulorum*, a native of the western half of the United States, makes a narrow pyramid of medium height. Many named selections of this species have been made by American growers, most of them silver-grey pyramids with an ultimate height of 20ft(6m) or thereabouts.

It will be clear by now that grey-green and grey-blue are the predominant colours of conifers, and *J. squamata* is no exception for there are some outstanding "blues" among its forms. 'Meyeri' grows fairly rapidly to a height of 10 to 12ft(3 to 3.75m) and is, perhaps, the finest of all blue conifers of moderate size. 'Blue Carpet', as its name suggests, is quite prostrate and 'Blue Star' is a slow-growing, compact shrub of 2 by 2ft(60 by 60cm), a true dwarf and a very good blue.

LARIX (larch) The larches, (members of the genus *Larix*) which are deciduous conifers, are beautiful, both in their spring green and golden autumn colour. The gardener should be aware, however, that all larches eventually grow to a large size and they are also the hungriest of trees.

METASEQUOIA (dawn redwood) The dawn redwood, *Metasequoia glyptostroboides*, is more than worthy of mention here. Like the larches, it is deciduous, and it requires a good moisture-retaining soil. Like the larches, too, the young growth is most attractive. The autumn colour is orange-brown and adds much to the garden scene at that time. This fossil-age tree was introduced into British gardens in 1948, having, as mentioned earlier, been re-discovered in China in 1941. The tallest trees in cultivation are now 60ft(18m) or so tall and narrowly pyramidal in outline.

PICEA (spruce) The spruces, *Picea* species, are all narrowly or broadly pyramidal in outline. Most species are very ornamental but, sadly, are unsuitable for smaller gardens. Several of the species have a number of forms in the smaller tree category, however, and there are numerous dwarf and slow-growing selections.

Picea abies, the Norway spruce (which is familiar to everybody as the Christmas tree), rapidly attains a height of 100ft(30m) or more and is widely planted by foresters. It has a very large number of dwarf and slow-growing forms ranging from the diminutive 'Little Gem', eventually 9 to 12in(23 to 30cm) high and 15in(38cm) across, to 'Remontii' which will grow to a compact 6ft(2m) with, needless to state, forms of every size and shape in between these two. Among the smaller, tall cultivars 'Aurea' is a pretty golden form; 'Cupressina', a distinctive narrow form; 'Finedonensis', a silver form of the greatest charm, and f. *pendula* 'Inversa', pendulous in habit.

Picea brewerana is always in demand, attaining eventually a height of 45ft(14m) or a little more. In Britain this species is rather slow-growing, compared with other species of spruce, and, if raised from seed, which is preferable, a juvenile state prevails (for up to 10 years) when the tree has the appearance of a dull, rather ordinary conifer. Patience will be rewarded, however, for when bearing its adult foliage it is a most remarkable, graceful, weeping tree. The alternative method of propagation, grafting, often results in a one-sided specimen, due to weak side branches being used for scions.

One of the "bread and butter" slow-growing conifers, *P. glauca albertiana* 'Conica' eventually attains a height of 6 to 8ft(2 to 2.5m). It has a densely branched, narrowly pyramidal habit and pleasing, bright green foliage.

The Serbian spruce, *Picea omorika*, is probably too tall for the smaller garden. It is, however, an extremely slim pyramid with an eventual height of 75ft(22.5m). A well-grown specimen is always attractive, with grey-blue downswept branches which may tempt even the "half acre" gardener to find a home for just one, perhaps as a special lawn specimen. There is a good dwarf form 'Nana', but keep the secateurs handy, for it will want to grow out of its normal 4 to 5ft(1.25 to 1.5m) size.

Picea orientalis is an almost perfect, finely branched, dark green spruce, but again of large size. There are two 25ft(7.5m) forms of the species which are suitable – 'Aurea', the young growths of which are an extremely pretty gold in spring, and 'Gracilis', a slower-growing green form.

Referring again to specimens for a lawn, the good blue selections of *P. pungens* have strong claim for such a position. There are many cultivars which have been selected in European nurseries, for blue conifers are very popular in northern Europe, and 'Hoopsii', 'Kosteri', 'Moerheimii', and 'Spekii' are all similar and all good. They will all develop reasonably slowly into trees of 45ft(14m). All have to be grafted; seed-raised stock is rarely as intense in colour. Choose an evenly branched specimen and not a one-sided tree – at least four strong buds should surround the leader bud.

PINUS (pine) Everyone will be familiar with the pines, particularly the Scots pine, *Pinus sylvestris*, which is one of our three native conifers, and without a doubt the finest of the three. Many of the species ultimately

32. Picea omorika

become large trees and provide us with some most attractive ornamentals for our bigger gardens, parks and so on. Others are high mountain dwellers and consequently are more suitable for the smaller garden. There can be no doubt that the genus is well to the fore among ornamental conifers. Pines are less demanding than the broader-leaved conifers; their needle-like leaves, which are held in bundles of twos, threes or fives, are especially designed to reduce transpiration. In the wild they are always to be found on the drier sides of mountain ranges and frequently growing in poorer soil and even, in some cases, in near-desert conditions. *P. aristata*, the bristle-cone pine, is indeed a native of such conditions in the south-western states of the United States. Specimens in the wild are reputed to be the oldest living things in the world. Seed-raised stock is available in the nursery trade which will grow into bushy gnarled specimens of great character. A pretty grey-blue they will eventually grow to 8 to 10ft(2.5 to 3m) in height if grown in full exposure in gardens.

The five-needled species are certainly the most attractive of the pines; sadly, most such species are too large for smaller gardens; *P. cembra*, the arolla pine, is a possible exception and should be considered for planting. It will eventually attain a height of 40ft(12m) and is columnar in habit. A few selections are offered occasionally, including a good blue, 'Glauca'.

Pinus densiflora is the Japanese red pine and is characteristically seen in photographs and paintings of the Japanese landscape as a bushy specimen, almost bonsai-like in general appearance. The species will become large in our conditions but there is an excellent slow-growing form, 'Umbraculifera', which eventually grows into an umbrella-like shrub of 6 to 8ft(2 to 2.5m) in height. It is a fine plant.

There is an ever-increasing number of selections of *P. mugo*, the dwarf mountain pine, many superb dwarfs of great charm and value which should be used, with care, in the rock garden and similar limited spaces. The species, when seed raised, is used in great quantities as a ground-cover subject by local authorities.

The five-needled *P. parviflora*, or Japanese white pine, is a superb smaller species of irregular outline. Once again the enthusiasts (in this case Japanese enthusiasts) have named countless forms, many differing but slightly and most with difficult Japanese names. Keep a look out for the best of these forms when visiting nurseries and garden centres.

Inevitably, our native Scots pine, *P. sylvestris*, has a number of selections to its credit, and many are really first-rate dwarfs, ranging from near prostrate forms to those attaining 6 to 8ft(2 to 2.5m) in height. *P. sylvestris* 'Aurea' is taller, very slowly attaining a height of 30ft(9m). It is a most attractive small, bushy tree. In summer a normal grey-green, as winter approaches it gradually changes colour over-all to a lovely clear gold, returning to its usual colouring in spring – a most exciting happening.

Pseudotsuga The mighty Douglas fir, *Pseudotsuga menziesii*, is an important forestry tree, particularly in areas of higher rainfall. There are dwarf and slower growing forms and one, a fine compact blue form, *P. menziesii* 'Fletcheri', will eventually grow into a flat-topped, irregularly rounded specimen of 6 to 8ft(2 to 2.5m) tall and wide. One or two other distinctive forms may crop up in the nursery trade from time to time.

Sequoia With its great size the giant redwood, *Sequoia sempervirens*, has no place here but it does have a form of considerably lesser stature, 'Adpressa', which will attain 50ft(15m) in height eventually. However, if the lead growth is removed when the plant is young and a little occasional pruning is practised, a desirable slow-growing conifer of 6ft by 6ft(2m by 2m) can be produced. The foliage is smaller than that of the type tree and the young tips are prettily marked with creamy-white. A reliable dwarf, *S. sempervirens* 'Prostrata' forms an attractive mound 4ft(1.25m) tall and wide, the leaves being typical of the species but a deeper blue.

TAXODIUM (swamp cypress) The swamp cypress, *Taxodium distichum*, provides, like those other deciduous conifers the larches and the dawn redwood, fine autumn colour. This species demands moisture and will even tolerate water around the base of the tree. It will slowly attain a height of 50 to 60ft(15 to 18m) and is slim in outline, particularly when young.

TAXUS (yew) The yews, *Taxus* species, have many merits; in particular their ability to tolerate shade, their good hedging qualities and, in the case of several which are low growing, their suitability for ground-cover. The predominant colour of the yews is a sombre black-green, which had a great attraction for the Victorians. It still has a place as a backcloth to lighter plantings, or to add "strength" to a planting. For contrast, there are a number of golden-foliaged cultivars. *Taxus baccata* 'Adpressa' is an attractive, small-leaved, densely branched shrub of which there are several variations, one an excellent gold colour. *T.b* 'Dovastoniana' is a wide-spreading small tree of 15ft(4.5m) or so, the branches of which are held horizontally. A well-grown specimen is particularly attractive and again there is a golden form. The Irish yew, *T.b.* 'Fastigiata' is a familiar large shrub, often seen in churchyards. It has a very real place in the garden where a formal column is required. There are also two golden forms of similar size, around 10 to 12ft(3 to 3.7m). A third golden form, 'Standishii', of smaller stature, makes a very pretty slim column and is ideal for the small garden. Several low, spreading cultivars have been named. 'Repandens' is most often encountered.

THUJA (arbor-vitae) The thujas have already been considered as hedging subjects (see p. 59). There are also a number of excellent species and cultivars which are suitable for planting as specimens. They are all similar to the chamaecyparis in general appearance and outline.

Thuja koraiensis, the Korean arbor-vitae, is a slow-growing species, ultimately 10 to 15ft(3 to 4.5m) tall with very pretty silver undersides to the branches. An extremely hardy species from the eastern half of North America is *T. occidentalis*. The cultivars of this species are numerous and all are suitable for the smaller garden. Most of the dwarfs are rounded bun-shaped, domed, or broadly pyramidal and the taller forms are slim. There are a few golden forms, 'Rheingold' being by far the best known. 'Lutea Nana' is a recent addition to British nursery catalogues, but not as dwarf as the name suggests for it will attain a height of 8ft(2.5m) or so. Most of the cultivars take on a striking additional bronze colouring in winter which is an added attraction for the golden forms and the following slim, green selections: 'Fastigiata', 'Holmstrup', 'Pyramidalis Compacta' and 'Spiralis'. All are in the 20 to 30ft(6 to 9m) range, and all are superb sentinels which can be chosen with confidence. *Thuja orientalis* is smaller growing than the previous species. Four golden forms, 'Aurea Nana' (the smallest of the four) 'Conspicua', 'Elegantissima' and 'Semperaurea' are all very special forms and all turn a bronze colour in winter.

Thuja plicata is a much larger species which hails from the great forests of the north-western United States. The timber which is produced in great quantities is the western red cedar, which is used widely for small buildings. Dwarf and slow-growing golden forms of merit are 'Collyer's Gold', 'Cuprea', 'Rogersii' and 'Stoneham Gold' and an excellent rounded green form, 'Hillieri', provides a pleasant contrast. Tall cultivars which are suitable for specimen planting or screening are 'Aurea', 'Semperaurescens' and 'Zebrina', all golden forms of 40ft(12m) or so; 'Atrovirens' and 'Fastigiata' are two useful tall green cultivars.

TSUGA (hemlock) Finally, keep a look out for some of the excellent dwarf forms of *Tsuga canadensis*, the eastern or Canada hemlock. American enthusiasts have named many, possibly far too many, and some appear in nurseries and garden centres from time to time. The best make exciting additions to our dwarf and slow-growing conifer collections. They vary in height from 1 to 10ft(30cm to 3m) and range from tight buns and prostrate forms to weeping forms and tall pyramids.

This chapter only scratches the surface of the wealth of conifers available, but hopefully it will whet the appetite of garden makers.

6.

Shrubs for Year-Round Display

Two of the ugliest garden words to have been given us by the Victorians are rockery and shrubbery. As far as the last is concerned it suggests and invariably is a border of any length in which shrubs are set willy-nilly without consideration for ultimate effect. It further suggests a garden backwater to which shrubs of dubious origin or value are relegated, a sort of free for all. Today, the shrubbery is a rarity mainly to be found in pre-war designed parks and London squares. New schemes deserving the name are, however, occasionally found in certain housing estates and the like where a shrub's ability to keep people in or out of a given area is considered more important than any aesthetic value.

True, in a wild situation shrubs are gregarious and actually enjoy the company of others, often forming tangled thickets or low scrub. Occasionally, when wandering through such wild areas one encounters an individual shrub which, by chance or accident, having found itself isolated and free from restriction, has developed its true habit. This is the situation one should strive for in the garden. To plant shrubs in a border is fine so long as their natural habit is known beforehand and they are planted accordingly and in a way that complements rather than competes. Given the choice, however, a shrub planted in isolation either in a bed or in a lawn enables one more easily to appreciate its individual characteristics. Thus, if planted in a bed or border, its companions should not be allowed to crowd it out. Shrubs interplanted with hardy perennials of the less robust kind, bulbs or ferns are acceptable in the right mixture and the right situation. Shrubs interplanted with trees can create a natural and pleasing, even impressive effect, again in the right mixture and situation. Unless the shrub is known to be tolerant of shade then avoid planting shrubs beneath a tree's canopy and be sure to check a tree's ultimate size and characteristics before planting it among or near to established shrubs. The ideal situation, perhaps, is one in which a shrub, known for its beauty of form or special feature, is planted as a specimen in isolation. It may be a small shrub in a small garden or a large shrub in a large garden, whatever the choice, so long as the balance is right, it will provide a feature to be enjoyed for years to come.

The choice of shrubs for specimen planting is a personal matter, but when considering that choice one should bear in mind the variety of features a particular shrub has to offer. The main ornamental features to be found in the shrub kingdom are habit, bark, leaf, flower, fragrance, fruit and autumn colour. Two of these – fruit and autumn colour – are autumn features though several shrubs fruit outside this season. Habit and bark are all-the-year-round features although often best seen and appreciated in winter. Flowers and fragrance, depending on the chosen shrub, can be had at any time in the year while leaves are a summer feature in deciduous shrubs and an all-the-year-round feature in evergreens.

It is possible to have shrubs with more than one feature – a holly for instance with attractive habit, evergreen leaves (plain or variegated) and colourful fruits; or preference may be given to a single-feature shrub such as *Forsythia × intermedia* 'Lynwood' whose only ornamental asset is its glorious flower display in April. There are shrubs to suit all tastes and in order to help make the choice a little easier the following is a selection of some of the more interesting and ornamental kinds, discussed on a seasonal basis.

Winter

Winter is often regarded as the back end of the year and a bleak season for shrub lovers, which is just not true. It is, for instance, the best time to admire those shrubs with coloured or otherwise ornamental barks. Few who have seen the blue-white stems of *Rubus cockburnianus* would deny that they are amongst the most striking of all shrubs for this feature. Two other species – *R. biflorus* and *R. thibetanus* – are quite as good, and providing their old shoots are cut clean away immediately after flowering they will continue to produce bright young shoots to see the winter through. Their only drawback is their aggressive suckering nature which can be curbed by the annual removal of unwanted suckers.

If the garden includes a pond or stream then a pollarded willow will provide a splendid winter feature. Although, strictly speaking, trees, such willows can be treated as shrubs by the annual or biennial pruning of shoots either to ground level or to a short stem. Favourites for this treatment include 'Chermesina' (orange-red shoots) and 'Vitellina' (yolk-of-egg yellow shoots), both of which are forms of the white willow, *Salix alba*. They may be planted singly or, if room allows, in bold groups.

There are many shrubs with attractive peeling bark including *Enkianthus perulatus*, *Olearia macrodonta*, *Deutzia pulchra*, *Fuchsia excorticata* (for mild areas) and *Dipelta floribunda*. Careful pruning will allow one to admire the stems of such shrubs without necessarily spoiling their overall effect.

Compared with spring and summer, winter has fewer flowering shrubs but these are all the more welcome and appreciated as a result. The genus *Viburnum* seems to have the lion's share of such flowers there being at least four species and several cultivars in cultivation. Of these *V. tinus* is possibly the most commonly planted especially as a hedge in coastal gardens. There are several named cultivars of this evergreen of which 'Eve Price' is possibly the best. Compact in habit, up to 8ft(2.5m) with comparatively small, neat leaves, the white, scentless flowers (red in the bud) are produced in autumn, opening throughout winter. It is a superb evergreen for formal effect although its compact habit suits it for many situations. Differing in several ways from the last are the deciduous *V. farreri* and *V. grandiflorum*. The former is well known for its erect twiggy habit and fragrant, pink-budded, white flowers but the latter is less often seen due, in the main, to it being less hardy even though its flowers are pink and individually larger than those of the other. Both species, however, are now eclipsed in gardens by their hybrid, *V. ×bodnantense*, which in its cultivars 'Dawn' and 'Deben' is hard to beat. Both have ample clusters of sweetly scented, pink and white flowers which, once noted, will never be forgotten. They appear intermittently over a very long season which, depending on prevailing conditions, can run from late autumn until early spring. Both are large upstanding shrubs and require plenty of room in which to develop.

Mention of scent brings another famous shrub to mind in the winter sweet – *Chimonanthus praecox*. It is, however, very much a patient gardener's shrub, young plants taking several years to reach flowering condition. When it does arrive, however, the fragrance of the purple-eyed, waxy-yellow, cup-shaped flowers has no equal (see also p. 81). Like the viburnums, winter sweet requires ample room for development and prefers a warm, sunny position to ripen its growths.

In recent years there has appeared on the garden scene a shrub which promises to be here to stay – its name is *Daphne bholua*, a native of the eastern Himalaya where it grows in woods and clearings up to 11,000ft(3,353m). Its flowers are borne in clusters at the tips of the shoots. They are white, stained rose-purple and impart a delicious fragrance to the air. Several forms are in cultivation, some deciduous and hardy, others evergreen and not so hardy. One of the most hardy and satisfactory of these is named 'Gurkha' and reaches 6 to 8ft(2 to 2.5m), flowering on the naked branches from January to March, earlier or later depending on prevailing conditions and shelter. Unlike most daphnes it appears to react to lime in the soil, its leaves becoming chlorotic in summer.

Another shrub which prefers an acid soil is the witch hazel, *Hamamelis*, of

33. Daphne bholua 'Gurkha'

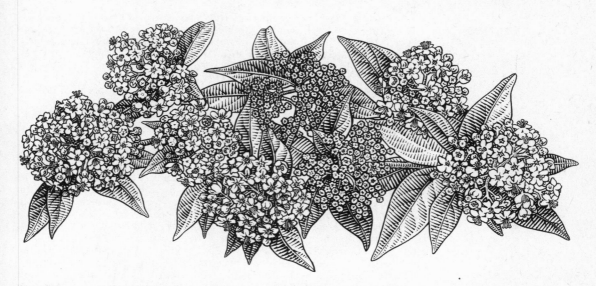

which there are several species and cultivars. One of the most commonly seen is the Chinese *H. mollis* whose golden, strap-shaped petals unwind like watch springs at the slightest hint of warmth. On any bright day between Christmas and February one can find the flowers clustered along the branches like colonies of golden spiders creating a bright splash and a sweet perfume. Although the type species is a first-rate shrub there is also a superb cultivar, 'Pallida', in which the flowers are larger and of a clear sulphur-yellow. Both eventually are large shrubs of wide-spread habit and demand plenty of space in which to develop. They associate well with blue-flowered bulbs such as *Scilla* and *Chionodoxa* spp. and are particularly dramatic when underplanted with the winter-flowering heaths, *Erica herbacea* (syn. *E. carnea*), *E. erigena* (syn. *E. mediterranea*), *E. × darleyensis* and their numerous cultivars.

It so happens that most shrubs which carry attractive fruits in winter are also evergreen – *Skimmia, Aucuba* and *Viburnum davidii* being three. Two shrubs of this category which come very close to being complete all-rounders are *Cotoneaster glaucophyllus*, especially its variety *serotinus*, and *C. lacteus*. Both are vigorous in growth – up to 10ft(3m) or more and have leathery, oval leaves which are white or blue-green beneath. Their white flower clusters are produced in late June and July – late, that is, for a cotoneaster – which means their dense clusters of small but bright red berries are correspondingly late to ripen, usually after Christmas. Like others of their genus they are easy and hardy in most soils.

It is a moot point as to whether the English holly and its cultivars should be classed as shrubs or trees. Theoretically, they are the latter but in practice they are often grown as shrubs, either by annual clipping or by choosing one of the slower growing cultivars of which there are several. In the last category comes the silver hedgehog holly, *Ilex aquifolium* 'Ferox Argentea' which is compact in habit and has purple twigs densely crowded with small leaves which are green and grey, margined creamy-white. The upper leaf surface is peppered with small cream-coloured prickles, hence the common name. It is a male form and does not produce berries. Its flowers, however, do produce abundant pollen which makes it an ideal pollinator for the best of the berrying cultivars such as 'Madame Briot', 'Handsworth New Silver', 'Pyramidalis' and 'J.C. van Tol'.

One evergreen which, in many gardens, provides the one bright sunny corner during winter is *Elaeagnus pungens* 'Maculata', a robust shrub, vigorous when once established and covered with large, dark green, silver-backed leaves the upper surface of which is marked with a bold golden splash. It will produce green-leaved reversions which must be cut

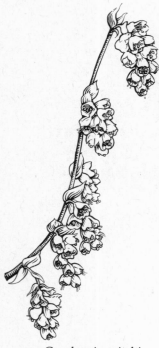

35. Corylopsis veitchiana

clean away without delay; otherwise this is an easy and hardy evergreen.

A winter evergreen which produces flowers as a bonus is *Garrya elliptica* from California. It is not satisfactory in the coldest areas but in most regions, especially in the southern half of Britain, the male form is spectacular when draped with its long grey-green catkins during January and February (see also p. 83).

All these winter shrubs are useful for cutting for indoors if pieces are carefully taken with sharp secateurs and only from an established plant. Those with flowers are particularly useful and may be cut when still in bud.

Spring

This season covers three of the most exciting gardening months, from the early awakenings in March to the mass blossoming of May. The choice of flowering shrubs is enormous and although the following are some of the most rewarding they are nevertheless but the tip of the iceberg. Related to the winter-flowering witch hazels are the *Corylopsis*. Their flowers, however, are more conventional, small, primrose yellow and cup-shaped, carried in drooping clusters along the slender branches in April or earlier in the case of *C. pauciflora*. The last-named is a dense, twiggy shrub with small sweetly-scented flower clusters. Because of its slow growth and compact habit it is more suitable for the small garden than any of the others although it does reach a height of 6ft(2m) eventually. It does not, however, thrive on limy soils. Such soils are no problem for the other species of *Corylopsis*, especially *C. veitchiana* which thrives in chalk or acid soils. It is a tall, vigorous shrub of up to 8ft(2.5m) with fresh green, oblong leaves and substantial racemes of yellow flowers from which peep brick-red anthers.

To bridge the gap between winter and spring one should consider the qualities of the evergreen *Mahonia japonica* which will, in time, form a broad mound of stout stems bearing ruffs of bold pinnate spine-toothed dark green leaves. From the tips of the shoots appear clusters of long, drooping racemes of small yellow flowers whose fragrance resembles that of lily-of-the-valley (*Convallaria majalis*). It is a tough, reliable and valuable shrub in sun or shade.

April is the month when *Magnolia stellata* floods its stark, leafless twigs with white flowers. Although it can reach 10ft by 10ft(3m by 3m) or more eventually, it is comparatively slow-growing and suitable, therefore, for small gardens. It makes an excellent lawn specimen and has the added quality of flowering when quite young. It is also unfussy as to soil so long as it is not waterlogged.

Osmanthus delavayi is often referred to as a shrub for the connoisseur. This does not mean, however, that it is in any way difficult to grow. It is an evergreen of neat habit with dark green, rounded, prettily toothed leaves and produces its clusters of sweetly-scented white flowers in April. Eventually it will reach a height of 8 to 10ft(2.5 to 3m) but not for many years. More vigorous and erect in growth is its hybrid with *O. decorus*, now known as *O. × burkwoodii*, which has longer, smoother leaves and is just as free flowering and fragrant.

Similarly erect but otherwise very different is the evergreen *Berberis × lologensis*, a hybrid of *B. darwinii* and *B. linearifolia*. It is strong growing and possessed of blackish-green, narrow, leathery leaves which are completely forgotten in April when the brilliant orange, red-budded flowers crowd the branches. No other berberis, excepting its parents, can match this splendid hybrid in its striking flower colour.

The family *Ericaceae* contains some of the most desirable shrubs for gardens on acid soils. Leaving aside *Rhododendron* and *Azalea*, which are dealt with elsewhere (see p. 205), there are still more than enough to occupy specialists for a lifetime. *Enkianthus perulatus* from Japan is the least known of its brethren in cultivation, which is difficult to understand, given its qualities. One of the smallest species, up to 6ft(2m), slow-growing and compact in habit, it seems custom-made for the small garden. Neither do its qualifications end there. In April its slender twigs are crowded with small, white, pitcher-shaped, nodding flowers while in autumn it offers rich crimson leaf tints and is reliable, too. As if this was not enough the bark of old stems peels and flakes creating an attractive piebald effect which careful pruning can enhance.

Camellias are one of the most prized groups of shrubs in garden history and the hundreds of named cultivars available today make the choosing of those most suitable for ones own garden, a difficult task. Camellia enthusiasts all have their own ideas of what constitutes a good cultivar, but for first-time buyers there are several which can happily be recommended for general cultivation. *Camellia × williamsii*, in a comparatively short time has produced several candidates for the above category. Perhaps the most popular is 'Donation' which is fairly hardy and reliable in its flowering. The large semi-double, orchid-pink blooms crowd the stems in April often causing them to bend under the weight. If it has one weakness it is the slender nature of the branches which tend to lean outwards and occasionally break in the wind. This can be controlled by careful pruning or by growing it against a wall or fence where it makes a splendid effect. More elegant in appearance is another hybrid, 'Cornish Snow', and especially the related cultivar 'Michael'. The slender arching or drooping branches of this 8 to 10ft(2.5 to 3m) tall shrub bear small, slender-pointed, glossy green leaves and quantities of small white flowers, larger in 'Michael'. Like most others of its clan it does best in a site sheltered from strong wind and protected from the early morning sun. The cultivars of *C. japonica* are legion, but if only one was to be chosen perhaps it might be 'Adolph Audusson' whose bold appearance and vigorous, upright growth have stood it in good stead for many years. The large, semi-double flowers are composed of blood-red petals and a handsome boss of yellow-tipped stamens, all of which is shown off to perfection against the dark, polished, green leaves.

Returning once more to the *Ericaceae*, consideration must be given to one or other of the *Pieris* species and cultivars which, on acid soils, have many qualities to commend them. *P. japonica*, in one or other of its named cultivars is fairly hardy and easy but if space allows of only one and the site chosen is sheltered from cold winds and frost, *P.* 'Forest Flame' is probably the best choice. The white, pitcher-shaped flowers are carried in substantial drooping clusters from the tips of the shoots, but this is only the beginning. With the opening of the flowers in May the brilliant red young growths appear, developing until long after the flowers have faded, during which time they have passed from red through pink to creamy-white and finally green. It is a large shrub – 10 to 15ft(3 to 4.5m) eventually, but has few equals for spring foliage effect.

Those who garden on chalk and are denied the pleasure of the last shrub may consider as a substitute *Photinia × fraseri* 'Red Robin' or 'Robusta', both of which have attractive coppery-red young growths from spring through to midsummer. Both are evergreen and fast growing reaching 15 to 20ft (4.5 to 6m) or more in a suitable site. Their growths also appear less liable to damage by frost. *Photinia glabra* 'Rubens' has young foliage of a glistening red and is less vigorous, more compact in habit occasionally attaining 10ft(3m) but usually much less. All these photinias produce flattened heads of small white flowers in spring, but not on young plants.

If one has a penchant for shrubs with coloured young growths but only a small garden the dwarf coral maple, *Acer palmatum* 'Corallinum', may provide an answer. Its young leaves are a brilliant shrimp-pink and create a display for several weeks before changing to a mottled green in midsummer. It is not, however, a shrub for those in a hurry, being extremely slow in growth and compact in habit. An old specimen of 40 years or more may only have attained 3ft(1m) in height which makes this shrub a good choice for the rock garden or raised bed.

For many people, April would not be the same without *Forsythia* creating its bright splashes of yellow in the suburban landscape. For others, however, the double yellow button flowers of *Kerria japonica* 'Pleniflora' are far more satisfying and this shrub has attractive green cane-like shoots as a bonus. It is a tall-growing suckering shrub up to 10ft(3m) tall and makes a loose mound of arching stems where space permits; otherwise it is normally grown against a wall. The single-flowered type is only half that height.

36. Paeonia lutea *var.*
ludlowii

Blue is a colour which contrasts effectively with yellow and although there is a preponderance of yellow flowers over blue in spring the latter colour is well represented by a large number of the ceanothus. For gardens in mild areas and where space will permit the planting of a large shrub, the most impressive is undoubtedly *C. arboreus* 'Trewithen Blue', whose comparatively large evergreen leaves are almost hidden in spring by the dense panicles of deep blue flowers. When thriving it will attain 10 to 15ft(3 to 4.5m) or more eventually and then is a spectacular sight. *C. thyrsiflorus*, meanwhile, has paler blue flowers and smaller leaves and is known for its comparative hardiness. It can attain 10ft(3m) or more when happy and produce its flowers from May into June. There are several evergreen hybrids of medium to large size which, in warm gardens certainly, will produce a bold display of bright blue flowers. They include *C. × lobbianus*, *C.* 'Cascade', *C.* 'Southmead', *C.* 'Delight' and *C.* 'Italian Skies'.

Attractive foliage and flower are important assets for a garden shrub and when both are combined they ensure for that shrub a special place in the garden. *Paeonia lutea* var. *ludlowii* is one such and although it requires plenty of space in which to develop its full potential those gardens with space enough to accommodate it should do so. The large boldly-lobed leaves are handsome in themselves and the cup-shaped, yellow flowers – like large kingcups – are borne on long stalks among the leaves in May. Although tolerant of some shade this peony flowers best in a well-drained, even dry, sunny site.

Some of the amelanchiers are dual-purpose shrubs with flowers and autumn colour. The most spectacular perhaps is *Amelanchier lamarckii*, which has been referred to as *A. confusa*, *A. arborea* and, most frequently, as *A. canadensis*. It is still found described under the last-mentioned name in most British nursery catalogues. In April the naked branches of this large bushy shrub or small tree are covered as if with snow as each shoot tip and spur produces a short raceme of white flowers. Again, in autumn, the shrub attracts attention with its brilliant orange and crimson tints.

Deutzia pulchra is possibly the most impressive of its clan and one of the earliest to flower. It will reach 8 to 10ft(2.5 to 3m) when thriving and has attractive exfoliating, warm orange-brown bark. The handsome, long-lasting, deep green leaves are lance-shaped up to 4in(10cm) long and, if this is not enough, the large bell-shaped, nodding, waxy-white flowers with orange anthers are borne in slender panicles like lily-of-the-valley in May. Truly, this is a stately shrub which needs a mild, sheltered garden and dappled shade to be seen at its best.

Uniting, in its flowering period, the spring and summer seasons, *Viburnum plicatum* var. *tomentosum* is one of those splendid shrubs combining an attractive habit, leaves, flowers, fruits and autumn colour. Broader than high its branches are carried in flattened tiers creating a table-top or wedding-cake effect when in flower. The pleated leaves are closely followed by flattened heads of white lacecap flowers which are carried from May into early June. They sit in two ranks along the upper sides of the branches and are followed by red berries turning eventually to black at which time, in a good year, the leaves are prettily tinted. The most commonly planted cultivar of the above is named 'Mariesii', while for those who prefer a more vigorous form there is a cultivar named 'Pink Beauty' in which the flowers turn to pink as they age.

Summer

After the mad rush of flowering shrubs in April and May things settle down to an easier pace during summer, the main flowering being shared between several large genera. *Philadelphus* provides a feast of flower and fragrance at this time with species and cultivars to suit most gardens. For small gardens the small-leaved, small-flowered *P. microphyllus* is a delight, rarely exceeding 4ft(1.25m) in height. It has a dense rounded habit. If it can be given a dry, sunny position it will flower its heart out in June and, at the same time, fill the air with its perfume. The next four hybrids of exceeding merit are worth a place in any garden. In order of size, and beginning with the smallest, they are: 'Sybille', 'Belle Étoile', 'Beauclerk' and 'Voie Lactée'. The first of these rarely exceeds 3ft(1m) but has a wide-spreading habit to 7ft(2.25m) across with arching branches weighted down in June and July with saucer-shaped, white flowers with a pale pinkish-purple basal stain. It is deliciously scented of orange blossom. 'Belle Étoile' is rather more erect, less spreading than the last up to 6ft(2m) high with powerfully fragrant flowers in June and July. The individual flowers are shallowly funnel-shaped, creamy-white stained purple at the base. Even the bark is attractive, being a rich mahogany-brown and peeling to reveal the pale fawn new bark. 'Beauclerk', too, will reach 6ft(2m) and will expand likewise, its gracefully arching branches weighted down in June and July with an abundance of large, sweetly fragrant flowers up to 3in(8cm) across. These are saucer-shaped at first, later flattening and have an unusual square outline shared by few others. They are white with a pale pink basal flush. 'Voie Lactée' is perhaps the finest of the single white hybrids. It attains 6ft(2m), is erect at first, later spreading, and bears large, slightly scented, saucer-shaped, white flowers which later open flat. All four are worth considering for the small garden even though the last three may need judicious pruning to contain them. All are lovely summer-flowering shrubs and without at least one of them the garden would be incomplete.

Closely related to the philadelphus and just as important from a garden point of view are the deutzias. There are many species, hybrids and cultivars and, as in the previous genus, one must choose one and admire the rest in other people's gardens. *Deutzia × hybrida* and its cultivars are bold shrubs of fairly erect growth with long, handsome leaves and substantial panicles of flowers which are mainly in the pink, rose, purple range. The cultivar 'Contraste' has pink flowers marked purple on the reverse while in 'Joconde' the larger flowers are white within when fully open. 'Joconde' is also a taller – 6 to 8ft(2 to 2.5m) – border shrub. Both flower in June and thrive best in dappled shade although an open situation is quite acceptable.

One of the most satisfactory species is *D. compacta*, which develops a compact mounded habit, eventually up to 6ft(2m) tall, with exfoliating pale brown bark, orange-brown on the reverse. Its small, creamy-white flowers are carried in flattened heads in July. It has a cultivar, 'Lavender Time', in which the flowers are pale lilac. For those who would prefer a white-flowered deutzia, hardy and vigorous as well, the hybrid group *D. × magnifica* has several contenders. If it had to be restricted to one, perhaps the cultivar 'Latiflora' would be most suitable. It is robust and easy to grow with large white flowers in dense panicles.

One of the glories of British gardens in June are the lilacs in their multiplicity of form and colour. The numerous cultivars of the common lilac, *Syringa vulgaris*, are most popular but there are several species and their forms which are more graceful and far better suited to specimen planting, especially in lawns. One of these is *S. reflexa*, a Chinese shrub up to 10ft(3m) or more with large leaves and long, densely-packed drooping panicles of rich, purplish-pink flowers, white within. These are produced from late May into June. Flowering over a similar period is *S. × josiflexa* which bears its fragrant rose-pink flowers in loose, plume-like panicles from the tips of the arching shoots. There are several cultivars of this Canadian-bred hybrid one of which, 'Bellicent', is quite outstanding. Smaller than any already described is *S. microphylla* which was introduced from China by William Purdom. It is a pretty shrub up to 6ft(2m) tall with small, pointed leaves and rosy-lilac fragrant flowers in June and again in September. The cultivar 'Superba' is freer-flowering with rosy-pink flowers from May intermittently until October. *S. meyeri* is even more suited to the small garden because of its slow growth and dense, compact, rounded habit. It eventually reaches up to 6ft(2m) in height. The leaves are rounded or diamond-shaped and of a velvety dark green. The pale lilac or lilac-pink flowers appear even on young plants from late May into June. This variable species is often planted on rock gardens where it forms a neat, attractive mound until, eventually, its size requires it to be moved or replaced.

Most gardens have at least one corner which can be described as sunny or warm. If the soil here is also well-drained or can be made so then a host of

37. Philadelphus 'Belle Étoile'

excellent flowering shrubs will vie for one's attention. Many of these happen to be dwarf shrubs such as × *Halimiocistus wintonensis*, which forms lovely low mounds of grey leaves and rewards one with flowers 2in(5cm) across which are pearly-white with a feathered and pencilled zone of crimson-maroon, contrasting with the yellow basal stains. These are produced in succession from May through June.

The rock roses *Cistus* spp. are one of the most rewarding groups of summer-flowering shrubs. Ranging in habit from low mounds to tall, erect shrubs, their single rose-like flowers appear all through summer offering a variety of colours. For planting on rock gardens or in small borders or raised beds there is *C. creticus* with flowers coloured purple to rose. *C. × lusitanicus* 'Decumbens', flowers white with crimson basal blotches, and *C. albidus*, flowers pale rose-lilac with a yellow eye, are easy and comparatively hardy. Of the taller-growing kinds *C. × cyprius*, flowers white with crimson blotches; *C. laurifolius*, flowers white with yellow centres; Peggy Sammons' and 'Silver Pink', both pink-flowered; and *C. × purpureus*, flowers rose-crimson with chocolate basal stains, are among the best. The last-named is less hardy than most but worth all the protection one can provide.

In sheltered gardens in the south and west of the British Isles one might try *Melianthus major* if only for its foliage which is large, deeply lobed and a delightful blue-grey in colour. It is a small, spreading shrub which needs a warm, sunny site and contrasts well with brickwork. Not all shrubs from Mediterranean climates are necessarily impossible in Britain and a visit to any well-known garden worth its salt will reveal at least one Mediterranean-type shrub in happy occupation. Tasmania, for instance has contributed a number of first-rate shrubs for sunny sites in British gardens. One of these is *Grevillea sulphurea*, a spreading shrub up to 6ft(2m) tall with long stems densely clothed with needle-like evergreen leaves. For many months during summer and autumn the slender canary-yellow flowers crowd the branches creating a bright and pleasing display. It is not, however, suitable for chalk or limy soils.

From the same Australian island comes *Ozothamnus ledifolius*, another evergreen but this time dense and compact in habit, forming a neat mound up to 3ft(1m). Its small, narrow leaves are green with golden reverse and form an unusual backing for the terminal clusters of white flowers, burnt sienna in bud which give off a pleasant honey-like aroma. It is ideally suited for rock garden or raised bed. Much taller – up to 6ft(2m) is *O. rosmarinifolius*, which is dense and erect in habit with narrow green leaves and red-budded white flowers in tight clusters. Full sun and a well-drained site are required by these last three, while in the coldest areas they require protection from frost. Even if frost should claim them they are easily rooted from cuttings and a stock should be kept in reserve for such happenings.

Hardier, and therefore more reliable for colder gardens, are the hypericums. Most gardeners plant *Hypericum* 'Hidcote' but there are several others worth considering among which *H. kouytchense* is a gem. Low in habit (3ft[1m]) its arching stems are covered with large yellow flowers in which the long bold stamens are prominent. These appear from June to October and are replaced by colourful bright red seed capsules. *H. forrestii* is taller growing 4 to 5ft(1.25 to 1.5m) similarly rounded and compact in habit and free flowering with saucer-shaped, golden-yellow flowers through summer into autumn. The yellow flowers of the hypericums contrast effectively with the blue flowers of *Ceratostigma willmottianum*, another low deciduous shrub and together they make colourful and satisfying late summer and autumn flowering groups to which may be added dwarf potentillas such as 'Tangerine', 'Elizabeth', 'Goldfinger' and 'Lady Daresbury' all yellow flowered, orange in the first named. Others which provide late summer flowers include *Penstemon* 'Garnet', a subshrub with erect panicles of drooping red tubular flowers; *Fuchsia magellanica* and its forms, as well as many hybrid fuchsias; and *Caryopteris × clandonensis* 'Heavenly Blue' with bright blue flowers.

Whilst most buckeyes are trees there is one which is most certainly a shrub although, in ideal conditions, its suckering propensities will eventually fill a large area with erect stems up to 10ft(3m). Its name is *Aesculus parviflora* and there can be few more attractive summer-flowering shrubs than this when its erect, cylindrical panicles appear like candles from the tips of the shoots. Each white flower is equipped with a brush of long, slender red-anthered stamens and the overall effect is quite breath-taking.

Anyone who has admired the yellow flowers of the broom in woodland rides and on native heaths will appreciate the value of such displays in the garden. The brooms, collectively encompass a wide variety of shrubs varying mainly in habit and flower colour. The majority flower in late spring or early summer but there are several which begin later, in late June or July. Of these, two are notable for their large size 10 to 15ft by 10 to 15ft (3 to 4.5 by 3 to 4.5m) eventually and elegant sprays of yellow pea flowers. *Genista tenera* (*G. cinerea* of gardens) is the first to flower in late June continuing into July. It is followed by the Mount Etna broom, *Genista aetnensis*, which is even more elegant with its slender, rush-like green branches dripping with small golden-yellow pea-flowers. Both are shrubs for the large garden and they are especially effective in the heather garden. Alternatively, they are superb lawn specimens.

For late summer flowering the cultivars of *Hibiscus syriacus* take a lot of beating. These are large, angular shrubs eventually and are long-lived in the right place. They are surprisingly cold-hardy and easy so long as the requirements of sun and good drainage are provided, and, once established, supply a succession of large, trumpet-shaped flowers from late summer into autumn. Of the many cultivars 'Bluebird', 'Woodbridge' and 'Diana' are the most desirable for their single blue, rose-pink and white flowers respectively. These shrubs are very late in leafing and impatient, inexperienced gardeners have been known to dig them up and throw them away in the mistaken idea that they had been killed by the winter.

Two shrubs which are not planted as much as their ornamental merit deserves are *Eucryphia glutinosa* and *Hydrangea heteromalla* 'Bretschneideri'. The first of these is large, up to 15ft(4.5m) or even a small tree to 25ft(7.6m) if allowed. Its attractive pinnate, dark, shining green leaves provide beautiful tints of orange and red in autumn while, in July and August, its branches are crowded with single, rose-like white flowers with yellow anthers. Although requiring an acid soil this is a most delightful and aristocratic shrub, well worth its place where space and soil conditions permit. It should be planted when small, preferably in a position sheltered from strong winds. The hydrangea is one of several which deserve a place in gardens. The lavender-blue flowered *H. villosa* and the lavender and white flowered *H. aspera* are two strong candidates for garden space but the merits of *H. heteromalla* 'Bretschneideri' are its erect stately habit to 10ft(3m), bold foliage and flaking purple-brown papery bark. Best of all, however, are its large, flattened lacecap heads of white flowers in July.

Autumn

Although many shrubs continue to flower in autumn there are several which only flower at this season. Principal among these is *Mahonia × media* and its several named cultivars. All are evergreens of stately appearance, erect-stemmed eventually to 10ft(3m) high (taller in ideal conditions) and carrying their long, pinnate leaves in bold rosettes towards the ends of the branches. The long racemes of yellow, slightly scented flowers appear in loose terminal clusters in November and continue for many weeks. Cultivars include 'Charity', 'Buckland', 'Lionel Fortescue', 'Underway' and 'Winter Sun'. All are hardy, robust shrubs with splendid dark, shining foliage eminently suitable for woodland, border or as lawn specimens.

Another autumn-flowering evergreen is *Fatsia japonica*. Although botanically related to the ivy it seems to deny the connection with its bold glossy leaves carried on long stalks and its conspicuous terminal panicles of creamy-white flower heads. It is worth growing for its foliage alone and is one of the best shrubs for creating a subtropical effect in a British garden. It thrives best in semi-shade and is specially effective in coastal gardens as well as those in towns and cities where it appears oblivious to dull skies or pollution. The flowers attract an interesting clientele of late flying insects

38. Hypericum forrestii (p.72, top)

39. Aesculus parviflora (p.72, bottom)

40. Hibiscus syriacus 'Woodbridge'.

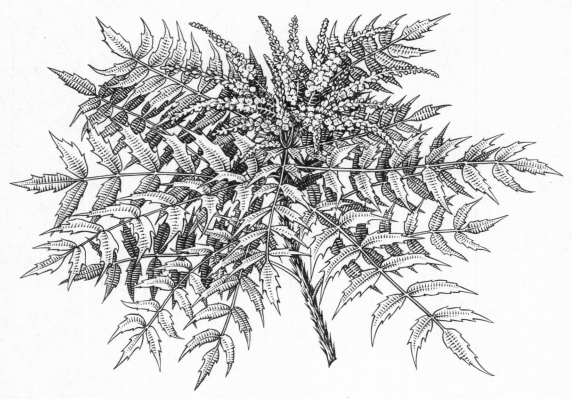

41. Mahonia × media
'Charity' (see p.73).

which add to rather than detract from its charms.

In the same family, though again quite different in general effect, is *Aralia elata*, the angelica tree. Left to its own devices it will develop a main stem branching in its upper half to form a small tree. It may, however, be hard pruned to ground level or at least to a short stem to encourage a more shrubby habit. So treated, the prickly stems in spring will put forth huge, much divided leaves, often a yard or more long. During September the large panicles of creamy-white flowers appear from the tips of the strongest shoots, lasting for several weeks until replaced by glistening black berries. There are two cultivars of this hardy shrub, one with creamy-white margined leaflets the other yellow-margined but becoming creamy-white later. They are sometimes hard to acquire but are well worth searching for.

Early in autumn *Clerodendrum trichotomum* is in full flower, its fragrant white flowers protruding from maroon calyces. These are followed by beautiful turquoise berries which last into winter. It makes a large shrub or a small low tree even and needs plenty of room in which to develop its spreading head. Requiring less space but unfortunately less hardy is *C. bungei*, a suckering shrub producing clumps of erect stems to 6ft(2m) or more clothed with bold, heart-shaped leaves and bearing dense terminal heads of rosy-red, fragrant flowers which attract any butterfly which happens to be passing. A cold winter will cut its stems to the ground but then it seems quite happy to behave as an herbaceous perennial.

Most deciduous shrubs, in a good year, will give autumn leaf colour. Many of the shrubs already discussed can be expected to contribute in this way to the garden in autumn, i.e., *Amelanchier*, *Enkianthus*, *Viburnum*. There are, however, a good number of shrubs whose main contribution to the garden is the colour of their autumn foliage and all but the smallest gardens should include at least one of these. A prime candidate for such an honour must be *Hamamelis vernalis* 'Sandra', an erect-stemmed shrub to 6ft(2m), eventually opening out. Its leaves emerge purple gradually turning green as they age. In autumn, while the leaves of the type turn clear yellow, those of

'Sandra' exhibit a brilliant mixture of red, scarlet and orange to create a striking bonfire effect. Few other shrubs offer the same intensity of colour. Like others of its clan it prefers an acid soil if it is to give of its best. Almost if not as brilliantly coloured are the leaves of the American *Fothergilla major*, whose creamy-white clusters of flowers in April, while attractive, are no match, in terms of attraction, for its autumn foliage in which yellow, orange and red combine. It also requires a lime-free soil in which to thrive and is then capable of reaching 8ft(2.5m).

The smoke trees or sumachs, *Cotinus* spp., are superb shrubs or small trees for autumn effect. *Cotinus coggygria*, the Venetian sumach, will form a large mound up to 10ft(3m) tall, and whether grown on a single or on several stems will create a brilliant splash of colour in which orange, crimson and purple predominate. The purple-leaved cultivars, including 'Royal Purple' and 'Notcutt's Variety', are just as satisfactory and have the additional attraction of summer foliage colour.

Rich autumn leaf colours are found in several of the spindles, *Euonymus* spp., the most famous perhaps being *E. alatus*, a slow-growing, dense bush up to 6ft(2m) tall with curiously winged stems and leaves that turn a rich crimson before falling. Other *Euonymus* spp. are dual-purpose and add ornamental fruits to their autumn leaf display. Among these are *E. oxyphyllus*, a large spreading shrub up to 10ft(3m) tall whose leaves in autumn turn to shades of red and purple when, at the same time, the branches are strung with carmine-red capsules which split to reveal orange-coated seeds. Similar in effect are the various forms of *E. hamiltonianus*, whose lemon and pink or darker autumn tints complement the coral-pink capsules which are borne in profusion. These forms are still grown in nurseries under various names of which *E. yedoensis*, *E. sieboldianus* and *E. maackii* are the most common. They develop into large shrubs up to 8 to 10ft(2.5 to 3m) tall on average, their colours adding immeasurably to the autumn scene. Few shrubs can match the viburnums and cotoneasters for autumn effect. Our native *Viburnum opulus* may be equalled but is certainly unexcelled by its Asian or American counterparts. The white lacecap flowerheads in summer are followed in autumn by large, drooping bunches of glistening red, translucent berries when, at the same time, the handsome maple-like leaves turn red and purple shades. 'Notcutt's Variety' is a selected form with larger flowers and fruits while 'Xanthocarpum' has fruits of a golden-yellow colour. For small gardens there are few rivals to *V. wrightii* 'Hessei', which rarely rises above 3ft(1m) and develops a dense, compact habit with broad, attractively veined leaves which are ideal backing for the sealing-wax-red fruits. This is one of the most reliable fruiting shrubs.

Cotoneasters have already been lauded for their fruiting qualities and such is their variety of size and habit that there cannot be a garden anywhere that will not accommodate at least one of their number. For large gardens the red-fruited *C. frigidus* and its yellow-fruited form 'Fructu-luteo' are virtually unbeatable. Both are large deciduous shrubs up to 15ft(4.5m) or more eventually, with bold foliage and an ability to grow in almost any situation, a character shared by many other members of the genus. Equally large, but developing a more wide-spreading habit with arching branches in more or less horizontal sprays, are the hybrids between *C. frigidus*, *C. henryanus* and *C. salicifolius*. The name *C. × watereri* is loosely used to cover this group but there are some outstanding named cultivars which are free-fruiting and semi-evergreen in nature. Of these two of the best with red fruits are 'Cornubia' and 'St Monica', while 'Exburyensis' and 'Rothschildianus' have yellow fruits, those of the former becoming pink-tinged with age. A single specimen of any one of these cotoneasters will make a bold feature in a lawn or border. Among those of medium size are the grey-leaved *C. franchetii* var. *sternianus* and the small-leaved, mound-forming *C. conspicuus*, both of which are evergreen and free-fruiting. Two of the best cotoneasters are *C. splendens* and *C. bullatus* var. *floribundus*. The first of these rarely exceeds 6ft(2m) and has small, neat leaves and a wealth of bright orange fruits, while the latter will reach 10ft(3m) and bears clusters of bright red fruits against handsome, conspicuously veined leaves.

7.
Climbing and Wall Plants

Walls of houses and out-buildings, as well as fences and trellises within the garden (or on the boundary) provide us with accommodation for an interesting range of plants – climbers, both shrubby and herbaceous, together with many of the more spectacular flowering shrubs of borderline hardiness, such as abutilons, the evergreen ceanothus and myrtles which, if grown away from the shelter and extra warmth of a wall, would not survive or would suffer considerable winter damage in colder districts. Indeed, house walls and porches in particular, as well as low walls or balustrading which makes divisions within the garden, provide an opportunity to grow many exotic, exciting and unusual plants (see select lists on pp. 85 to 89).

Tree stumps, posts, tripods and pergolas can all provide a home for well-chosen climbing plants, such as akebia, clematis, honeysuckles or climbers of like character. There are a number of vigorous vines and roses as well as such familiar and lusty climbers as wisteria and Russian vine, *Polygonum baldschuanicum*, which will festoon decrepit trees. Some are equally appropriate for smothering an unsightly building or garden shed or, trained on trellis, to screen an eyesore, such as a domestic oil-storage tank.

Difficult, unmowable banks may be rapidly and attractively clothed in a labour-saving manner with rambler roses or suitable climbers. These include such larger-leaved ivies as *Hedera colchica* and *H. canariensis* and their cultivars, and such honeysuckles as *Lonicera etrusca* and *L. japonica*.

Less vigorous climbers, such as cultivars of *Clematis texensis* and *Tropaeolum speciosum* can contribute welcome colour and variation of flower and leaf when trailing over heathers or non-flowering hedges. The uses of climbers and wall shrubs within the garden are indeed many and varied; it is, however, necessary to consider their individual requirements in order to choose the right plant for the right wall or other specialized position.

FURNISHING HOUSE WALLS AND PORCHES, BOUNDARY WALLS AND FENCES The space between windows, as well as the height of walls (particularly in the case of bungalows) is often a limiting factor. Wall shrubs rather than climbers are frequently the best choice in such circumstances (see select list p. 86 for suitable subjects). Most climbers, and especially the more vigorous vines, honeysuckles and clematis, have a tendency to grow rapidly to the highest point, and, in so doing, often become a nuisance, blocking gutters and growing under roof tiles, while the lower part of their stems become bare and unfurnished. Here, well-trained and well-pruned wall shrubs are often to be preferred and south- or west-facing aspects give the opportunity to grow some interesting and colourful exotic wall shrubs, such as *Abelia, Abutilon, Callistemon, Coronilla glauca, Cytisus battandieri, Piptanthus laburnifolius* and *Punica granatum*. There are many others from which to make a choice.

However, some climbers such as large-flowered hybrid clematis, honeysuckles, loniceras and the more vigorous climbing roses are much loved and people tend to plant them in the most unsuitable places. To some extent, this problem can be tackled by timely pruning (see "Mastering the Craft of Pruning", pp. 311 to 318), but the scene can often be satisfactorily transformed by the use of low-growing shrubs to mask effectively the lower parts of stems and bare areas of wall. Particularly effective for this task are

42. *Rustic tripods with an open top – the posts are linked with short cross pieces – make ideal supports for clematis, climbing roses and other plants which, by adding height to a border, provide additional interest. The clematis is led up through the middle to festoon down from the top.*

Potentilla, Cistus, Coronilla, Phlomis, Fuchsia (hardy), *Santolina, Rosmarinus* (rosemary) and *Lavandula* (lavender).

The access path which surrounds most houses usually creates bays and borders of varying widths which, if well cultivated, provide good growing conditions for climbers, wall shrubs and associated foreground shrubs; plants which, if well chosen, can blend together harmoniously. Care should be taken to choose only shrubs of dwarf habit for positions under windows. Provided a border width of at least 2ft(60cm) is available, any of the plants mentioned in the previous paragraph will be useful in this position against a sunny wall while *Daphne, Hebe, Skimmia* and *Sarcococca* can be used in similar situations near a shaded wall.

Planting may be considerably restricted when paths or paved areas are carried right up to the house wall. In such circumstances, it is certainly worth removing paving to form at least a 2ft(60cm) wide border – even a single slab, say 2ft by 2ft(60cm by 60cm) lifted from a suitable position against the house wall in the patio area will enable a well-prepared site to accommodate a climbing plant, perhaps a clematis, with a potentilla, hebe or hardy fuchsia at its feet to mask its leggy stem and shade its roots.

Boundary walls or fences are usually between 5ft and 8ft(1.5m and 2.5m) in height and have no windows and are therefore less restricting, but it may be necessary to choose hardier subjects away from the warmth of house walls – pyracantha, climbing roses, jasmine and so on.

MEANS OF SUPPORT In practical terms climbers and wall shrubs may be divided into two broad sections: climbers which adhere to walls by means of aerial roots or by tendrils tipped with adhesive discs, and climbers which climb by means of twining stems, curling leaf stalks or curling tendrils.

Examples of climbers with aerial roots include the ivies (hederas) and the climbing hydrangea, *Hydrangea petiolaris*. An example of a climber with tendrils tipped with adhesive discs is Virginia creeper, *Parthenocissus quinquefolia*. Once established and growing strongly, these climbers should be completely self-supporting. They often, however, require some assistance to induce their tendrils or aerial roots to adhere to the wall or climbing surface. In the case of newly planted young climbers of this type, lead-headed wall nails (as used to secure telephone cables) are useful to press stems against the climbing surface until the aerial roots or adhesive discs take over. A tall, large wall of rough-textured finish not requiring further decoration is preferable for these plants. Ivies and similar climbers, if they are removed at a later date, can loosen mortar or pointing of old brick walls or similar surfaces.

Climbers which climb by means of twining stems include wisterias and honeysuckles; those with curling leaf stalks, clematises, and those with curling tendrils, the vines or vitises. These are not self-clinging and they require support, as do all climbing roses and wall shrubs. Most will require careful training and securing to galvanized wire (12 gauge is best) supported by vine eyes in the case of larger areas of wall or fence. In smaller wall areas, it is better to use plastic mesh trellis in green, brown or white secured to suitable battens. This method is particularly useful for restricted areas between windows, etc. Decoration of the wall or fence is possible in both cases. Vine eyes 3 or 4in(8 to 10cm) long are pointed strips of galvanized metal with a hole at the broad end through which the wire is drawn. They should be driven into the wall, preferably at joints (sometimes it is necessary to use an electric drill in advance) at about 3ft(1m) intervals in ranks either up or down and about 1 to 1½ ft(30 to 45cm) apart. Screw-in type vine eyes are available for fences, pergola posts, etc.

PERGOLAS AND RUSTIC TRIPODS Pergolas constructed of brick, stone or wooden uprights and wooden cross-members often span a path and makes a feature in many gardens. Climbers such as wisterias and vines and strong-growing honeysuckles and clematis are ideal for furnishing roof beams while less vigorous climbers or shrubs are secured to the uprights (say *Clematis macropetala, Ceanothus* 'Gloire de Versailles' or *Actinidia kolomikta*).

43. *The training of a young* Hydrangea petiolaris. *Lead-headed wall nails are used to start adhesion of this self-clinging climber -- it adheres by aerial roots – which is suitable for clothing a tall north- or east-facing wall or fence.*

44. *Lead-headed wall nails.*

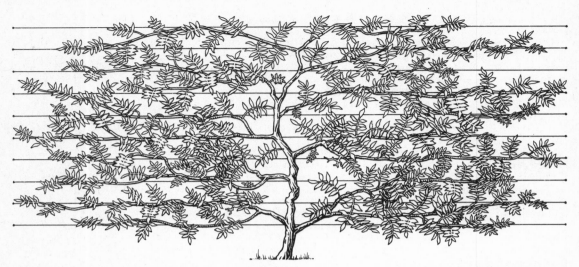

45. *With climbers like Wisteria it is important that they should be trained to form a well-spaced branch system.*

In shrub and herbaceous borders an occasional rustic tripod will provide support for climbing roses, clematis, jasmine or the bright yellow leaves of the golden hop, *Humulus lupulus* 'Aureus'. It is worth preserving the base of each post with green Cuprinol, ensuring that this preservative extends at least 6in(15cm) above ground level – the point where wooden posts quickly rot. Construct the tripod with an open top, linking the posts with short cross pieces (see Fig. 42). Lead the climber up through the middle to festoon down from the top. Such tripods can make a most effective feature and add height to a border, emerging through dwarfer shrubs and ground-cover plants growing around about them.

Single rustic posts (at least 4 to 6in[10 to 15cm] in diameter) positioned 6 to 8ft(2 to 2.5m) apart can be linked by rails of 2 to 3in(5 to 8cm) in diameter, perhaps supporting plastic or wire mesh trellis. Such an arrangement forms an excellent support for climbing roses and so on, and makes a good background for rose or shrub borders.

SITE PREPARATION, PLANTING AND AFTER-CARE The soil against walls, particularly of new buildings, is frequently poor and sometimes heavily adulterated with builders' rubble; it is often hard-packed. In older gardens, growing conditions may be little better if the borders have long been occupied and the soil exhausted by decrepit climbing or wall shrubs. For the best results, it is worth trenching the entire border area 1½ ft(45cm) deep, removing the rubble, chalk, gravel or sub-soil encountered, together with roots or stumps from any previous planting, and replacing this with good fresh top soil. This top soil should consist ideally of top spit loam, particularly in those places where new specimens will be planted. At second best, individual site preparation in borders or paved areas should be at least 1½ft(45cm) deep and 2ft(60cm) square. Well-rotted farmyard manure or good mature compost should be dug into the lower spit before any re-soiling is carried out to aid rapid establishment and growth.

Equally generous site preparation is necessary when plantings are being made to clothe pergolas and tripods, and particular care is necessary when preparing sites for climbers to grow through trees. Here, due regard must be given to competition with the feeding roots of the tree. These are usually some distance away from the trunk, in the vicinity of the outer edge of the canopy of the tree. If fibrous feeding roots are encountered it is a good idea to seal them off from the new climber by means of an open-bottomed box of wood, tile or slate, say 2 to 3ft(60cm to 1m) square, in which the new plant is established in a good depth of fresh soil and compost. However, it is best to select a host tree for this purpose which has a thin, narrow crown rather than one which is broad and dense so that adequate light and rain can reach the climber.

PLANTING Apart from climbing or rambler roses, the majority of wall shrubs and climbers are provided by good nurserymen as pot- or container-grown plants which can be planted at almost any time of the year, providing that there is adequate attention to watering and after-care (climbing or rambler roses and open-ground shrubs are normally planted between the end of October and March during open weather conditions).

First, ensure that pot-grown plants are thoroughly moist before planting. If necessary, immerse the pot in a bucket of water until it is adequately moist; it is most difficult to introduce water to a dry root ball once planted. Excavate the prepared site to an adequate depth and incorporate plenty of peat, composted bark or garden compost with the soil in the vicinity of the planting hole. Plastic pots or containers must be carefully removed or cut away before planting. After positioning the plant, with the top of the root ball on the surface of the growing compost no more than 1in(2.5cm) below the general soil level, top up with fine soil, peat or composted bark and firm very thoroughly with the full weight of the body behind the heel. Slight 'basin' planting (leaving a shallow depression in which water can collect) is desirable in dry areas, and against walls where rain often has difficulty in penetrating. Dryness in borders against walls is something to keep in mind at all times. Lightly rake in a top-dressing of good compound fertiliser – rose fertiliser containing magnesium is as excellent for shrubs and climbers as it is for roses and should be applied as recommended for the last-mentioned.

Subsequent attention to watering is vital, particularly in the first and second springs following planting, and during all periods of drought (particularly in spring) for several years thereafter. In such circumstances, several bucketfuls of water per plant may be necessary; climbers and wall shrubs on south- and east-facing walls are particularly at risk in drought conditions. However, mulching material, such as pulverized bark fibre, straw, leaves, coarse peat or chopped bracken, well-rotted farmyard manure or a mixture of these is an ideal means of conserving moisture and

46. *A pergola spanning a path can be an extremely attractive garden feature, clothed, perhaps, as here, with a rambler rose and an ornamental vine,* Vitis coignetiae *(see pp. 88 and 89).*

maintaining a cool root run in hot weather. Do not pile heavy mulches, particularly manure, against stems and trunks; leave a small gap, otherwise rots and fungal troubles may occur on stems near ground level. Now you can rest until growth starts, with the training of the plants against wall, trellis or pergola the next move to consider (see pruning chapter, p. 311).

PROTECTING TENDER PLANTS In areas where severe frosts and cold, penetrating winds are experienced some winter protection may be necessary, particularly for newly planted half-hardy wall shrubs and climbers. In most districts, however, severe winter weather is rarely encountered before the turn of the year, and the longer the covering is delayed the more hardened the new plant will become to local conditions. Half-hardy subjects may be planted from pots in the late spring or, if available, in the summer months, but ideally no later than September, in order that they make some root growth and at least partially establish themselves before the onset of winter. This applies to such plants as *Abutilon*, *Ceanothus*, *Cestrum* and *Myrtus*, which should be afforded winter protection about Christmas time, using suitable porous material, which allows air to circulate, but still protects from hard frosts and cold winds. Useful for this purpose are cut bracken fronds, long straw, dead tops of herbaceous border plants (such as Michaelmas daisy) or the cut branches of evergreens (such as laurel and cypress). This material can be held in place by a few stout canes and if severe weather is forecast in January and February it may be desirable to provide additional cover with hessian or polythene.

PLANTING FOR SEASONAL EFFECTS

Most gardeners use wall shrubs and climbers to provide reasonable coverage of house walls or the walls and fences within the garden. Evergreen plants should be evenly distributed and most garden owners are seeking colour and interest at all seasons, through the medium of flowers, foliage and perhaps berries.

SOUTH- AND WEST-FACING WALLS AND FENCES Let us consider suitable subjects for walls and fences with a south or west aspect and a run of some 50ft(15m). We will assume that the soil is fertile. Such a length of wall or fence would need about eight subjects to provide it with average coverage.

For spring effect include an evergreen ceanothus; of the many available a hardy, popular and reliable cultivar to choose is 'Brilliant'. Rich mid-blue flowers are produced in quantity in May and June against a background of small glossy leaves. *C. impressus* 'Puget Blue' is slightly less hardy, but is particularly notable for its deeply impressed leaves and deep blue flowers. Pruning back after flowering will ensure a neat coverage of fence or wall. With the ceanothus might be associated that charming small evergreen shrub *Coronilla glauca*. Its bright yellow pea flowers are produced in the greatest profusion in April and May, although bloom is often much in evidence throughout a large part of the year and is seen to good advantage against the glaucous evergreen leaves. Usually quite small, *C. glauca* will adapt well with little pruning under a window which is about 3ft(1m) above ground level.

There is no shortage of plants for summer effect. Although its best display is in summer and autumn, *Abutilon megapotamicum* is often in flower for much of the year. It is an indispensable plant and very successful in all but the coldest areas, the hanging red and yellow fuchsia-like flowers may indeed be enjoyed at all seasons if it is sited so that the slender branches arch over a window or patio door. The Moroccan broom, *Cytisus battandieri*, is a handsome hardy species from the Atlas Mountains and if unrestricted will reach 15ft(4.5m) or more on a wall. One of the most impressive of all the brooms, it is grown as much for its handsome, silky-hairy, silvery-green leaves as for its terminal clusters of bright yellow, pineapple-scented flowers produced in June and July. This is one of those shrubs with which it is appropriate to associate a large-flowered hybrid clematis of moderate vigour – perhaps the beautiful soft rose-pink 'Comtesse de Bouchaud' or the broad sepalled sky-blue 'Perle d'Azur', for these are very telling when seen against the silvery leaves of the broom and will produce flowers until the autumn. Prepare a site for the clematis a little away from the host's roots.

To provide a display in autumn on our south or west wall, there is no better plant than *Solanum crispum* 'Glasnevin' (syn. *S.c.* 'Autumnale'). This is the best form and a spectacular plant, producing 6in(15cm) wide clusters of purple-blue flowers with bright yellow stamens. This Chilean climber is remarkably hardy, semi-evergreen and appropriate for a tall wall or fence, or for scrambling over a shed or similar structure. Equally effective and less frequently planted is the evergreen *Escallonia* 'Iveyi', (*E. bifida* × *E. exoniensis*). Its large, handsome, dark green foliage makes the perfect background for the large panicles of pure white flowers which attract butterflies in the autumn. This is a large shrub, but it adapts well to wall cultivation.

As a winter-effective subject for this aspect and for all soils, including chalky ones, we could consider *Chimonanthus praecox*, the winter sweet. It is grown primarily for its sweetly scented flowers produced in open weather during January or February on the leafless branches. A medium-sized shrub, this needs pruning back immediately after the flowers fade to ensure that it retains a compact habit. 'Grandiflorus' is the best form with deep yellow cup-shaped flowers with a prominent red or purple stain, while f. *luteus* has larger, unstained, translucent pale yellow flowers which open a fortnight later than the type. As this shrub is not effective during summer, it is best to use it to provide support for one of the many large-flowered garden clematis such as the reliable purple-blue 'The President' or 'Ville de Lyon', the best of the reds, which often flower from July to October.

Lofty walls, often at the gable end of a house, frequently incorporate a chimney which, if in use, will give off warmth to foster the tender climber or wall shrub. If such a wall is south- or west-facing, there is a grand opportunity to grow vigorous, often spectacular plants which would be unsuitable for growing against lower walls, probably incorporating windows. Most plants of this kind need plenty of room, and if more than one is planted they should be at least 8ft(2.5m) apart. Again, with regard for seasonal effect, the choice could be made from the following, assuming the availability of a sunny wall and fertile, well-drained soil. The evergreen *Ceanothus arboreus* 'Trewithen Blue' originated in a notable Cornish garden and is a large and spectacular spring-flowering shrub with leaves larger than the average and great panicles of slightly fragrant, deep blue flowers. In a recess by the chimney breast, the silver wattle, *Acacia dealbata*, the popular florists' mimosa, is worth a trial. It would benefit from the warmth of the chimney, and needs height to show off its silvery-green, fern-like foliage and golden mimosa-like flowers. In favoured areas it can reach tree-like proportions. Slightly hardier and requiring a similar site is the all too infrequently planted New Zealand kowhai, *Sophora tetraptera*. The best form 'Grandiflora' displays in May and June remarkable golden-yellow flowers, pea-shaped, but somewhat tubular. Each of these flowers is at least 1½ to 2in(4 to 5cm) long and they are borne in drooping racemes of four to eight flowers. This is a large shrub or even small tree with spreading branches and pinnate leaves and shoots. The flower and leaf stalks are covered when young with an unusual tawny down. The kowhai is an intriguing and beautiful plant, well worth a trial.

A high south- or west-facing wall is essential for *Fremontodendron* (*Fremontia*) 'California Glory' (*F. californica* × *F. mexicana*). This splendid and floriferous hybrid seems to be hardier than either of its parents. The bright yellow flowers are at least 2in(5cm) across and are freely produced all summer. Perhaps the most distinguished and magnificent of all evergreens for growing as a wall shrub is *Magnolia grandiflora*. Here again a tall wall is essential and a good depth of rich, loamy soil to obtain the best from this fine shrub. 'Exmouth' is the best cultivar with 6 to 10in(15 to 25cm) leaves, long, polished green above and rust-felted beneath. These give the plant its nobility and makes a perfect background for the immense and richly fragrant, globular flowers, creamy-white in colour and 8 to 10in(20 to 25cm) across. These flowers usually appear in summer and autumn, for the first time perhaps six to ten years after planting.

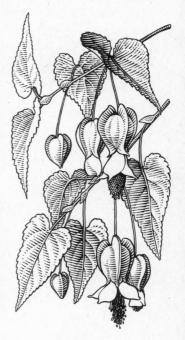

47. *The handsome red and yellow fuchsia-like flowers of* Abutilon megapotamicum *make it a natural choice for a south- or west-facing wall or fence. Its main display period is summer and autumn but it also flowers at other times as well.*

NORTH- OR EAST-FACING WALLS OR FENCES For a 50ft(15m) run or thereabouts of north- or east-facing wall or fence, early spring flowers could be provided by one of the many cultivars of *Chaenomeles* (syn. *Cydonia*), the ornamental quinces, commonly known as "Japonica". Well pruned and trained specimens can be most spectacular, the waxy flowers lasting over a long period. Lateral shoots should be pruned back to two or three buds immediately the flowers fade so that the plant will have a compact habit and provide adequate wall coverage. A selection of the best, readily available cultivars or hybrids of *C. speciosa* (syn. *C. lagenaria*) includes: 'Crimson and Gold', deep red with golden anthers; 'Moerloosii', pink and white, and reminiscent of apple blossom; 'Knaphill Scarlet', with orange-scarlet flowers borne over a long season; 'Nivalis', the best, large white; 'Simonii', semi-double blood red flowers, low growing and excellent for planting under a window; and 'Rowallane', a large crimson flowered cultivar. The variegated form of the Canary Island ivy, *Hedera canariensis* 'Gloire de Marengo' is a superb wall covering for a shady sheltered aspect and is, of course, effective at all seasons of the year, and particularly in the spring when fresh growth is being produced. The large leaves are deep green overlaid with silvery grey and margined with white; it is the fastest growing, but not the hardiest, of the variegated ivies.

For high walls the climbing *Hydrangea petiolaris* is a frequent choice. It will, after it has been established for a few years, be most conspicuous at mid-summer when it displays its large corymbs of white, sterile florets. This self-supporting deciduous climber is also most decorative in winter with its bright cinnamon-coloured peeling bark. Alternatively, the evergreen climbing hydrangea, *Pileostegia viburnoides*, could be found a place here. This is slower growing but equally self-supporting; its handsome, prominently veined leaves are up to 6in(15cm) long, and its panicles of creamy-white flowers appear, rather later than those of *H. petiolaris*, in August and September.

Slower growing than *H. petiolaris* but very worthy of consideration are either of the two species of the small genus *Schizophragma*, which is closely allied with this hydrangea. *Schizophragma integrifolium* is the more magnificent of the two species (the other is *S. hydrangeoides*), having broadly ovate, slender-pointed leaves up to 7in(18cm) long. The flower heads may be as much as a foot (30cm) across and are remarkable for the large, white, ovate, conspicuously veined bracts of up to 3½in(9cm) in length which terminate each division of the inflorescence. This choice species was introduced around the turn of the century by the distinguished plant collector E.H.Wilson. *Drimys winteri*, the winter bark, adapts well to being grown against a tall, shaded wall. Its leaves also are very handsome, 5 to 9in(13 to 23cm) long, evergreen, leathery and glaucous beneath; umbels of fragrant ivory-white flowers open in May. This distinguished shrub deserves to be more frequently planted.

Another excellent evergreen wall shrub producing its bright yellow, laburnum-like flowers in early summer is the evergreen laburnum, *Piptanthus laburnifolius* (syn. *P. nepalensis*). Its handsome, dark green, trifoliate leaves are glaucous beneath and may fall in severe winters. It is an excellent wall shrub worthy of wider planting. Alternatively, if another climber rather than a wall shrub is appropriate, the choice honeysuckle, *Lonicera tragophylla* is well worth wall space. This grows and flowers well in almost complete shade. Its bright golden-yellow scentless flowers are produced in June and July. Crossed with *L. sempervirens*, it has given us the hybrid *L.× tellmanniana* which is equally showy and desirable; its flowers are flushed red at the bud stage and open to yellow with a coppery tint.

A fascinating and all too infrequently planted wall shrub is the evergreen *Itea ilicifolia*. This is conspicuous in the early autumn when it is carrying its long, drooping, catkin-like racemes of fragrant green-white flowers, viewed against elegant, holly-like foliage. This is a striking, unusual and reasonably hardy shrub.

Less hardy and demanding a lime-free soil is the choice and beautiful coral plant, *Berberidopsis corallina*. This is well worth a place where there is adequate moisture and the site is shaded. This is undoubtedly one of the most remarkable and spectacular of climbing plants. Its heart-shaped, fine-toothed leaves are blue-white beneath and in late summer and autumn are borne drooping racemes of deep crimson flowers at least 4in(10cm) long. The firethorns, *Pyracantha*, are familiar and perhaps rather overplanted as wall shrubs. They are hardy and can be allowed to develop their natural shape and size in a free-standing position. However, they provide excellent evergreen cover for a shaded wall, and if long, lateral growths are pruned back immediately after the white flowers fade, a neat habit is maintained. In recent years some new cultivars reaching us from the United States are said to be resistent to fireblight and scab, troublesome diseases which have caused die-back of pyracanthas. All of them produce spectacular displays of berries in the autumn, these persisting into winter. These newer cultivars include 'Golden Charmer', 'Mohave' (with large orange-red fruits), 'Orange Glow' and 'Tetron' (which has a narrow, upright habit and yellow fruits).

For reliable winter flowering, one cannot exclude the yellow winter jasmine, *Jasminum nudiflorum*. Its bright yellow flowers appear in open weather from November to February and are invaluable if branchlets are cut and brought into the house in bud, to open on the dullest of winter days. Although excellent as ground cover on difficult steep banks, it makes a fine wall shrub and may be trained up quite a tall wall, if desired, to festoon down most attractively. Cut back long growths immediately after flowering has finished to maintain a neat, compact wall coverage. *Garrya elliptica*, particularly in its best male form 'James Roof', is a magnificent spectacle during January and February when hung with its long grey-green catkins. This is a magnificent, wind-resistant evergreen but the leaves can be "scorched" in severe weather. The female plant, although its catkins are shorter, has interesting deep brown-purple fruits in long clusters. For summer and autumn effect a garrya can play host to a good clematis species, such as *C. tangutica* with its numerous bell-shaped yellow flowers and silky seed heads. If you have a lime-free soil, you can also associate with it the scrambling Scotch creeper, *Tropaeolum speciosum*, which usually establishes well in cool, shady conditions, particularly in the north of England and Scotland. When growing well, it is sensational with its scarlet nasturtium flowers 1½in(4cm) across, produced freely from June onwards.

Given lime-free soil, one of the many camellias can be trained as a wall shrub, either against a north-facing wall or a west-facing one. In such situations they are less likely to suffer from summer drought (which causes bud drop) or to have their flowers damaged by early morning spring sunshine following frost. By reason of their winter or very early spring flowers, and in certain cases their habit of growth, some are particularly appropriate for wall cultivation. A choice might be made from the very free-flowering 'Inspiration' (*C. reticulata*×*C. saluenensis*) with large, semi-double, deep pink blooms; *C. japonica* 'Nobilissima', paeony-form, white and very early flowering; *C. japonica* 'Sylva' rose-red; and 'Leonard Messel' (*C. reticulata*×*C.*×*williamsii* 'Mary Christian') a remarkably hardy cultivar with large, semi-double, coral-pink flowers.

One of the most worthy of space is *C. sasanqua* 'Narumi-gata', perhaps the only cultivar of this beautiful winter-flowering species that performs reliably in the British Isles. It produces its large pink-tinted white flowers with reasonable regularity on established plants. Members of the *C.*×*williamsii* (*C. japonica*×*C. saluenensis*) group of hardy hybrids are also very adaptable to wall cultivation, flowering freely and reliably from November to May. 'Donation' produces quantities of very large semi-double, beautifully veined pink flowers and is reliable and spectacular if now somewhat over planted. 'E.G. Waterhouse' is of more recent introduction and has formal double, pale pink flowers, while 'J.C. Williams', compact in habit and free-flowering, bears single, rose-pink flowers. This last is often considered the finest of all camellias. 'November Pink' is very early coming into flower and continues intermittently throughout winter and spring, as the weather allows.

CHOOSING AND GROWING CLEMATIS These delectable and well-known climbers are, with the possible exception of the rose, the most colourful,

49. Ceanothus 'Delight', a fine spring-flowering hybrid which bears rich blue panicles of flowers (top, opposite page).

48. Clematis tangutica is an indispensable climber furnishing for low walls, hedges and tripods, the yellow flowers being borne in late summer and autumn and, in the later stages, in conjunction with the silky seed heads, shown above.

charming and (often) spectacular hardy plants that can be grown in gardens – hence their singling out for special mention. They are remarkably adaptable and will adorn all types of walls, fences, pergolas, trellis and tripods; they will also scramble through trees, climb among roses or over hedges and through plantings of heathers or even weave their way among boulders.

To give of their best against a wall or fence, the large-flowered garden clematis need to be planted in a sunny site where the root area will be shaded by dwarf shrubs or other plants. For the best results a well-cultivated and well-drained, rich, loamy soil is desirable. They are excellent for growing on chalk or limestone and respond to generous annual feeding; thorough watering may be necessary, particularly at times of drought.

The species are particularly successful when festooning pergolas or wooden tripods. Among the most reliable and desirable of these in general cultivation are *Clematis alpina* which bears solitary, powder-blue nodding flowers in April and May. This is a charming dwarf to scramble over a low wall or boulder. *C. alpina* 'Frances Rivis' (syn. 'Blue Giant') has larger, freely produced flowers up to 2in(5cm) long with conspicuous white centres. *C. armandii* is the best evergreen species, and this is generally available in two cultivars, 'Snowdrift', with clusters of pure white flowers, and 'Apple Blossom', white, shaded pink. These flower in April and early May. The long, leathery leaves provide an effective and unusual year-round wall coverage. *C. chrysocoma* is, in effect, a refined, less rampant *C. montana* with soft pink flowers produced in May and June. Ideal for a pergola upright is *C.×durandii (C. integrifolia×C. × jackmanii)*, an unusual semi-herbaceous hybrid with spectacular violet-blue flowers measuring 4in(10cm) across. These are produced all summer.

Equally desirable and slightly more robust is *C. macropetala*. This is like a double-flowered, violet-blue *C. alpina*; its shell-pink cultivar, 'Markham's Pink', (syn. 'Markhamii') is especially lovely.

Popular, vigorous and beautiful *C. montana* and several of its cultivars are very well known and perhaps some are rather over-planted. They will succeed in most aspects and are particularly useful for covering trees and outhouses. Among the most notable cultivars are 'Alexander' with large well-scented, creamy-white flowers; 'Grandiflora', perhaps the best white-flowered form for general planting; var. *rubens*, the popular rose-pink form with red-purple shoots and leaves; and the newer 'Tetrarose', which is less rampant and very striking with its lilac-pink flowers up to 3½in(9cm) across.

Clematis tangutica is undoubtedly the best yellow-flowered species and an indispensable plant for every garden. It is excellent for clambering over low walls, hedges or tripods, the distinct bell-shaped yellow flowers appearing in late summer and autumn and mingling effectively in the later stages with the silky seed heads. *C. viticella*, the true virgin's bower, is a useful and effective, moderately vigorous species for pergola or tripod, best represented by its cultivars or hybrids, notably 'Alba Luxurians', white, tinted mauve, 'Kermesina', crimson, and 'Royal Velours', deep purple.

The large-flowered garden clematis are frequently planted with climbing roses, ceanothus, garrya or other wall shrubs which are out of flower in the summer months. Be careful, however, not to plant in close competition with the roots of the host plant. Some shade is desirable for pale pink cultivars, such as 'Nelly Moser', which tend to fade quickly in hot sunlight.

There is a troublesome fungal disease, clematis wilt, which can be very distressing when it occurs as it causes the sudden overnight collapse of apparently healthy plants, often full of bud and flower. If this occurs, affected shoots (if need be the whole top of the plant) should be removed; cut back to below soil level if necessary until live healthy tissue is encountered. Even small wounds should be sealed with Arbrex or a similar fungicidal tree paint, and any remaining top shoots – and new shoots as they occur – should be sprayed, at about fortnightly intervals, with Bordeaux mixture or a liquid copper fungicide. Given this treatment the plant will, hopefully, recover. It is worthwhile spraying all clematis plants with a copper fungicide in the autumn and again in the spring when the shoots are developing, concentrating particularly on the base of the plant in an effort to prevent attacks by this disease.

A short list of reliable cultivars with a wide range of colours might include 'Comtesse de Bouchaud', one of the best pinks; 'Daniel Deronda', a very beautiful violet-blue cultivar with a paler centre; and 'Hagley Hybrid', an exciting newish cultivar with deep shell-pink flowers with purple anthers. 'Henryi' is the finest white with very large flowers; 'Jackmanii Superba', strong growing and free flowering with rich violet-purple flowers, and a form of the original large-flowered hybrid between *C. lanuginosa* and *C. viticella*, produced in 1860 at Jackman's Nurseries, Woking, Surrey; and 'Ville de Lyon', perhaps the best red with the beautifully veined crimson flowers having prominent golden anthers. All the above cultivars are effective between June and October.

CLIMBING AND WALL SHRUBS FOR VARIOUS PURPOSES

Those mentioned are suitable for general planting and are usually available from nurserymen and garden centres. A few of those listed are less frequently planted and may be available only from nurseries specialising in unusual plants. Many such plants are worthy of wider recognition.

Key
* = suitable for narrow positions between windows, etc.
† = not fully hardy – will require protection in severe weather until well established, other than in mild areas.
ev = evergreen   × = of hybrid origin
‡ = acid soil essential   spp = species
cv = cultivar   (t) = for tall walls
Most will require the support of wire or trellis, but those climbers marked ø are self-clinging.

South- and West-Facing Walls and Fences of 6ft(2m) or more in height

Plant generally 6 to 8ft(2 to 2.5m) apart on walls and fences.

Climbers		Wall Shrubs	
*	*Actinidia kolomikta*	†*	*Abelia floribunda*
*†ev	*Araujia sericofera*	ev	*Abelia × grandiflora*
	Campsis grandiflora	†*	*Abutilon megapotamicum*
ø	*Campsis radicans*		*Abutilon vitifolium*
	Clematis – most species		'Veronica Tennant' (t)
	(see opposite page)	ev	*Acacia baileyana* (t)
	Clematis – large flowered	ev	*Acacia dealbata* (t)
	hybrids (see above)		*Buddleia colvilei* 'Kewensis'
*	*Eccremocarpus scaber*		*Buddleia crispa*
	Jasminum officinale and cvs.	†	*Caesalpinia gilliesii*
ø	*Parthenocissus* species and cvs.	ev	*Callistemon linearis*
†	*Mandevilla suaveolens*	ev	*Carpenteria californica*
†ev	*Passiflora caerulea*	ev	*Ceanothus*, many spp and cvs.
	'Constance Elliott'	ev	*Cestrum* 'Newellii'
*	Roses – climbing spp. and		*Chimonanthus praecox* f. *luteus*
	cvs. of moderate growth		*Cytisus battandieri*
		†	*Cytisus* 'Porlock'
		*	*Daphne bholua*

spp.	cvs.		
banksiae	'Casino'	†ev	*Dendromecon rigida*
'Lutea' (t)	'Guinée'	ev	*Escallonia* 'Iveyi'
ecae	'Handel'	†ev	*Feijoa sellowiana*
laevigata	'Schoolgirl'	ev	*Fremontodendron*
'Anemonoides'	'Swan Lake'		'California Glory' (t)
		†	*Hypericum* 'Rowallane'

	Schisandra grandiflora rubriflora	†‡ev	*Leptospermum scoparium* cvs.
	Solanum crispum	ev	*Magnolia delavayi* (t)
	'Glasnevin' (t)	ev	*Magnolia grandiflora* (t)
†	*Solanum jasminoides* (t)	†ev	*Myrtus communis* and cvs.
*ev	*Trachelospermum asiaticum*	ev	*Olearia avicenniifolia*
†ev	*Trachelospermum jasminoides*	†ev	*Olearia × scilloniensis*

50. *Actinidia kolomikta, a climber for a south- or west-facing wall or fence of 6ft (2m) or more in height. Its variegated leaves are an extremely attractive green and the lower part white with pink flushing.*

Climbers		Wall Shrubs	
†	*Wattakaka (Dregea) sinensis*	†	*Punica granatum* and cvs.
	Wisteria sinensis and cvs.	†ev	*Sophora tetraptera* 'Grandiflora' (t)
		†ev	*Teucrium fruticans*

North- and East-facing walls and fences of 6ft(2m) or more in height

Many are equally successful on south- and west-facing surfaces. Note that camellias are suitable for north- or west-facing walls only.

Climbers		Wall Shrubs	
ev	*Akebia quinata*	ev	*Azara microphylla* (t)
†ev	*Berberidopsis corallina*	‡ev	*Camellia japonica* cvs.
øev	*Decumaria sinensis*	‡ev	*Camellia sasanqua* 'Narumi-gata'
øev	*Hedera canariensis* 'Gloire de Marengo'	‡ev	*Camellia × williamsii* cvs.
øev	*Hedera helix* and cvs.		*Chaenomeles speciosa* cvs.
ev	*Holboellia coriacea*	ev	*Choisya ternata*
ø	*Hydrangea petiolaris*	††ev	*Crinodendron (Tricuspidaria) hookeranum* (t)
	Lonicera – most spp. and cvs., particularly:	ev	*Drimys winteri* (t)
ev	*Lonicera japonica*	ev	*Eriobotrya japonica* (t)
	Lonicera tragophylla	ev	*Garrya elliptica* 'James Roof'
ø	*Parthenocissus henryana*	ev	*Illicium anisatum*
ø	*Parthenocissus tricuspidata* 'Veitchii'	ev	*Itea ilicifolia*
øev	*Pileostegia viburnoides*	ev	*Jasminium humile* 'Revolutum'
ev	*Rubus henryi* var. *bambusarum*		*Jasminum nudiflorum*
ø	*Schizophragma hydrangeoides* (t)	*	*Kerria japonica* 'Pleniflora'
	Schizophragma integrifolium	ev	*Mahonia × media* cvs. 'Charity' and 'Winter Sun'
	Vitis – several spp. and cvs.	ev	*Piptanthus laburnifolius* (syn. *P. nepalensis*)
		ev	*Pyracantha* – most spp. and cvs. (t)
		ev	*Viburnum tinus* and cvs.

Balustrades, Low Walls and Positions Beneath Windows

Vigorous, tall-growing shrubs and climbers are quite unsatisfactory in such situations and need continual heavy pruning to restrict them. The plants listed below are suitable for such positions. While climbers will require support, most of the dwarf shrubs referred to here can be planted near the wall and should not need more than light pruning to keep them within bounds. The climbers listed are, in the main, more appropriate for balustrades and low, free-standing walls within the garden than for positions under windows.

SOUTH- AND WEST-FACING POSITIONS (LOW WALLS)

Climbers		Wall Shrubs	
†ev	*Billardiera longiflora*	ev	*Abelia* 'Edward Goucher'
	Clematis alpina and cvs.		*Abelia schumannii*
	Clematis tangutica		*Abeliophyllum distichum*
†ev	*Clianthus puniceus*	†	*Aloysia triphylla* (syn. *Lippia citriodora*)
†ev	*Eccremocarpus scaber*		
†ev	*Sollya heterophylla*	†	*Artemisia arborescens*
	Vitis vinifera 'Incana'	†ev	*Calceolaria integrifolia*
	Vitis vinifera 'Purpurea'		*Caryopteris × clandonensis* 'Heavenly Blue'
		ev	*Cistus* spp. and cvs., particularly 'Silver Pink',

Wall Shrubs

†	*Cistus* × *purpureus* and *C.* × *skanbergii*
†ev	*Convolvulus cneorum*
ev	*Corokia cotoneaster*
†ev	*Coronilla glauca*
	Cotoneaster horizontalis 'Variegata'
ev	*Cotoneaster microphyllus* and cvs.
†ev	*Lavandula dentata*
ev	*Phlomis fruticosa*
	Phygelius capensis 'Coccineus'
†	*Punica granatum* var. *nana*
†	*Salvia microphylla* (syn. *S. grahamii*)

51. Lonicera japonica halliana, *a climber for low east- and north-facing walls.*

EAST- AND NORTH-FACING POSITIONS (LOW WALLS):

Climbers

øtev	*Ficus pumila* 'Minima'
ev	*Hedera helix* – variegated cvs. particularly: 'Glacier', 'Goldheart' and 'Tricolor'
ev	*Hedera canariensis* 'Gloire de Marengo'
ev	*Hedera colchica* 'Dentata' and *H.c.* 'Dentata Variegata'
	Jasminum nudiflorum
ev	*Lonicera japonica halliana*
ev	*Lonicera japonica* 'Aureoreticulata'
	Lonicera periclymenum 'Serotina'

Wall Shrubs

	Chaenomeles speciosa 'Simonii'
ev	*Choisya ternata*
ev	*Daphne odora* 'Aureomarginata'
ev	*Daphne* × *hybrida*
ev	*Euonymus fortunei* 'Silver Queen'
ev	× *Fatshedera lizei*
	Fuchsias – hardy cvs.
	Hydrangea 'Preziosa'
	Hydrangea quercifolia
	Hydrangea serrata cvs.
ev	*Ribes laurifolium*

Climbers for Pergola uprights, tripods, arches, etc.

	Actinidia kolomikta
	Clematis - most large-flowered hybrids and spp. of moderate growth, particularly: *Clematis chrysocoma*, *C.* × *durandii*, *C. macropetala* and *C. montana* 'Tetrarose'
ev	*Hedera helix* cvs.
	Humulus lupulus 'Aureus'
	Lonicera caprifolium 'Pauciflora'
	Lonicera 'Dropmore Scarlet'
	Lonicera × *heckrottii* 'Gold Flame'
ev	*Lonicera implexa*
	Mutisia oligodon

Climbing Roses of moderate growth, particularly:
'Aloha'
'Dublin Bay'
'Golden Showers'
'Pompon de Paris'

†ev	*Trachelospermum jasminoides*
	Tropaeolum speciosum
	Vitis davidii cyanocarpa
	Vitis labrusca
	Vitis vinifera 'Apiifolia'

Climbers for Pergola Roof Beams

    Actinidia chinensis
    Aristolochia macrophylla
      (syn. *A. sipho*)
    Clematis montana and cvs.
ev   *Hedera colchica* 'Dentata
      Variegata'
    Jasminum officinale
    Lonicera × americana
    Lonicera etrusca
    Roses, particularly:
      'Crimson Conquest'
      'Easlea's Golden Rambler'
      'Madame Alfred Carrière (white)
      'Madame Grégoire Staechelin'
      'Mermaid'
    Vitis vinifera 'Brant'
    Vitis coignetiae
    Wisteria floribunda 'Multijuga' (syn. *W. floribunda* 'Macrobotrys')
    Wisteria sinensis and cvs.

Vigorous Climbers to climb into Trees or smother Stumps, old Sheds, Steep Bankings, etc.

ev   *Akebia quinata*
    Aristolochia macrophylla
    Celastrus orbiculatus
    Clematis montana and cvs.
    Clematis rehderiana
ev   *Holboellia coriacea*
ø   *Hydrangea petiolaris*
    Lonicera caprifolium
      'Pauciflora'
ev   *Lonicera japonica* and cvs.

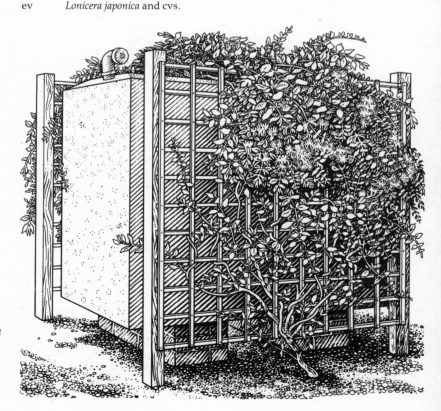

52. *A domestic oil tank can be quite easily screened by growing an evergreen climber, such as* Lonicera japonica halliana, *over trellis-work.*

ø	*Parthenocissus quinquefolia*
ø	*Parthenocissus tricuspidata*
	'Veitchii'
øev	*Pileostegia viburnoides*

Polygonum baldschuanicum
Rosa 'Complicata'
Rosa filipes 'Kiftsgate'
Rose 'Wedding Day', and
    vigorous rambler roses (particularly for bankings):
        'Albéric Barbier' (cream)
        'Albertine' (pink)
        'Crimson Shower' (crimson)
        'Macrantha' (pink)
        'Veilchenblau' (purple)
Rubus ulmifolius 'Bellidiflorus'
Vitis coignetiae
Wisteria sinensis and cvs.

Screening a domestic oil tank

Support these climbers on trellis. All are evergreen (or semi-evergreen) and shade-tolerant as the oil tank is usually on the north side of the house. Select one or two from the following pairs:

ev	*Hedera colchica* and/or *H.c.* 'Dentata Variegata'
ev	*Lonicera japonica repens*
	and/or *L.j. halliana*
ev	*Akebia quinata* and/or *Lonicera japonica*
	'Aureoreticulata'

In mild areas try:

ev	*Clematis cirrhosa* (syn. *C. balearica*)

53. *A vigorous rose like* Rosa *'Kiftsgate', allowed to climb into a tree, is spectacular when bearing its white flowers in late June and July.*

8.

Hedges and Screens

Hedges and screens define a garden and special areas within a garden. They are often needed to exclude intruders, and may be useful in restraining children and family pets from wandering. They can, when properly maintained, provide a background of uniform green – or yellow in the case of a conifer like × *Cupressocyparis leylandii* 'Castlewellan' – against which plants and plant groupings can appear to better advantage than when distracted by unwanted views. Most important, in many gardens they provide shelter from wind and thus improve the micro-climate in which favoured, but perhaps rather tender, plants can be grown without damage and to better advantage. A hedge, screen or fence is almost essential around every garden and is desirable within all but the smallest.

The effect of wind is an underrated aspect of the environment in which we garden. We water plants to combat droughts, and drain soils to remove surplus water. We protect plants from frost and give shade to those that dislike too much sun. Winds are equally damaging to plants. Even light breezes reduce temperatures, remove moisture and disturb growth. Stronger winds break leaves and branches, rock and damage roots, prevent pollination and produce windfalls of fruits. 'Windfall' is one of the few gardening terms indicating damage by this ever-present aspect of the climate. A windswept garden is almost always untidy and less attractive than one with adequate shelter. In gardens with adequate shelter its value is rarely appreciated until a large tree disappears in a gale or a sheltering hedge becomes overgrown and sparsely furnished at the base, letting in strong winds.

Before providing shelter it is as well to study the behaviour of wind in the open and where some shelter is present. A knowledge of this subject is invaluable even when considering the planting of a new hedge in the smallest garden. Prevailing winds, as every gardener knows, can be the most damaging, but the atmosphere is under pressure from all directions, and winds, which are bodies of air under pressure, flow from all directions. Thus all-round protection is needed in every garden, and, unless it is provided naturally it needs to be provided by plants or structures if a successful garden is to be created.

Over a perfectly level surface such as water or a large flat plain, air flows direct and unhindered from high to low pressure areas and only changes direction as the areas of pressure alter. However, no garden is completely flat and every solid projection distorts the flow of air. Hills, houses, forests and so on down to the smallest plants change the direction of the wind to a greater or lesser extent. The flowing air may rise above or go round each obstacle. This tends to increase the wind speed close to the top or side of the obstacle and slightly reduce it on its lee side. A small degree of vacuum is created in the lee of solid barriers and the turbulence that ensues is frequently noticed when dry leaves or snow are there to indicate the swirling effects that are produced. In the same way the higher wind speeds at the corners of buildings and between two solid barriers are often noted.

PRACTICAL OBJECTIVES Solid barriers, as we have seen, create their own problems of changing wind direction, increases of speed above or beside them and turbulence behind them. Open screens and thin hedges filter the air flow and thus reduce the turbulence. Such screens reduce the wind speed and allow some air to flow through and fill the vacuum that otherwise might be created.

We can arrange for, on the one hand, complete diversion of the wind with consequent turbulence on the lee side of the barrier or, at the other extreme, have a very open screen which has very little effect on wind speeds. For the gardener the optimum amount of reduction in both wind speed and turbulence is provided by screens that have a ratio of about 60 per cent solid to 40 per cent aperture. Thus 2½in(6cm) planks spaced 1½in(4cm) apart would come near the optimum for use as a screen to prevent damage by wind. Lath fences made of 1in(2.5cm) laths spaced 1in(2.5cm) apart and mounted on 2in(5cm) timber with diagonal cross branching, are a most satisfactory, practical design. These have long been used in windy districts. It is more difficult to measure the effectiveness of living hedges as windbreaks; they vary in permeability according to the season and the stiffness or flexibility of their branches and twigs, while deciduous plants are obviously more permeable in winter than in summer. A rough general rule is that a suitable shelter hedge is one where movement can be distinguished when looking through it but the identity of the moving objects cannot be distinguished.

Such permeable screens and hedges allow enough air to filter through, avoiding anything approaching a vacuum that creates turbulence. Wind speeds are at the same time adequately reduced for practical purposes.

CAUSE AND EFFECT The next aspect of the wind behaviour that needs consideration is the extent of the effect of barriers or shelter on wind speed and direction. Taking 'H' as the height of the barrier, the speed of wind striking a barrier at right angles is reduced to a distance of some 30 H to leeward and some 5 H to windward. In other words, if no other barrier is present the wind reaches its original speed at 30 H to the lee of the barrier, but there is only a noticeable reduction up to about 7 H. Thus a screen 10ft(3m) high will considerably reduce the speed of the wind up to some 70ft(21m) and the wind will steadily increase in speed up to 300ft(90m) when the original speed will be regained (see Fig.54).

An understanding of the theory of wind behaviour is necessary to plan new hedges or screens to best advantage if there is a choice of planting

*54. **A.** A cross-section, to scale, of a hedge standing at right-angles to the direction of the wind. The figures show the percentages of the original wind speed to windward and leeward of the hedge with H representing the height of the hedge; e.g. 5H = five times height of hedge.*
***B.** The effect of a relatively short length of hedge on wind speed. The figures relate to percentages of the original wind speed.*
***C.** A plan of the ground surrounding a hedge with the wind blowing at an angle of 45 degrees to it. Indicated are the percentages of the original wind speed in relation to the distance from the hedge, with H representing the height of the hedge. The measurements of the wind speed are taken along the line of the original direction of the wind and not at right angles to the hedge. Note the increase in wind speeds at the ends of the hedge and on the windward side when the wind strikes at an angle.*

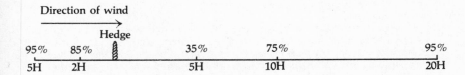

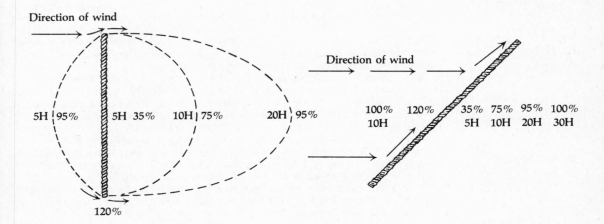

plans. Such knowledge can be put to good use when planning new plantings or deciding whether to move or uproot existing plants. Most gardeners will also want to take into account the overall design of the garden – the need to hide particular eyesores, provide backgrounds and fill gaps between buildings or established plants.

NOISE SUPPRESSION   In addition to the advantages already referred to, hedges and screens can reduce noise to a limited extent but as noise and wind barriers they need very different properties. Wind barriers are best when slightly permeable and sited close to the area to be sheltered. Noise barriers are best when broad, solid and thick and near the source of the noise. But one must state that trees are not very efficient in this respect. Nevertheless, all hedges and screens muffle some sound and may reduce the distress caused by noise if only by the psychological effect of shutting out the sight of the source of the noise. Recent research, repeated in this country, has shown that to be effective a very wide filter screen of trees is needed, certainly not less than 45ft(14m) and probably up to 150ft(45m). Shrubs – particularly evergreens – by providing thicker cover low down can be more effective than trees with bare trunks low down.

NATURAL AND MAN-MADE BARRIERS   What can be done to provide such hedges and screens? They can range from the formality of artificial fences and severely clipped hedges to lines or groups of trees or shrubs of a single or several similar species. All need to be able to withstand the strongest winds to be expected on the site. Loss of shelter during a violent storm not only causes annoyance and involves the cost of replacement but can result in the loss of the cherished plants that were being protected.

Wooden fences and trellis of assorted types are available in most districts and can form useful temporary screens against which more permanent screens of trees or shrubs may be raised. Their life span varies but few can be termed even semi-permanent. Those constructed of solid timber, treated with wood preservative before erection and set deeply in the ground or in solid bases, can last for some years. They are then useful as supports for climbing or trailing plants that add to the attraction of the garden and that may be the chief reason for their use. It must be remembered that the more solid the fence or screen the greater the wind turbulence on the sheltered side and the greater the difficulty in keeping such structures erect in the strongest gales.

Wire or plastic netting or strips of plastic on metal or wooden uprights are purely temporary means of providing shelter from wind, defining a boundary or screening an eyesore. They may provide support for temporary climbing plants or protection for a more permanent hedge but they are nearly always unsightly and better avoided wherever possible.

Walls of brick or concrete, solid or open and in a range of designs, are much more permanent and can fill many requirements in suitable situations, such as when they form extensions to the house or other buildings or enclose the most formal parts of the garden. There, they may cut off the winds that whistle round corners, screen ugly outbuildings or unsightly views. They may be better for these purposes than even the toughest trees or shrubs which may be impossible to grow in such circumstances. Many old walls remain in older gardens, and, like those more recently erected, they not only provide shelter but valuable space against which to plant and on which to train fruiting plants which thrive better in such conditions. They may also provide protection for many climbers, trees and shrubs which would be unlikely to survive without such shelter and support.

The importance of providing artificial screens with adequate support must be emphasised again if these are to do their job properly and remain upright in the strongest of gales. All types of fences need strong posts set in solid foundations and adequate ties. Additional buttresses may often be needed for single walls and all must be set on solid foundations.

In many situations living hedges and screens are better than artificial barriers. Patience is needed while they mature, but many can last a lifetime and add beauty to the garden.

CULTURAL CONSIDERATIONS The detailed needs of each plant will be considered when discussing their uses, but in general it can be said that the greater the depth of soil the better the growth and the longer the life of a hedge. For all but a very few species adequate draining to prevent waterlogging is essential. Where drainage is suspect and wet conditions are likely it is often better to limit the plant choice to those that thrive in such conditions rather than to struggle to drain the ground and still run the risk of failure.

For all hedges proper soil preparation is necessary in order to provide good rooting conditions. All weeds must be removed. This will ensure early and uniform growth. Suitable early training and regular trimming will then lead to the development of a successful hedge.

In garden conditions it may be desirable to dig a strip up to 6ft(2m) wide for each new hedge. Compost or farmyard manure can be incorporated to improve the soil and the roots of perennial weeds can be removed. Annual and herbaceous perennial weeds can be a nuisance to newly planted hedges and cause poor bottom growth, but other shrubs, climbers and scramblers are the worst 'weeds' of hedges. They are mostly natives that spread from roots left in the soil during site preparation or by seeds from neighbouring plants. Among the worst offenders are elder, hawthorn and sycamore among the trees, and brambles, bindwood and dog rose that scramble through and damage both young and established hedges. All of these and other invaders need to be looked for each year and removed before a length of hedge has been damaged beyond repair.

If soil preparations are adequate such dominant hedge weeds should not be troublesome in the first years, and the ordinary garden weeds can be dealt with by hoeing or the use of herbicides (see Chapter 38, ''Weed Control'', pp.332 to 339).

Just as most hedges compete with neighbouring plants for food and water and thus cause loss of vigour in such crops, so, in the first year or two, young hedges may suffer from competition by weeds, or from lawns or other plants growing nearby. Weeds can be controlled but with newly planted hedges the effects of competition may need to be offset by additional feeding and watering if good early growth is to be obtained.

When growth commences, training and trimming need to be started. All but very few hedge plants are better when trained to form a broader base and narrower top than the traditional perpendicular or more common rounded hedge pattern. A narrow-based isosceles triangle is the ideal sectional shape for most hedges. With such a slightly wider base the lower branches will not be killed by lack of light and the hedge will remain green to the ground. It seems so much easier to trim the lower branches too hard and thus produce a rounded sectional pattern to the hedge. A positive effort has to be made to leave the base lightly trimmed or untouched in order to encourage the suggested wider base and narrower top. For once inhibited by heavy trimming or by competing weeds or near by cultivated plants few hedge plants produce new growth at the bottom and the hedge remains for ever inadequate and unsightly. The advantages of narrow-topped hedges are in their greater permeability and in the limited space available on which snow can settle. The greater permeability allows the wind to filter through and reduces turbulence, while the limited snow cover reduces the risk of breaking open the hedge and damage to branches that can be almost irreparable.

The frequency of cutting will, of course, depend on the subject which has been chosen for hedging, but a few general points are worthy of note. Except for conifers and a few trees such as beech and hornbeam, most shrubs make better hedges when the leading shoots are removed to encourage side growth and establish a useful base. Most also make a better and quicker hedge when trimmed rather more frequently than usual in the first two or three years. Thereafter, annual trimming may be sufficient for most species although some make more formal hedges when cut two or three times each summer.

When planting it is almost a necessity to use a garden line to ensure a straight run of hedge or to achieve a predetermined curve. A single line of plants is to be preferred as weeding or hoeing is then easier and the final growth and appearance better than with a double row of plants. Spacing of the plants depends on their vigour, on the intended ultimate spread of the hedge and on the cost of the plants. Some, such as Leyland's cypress, × *Cupressocyparis leylandii*, make perfectly good hedges when planted at 3 or 4ft(1 or 1.25m) apart and when trimmed to a broad base of similar width. Others, such as privet, *Ligustrum ovalifolium*, and its forms, or escallonias in the milder districts, make good hedges very quickly from cuttings struck in lines at 9 or 12in(23 or 30cm) apart where the hedge is to be grown. Similarly planted seedlings of quickthorn will produce useful hedges in a very few years.

The provision of slight shelter for the new hedge by planting against fine mesh wire netting or, in very exposed situations, lath fencing, can produce a good screen more quickly. If really necessary, the young growths can be tied to the fence in order to encourage upward growth. Such temporary fencing can be left within the new hedge and thereby provide some stability in the early years and prevent the passage of unwanted animals.

PLANTING RECOMMENDATIONS

Almost any shrub or tree can be planted in rows to produce an informal screen, but the number of species suitable for the production of formal hedges is more limited. Plants for use as formal hedges need certain characteristics: an ability to withstand regular annual – or more frequent – clipping; and a main stem, or stems, from which grow many branches that remain alive as the tree or shrub grows upwards. The more restricted the root run the more acceptable the hedge plant as it is then less competitive with plants in neighbouring beds or borders and with the grass in adjacent lawns. Evergreens, or those deciduous shrubs which retain their dead leaves through the winter, have an advantage in many situations. The most satisfactory will now be examined.

Conifers for Hedging

The common English yew, *Taxus baccata*, forms the background and frame of many of the stately gardens of this country. It is the standard formal hedge with which others are compared and is still worthy of consideration where such conditions are desired. Its branches stand regular clipping and even with perpendicular sides they remain alive and green for many years. Although not often necessary, yew trees have a great ability to produce fresh growth from very old wood, and an irregular hedge, or one of the wrong height or width, can be trimmed back to a desired size or shape. Such drastic pruning may best be done in the spring but the normal regular clipping is a task for July and early August. Well maintained a yew hedge, with its dull surface, is the ideal foil for borders or flower beds or as screens for walks or formal lawns where privacy is desired. It is also the ideal plant for the most intricate topiary. Quite tall plants can be used to produce a hedge in a short time but it is cheaper and almost as quick to plant young plants of about 1ft(30cm) in height at from 1½ to 2ft(45 to 60cm) apart.

× *Cupressocyparis leylandii*, the Leyland cypress, was first found growing as a natural seedling almost one hundred years ago. The seed was from *Chamaecyparis nootkatensis* that had been pollinated by *Cupressus macrocarpa*. In recent years the cross has been deliberately repeated and several distinct clones have been selected. Being propagated vegetatively each batch of plants should be uniform in vigour and appearance. It makes rapid top growth that is not always balanced by equally vigorous root growth unless planted very young.

For the best results Leyland cypress should be planted as newly rooted cuttings as this allows a good root system to be produced before the aerial growth and with it a fair chance that the plants will remain upright in all but the most exposed conditions. It is very frost-hardy and withstands all but the most severe coastal gales. This hybrid withstands trimming far better than either parent; it bears some comparison with the yew and reaches a satisfactory height more rapidly. Unless the base is left wider than the top or is otherwise exposed to full light the lowest branches will die off and will not be replaced. 'Castlewellan', a cultivar with golden foliage, can be made into an attractive hedge for the right situation where a light rather than a dark background is needed.

Chamaecyparis lawsoniana, the Lawson cypress, is one of the best known of all conifers. The many forms of this erect-growing conifer make useful untrimmed screens but as clipped hedges can bring certain problems. All reach a considerable height in due course but some, such as certain golden forms, do so less rapidly. The tops of each plant may be removed to restrict upward growth and preserve a limited hedge for several years, but they are all better as untrimmed rather than formal hedges. All have a tendency to become thin at the bottom, and they then need low shrubs in front of them to hide their ugliness while allowing the upper branches to screen unwanted views or provide a background or shelter from wind.

Cupressus macrocarpa, the Monterey cypress, is even less tolerant of trimming than other conifers and more likely to lose its bottom branches. It is not entirely frost-hardy, but untrimmed in the milder climates it grows rapidly and to a considerable height and, coming as it does from the edge of the sea on the Californian coast, it is very tolerant of salt-laden winds. Indeed, as a shelter belt – rather than a trimmed hedge – in mild areas it is equal to any of the conifers normally used for the purpose.

Thuja plicata, the western red cedar, is another conifer with several forms that can be lightly trimmed as a hedge but which ultimately grows to a considerable height. It is better used as a screen which can be topped at the required height or left to go to its natural height as a screen or windbreak.

Cedrus atlantica f. *glauca*, the blue cedar, *Tsuga mertensiana*, the hemlock, and *Metasequoia glyptostroboides*, the dawn redwood, have been trimmed, at Wisley and elsewhere, into attractive hedges. Each has its own special feature and it will be interesting to see how long each can be maintained as a useful hedge. *Cedrus atlantica* f. *glauca* has distinctive blue-grey foliage and, carefully pruned, it quickly produces a narrow hedge. Untouched, it grows quite quickly upwards and outwards and, so left, it is entirely unsuited to all but the largest gardens. *Tsuga mertensiana* has fine foliage similar to that of the yew but it has to be shown how long it will withstand persistent clipping. *Metasequoia glyptostroboides*, the third of this group, arrived from China in 1948. It grows rapidly in moist soils but tends to form a huge butt or bole in many situations that would make it unsuitable as a hedge. Its leaves change to a pleasant yellow in autumn before falling and it is more likely to become a useful ornamental or possible untrimmed shelter where winter shade is not wanted.

Many other conifers can be planted to form useful untrimmed screens but many tend to be too spreading for the average garden. For larger gardens and public parks a few are among the best for the production of shelter belts, being firm of root and resistant to the worst gales.

Pinus radiata, the Monterey pine, from the same part of California as *Cupressus macrocarpa*, grows rapidly to a massive tree that is extremely root firm in all but the thinnest of soils. Several other pines are almost as useful as are several spruces and firs (*Picea* and *Abies*, respectively) while the massive monkey puzzle, *Araucaria araucana*, can stand bold in most wind-swept situations.

Other Options

Turning now to broad-leaved or flowering plants the choice for formally trimmed hedges is not very great but, as already suggested, almost anything can be planted in a row to form a lightly pruned or untrimmed screen.

The privets, *Ligustrum ovalifolium* and its golden and silver forms and related species, have been so widely planted as to become common and looked down upon. They are cheap, coming easily from cuttings struck in the open; they are quick growing and can be trimmed to make quite neat hedges, mostly clothed from top to bottom for many years. In very cold and windy winters they tend to be deciduous, but they can be very effective hedges in many situations. Clipping twice a year, in May-June and August, produces a better hedge than annual clipping and three or four cuts during the summer can be even better.

Crataegus monogyna, the native quickthorn, hawthorn, whitethorn or May – and the closely related *C. oxyacantha* – is equally cheap, comes easily from seed, and are the basis of most farm or country hedges. Properly trimmed once a year, in July, it can soon make an animal-proof hedge that will withstand all frosts and all but the most severe salt-laden gales. The rounded shape of the farm hedge need not be copied. That shape comes from hedge-bottom weeds and the old methods of trimming. Perfectly satisfactory erect or broad-based hedges can be produced if care is exercised from the start. This common hedge is, of course, deciduous and because of its ubiquity is not considered very attractive, but it has its place as a boundary hedge.

Several cultivars of *Ilex aquifolium*, the common holly, and a number of its exotic relations have much to commend them as boundary and internal hedges to provide year-round cover. The native species raised from seed may not be entirely uniform but it will be sufficiently so to form a useful hedge. Specimens raised from cuttings can be relied upon to have completely even growth and appearance, if the soil and its preparation have been satisfactory. Although it is not quick growing, a foot (30cm) of growth each year after establishment will soon produce a useful hedge that will stand for years at almost any height and width; and several clones of the hybrid *Ilex × altaclarensis* such as 'Atkinsonii' and 'Hodginsii' can do better than that. For those who like them there are variegated-leaved forms with yellow or white margins or centres. They will provide extra light and colour on dull winter days. Plant at least 18in(45cm) apart and trim annually in August.

Berberises, or barberries, are also prickly subjects that make useful garden hedges. *Berberis darwinii* and *B. × stenophylla*, both evergreens, are the most commonly seen as full-size hedges. Both have the added advantage of bright yellow flowers in spring if the annual trimming is done soon after flowering and the resulting short growths are not again removed. Several other members of this genus can make less formal hedges from 3 to 8ft(1 to 2.5m) in height and some of them have the added advantage of red berries and coloured foliage in the autumn.

The small-leaved shrubby honeysuckles, *Lonicera nitida* and its near relations, became popular hedge plants some years ago. They are evergreen and very cheaply propagated by cuttings but do not reach or remain erect at any great height – 4ft(1.25m) is really an effective maximum, and they must be closely clipped very frequently from early May to late August. With such attention a neat little hedge can be produced for the right place in the garden but it is asking a lot from any gardener to be so regular with his machine or shears. Failure to clip regularly soon produces uneven shapes and ugly dead patches and there are probably several better alternatives.

The boxes *Buxus microphylla* and *B. sempervirens* can be well used for smaller hedges, from the tiny box edging used in the formal gardens of long ago to the useful dividers between beds and borders where it is desirable to separate one group of plants, or style of planting, from another. There are many cultivars and since the aim of such plantings will normally be for uniformity it is desirable to see that all the plants in a single hedge are from the same source. Planting the smallest from 6 to 9in(15 to 23cm) apart and the larger ones up to 18in(45cm) will produce useful hedges that only need annual trimming to maintain their formality.

Two of our native trees are among the most useful for formal hedges. The beech, *Fagus sylvatica*, and the hornbeam, *Carpinus betulus*, can be trained into some of the best of the larger garden hedges as the longest established hornbeam hedges at Wisley demonstrate. Both retain their brown leaves through the winter when young and when regularly trimmed. The two native oaks, *Quercus petraea* (the sessile oak) and *Q. robur* (the common or English oak), also behave in the same way and with the evergreen oak, *Q. ilex*, can be trained as large solid hedges for suitable situations. Planted 18in to 2ft(45 to 60cm) apart and trimmed with vertical sides or slightly wider bottoms all take a year or two before they start into effective growth, but they then grow steadily at 1ft(30cm) or so a year to the desired height.

Shelter for Seaside Gardens

No chapter on hedges could omit reference to the needs and problems of shelter for seaside gardens. Salt resistance usually, and obviously, comes in plants that are native to such conditions. Those from New Zealand and the coastal regions of South America produce some of the best hedges for this purpose, but not all are entirely frost-hardy. *Escallonia macrantha,* and two Cornish-raised cultivars, 'Crimson Spire' and 'Red Hedger', come nearest to being resistant to both salty gales and sharp frosts. Some other members of this genus also make useful hedge plants but some are too thin or straggling to be useful. The easiest way of producing a quick hedge of these plants is to insert them 8 to 12in(20 to 30cm) apart in a single row where needed. Cuttings inserted at any time between October and March will usually root if at least two-thirds of their length is in the soil. In good conditions the two cultivars will produce 1ft(30cm) of growth in the first summer and at least 2ft(60cm) each year after that. The species *E. macrantha* is rather slower but forms a massive hedge with rather less trimming. All can be trimmed two or three times each summer to produce almost privet-like solidity or, after a single cut in June-July, will bear short branchlets that produce attractive red flowers in early summer.

Several olearias are also very salt-tolerant, but many were cut down during a recent cold winter in gardens where they had grown for many years. They are probably worth planting again in the mildest seaside gardens. *Olearia macrodonta,* with rather dull green, holly-shaped leaves, and *O. solandri,* with golden leaves not unlike those of a coarse heather, can be trained into reasonably neat hedges that grow to 8ft(2.5m) or more in height. For sheltering the very mildest corners *O. traversii* is as quick-growing as any shrub. Unfortunately, it outgrows its roots and to produce a good shelter it is necessary to cut back the branches by at least a third at the end of the first two or three summers. This reduces the top hamper and allows the roots to become firm before the full growth is exposed to the force of the autumn and winter gales.

Griselinia littoralis has lovely pale green shapely leaves that resist most winds and, in due course, grows to 30ft(9m) or more if left untrimmed. It can be trained to make formal hedges, but, like some of the other New Zealanders, it recently suffered badly in a series of sharp frosts after a very mild autumn.

The various forms of *Fuchsia magellanica* make graceful informal hedges with masses of red flowers through the late summer and into the autumn, but only in the mildest districts. They survive and behave as perennials elsewhere and thus can only be used as dwarf, untrimmed hedges in such gardens.

Almost any other shrub or small tree can be planted in lines to form partially pruned or completely informal screens, Local gardens, public parks and nursery gardens can be useful sources of information about the behaviour of plants in the locality and the adventurous gardener may wish to try something quite out of the ordinary after seeing some particularly vigorous shrub doing well in a similar situation to that of his own garden. At Wisley there is an interesting and varied collection of specimen hedges which is of great value in selecting the right subjects for a particular location or purpose.

9.

Herbaceous Perennial Plants

Long ago, in the late 16th century, when numerous plants new to gardening in this country were being introduced from the Middle East, the Cape and North and South America, the principal enjoyment to gardeners was the growing of all sorts of plants in mixture. Bulbs and other herbaceous plants, annuals and shrubs, fruits and herbs were accorded equal status. As the fashion of garden designing took ever greater importance in the minds of the great, the powerful and the rich, the plants were relegated to what became the kitchen garden. For 300 years the craft of gardening was mainly concentrated on this type of work as the very extensive walled gardens of the 19th century show; cottage gardening, on the other hand, did not change. But with the ever-growing collection of plants in our gardens a new awareness of the value and beauty of plants came to the fore, mainly through the writings and examples of William Robinson and Gertrude Jekyll. The latter is particularly remembered as the arch-exponent of the herbaceous border. She used her herbaceous plants – augmented by annuals and shrubs – to create garden pictures of advanced sophistication. This was all very well when garden staff were easy to obtain, but today, when most garden owners are their own head gardener and garden boy rolled into one, and when the taste and desire for plants has almost exceeded all other aspects of gardening, we have to look again at the values and uses of trees, shrubs and plants in an endeavour to plant them so that they each give of their maximum to make the garden beautiful, easy to maintain and restful and enjoyable to the senses. To this ideal every plant should and can play its part, and it will be found that practically every garden owes its beauty to its mixture of plant form – just as it did in early days but with much more stress on arrangement. Lovely though a true herbaceous border may be during the summer months, it is not perhaps the ideal way in which to use herbaceous plants. They are needed to knit together the single specimens of shrubs and trees – all that most of us are permitted today – by under-planting and grouping to create garden pictures, besides the fact that the herbaceous plants in general flower after the majority of flowering shrubs. They therefore provide floral colour mainly from June to September before the onset of autumn with its additional bonus of leaf-colour and berries from shrubs and trees.

The fundamental idea of a garden is a space from which to enjoy the plants. The more trees and shrubs are included the more areas there are for shade-loving plants, an added luxury dealt with elsewhere in these pages (see p.150). Let us then visualise an open plot of almost any size whose boundaries – walls, fences or hedges – need screening and that one will step from the living room onto a paved area and then onto the lawn. For the herbaceous plant enthusiast this will be a heaven-sent opportunity to indulge in island beds which have proved in the capable hands of Alan Bloom so successful for the growing of the shorter plants. But unless handled very carefully within the scheme island beds can clutter up the one and only space upon which we depend for our serenity. We are all enthusiasts in one way or another and this is what makes each garden of different character and appeal. Perhaps our main aim is to grow prize delphiniums; if so we must first be sure that the site is right, open and sunny and if possible protected from gales. No plant can compete with delphiniums in their majesty and range of colouring. They need what might be described as good kitchen-garden cultivation. Their colours today embrace white, cream, pink and purple besides the most valuable of all the splendid pure blues. Paeonies also need all the sun, air and good cultivation they can get, and only to a lesser degree do they contribute the glory of their bowls and bosses of magnificent colours. Some of the single-flowered species open in late spring; pale yellow *Paeonia mlokosewitschii*, magenta *P. arietina*, pure white *P. emodi* and others. They appear before the old double red *P. officinalis* which is followed by a huge range of doubles and singles descended from *P. lactiflora*, from white through pink to darkest crimson. The foliage of all is large-lobed and lasts in beauty for most of the summer. Few people today plant a border of Michaelmas daisies, partly because they suffer from mildew. But it is as well to add here and now that all highly developed and selected strains of plants are more troublesome when it comes to pests and diseases than are nature's wildings. And so, leaving special areas of the garden set aside for carnations and delphiniums, paeonies, dahlias and the like we will return to the perennials which can be grown in mixture with shrubs and other plants in varying situations and with varying effect.

TALLER PLANTS Taking them as a whole perennial plants are of less weighty calibre than shrubs and, of course, almost all die to the ground every winter. Even so we should bear in mind that there are a few very tall plants – of 6ft(2m) or so – which in their season can dominate everything. For instance, the magnificent foliage and spires of yellow of the garden plant known as *Verbascum vernale* – a mullein of great value, starting to flower in June. Also for early summer there is that huge cloud of white from *Crambe cordifolia* and the light yellow scabious-flowers of *Cephalaria tatarica*. Soon after these the lobed glaucous leaves of *Macleaya microcarpa* appear, borne all the way up the stems which support the sprays of tiny flowers giving the name of plume poppy. This is a rather invasive plant; the closely related *M. cordata* is far more compact, with white instead of flesh-coloured flowers. And in August there are the giant *Rudbeckia laciniata* 'Golden Glow' and *R. nitida* 'Herbstsonne', daisies of bright brassy yellow, the one double and the other single. In September come the white Hungarian daisies of *Chrysanthemum uliginosum*, so telling when used with the spires of lavender-blue of *Aconitum carmichaelii* var. *wilsonii* 'Barker's Variety', a monkshood of special excellence. But these, together with the tallest of big red hot pokers, certain cimicifugas and the goat's beard, *Aruncus dioicus* (*A. sylvester*), are only for large gardens – or at least large borders. As a general rule it will be found that the height of plants used should not exceed half the width of the border. Let us then return to the plants which achieve 1ft to 4ft(30cm to 1.25m), or thereabouts, and which will prove so useful and effective when grouped among perhaps dwarf shrubs like potentillas, hebes, lavenders and the like to make a rich and varied assembly, to flower in their turn for many months. Few of them will need supporting, and, when once established, they are true perennials increasing in beauty yearly.

PLANTING PATTERNS Visualising that perennials grow from ground level each year, it is a good idea to put early flowering plants towards the back. Here such things as the royal blue anchusas, oriental poppies, orange and pink alstroemerias, lupins, bearded irises, *Dicentra spectabilis* (bleeding heart or lady-in-the-bath, an exquisite spring flowerer) and blue *Geranium sylvaticum* – none of which is particularly impressive after flowering – will be obscured by the growth of later flowering plants. On the other hand the front of the bed or border need not be flowerless; we have a different class of plant to choose for this, the early flowering plants whose foliage remains beautiful for the rest of the season, such as the heucheras, whose airy spires of scarlet or pink over neat rounded leaves give such joy in June, alongside the pink or crimson daisies of pyrethrums (technically *Chrysanthemum coccineum*) and the columbines or aquilegias, in a large range of tints, easily raised from seeds. Quite early, too, are *Euphorbia polychroma* (*E. epithymoides*) in the usual "greenery-yallery" of the spurge family, and the grey-white

55. Dicentra spectabilis, *bleeding heart or lady-in-the-bath.*

56. Dictamnus albus, *the burning bush.*

spires of *Veronica gentianoides* ascending over mats of dark green or variegated leaves. A little later *Alchemilla mollis* or lady's mantle produces its clouds of tiny sulphury green stars, a good contrast to *Geranium* 'Johnson's Blue' and the taller, perennial yellow foxglove, *Digitalis grandiflora*, with white or lilac-blue from *Campanula latiloba*. The vivid cerise-crimson of *Lychnis* 'Abbotswood Rose' may not appeal to everyone but its fierce colour is tempered by its velvety grey leaves, while intriguing pinky-white tubular flowers borne on prickly spikes of *Morina longifolia* will enhance any planting. There are two grassy-leaved plants for contrast, the little white St. Bernard's lily (*Anthericum liliago*, whose best form is known as 'Major' or 'Algeriense') and the lemon-yellow day lily, *Hemerocallis flava*, with inexpressibly sweet scent.

Seldom seen but of special excellence is the long-lived clump-forming burning bush, *Dictamnus albus*. The white is more attractive, I find, than its subdued lilac-red form *purpureus*. Elegant flowers with long stamens are carried in spikes; the whole plant is aromatic, so much so that the red-brown oily seed pods will produce a puff of flame if a lighted match be held beneath them on a hot still day in August. Something quite "different" for early summer are two other spurges, *Euphorbia palustris* and *E. griffithii*, the first in lime-yellow and the second in brick-red; both last long in flower followed by beautiful foliage. The earliest of the red hot pokers flowers with them; often known today as *Kniphofia* 'Atlanta', it is probably nothing more than the old garden plant *K. tuckii*. Stalwart pokers are borne freely, coral-red in bud opening to cream.

FOLIAGE EFFECTS   Some taller plants of good long-lasting foliage are the magenta-crimson *Geranium psilostemon* whose black centres do so much to give it character, the double blue forms of *Geranium pratense* 'Plenum Caeruleum' and 'Plenum Violaceum', *Salvia* × *sylvestris* 'Mainacht' in dusky violet, *S. haematodes* in light lavender, and *Thalictrum aquilegiifolium* whose fluffy heads of bloom, pink-lilac, purple or white are held above elegant columbine-like foliage. A lupin-relative should be borne in mind; it is *Baptisia australis* whose soft blue pea-flowers give way to black pods among wiry stems of divided leaves. Right in front can be placed catmint (*Nepeta* × *faassenii*) which is in flower from June onwards, and *Bergenia* 'Morgenrote'. This plant has the added value of producing a second crop of its pink flower heads in June, well after the spring crop, and, of course, all the bergenias are first class for giving solidity to the front of the border or bed; their broad, rounded leaves are an excellent foil for masonry or gravel besides being a contrast to almost everything else.

Foliage it will be seen plays a very important part in garden display. After all, even the deciduous plants bear leaves for six months and the value of the few evergreens among perennials cannot be stressed too strongly, such as *Campanula latiloba*, bergenias, the glaucous trails of *Euphorbia myrsinites*, London pride and thrift to name but a few. They go a long way to knitting the perennials to the shrubs in winter. Almost without exception it is the height of the foliage of a plant which dictates its position in the border. *Campanula latiloba*, for instance, grows to some 3ft(1m) in flower, but its evergreen rosettes of leaves demand a frontal position. Good crisp covering of frontal leaves of any colour give great tidiness to a border, besides solidity. In fact, a border can be made or marred by its frontal appearance, and where these solid plants can be allowed to spread over a gravel or paved path – or paved verge of a lawn – their value is enhanced.

COLOUR COMBINATIONS   In the early months we so avidly await every bloom that opens, that colour from flowers or foliage is accepted at face value. By June some splendid pictures will arise, and by July, when we are in the full spate of bloom from perennials, we can pause and look around for long-lasting colour combinations. Spring flowers come and go fairly quickly; summer brings us the full value of some flowers which can be coupled with the background of shrubs whose foliage and flowers last for weeks. By the end of August one should be able to go round the garden and note plants which need moving to places where their colour or stance will

57. Hemerocallis, *the day lily*.

have greater effect. The shrubs, if they have been carefully chosen, should dictate the colour of the accompaniment of perennials. Take, for instance, shrubs of bright yellow colouring (hypericum), yellow variegated foliage (*Elaeagnus pungens* 'Maculata'), or coppery-purple foliage (*Berberis × ottawensis* 'Purpurea'); all would make a splendid background for flowers of red, orange and yellow, whereas a totally different colour scheme could be contained by trees and shrubs of greyish foliage (*Pyrus salicifolia* 'Pendula'), white variegated *Cornus alba* 'Elegantissima', to which could again be added the coppery-purple foliage of perhaps *Cotinus coggygria* 'Foliis Purpureis'. Against them could be grouped the paler colours, pink, lavender-blue, palest yellow and even white: "even white" because pure white, like scarlet, does not blend easily with anything and tends to stand out in the distance and to dazzle near at hand. Although not a herbaceous plant, the tree lupin, *Lupinus arboreus*, makes a good though short-lived bush with abundant spikes of canary-yellow flowers in June, ideal with a coppery purple background.

There is no shortage of brilliant flowers for the first scheme. Splendid flat heads of yellow achilleas in several heights; yellow or sulphur daisies of *Anthemis tinctoria*; dazzling orange and red of *Crocosmia masonorum* or *Curtonus paniculatus* and their hybrids and relatives; the hard vermilion of *Lychnis chalcedonica*; the browns, oranges and yellows of heleniums; bright yellow of sunflowers (*Helianthus*) and also of *Heliopsis*; orange-scarlet tubular flowers in large sprays of *Phygelius capensis* (really a shrub but admirable when pruned down every spring), and the red-and-yellow spikes of that brightest of red hot pokers, *Kniphofia* 'Royal Standard'. For the foreground there are herbaceous potentillas of mahogany-red, scarlet or yellow; the yellow *Oenothera tetragona* in its several varieties, and the yellow daisies of *Inula ensifolia*. To this little assembly could be added some dwarf purplish-copper foliage such as *Berberis thunbergii* 'Atropurpurea Nana' and *Sedum maximum* 'Purpureum'. Try them with red-and-yellow *Gaillardia* cultivars.

Into this particular grouping come the numerous day lilies, *Hemerocallis*.

58. Platycodon
grandiflorus *'Mariesii'*.

Except in very cold northern gardens they are thoroughly at home, making ever-greater clumps of their graceful, broad grassy foliage, particularly valuable in early spring when their bright green lights up the garden in a way that few plants do. We have already looked at the best early species, *H. flava*; this is closely followed by the soft terra cotta of tall *H. fulva*, and later by the ancient 'Kwanso Flore Pleno' with double, long-lasting flowers. The fact that the flowers of the singles last only for a day is no great disadvantage for there is a long succession from every stem. Many hybrids have been raised and I think there is no doubt that the lemon-yellows such as 'Dorothy McDade' and 'Marion Vaughn' are the most telling in the garden landscape. There are two splendid rich mahogany-reds, 'Alan' and 'Stafford', and a whole range of pale orange, orange-red, buff, peach and delicate two-toned flowers to choose from. On the whole, the flowers showing one colour only are the most effective although at close range the varied tints and markings of others are intriguing.

SOFTER COLOURS   For the softer colour scheme there is an equally large range to choose from. In the front could be placed a little white everlasting flower, *Anaphalis triplinervis*, which has the additional asset of greyish foliage; the pink masterwort, *Astrantia maxima*; *Calamintha nepetoides*, a bee-loved plant with tiny blue flowers borne for many weeks; the strange grey-blue of *Campanula* 'Burghaltii' (which if cut over after flowering will present another crop of flowers in September), and a sweet sultan in pink *Centaurea hypoleuca* 'John Coutts' and the much larger, imposing C. 'Pulchra Major'; the foliage of both is glaucous-white beneath. The daisy-flowered erigerons are available in a whole range from near white to darkest purple; *Scabiosa caucasica*, *Stokesia cyanea* and *Platycodon grandiflorus* 'Mariesii' all in lavender-blue or white; and as a contrast there are the flat pink heads of *Sedum spectabile*, chosen by tortoiseshell butterflies for their nectar without due regard to the clash of colours! And, of course, one must not forget *Stachys byzantina* (*S. lanata*), or lambs' ears, in one of its forms, in front, with the silvery foliage, also, of *Veronica incana* contrasted by its blue spikes.

   For plants of greater height in soft colours there is no lack. Blue is always sought for in gardens and we might start, therefore, with this colour, though true blue is not freely available; most verge towards lavender-blue. The summer-flowering monkshoods, *Aconitum* 'Newry Blue', 'Bressingham Spire' and 'Spark's Variety' form an impressive trio difficult to separate botanically, but providing from their spires of hooded flowers dark colours – purplish or navy blue – which are admirable to contrast with the pale tints. *A. bicolor* has flowers of white and blue, but is apt to strike a bizarre note. Any tint from white to dark blue is found among the forms and hybrids of

59. Clematis
heracleifolia *var.*
davidiana.

60. Eryngium alpinum

blue African lilies; the hardy ones – known collectively as the Headbourne Hybrids – belong to *Agapanthus campanulatus* and the trials at Wisley brought forth some splendid named forms which should soon become available.

Aster amellus and its named forms provide short large-flowered daisies of violet, blue and pink although eclipsed in the hybrid *Aster × frikartii* 'Mönch', whose clear lavender-blue flowers are produced for about three months on plants 3 to 4ft(1 to 1.25m) high; it is thus one of the most valuable of all plants. All these asters need some support. About midsummer it would be difficult to do without *Campanula lactiflora* in one of its forms, lavender-blue, pinkish or violet. It does, however, create a horrible gap later and late summer or early autumn flowers should therefore be grown in front of it. There are two very good blue herbaceous clematis, *Clematis heracleifolia* var. *davidiana* whose flowers, shaped like those of a hyacinth, are borne in sprays over a leafy sprawling bush, taking up some 4ft(1.25m) square when established, and *C. × durandii*. This last, a beautiful hybrid of *C. × jackmanii*, has large indigo-violet blooms and is best when trained up over a spring-flowering bush at the back of the border. Prickly foliage and flowers come from the sea hollies, species of *Eryngium*, such as the large-flowered *E. alpinum*, the small-flowered garden plant known as *E. tripartitum* and the several good hybrids, and the globe thistles, of which I should choose *Echinops ruthenicus* or *E. ritro*. Their knobs of steely blue are very effective over the dark green, silver-backed leaves. *Nepeta* (or *Dracocephalum*) *sibiricum* is a charmer with spires of Spode-blue sage-like flowers, with a darker tint echoed in the masses of flowers of *Polemonium foliosissimum*.

In this splendid grouping of lavender-blues we also have the spiderworts (*Tradescantia × andersoniana*, hybrids of *T. virginiana*) whose purplish-blue flowers may be pale or dark, or they may be white or verging to crimson; they are imperturbable plants and please except for their untidy foliage; powder blue from *Veronica longifolia*, a less good plant than *V. exaltata*; the

61. Agapanthus campanulatus

62. Tradescantia ×
andersoniana *(see p.103).*

comparatively new Russian sage, *Perovskia* 'Blue Spire', which is semi-shrubby and should be cut right down every spring, producing when fully established sheaves of lavender flowers over fragrant leaves and stems; and those two stalwarts of the border, *Salvia nemorosa* 'Superba' and *Phlox*. The salvia long known as *S. virgata nemorosa*, gives us rich purple spikes which, if reduced when their colour has gone, will produce more. In addition to the usual plant of 3 to 4ft(1 to 1.25m) there are two useful short ones, 'Lubeca' and 'East Friesland'.

When it comes to the cultivars of *Phlox paniculata* one has to take a deep breath. Besides lavender-blue and violet-purple, there are many other tints from white to crimson. The eyes of some are darker, others lighter, than the main tint of the petals. Some of the newer crimsons and reds are so bright that they are better placed among the brilliant yellows and reds of the earlier list. Unfortunately modern phloxes are overbred and succumb to the attacks of eelworm which is evinced by a twisting of the leaves. Another species, *P. maculata*, only available in paler colours, is not so prone. Taking them as a group they provide a splash of solid colour scarcely equalled by any other hardy perennial, and their fragrance is soft and rich. Even so their appearance is tinged with sadness for they usher in the late summer flowers. Give them good soil with plenty of humus and they will often thrive.

WIDENING THE REPERTOIRE   After such a feast of blues and purples the phloxes alone bring us strong pinks and crimsons and good whites. It is not only the blue flowers that appear in such plenitude in July; pink is also much more evident than earlier. Like the phloxes, *Sidalcea malviflora* also requires good soil, so that the tall pink spikes of silky, small, hollyhock flowers can show above lesser fry: 'Sussex Beauty', 'Reverend Page Roberts' and 'Elsie Heugh' form a trio hard to beat, but some shorter ones like 'Oberon' and 'Puck' are useful to the hard-pressed garden owner of today who has little time for staking. Closely related is a shrubby – though short-lived – plant, *Lavatera olbia* 'Rosea', a large plant with a very long succession of beautiful flowers borne in long sprays. *Physostegia virginiana* is available in pink or white, with a dwarf pink variety 'Vivid'. The flowers are borne in stiff spikes on mobile, "stay-put" stalks for which reason it is known as the obedient plant. The roots are invasive. For moister borders the spires of magenta-pink from the purple loosestrife, *Lythrum salicaria* and its close ally *L. virgatum*, are difficult to leave out because they last so long in flower. The daisy family contributes that noble plant *Echinacea purpurea*, whose petals of rich carmine-pink are surmounted by a large boss of orange-brown – a most unusual combination; 'Robert Bloom' is a splendid rich-coloured cultivar and there is also 'White Lustre' again with the prominent centre.

The big lax plants of *Polygonum amplexicaule* and *P. bistorta* are at times rather unmanageable, but their rat's-tail flowers are produced over a long period and their foliage subdues all weeds. *P. amplexicaule* 'Firetail' is the brightest, up to 4ft(1.25m) or so tall, while *P. bistorta* 'Superbum' is a clear pink and shorter.

For other light colours for the softer schemes we can turn to the statuesque *Veronicastrum (Veronica) virginicum* in white, pale blue or pinkish-lilac; the 5ft(1.5m) *Verbena patagonica* (syn. *V. bonariensis*), which will seed itself galore but is so free and so long in flower that its open sprays can be forgiven – and, it may be added, it can be quite insignificant unless grown in quantity, among, perhaps, earlier flowering plants. We also have that great delicacy *Thalictrum delavayi*, for many years known as *T. dipterocarpum*. Stout stems with elegant, lobed foliage bear airy-fairy tiny flowers of lilac or white with cream stamens. 'Hewitt's Double' is very effective though lacking the stamens. They are not easy to establish and are best planted when young in depressions and earthed up as they grow. A totally different plant is *Selinum tenuifolium* which is a most refined cow-parsley in snowy-white.

One cannot make a border satisfactorily with only blues and mauves and pinks; one needs the dark purples and crimsons, the whites and pale yellows. White for July and August is provided by phloxes and the forms of

9.   *A tall wire waste-paper basket forms the basis of this highly attractive and novel display of nemesias and lobelias in the Garden for the Disabled at Wisley. Other annuals (see pp. 122 to 128) could quite easily be grown in a similar manner, perhaps to brighten a sunny patio.*

10. *The elegant white saxifrages in the trough frame beautifully the superb container of the South African* Rhodohypoxis baurii *(see pp.138 to 144).*

11. *Orange sun roses (a form of* Helianthemum nummularium *), pinks,* Penstemon pinifolius, *a miniature rose, a golden form of* Calluna vulgaris, *housleeks, the grey-leaved* Artemisia schmidtii 'Nana' *and sedums give this raised scree bed much interest. It is the kind of feature which can be incorporated successfully in many garden scenes (see pp.138 and 139).*

12. *The dry wall at the entrance to Wisley Garden which has given so much pleasure to countless numbers of people in spring over many years. The three-tier effect of the tulips, the alyssum, iberis and aubrieta, and the polyanthus creates a riot of colour.*

Chrysanthemum maximum. The latter have yellow centres (except the true doubles) and thus are not so coldly white as the phloxes. We have seen dark purples among our earlier paragraphs, but little crimson. It is found best in *Monarda didyma* 'Cambridge Scarlet', and some of the other forms which range through pink and purple; also in phloxes and *Knautia macedonica* (syn. *Scabiosa rumelica*). This is best left to sprawl, covering some 3sq ft(1m²), producing a long succession of true crimson scabious-flowers. (To make the most of the space they can be surrounded by spring bulbs.) With regard to pale yellow, so useful for contrasting happily with the softer colours, great value is found in *Thalictrum speciosissimum*; the fluffy citron yellow flowers appear on 6ft(2m) stems in late June, after which they should be removed so that one can enjoy the elegantly lobed glaucous foliage. There is also a light yellow sweet sultan, *Centaurea ruthenica*, whose deeply cut leaves of dark green contrast with the clear flower tint. And here and there among this assembly of soft tints one needs the silver-grey of *Artemisia ludoviciana* and its relatives – all colonisers, so beware! – and blue rue, the great glaucous leaves of seakale, with *Anthemis cupaniana*, *Artemisia canescens* and pinks in the foreground.

FROM AUGUST ONWARDS   As intimated phloxes do not appear without a touch of sadness at the passing summer. The same may be said of the Japanese anemones; first to open is *Anemone tomentosa* (often labelled *A. vitifolia*) in August, followed soon by the ordinary single pink *Anemone × hybrida* and its superlative ordinary white 'Honorine Jobert'. Very few plants have the quality of leaf, flower and port exhibited by these two stalwarts, invasive though they are. Their beauty carries us through September, into the main Michaelmas daisy period, while *Aster × frikartii* is still in flower, to the tiny flower sprays of *A. ericoides*, its forms and hybrids, the wiry dark bushes of *A. laterifolius* 'Horizontalis', the exquisite *A. turbinellus*, until the garden plant known as *A. tradescantii* effectively closes the season in November. Late-flowering wands of white from *Cimicifuga simplex* will be produced in sun or shade, and in a warm corner the violet-blue of *Salvia guaranitica* will light up the yellow flowers of the shrub *Hypericum* 'Rowallane'. A rather unusual note is struck by *Cautleya* 'Robusta', whose handsome green blades are surmounted by spikes of red calyces from which emerge dark yellow flowers followed by blue berries. In sunny, but not dry, borders the kaffir lilies will thrive, running freely and producing amid grassy foliage elegant spikes of small gladiolus-like flowers; *Schizostylis coccinea* 'Major' in gorgeous crimson, and its counterpart in clear pink, 'Sunrise', are the two best. While *Sedum spectabile* is losing its chalky pink colouring the hybrid *S.* 'Autumn Joy' produces large flat heads of rich pink turning to crimson-bronze, with the usual fleshy leaves of the type. And as a foreground plant for late summer and autumn, nothing is so prolific and charming as the nemophila-blue *Geranium wallichianum* 'Buxton's Variety'. After settling down for a year or two it will annually make a large clump a foot high. Its blue is just right as a complement to *Fuchsia* 'Mrs. Popple' and the pale yellow 4ft(1.25m) *Nepeta govaniana*. A fourth companion would be *Geranium* 'Russell Prichard' whose greyish mats of foliage are bespangled with soft lilac-rose flowers from July until the autumn.

The red hot pokers, whether they are "red hot" or not, are generally looked upon as autumn flowers. The well-known old *Kniphofia uvaria* certainly is, but it is a bit too coarse for the average border. There are, however many smaller, even dainty, kinds which owe their origin to *K. triangularis* (*K. galpinii*) and similar species. Being only 2 to 3ft(60cm to 1m) high, their foliage is fine and grassy, in keeping with their small spikes of flowers. Scarlet, salmon, coral, peach and cream will be found among the several kinds available; 'Macowanii', 'Nelsonii', 'Sunningdale Yellow', 'Bressingham Glow' and 'Enchantress' are a few of the best.

The list is long, the variety is great. Nothing has been said about the stately foxtail lilies, species and varieties of *Eremurus*; nor the hardy arums, particularly *Zantedeschia aethiopica* 'Crowborough' and 'White Sail', whose striking white flowers and handsome foliage, lasting through until autumn,

63. Schizostylis coccinea 'Major'

64. Gentiana lutea

are such an asset in any garden. June welcomes the purple spikes of hardy orchids, *Dactylorrhiza elata*, *D. foliosa* and *D. latifolia*; they are splendid perennials and assort well with the lemon-yellow hooded flowers of *Roscoea cautleoides*. Nor the statuesque *Gentiana lutea* and *Phlomis russeliana*, both providing whorls of soft yellow flowers over handsome leaves. Nor, if a border were moist, could a *Rodgersia* or two be omitted, particularly the pink *R. pinnata* 'Superba'; and a home must be found for the spring-flowering fair maids of France, *Ranunculus aconitifolius* 'Flore Pleno' with its elegant leaves and white flowers in tight rosettes of petals; it overlaps with the early-flowering *Doronicum* species, or leopard's bane, which do so much to fill the gap made by the fading daffodils.

THREE FURTHER COUNSELS   Spread before you is a brief survey of the riches that we have at hand from herbaceous plants; it is for you now to make your selection for each part of your garden where you want several plants to act as a fore-ground to the greater shrubs; under the latter may be grouped spring bulbs and shade-loving plants for spring flowering such as hellebores and lungworts. By so doing you will be extracting the maximum amount of flower per square yard. There are three further counsels to be offered to you: remember always that it is the *plant* that counts, not just the flowers. If the whole plant looks respectable during its growing period, apart from its flowers, your garden will gain immeasurably. But returning once again to delphiniums, they can be grown and enjoyed in the mixed border – or anywhere in the garden – and an old dodge of Miss Jekyll's was to plant a perennial pea, *Lathyrus latifolius*, in its white or puce form, so that with support it could be trained up to cover the barren stems. Likewise she used *Gypsophila paniculata* to plant behind oriental poppies so that the former took the place of the poppies in summer when they had died down. These expedients prove that even with plants which do not remain in beauty through the season there are ways and means. Another point is directly concerned, once again, with foliage. Nowadays there are many variegated plants on the market; they are irresistible in a garden centre – particularly if they are evergreen – but a source of embarrassment when one takes them home. An occasional plant with "coloured" foliage can work wonders, in fact they are valuable to enhance colour scheming; but too many become wearisome and unsettling and one longs for quiet greens. Here the beauty of one variegated plant must be extolled! *Tovara virginiana* var. *filiformis* 'Painter's Palette'; it slowly forms a clump of leaves whose colours include green, cream and brown.

Thirdly, the shape of foliage is the most important thing; let its colour be green as a general rule so long as shape and texture are different from that of the next. This, of course, applies as much to shrubs as it does to plants, and to trees as well if one is thinking in landscape scale. Today grey foliage is very popular and it has not the unsettling effect of variegation; it was used considerably by Miss Jekyll. She used the round blades of bergenias to contrast with the sword-shaped leaves of yuccas and day lilies, crinums and the rest. Both shrubs and herbaceous perennials can appear heavy in the mass but we have the constant uplift of the narrow grassy leaves of day lilies, pokers and irises. To these we will add the grasses, a class of plant into which we have yet to delve. They are available in every size: the tall pampas grass, *Cortaderia selloana*, in silvery cream or silvery-pink ('Rendatleri') is only for the largest gardens, outdoing all but the cardoon and *Macleaya* in size. A more compact form is 'Pumila'. Grassy though the long leaves are, the pampas grasses are planted more for their great foxtail-blooms than for their foliage, whereas an equally tall plant, *Miscanthus* 'Silver Feather' is good in foliage and flower. The forms of *Miscanthus sinensis* – particularly the white striped *M.s.* 'Variegatus' and yellow cross-banded 'Zebrinus' – are useful to add lightness to the largest of plantings. Bowles' golden grass (*Milium effusum* 'Aureum') is best in shade but Bowles' golden sedge (*Carex stricta* 'Aurea') will thrive and add brilliant yellowish tone to a frontal group, not exceeding 2ft(6cm) in height. Compact also and valuable in its glaucous grey is *Helictotrichon sempervirens*, although the flowering sprays, equally grey, are considerably taller but can be removed in good time. Its glaucous tone is echoed in *Festuca glauca*, a neat tuffet for the foreground while equally dwarf, but gracefully arching is the brilliant yellow *Hakonechloa macra* 'Aureola'. For autumn effect we have the purplish flowers of that neat clump-former *Molinia caerulea* 'Variegata', and for summer effect *Pennisetum orientale* with its soft bottle-brushes of mauve-grey. *Stipa gigantea* has done as much as any grass in recent years to call attention to neglected beauty; it is a giant oat of 6ft(2m) or so, very resistant to wind. The variegated forms seem to be stressed, in spite of advice in an earlier paragraph, but these all can add so much to groupings of other plants, and the same may equally well be said of the numerous green species. None of those mentioned is of a running nature; all may be trusted in the tidiest garden. It should be borne in mind that grasses, like silvery-grey plants, are best planted in warm spring weather.

RE-ASSESSMENTS Some of us are commuters, in other words summer evenings are times of full enjoyment; and it is then that all the pale colours shine at their best. It is then, too, the time to take out pencil and paper to note plants which are not giving full satisfaction. This may be due to ill health – unsuitable soil or position, too dry or too wet; or to poor placing – bad neighbours, or the wrong colour, contrasting when it should be complementary or vice versa, weakness when there should be boldness, or flower shapes too much alike. Everyone has different ideas, fortunately, but in creating colour groups part of the spectrum is better than the whole and all will go well if the division of colour is made central to the reds. It is the reds verging towards yellow that are so inimical to the reds verging towards blue. All else can be happily resolved with the huge resources on our palette.

CULTURAL POINTERS Plants purchased in containers are generally successful and will reveal their beauty even in the second season; open-ground plants take perhaps a year longer. If plants arrive in autumn or winter when the soil is sticky, or just cold and wet, it is a good plan to establish the new plants in pots or boxes of prepared potting soil, and store in a light, airy shed or cold greenhouse or frame, ready for planting in spring. Soil has scarcely been mentioned; we all are apt to think our soil is normal and fertile, but new plants do benefit from a thorough preparation of the soil with admixture of peat and Growmore; in time they may need lifting, dividing and replanting with the same sort of assistance. It is very necessary to be quite sure about the placing of shrubs in the first instance for they are troublesome to move when large, whereas perennials are comparatively easy to transfer from one position to another. As shrubs grow above ground, so do their roots spread below ground; it is a wise step to sharpen a spade and to cut vertically downwards, severing the roots from shrubs or hedge where they may be invading the areas given to perennials.

10.

Bulbous Flowers

The term "bulbous flowers" used in its widest sense opens up a Pandora's box for the gardener as it covers not only the conventional bulb of the botany textbook but a multitude of plants that use some form of swollen rootstock as their food-storage system. Rhizomes and tubers of all shapes and sizes fall within the gamut of the bulb enthusiast and although many of the species grown belong to the monocotyledonous families, *Amaryllidaceae*, *Iridaceae* and *Liliaceae*, such diverse dicotyledonous genera as *Anemone*, *Corydalis*, *Cyclamen* and *Tropaeolum* include species with swollen rootstocks which fit neatly into the same garden situations as the true bulbs.

If one looks at the distribution patterns of bulbous plants in the wild it quickly becomes clear that they occur mainly in situations where for a period of the year they undergo climatic extremes or conditions for growth are for some other reason unfavourable. This may be due to drought or severe cold or adverse light conditions and in order to survive they "go underground" during the unfavourable period. Their survival mechanism is by means of some form of swollen rootstock which contains sufficient foodstore for the plant to sit out the difficult period and provide the rapid boost to root and shoot growth required as soon as suitable conditions of temperature and moisture in the ground allow.

In some cases bulbous plants have become very sophisticated in their growth patterns. Certain temperature·regimes, for instance, are critical to the development of flower buds for the following season, particularly in various members of the *Amaryllidaceae*, and when brought into cultivation and not given similar conditions to those in which they grow naturally they refuse to flower. Others adapt astonishingly well to cultivation in very different conditions from those in their natural habitat and many species that normally undergo a dormant period of summer drought cheerfully thrive out of doors in the variable weather of a British summer.

It is always important when growing any plant you have not tried before to find out the growth pattern and climatic conditions of its natural habitat. In most cases this is a great help in deciding where and how to grow the plant and, blended with information from the experienced grower, usually results in the successful establishment of the plant concerned.

The writer remembers the astonishment of seeing *Crinum campanulatum* growing and flowering well in pools in a most unbulb-like manner in South Africa. The pools gradually dry up during the summer and the mud then provides ideal germinating conditions for the fleshy seeds while the dormant bulbs nestle cosily in the baked mud and patiently wait for the winter rains before starting growth again. Similarly in Turkey *Colchicum szovitsii* and *Crocus gargaricus* both flower abundantly in squelchy meadows, often in pools of water – conditions that contradict totally the conventional "well-drained compost" of the books. Both, however, undergo the other part of the normal bulb recipe, "the summer baking", in nature, but luckily, in cultivation, do not insist on being saturated when in growth!

The purpose of this chapter is not to provide a treatise on the cultivation of bulbous plants – nor would it be remotely possible to deal adequately with the many hundreds of species that can be obtained and grown. It is a selection of some of those for which the writer has a personal liking together with a number of uncommon species that are ignored by most nurserymen

65. Fritillaria imperialis, *the crown imperial.*

dealing with bulbous plants but are nevertheless attractive and easy to grow. As the value to individual gardeners will depend in some cases on the garden conditions they can provide, I have also grouped those requiring more or less similar treatment together. These categories should be regarded merely as guides, for many species will grow very satisfactorily in several different garden situations. As will be realised, the popular daffodils, tulips, hyacinths and lilies are not considered in this brief survey.

For general cultivation

Perhaps the most satisfactory for general cultivation are those bulbous plants that, given good soil drainage, a reasonably fertile soil and an open position will flower and increase happily without more care than would be given to any ordinary herbaceous plant.

The stately crown imperial, *Fritillaria imperialis*, native from Turkey to the western Himalayas is a most effective early border plant, but is a gross feeder and may not flower on poor, sandy soils unless its appetite is assuaged by top dressings of well-rotted manure or the equivalent each season. In April the 3ft(1m) flower stems are topped with whorls of pendent, bell-shaped orange, red or yellow waxy-petalled blooms each 2 to 3in(5 to 8cm) across. In the border it is best placed where its rapidly dying foliage is hidden behind the growth of a later-flowering neighbour.

Uncommon but equally hardy is the closely related, March-flowering *F. raddeana* from Iran and nearby areas of the USSR. It differs in its more slender habit and more open pale yellow, green-tinted blooms. In recent years a very vigorous form of *F. persica* known as 'Adiyaman' has become available and makes a fine clump in the border with 10 to 20 dark-hued, plum-purple flowers on 3ft(1m) stems. The shoots emerge early from the soil in spring and may sometimes suffer from frost damage so are best covered with dry bracken as soon as they appear. Very seldom seen, but easily raised from seed, is the sturdy *F. pallidiflora*, native to Russia and quite hardy in Britain. It reaches 1 to 2ft(30 to 60cm) in height and produces three or four squarish yellow bells, spotted red inside, during April. Many other *Fritillaria* species are now available, particularly for the alpine house, but for those with no facilities to grow or inclination to try these more specialist plants, add to the species mentioned above *F. acmopetala*, *F. pontica*, *F. pyrenaica* and *F. verticillata* which put up uncomplainingly with a minimum of attention in my own garden and flower each season.

Valuable too is *Galtonia candicans*, a showy South African, which from a basal cluster of erect leaves produces in late summer 3 to 4ft(1 to 1.25m) scapes bearing up to 15 pure white pendulous, slightly scented, bells. In the herbaceous or shrub border, placed with a background of dark foliage, it is extremely effective and in spite of its origin appears hardy in most parts of Britain. Another South African, the orange-flowered *Crocosmia masonorum*, begins its flowering season in July and, although only relatively recently introduced, has rapidly established itself in gardens. It is a free-flowering species which is easily raised from seed and unlike some of its beautiful montbretia relatives appears totally hardy.

Also beginning their long flowering season in July are the various forms of *Crinum × powellii* with long strap-shaped leaves and stout, 3ft(1m) stems surmounted by large trumpet-shaped flowers in various shades of pink. A most beautiful pure white form is also available. There are few more rewarding plants for garden decoration than this hybrid which continues to bloom until late September – although it is not the easiest plant to transplant or to give away, requiring a major operation before the thick, fleshy rootstock yields to brute force!

The foxtail lilies, species and hybrids of *Eremurus*, are sadly neglected nowadays although anyone who saw the magnificent stands growing in the chalky warm soil of the late Sir Frederick Stern's garden at Highdown near Goring, Sussex was immediately galvanised into trying to grow them. The 8ft(2.5m) spikes of yellow, orange, peach, pink or white blooms make a magnificent spectacle on the rare occasions they are now seen but as growth begins very early in the year a dry bracken covering is advisable to protect

66. Fritillaria persica
'Adiyaman'

the large basal leaves as they develop. A few, such as the yellow *E. bungei*, only aspire to 2 to 3ft(60cm to 1m) and are more suitable for the small garden but all are well worth trying in a sunny, open position where the fleshy, brittle roots remain undisturbed by the compulsive hoe of the tidy gardener.

The ornamental onions are also very decorative and in a genus of over 500 species there are plenty to choose from – and plenty to reject in view of their weedy character! Tall species like *Allium altissimum* with bright pinkish-purple drumstick flower heads and the wine-red *A. atropurpureum* are almost dwarfed by the striking *A. giganteum* which lives up to its name in reaching 4 to 5ft(1.25 to 1.5m) when showing off its lilac-purple 4 to 5in(10 to 13cm) flower heads. It is rivalled by the purple-flowered *A. rosenbachianum* but more spectacular to many and particularly useful for dried arrangements is *A. christophii* (*A. albopilosum*) with huge umbels, 6 to 10in(15 to 25cm) across, of starry purple-blue flowers which become hard and spiny in fruit.

All the ornamental onions mentioned require sunny open well-drained conditions to flower and increase but once established make fine border plants which seldom if ever become a nuisance by seeding indiscriminately. The same cannot be said of "old gas-bags", *Allium* (now *Nectaroscordum*) *siculum* for which I have a peculiar, if unreasoning, affection in spite of the revolting smell emitted by the bulbs and broken leaves. Its 4 to 5ft(1.25 to 1.5m) stems are topped with loose umbels of angled bell-shaped green, purple and white flowers, akin to those of a fritillary in shape, followed by straw-coloured erect seed-pods which are virtually scentless when dried for winter decoration. It spawns prolifically and can become a pest in some gardens.

Unusual but, in my experience, quite hardy are several species of *Eucomis*, members of the lily family from South Africa, sometimes known as pineapple flowers from the topknot of leaves which surmounts the flower spikes. The naming of the various species in cultivation is somewhat inexact but all those available are fine late-flowering plants that increase quickly and bloom freely each year in late summer. *E. comosa* (*E. punctata*) flowers in July or August producing 2ft(60cm) stems with 1ft(30cm) long spikes of creamy-green starry flowers that remain attractive as the fruits develop. Similar, but with shorter flower stems and purple-edged flower segments is *E. bicolor* whilst *E. pallidiflora* reaches 3 to 4ft(1 to 1.25m) with handsome spikes of creamy-yellow. All may be readily raised from seed and certainly in the Wisley area seem totally unaffected by even the severest winter weather with little or no protection.

Leucojum aestivum is native to Britain and although preferring damp, heavy soils will grow and flower freely in any reasonable garden conditions. The vigorous clone 'Gravetye Giant' reaches 1½ to 2ft(45 to 60cm) when in bloom, producing its pendulous, bell-shaped, white, green-tipped blooms in April or May. Its common name, summer snowflake, is scarcely apt as to season but serves to distinguish it from the early-flowering *L. vernum*, the spring snowflake, a dwarfer version of equal merit that blooms in February and March. Both increase readily from offsets and grow well naturalised in grass provided the daffodil-like foliage is allowed to die down naturally.

The kaffir lily, *Schizostylis coccinea*, which blooms from September to November is another adaptable and usefully variable species. It requires fairly moist, rich soils to give of its best and then produces masses of its gladiolus-like spikes of open, bright red or pink flowers until the frosts finally deter its impudence. Various named clones are available, all apparently hardy and prolific, rapidly forming clumps by sending out short, couch-grass-like rhizomes from the main corms to form new corms at the tips.

One of the most elegant of border plants is *Dierama pulcherrimum*, the "angel's fishing rod", with graceful, arching 4 to 5ft(1.25 to 1.5m) stems and pendulous, bell-like flowers varying from deep wine-red through purplish-pink to white and surrounded by silvery, papery bracts. Easily raised from seed, *D. pulcherrimum* produces narrow, wiry leaves which are virtually evergreen so the corms should never be allowed to dry out completely as this may cause the foliage to die back and weaken them. The fine selected

67. Galtonia candicans
(see p.109).

68. Allium christophii

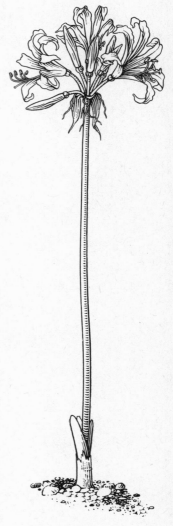

colour forms raised by the Slieve Donard nursery in Northern Ireland and named after birds, sadly, have disappeared from the nursery lists but are well worth obtaining if the chance occurs. Dieramas generally sulk if transplanted when mature and prefer to be left alone to form strong clumps which are also able to resist better the occasional very severe winter that may otherwise betray their South African origin.

Bulbs for warm borders

Borders which are situated under south- or west-facing walls suit many bulbs requiring a warm microclimate to flower well out of doors in Britain. From September to November the beautiful, funnel-shaped, bright pink and white, delicately scented blooms of *Amaryllis belladonna* appear. It flowers most freely when the bulbs are subjected to a warm, sunny, dormant phase – not always possible, of course, during the British summer. As active growth begins it should be given ample water and in poor soils a sprinkling of a balanced fertiliser such as Growmore, annually, applied as the leaves start to develop. If the only results of your labours are luxuriant leaves and no flowers, a dressing of potassium sulphate at $\frac{1}{2}$ to 1oz per sq yd(14 to 25g per m^2) or a high potash fertiliser applied at the beginning of leaf development and thoroughly watered in should redress the balance. This is a treatment that is often helpful in inducing non-flowering plants to bloom. 'Hathor', an uncommon white-flowered clone, and 'Kewensis' with deep rosy-red, white-throated flowers, are fine selections occasionally to be obtained in addition to the more usual pink-flowered forms but regrettably they seldom appear in trade lists.

Flowering over the same period is *Nerine bowdenii*, prolific of increase and apparently hardy throughout Britain although blooming most abundantly in warm sunny positions. 'Fenwick's Variety' is the most robust, free-flowering clone generally available but various other colour forms are sometimes offered including a white, faintly pink-tinged clone which is

69. Nerine bowdenii

70. Dierama
pulcherrimum *(see p.110)*

particularly attractive as a cut flower. The pure white *N. flexuosa* var. *alba* with wavy, crisped perianth segments will grow well in similar positions in the South but is generally considered to need cool glasshouse conditions elsewhere in Britain. Numerous named hybrids are available (mainly with *N. sarniensis* as one parent) for greenhouse decoration as well as a range of species including the delightful dwarf rose-pink *N. filifolia* and the paler pink, rather taller *N. appendiculata*, both of which I have seen grown successfully out of doors in Northamptonshire although in severe winters a few bulbs should always be kept in a frost-free greenhouse as an insurance policy.

September and October are also the months when the South American *Zephyranthes candida* and *Sternbergia lutea* from southern Europe are at their best. The former species comes from Argentina and Uruguay where it occurs in damp grassy habitats yet adapts readily to our climate producing its white, crocus-like blooms on 2 to 3in(5 to 8cm) stems regularly each autumn. *Sternbergia lutea* grows wild on sunny, limestone hillsides and sometimes is reluctant to bloom although increasing rapidly from offsets. Warm, sunny borders with wall protection will usually provide ideal flowering conditions for both plants but should *S. lutea* itself persistently refuse to bloom, grow its narrow-leaved relative, *S. sicula*, which seldom fails to produce its clusters of golden, crocus-like goblets annually each autumn.

Less reliably hardy, but exotic in appearance, is the summer-blooming *Tigridia pavonia*, the tiger flower, an iris-relative that grows wild in Mexico and some areas of central America and is easily raised from seed. The individual flowers, borne on 12 to 15in(30 to 38cm) stems, are over 4in(10cm) across orange, red, yellow or white and variously stippled or spotted in the centre. Cold winters will kill the corms even under a sunny protected wall but as they will often flower within a year of seed being sown casualties may soon be replaced.

Most of the peacock flowers, species of *Moraea*, a genus very closely related to *Iris*, are not hardy in Britain but *M. spathulata* and *M. moggii*, both producing yellow flowers on 3ft(1m) stems in late summer, seem quite unaffected by our winters given the sunny border conditions prescribed for *Amaryllis* and *Nerine*. The Californian *Calochortus barbatus* with pendulous yellow, brown-marked bells on wiry, flexuous, 1ft(30cm)-long stems has flowered regularly in late summer in the writer's garden for the last 10 years unprotected and increases steadily by means of bulbils borne in clusters in the leaf axils. It is sadly the only species of the genus that it has proved possible to grow out of doors at Wisley, other species insisting on frame or alpine house culture to exist.

Bluebells are not usually regarded as plants requiring warmth and hot summer conditions but *Scilla peruviana* (which in spite of its name comes not from Peru but from Spain and Italy) is an exception. The large bulbs produce rosettes of fleshy broad leaves from the centre of which appear in summer very broad, conical sprays of deep blue (or in one form white) starry flowers on stems 9 to 12in(23 to 30cm) high. Like many of its relatives it rapidly increases by offsets and is also very readily raised from seed.

Arum creticum, although perfectly hardy, is another candidate for the warm border. The bright yellow spathes, like those of our native lords and ladies in shape, are sweetly scented and are produced during March and April with the foliage. It increases quite freely from offsets but seldom seems to produce seed in our climate, unlike *A. italicum* with its greenish or creamy-white spathes and the less common purplish-black *A. nigrum*, both of which fruit freely.

The Natural Woodlanders

Many bulbous plants that grow in woodlands in nature adapt very well to garden conditions provided they can be given the dappled shade, reasonable drainage and leaf-rich soil approximating to that of their normal environment. They thrive in the layers of leafmould laid down by the deciduous trees each autumn, resting during the summer in relatively cool, dry soil that the top canopy of tree foliage arranges for their benefit. A considerable number, like the snowdrops and winter aconites, may be grown perfectly well in the open garden but others prove less accommodating and require at least partial shade and a surface mulch of leafmould or mushroom manure to become adapted to cultivation.

At the turn of the year the fresh young shoots of various snowdrops are always a welcome sight and *Galanthus nivalis*, the common snowdrop in its various forms, some double-flowered others with green-tipped outer segments, are easy and prolific growers in most soils and situations. The later-flowering *G. nivalis* 'Scharlockii', the donkey's ear snowdrop, is an attractive oddity with long bracts extending well beyond the flower. It is not always quick to establish but once satisfied with its garden accommodation will form dense clumps and thrive for many years. *G. elwesii*, which occurs wild in western Turkey and parts of the Balkans, is more demanding and prefers rather heavier soils although its close relative *G. caucasicus* is less pernickety and grows well even on the sandy Wisley soil provided its annual mulch of leaf-mould is not forgotten. Both have broad glaucous leaves and differ basically only in the green markings of the inner segments which are at the apex in *G. caucasicus* and both apical and basal in *G. elwesii*. Many other very good hybrids such as 'Atkinsii', 'Sam Arnott', 'Magnet', 'Mighty Atom' and 'John Gray' are grown by enthusiasts but only a few are stocked by bulb nurserymen at the present. Stocks of the autumn-flowering *G. nivalis* ssp. *reginae-olgae* (which now includes *G. corcyrensis*) from Greece and Sicily, however, have become more readily available in recent years and, provided they are grown in a site where the bulbs can remain reasonably dry in summer, will settle down and bloom regularly and freely to add a touch of spring to the autumn scene.

Woodland conditions are also ideal for various *Anemone* species that perennate by means of rhizomes or tubers. *A. blanda* which grows wild in Turkey and south-eastern Europe is normally a mountain plant growing in light woodland or in the shade of rocks or low scrub. Variable in colour from deep blue through pink to white in nature, it proves very amenable in cultivation particularly in hot, dry, chalky soil like that of Highdown near Goring where it flourishes and seeds freely to form a blue ground haze among the shrubs during February and March. The closely related *A. apennina* is no less accommodating producing delicate ferny foliage topped by blue starry flowers in March or April. It spreads freely by means of its blackish, slender rhizomes in leafy woodland soils but is equally at home naturalised in grass or under shrubs. Our native wood anemone, *A. nemorosa*, has produced a number of variants such as the blue-flowered 'Allenii' and 'Robinsoniana' and the sumptuous, large-flowered white 'Wilks's Giant' which make fine garden plants. The conspicuous tuft of stamens in the centre of the blooms of the pure white 'Vestal' give it the appearance of having doubled flowers like neat pom-poms and, as with most forms of *A. nemorosa*, it will naturalise well in short grass.

The yellow-flowered *A. ranunculoides*, a European woodlander, thrives in leafy or peaty soils and although small-flowered provides welcome splashes of bright yellow to accompany the wood anemones. A semi-double form also makes a pleasant carpeter for similar positions with the hybrid between *A. nemorosa* and *A. ranunculoides* known as *A. × seemannii* providing a variation in pale primrose-yellow.

Most of the species of *Erythronium*, known in Britain as dog's-tooth violets and in North America as trout lilies, will make themselves thoroughly at home in the woodland garden. *E. californicum* with creamy-white flowers and glossy leaves, the pink-flowered *E. revolutum* with beautifully brown-mottled foliage and the similar but white or cream-flowered *E. oregonum* rapidly form colonies and when thoroughly happy will seed around gently. One of the most tolerant is *E. tuolumnense* which will flower freely under near starvation conditions in sandy soils but is equally as successful in damp woodlands where the yellow flowers, reflexed at the tips, as in all the species, like miniature turk's-cap lilies, appear during April. It has given rise to two exceptionally vigorous hybrids, 'Pagoda' and 'Kondo', which have marbled leaves, paler yellow blooms and the tolerance of *E. tuolum-*

71. Sternbergia lutea

72. Scilla peruviana (see p.112)

73. Anemone blanda (see p.113)

nense to varying conditions of cultivation. Equally as prolific is 'White Beauty', thought by some to be a hybrid of *E. oregonum* while others consider it to be a vigorous selection from the species. Whatever its antecedents its regular production of an abundance of white, russet-marked blooms in early spring assures its place in gardens as one of the finest and easiest dwarf bulbs available. Unlike most of the North American species the variable *E. dens-canis*, the European and Asian dog's-tooth violet, is often found naturally in open areas of turf pushing its mottled leaves and nodding purple, pink or white flowers above the flattened grass as the snows melt. Naturalised in grass or grown in woodland it presents no difficulties but does not display its low-level blooms as effectively as do its transatlantic relations with their taller flower stems.

Cool, leafy, well-drained soils in dappled shade provide a good general recipe for all the species and hybrids generally grown which are among the most satisfying and attractive of all bulbs available for our gardens.

May sees the appearance of one of the loveliest of woodland plants, *Trillium grandiflorum*, the wake Robin or trinity flower of the North American woods. The neat whorls of three broadly egg-shaped leaves form mounds of foliage a foot or so high above which the showy upright, white or, very occasionally, pink flowers appear on short stems during late spring. A beautiful but still uncommon fully double-flowered form is very occasionally offered in the trade, its long-lasting blooms reminiscent of the florists' gardenias in texture and shape. Equally as attractive is *T. sessile*, the toad trillium, with stemless scented, maroon-purple flowers that crown tight whorls of mottled leaves. It appears to be inextricably mixed up in gardens with *T. cuneatum* which should have brownish-purple, wider segmented flowers and a somewhat squatter habit. Both species grow well in leaf-rich soils but the very beautiful painted lady, *T. undulatum*, with white or pale pink, red striped blooms is less easy to satisfy, preferring more acid, cool, peaty conditions, ample water in the growing season and sharp drainage to prevent the rhizomes rotting during the dormant season.

Flowering at the same time and enjoying similarly leaf-rich soils are the various species and hybrids of Solomon's seal of which the most satisfactory and commonly grown is the vigorous *Polygonatum* × *hybridum* which has largely replaced its parents *P. multiflorum* and *P. odoratum* in gardens. The stout, spreading rhizomes form large interwoven clumps just below soil level and produce elegantly arching 4ft(1.25m) stems clothed in neat, ovate leaves with clusters of pendent, white, 1in(2.5cm) long tubular flowers in May and June. Comparable in habit and flowering season is the related *Smilacina racemosa* which differs in producing terminal inflorescences of dense, creamy-white, starry blooms followed by red, speckled berries in autumn.

Both the common bluebell and the Spanish bluebell naturalise readily in woodland areas but less frequently seen is *Scilla lilio-hyacinthus*, a bluebell from woodlands in western Europe which produces neat rosettes of glossy, broad leaves from which foot-long flower spikes of deep blue (or occasionally white) flowers appear in late May or June. Slightly earlier in the year the fragrant pink flowers of the Greek *Cyclamen repandum* with its dark green often silver-splashed leaves make a colourful carpet in the warmer areas of the country although it is not reliably hardy throughout Britain. The well-known autumn-flowering *C. hederifolium* (formerly *C. neapolitanum*) and the scented late summer-flowering *C. purpurascens* (*C. europaeum*) will also seed around in leafy soils with the very variable *C. coum* filling the winter gap with its squat, carmine, rose or white blooms which appear in January and February out of doors.

In summer the dwarf *Corydalis cashmeriana* will form pools of brilliant blue in the gardens of those fortunate gardeners who are able to provide the conditions this most beautiful species requires. Cool moist peat in partial shade is essential to its well-being but in southern Britain it is by no means easy to produce the degree of summer humidity it seems to insist upon to thrive although in some Scottish gardens it forms dense colonies, spreading rapidly by seed in conditions akin to those of its high Himalayan homeland. Less fussy are the spring-flowering tuberous *C. bulbosa* and *C. solida* with ferny, dissected foliage and sprays of rosy-purple flowers on 6in(15cm) stems. They increase readily from offsets and seed and ask for no more than to be left to spread naturally without disturbance.

Although a plant of meadows and grassland in the Pyrenees, *Crocus nudiflorus*, one of the few species which increases by stolons, is perfectly at home in woodland. The slender, purple flowers are produced before the leaves in September or October slightly before those of *C. banaticus* which is naturally a woodland plant from Roumania and Hungary. The rich lilac-purple flowers are unusual in the genus in having three, large outer segments and three much smaller inner segments with deeply divided, feathery lilac styles. Although seldom offered, *C. banaticus* (also grown as *C. iridiflorus* and *C. byzantinus*) can be increased readily by offsets and in the writer's own garden also self-seeds happily into the peat blocks of a small peat garden on the north side of the house. The secret is not to allow the corms to dry out during the dormant season as they will not tolerate the baking which many other *Crocus* species enjoy.

Bulbs for the Rock Gardener

Bulbous plants for the rock garden, raised bed, bulb frame and alpine house are legion. The basic requirement is an open, sharply drained compost which is sufficiently rich in nutrients to allow the bulbs to grow and flower well for a few seasons without the need for further feeding, whether in pots or the open ground. Slow-release fertilisers are mainly used for commercial shrub and pot-plant production but they are extremely useful also for bulbs or rock garden plants grown in pots or in raised beds. If they are incorporated into the potting compost it avoids the need to apply additional nutrients in liquid or granular form the following season. The regular but slow release of nutrients is particularly suitable for many bulbs and rock garden plants where steady growth is required. The John Innes No. 2 potting compost to which extra grit and slow-release fertiliser have been added suits the vast majority of bulbous plants providing the sharp drainage and balanced food supply they require to succeed.

The following selection merely skims the surface from the vast pool of species and cultivars that can be grown but all of those chosen have one feature in common, the ease with which they grow and increase.

Many *Crocus* species whether grown in pots or in the open provide a superb display both in spring and autumn. Spring-flowering species like *C. chrysanthus* and its numerous named offspring with *C. biflorus* in yellow, blue, white, purple and bronze, strongly scented and variously stippled and feathered externally are difficult to equal for their prolific display in February and March. 'Cream Beauty' and 'Ladykiller', with its glistening purple exterior and white interior, are personal favourites among these hybrids while the bright orange-yellow waisted flowers of some wild forms of *C. chrysanthus* match their progeny both in beauty and in ease of cultivation. Similar in flower colour is *C. flavus* (*C. aureus*) from the Balkans and Turkey, a free-seeding species that has given rise to the large-flowered 'Dutch Yellow' of the nursery trade. It will also naturalise well in short grass as will the yellow-throated, lavender *C. sieberi* from the Greek mainland, although the Cretan forms are more difficult to acclimatise, even to pot culture.

Although the autumn-flowering *C. speciosus* and *C. kotschyanus* (syn *C. zonatus*) are frequently grown several other species that flower at the same period are equally as amenable. *C. niveus*, white or pale lilac with a yellow throat, the long-tubed, globular-flowered *C. goulimyi* and *C. cartwrightianus*, the wild ancestor of the saffron crocus with deep purple, darker veined petals and bright orange-red stigmata, all come from very restricted areas in Greece, yet multiply rapidly and flower profusely in cultivation.

Autumn also is the peak flowering time for *Colchicum* species and hybrids many of which produce their red-purple or white blooms in September or October, whilst the leaves do not develop until the late winter or spring, a growth pattern that gives rise to the common name "naked ladies" which is applied to our native *C. autumnale*. The large goblet-flowered, purple *C.*

74. Cyclamen hederifolium

75. Crocus banaticus

76. Crocus goulimyi (see p.115)

77. Crocus niveus (see p.115)

78. Crocus cartwrightianus (see p.115)

speciosum and its pure white form, which is amongst the most beautiful of all bulbous plants, *C. cilicicum* with up to 20 rosy-lilac blooms from each corm, the similarly floriferous *C. byzantinum* and the named hybrids like 'The Giant' and the double-flowered 'Waterlily' are trouble-free and prolific of increase in any but poorly drained soils but are perhaps more suited to the shrub border than the rock garden where their large glossy foliage can develop fully without swamping more delicate neighbours. On the rock garden or raised bed *C. agrippinum* with purple-red chequered flowers and the lovely but rare *C. boissieri* which produces its deep purple-pink globular, green-throated flowers from horizontal, rhizome-like corms are much more at home, their neat foliage presenting no danger to smaller plants nearby.

The slender 6in(15cm) racemes of the pink-flowered *Scilla scilloides* (syn. *S. chinensis*) from China and Japan also appear in autumn, somewhat surprisingly in a genus noted mainly for its spring display. The brilliant blue dwarf *S. sibirica* and paler blue, dark striped *S. tubergeniana* (now merged with the tongue-twisting *S. mischtschenkoana*) open their flowers as they emerge from the ground in February and March with the more bluebell-like *S. italica* and *S. amoena* usually delaying their appearance until April.

Glory of the snow is the common name applied to species of *Chionodoxa* which produce their clear blue flowers as the snow melts on their mountain homes in Turkey, Cyprus and Crete. The well-known *C. luciliae* (of nursery catalogues) with six to ten, white-centred, blue flowers, *C. gigantea* with similar but fewer and much larger flowers, and the dark blue *C. sardensis*, all March-April flowering, are fairly generally available and thrive in Britain in virtually any well-drained site, looking particularly effective when naturalised amongst shrubs. The naming of the species in cultivation is open to doubt and for convenience the names used in bulb catalogues are retained here.

The hybrid × *Chionoscilla allenii* (*Scilla bifolia* × *Chionodoxa luciliae*) occurs wild in nature and is an extremely effective and prolific plant for the rock garden. The deep blue flowers, intermediate between those of its parents, appear in March or April on two or three stems but regrettably this very fine hybrid is seldom commercially available.

Many of the dwarf daffodils from Spain and Portugal have much to offer to the rock gardener and some like the variable but always attractive *Narcissus bulbocodium*, the hoop petticoat daffodil, may spread rapidly by seed as on the alpine meadow at Wisley where they flower profusely in late March and April. The funnel-shaped flowers on stems 3 to 4in(8 to 10cm) high vary from deep yellow to primrose and seem perfectly at home naturalised in short grass or growing in the rock garden. Some forms such as subsp. *romieuxii*, pale lemon and winter-flowering, and the related *N. cantabricus* with white flowers, frilled and more open on var. *petunioides*, are best grown in the alpine house as they appear to prefer a definite summer baking. *N. cyclamineus* with its straight-sided, narrow yellow trumpets and swept back "wings", however, grows well in rather damper conditions and like *N. bulbocodium* will seed around happily when suited. The "angel's tears daffodil", *N. triandrus*, is equally as effective, flowering slightly later, with graceful, pendent, creamy-white flowers on 6in(15cm) stems. It can be grown in almost any well-drained soil, at Wisley being happy in such diverse situations as the shade of Scots pines, in a hazel hedge and on the open rock garden. The miniature trumpet daffodils, *N. asturiensis* and *N. minor*, also flourish under rock garden conditions flowering in March and April. As they seldom exceed 4 to 6in(10 to 15cm) in height they are ideal for pan culture or for raised beds, again demanding no more than good drainage and a reasonably fertile soil to provide a regular display each season.

Of the *Allium* species suitable for rock gardens *A. beesianum* with bright blue bells, the very ornamental *A. karataviense* with glaucous, purplish leaves and large white, rounded flower heads, the small-flowered blue *A. caeruleum*, the wine-coloured *A. cyathophorum* var. *farreri* and the reddish-pink *A. narcissiflorum* are reliable and easily grown dwarfs of 6 to 9in(15 to 23cm) increasingly gently but seldom spreading beyond their allotted space unlike some of their relatives.

The scent typical of onion foliage is also to be found in *Ipheion uniflorum*, an attractive, clump-forming species from Argentina and Uruguay which is completely undeterred by British winters. The open, star-shaped flowers which vary from deep purple-blue to white in colour are an inch or so across and several 6in(15cm) flowering stems with one, or rarely two, blooms each are produced by each bulb in early spring. The related genus, *Triteleia*, provides several good rock garden species of which *T. ixioides* with 1ft(30cm)-long stems and sprays of yellow, purplish-striped flowers and the deep blue *T. laxa* prove reliable and floriferous during early summer.

The very limited range of bulbs mentioned here provides only a taste of the many that may be grown on the rock garden or in the alpine house. It is possible to maintain a virtually unbroken succession of flowering bulbs throughout the year even in relatively small gardens by careful selection, particularly if a supplement of summer-flowering species like the lovely white, pink-flushed *Arisaema candidissimum*, the yellow, orchid-like *Roscoea cautleoides* and its purple counterpart *R. procera* can be included in the planting schemes.

Bulbs for the Greenhouse

In addition to the many bulbs like daffodils and hyacinths brought into greenhouses to flower in pots, there are numerous beautiful and relatively easily cultivated species which require cool or temperate greenhouse conditions. Several of these are South African in origin and one of the most tolerant is *Vallota speciosa* (*V. purpurea*), a member of the *Amaryllidaceae* sometimes known as the Scarborough lily, which was apparently cultivated widely in Scarborough when bulbs from a wrecked Dutch ship were washed ashore near the town. The strap-like leaves are more or less evergreen and in August or September the 1ft(30cm)-long stems bearing four or five scarlet 4in(10cm), open, bell-shaped blooms appear. The equally attractive pink-flowered form var. *delicata* is also grown in Britain. Although it will survive in very protected positions in sheltered gardens in Britain, it seldom flowers well; but it thrives as a window-sill plant, blooming freely even when the small offset bulbs are spilling over the sides of the pot.

Closely related is the genus *Cyrtanthus*, again African in origin, but differing in the flower shape which in many of the species is tubular. There are, however, one or two species like *C. sanguineus* which has red flowers more nearly approaching those of a *Vallota* in shape. The most striking species is *C. obliquus* with upright, twisted, greyish-green leaves and stout stems, 1 to 2ft(30 to 60cm) high, bearing in late autumn or winter eight or nine pendent, 3 to 4in(8 to 10cm) red, green and yellow tubular flowers. Less flamboyant, but as tolerant as *Vallota* in its requirements, is *C. mackenii* with slender foliage and narrow creamy-yellow tubes, borne at any time of the year in the greenhouse but July or August-blooming in its native Natal.

Equally as unpredictable in its flowering time in Britain is *Sprekelia formosissima*, the Jacobean lily from Mexico and Guatemala. It is a most decorative plant in flower with one, or occasionally two, deep crimson, irregularly shaped flowers about 4in(10cm) across and can in sheltered gardens be grown outdoors although, experience proves, it is then shy-flowering.

One of the best winter-flowering bulbs for the greenhouse is *Veltheimia bracteata*, sometimes grown under the name *V. capensis*, a related species. It is a vigorous plant and like *Vallota* remains undeterred by confinement in what appear to be starvation conditions for a year or two if repotting is overlooked. It blooms regularly and freely in December or January in coolhouse conditions, the dense spikes of tubular pinkish-red flowers, speckled green and white, lasting for several weeks before giving way to the seed pods and the winged seeds from which it is very readily propagated. A clone known as 'Rosalba' with yellower flowers is also available and equally as robust.

Another genus of easily-grown winter or early spring-flowering South African bulbs is *Lachenalia*, frequently and widely grown earlier this century but now seldom offered or seen. All the species grown are small, fleshy-

79. Narcissus bulbocodium

80. Narcissus cyclamineus

leaved bulbs with 6 to 12in(15 to 30cm) stems of pendulous or semi-erect blooms similar to those of the English bluebell in shape. *L. aloides* (*L. tricolor*) is normally red and yellow-flowered but with green and red-purple added to the mixture produces the cultivar 'Quadricolor'. It may also have orange and yellow variations. Less commonly seen, but equally beautiful, are *L. rubida* with bright red, green-tipped tubes, and the pale blue, ghost-like *L. glaucina*.

Haemanthus, known as "torch lilies" or "blood flowers" in Africa, again make excellent pot plants as they require relatively little care once established. *H. coccineus* with scarlet flowers and *H. albiflos* in white, produce dense shaving-brush-like inflorescences a few inches above the bulb usually just as the leaves develop. Normally they bloom in late autumn or winter in Britain but are not too regular in their habits and sometimes come into flower at other seasons. The taller *H. katharinae* with bright scarlet tennis-ball-sized inflorescences, *H. magnificus* with 6in(15cm) orange-scarlet globes on 1ft(30cm)-long stems and the orange or red *H. natalensis* are occasionally available and certainly worth obtaining if at all possible.

The daffodil family, *Amaryllidaceae*, provides a number of South American genera which, like hippeastrums, are easily grown pot plants for the coolhouse. *Stenomesson variegatum*, nowadays considered to include plants at one time grown as *S. incarnatum* and *S. luteoviride*, is extremely variable in flower colour and may be greenish-yellow or yellow with red markings, pink with deep banding or self coloured in scarlet or rose. The flower stems may reach 2ft(60cm) in height and during autumn or winter carry an umbel of four to eight, more or less pendent, tubular flowers 2 to 3in(5 to 8cm) in length.

Similar in growth are *Urceolina peruviana* with red or orange-red, 1 to 2in(2.5 to 5cm) urn-shaped hanging blooms and *Phaedranassa carmioli*, its 2 to 3in(5 to 8m), narrowly trumpet-shaped flowers an exotic mix of crimson and green. Their cultural requirements are very similar to those of *Vallota*, flower production appearing to be increased as the bulbs fill and begin to outgrow the pot allotted to them.

A small group of bulbous plants have developed a climbing habit as an adaptation to their particular environment in the wild and among them are several beautiful, easily grown plants mainly for greenhouse culture. The swollen tuberous rootstocks produced by several species of *Tropaeolum* bring them into my definition of bulbous plants and two of these, *T. tricolorum* and *T. tuberosum*, are extremely attractive as well as easy to grow. *T. tricolorum* from Bolivia and Chile begins its growth in the autumn sending up its slender, fresh green shoots in October. As the shoots appear they require the support of a network of slender twigs, 18in(45cm) or so high, over which they scramble before producing their delightful scarlet, black-tipped blooms. The tubers are best planted in a slightly acid, well-drained compost in deep pots or in the greenhouse border and provided frost is just excluded the plants will flower abundantly for several weeks during late winter and early spring.

The orange-flowered *T. tuberosum*, also South American, blooms during the summer and autumn out of doors if the dormant tubers are planted 9 to 12in(23 to 30cm) deep in the early spring so that they do not suffer from frost damage. Recent introductions appear to be summer-flowering and hardier than the usual nursery stocks available which also tend not to flower until early autumn. Grown in a greenhouse border *T. tuberosum* will reach 10ft(3m) or more in height and flower for much of the winter, but if grown outside in the garden it is as well to harvest a few of the tubers and store them in dry, cool, frost-free conditions over winter. The tubers, like those of potatoes, are edible and close to the soil surface so may be killed in severe weather.

Three genera of the lily family from Africa also provide us with climbers for the cool greenhouse. *Gloriosa* is a genus represented in tropical and subtropical Africa (and India) by a number of variations on a similar theme of red and yellow. A number of species has been described but botanists nowadays tend to regard these as forms of one very variable species, *Gloriosa superba*. In its "typical" form it has deep orange-red or yellow, nodding flowers several inches across and climbs to a height of 3 to 4ft(1 to 1.25m) by means of leaf tendrils. Equally vigorous is the beautiful *G. rothschildiana* with bright red, yellow-based blooms with undulate margins.

Sandersonia aurantiaca from South Africa (the only species of its genus) has finger-like tubers that produce scrambling stems and tendril-tipped leaves much like those of *Gloriosa*. It grows to about 3ft(1m) in height and bears singly, in the upper leaf axils, pendulous, bright orange flowers about 1in(2.5cm) across and shaped like the old-fashioned, waisted gas lamp mantle of the Victorian era. Very similar in growth habit is *Littonia modesta* from Natal, differing mainly in its more open, bell-shaped flowers, rich orange in colour and borne on stems scrambling to 6ft(2m) or so in height.

All three genera require very similar cultural conditions and prefer a well-drained, fairly rich compost such as John Innes No. 2. The dormant tubers should be potted into 10in(25cm) or 12in(30cm) pots in February and brought into a warm greenhouse to start them into growth. Ample water and rather cooler conditions should be provided once they are growing well. After flowering watering should be reduced as the leaves begin to yellow and when dormant the tubers should be kept dry until required for repotting again the following spring.

The diversity and variation of bulbous plants, together with the ease with which many of them may be grown, provide infinite scope to use them in many garden situations although in this chapter it has regrettably only been possible to mention a very few of the numerous species and cultivars that are available and deserving of wider cultivation for their beauty and adaptability to our garden needs.

11.

Annuals and Biennials

Annuals and biennials are the ephemera of the garden and of special value precisely because they are so readily and inevitably disposable. They contribute nothing to the garden's permanent furnishing but they can add a great deal to its seasonal colour and variety. Although borders exclusively planted with annuals are much talked about and are much admired features of some large gardens, such as Wisley and that of the Northern Horticultural Society at Harlow Car, it is unlikely that they will ever become really popular with home gardeners since few can spare the space for a feature that leaves the ground bare for so many months of the year. In small gardens every inch of space must be made to contribute something of interest most of the time. This implies a framework of more or less permanent plants, mainly shrubs and perennials supplemented by trees, climbers and semi-permanent bulbous plants which have the convenient habit of appearing at certain times and then dying down to make way for other things. In this kind of garden regime annuals of all kinds, flowering and foliage, creeping, upright or climbing, have a very important role to play, appearing, like the bulbs, at specific seasons but, unlike them, disappearing completely when their display is over leaving nothing below ground to be accidentally damaged when the beds are being cleaned or new things are being planted.

MAJOR GROUPINGS For purposes of cultivation it is convenient to divide annuals into two major groups, hardy and half-hardy. One could make a third section of tender annuals but they are outside the scope of this chapter since they are for greenhouse cultivation only in all but exceptional circumstances. What is important to grasp is that no hard and fast dividing line can be drawn between these groups. What is hardy in one garden may be half-hardy in another or plants normally regarded as half-hardy may prove to be hardy in a year in which there are few late spring frosts. At the extremes one can be certain but in the middle there is a considerable grey area about which individual gardeners must make up their own minds according to their own or their neighbours experience. When these terms are used in the following pages it is precisely in this way and they are personal judgements made as a result of observations over half a century, mainly in the south-east of England which, contrary to widespread belief, can have a climate as cold and treacherous as any in the country.

Hardy annuals are those that can safely be sown outdoors in spring where they are to flower. This definition allows the common nasturtium to be included although its rather succulent growth is destroyed by any severe or prolonged frost. The explanation is that its large seeds do not germinate until the soil is quite warm, usually some time in May, and so even if sown several weeks earlier there will be no growth to be damaged until danger of serious frost is past. The very hardiest of the hardy annuals can also be sown in September to germinate before the winter and restart into growth the following spring, but nasturtiums certainly do not qualify for that category.

Half-hardy annuals are the ones which must usually be germinated in an artificial climate, in greenhouse, frame or sunny room, in order to get plants sufficiently early to make a good display before autumn cold destroys them.

Yet here again there are differences and some odd anomalies such as that the single annual asters can be sown outdoors in early May with good prospect that they will flower well, but the double-flowered cultivars are rarely satisfactory in this way and are better sown in a temperature of about 60°F(16°C) in March or early April. Most half-hardy annuals prefer to be sown a little earlier than that and, in a higher temperature, between 60 and 68°F(16 and 20°C).

In addition to genuine half-hardy annuals there are plants usually treated as such though they are half hardy perennials. These mostly have a slower rate of growth than the true annuals and so need to be sown earlier, in January or February rather than in March or early April. They include such popular plants as antirrhinums, bedding begonias, cultivars of *Salvia splendens*, verbenas and zonal pelargoniums which, at least by public authorities, are increasingly being grown from seed and discarded in the autumn to save the expense of overwintering stock plants in a heated greenhouse. It seems unlikely that this particular development will be much used by home gardeners because of the difficulty of getting seedling geraniums into flower sufficiently early the first year without the use of chemicals which are not readily available to amateurs.

BIENNIALS True biennials die like annuals after they have flowered and seeded but they spread their life over two years. In practice they are not a very clearly defined class since many of the plants cultivated as biennials, wallflowers for example, pansies and sweet williams, are really perennials which are most conveniently treated as biennials. Others like the foxglove, the common forget-me-not and some verbascums, usually behave in the biennial way and yet on occasion live on to flower a second or even a third time. In the garden it is best to ignore these vagaries and grow them all as biennials, re-sowing them each May or June either in a seedbed outdoors or in pans or seed trays in a frame or unheated greenhouse. The seedlings are then planted out 6 to 8in(15 to 20cm) apart in a reserve bed and are moved into their flowering positions in September or October. They can often be used very conveniently to fill the gaps left by the removal of annuals and summer bedding plants.

TECHNIQUES AND DEVELOPMENTS Parks superintendents and others who garden in public places nearly always use annuals and bedding plants by themselves for massed displays. In big beds planted for a pattern of solid colour it is important that each plant behaves in a uniform way. If it is a little taller, shorter, bushier or leafier than the norm or even a very little different in colour it may spoil the whole effect. With plants constantly renewed, generation after generation, from seed the easiest way to ensure such uniformity without seriously weakening constitution by in-breeding is to produce first generation (F_1) hybrids. The parent lines from which these are produced can be as inbred as may be necessary provided vigour returns in the hybrid generation. They can even be replaced from time to time by new parent lines provided these produce an indistinguishable result and since the parent lines never leave the breeder's nursery no one but he and his staff know precisely what they are or whether they have been changed. For the customer the F_1 hybrid produces uniformity with good constitution and for the raiser an unbreakable copyright since no one else possesses the parents from which the hybrid is made.

It is no wonder that this genetical trick has flourished but it is a little surprising that it has succeeded almost as well with private as with public gardeners. For, partly because F_1 hybrids are expensive to produce, partly because they are a monopoly product, their seed costs a lot more than that of comparable open-pollinated varieties. For the extra money the public gardener gets a quality that he finds very valuable. It is doubtful whether absolute uniformity has any comparable value for most home gardeners. If plants are not used in large masses, but instead are required to provide splashes of seasonal colour amid a framework of more permanent plants, it matters little if there is some variation among them provided it does not go too far – and that can be taken care of by careful selection of the seed-bearing plants without any costly hybridisation being involved.

Two techniques which are probably of more genuine value to home gardeners than F_1 hybrids are formula mixtures and hermetically sealed seed packets. Most owners of small gardens prefer to have annuals in mixed colours. Ordinary mixtures are made by growing a representative selection of colours together and harvesting the seed from them as it comes. Since some colours may produce seed more freely than others the balance in the next generation can be markedly different from that in the cropping fields. Formula mixtures are produced by growing each colour in isolation and then blending the seed in proportions which the seedsmen believes will give the most pleasing effect. The formula can be repeated year after year with little or no variation.

Hermetically sealed seeds are put into their foil and plastic packets in rooms with accurately controlled humidity so that the air inside the packet is just right to keep the seeds in good condition for as long as possible. Of course, once the packet is opened the benefit is lost but the shelf life of hermetically sealed seeds is much longer than that of seeds in traditional paper packets and this is an added guarantee of good germination.

ASSESSING THE GENERA

It is an odd fact that more time and money have been spent on breeding a limited range of annuals and bedding plants than on any other ornamental plants, even roses though these rank an easy second. It is the kinds that are popular with the public authorities and with the large scale producers of box plants that have been most assiduously developed and the rest are comparatively neglected though some may be of equal or even greater value for home gardeners with their very different requirements. It is important that amateur gardeners should keep on asking for annuals that they really like and not meekly accept those that have been bred for another purpose, for only by doing so can they ensure that there will be sufficient demand to encourage someone to produce the necessary seed. Let us look a little more closely at what is, or at any rate should be, available.

Adonis aestivalis is one of those that might easily disappear, for the public parks do not need it at all and I doubt whether many home gardeners buy it, pretty though it is. A true hardy annual, it is a member of the buttercup family with finely divided leaves and crimson, cup-shaped flowers on 1 to 1¼ft(30 to 38cm) stems. There is not the slightest danger that ageratums might be displaced for they are among the most popular of groundwork annuals. Strictly speaking, they are perennials and were once grown from spring cuttings but only older gardeners will remember that. Now seed firms vie with one another in producing even more uniform F_1 hybrids. The names may change but the plants, smothered in fluffy blue flower heads, alter very little.

Alonsoa is on the danger list despite the brilliance of its small but numerous scarlet-spurred flowers. *Alonsoa warscewiczii* is the best and it used to be called *A. compacta*, which emphasises its neat habit. It is really perennial but is grown as a half-hardy annual for sunny places. The alyssums, now correctly known as *Lobularia*, are in no danger at all and have been improved by the production of even flatter, more carpet-forming varieties. All the same, there are places in which an old-fashioned, sprawling alyssum is best. *Amaranthus* comes in two totally different guises; as *A. caudatus*, the love-lies-bleeding, with long chenile-like trails of beetroot-purple or lime-green flowers, and as *A. tricolor* with astonishing leaves as richly coloured and variously shaped as those of crotons. The first is a hardy and the second a half-hardy annual. *Anchusa capensis* is said to be a biennial but is almost always grown as a half-hardy annual. It looks like a very fine forget-me-not flowering in summer. Much the same could be said of *Cynoglossum amabile*, another biennial usually grown as a half-hardy annual.

Antirrhinums need neither recommendation nor description. They are perennials and really do behave as such in suitably warm and well-drained places but are normally grown the half hardy way. Cultivars are legion and

F_1 hybrids abound but there are also many excellent open-pollinated varieties at around a quarter the price. Heights range from 6in to 1ft(15cm to 30cm) or even more. *Arctotis* is among the loveliest of South African daisies. The kind sold as *A. grandis* has silvery-white flowers with a steel blue centre and is a half-hardy annual. Those listed as *A. × hybrida* are, on the whole, shorter, contain rich as well as delicate colours and some plants may live a year or so in the right environment. Annual asters or *Callistephus* have been wonderfully extended in habit and flower form. It is the shorter-stemmed cultivars and those with single flowers that are best for garden display, the long-stemmed doubles being more suitable for cutting.

Bartonia aurea is a showy hardy annual with yellow flowers that has never made much mark with gardeners and could easily drop out of the lists if there is no rise in demand for it. Its correct name is *Mentzelia lindleyi* and it has the attractive popular name blazing star. *Begonia semperflorens* is the most popular of its genus for outdoor planting, really a perennial but almost invariably grown as a half-hardy annual. No plant flowers more persistently but its colour range is limited to pink, red and white with green or bronze-red foliage. To be successful it needs to be sown in warmth in January or February and, since the seeds are dust-like and the seedlings are tiny when in need of pricking out, many amateurs prefer to leave the raising to professionals and buy box plants in early summer ready for planting out.

The pretty Swan river daisy, *Brachycome iberidifolia*, is another that could easily disappear for lack of demand. It grows 8in(20cm) high and produces small blue or white daisies. It needs to be raised in a greenhouse.

It is probably the demand from flower arrangers that keeps *Cacalia coccinea* (*Emilia flammea* or *E. sagittata*) alive in the seed lists. Known as the tassel flower, it has sprays of little orange-red daisy flowers, all centres and no ray petals. It can be grown as a hardy or half-hardy annual. Calendula needs no recommendation, only the warning not to rely too much on self-sown seedlings which can appear in hundreds but will rapidly revert to the wild single type of flower.

There are now numerous races of carnation which can be grown as half-hardy annuals including some F_1 hybrids which have flowers of astonishingly good quality. Celosias are happiest under glass but in sunny years they can be grown outdoors and their glistening plumes of carmine, crimson or yellow flowers are spectacular. They need to be started early in genial warmth.

The tall cornflowers, cultivars of *Centaurea cyanus*, can provide some of the best blues in the garden and are easily grown hardy annuals but they need support. Other colours are available and there are also short cultivars ideal for edging and ground cover. The sweet sultan is also a centaurea, derived from *C. moschata*. It is most attractive when well grown but needs sun, warmth, good soil and good drainage.

Annual chrysanthemums come in several distinct races, easily the most spectacular being those sold as 'Tricolor' (they are really cultivars of *C. carinatum*) with single or semi-double flowers zoned with white, red and yellow. For those who prefer their colours plain there are excellent single and double-flowered forms of *C. coronarium* wholly yellow. All are hardy annuals. Clarkias are just as easy to grow but lack the wide utility of the chrysanthemums. Nevertheless they can look very attractive spearing their slender spikes of rose or carmine through lower-growing plants. *Cleome hassleriana* (*C. spinosa*) is the spider flower, a half-hardy annual sufficiently large and distinctive to be used as a key feature. Its purplish colour is variable and the clearest pink forms are the most attractive.

Cobaea scandens is one of the fastest-growing climbers, so fast that it can be grown as a half-hardy annual and will still cover a large screen by the end of the summer. The purple or white flowers resemble Canterbury bells. The annual *Convolvulus* is an ideal sprawler for a sunny place. Careful selection has fixed the most effective deep blue colour with white and yellow centre. Lighter mauve and purplish-pink forms are also available. All are sufficiently hardy to be sown out of doors. Gardeners usually call the hardy annual *Coreopsis drummondii Calliopsis*, presumably to distinguish it from the perennial kinds. All cultivars combine yellow and chestnut-crimson in

81. Chrysanthemum 'Tricolor' (cultivars of C. carinatum)

82. Dimorphotheca, *the star of the veldt*

varying proportions and look best when grown in fairly large groups.

Cosmos has benefited from breeding to make it less tall and leafy and more ready to start flowering freely quite early in the summer. A second species, named *C. sulphureus*, has added yellow and orange to the predominantly white, pink and crimson *C. bipinnatus*. It is also a stiffer plant which always displays its flowers well. All need to be grown the half-hardy way. *Cuphea miniata* is a half-hardy annual relative of the cigar plant, *C. ignea*, and has similar little tubular scarlet flowers but without the black tip. It is occasionally available.

Gardeners always call the hardy annual delphiniums derived from *D. ajacis* larkspurs, which no doubt saves confusion. They can be sown outdoors in September for extra early flowers and the colour range includes good reds and pinks as well as blues, purples and white. There is now a shorter-stemmed race which needs no support. The annual pinks are varieties of *Dianthus chinensis* and its variety *heddewigii*. They are very showy plants and the great demand for them has produced all manner of F_1 hybrids, some very good indeed. Less expensive open pollinated mixtures such as 'Persian Carpet' and 'Baby Doll' are usually sufficiently good to meet the requirements of the private gardener.

Dimorphotheca is the star of the veldt, another of the beautiful South African daisies. Like *Arctotis* its petals are long and narrow, the central disk small and neat. Colours are both rich and delicate. Surprisingly, these are hardy in many places, but in cold damp districts it is wise to raise them under glass.

Eschscholzia, the Californian poppy, has petals with a satin sheen that enhances the naturally bright orange-yellow colour. Breeding has added pinks and carmines as well as double flowers which further increase the effectiveness of the dazzling display. *Euphorbia marginata* is a hardy annual spurge with bright green leaves edged with white. It is mainly the interest of flower arrangers that has ensured its continued availability.

Gilias can be confusing for some go under their own name while others are falsely listed as *Leptosiphon*. It is these last that are most popular; dainty little plants with small flowers like multi-coloured confetti. *Gilia capitata* has pincushion clusters of blue flowers and *G. tricolor* is stiffer, more branched with ferny leaves and lavender, yellow and pink flowers. All are hardy annuals. There is no difficulty with godetias which are easy to grow and as easy to buy. The most popular race is fairly short and bushy with quite large double or semi-double flowers rather like azaleas. A taller more slender race has its uses, especially in mixed borders. All are hardy.

Everlasting flowers of all kinds are back in favour after a period of some neglect. This is partly due to the great improvement of *Helichrysum bracteatum* which has been changed from a rather coarse plant to a compact and free-flowering one in such cultivars as 'Bright Bikini' and 'Dwarf Spangles'. *Acroclinium* and *Rhodanthe*, names now considered synonymous with *Helipterums* and also *Xeranthemum*, all have smaller flowers and a more slender habit. There are also numerous statices, really cultivars of *Limonium bonduellii*, *L. sinuatum* and *L. suworowii*. All of these are best grown as half-hardy annuals, although those everlasting flowers listed as *Acroclinium* and *Xeranthemum* cultivars are sometimes sown outdoors in spring.

Felicia bergerana, the charming little kingfisher daisy with blue, yellow-centred flowers, is now only available from a few seedsmen yet it is one of the prettiest half-hardy annuals for a sunny rock garden. *Charieis heterophylla*, which is always marketed as *Kaulfussia*, is another dainty blue daisy that is getting scarcer and more difficult to find.

Annual gaillardias for the garden are double-flowered cultivars of *G. picta* and are also sun-lovers which need to be grown as half-hardy annuals. *Gypsophila elegans* is grown commercially as a cut flower and so is freely available in both white and pink varieties. These can be sown outdoors where they are to flower.

Hollyhocks are perennials which are commonly grown as biennials, but 'Summer Carnival' flowers so early in life that it can be treated as a half-hardy annual. The flowers are semi-double and include all the familiar hollyhock colours.

83. Lavatera trimestris 'Silver Cup'

The annual sunflowers, are not all golden giants although all are derived from one species *Helianthus annuus*. There are also shorter, more manageable cultivars, some with the typical golden flowers, others splashed or almost covered in bronzy-crimson. All can be sown where they are to flower, which should be a sunny and warm place. The dainty blue and white *Heliophila* seems already almost to have disappeared, driven out, no doubt, by more showy and robust plants. However, *Ionopsidium acaule*, the violet cress, with tiny mauve flowers, lives on because it is an excellent carpeting plant which can be sown where it is to grow.

The two hardy annual species of iberis, always marketed as candytufts, present no problems. *Iberis coronaria* carries its flowers in dense spikes and is always white. *I. umbellata* produces its flowers in little flat clusters and may be white, purple or mauve. *Impatiens wallerana* is the plant gardeners call busy lizzie because, provided the temperature keeps up, it hardly ever stops flowering. It is a perennial but nowadays is grown in vast numbers as a half-hardy annual thanks to the production of much shorter, denser, more wide spreading cultivars which make ideal ground cover, will flower even in moderately shady places and come true from seed. The balsams, which are varieties of *Impatiens balsamina*, are happier under glass although the new dwarf cultivars can be used for outdoor display as well. All need a good deal of warmth for successful germination.

Ipomoeas are also a little tricky to manage when young. The seeds should be soaked for 24 hours before sowing and germinated in a temperature of at least 65° to 68°F(18.5 ° to 20°C). Leaves often go white when the seedlings are young, and again it is low temperatures that are most likely to be the cause. 'Heavenly Blue' is a well-named and favourite cultivar – but other colours are available.

Kochia trichophylla is one of the few annuals grown solely for its foliage. It looks like a small bright green cypress until, in autumn, its leaves turn to coppery-crimson. It is sometimes listed as hardy but is better raised under glass.

Lavatera trimestris took a leap forward in popularity with the introduction of two fine cultivars, gleaming pink 'Silver Cup' and pure white 'Mont Blanc'. These, and the old 'Loveliness', are all easily grown hardy annuals which make big bushy plants and look well in the company of hardy perennials. *Malope trifida* is similar but cruder in colour and it has not been improved. *Limnanthes douglasii* is one of the first annuals to flower, especially if sown in September. Its low mounds of ferny yellowish leaves are the perfect groundwork for the saucer-shaped yellow and white flowers. *Layia elegans* also combines yellow and white but its flowers are of the daisy type and the white makes a ring around them for which reason it is called tidy tips. It is a hardy annual. *Linaria maroccana* is the annual toadflax and looks like a tiny antirrhinum with flowers in rich and varied colours. It can be sown where it is to flower.

The annual flax, *Linum grandiflorum*, has flowers of such a vivid scarlet that no one has ever tried to improve them. There is a white cultivar which retains a central spot of red. The display is short-lived, but successional sowings can be made where the plants are required. Lobelias have been top favourites for generations both for carpeting and trailing over walls and from window boxes and hanging baskets. Despite all the breeding some of the very old cultivars remain among the best including dark blue 'Crystal Palace', and blue and white 'Mrs Clibran'. These need half-hardy treatment.

Lunaria biennis is, as its name indicates, a true biennial. It is a fine plant which usefully bridges the gap between spring and summer with its magenta or white flowers and these are followed by the distinctive parchment-like seeds pods so useful for winter decoration. There is a variant with cream-variegated leaves, the colour coming as the plants mature, but this is handed on between amateurs and does not seem to reach the seed lists.

The annual lupins are not particularly attractive, but their rather excessive leafiness has been restrained in some short-stemmed cultivars such as 'The Pixie'. Marigolds have been overdeveloped to the point of confusion. Thousands of varieties have been named yet there is only market room for a

84. Ipomoea *'Heavenly Blue'*

85. Mesembryanthemum
criniflorum (correctly
Dorotheanthus
bellidiformis)

86. Nemophila insignis,
baby blue eyes

few dozen at most. The breeders greatest achievement has been in combining the neat flowers and bronzy-red markings of the French mari-golds, derived from *Tagetes patula*, with the greater vigour of the African marigolds, derived from *T. erecta*. There is now every imaginable size from 6in(15cm) pygmies to 3ft(1m) giants with flowers that may be single, semi-double or fully double in the small cultivars but are always huge balls in the large ones. Even the strong smell of the leaves, unpleasant to some people, has been eliminated from some cultivars and there are marigolds with white flowers. Colour advances have also been made in little *Tagetes signata*, a delightful cushion-forming plant with ferny leaves and small but abundant flowers which may be lemon, yellow or orange-red.

Chrysanthemum parthenium (*Matricaria eximia*) is a pretty but not very permanent perennial which is almost invariably grown as a hardy annual. It has finely divided leaves and dense sprays of white or yellow flowers which, in the cultivated varieties, are always double. *Mesembryanthemum criniflorum* is correctly known as *Dorotheanthus bellidiformis*, but it would be useless to look for that name in seed lists. No carpeter exceeds this in brilliance, the superficially daisy-like flowers embracing carmines and crimsons which seem almost artificial in their intensity as well as subtler shades of apricot and buff. It is half-hardy and needs to be sown at least twice for continuity.

There are no problems with mignonette, an age-old favourite which can never be spectacular but is loved for its sweet perfume and makes a cool contrast to the gayer colours around. The showy monkey flowers or *Mimulus* with yellow or orange flowers splashed with pink or crimson are really short-lived perennials, but they are grown as half-hardy annuals and they like moist places.

Molucella laevis is the graceful bells of Ireland or shell flower, much used by flower arrangers and so freely available. It is half-hardy and not very easy to germinate. Do not throw away the seed pans too quickly as late seedlings may appear long after most have been pricked out.

The common bedding forget-me-nots are always grown as biennials and for best results seed should be purchased annually since self-sown seed-lings quickly revert to type. Yet this is such a lovely plant that in wild places or where forget-me-nots are naturalised it is not necessary to have carefully selected garden cultivars and plants can be left to seed themselves freely.

Nasturtiums, which are really cultivars of *Tropaeolum majus*, have been taught to carry their flowers above their leaves and some cultivars have been deprived of their slender nectar-filled spurs which seems to have little advantage unless it is held that bees spoil the flowers. More useful is a cultivar named 'Alaska' with heavily cream-variegated leaves. *Nemesia* seems to be attracting less attention, maybe because commercial producers of box plants like to market everything in bloom. There is no difficulty in getting nemesias into flower so early but it is fatal to success since the plants become starved and seldom grow away freely when planted out.

Nemophila insignis, popularly known as baby blue eyes because of its light blue, white-centred flowers, continues to be sold unimproved, which is just as well since it is difficult to see what change could be advantageous to this charming little mat-forming hardy annual. A few efforts have been made to popularise *Nicandra physaloides* mainly on the score that it is supposed to keep flies away but it is a coarse and rather unattractive annual which has found few buyers. It can be sown outdoors or under glass.

Nigella damascena is the love-in-a-mist with cornflower-blue flowers sur-rounded by veils of green filaments. Lavender, purple and pink cultivars are also available in a selection known as 'Persian Jewels'. All are hardy and very easy to grow.

Pansies and violas have become so intermingled that even the experts cannot give any logical method of distinguishing one from the other. All are really perennials but are increasingly grown either as biennials sown outdoors in June-July or as half-hardy annuals sown in a greenhouse or frame in February-March.

Petunias are legion, in fact there are now probably as many cultivars of them as there are of marigolds. In hot, dry summers there are no better or more prolific plants but wet weather soon has them bedraggled. For this reason the Resisto cultivars, bred to recover quickly from rain damage, are the most reliable in most parts of Britain. All petunias must be raised under glass and benefit from February sowing if 65°F(18.5°C) can be maintained.

Phacelia campanularia is one of the bluest of flowers, a very fast-growing hardy annual but with a rather short season. By contrast the annual phloxes flower for a long time and are first-class for edgings and ground cover. All are derived from the Texan *Phlox drummondii* and so it is not surprising that they love sun and warmth. They are half-hardy annuals.

There are two races of annual poppies, one selected from the common field poppy, *Papaver rhoeas* and marketed as Shirley poppies, the other derived from *P. somniferum* and sold as carnation-flowered or paeony-flowered. These have larger flowers, a wider colour range and heavier grey-green foliage. Iceland poppies, derived from *P. nudicaule*, are short-lived perennials grown as biennials. They make splendid cut flowers and are available in lovely shades of yellow, orange, pink, apricot and white.

Polygonum capitatum comes and goes in the seed lists. It is an unspectacular but attractive carpeter with bronze marked leaves and small pink flowers. Really a perennial, it is nearly always grown as a half hardy annual. *Portulaca grandiflora* is a small but dazzling annual succulent for hot, sunny places. Double-flowered cultivars are best and mixtures are available giving white, yellow, pink, rose, scarlet and purple flowers. *Ricinus communis* is the castor oil plant, a big, branching half-hardy annual grown for its large deeply lobed leaves which have a very tropical appearance. They can be green, bronze or reddish-purple and mixtures are available.

Annual rudbeckias have increased greatly in popularity since the introduction of fairly short, well-branched cultivars such as yellow-flowered 'Marmalade' and yellow and bronzy crimson 'Rustic Dwarfs'. The gloriosa daisies are of similar origin but are taller and include double-flowered as well as single cultivars. All are biennials or even short-lived perennials but are generally grown as half-hardy annuals.

The intricately veined and pencilled trumpet flowers of *Salpiglossis* are beautiful but are seen at their best in the shelter of a greenhouse. Outdoors plants should be given a sunny, protected position. They are half-hardy annuals.

The scarlet salvia, *Salvia splendens*, can now be bought in pink and purple cultivars but scarlet remains far and away the most popular colour. These plants rival bedding geraniums in the continuity of their flowering but need to be sown early, in January if possible, in a temperature of around 68°F(20°C). *S. farinacea* is a totally different plant, a perennial usually grown as a half-hardy annual, with slender spikes of lavender-blue flowers which last a long time. Two more species much in demand are *S. horminum*, in blue, pink and purple cultivars, a hardy annual usually listed as clary, a name which really belongs to *S. sclarea* which is biennial and in its best form, *turkestanica*, has densely grey downy leaves and soft pink flowers.

Sanvitalia procumbens is a gay little yellow and black hardy annual daisy occasionally available and useful as ground-cover in sunny places. *Saponaria vaccaria* is an easily grown, sprawling annual with masses of small pink flowers suitable for sunny rock gardens or banks, and the same is true of *Silene oculata* which is always sold as *Viscaria*. *Silene pendula* is quite a different plant, also an annual, though less hardy, and even more showy especially in its double-flowered forms but much more difficult to buy. The so-called annual scabious (it is really a slightly tender perennial) is readily available in excellent selections of mixed colours including very deep crimson as well as lighter carmines, pinks and lavender-blues.

One of the best things that ever happened to the annual stocks, sold as Ten Week, which is a little optimistic if it signifies time from sowing to flowering, was the linking of a light green leaf character with doubling of the flowers so that the desirable double-flowered plants can be selected at the pricking out stage. Beauty of Nice stocks, which will flower under glass in the short winter days, have been similarly endowed but the feature does not seem to have been added to the biennial spring-flowering stocks sold as East Lothian and Brompton.

87. Molucella laevis, *bells of Ireland*

88. Papaver nudicaule, *the Iceland poppy*

89. Rudbeckia 'Rustic
Dwarfs' (see p.127)

Tall sweet peas remain very much a British preoccupation, the overseas
market, such as it is, being dominated by the shorter Knee-hi and Jet Set
strains which are wonderfully free-flowering and make a fine display in the
garden without needing a great deal of support.

Sweet william is the popular name of *Dianthus barbatus*, a showy perennial
which gets straggly with age and so is usually grown as a biennial. Dwarf
cultivars as short as 6in(15cm) have now been added to the familiar races
averaging 15 to 20in(38 to 50cm) in height. The frilly flowered, yellow
canary creeper continues to be sold as *Tropaeolum canariense* and does not
find a place with the nasturtiums to which it is related. It can be grown in
the same way. Occasional efforts are made to popularise *Tithonia rotundifolia*
which looks like a very coarse zinnia but it has never really caught on.

More South African daisies are the cheerful orange ursinias, now usually
sold as hybrids between the several very similar species. *Venidium fastuosum*
is much larger and coarser with big yellow, black-zoned flowers. All are best
grown as half-hardy annuals. Bedding verbenas have also for the most part
lost their specific status and become merged as colourful hybrids ideal for
groundwork and for spilling over the edges of window boxes, plant
containers and so on. Although perennial they are commonly grown as
half-hardy annuals but benefit from an early start. Wallflowers are also
perennials but they get straggly and unreliable with age and so are grown as
biennials. Shorter, 1ft(30cm) tall, cultivars are now available for places
where the normal 15 to 18in(40 to 45cm) height would be difficult to
accommodate.

Common maize, *Zea mays*, can be obtained in cultivars which produce
variously coloured cobs useful for winter decoration. The broad leaves also
give a tropical effect to borders in summer. Maize seedlings transplant badly
and so seed is best sown singly or in pairs in small pots in early May and the
resulting plants set out undisturbed in early June.

Zinnias have been highly developed, mainly for the American market,
and a good selection is always available here for those who can grow them
well.

12.

Ground-Cover Plants

Ground-cover planting provides an essential element in labour-saving gardening, other elements being trees, shrubs and bulbs generally. Thus it follows that for effective ground cover leaves will be more important than flowers, and that dense-growing, leafy evergreens which need little or no attention are ideal. Contrast will be provided by the texture and colour of the leaves, through all the various shades of green from the palest yellowish-green to the darkest blue-greens. In addition, there are many plants with variegated leaves and others with leaves of yellow, grey or purple shades.

Ground-coverers are usually regarded as flat growing, but many medium-sized and large-growing plants produce such a dense canopy of leaves, in some cases on pendulous branches, that they make their own cover. The evergreens *Choisya ternata*, *Cotoneaster salicifolius* var. *floccosus* and, on a small scale, *Mahonia japonica*, are good examples, as are the deciduous berberis, hydrangeas (not the *paniculata* types) and *Rosa* 'Canary Bird'. Ground-cover plants, set close to each other, help each other to grow; and they assist many taller plants to grow as the thick cover of vegetation they form conserves soil moisture and helps to keep the roots cool.

Aesthetically, too, a well-clothed leafy border is always preferable to one with tracts of bare soil. From the design point of view, ground cover links and defines spaces without impeding views and acts as a background for "accent" planting; the juxtaposition of plants is the essence of all planting design. Bold drifts of ground-cover plants avoids any suggestion of spotti-ness. The junction of vertical and horizontal lines can be masked effectively by allowing ground-cover plants to run up to the base of plants with greater height.

TYPES OF GROUND COVER Ground-cover plants fall into two categories depending on their nature of growth:
(a) Plants which quickly become really effective weed smotherers, growing virtually anywhere and needing little, if any, maintenance. Examples include the large-leaved ivies (*Hedera*), *Hypericum calycinum* and *Galeobdolon argentatum* (syn. *Lamium galeobdolon* 'Variegatum'). A disadvantage of this group is that they may be rampant colonizing invaders which can become "weeds", and they can crowd out more choice but less vigorous plants. Others in this category seed themselves freely, but generally the seedlings can be pulled up easily when small – e.g., *Alchemilla mollis* and *Viola labradorica*.
(b) Plants which will need some attention in the early years and are not so adaptable to a wide range of soils; also, they may be slower growing. In this category will be found many plants which will provide a wider range of texture, leaf shape and colour. Prominent in this category are ajugas, epimediums, hostas, pachysandras and dwarf conifers. Examples of good ground-coverers can be drawn from free-standing shrubs, including species roses, climbing shrubs, conifers, herbaceous plants, alpines and ferns. While shrubs provide the most long-lived ground cover there are some excellent herbaceous plants such as geraniums, hemerocallis, polygonums and tiarellas which will rarely need any attention. On the other hand, there are many others which, while keeping most weeds at bay – for example,

astilbe, aubrieta and sedum – will always need some attention.

Some plants, of which bush roses and irises are examples, will always need hand-weeding or hoeing. The keen gardener will not wish to forego growing all those plants which need hand-weeding but he or she may wish to devote the larger areas to those plants which give reasonably effective ground cover. If the *raison d'être* for ground cover is the complete absence of weeds and weeding once the plants are established, then the choice must be made from a narrower range of plants. It is this range of plants which is described later in this chapter.

Where the planting is to be under young trees the choice must be made with particular care, for in the early stages there will be plenty of light, but as the trees grow the ground-cover plants will be in shade. Ground-coverers tolerant of changing conditions include *Hypericum calycinum* and *Vinca minor*. Ground-coverers planted under mature trees may be required to withstand dry shade and drip from the leaves as well as competition from the tree roots. The addition of humus during the thorough preparation of the soil is essential.

Cultural Attentions

GROUND PREPARATION: No matter which ground-cover plants are chosen none of them will win a battle against pernicious weeds and it is folly to think otherwise. Thorough preparation of the soil in advance of planting to achieve a high level of fertility and cleanliness is absolutely essential. Do remember that once the plants are established the removal of weeds (especially couch grass) from among the plants will be difficult. Fortunately chemical weed control takes out much of the tedium of cleaning the land (see Chapter 38, "Weed Control", p.332 to 339) but, where perennial weeds are growing, be sure that almost a year is allowed for the job. Among the most persistent perennial weeds are bind-weed, couch grass, creeping thistle, ground elder and mare's tails, the destruction of which should be started in January/February in readiness for new planting to take place in the autumn. Then the long-term residual weedkiller, Casoron in granular form, should be applied when the top growth may not be visible. On re-growth, use the systemic herbicides Tumbleweed or Dalapon, two applications of the latter being most effective against couch grass. Annual weeds can be controlled with a contact herbicide such as Weedol (containing paraquat and diquat) with one or two applications during the growing season.

The method of cultivating the site depends on the type of soil and on the drainage. If it lies wet even in dry weather then a system of land drains will probably be needed. However, much can be done by forking or digging the top spit and breaking the sub-soil (bastard trenching). Coarse sand and partially rotted strawy manure, coarse peat or composted bark should be mixed into both spits as work progresses. Where the drainage is adequate and the soil is in good condition the top spit can be forked or dug. If it is to be mechanically cultivated then pernicious weeds *must* have been treated chemically beforehand. Ground-cover plants appreciate a dressing of a slow-release fertiliser such as bone-meal or superphosphate, or a proprietary fertiliser such as Osmocote or Vitax Q4, both of which contain trace elements. This should be applied, for preference, to a layer of peat or compost spread over the soil surface, which is then lightly forked in. Nitro-chalk is beneficial on acid soils. The soil should be left to settle for a week or two, or if the soil is light it can be trodden firm with the feet. Such treading is not advisable on heavy clay soils which will quickly go hard.

FEEDING: Until the plants form a complete carpet it will help to apply an annual dressing in early spring of a slow-release, well-balanced general fertiliser in granule form, e.g., Vitax Q4. Thereafter the occasional application of a liquid fertiliser in late spring or early summer will be beneficial.

WEEDING: It is vital that weeds should not be allowed to gain a hold in new planting so, at first, hoeing (taking care not to damage the young roots) and hand weeding will be necessary. Chemical weedkillers cannot usually be used around herbaceous perennials or conifers, but can be used, with care, around most shrubs and roses, even immediately after transplanting.

PRUNING: Any plants which become straggly can be cut back hard to encourage new bushy growth. This is generally best done in late winter.

THINNING: Periodically it may be necessary to lift and divide herbaceous plants, retaining only the young outer parts of the clumps. Removal of shrubs may be necessary depending on the density of the original planting.

AFTER-CARE: Newly planted stock may need watering in the first spring and early summer, especially if the stock was planted in late winter or spring. In dry areas spraying overhead on warm, still days increases humidity, thus encouraging growth.

MULCHING: A mulch will help to conserve soil moisture, improve the soil condition and keep down the weeds. It is best applied in early spring while the soil is still moist. A layer of 2 to 3in(5 to 8cm) deep of humus-forming material such as well-rotted compost, farmyard manure, leaf mould, pulverised or shredded bark or peat will be especially valuable if applied in the spring following planting. Annual mulching thereafter will also help.

SETTING OUT: Better cover results from planting numerous small, well-rooted plants than from fewer, larger clumps. On limy soils, closer planting to hasten the eventual cover is advisable. The number of plants required per square yard (square metre) depends on growth rates – the faster the growth and the bulkier the plant the fewer which are required, and conversely the weaker the growth rate the more will be needed. Recommended planting distances are given in the descriptive lists. By planting wider apart (within reason) equally good ground-cover will be obtained, but over a longer period and with more labour in weeding the bare ground. Some transplanting, especially of herbaceous subjects, may be necessary on the closer plantings. To find the distance to be left between plants of different sorts, add the expected spread of each, then divide by two.

On a small scale, an informal planting arranged by eye will suffice, but on a larger scale subtle effects can be created by staggering the plants asymmetrically avoiding straight lines. There are an infinite number of variations to consider; planning the layout on paper is worthwhile.

CONTAINER- AND POT-GROWN PLANTS: These have the advantage over bare-root plants in that there should be a reservoir of nutrients and moisture in the potting soil which will sustain the plant while new roots extend into the surrounding soil. The plastic pots or bags should be removed carefully, taking care not to damage the roots. Plants in peat pots should be planted as they are, as the roots will penetrate the walls of the pots, which will disintegrate.

Habit of Ground-Cover Plants

The habit of ground-cover plants can be classified as follows:

CARPETERS: These form a carpet by means of runners, or a prostrate growth habit, many having surface-rooting stems. Examples include *Cotoneaster dammeri*, *Vinca* and *Galeobdolon argentatum*.

CLUMP-FORMERS: Mainly herbaceous plants, these form clumps from a central rootstock, e.g. *Bergenia*.

HUMMOCKS: These are usually provided by shrubs such as *Erica* (heather) and *Hebe*; they need to be planted fairly close together to make good cover.

SPREADERS: These increase their size by underground shoots or roots. Examples include *Hypericum calycinum* and *Pachysandra terminalis*.

SPRAWLERS: These are shrubs of floppy habit with both erect and drooping stems; e.g. *Euonymus fortunei* 'Colorata'.

GROUND-COVER PLANTS NEEDING MINIMUM MAINTENANCE

All plants described in the following lists are ground-coverers which, when established, will require minimum maintenance.

To make reference easier, the first mention of any genus is denoted by the use of italic capitals.

Shrubs

All plants are deciduous unless marked ev, *which denotes evergreen.*

ARCTOSTAPHYLOS (ev) Carpet-rooting evergreens allied to rhododendrons. They need lime-free, fertile soil; full sun or partial shade. Both bear tiny "bells" in spring, then red berries.

A. nevadensis Prostrate shoots with small, dark green, pointed, glossy leaves. 6in(15cm). Plant 4ft(1.25m) apart.

A. uva-ursi, bearberry This native, creeping alpine shrub makes long trails with blunt, dark leaves. 6in(15cm). Plant 2ft(60cm) apart.

BERBERIS, barberry Dense hummock-forming bushes making excellent cover. Easily grown but the smaller forms are rather slow.

B. 'Amstelveen' (ev) Beautifully arching branches, dense habit and faster growth. 2½ft(75cm). Glossy fresh green leaves with blue-white undersides. Plant 2ft(60cm) apart.

B. candidula (ev) Excellent, evergreen ground cover of hemispherical habit, slowly attaining a height and spread of 1½ by 4ft(45cm by 1.25m). Small, dark green glossy leaves with silvery-blue reverse. Plant 1½ft(45cm) apart.

B. gagnepainii (ev) Shapely dense bushes of erect-growing branches with three-part spines. 4ft(1.25m). Long, narrow, crinkled leaves. Plant 2½ft(75cm) apart.

B. 'Parkjuweel': A semi-evergreen ground-cover of dense prickly habit. 2½ft(75cm). Medium to large, obovate, almost spineless leaves colouring well in autumn. Plant 3ft(1m) apart.

B. verruculosa (ev) Sturdy evergreen with firm yet arching branches. 3 to 4ft(1 to 1.25m). Exceptionally glossy, small to medium-sized, leathery leaves. Plant 3ft(1m) apart.

Calluna vulgaris (ev), heather or ling Requiring lime-free soil with humus, they like full sun or partial shade. Many cultivars are available but the compact growers are best for ground cover, making hummocks 1½ft(45cm) high. Plant 1½ft(45cm) apart. 'County Wicklow': Double, shell-pink flowers, August-September. 'Gold Haze': Bright golden foliage all year round. White flowers August-September. 'Golden Feather': Golden feathery foliage in early summer, gradually turns to soft shade of orange in winter. 'J.H. Hamilton': Double bright pink flowers, July-August. 'Mullion': Semi-prostrate with numerous branches. Deep pink flowers August-September. 'Robert Chapman': The spring foliage is gold; it changes to orange and to red later. Soft purple flowers, August-September. 'Sunset': Foliage in shades of yellow, gold and orange. Pink flowers, August-September.

CEANOTHUS thyrsiflorus repens (ev), creeping blue blossom Quickly forms a mound of dense evergreen foliage which is literally covered with mid-blue flowers in May. 2ft(60cm). Plant 4ft(1.25m) apart.

CHAENOMELES, cydonia or flowering quince Very hardy, also free flowering and early.

C. japonica Low spreading, thorny shrubs reaching 3ft(1m). Abundant dark red flowers followed by yellow quinces. Plant 4ft(1.25m) apart.

C. × superba 'Crimson and Gold' Hummock forming, reaching 3 to 4ft(1 to 1.25m). Single flowers with crimson petals and gold anthers, February-March. Plant 5ft(1.5m) apart.

CISTUS (ev) The smaller-growing rock roses make hummock-like bushes; they are best in full sun and on well-drained soil. The following are among the hardiest:

C. × corbariensis Reaches 2 to 3ft(60cm to 1m). Small to medium-sized dark green leaves give winter interest. Rosy-pink buds and slightly cup-shaped white flowers in June. Plant 3ft(1m) apart.

C. palhinhae Broad and rounded. 2 by 3ft(60cm to 1m). Dark green, glossy, sticky leaves. White flowers nearly 4in(10cm) across. Plant 3ft(1m) apart.

COTONEASTER There is a suitable cotoneaster for virtually any site and soil. White flowers open in June to be followed by abundant crops of berries, mostly orange or red.

The following cotoneasters are all prostrate ground-covers, thriving in full sun to deep shade:

C. dammeri (ev)   Carpeting shoots root where they touch the soil, spreading indefinitely about 2ft(60cm) a year. On banks growth turns downwards. Bright red berries. Plant 2ft(60cm) apart.

C. 'Hybridus Pendulus' (ev)   Strong arching shoots spread about 3 to 4ft(1 to 1.25m) a year with the central part arching up to 2ft(60cm) high. Narrow, glossy leaves. Bright red berries. Plant 6ft(2m) apart.

C. salicifolius 'Repens' (syn. 'Avondrood') (ev)   A prostrate ground-coverer with medium-sized, narrow leaves. Red berries. Plant 3ft(1m) apart.

C. 'Coral Beauty' (ev). The prostrate, wide-spreading habit makes this a first-class ground coverer. 1ft(30cm) high. Small, evergreen leaves back the large, bright orange fruits in autumn. Plant 4ft(1.25m) apart.

Low to medium-growing cotoneasters, mostly small-leaved. Partial or full shade is ideal:

C. conspicuus var. *decorus* (ev)   Quickly forms a dense 2½ft(75cm) mound of gracefully arching branches. Dark green leaves, grey woolly beneath. Shining scarlet berries. Plant 3ft(1m) apart.

C. horizontalis, fish-bone cotoneaster   Fan-like branches are ideal for carpeting banks or against a wall. 2 to 5ft(60cm to 1.5m) high, according to site. Very small, dark green leaves turn orange before falling to reveal prolific scarlet berries. Plant 6ft(2m) apart.

C. microphyllus (ev)   Hummock-forming shrub 1½ to 2ft(45 to 60cm). Slender but rigid branches arch over to run along ground. Tiny dark green leaves, large bright crimson berries. Plant 6ft(2m) apart.

C. salicifolius 'Autumn Fire' (syn. 'Herbstfeuer') (ev)   Strong growing carpeters, 1 to 1»ft(30 to 45cm). The only one in this section to have large leaves; these are willow-like. Large red berries. Plant 6ft(2m) apart.

DABOECIA cantabrica (ev) Irish heath   Hummock-formers, closely related to erica. Lime-free soil is essential 1½ to 2½ft(45 to 75cm). Plant 1½ft(45cm) apart.

ERICA (ev)   There is a wide range from which to choose and fortunately among the best for ground cover are the winter-flowering forms which, unlike the remainder, are tolerant of limy soil, well-enriched with humus.

E. herbacea (syn. *E. carnea*)   All produce pink, red or white flowers in winter and there are golden-foliaged forms. 6 to 12in(15 to 30cm) high. Plant 1 to 2½ft(30 to 75cm) apart according to cultivar.

EUONYMUS fortunei (syn. *E. radicans* var. *acutus*) (ev)   Tolerant of a wide range of soils including chalk, this group of sprawling or hummock-forming evergreens make dense ground cover and some will climb walls. 'Colorata' (ev): Trails rising to 2 to 3ft(60cm to 1m) or climbs. Glossy green leaves assume purplish tints throughout winter. Plant 3ft(1m) apart. 'Dart's Blanket' (ev): Evergreen ground cover; flat-growing leaves, reddish-purple in autumn. Extremely tolerant of salt spray. Plant 3ft(1m) apart. 'Kewensis' (ev): Slowly forms a small hummock 6 to 9in(15 to 23cm) high, or will climb if given support. Minute leaves on prostrate stems. Plant 9in(23cm) apart. 'Silver Queen' (ev): As a shrub makes a hummock 1 to 2ft(30 to 45cm). Also will climb slowly. Creamy-white and green variegated foliage. Plant 3ft(1m) apart. 'Vegetus' (ev): As a semi-prostrate shrub 2 by 6ft(45cm by 2m), or will climb if encouraged. Plant 3ft(1m) apart.

GAULTHERIA (ev)   Lime-free, light, dry soil is required. Shade tolerant.

G. procumbens   Makes a dense spreading carpet 6in(15cm) high. Plant 1½ft(45cm) apart.

G. shallon   Thicket-forming 5 to 6ft(1.5 to 2m) high. Invasive. Plant 3ft (1m) apart.

GENISTA   Like the closely related *Cytisus* they also like sunny banks and light soil. The densely packed twigs or spines give an evergreen effect.

G. hispanica, Spanish gorse   Hummock forming 2ft(60cm). Plant 2ft(60cm) apart.

G. lydia   Forms a hummock of wiry grey-green arching shoots. 2ft(60cm). Plant 2ft(60cm) apart.

G. pilosa   Makes a dense grey-green, twiggy carpet. 8in(20cm). Plant 2ft(60cm) apart.

G. sagittalis Foot-high (30cm) hummocks of broadly winged, prostrate branches; yellow flowers in summer. Plant 2ft(60cm) apart.

HEBE (ev)   The shrubby veronicas like well-drained soil; they are hardy in most areas. Hummock formers, they achieve 9 to 24in (23 to 60cm) in height.

HEDERA, ivy (ev)   The ivies thrive almost anywhere, even in dense shade. They do best in partial shade and in soil which is neither very wet nor hard and dry. Much interest is provided by the leaf colour and shape. All make veritable carpets.

H. canariensis   Broad, rounded dark green leaves. Plant 4ft(1.25cm) apart. 'Gloire de Marengo' (syn, *H.c.* 'Variegata'). Large, shield-like olive-green leaves with silver and white irregular edging. Plant 3ft(1m) apart.

H. colchica, Persian ivy   Very large-leaved. Dense ground cover. Plant 4ft(1.25cm) apart. 'Dentata Aurea': Large, leathery, polished leaves; soft green with pronounced deep yellow variegation. Plant 3ft(1m) apart.

H. helix var. *hibernica*, Irish ivy   Rampageous ground cover with dark green, five-lobed, large leaves. Plant 4ft(1.25m) apart.

LONICERA pileata   Horizontally branched and hummock rooting. Reaches 2ft(60cm). Plant 3ft(1m) apart.

MAHONIA aquifolium (ev), holly-leaved berberis   Spreads slowly by underground suckers. Rich, shiny evergreen foliage. Plant 2ft(60cm) apart.

PACHYSANDRA terminalis (ev), Japanese spurge   Almost prostrate evergreen carpeters. 8in(20cm). Best in light, lime-free soil. Plant 1½ft(45cm) apart.

POTENTILLA   Easily grown, long-flowering, hummock-forming shrubs. Best in full sun. Height 1» to 3ft(45cm to 1m). Small leaves, dense twiggy growth; single flowers, mostly yellow shades. Plant 2 to 3ft(60cm to 1m) apart.

PRUNUS laurocerasus (ev), laurel   There are two laurels used for dense cover, 'Otto Luyken' and 'Zabeliana': Both flower freely.

P. laurocerasus 'Otto Luyken':   Compact, horizontal habit with erect stems up to 3ft(1m) carrying dark leaves. Plant 3ft(1m) apart. *P.l.* 'Zabeliana': Low and obliquely branched, reaching 4ft(1.25m). Almost willow-like, long, shining leaves. Plant 4ft(1.25m) apart.

ROSA   The following roses will, in time, provide complete cover and are easy to grow in most conditions: 'Max Graf' (Rugosa hybrid): The prostrate shoots, which root as they spread, are clothed with glossy leaves. Richly scented, single pink flowers. Plant 6ft(2m) apart.

R. nitida   Forms an ever-widening thicket up to 2ft(60cm). Scented, single, bright pink flowers, then showy round hips. Good autumn colour; the brownish-red colour of the stems is outstanding. Plant 2ft(60cm) apart. 'Nozomi': Forms an attractive carpet of single pearl-pink blooms which provide an almost continuous display over many weeks. Not, however, recurrent. Small glossy leaves smother the stems. Plant 3ft(1m) apart. *R. × paulii*: Splendid cover with long, trailing, excessively thorny leafy shoots. Single white flowers. Plant 6ft(2m) apart.

A new race of fairly prostrate ground-cover roses reaching 2½ to 3ft(75cm to 1m) in height was introduced in 1980. All have single or semi-double small flowers; perpetual. Dense glossy foliage is remarkably disease resistant. Plant 3ft(1m) apart. Cultivars include 'Red Blanket', rose-red; 'Rosy Cushion', rose-pink with ivory centres to flowers; and 'Smarty', pale pink, with golden stamens.

RUBUS tricolor (ev)   A benign galloper. One foot (1m) high, it roots readily on contact with the ground and is possibly the fastest of all ground-coverer carpeters in shade. Plant 6 to 8ft(2 to 2.5m) apart.

SALVIA officinalis (ev), sage   This species and its coloured forms are hummock rooting, densely-leaved shrubs, reaching 2ft(60cm). They prefer light soil. Plant 2ft(60cm) apart.

SANTOLINA chamaecyparissus (ev), cotton lavender   Dainty grey or green foliage. Needs light, well-drained soil. Plant 1 to 2ft(30 to 60cm) apart.

SARCOCOCCA humilis (syn. *S. hookeriana* var. *humilis*) (ev)   Dense thickets of short stems make good ground cover up to 1½ft(45cm). Scented flowers in winter. Needs fertile soil. Plant 1 to 2ft(30 to 60cm) apart.

SENECIO (Dunedin Hybrid) 'Sunshine' (syn. *S. laxifolius*) (ev) Forms dense, broad hummocks up to 3ft(1m). Silvery-grey foliage. Plant 4ft(1.25m) apart.

STEPHANANDRA incisa 'Crispa' An incomparable cover reaching 2ft(60cm). From a dense central hummock flow arching twigs clothed with very attractive, small, crinkled pointed leaves. Plant 3ft(1m) apart.

SYMPHORICARPOS × *chenaultii* 'Hancock' A very easy, dense spreading ground-cover ideal under trees. Reaches 1 to 2ft(30 to 60cm). Small, rounded leaves. Plant 4ft(1.25m) apart.

VIBURNUM davidii (ev) Forms dense, low mounds to 2½(75cm). Deep green distinctly three-veined leaves. Bright blue berries. Slow but very attractive. Plant 2½ft(75cm) apart.

VINCA (ev), periwinkle Easily grown, evergreen carpeters. *Vinca minor* may take three years before becoming effective, trouble-free ground-cover. Plant *V. major*, and forms, 2ft(60cm) apart; *V. minor*, and forms, 1 to 1½ft(30 to 45cm) apart.

Conifers

JUNIPERUS, juniper One of the most useful groups of conifers – tough, hardy and tolerant of chalky soil, the junipers withstand drought better than most conifers, but prefer sun to dry shade. Sometimes the finely divided branchlets carry both adult and juvenile foliage which adds to the attraction.

Prostrate Cultivars:
J. communis 'Depressa Aurea': Densely foliaged; reaches 1½ft(45cm). Butter yellow in summer, bronze in winter. Plant 3ft(1m) apart. 'Hornibrookii': At first a completely prostrate mat, later building up in the centre to cover a large area in time, adjusting itself to whatever shaped object it is covering. Young twigs turning bronze later. Plant 3ft(1m) apart. 'Repanda': Strong-growing, dense, prostrate form building up with age. Foliage sprays – some flat, others upright, with leaves lying close to the shoot – are dull green, bronzing slightly in winter. Very effective with other colour forms. Plant 3ft(1m) apart.

J. horizontalis 'Emerald Spreader': Completely flat, ground-hugging spreader, 2 to 4in(5 to 10cm) high. Emerald-green foliage. Plant 2ft(60cm) apart. 'Glauca': Completely prostrate, carpet-forming plant building up with age to make mounds 4 to 8in(10 to 20cm) high. Long, straight branches well clothed with densely set blue-green leaves giving a "whip-cord" effect. Plant 3ft(1m) apart. 'Wiltonii': Almost identical to 'Glauca' but slightly flatter and slower in growth reaching 2 to 4in(5 to 10cm). Foliage rather more of a silver-blue hue. Plant 2ft(60cm) apart.

J. sabina var. *tamariscifolia*, Spanish juniper: Dense, prostrate habit, the branches building up layer by layer to 1ft(30cm) or so. Feathery, bright green foliage, greyish-green when young. Plant 2½ft(75cm) apart.

Spreading Cultivars:
J. × *media* 'Pfitzerana' (syn. *J.* × *chinensis* 'Pfitzerana') Strong-growing branches at an angle of 45 degrees to the ground, the tips curving gracefully. 6ft(2m) or more. Greyish-blue foliage. Plant 5ft(1.5m) apart. *J.* 'Pfitzerana Aurea': Irregular yet graceful with branches dotted with golden foliage at an angle of 30 to 45 degrees to the ground. Slower growing than 'Pfitzerana'. Plant 4ft(1.25m) apart.

Herbaceous Perennial Plants

ACANTHUS, bear's breech Handsome, dark green, deeply divided leaves of architectural merit. 3ft(1m). Plant 3ft(1m) apart.

AJUGA (ev), bugle Good carpeter in ideal conditions and thrive in sun or partial shade. There are green and coloured-leaved forms. 2 to 3in(5 to 8cm). Plant 1½ft(45cm) apart.

ALCHEMILLA mollis, lady's mantle Clump-forming plants for sun or partial shade, they sport greenish-yellow flowers. 6 to 12in(15 to 30cm). Plant 1 to 2ft(30 to 60cm) apart.

ARABIS, rock cress   Carpeters which freely produce white flowers in spring. They thrive in any reasonable conditions. 4 to 5in(10 to 13cm). Plant 12in(30cm) apart.

ASTRANTIA, masterwort   Spreaders or clump-formers for sun or partial shade; avoid extremes of wet and dry soil. Lobed foliage. 9in(23cm). Plant 1 to 1½ ft(30 to 45cm) apart.

BERGENIA (ev)   Clump formers for sun or partial shade; large, dark green leaves make invaluable cover. The flowers, borne in early-late spring, are welcome. *B. cordifolia* and its cultivars are the most suitable. 12in(30cm). Plant 1½ ft(45cm) apart.

BRUNNERA macrophylla   Spreading clumps of large, rounded, dark green leaves are topped with forget-me-not-like flowers blue in spring. 12in(30cm). Plant 2ft(60cm) apart.

CAMPANULA, bellflower.   Several of the spreading or clump-forming bell-flowers make good cover. They have blue or white flowers. 6 to 12in(15 to 30cm). Plant 1 to 1½ ft(30 to 45cm) apart.

CERASTIUM tomentosum (ev), snow in summer   This is an invasive spreader, good in rough conditions. It forms silver-grey 9in(23cm) tall mats. Plant 2ft(60cm) apart.

COTULA (ev),   Carpeters for sun or shade, these provide a foil for miniature bulbs. 2in(5cm). Plant 2ft(60cm) apart.

EPIMEDIUM   Spreaders which do well in sun or shade in fertile soil. Two are evergreen. 12 to 15in(30 to 38cm). Plant 15in(38cm) apart.

EUPHORBIA, spurge   The spurges are important here because all forms thrive in sun or partial shade. *E. robbiae* (ev) is most accommodating; *E. griffithii* thrives in heavy soil. The clump-forming *E. polychroma* has 1ft(30cm) high, fresh green erect stems. Plant 1½ ft(45cm) apart. *E. griffithii* and *E. robbiae* are spreaders reaching 2ft(60cm) and 1½ ft(45cm) respectively.

GALEOBDOLON syn. *Lamium* (ev).   In full or partial shade and in most soils, *Galeobdolon argentatum* syn. (*Lamium galeobdolon* 'Variegatum') is a benign galloper best planted under trees or large shrubs or on a bank. Dark green leaves are marbled white. It reaches 1ft(30cm) in height. Plant 3 to 6ft(1 to 2m) apart, depending on how quickly cover is required.

GERANIUM, crane's bill   The geraniums are invaluable ground-coverers with attractive foliage and flowers. Most do well in full sun and all excel themselves in partial shade. Of the clump-formers, the following are outstanding: *G. endressii*, with pink flowers, which reaches 18in(45cm); *G. ibericum*, with violet-blue flowers and a little taller than the last, and the smaller *G. renardii* with grey-green, velvety leaves and white flowers. Plant at 1½ ft, 2ft and 1ft(45cm, 60cm and 30cm) apart respectively. The carpeters include *G. macrorrhizum* with light green foliage and lavender-blue flowers; plant 3ft(1m) apart. *G. sanguineum* and its form are low spreaders and all have dark leaves which make a good foil for the small white, pink or crimson flowers. Plant 1 to 2ft(30 to 60cm) apart according to cultivar.

HELLEBORUS (ev), hellebore   Ideal in full or partial shade, they like well-prepared rich soil. The best known of these clump-formers, the 1ft(30cm) tall *H. niger*, the Christmas rose, likes limy, well-drained soil. Very dark, evergreen leaves show off the large, white flowers in winter. *H. foetidus*, another evergreen, bears small ''bell'' flowers in late winter. Plant both 1½ ft(45cm) apart.

HEMEROCALLIS, day lily   Easily grown, mainly clump-formers with long, grassy leaves growing quickly in early spring. There are numerous hybrids available with yellow and pinks predominating. Reaching 3ft(1m) high, they should be planted 3ft(1m) apart.

HOSTA, plantain lily   Grown in full or partial shade and deep rich soil, these should be at their best, but they are surprisingly tolerant of less moist conditions. Almost all are clump-formers reaching 12 to 18in(30 to 45cm) in height with lily-shaped flowers being borne in summer on erect, 2ft(60cm) tall stems. The handsome leaves, green, glaucous or variegated according to cultivar, give effective ground-cover. Favourite forms include: *H. fortunei* 'Albopicta', *H. sieboldiana* var. *elegans* with glaucous blue leaves, and 'Thomas Hogg' which has rich green leaves with a broad white edge. Plant 1½ ft(45cm) apart.

13. *At its best,* Nyssa sylvatica, *the Tupelo – photographed at Wisley – is unrivalled for autumn colour. It makes a tree up to 40ft(12m) tall (see p.48).*

14. *Ornamental maples in all their autumnal finery at the Westonbirt Arboretum, Westonbirt, Tetbury, Gloucestershire. On a more modest scale autumn colour from Japanese maples (Acer palmatum cultivars) can be used to good effect in even small gardens.*

15. *The recently introduced Hamamelis vernalis 'Sandra', one of the finest medium-sized shrubs for autumn colour (see p.74).*

16.   *The yellow-flowered* Clematis tangutica *(see p.84) in fitting company
with the large-flowered clematis hybrids 'Ernest Markham' (petunia-red) on one
side and 'Mrs. N. Thompson' on the other.*

LAMIUM L. maculatum is much more cautious in its wanderings than the related *Galeobdolon* so can be let loose in quite small areas. *L.* 'Beacon Silver' has silvery-white leaves and pink flowers. Plant 1 to 3ft(30cm to 1m) apart.

LYSIMACHIA nummularia, (ev), creeping Jenny   This is a dense carpeter which likes partial shade and moist soil. The golden form should always be grown in partial shade. All reach about 1in(2.5cm) in height. Plant 15in(38cm) apart.

NEPETA × faassenii (syn. *N. mussinii*), catmint   This almost evergreen clump-former likes full sun and well-drained soil. It has grey-green, small woolly leaves and lavender-blue flowers borne in sprays. Plant 1½ft(45cm) apart.

POLYGONATUM multiflorum, Solomon's seal   This is a spreader liking full or partial shade and rich soil. Arching stems reach 3ft(1m) in height and bear lush foliage and greenish-white "bell" flowers in May-June. Plant 1ft(30cm) apart.

POLYGONUM, knotweed   Easily grown in sun or shade, there are knotweeds of all sizes from 2in to 8ft(5cm to 2.5m). Among the most effective are:

P. affine   Carpet-rooting, reaching 1 to 2ft(30 to 60cm) with bright green leaves and pink flowers. 'Darjeeling Red' and 'Donald Lowndes' have vivid crimson and red flower spikes respectively. Plant 1½ft(45cm) apart.

P. amplexicaule 'Atrosanguineum'   This forms 3ft(1m) high leafy clumps and bears crimson flowers from June to October. Plant 2ft(60cm) apart.

P. reynoutria   Reaching 2ft(60cm) in height, this spreader has dark green, rounded, leathery leaves and pink flowers borne in clusters. Plant 2 to 3ft(60cm to 1m) apart.

P. vacciniifolium   Carpeting plants up to 3in(8cm) tall with rich green leaves and pink flower spikes 6in(15cm) tall. Plant 1½ft(45cm) apart.

POTENTILLA alba, cinquefoil   This is a carpeter for sun or shade in well-drained soil. White flowers are borne on prostrate stems all summer. Reaches 4in(10cm) in height. Plant 12in(30cm) apart.

PRUNELLA, selfheal   Carpet-rooters easily grown in most soils. 'Loveliness' has dark green leaves and pink flowers. Plant 1½ft(45cm) apart.

PULMONARIA, lungwort   A perennial for full or partial shade and cool, moist soil. Clump forming. *Pulmonaria angustifolia* forms reach 6in(15cm) in height and the evergreen *P. picta* (syn. *P. saccharata*) forms grow 8in(20cm) tall. Flowers of blue, pink and, in some cases, red in spring. Deep green leaves, in some cases with white marbling. Plant 1½ft(45cm) apart.

SAXIFRAGA × urbium London pride (ev) and the related *S. umbrosa*   Evergreen rosettes of rounded, leathery leaves make carpets up to 8in(20cm), with pinkish-white flowers in sprays 1ft(30cm) high in early summer. Plant 1ft(30cm) apart.

STACHYS byzantina (syn. *S. lanata*), (ev), lamb's ears   This plant prefers a sunny position and well-drained soil. The non-flowering form 'Silver Carpet', 4in(10cm) is invaluable. Plant 1½ft(45cm) apart.

TELLIMA grandiflora (ev). For full or partial shade   This easily grown clump-former up to 1ft(30cm) tall, spread quickly. Bright green leaves. Small creamy, bell flowers in late spring. Plant 1½ft(45cm) apart.

TIARELLA cordifolia (ev), foam flower   In some shade and good soil it makes an 8in(20cm) high, dense mass of heart-shaped evergreen leaves, topped in spring by white, feathery flower spikes. Plant 1½ft(45cm) apart.

VIOLA labradorica (ev)   Well-drained, cool conditions are needed for this carpet rooter which reaches 4in(10cm) in height. Lavender-blue, scentless flowers appear in spring. Plant 1ft(30cm) apart.

WALDSTEINIA ternata (ev)   This carpeter will make ideal cover up to 4in(10cm) high in sun or shade, in dry or moist soil. Spikes of bright yellow flowers are borne on 4in(10cm) stems in spring. Plant 1½ft(45cm) apart.

Part II

PLANTS FOR SPECIAL PURPOSES

13.

Ways with Alpines

Growing alpine plants, as with all other forms of gardening, is subject to continual if gradual change. The rock garden had its heyday between the two world wars: remember the splendours of the rock gardens on the bank at the Chelsea Flower Show? They were often "sold" several times over, but today only their ghosts haunt the hallowed bank. Rock gardens began to die when the acres of the typical garden of the 1920s shrank to the rectangular plot of the 1930s, and ended up with the miniscule patch or even patio of today. They died when the skilled professional gardener of the 'thirties was replaced by the owner-plantsman, who quickly learned that rock plants do not need a rock garden, that hundreds of alpines can be accommodated in a small, easily managed space, and that colour can be enjoyed in almost every month of the year if the right conditions are provided. Foremost among these are the wide range of growing conditions to which the raised bed can be adapted.

THE RAISED BED This supreme alpine maid-of-all-work is based on the theory that alpines – by which is meant the smaller plants of the mountains rather than the billowing colour masses which need no special conditions – like a free-draining compost such as can be provided in a bed raised as little as 9 to 12in(23 to 30cm) above ground level. Or it can be raised to 3ft(1m) high for those with backaches who do not want to bend down, or those who wish to take advantage of the additional dimension of vertical planting. It is infinitely variable for any environment. If, as is most suitable, it is built of dry walling stone, it is fully adaptable to shape and aspect, for it can be curved, rectangular or right-angled as space permits. It can – and should – have both sunny and shady aspects, the latter being provided perhaps by the corner of a house or a tree (not overhanging, of course). Typical of the low-built raised beds are those behind the alpine house at Wisley, while on each side of the alpine house are other variants, the raised peat bed and the tufa wall. Dry stone walling should not be vertical, but tilted slightly toward the bed (see Fig.90) and vertical planting is best carried out during construction. A popular variant of this type of bed is the provision of a retaining wall some 2½ to 3ft(75m to 1m) from an existing boundary wall. To avoid subsequent frost damage, a sheet of heavy gauge plastic should protect the boundary wall from the soil filling. Such retaining walls may be made of brick (leaving planting holes), or the rather unsightly breeze or concrete blocks. The skilful use of railway sleepers can be seen in Valerie Finnis's superb raised beds at the Dower House, Boughton House, near Kettering, Northamptonshire, when this is opened to the public. Let us now consider various adaptations of the raised bed, the growing media and a few suggestions as to suitable plants for each type of bed.

THE RAISED SCREE BED No two alpine gardeners agree as to what constitutes the ideal soil mixture, but possibly the solution lies somewhere between two extremes of washed pea gravel and nothing else (Joe Elliot) and a 50/50 mix of ½in(.5cm) chippings and John Innes No 1 potting compost or its equivalent (Roy Elliott). Few alpines really need lime, but for those that do (and *Omphalodes luciliae*, *Daphne arbuscula*, *Phyteuma comosum*, *Polygala calcarea* and *Lithodora oleifolia* spring to mind), there are two alternatives. A portion of the scree can be made up of limestone chippings, or a few tufa rocks can be embedded in the scree surface and surrounded with crushed tufa in which such plants will live happily. Most scree plants relish full exposure to sun, but the plantsman will wish to contrive shady aspects for those that do not, such as lewisias, haberleas, ramondas and petrophytums. There are two golden rules to planting. First, one should not waste valuable space by planting rampant growers like the larger campanulas, geraniums and alyssums. Secondly, one should choose plants which will spread colour and interest over as long a season as possible. A few carefully selected bulbs will help here. The choice of plants is infinite, but a few suggestions would be: *Anchusa caespitosa*, *Asperula suberosa*, *Campanula nitida* var. *alba* and C. 'Haylodgensis', *Androsace jacquemontii*, *Erinacea anthyllis*, *Gentiana acaulis* and G. *verna*, *Thymus* 'Elfin', *Hebe* 'Boughton Dome', *Oxalis laciniata*, O. *enneaphylla* and O. *adenophylla*, *Chamaecytisus pygmaeus*, *Azorella gummifera*, *Juniperus communis* 'Compressa', the smaller "silver" saxifrages, European primulas and so on.

THE RAISED PEAT BED The traditional peat bed, where the supporting walls are made of large blocks of top spit peat, is so wholly dependent on a supply of the right sort of peat block that the average amateur would do well to consider the bed described above, with a peaty compost within the retaining walls. Many a good peat wall has had to be abandoned to invasive mosses, bracken and ling. A good quality sphagnum peat is preferable, though shredded wood bark is favoured by some people, but either medium should be thoroughly moistened before making up a compost, and, since both media are without nourishment, they should be mixed with good organic compost, woodland soil or leafmould if obtainable. Drainage should be provided by the addition of sharp sand; that used for swimming pool filters is superb, if expensive. The site must be chosen with care, for part shade is as vital to the peat bed as full sun is to the scree. A few suggestions for planting would be: dwarf rhododendrons for spring colour and Asiatic gentians and their hybrids for autumn. Almost all *Cassiope* species, epigaeas, phyllodoces, kalmiopsis, jeffersonias, trilliums, irises of the Evansia section, the smaller species of *Aciphylla* and *Andromeda*, the woodland phlox, erythroniums and every variety and species of *Shortia* that the fortunate can lay hands on. Interplant with shade-loving bulbs like the erythroniums, *Narcissus cyclamineus*, and many of the anemones.

90. *A raised bed – "the alpine maid-of-all-work". Dry stone walling should be tilted slightly towards the bed with vertical planting being best carried out during construction.*

THE RAISED FRAME This, for the real plantsman, is what the alpine house is to the rock gardener, a place to grow favourite plants which, for divers reasons, are best given winter protection. An ideal site would be a south-facing raised bed against a boundary wall, and a width from the inside of the boundary wall to the inside of the retaining wall of 4ft 5in(1.38m) would enable standard Dutch lights (2ft 7½in by 4ft 11in or 78cm by 1.53m) to be used for winter cover (see Fig.92). Means must be provided for fastening the lights down, for a gale can prove very costly. An alternative structure is described in the following section ("The raised bulb bed").

However, if both these suggestions seem unnecessarily complex or expensive, winter protection can be given by Dutch lights fastened in winter to square stakes hammered into the bed. The list of suitable plants is enormous, so let us consider the requirements of various categories. Firstly, the Kabschia saxifrages, all perfectly hardy yet whose early (February-March) flowers are easily damaged by rain and snow. Then there are the woolly-leaved plants like *Verbascum dumulosum*, *Origanum dictamnus* and *Helichrysum coralloides* which strongly resent winter wet on their leaves. There are the precious high alpine cushion plants so beloved of the alpine plantsman, the drabas (*Draba mollissima*, *D. polytricha* and *D. dedeana* are amongst the best), the dionysias, Aretian androsaces and indeed any of the delightful plants that miss the winter snow cover of their native land. Then there are the slightly tender plants like some of the finest thymes (*Thymus membranaceus* and *T. cilicicus*, the forms of *Campanula isophylla* from the Maritime Alps and *Rhodohypoxis* from the Drakensberg. Finally there are the "difficult squad" which need coddling; such are the delightful *Primula allionii*, its forms and hybrids, *Calceolaria darwinii* with its elfin charm, and *Pulsatilla vernalis*, whose soft furry buds are so easily rotted by our damp winters.

THE RAISED BULB BED Before embarking upon this venture, the gardener must have a clear picture of his or her requirements because there are two distinct methods. The long, frame-covered bulb beds outside the alpine house at Wisley are typical of the highly effective and extremely ugly method of growing bulbs in sections according to flowering period, and covering them over for the rest of the year to dry out. This is ideal for the gardener who wishes to grow rare and difficult bulbs, or who wishes to grow winter-flowering delights like *Narcissus bulbocodium* ssp. *romieuxii*, *N. cantabricus* and its forms, or some of the more tender *Cyclamen* species. The ordinary mortal is content with a typical, well-drained raised bed devoted to bulbs, where the flowering seasons can be mixed and the species planted are those that do not require drying off. In either case the bed needs full exposure to sun and, in the first case, to be hidden from view. The cardinal rule for both types of bed is never to plant any bulb without careful research into its habits, and to avoid free-seeding species like the plague. However carefully bulbs are chosen, some grow and spread faster than others; some tend to go downwards and some to rise to the surface and sooner or later the problem of re-planting arises. Here the trouble comes.

There are two methods of segregation. The best method is to plant each bulb or group of bulbs into the sort of trellis-work plastic pot used to grow aquatic plants: this enables particular bulbs to be thinned out when necessary, or even to be lifted annually for drying out. The second, but less satisfactory, method is to keep similar bulbs apart. Thus *Crocus* species should be kept apart by *Iris* species or *Galanthus*, or indeed any bulb or corm or tuber having differing characteristics.

Those who delight in the raised bulb bed will be well aware of the vast number of available bulbs for winter, spring and autumn flowering, but it should be remembered that for year-round interest, a few summer-flowering species should be planted and species from the following genera, if carefully chosen, will fit the bill. The term "bulb" is used in its widest sense: *Albuca*, *Allium* (choose especially carefully!), *Anoiganthus*, (now included in *Cyrtanthus*), *Brodiaea*, *Calochortus*, *Hypoxis*, *Lapeirousia*, *Oxalis* (again choose especially carefully!) and *Rhodohypoxis*.

91. *A raised tufa bed. Tufa is "The finest growing medium for lime-loving fibrous-rooted alpines of almost any degree of difficulty".*

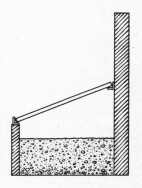

92. *A raised frame – "a place to grow favourite plants which, for divers reasons, are best given winter protection" (see p.140).*

93. *The Dutch lights on the raised frame are held in position by angle irons, as shown.*

THE RAISED TUFA BED OR CLIFF The finest growing medium for lime-loving, fibrous-rooted alpines of almost any degree of difficulty is tufa, the plants taking root in the "rock" itself. Tufa is not in fact a rock, but a deposit (c.f. stalactites and stalagmites) where water, leaching down through lime-rich hill or mountainsides, takes in soluble calcium bicarbonate: when it seeps out into the carbon dioxide of the atmosphere it slowly deposits a gradual build-up of solid calcium carbonate. It is costly to obtain from the available commercial sources, but there must be many unknown hidden deposits if we could only find them.

When first quarried the tufa is soft, easily shaped or cut with a saw, and somewhat liable to frost damage. It can be cut or chopped into a close-fitting vertical cliff such as the one at Wisley against the rear wall of the alpine house (Derbyshire tufa) or the high well-established, glass-roofed cliff (Welsh tufa) in the writer's garden in Handsworth (see Fig.91). Both the brown (Derbyshire) and the white (Welsh) varieties quickly acquire a patina and harden on exposure to the elements. Tufa absorbs water like a sponge, and planting is best done by drilling a 1in(2.5cm) hole at a slightly downward-pointing angle, dibbling in newly-rooted cuttings or small seedlings, pouring in dry sand to fill the hole and surround the roots, and watering. It is surprising how quickly the roots spread from the sand into the tufa and, provided the aspect is right, even "impossible plants" like *Jankaea heldreichii* can – if protected from winter wet – be regarded as permanent. For this reason it is best to devise a method for covering the cliff or wall with frame lights to protect plants in winter and also to lessen frost damage when newly-constructed. If this can be done, suitable plants for such a cliff or vertical wall might well include the following, though it must again be stressed that such plants will only succeed well if the roots are fibrous rather than thong or tap rooted, and of course acid-loving plants must be avoided at all costs: *Lithodora oleifolia*, *Verbascum dumulosum* and *V. pestalozzae*, all "silver" saxifrages but especially *S. longifolia* and *S.* 'Tumbling Waters', *Iris cretensis*, all ramondas and haberleas, *Silene acaulis*, *Vitaliana primuliflora*, *Omphalodes luciliae*, *Campanula isophylla*, many small hypericums – the possibilities are endless providing the rules are observed. For instance, aspect: *Iris cretensis* will flower ceaselessly from Christmas until March in fullest sun, while the ramondas and haberleas will form solid clumps, completely hiding the tufa, in a position of part shade. The provision of these differing aspects is the key to growing a wide range of alpines – yet it is by no means easy to provide such aspects in a raised bed in a small garden, and there are many who believe that the ideal way of overcoming this and other problems is to grow plants in troughs, sinks and other containers. This method is of particular value in the small, labour-saving garden where a paved area or patio replaces the gardener's beloved lawn.

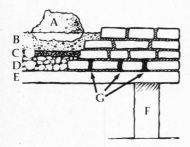

94. *Cross-section of a slab garden.* **A**, *tufa;* **B**, *growing medium;* **C**, *peat/turves;* **d**, *drainage layer;* **E**, *slab/tombstone;* **F**, *stone support;* **G**, *drainage slits*

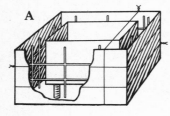

95. *Making a trough. Boxes made out of stout cardboard can be used for the shuttering* (**A**) *with certain advantages as explained in the text, opposite.*

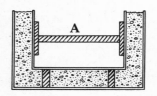

96. *Make full provision for drainage and, after inserting Hypertufa, reinforce the trough on the outside with wire netting and wire binding and with wooden struts* (**A**) *on the inside. Hypertufa sets slowly. (See text, opposite.)*

SINKS, TROUGHS AND OTHER CONTAINERS These only constitute a trouble-free way of growing alpines if the chosen container is a suitable one. The shallow sink with an overall depth of around 6in(15cm) needs at least 1in(2.5cm) of drainage material in the bottom, and the remaining 5in(13cm) – even if the sink is "built-up" with rocks – leaves all too little depth for the deep-delving roots of plants from the mountains. Such a container will need constant watering in hot weather if placed in an exposed position; therefore the deeper the container the easier it is to grow plants. The old stone trough, so beloved of alpine gardeners, has become almost impossible to acquire and alternatives must be found. This is where a do-it-yourself medium known as Hypertufa comes into its own, for not only can it be used to coat an ugly glazed sink to a semblance of natural – or fairly natural – stone, but it can be used as a cement for binding the rock edges of a slab garden (see Fig.94), and, indeed, for the actual fabrication of complete troughs. The ingredients of Hypertufa – which is not, like cement, inimical to plants – is as follows: cement, one part by bulk; sand, one part by bulk (the colour of the sand can affect the colour of the finished article); and peat, two parts by bulk, moistened and sifted. Sphagnum peat is best.

The components should be thoroughly mixed when dry (the peat, of course, *must* be damp), and the amount of water added depends upon the use to which the Hypertufa is to be put. Suppose, for instance, it is to be used to disguise an ugly glazed kitchen sink; first the glaze must be carefully painted over with a bonding adhesive such as Unibond or Polybond. Sufficient water is then added to the mixture to make a firm paste, which is plastered over the treated surface to a sufficient depth (say 2in[5cm]) to enable the surface to be patterned with a chisel to give a "natural" appearance. This should be done before the mixture is completely hard.

Reverting now to our slab garden, the ideal base would be a slab of York stone (old tombstones are ideal) and surrounding walls of the same stone can gradually be built up using Hypertufa as the bonding material. Drainage, as always, is vital and if a single slab is used as a base, several drainage holes must be made on each side and a layer of gravel or chippings used to cover the base up to and slightly above the drainage holes. This layer should be covered with unsifted peat or coarse bark fibre, and the growing medium then placed on top. If necessity demands the use of a concrete slab as a base, the edge of the concrete should be treated with Hypertufa paste as in the case of a glazed sink. Modern stone-coloured artificial facing bricks can also be used. Whenever troughs, slab gardens or so on are used, they should be mounted on stone supports, for this helps to keep slugs and so on at bay; such supports can also be prefabricated easily and effectively from Hypertufa, using simple shuttering. Mounting troughs in this way in a paved section of the garden is also invaluable in that the shadow cast by the troughs can be used for shade-loving paving plants, and such planting spaces should always be prepared with the utmost care when paved areas are laid down.

The making of troughs of all shapes and sizes out of Hypertufa can be a fascinating occupation, and the illustrations (Figs.95 and 96) give a clear idea of how the simplest trough can be made. There are those who favour elaborate wooden shuttering for the inside and outside of the trough, but the writer prefers to use boxes made out of really stout cardboard because these tend to get slightly out of shape under the weight and pressures of the Hypertufa and so avoid the rather formal outlines given by wooden shuttering. The essential (and a visit to the grocer or local wine merchant will help here) is to find two strong cartons which, when placed one inside the other, will leave a cavity of about 3in(8cm) between the two. Drainage holes are important, so stand the inner carton upon four supports (3in[8cm] sawn-off pieces of broom handle will do). Cut some wire netting to reinforce the trough, especially round the corners, and bind some wire tightly round, and over, the outer carton to prevent excessive "bellying". For the same reason, it is important to fit a few wooden struts end to end and side to side across the inner carton. Finally, remember that Hypertufa sets slowly. After 24 to 48 hours the outer carton, now soft and soggy, may be tentatively removed in order that corners may be rounded off and a pattern (shades of

the stonemason's chisel!) made into the surface before it fully hardens. But under no circumstances should the finished trough be moved, or the inner carton disturbed, for at least a week.

Another interesting experiment is the large, solid block of tufa, where the planting is done in the manner described in the earlier reference to tufa (see p. 141). Here, however, an exception should be made to mounting on a pedestal, for tufa dries out too quickly. Such a block should have its base 6in(15cm) into the ground so that water may be absorbed from below by capillary attraction.

Planting sinks and troughs There is little doubt that the popularity of sinks and troughs is due very largely to the fact that they provide a really good "way of growing", and the reason for this is that alpine plants revel in root association and quite often in root restriction, both of which are more easily provided in a trough than in a raised bed. Even difficult plants, for which alpine house treatment is often advocated, can be grown in troughs where they are less liable to be plagued with aphis and red spider and where, with a little ingenuity, they can be protected from winter wet by having a pane of glass or clear plastic slanted over them. The essential thing is that they should look attractive, and for this reason rocks, or better still tufa, should be used to give both height and form to the filled trough (see Fig.97). But however much a trough is built up, the growing medium at the periphery must be below the level of the rim, or watering will become difficult in hot weather.

Dwarf conifers make good trough subjects for architectural effect, and shrubs – especially those that are both dwarf and evergreen – are an essential part of the trough's "landscape". Of the first-mentioned those which spring to mind are: the really dwarf forms of *Chamaecyparis obtusa* 'Nana'; *Juniperus communis* forms such as 'Compressa' and 'Echiniformis', the dwarfer spruces such as *Picea mariana* 'Nana' and 'Pygmaea', and *P. abies* 'Little Gem' and 'Gregoryana'. Only the smallest and most slow-growing of

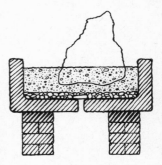

97. *A trough garden provides excellent conditions for alpine plants for they "revel in root association and quite often in root restriction". The cross-section of a trough shown above depicts the rock or tufa placement, the drainage material in the base and the correct level of the growing medium.*

shrubs are to be recommended, such as *Hebe buchananii* 'Minor', *Carmichaelia enysii, Convulvulus boissieri, Daphne petraea, Genista villarsii, Helichrysum coralloides, Ilex crenata* 'Mariesii', *Salix myrsinites* 'Jacquinii' – indeed, the list is so never-ending as to make casual mention of so few seem almost pointless.

In conclusion, let us remember that these are just a few of the "ways of growing" alpines, for the writer has seen many others: sempervivums grown in "strawberry pots", pseudo-lead plastic troughs, window boxes and even – horrible to recall – a block of polystyrene in which the plants were growing beautifully, but possibly shamefacedly, for beauty, be it only in miniature, must surely be the gardener's *raison d'être*?

14.

The Alpine House

Once inoculated with an affection for alpine plants, and having passed through the initial stages of becoming acquainted with the commoner – but no less desirable – kinds, the time will assuredly come when there is a desire to move into a higher sphere and to accept the challenge offered by some of the more temperamental and exquisitely lovely denizens of the high mountains. These are mostly cushion-forming plants, forced by their austere environment to adopt a lowly habit of growth and to spend the greater part of their dormant winter resting period beneath a blanket of snow.

To accommodate these treasures and provide the conditions under which they are most likely to succeed in cultivation it is desirable – even essential – to invest in an alpine house, a term which has come to be used for a greenhouse adapted or specially built for this particular purpose. A notable advantage of such a structure in these days of very expensive fuel and energy supplies is that it needs no artificial heating.

There are custom-built alpine houses, one or two horticultural builders will construct them to a design originally specified by expert growers. The particular features are a low "pitch", which brings the plants closer to the maximum light, *continuous* ventilation along each side of the roof and also along each side of the house at bench level. Ideally, an alpine house will run north and south with the door in the southern end.

Conventionally, the staging, or benching consists of open-slat wooden staging and this is satisfactory up to a point, but some adaption is desirable. Sheets of asbestos or thin galvanised iron can be placed on the benches and covered with a layer of sharp sand or ashes. Alternatively the bench can be made into a "box" about 6in(15cm) depth which is filled with sand or fine ashes, into which the pots and pans are plunged. The latter method, although it reduces the amount of individual watering required, has the disadvantage of encouraging the plants to root into the plunging material, a habit which can pose problems if it is desired to move plants with any frequency.

Clay or plastic pots? Controversy exists as to the advantages or disadvantages of clay pots and pans compared to plastics. Clays are traditional and many people prefer them because they are porous and allow the soil to "breathe" whereas the plastics are impermeable. Given the willingness to learn a different technique in watering the use of plastics is no bar to success. The compost used in plastic pots should also contain a higher proportion of "grit" than that used for clay ones. The moisture in a plastic pot or pan does not evaporate as quickly as that in a clay pot and there is a risk of over-watering. The additional grit ensures that water passes more rapidly through the compost and does not linger about the roots – a condition which alpines detest.

Compost mixtures The compost used for alpine house plants will vary according to the particular needs of individual kinds, but a mixture for overall use would consist of two parts of loam – or good top-spit garden soil – one part of fine-grade moss peat and one part of sharp sand or fine grit. Should moss peat not be available its place can be taken by leafmould or well-rotted garden compost. Should leafmould be used it is advisable to be aware of its source, since, if it were to be from the leaves of trees growing over chalk, it is probable that it will have a lime content and would not be suitable to use for lime-hating plants. If plastic pots are used the grit or sand content should be increased by 50 per cent.

With this basic compost available it can be altered to suit the special needs of plants which ask for special treatment. The loam or garden soil should be tested to discover its pH value. The pH scale runs from nought to 14. Up to pH 7 it is acid to neutral, above that figure it is alkaline and contains lime. Simple soil-testing kits are available from chemists. It is advisable that the basic compost should be as near neutral as possible so that the acidity or alkalinity can be increased as desired.

Watering and ventilation   The general care of an alpine house consists of common-sense watering and the maintenance of full ventilation at all possible times. The ventilators should seldom be completely closed although it may be desirable from time to time to close or partially close those which are exposed to particularly vicious weather conditions. Watering during the growing season should be liberal and cautious during the winter. When a plant obviously needs water, apply it liberally. A mere "sprinkle" will do more harm than good. A good basic maxim for watering is "when in doubt, don't". A plant which has been too dry will usually recover but one which has been saturated will not.

THE PLANTS

While the primary purpose of an alpine house is to provide a suitable environment in which to grow the less common plants which have special needs, there is no reason at all why other, more ordinary kinds should not accompany the rarities. It is highly desirable that the alpine house should provide beauty and interest over the whole year, a feature which is of special importance during the winter months, when conditions in the open garden are either unpleasant or even impossible. Among the plants which will be described in subsequent paragraphs there will be several which in no way demand alpine house treatment, but which will make a welcome contribution therein and add to the variety and interest of what can become an exhilarating bypath of alpine gardening.

The choice high alpine cushion plants, such as Aretian androsaces, drabas, dionysias and those with very hairy, woolly foliage, are not very fond of overhead watering and need to be watered with care, either soaking them from below by standing their containers in water up to the rim until they have soaked up water by capillary action, or by applying water carefully around but not on them. During the height of summer some form of shading is advisable, either in the form of sun-blinds, or by a light spray of liquid shading on the glass. Blinds are preferable as they can be removed on dull days when maximum light is important.

The genus *Lewisia* has, during recent years, made an important contribution to rock gardening. There are numerous species, but it is the colourful hybrid strains which predominate, with one or two notable exceptions. Lewisias can be grown in the open if they are given lime-free soil and either placed in narrow crevices or on a slope. They dislike growing on the flat in the open. In the alpine house they make a brave display of mixed and vivid colours early in the year. Most of them have finished flowering by June, but the hybrid L. 'George Henley' is an invaluable exception as it continues to produce its 9in(23cm) sprays of purple-red flowers from spring until late in the autumn. The most spectacular of the species, and one which is happier when confined to an alpine house, is *L. tweedyi*. Like all *Lewisia* species it comes from North America and makes bold clumps of wide, fleshy leaves and, singly on 6in(15cm) stems, carries large flowers of a colour difficult to describe, being a suffusion of yellow, pink and apricot. All lewisias relish a drying-off period after they finish flowering – not arid, but kept well on the dry side for several weeks.

Scattered about the world are some very lovely species of *Ranunculus* and,

98. Lewisia *'George Henley'*

from the Atlas Mountains of North Africa comes *R. calandrinioides*, which is an absolute "must" for the alpine house. It dies down after flowering and has a resting period, from which it rises in the autumn, producing long, wide ash-grey leaves and 9in(23cm) stems carrying large, saucer-shaped blossoms of white, often shaded gently with pink. It begins to flower soon after Christmas and, soon after setting its seeds, dies down to rest. The seeds fall while still apparently green and unripe and should be sown immediately. It is a lusty grower and appreciates repotting in fresh soil at least every other year, an operation best carried out in the late autumn, just before growth begins. It is hardy and unfussy about soil, but it flowers so early in the year, and its petals are so delicate, that they may be weather-damaged in the open.

The delightful, cushion-forming Aretian androsaces are among the aristocrats which are seen at their best in an alpine house. They all resent overhead watering and should be given the extra care advocated earlier (see p.146). Mostly cliff-dwellers in nature, they like being tightly wedged between small pieces of stone and surrounded by a layer of pure washed grit or fine stone chippings. Although not all that easy to please they are so rewarding that any effort is justified that will persuade them to make their fascinating dense domes and pads of tightly congested rosettes of wee, usually hairy, soft leaves, which disappear in spring beneath the countless white, stemless and often fragrant flowers. Three of the best with which to make a start are *A. vandellii* (syn. *A. imbricata, A. argentea*) from the Central and Southern Alps, and *A. pyrenaica* and *A. pubescens*, both from the Pyrenees. *A. vandellii* should be given lime-free soil, the others are more tolerant and will take an alkaline compost.

99. Stachys candida

Although still a rarity in cultivation, *Stachys candida*, from Grecian mountains, is gradually spreading around and is available from specialist growers. Another cliff-dweller it appreciates a confined root-run and a measure of austerity. The roots are woody and vigorous so that it should be given a fairly deep container. Its short, rather brittle stems are dressed in rounded leaves felted with silver hairs, and the quite large, hooded flowers are white, delicately veined with pink and appear during the summer months. It is a comparative newcomer, and well worth seeking out. It is unlikely to flourish in the open.

Equalling the androsaces in charm, and related to them as both genera belong to the *Primulaceae*, are the cushiony dionysias, mostly from Iran and Afghanistan, where they dwell at great heights, in rock crevices and often in areas where rainfall is so infrequent that almost the only moisture they receive is from low clouds, or from nightly precipitations in the form of dew. There are 30 or more known species of *Dionysia*, but only a very few of them are firmly in cultivation. They prefer a gritty, limestone soil and demand very sharp drainage and great care with the watering can. The easiest, and most readily available is *D. aretioides*, which makes high-domed cushions of closely packed rosettes of small, hairy, grey leaves, liberally studded in earliest spring with stemless golden, primrose-scented flowers. Also reasonably amenable is *D. curviflora*, which is of a different habit, forming flat pads of densely packed, small, green leaves over which hover many long-tubed flowers, yellow-eyed and rich pink in colour, but lacking the fragrance of *D. aretioides*.

Thalictrums are usually valued as tall plants for the herbaceous border, but there is a precious dwarf from Japan, *Thalictrum kiusianum* which seldom exceeds 6in(15cm) in height and makes a delightful specimen for the alpine house. It can also be grown in the open. From a wiry, running root it emits stiff, wiry, branching stems carrying typical but tiny thalictrum foliage and clouds of small purple flowers. It is an airily dainty little plant and is of the most accommodating disposition, asking only for any well-drained soil.

Invaluable, not only for their beauty, but because they flower in high summer when the first flush of spring-blossoming alpines is over, are the innumerable campanulas, many of which are invaluable alpine house subjects. Greatly daring – and if it can be obtained – one might try *Campanula cenisia*, a lime-hater from great heights in the European Alps. Give it very, very gritty soil in a shallow pan and it may decide to spread by

100. Thalictrum kiusianum

101. Campanula arvatica

its thread-fine underground stems, erupting here and there with tufts of round, glaucous leaves and funnel-shaped slaty-blue flowers.

Much easier is *C. arvatica*, a Spaniard. In nature it is usually a cliff dweller but in cultivation it is happy enough in gritty soil, either alkaline or neutral. Over its low mats of tiny notched leaves are 3in(8cm) stems each carrying several upturned, star-shaped flowers of rich violet-blue. It also has a very charming albino with pure white flowers. From Armenia comes lovely *C. betulifolia*, a rather taller plant whose smooth wedge-shaped leaves are toothed at the edges. The branching stems carry galaxies of crimson buds which expand into white or soft pink flowers. A specimen in full flower is quite sensational.

Of the utmost importance are the early-flowering saxifrages, of which there is a host from which to choose. One of the most exciting is *Saxifraga grisebachii*, seen at its magnificent best in the cultivar 'Wisley'. From its neat rosettes of ensilvered leaves rise, in early spring, central stems, clothed in crimson bracts, which elongate into arching croziers. The small flowers are tucked between the colourful bracts. At the same season come the several forms of *S. burserana*, a cushion-forming species whose narrow, hard grey leaves are compressed into tight pads, over which hover innumerable flowers, the whiteness of the petals enhanced by the, usually, red flower stems. There is also a hybrid, not very accurately named *S.b.* 'Lutea', which has soft yellow flowers. The type, and all the forms are desirable, but the most handsome are 'His Majesty' and 'Gloria'.

Very similar in appearance, and either easily taking the place of the other, are *S.* 'Irvingii' and *S.* 'Jenkinsae'. Dense cushions of closely packed, tiny, grey-green leaves form the base for innumerable, very short-stemmed pink flowers. All these are low-growing and compact, but the glory of the saxifrage family is undeniably *S.* 'Tumbling Waters'. If moved into a slightly larger pot each year this splendid plant will eventually make a rosette of strap-shaped silver-grey leaves 12in(30cm) in diameter, and will then erupt into an arching inflorescence carrying hundreds of pure white flowers. The flowering rosette always dies after it has blossomed but almost always makes a few side-rosettes which can be rooted as cuttings. It does set seeds, but these will not produce the true plant as it is of hybrid origin.

Not to be thought of as a flowering plant, but extremely attractive as a dwarf shrub, is *Helichrysum coralloides*, a New Zealander whose erect branches are densely covered with scale-like green leaves, each with a slightly protruding "edging" of the silver "wool" which lies beneath the leaves. It has all the appearance of a piece of branching coral and never fails to arouse interest and admiration. Very different in appearance is *H. marginatum*, which comes from the high Drakensburg mountains of South Africa. It grows as a flat carpet of softly silver-haired leaves upon which sit

102. Helichrysum coralloides

cone-shaped crimson buds, expanding into white, papery-petalled flowers.

No alpine house should lack a few pans of pleiones, near-hardy terrestrial orchids. They ask for no special "orchid" composts and are quite content if given a standard potting compost, to which has been added a little extra humus in the form of peat or leafmould. From the sturdy pseudo-bulbs come, first of all the lovely flowers, followed by the large, aspidistra-like foliage. Most of those easily available are forms of *Pleione bulbocodioides* and the colour of their flowers ranges through shades of rose-red, red-purple and pink, the throat and "lip" of the flowers being marked and striped with various colours. After blossoming, when the leaves begin to turn yellow and fall, pleiones like to be given dry treatment during their dormant period – never completely arid, but watered only occasionally and with discretion. As soon as the growths which herald the flowers are visible in the spring, they should be watered liberally. There are a few with wholly white flowers which are equally desirable.

The autumn can be enlivened by *Cyclamen hederifolium* (syn. *C. neapolitanum*), whose marbled, ivy-shaped leaves are preceded in late August by the rich pink flowers. There is also a handsome albino. Any or all of the cyclamen species, such as *C. purpurascens* (syn. *C. europaeum*), *C. repandum*, *C. graecum* or *C. coum* are welcome additions to any alpine house collection, and a selection of them will provide flowers at various times from spring until winter.

Erigerons are usually regarded as plants for the flower border, but there are several alpine species, and one which is especially desirable for the alpine house is tiny *E. aureus* from the Rocky Mountains of North-west America. Its softly hairy leaves are feathered into little tufts from which rise 3in(8cm) stems, each bearing a golden "daisy" flower. It will blossom continuously throughout the summer. It prefers lime-free, rather gritty soil.

No lover of alpine plants could live without gentians. They are all hardy enough to be grown in the open, but in the early spring, a pan of *G. verna* is a joy to behold when it displays its clear blue flowers on very short stems. For the late summer and autumn, and always in soil which is guaranteed to be lime-free, a few pans of *G. sino-ornata* will greet the dying year with sheets of azure trumpets. As a complete contrast, with pure white flowers over dark stems and leaves, is New Zealand's gift to the family, *G. saxosa*, which is early summer flowering.

15.

Plants for Shade

If shady parts of the garden do not occupy too much of the total area there is every reason to count them a blessing, with one proviso – that the shade should be light rather than heavy, and, in some cases, taking the form of partial shade when direct sunlight has access for a few hours each day. A host of plants of character and beauty either do well in, or actually need, such conditions. There is, moreover, another quite different consideration if your aim is to create a garden with a strong persona. Well planted, shady areas of a garden exude tranquility thus providing both a contrast and a balance to the open, sun-drenched areas which, for a good part of the year at least, can be expected to be vibrant with colour and have dash and sparkle. The colours are there all right in shade but usually on a somewhat lower key, excepting, perhaps, in the shape of such lovers of light shade as the rhododendrons and camellias, astilbes and candelabra primulas.

Of course, there is shade and shade. Most appealing of all – both to the observer's eye and the plants themselves – is the kind of light dappled shade associated with sunlight filtered obliquely through high-branched trees or the kind of partial shade referred to earlier. Most difficult to cope with is the shade found under the canopy of trees with heavy leaf cover, and a thirst for soil moisture which inevitably proves too severe a challenge for all but the most adaptable of shrubs and perennials, when the desire is to make under-plantings. Planting suggestions for such positions are made on p. 155.

A form of shade which is usually of a degree which many plants find amenable, although it can be dense on occasions, is that found on the north side of high walls (of the home, outbuildings, even high boundary walls) and tall, close plantings of conifers and large broad-leaved evergreen shrubs such as laurels. Such planting areas, together with those outlined earlier, span the extremes of shade which are likely to be encountered. The subtle variations of shade between one type and another and, for that matter, within each type, make it necessary for each one of us to form our own judgement on what is and what is not desirable from a planting point of view. Nature refuses to be shackled and slotted into neat categories just for our convenience. Above all, one avoids doing stupid things, like expecting shade-loving calcifuges such as rhododendrons and camellias to survive in alkaline soils, or moisture-loving plants like astilbes and primulas to do well in dry soils. That is no more than common sense, but it is surprising how often we are tempted to do unwise things just because a particularly engaging plant, seen elsewhere, arouses our acquisitive instincts.

HERBACEOUS PERENNIAL PLANTS Various influences have been at work in recent times to heighten our interest in, and change our attitudes towards, herbaceous perennial plants. The move towards a more naturalistic style of gardening; the informal use of plants to create patterns of colour, shape and texture have given these fascinating plants a new lease of life. It is all very exciting, and, of course, involves also the use of shrubs, bulbous flowers and annuals. It also has as much relevance for shady parts of the garden as in more open situations.

Few would, one imagines, disagree at the hostas, or plantain lilies, being called the shade plants *par excellence*. They, and other fine foliage and flowering plants, like the lovely lady's mantle, *Alchemilla mollis*, were in the vanguard of the changes just referred to. Of the many hostas available a general favourite is *Hosta crispula*, elegance personified with its sharp-pointed, wavy margined leaves of dark green, edged prettily with white. Lilac-coloured flowers are borne in mid-summer. Its height of 2ft(60cm) makes it suitable for planting in many situations. Make a point of seeking out, too, a fine trio of hostas from the United States – 'Royal Standard' and 'Honeybells', both hybrids, and 'Frances Williams' which is a cultivar of the well-known *H. sieboldiana*. All are from 2½ to 3ft(75cm to 1m) tall. 'Royal Standard' has fresh-green, heart-shaped leaves with wavy margins and fragrant white flowers in August-September; 'Honeybells' has pale green, wavy-edged leaves and lilac-mauve, fragrant flowers in July-August; and 'Frances Williams' has its parent's large, bluish-grey, deeply veined leaves, edged with yellow in this form – and white, mauve-flushed flowers which it bears from late June to August. All hostas need plenty of moisture at the roots to prosper, and a good soil. They are not, however, demanding plants.

103. Hosta crispula

How welcome it is, too, to see the greatly increased interest in the herbaceous geraniums, perennials with fine decorative qualities which include so many suitable for either sunshine or shade, or both. One of the finest is *Geranium psilostemon* (syn. *G. armenum*), some 4ft(1.25m) tall and quite beguiling with its handsome, deeply cut foliage and display of magenta-red flowers with black centres in early summer. It has to be said that, while it flowers well enough in shade, the really stunning perform-ances are put on in sunny positions. The foliage is always a joy.

Excellent in shade are the varieties of *G. endressii* (notably 1ft[30cm] tall 'A.T. Johnson', which has silvery-pink flowers, and 'Wargrave Pink', a little taller, which are in bloom for most of the summer) and July-September flowering *G. wallichianum* 'Buxton's Variety', also 1ft(30cm) tall and spread-ing in habit, with imposing deep blue flowers. Everybody's favourite, too, is that excellent "doer" 'Johnson's Blue', 1ft(30cm) tall and usually good for a display from June to September. Lastly, mention of a very different geranium, the so-called mourning widow, *G. phaeum*, which has the ability to do well in quite heavy shade. Its common name comes from the very dark colour of the small flowers, a soft purple; and very beautiful these look against the delicate green of the leaves. Its flowering period is May-June.

Aruncus dioicus (syn. *A. sylvester*) is a grand plant for light shade and a moist position where the soil drainage is efficient. Plumes of creamy-white flowers borne on 4 to 5ft(1.25 to 1.5m) stems above fern-like foliage delight the eye in June, especially if it is associated with softly coloured shrub roses like the cream 'Gold Bush'. Its smaller cultivar, *A. d.* 'Kneiffii' only half as tall, has the same kind of flowers and could be a more suitable choice for small gardens. The related *Filipendula palmata* (both it and the *Aruncus* belong to the *Rosaceae* family and were once included in the genus *Spiraea*) needs much the same growing conditions and is a very useful plant for summer display with its pink plumes of flowers borne on 3 to 4ft(1 to 1.25m) stems and its handsome lobed leaves.

For early colour, in May-June, there are few perennials to compare with *Polygonum bistorta* 'Superbum', the polygonums being the knotweeds which include a selection of outstanding border plants and not a few which are little better than weeds. This plant throws up bright pink poker-like flower heads above a mat of rather large, coarse-looking foliage and it is a lovely plant to associate in light shade with the very pretty, early-flowering pulmonarias (lungworts) with their mottled foliage and blue and pink flowers, spindly stemmed little epimediums and *Brunnera macrophylla* 'Variegata', this last so attractive in May-June with its delicate-looking little sprays of bright blue, forget-me-not-like flowers borne above heart-shaped leaves splashed with cream.

For a moist position consider planting, too, the willow-leaved gentian, *Gentiana asclepiadea*, for its rich blue, funnel-shaped flowers borne on arching stems are the source of much pleasure in the second half of summer. Also, of course, the astilbe hybrids, grouped botanically under the name *A.×arendsii*. Their panicles of upstanding blooms in bright colours

104. Pulmonaria
saccharata 'Pink Dawn'

and their fern-like foliage endear them to many gardeners. Fine cultivars include the rich red 'Fanal', bright pink 'Bressingham Beauty', white 'Irrlicht' and brick-red 'Red Sentinel', variously making their display between June and August. Don't overlook either the dwarf hybrids – 1 to 1½ft(30 to 45cm) tall against the 2 to 3ft(60cm to 1m) of the tall cultivars – for these include excellent offerings like shell-pink 'Sprite', rose-pink 'Bronze Elegance' and salmon-pink 'Dunkellachs', all with dark-coloured foliage which adds to the dramatic effect.

Wonderfully shade tolerant – it will grow well under tree canopies – is the decorative *Euphorbia robbiae*, 1½ft(45cm) tall and with rosettes of dark green leaves topped in May-June by yellow bracts. All the euphorbias will do well in less exacting shade conditions, including the very showy *E. characias* with its bold heads of green, purple-eyed flowers borne on a bushy plant some 4ft(1.25m) tall.

The handsome hellebores are also, of course, superb shade plants, and what delight they bring in the dark months, beginning with the Christmas rose, *Helleborus niger* (whose white flowers on 1ft[30cm]) stems are much the better for being protected with a cloche or other temporary covering against the vagaries of the weather at the turn of the year). Then, from winter into spring, we can enjoy the white to purple blooms of the Lenten roses, forms of *H. orientalis*, and the handsome stinking hellebore, *H. foetidus*, its dark green much-divided leaves accompanied then by pale green, maroon-fringed flowers. Best of all, though, many of us would say, is *H. corsicus* with its heads of pale green, cup-shaped flowers carried proudly above extremely handsome, spiny, tripartite leaves in early spring.

Then there is *Kirengeshoma palmata* from Japan, long-resident here but much neglected 3ft(1m) of loveliness with its palmately-lobed, maple-like leaves playing host in late summer and early autumn to nodding, pale yellow, bell-flowers which are borne in groups of three. This plant is at its most decorative in September and is best suited for light dappled shade where the soil is of a humusy nature, keeps nicely moist but is free-draining.

As already indicated, the primulas generally are moisture-loving plants which do exceedingly well in light shade. Especially lovely for May-July colour is the Bartley Strain of *Primula pulverulenta*, some 2ft(60cm) tall and carrying whorls of soft pink flowers. Another member of the Candelabra group, *P. japonica*, is of much the same height as the last, has a similar flowering period and offers excellent cultivars such as 'Miller's Crimson' and 'Postford White'. Then there are the foot-high(30cm) drumstick primulas, forms of *P. denticulata*, with their ball-like flowers in shades from white through shades of pink and red to purple, and, in the primrose section of the genus, the pretty and useful *P.* 'Wanda', (a *juliae* hybrid grouped as *P.×pruhoniciana*). This fine hybrid is a lovely sight in spring (and even, on occasions, earlier than that). It will colonise readily under small trees like *Prunus* and *Malus*. So will the charming *Tellima grandiflora* with cream bell flowers of small size borne on 2ft(60cm) stems in May above fresh green rounded leaves. The evergreen leaves take on bronzy hues in winter.

Mentioned earlier in passing were the pulmonarias, or lungworts, delightful shade plants for spring flowering which seem now to be attracting more interest. One of the finest of these is *Pulmonaria saccharata* 'Pink Dawn', its leaves of rich green marbled with white and with rose-pink flowers borne in April and May. The species itself is very lovely, however, with the amalgam of pink and blue in the flowers as they age. So long as they remain cool at the roots and have adequate supplies of moisture in the growing season they are very easily pleased plants.

BULBOUS FLOWERS   For advice on a splendid selection of bulbous flowers for growing in dappled shade turn to the section of the chapter on bulbous flowers entitled "The natural woodlanders" (pp. 112 to 115).

It is not putting it too strongly to say that we hunger for the gay colours of the garden daffodils and narcissi in late winter and spring. All, or almost all, do well in light shade, just as they will revel in sunny positions. One of the most delectable of the dwarf kinds is *Narcissus cyclamineus* only 5in(13cm) tall and with its deep yellow, long and narrow trumpets subtending swept-back petals which give the flower such a very distinctive appearance. It is a lovely narcissus to have in a raised bed near the house for it can be in flower in February and will certainly be there to be enjoyed in March. Even more important than *N. cyclamineus* itself, though, from a garden display point of view, is the range of *cyclamineus* hybrids which have resulted from crossing this species with trumpet cultivars. These are mostly between 8 and 15in(20 and 38cm) tall and they are ideal for brightening up shrub borders which are possibly a little dull in the last days of winter and the start of spring. Bright yellow and orange 'March Sunshine' is one of the most attractive of this group of hybrids, likewise 'Peeping Tom', both March flowering; numerous others include cultivars such as primrose-yellow 'Jenny', canary-yellow 'Charity May', creamy-white and yellow 'Jack Snipe' and, of course, 'February Gold', as the name suggests very early flowering, and long-lasting, too.

What can be lovelier, too, than naturalising daffodils in grass areas. Mixtures of cultivars are offered at advantageous prices for this purpose, and to create the most natural effect scatter these at random and plant them where they fall, some 4in(10cm) deep.

Hyacinths which have been flowered in the home can afterwards be planted out in the garden, not necessarily in shade although they will cheerfully put up with it without any protest. They can look very attractive, for instance, in small groups around shrubs. All lilies like to have a cool root run – such as can be provided by low-growing shrubs or leafy herbaceous plants – and their heads in sunshine. Appreciative of light, dappled shade are *Lilium pardalinum giganteum* – excellent for growing in thin woodland – some 6ft(2m) tall and with beautiful turk's cap flowers of vermilion-red shading to orange-red and with yellow centres; the 4ft(1.25m) tall *L. martagon*, a turkscap type with reddish-purple to purple blooms which are borne in July, and *L. henryi*, another tall (6 to 7ft[2 to 2.25m]) lily with beautiful recurved blooms of orange-yellow, spotted brown, which are borne in late summer. The rightly popular July-flowering regal lily, *L. regale*, will also do well in such conditions although it prefers sunshine. Its funnel-shaped blooms are white on the inside and stained with purple without; the centres are yellow. The Olympic and Bellingham hybrids also do well in such conditions.

SHRUBS AND CLIMBERS One of the finest of all garden shrubs for lightly shaded positions is *Mahonia* 'Charity' (it does equally well, it should be said, in full sun) which produces its terminal racemes of fragrant yellow flowers from November into the new year and until as late as February in some gardens. With its glossy, rich green leaves each comprising of up to 21 spiny leaflets this is an evergreen which holds the attention, and the flowers just referred to are borne up to 20 together in arching trails. Its usual height is about 10ft(3m) and its spread perhaps 6ft(2m) but it can be considerably more. However, if space is a problem it can be pruned in early spring.

If soil moisture is available in adequate quantities and your garden has a lime-free soil, then there is an opportunity to grow a selection of *Camellia japonica* cultivars or, even better, those of *C.* × *williamsii* – like the well-known double, pink 'Donation' and 'J.C. Williams' of similar colouring – which, in addition to their other fine qualities, drop their spent blooms, which the others do not, this giving the plants an untidy appearance unless they are picked over at regular intervals in the flowering season. With lime-free soil you can take your pick, too, of the vast rhododendron tribe, perhaps paying particular attention to the many lovely small-growing cultivars now available, and in particular, perhaps, the *R. yakushimanum* hybrids which are tailor-made for shade with their compact habits and beautiful flowers which appear, depending on cultivar, from April to June. The same applies to the various pieris and pernettyas, which, like the rhododendrons, belong to the *Ericaceae* family. One of the best choices in *Pieris* is the cultivar 'Forest Flame' which will make a large shrub in time but is more compact than some. Its glory is the colouring of the young leaves in spring which start off bright red and later pass to pink, then creamy-green

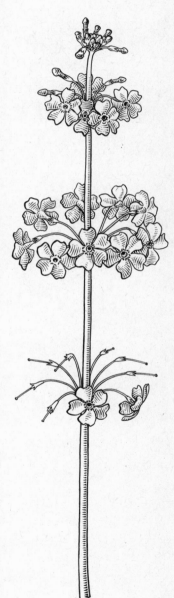

105. Primula
pulverulenta *Bartley
Strain*

106. Hydrangea
macrophylla *'Bluewave'*

and finally green. Panicles of creamy-white, lily-of-the-valley-like flowers
are borne with the eye-catching red leaves in May. This and other pieris
need a sheltered position and the kind of dappled shade which would be
provided for rhododendrons.

Again, with soil moisture no problem, there is the splendid old *Viburnum
tinus*, or laurustinus, to call on for winter flower from around the turn of the
year until April, preferably in its excellent and more compact cultivar 'Eve
Price', or 'Gwenllian' which has the added attraction of not only producing
flowers but small blue fruits in addition. Well worth growing as a foliage
shrub of low stature, too, is *V. davidii* (some 3ft([1m] tall and more wide). If
male specimens are planted with the females the latter will often produce
good crops of bright blue berries.

Fuchsias are ideal plants for light shade, just as they are for sunny
positions, either in the shape of *Fuchsia magellanica* cultivars – like 'Riccartonii', with red and purple flowers, and 'Versicolor', with dainty flowers of
similar colouring and very pretty leaves of grey-green, tinted pink at first
and with creamy-white variegation – or the hardiest of the named hybrids of
mixed parentage. All are suitable for permanent planting in sheltered
positions if the crowns are given winter protection in the form of dry litter.
If cut back by hard weather they will usually break freely from the base. (See
Chapter 20, "Fuchsias", pp. 185 to 188.)

Also ideal for light shade in milder parts of the country are the Hortensia
and Lacecap hydrangeas – forms of *Hydrangea macrophylla* – which are so
pleasing when in flower from July to September. Always make sure,
however, that they are given a nicely moist but well-drained soil in which to
grow for they have a great thirst in hot weather. Plant them also in sheltered
positions. They mostly grow 4 to 6ft(1.25 to 2m) tall although they can be
more in especially favoured climatic conditions.

On alkaline soils the blue-flowered cultivars turn to shades of pink and
red, a trait which can be counteracted to a certain extent by the application
of a proprietary blueing agent to the soil in the growing season. Much
depends on the degree of alkalinity of the soil. Superb cultivars of the
mop-headed Hortensia type include 'Génerale Viscomtesse de Vibraye',
blue or rose-pink; 'Hamburg', medium blue or rose-pink; and 'Madame E.
Mouillière', pure white. Of the Lacecap cultivars, so attractive with their
centrepieces of small fertile flowers surrounded by rings of ray florets, the
following are highly decorative: 'Bluewave', blue or pink; 'Whitewave', blue
or pink centres, white ray florets; and 'Mariesii', blue or rosy-red.

Another splendid hydrangea is the hybrid 'Preziosa', a cross between *H.
macrophylla* and *H. serrata*. This has flowers of the mop-headed type which
start off salmon-pink and gradually deepen in colour as the season
progresses. Also, the leaves and stems are tinged with purple. Its usual
height is 4 to 5ft(1.25 to 1.5m).

Excellent small evergreen shrubs for winter colour through their berries
are the skimmias, mostly 3 to 4ft(1 to 1.25m) tall and much the same in
width. The majority of skimmias bear male and female flowers on separate
plants, so both sexes must be planted to obtain a crop of berries, but with
the hermaphrodite *Skimmia reevesiana* this is not necessary. It bears its oval,
crimson berries in abundance above a mat of attractive, narrowly elliptic
leaves. Its height is usually around 2ft(60cm) with a spread of about
4ft(1.25cm) and it delights in light shade. This species, however, will not
grow on limy soil.

The snowberries or *Symphoricarpos*, which make medium-sized shrubs of
5ft(1.5m) or so are also good plants for shade, given adequate soil moisture,
these including *S. × doorenbosii* 'Mother of Pearl' with white, rose-flushed
berries borne on arching branches from autumn until deep into winter.

All the shrubby cornus with brightly coloured stems in winter will do well
in light shade in moist or reasonably moist conditions, like such interesting
shrubby willows as the Japanese *Salix sachalinensis* 'Sekka' with its flattened
or fasciated reddish-brown stems and handsome catkins.

That house-cum-garden shrub *Fatsia japonica* should also not be forgotten
for it is an extremely handsome foliage plant with its large palmate leaves
some 15in(38cm) across, rich, deep green and glossy and a magnificent foil

for the white flower heads which appear in early autumn. Give it a sheltered position, perhaps in a shady corner of the front garden, or on the patio or terrace. It can be expected to grow some 8ft(2.5m) tall but it could be considerably more if it liked especially the conditions offered.

For advice on suitable climbers and wall shrubs turn to Chapter 7, pp. 82, 83 and 86 and 87, where information will be found on those suitable for growing against north walls with their lower light values and generally cooler conditions. Just to elaborate on one of the recommendations there, namely *Parthenocissus henryana*, this remarkably handsome and very slightly tender climber – it needs shelter from cold winds without exposure to bright sunshine – is a joy on such a wall face. The leaves each consist of three to five leaflets, dark green in colour and, when grown in light shade, with prominent silvery-white leaf veining. The leaves turn red in autumn before falling. It is a good example of the many choice plants which do well in seemingly unpromising situations. The charms of the ivies (species and cultivars of *Hedera*) should also be exploited to the full.

COPING WITH DRY SHADE One of the finest of all shrubs for coping with dry shade is the evergreen *Mahonia aquifolium*, which will grow in any reasonable soil and produces colourful yellow flowers in clusters in spring. Its good nature and grow-almost-anywhere ability make us tend to under-estimate its value. It grows some 3ft(1m) tall and more wide. Another very easy ground-coverer (for lime-free soils) is dwarf *Pachysandra terminalis*, also evergreen and with small, toothed, diamond-shaped leaves of bright, glossy green. Scented white flowers are borne in early spring. It is a useful shrub for planting under trees. So is the creeping *Rubus calycinoides* which has dark green and glossy small, broadly ovate leaves with wrinkled surfaces. This will grow around tree boles quite happily. Very accommodating, too, are many of the cotoneasters, including such useful ground-coverers as *Cotoneaster dammeri*, prostrate-growing and red-berried, and wide-spreading and low-growing 'Skogholm', a cultivar with coral-red berries. Both of these are evergreen.

Hedera colchica 'Dentata Variegata', the variegated Persian ivy, is extreme-ly attractive with large, broadly ovate leaves an amalgam of green and grey margined with soft yellow. It will grow virtually anywhere without show-ing any displeasure. Likewise the numerous cultivars of the common ivy, *H. helix*, which have come so much to the fore in recent years. Their leaf shapes and colourings can be highly attractive as in 'Goldheart' with its dark green leaves coloured golden-yellow in the centre; 'Cristata', in which the leaves have distinctive wavy, crimped edges; and 'Silver Queen' with its cheerful green and white variegated leaves.

There is nothing quite to equal the variegated dead nettle, *Galeobdolon argentatum*, for colonising the ground under trees, and very pretty it is with its white markings on the leaves. This used to be known as *Lamium galeobdolon* 'Variegatum', and will be found in most nurserymen's catalogues under this name. But with its enthusiasm for territorial conquest beware of letting this perennial loose elsewhere in the garden.

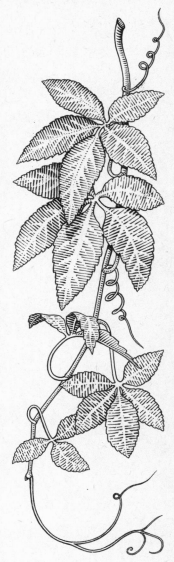

107. Parthenocissus henryana

16.

Plants for Dry, Sunny Positions

There are very few parts of any garden where plants will not grow, for plants, like man, are very adaptable and a wealth of material can be found for growing in dry, sunny positions. In the wild, plants have adapted themselves to withstand dry, sunny positions by producing thickened leaves and stems to retain their moisture; others, to prevent moisture loss, have coated their leaves with hairs or felt and some have even reduced their leaves to spines or prickles. Plants for dry, sunny positions come in all shapes and sizes from trees to very small alpines, so despite the size of the garden one is always able to find suitable planting material. In the British Isles, with its varying climatic and soil conditions, dry, sunny gardens tend to be found on the lighter, sandy soils, and even drier conditions are associated with undulating and sloping sites. The majority of plants suitable for this position will tolerate a wide range of soil types and are not demanding as to alkalinity or acidity.

Soil is important to support plant life, for not only does it provide water, nutrients and oxygen but it is also important to give anchorage to the roots. Under dry conditions there are two great disadvantages; first, the inability of a light soil to retain moisture which is so essential for the establishing of young or newly transplanted plants, and secondly the lack of nutrients, so essential for healthy growth, which are readily leached from the soil. The advantages of such soils is that they are easy to work, particularly during the autumn and winter; they also warm up more quickly in the spring and are not cold and wet during the winter, which can kill plants. Initial soil preparation is very important, and the site must be free from perennial weeds. It is well worth spending time at the beginning to rid the soil of such weeds, using herbicides or the digging fork. Organic matter should be added in the initial preparation, to improve the texture and moisture retention of the soil.

With plants suitable for such conditions, particularly those from the Mediterranean areas, it is essential that the soil should not be too rich in nutrients or the true character of the plant will be lost. A light dressing of farmyard manure or garden compost can be used as can peat. On heavy soils, a 2in(5cm) layer of coarse washed river sand or ⅛in(2.5mm) grit worked into the top spit will make it possible to grow many of them.

Planting can either be carried out in the autumn or spring, but it is possible to plant containerised plants at almost any time of the year. It is preferable to plant trees, shrubs and the larger herbaceous plants in the autumn and the smaller subjects in the spring. Firm planting is essential and it will be necessary to irrigate the area for the first season after planting, but in subsequent years the plants are better left to fend for themselves, allowing their roots to penetrate deeply to look for moisture. Mulching not only greatly improves the look of the garden but it helps to prevent moisture evaporation from the soil and has the effects of suppressing weed growth. Materials which can be used for a mulch include peat and composted (processed) bark, but for the smaller alpines in particular, which resent winter dampness around their necks, a mulch of pea gravel is best; this should be tucked under the plants right up to their necks.

Trees and shrubs form the backcloth of any garden whether it be large or small but, with the modern tendency towards smaller gardens, trees and the larger growing shrubs have to be chosen with more care if they are not quickly to out-grow their position. When making the choice bear in mind the merits of the plant – whether or not the foliage is attractive; the flowering period; the potential of any fruit or seed heads; and possible autumn tints it may provide, as well as bark and twig effect, particularly during the winter months.

TREES AND CONIFERS Among a selection of trees suitable for dry, sunny gardens *Robinia pseudoacacia* 'Frisia' is among the best with its golden-yellow pinnate leaves from spring until autumn and, when sited against a dark background, the colour of the foliage is intensified. Being a small to medium-sized tree it can be accommodated in most gardens, but if space is restricted it can be pruned hard back in the early spring and allowed to grow as a shrub. Also belonging to the family *Leguminosae*, and having a similar appearance with its bright yellow young leaves, is the honey locust, *Gleditsia triacanthos* 'Sunburst'. This can be used but the leaves turn green as they age. For the larger garden the tree of heaven, *Ailanthus altissima*, which is fairly fast growing, makes a very imposing specimen with its ash-like leaves which, when young, can be up to 3ft(1m) in length. The fruit is also like that of the ash. As a rule male and female plants can be grown but the female form is to be preferred to that of the male because of the evil-smelling flowers, but occasionally male and female are produced on the same tree.

While the birch will tolerate a wide range of conditions it is worthy of mention, particularly those kinds with striking bark effect during the winter, and when used for this purpose a multi-stemmed plant is to be preferred to a single stem. Birches are very easy to grow from seed but it should be remembered that it takes a few years for the tree to produce its bark colour. It should also not be forgotten that they are useful for autumn tints. Among the best for white bark effect are *Betula costata*, *B. jacquemontii*, *B. × koehnei*, *B. papyrifera* and *B. platyphylla*, while our own native *B. pubescens* should not be forgotten; *B. albo-sinensis* and *B. ermanii* are useful additions with pinkish bark. The Judas tree, *Cercis siliquastrum*, is another member of the pea family, *Leguminosae*, which is easily grown from seed. It is essential that young pot-grown plants should be positioned correctly in the first place because, like other members of the family, they resent root disturbance and will not transplant. The purplish-rose flowers are produced in clusters from the old wood and the seed pods hang on well into the winter; it should be said that it grows much better in the south but is a great challenge to northern gardeners.

Turning to conifers, these can add variety to the garden, whether it be for their upright or low spreading forms. There is a wide variety of material to choose from among the junipers, especially the prostrate forms which are very useful for clothing slopes and even for covering up unsightly manhole covers. Where an upright focal point is required in the garden the Irish yew, *Taxus baccata* 'Fastigiata', and its golden form, 'Fastigiata Aureomarginata' although relatively slow growing, can be made use of to give a vertical line, particularly when underplanted with other low-growing subjects.

SHRUBS AND SUB-SHRUBS From the *maquis* areas of the Mediterranean, which has resulted from the felling of the trees, come many shrubs well adapted to withstand hot, dry conditions, their main drawback under British climatic conditions being that, in the event of severe winters, some can be totally killed or their branches killed due to frost or cold north winds. Fortunately, many of them are very easy to propagate from cuttings, and with many of the cistus in particular flowering is better on younger plants, so it is probably a good policy to plan to replace them every five to seven years. *Cistus purpureus* is one of the more spectacular of these with large, rosy-crimson flowers with a chocolate basal blotch. Growing with the cistus are the familiar lavenders and rosemaries used for their herbal qualities in the kitchen.

The brooms are among the best of sun lovers and, if there is space, consider growing the rather tall-growing Mount Etna broom, *Genista aetnensis*, which makes a stately shrub up to 15 to 20ft(4.5 to 6m) high, or the

108. Cistus purpureus

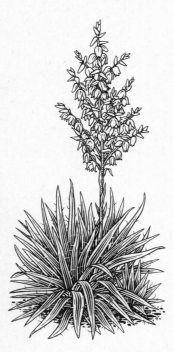

109. Yucca filamentosa
'Variegata'

slightly smaller Spanish broom, *Spartium junceum*, with its rush-like stems and longer flowering period from summer through to early autumn. For those who garden near the sea, this last is an excellent shrub for it is tolerant of salt spray.

The genus *Cytisus* contains many brooms from prostrate shrublets to small trees. *C. ardoinii* is small enough to be found a home in the rock garden while the common broom, *C. scoparius*, of which there are a number of named clones, are useful additions to the shrub border, flowering in May and early June. Over-vigorous plants can be pruned immediately after flowering but care must be taken not to prune back into old wood. For those wishing to produce a low, impenetrable mound which is animal- and child-proof as well as providing nesting sites for birds, *Genista hispanica*, the Spanish gorse, can be used to good effect. *G. lydia* is a favourite for growing on the top of dry walls and can also be planted in cracks in the side of walls, but it is easier to plant as the wall is being built rather than trying to ram the root ball in between two stones at a later date.

To give a really sub-tropical look as well as an architectural feel to the garden, the yuccas are a group of plants which can be used as focal points. One of the best for a small garden is *Yucca filamentosa*, which has white threads clothing the margins of the leaves and also produces creamy-white flowers on 3 to 6ft(1 to 2m) stems. Equally valuable, particularly during the winter months, is *Y.f.* 'Variegata', which also produces clumps of sword-like leaves with yellow stripes.

Two Californian sub-shrubs worthy of mention are *Romneya coulteri* and *Zauschneria californica*. The tree poppy, *Romneya coulteri*, is well worth growing for the glaucous appearance of the stems and leaves as well as its white, poppy-like flowers with a central mass of yellow stamens. It is sometimes difficult to establish but once this has been achieved it spreads by underground rhizomes and, when near to a building, it has been known for it to spread under the floor boards. *Zauschneria californica*, the Californian fuchsia, is very useful in that the red flowers are produced during the latter part of the summer and early autumn and it is useful for growing in the side of a dry stone wall or can even be grown in a rock garden of sufficient size.

WALL PLANTS When furnishing the garden, the walls of the house and buildings should not be forgotten for these offer the right kind of dry, sunny positions. A well-flowered specimen of the trumpet vine, *Campsis radicans*, is a sight to be remembered; it is rather strong growing and can be allowed to clothe the roof of an out-building. *Cytisus battandieri* can be trained against a wall as well as making a fine tall shrub with its fragrant, pineapple-scented, yellow flowers. Other shrubs worthy of a place include *Buddleia crispa* and many of the abutilons, callistemons and ceanothus.

SMALLER PLANTS To complete the garden picture, smaller plants are required and one can turn again to the Mediterranean flora from the *garigue* areas, which are a step further from the *maquis*, where there may be hardly any soil at all after man's familiar sequence of grazing, cultivation and neglect. Here, familiar plants are to be found such as rue, sage and garlic and, these, together with some of our familiar bulbs like fritillaries, tulips and crocuses, can be grown in the kind of conditions we are dealing with here. It is surprising how many plants with herbal qualities are able to withstand hot, sunny conditions, like rue, *Ruta graveolens*, of which it is best to grow 'Jackman's Blue'. *R. graveolens* 'Variegata' is very effective in the early part of the summer but, with age, the leaves gradually turn green, and some gardeners can get a nasty rash after pruning this plant. Sage, the sub-shrubby *Salvia officinalis*, can become leggy with age and benefits from the light, regular pruning it receives for use in the kitchen. The more decorative varieties, 'Icterina', 'Purpurascens' and 'Tricolor' are to be preferred for general garden display. One other salvia worthy of mention, herbaceous in this case, is *S. argentea*, grown for its woolly-white leaves. It will self-seed itself around the garden.

The cardoon, *Cynara cardunculus*, is one of the most stately of herbaceous plants, closely related to the globe artichoke, and with silvery-grey leaves 3 to 4ft(1 to 1.25m) long, pointed and deeply toothed. The flowers are large, purple and thistle-like, and if not required these can be removed and the plant be grown for its foliage effect alone. Also useful for foliage effect is the fennel, *Foeniculum vulgare*; with its frothy appearance it will associate well alongside *Iris pallida* 'Variegata' and *Bergenia cordifolia*. Euphorbias are essential for such a position, especially *E. polychroma*, with its yellow spring flowers, and the larger-growing *E. characias*, whose green flowers have dark brown centres. Other plants worthy of mention include the perennials *Acanthus spinosus*, *Agapanthus*, *Echinops*, *Liatris*, *Limonium latifolium*, *Oenothera* and *Perovskia* 'Blue Spire', a shrub which tends to die back in winter and needs cutting hard back in spring.

GRASSES These form an important part of the garden, usually in the form of a lawn, but in the dry, sunny garden it may not be practical to have a lawn. Nevertheless, ornamental grasses can be grown. Although *Stipa pennata* may not be totally reliable as a perennial it is well worth raising plants from seed to have its long feathery, white seed heads dancing in the breeze. In contrast, the hardy *Festuca glauca* is compact with steel-blue leaves giving colour and contrast throughout the year. If a taller grass is required then the 3ft(1m) tall *Helictotrichon sempervirens* can be used to good effect, forming dense clumps.

SILVER AND GREY FOLIAGE When confronted with a dry, sunny situation one tends to turn to plants with silver and grey foliage which are native to hot, dry areas, where they have had to adapt to the conditions by covering their leaves with hairs in order to survive. It is, of course, the density of the hairs which gives the plant its typically silver or grey appearance. If silver-leaved plants are planted in a shady position, their leaves will remain a dirty green throughout the summer, whereas specimens of the same plants grown in full sun will provide a clear silver or grey effect. In their native habitat, nearly all are to be found growing on limestone formations although they will tolerate a wide range of soils. It is probably true to say that they are a better colour when grown in chalky areas. A well-drained soil is essential if plants are to come through the winter safely because, if they remain damp around the neck throughout the winter, frost will crack and lift the bark from the stems, thus killing them. It is often safest to propagate a few plants as an insurance. Cuttings are best taken at the end of August; then, after potting, they can be placed in a cold frame to overwinter, but ensure that the pots are kept on the dry side, only increasing the amount of water given as the weather improves in spring. As they are chiefly grown for foliage effect rather than their flowers, it is a good policy to remove the flowers regularly for this helps to keep the colour in the foliage. Plants which are allowed to flower lose some of their lustre, taking on a dull, grey appearance.

Some of the taller-growing silver-foliaged plants benefit from pruning but they should not be pruned hard back, merely shaped and tidied in April or May. Artemisias are very useful, particularly *Artemisia absinthium* 'Lambrook Silver', which is a form of our native wormwood. *A.* 'Powis Castle' appears to be very hardy, making spreading mounds about 2ft(60cm) high.

For gardeners looking for flower as well as foliage effect, *Gazania* 'Silver Beauty' with its yellow and black flowers is effective, but it should be remembered that the flowers close up in dull weather. The curry-like aroma from the leaves of the shrubby *Helichrysum angustifolium*, one of the best silvers, is an added interest. A number of helichrysums are worth growing, including *H. petiolatum* which can be used to great effect as a trailing plant in hanging baskets or window boxes. *Santolina chamaecyparissus* is often left neglected and becomes woody, but when it is kept pruned it is a first-rate plant. Young plants should be frequently stopped to keep them bushy. Lambs' ears, *Stachys byzantina* (syn. *S. lanata*) is one of the most common border perennials and very easy to grow. Where space is limited, the sub-shrub, *Tanacetum densum-amanum* is exceedingly useful with its slowly spreading mats of white, feathery leaves, and it will even brighten up a sunny corner in the rock garden.

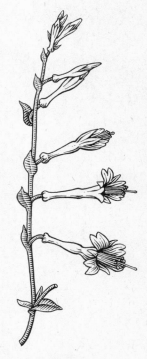

110. Zauschneria californica

111. Sempervivium
arachnoideum

ROCK GARDEN PLANTS Many alpines, or plants suitable for growing in
rock gardens, can also be found for dry, sunny places in such a garden
feature. It is amazing how the houseleek or sempervivums can survive on
the roof of a building. To see *S. arachnoideum* in the wild, clinging on to bare
rocks and with the morning dew clinging to its web-like hairs is something
to be remembered. Aethionemas are very useful in the rock garden because
of their summer flowering and help to extend the flowering period as the
bulk of alpines flower earlier in the season. The light pink flowers are set off
well against the blue-grey foliage. Others worthy of consideration include
Geranium subcaulescens; helianthemums, which are available in a wide range
of colours; *Phlox douglasii* and *P. subulata* cultivars; *Raoulia australis*; *Saponaria
ocymoides* and *Thymus herba-barona* and *T. lanuginosus*.

BULBOUS PLANTS A brief survey of this kind would not be complete
without including some bulbs. *Allium karataviense* is very ornamental, not
only for its foliage and cricket-ball sized head of flowers but also for the
dried seed heads. The well-known crown imperial, *Fritillaria imperialis*, is
worthy of a place, but beware of the pungent scent from the flowers. Other
attractive fritillarias include *F. acmopetala*, *F. persica*, *F. pontica* and *F.
pyrenaica*. *Galtonia candicans*, which flowers in the summer, is very useful for
mixing with low-growing herbaceous plants with its 4ft(1.25m) flower stems
carrying numerous drooping white bells. In the autumn *Nerine bowdenii* is
very attractive and, for spring flowering, there are many crocuses, irises and
tulips to choose from.
    Naturally, there are plenty of other plants suitable for dry, sunny
positions, but hopefully those mentioned here will provide you with ideas if
such conditions are to be found in your garden.

112. Allium karataviense

17.

Plants for Pools

The essentials for the successful cultivation of ornamental aquatic plants are strong light, adequate soil, and water, static or nearly so, of suitable depth.

THE SITE Algae, the simple plants which constitute the major weeds of the water garden (whether as the microscopic single-celled forms that turn the water green, or the filamentous type called silkweed) are encouraged by sunlight. But siting a pool in the shade to avoid these nuisances drastically reduces the flowering potential of the ornamental water plants. The dilemma is resolved by siting the pool where it will get all the sunshine possible and by covering half to two-thirds of the water with foliage which prevents sunlight from penetrating below the surface. Thus, ornamental plants are encouraged and they, in flourishing, inhibit algae.

POOL SIZE AND SHAPE The greatest difficulties are always experienced with the smallest pools. The larger the pool the more stable the environment, to the benefit of both plants and fish. At least 50sq ft(5m²) of surface area should be the aim, with as much more as circumstances permit. The surface shape, formal or irregular as required to match its setting, should in any event be kept simple and open. Canals, narrow waists and complicated shapes are awkward to construct, difficult to plant and lack the impact of an open stretch of water. A circle, or something near to it, displaying its full width from every angle of view, is the best shape.

POOL DEPTH To minimise labour in construction and maintenance the pool should be no deeper than is necessary. A depth of 3 or 4ft(1 to 1.25m) is not necessary, either for the safety of fish in winter, or to permit the cultivation of the largest water lilies. Water lilies certainly vary greatly in vigour, but a study of the figures given for each of the seven groups into which they may conveniently be divided (see p. 163) reveals that a water depth over the crown of 12 to 15in(30 to 38cm) comes within the depth tolerance of the majority. Add 6 to 9in(15 to 23cm) for soil depth and it is seen that maximum pool depths of 18 to 24in(45 to 60cm) are adequate. The 24in(60cm) depth is preferred because it confers greater volume in relation to surface area, making for greater stability and less liability to algae problems.

Apart from this main depth only one other planting level is needed. This is to accommodate the marginal plants (e.g., iris and reed mace) which grow in shallow water. Assuming container planting, they can be catered for by incorporating a shelf 10 to 12in(25 to 30cm) wide and 8 to 9in(20 to 23cm) below water level. Any fine adjustments to suit particular plants can be made by supporting the containers on a tile or two.

MATERIALS The traditional pool-making material, concrete, is still favoured by many for the sake of its satisfying texture and finish. Concrete, unfortunately, is inflexible and liable to crack under the strains imposed by an expanding ice sheet or an unstable subsoil. Once cracked it can seldom be made watertight again. Plastic materials take some of the backache out of pool construction and are unaffected by the stresses that are so damaging to concrete. A well-made glass-fibre pool has an almost unlimited life; regrettably, most of the designs available are unsatisfactory in both size and shape, only two of the largest coming anywhere near the surface area recommended. A flexible plastic sheet which, when draped in a hole and filled with water, moulds itself faithfully to the shape of the excavation, is now the favoured material for pool construction. The technique offers freedom in design and there is virtually no size limit. Laminated PVC, which may reasonably be expected to last 15 years, and butyl synthetic rubber, which is said to last 50 years or more, are the two widely available alternatives. Both can be accidentally punctured but are simply repaired. Polythene sheet is vulnerable, irreparable, and not recommended for serious pool construction.

MOVING WATER   Water lilies give of their best only in still, warm water. Any water movement will, to some extent, inhibit flowering; currents of cold water inhibit growth as well as flower. Nevertheless, the splash of water is aesthetically pleasing and of practical benefit to fish. Provide enough movement to make a splash then, but take care to minimise its adverse effects. It must never be created by a constant inflow of cold mains water, but only by circulating water from the pool itself. A fountain reduces the space available for water lilies. A modest waterfall or spouting ornament would be a better choice since either would disturb a smaller area than a fountain. Above all, the pump position must ensure that water is taken out of the pool as close as possible to where it is returned, thus minimising currents. The turnover rate should not exceed the volume of the pool in an hour.

PLANT SELECTION

Aquatic plants fall into several categories which have ornamental value and practical usefulness in varying degrees. Although only oxygenators and water lilies are essential in practical terms, some floating and marginal types are needed to create a plant community of maximum attractiveness and interest.

Water Lilies

Pride of place in any water garden must go to the hardy members of the genus *Nymphaea*, the water lilies. They produce flowers of outstanding beauty over a long season and their leaves play a major part in the suppression of algae by cutting off light at the surface. Tropical water lilies require conditions of consistently high summer temperature that cannot be provided outdoors in Britain.

The comments and lists that follow are concerned only with hardy perennial kinds that require no winter protection outdoors in Britain. They flower from June to October and become dormant in winter. They vary considerably in size, in vigour, and in the surface spread of their foliage. They vary also in price; the cheaper variety will not necessarily be an inferior one, but it will certainly be a strong grower, easily propagated. It is axiomatic that a cheap unnamed lily will be a very vigorous one, probably culled from lake stock; it is likely to be capable of covering most, if not all, of a 50sq ft(4.6m^2) pool within two seasons. Some discrimination is required if the pool is to be planted with varieties that are in proportion, and if maximum interest is to be achieved, by planting several moderate-growing varieties of different colours in the same space that would be occupied by a single giant.

To facilitate selection it is convenient to divide the water lilies into seven groups, for each of which a suitable planting depth and the surface area covered by the foliage on an established plant is indicated (see chart). The surface cover provided by the foliage of water lilies belonging to the various groups can only be approximate since so much depends on the type of soil and planting method. The figure for planting depth refers to the depth of water over the crown and does not include soil.

	Planting Depth	Surface Cover (approximately)		Soil volume per plant*
		Spread	**Area**	
Group I	3–9in(8–25cm)	15–18in(38–45cm)	.14sqyd(.12m²)	2qt(2.5l)
Group II	5–12in(13–30cm)	2ft(60cm)	.35sqyd(.3m²)	4qt(4.5l)
Group III	7–15in(18–38cm)	3ft(1m)	.8sqyd(.66m²)	8qt(9l)
Group IV	9–18in(23–45cm)	4ft(1.25m)	1.4sqyd(1.2m²)	16qt(18l)
Group V	9–24in(25–60cm)	5ft(1.5m)	2.2sqyd(1.8m²)	16qt(18l)
Group VI	12–30in(30–75cm)	6ft(2m)	3sqyd(2.5m²)	24qt(27l)
Group VII	15–36in(38–90cm)	8ft(2.5m)	5.6sqyd(4.7m²)	32qt(36l)

*The soil volumes quoted assume that soil will be completely renewed after three years.

HARDY WATER LILIES

In the following list 51 hardy water lilies (nymphaeas) are described under four headings according to colour. Within each colour group they are listed in order of size, starting with the smallest varieties.

White water lilies

Nymphaea pygmaea var. *alba* Starry white flowers and small green leaves make this a charming subject for cultivation in sinks and shallow ponds. Group I. 'Candida': The ideal water lily for most glass-fibre and other small ponds. The cup-shaped flowers are 3 to 3½in(8 to 9cm) across. Group II. *N. odorata* 'Minor' A dwarf form with scented white blooms up to 3in(8cm) across. The apple-green leaves are reddish beneath. Group II. 'Hermine': Very white starry flowers. The ratio of blooms to leaves is above average. Excellent water lily for a small pond. Group III. 'Gonnère': A superb variety combining very double 5 to 6in(13 to 15cm) goblet-shaped flowers with a comparatively small leaf spread. Group IV.
N. odorata var. *alba* Admirable for lake margins where it has elbow room in fairly shallow water. The 4 to 5in(10 to 13cm) flowers are pleasantly scented. Group V. 'Albatross': Pointed petals give the dazzling white blooms a spiky appearance. The young leaves are purple-tinted, becoming dark green. Group V. 'Marliacea Albida': Probably the most widely planted of all water lilies, often in ponds too small for it. It is tough, reliable, beautiful and very vigorous. Group VI.
N. alba This variety has the largest flower, 4 to 5in(10 to 13cm) across, of any British native plant, and is capable of growing in cold water as much as 10ft(3m) deep, but has little to recommend it for garden pools. It should not be confused with 'Marliacea Albida' (see above), a far better flowering plant. Group VI.
N. tuberosa 'Richardsonii' Ideal for natural ponds where it will develop from a depth of 2ft(60cm) or so into deeper water. Large, globular, semi-double white blooms. Group VII. 'Colossea': An initial tinge of flesh pink is soon lost to leave the 8in(20cm) flowers completely white; the usual listing of this variety among the pinks is not justified. Vigour and flower production are both impressive. Group VII. 'Gladstone': A massive producer of huge leaves and 8in(20cm) flowers of splendid form and substance, this very vigorous lily grows best in 2 to 3ft(60 to 90cm) of water. If shallower it soon pushes leaves well above the surface, obscuring the flowers. Group VII.

Pink water lilies

'Joanne Pring': An outstanding miniature water lily with blooms little more than 2in(5cm) across. The petals are wide and deep pink, tapering to paler points. Group I. 'Laydekeri Lilacea': Very satisfactory for small pools, this variety has cup-shaped blooms that mature from pale lilac to a bright carmine pink. Group II. 'Pink Opal': An outstanding variety for small pond cultivation. The fragrant, cup-shaped blossoms are a uniform deep salmon-pink. The leaves have a bronzy cast. Group III. 'Fire Crest': Red-tipped stamens make a conspicuous centre to the wide-opening pink flowers; they have the typical *N. odorata* fragrance. Group IV.

N. odorata 'Turicensis'   A free-flowering medium grower with scented, soft rose-pink blooms. Group IV.

N. odorata 'W.B. Shaw'   A very attractive lily whose flowers are held well above the surface. They are pink at first, paling as they age. Group IV. 'Rose Arey': One of the most beautiful of all water lilies. The flowers, rich silvery-pink and fragrant, have an unrivalled elegance of form. They may be as much as 8in(20cm) in diameter. Group IV. 'Mme. Wilfron Gonnère': With double, goblet-shaped flowers and moderate leaf growth, this is almost a rose-pink version of 'Gonnère', although the petals are broader and their arrangement more formal and less crowded. Group IV. 'Masaniello': A fine variety with big, solid blooms, rose-pink stained with carmine. The flower centre matures to strawberry red. Group V. 'Marliacea Carnea': This might be listed among the white varieties except for the blush that tinges the base of the sepals and petals when the plant is established. Most unnamed "pink" lilies turn out, disappointingly, to be 'Marliacea Carnea'. Group VI. 'Marliacea Rosea': Although very pale at first, this variety produces genuinely pink flowers, large and beautifully shaped, when the plant has been established for a year or two. Like 'Marliacea Carnea' it is tough, vigorous and virtually foolproof. Group VI. 'Amabilis': Wide-opening tapering petals form very large salmon to rose-pink blooms. Group VI. 'Mrs. Richmond': This variety has very large pink flowers, the centres becoming deeper with age. Group VII.

N. tuberosa 'Rosea'   This water lily raises fragrant 4 to 5in(10 to 13cm) soft pink flowers above the surface. Spreading growth; ideal for lake margins. Group VII.

113. Nymphaea 'Rose Arey'

Red water lilies

N. pygmaea 'Rubra' The blooms start pale pink and mature to deep red. Larger in leaf and flower than the other *pygmaea* forms. Group II. 'Ellisiana': Scarce, and well worth searching for. The blooms are dark red, almost purple towards the centre. Group II. 'Froebelii': A reliable, compact, and free-flowering variety, ideal for small ponds. The petals are bright deep red, contrasting with the pale inner sepals. Group III. 'Laydekeri Fulgens': Larger in leaf than the last but still suitable for tubs as well as ponds. Exceptionally prolific in the production of its rosy-crimson flowers. Group III. 'James Brydon': An exceptional variety. The 5 to 6in(13 to 15cm) deep goblet blooms are rich carmine-pink with a silvery sheen. The leaves are bronzy purple becoming green, uncrowded and relatively small. Group IV. 'Gloriosa': A prolific red variety of restrained growth that is highly praised in the United States but which is not yet widely known in Britain. Group IV. 'Atropurpurea': Dark crimson-purple blooms up to 8in(20cm) across open wide and flat to show off the lax golden stamens. Group V. 'René Gerard': Although moderate in leaf spread, this variety produces 8 to 9in(20 to 23cm) flowers profusely. They are pink and crimson deepening to dark red at the centre. Group V. 'William Falconer': Dusky red flowers almost as dark as those of 'Atropurpurea': They are more cup- than saucer-shaped and 6 to 7in(15 to 18cm) in diameter. Group V. 'Conqueror': A robust variety whose leaves do not spread excessively. The flowers are broad-petalled, substantial and deep red with paler touches. Group VI. 'Escarboucle': The most popular red water lily. The flowers are beautifully shaped, bright crimson and produced very freely over a long season. Group VI. 'Charles de Meurville': A vigorous grower that produces very large leaves and claret red blooms up to 9in(23cm) in diameter. Group VII. 'Attraction': This needs room for the unrestricted spread of both leaves and roots; it is ideal for lake planting. The flowers, up to 10in(25cm) across if well nourished, develop from pink to dark red as they age and are flecked or streaked with white or pale pink at all stages. Group VII.

Yellow, orange and coppery water lilies

N. pygmaea 'Helvola' The most popular of the miniature lilies. It produces mottled 3 to 4in(8 to 10cm) leaves and profuse 2in(5cm) primrose yellow flowers. Group I. 'Aurora': An appropriate name for a flower of mixed and changing colours – creamy-yellow to orange-apricot to deep red. Prolific. Group II. 'Graziella': Although generally described as orange the 3in(8cm) blooms are a blend of subtle shades from pinkish-apricot to pale copper. Group III. 'Comanche': This cultivar raises 4 to 5in(10 to 13cm) flowers well above the surface. They mature from apricot-pink to deep coppery-orange. Group III. 'Indiana': A water lily which runs the gamut of 'sunset shades' from pink, flushed orange to rich coppery-red. The leaves are spotted and mottled with purple. Group IV.
N. odorata 'Sulphurea Grandiflora' A clear yellow variety of charming character. The large, many-petalled flowers are raised well clear of the marbled leaves. Group IV. 'Moorei': This cultivar produces light yellow flowers some 6in(15cm) across. It is similar to 'Marliacea Chromatella' except for a spotted leaf and more restrained growth. Group V. 'Sunrise': While this water lily responds to sunshine with superb yellow blooms some 10in(25cm) or more across, lifted high above the water, it can be inhibited by cool British summers. Group V.
'Marliacea Chromatella' Like the other hybrids of its group, tough, robust, reliable and free-flowering. The blooms are creamy-yellow, the leaves handsomely marbled with chestnut. Group VI. 'Colonel A.J. Welch': A vigorous, leafy variety. It has narrow-petalled, up-lifted yellow blooms and a poor flower-to-foliage ratio. Group VII.

OTHER SURFACING PLANTS

APONOGETON DISTACHYUS, water hawthorn Waxy white flowers with black anthers and a pervasive scent are borne profusely in spring and

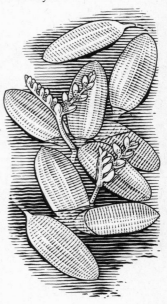

114. Aponogeton distachyus

autumn, sporadically in summer and winter. Every pool should have it. Planting depth (hereafter referred to as PD), 6 to 24in(15 to 60cm).

NYMPHOIDES PELTATA (syn. *Villarsia nymphaeoides, Limnanthemum peltatum*), water fringe   Leaves like a small water lily; deep yellow flowers. Rampant in muddy shallows. PD 4 to 12in(10 to 30cm).

NUPHARS. NUPHAR LUTEUM, N. ADVENUM, N. JAPONICUM, spatterdocks   The massive leaf spread and 2in(5cm) yellow flowers are not worthy of space that could be occupied by hybrid water lilies.

ORONTIUM AQUATICUM   Silvery blue-green leaves float or stand out of the water, depending on the planting depth. Long, white-stemmed, yellow flower spikes inspire the name golden club. PD 2 to 18in(5 to 45cm).

OXYGENATING PLANTS

In daylight all the plants in the pool produce oxygen. Those whose leaves are on or above the surface discharge it into the air. Submerged oxygenating plants put oxygen directly into the water. However, the production of oxygen is only one of their functions, and not the most important, since the absorption of oxygen through the water surface normally provides all that is required.

The real value of oxygenators is in filtering, clarifying and purifying the water. In building up their rapid summer growth oxygenators consume carbon dioxide and dissolved mineral salts. This competition for essential nutrients starves algae and is a vital factor in keeping the water clear.

Oxygenators do not maintain water clarity by themselves. The partnership of plants such as water lilies, whose leaves spread on the surface and deprive algae of light, is essential. Oxygenators themselves need light and they should be concentrated in areas not covered by surface foliage. Canadian pondweed and willow moss are the best choice for shaded areas.

Although most oxygenators grow rapidly it is not practicable to plant one or two and wait for them to spread. It is in the mineral-rich waters of a new pool that their services are most urgently needed. One for every 2 to 3sqft (.2 to .3m^2) of surface area is recommended for pools up to 100sqft (9m^2); beyond that one for every 4 to 6sqft(.4 to .6m^2).

Most are supplied as bunches of unrooted cuttings. Whether planted upright with 2in(5cm) of the stems buried, or laid flat with a stone to hold them down, they will quickly develop roots. Since these are primarily for anchorage rather than feeding, coarse sand (or fine gravel) is as acceptable a medium as soil, and less likely to discolour the water. A plastic seed tray is adequate for planting five or six bunches. Larger planting areas can be created within a line of bricks containing coarse sand or pea shingle 2in(5cm) deep. A circle 4ft(1.25m) in diameter will take 50 oxygenators planted 6in(15cm) apart – and requires 200lb(90.72kg) of gravel.

If oxygenators are 'simply dropped in', some of the drifting fragments will root, but the method is wasteful. It is recommended only for hornwort. Which oxygenators will best suit a pool can only be determined by experiment. It is advisable to plant a mixture, as offered by most specialist suppliers.

Until newly planted oxygenators have had time to root they are extremely vulnerable to dislodgement and destruction by fish. No fish should be allowed in the pool (other than insectivorous Golden Orfe) for a month after planting. If fish are already present the oxygenators must be protected with a cage of small-mesh wire netting.

Most oxygenators decline rapidly after the burst of summer growth and they perform no useful function in autumn and winter. Indeed they contribute to the pool's problems if their bulk is allowed to decay in the water. To avoid this they should be cut back to a few inches in August or early September or, in the case of hornwort, thinned by raking. Exceptions are water violet and autumnal starwort, which are at their best between autumn and spring.

CALLITRICHE AUTUMNALIS (syn. *C. hermaphroditica*)   The best oxygenator among the starworts since it grows submerged.

CALLITRICHE PLATYCARPA (syn. *C. verna*)   This species and *C. stagnalis*

115. Hottonia palustris

grow in shallow water, making attractive surface rosettes of pale green leaves.

CERATOPHYLLUM DEMERSUM (hornwort) This has somewhat bristly foliage, less vulnerable to fish than the rest. It need not be planted.

ELODEA CANADENSIS (syn. *ANACHARIS*) This can be a rampant grower in a new pool. After a season or two it usually settles down to tidy, short, carpet-like growth.

ELODEA CRISPA (syn. *Lagarosiphon muscoides* 'Major') This makes long dark green ropes of growth with tight curved leaves.

FONTINALIS ANTIPYRETICA, willow moss This makes dense clumps of very dark green. It is happiest under bridges and in other shady places, attached to stones.

HOTTONIA PALUSTRIS, the water violet A plant with attractive light green, ferny foliage and pale lavender flowers. It is at its best and most plantable in autumn and early spring.

MYRIOPHYLLUM SPICATUM, water milfoil This has thin reddish stems and fine leaves of olive green. *M. verticillatum* has green stems.

POTAMOGETON CRISPUS Bronzy-green oblong leaves with wavy edges. *P. PECTINATUS* has thread-like leaves while *P. lucens* and *P. perfoliatus* both have very large translucent leaves.

RANUNCULUS AQUATILIS, water crowfoot This plant has finely dissected submerged leaves and broadly lobed floating foliage. White flowers are held above the surface.

FLOATING PLANTS

The plants, which need no planting, are a diverse assortment, generally more interesting than ornamental. If the surface-shading function is adequately performed by water lily foliage, floating plants can be dispensed with.

AZOLLA CAROLINIANA, fairy moss It spreads a shaggy pastel carpet across the surface. Rampant until frosted.

HYDROCHARIS MORSUS-RANAE, frog-bit. Makes surface runners with miniature water lily pads and a small white flower. A martyr to snails.

LEMNA TRISULCA, duckweed This is the only tolerable duckweed, its translucent leaf fragments floating submerged – in effect it is an oxygenator.

LEMNA GIBBA, *L. MINOR* and *L. POLYRRHIZA*, duckweeds These are very hard – or impossible – to control. Their bright green specks can quickly form a solid wall-to-wall surface carpet.

STRATIOTES ALOIDES, water soldier A rosette of spiky saw-edged leaves, like the top of a pineapple, sits in mud on the bottom until it is time to rise to the surface and open a white flower.

UTRICULARIA VULGARIS, bladderwort This forms a brownish tangle of thin stems festooned with tiny daphnia-trapping bladders. Miniature yellow snapdragon flowers above the surface. Interesting but inconspicuous, it needs acid water.

EICHHORNIA, water hyacinth; *TRAPA*, water chestnut and *PISTIA*, water lettuce Excellent ornamental floating plants in a greenhouse but are disappointing and short-lived outdoors in Britain.

CERATOPHYLLUM A submerged floating plant, is described under Oxygenating Plants (see above).

MARGINAL PLANTS

Although they are not essential to pool balance, marginal plants have a diversity of form and flower that can contribute beauty and character to the ornamental pool. Many species offered commercially are deficient in beauty and weedy in character; the following is a selective list. Descriptions include the approximate height of the plant; the PD (planting depth) figure refers to the depth of water over the soil.

ACORUS CALAMUS 'Variegatus' This has iris-like leaves striped green and cream. 30in(75cm). PD 0 to 2in(0 to 5cm).

BUTOMUS UMBELLATUS, flowering rush Clusters of pink flowers with dark red stamens. 3 to 4ft(1 to 1.25m). PD 2 to 6in(5 to 15cm).

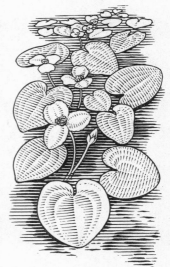

116. Hydrocharis morsus-ranae

117. Calla palustris

CALLA PALUSTRIS, bog arum Glossy broad leaves and small white 'arum-lily' spathes in June. Spreading. 6in(15cm). PD 0 to 2in(0 to 5cm).
CALTHA The indispensable marsh marigolds do best in soil barely covered by water.
CALTHA PALUSTRIS 12in(30cm), has shiny single flowers; *C. palustris* 'Plena'. 9in(23cm), has very double blooms. They flower for six weeks or more. *C.p.* var. *alba*, 12in(30cm), is the white form. *C. polypetala*, 24in(60cm), has large single yellow blooms; it sprawls.
CYPERUS LONGUS A graceful foliage plant for the background in large pools. 4ft(1.25m). PD 2 to 6in(5 to 15cm). *C. vegetus* is a better choice for the average pool. 2ft(60cm). PD 0 to 2in(0 to 5cm). Both are invasive.
ERIOPHORUM ANGUSTIFOLIUM, cotton grass The common name aptly describes the pendent, silky, white tufts on thin stems. June to August. 18in(45cm). PD 2 to 4in(5 to 10cm).
IRIS LAEVIGATA, the blue water iris This species and its cultivars make a superb show in June. *I.l.* var. *alba* is white; *I.l.* 'Albo-purpurea' is white mottled with blue; *I.l.* 'Atropurpurea' is deep violet-blue; *I.l.* 'Sorrento' has double, purple flowers. *I.l.* 'Variegata', in which light blue flowers are allied to the summer-long attraction of cream-variegated leaves, is one of the best of all marginals. 24 to 30in(60 to 75cm). PD 2 to 4in(5 to 10cm).
IRIS PSEUDACORUS, the common yellow flag iris This grows 3 to 4ft(1 to 1.25m) tall. *I.p.* 'Variegata' is a neater form (24 to 30in [60 to 75cm]) with leaves striped green and yellow, becoming green.
LOBELIA FULGENS This plant has plum-red foliage and vivid red flowers from August to October. 3 to 4ft(1 to 1.25m). PD 2 to 6in(5 to 15cm).
LYSICHITUM These bear striking 2ft(60cm) spathes in April, followed by enormous leaves. They need very deep, acid, boggy soil and are not suitable for container cultivation. *L. americanum* has yellow spathes whilst those of *L. camtschatcense* are white.
MENYANTHES TRIFOLIATA, bog bean Pinky-white fringed flowers held over spreading leaves. 9in(23cm). PD 0 to 3in(0 to 8cm).
MIMULUS GUTTATUS This is the *M. luteus* of nurseries and it bears red-spotted yellow flowers all summer. 12in(30cm). PD 0 to 1in(0 to 2.5cm). *M. ringens* is deep lavender blue. 18in(45cm). PD 2 to 4in(5 to 10cm).
PONTEDERIA CORDATA Spikes of lavender-blue flowers from July to September and large, glossy leaves make this one of the best aquatics. 30in(75cm). PD 2 to 4in(5 to 10cm).
RANUNCULUS LINGUA 'Grandiflora', spearwort This has buttercup flowers between June and August on 4 to 5ft(1.25 to 1.5m) stems. A rampant coloniser. PD 2 to 6in(5 to 15cm).
SAGITTARIA, arrowhead. The common name is apt for the large three-pointed leaves. *S. japonica* has yellow-centred, single, white flowers. *S. japonica* 'Plena' has very double blooms. *S. sagittifolia* has white, single flowers with dark centres. 24 to 30in(60 to 75cm). PD 4 to 6in(10 to 15cm).
SCIRPUS LACUSTRIS, the true bulrush It is too coarse and invasive for ornamental pools. *S. albescens*, although 4 to 6ft(1.25 to 2m) tall, is better behaved; the rushes are vertically striped green and cream. *S. zebrinus* (porcupine rush) has quills alternately banded green and white. 3 to 4ft(1 to 1.25m). PD 4 to 6in(10 to 15cm).
TYPHA Wrongly called bulrushes; should be called reed maces.
T. latifolia, 6 to 8ft(2 to 2.5m) tall, is too overpowering for most pools.
T. angustifolia and *T. laxmannii* (syn. *T. stenophylla*), have slender leaves to 4 or 5ft(1.25 to 1.5m). *T. minima*, the dwarf reed mace, has plump brown bosses on 18in(45cm) rushy stems. PD 2 to 6in(5 to 15cm). All typhas are invasive.
ZANTEDESCHIA AETHIOPICA, arum lily Superb white flowers and lush foliage. Will over winter safely on the pool floor. 24 to 30in(60 to 75cm). PD 6 to 12in(15 to 30cm).

PLANTING POOL PLANTS

Aquatic plants are moved when actively growing, not when they are dormant. The season begins with some marginals and oxygenators in April;

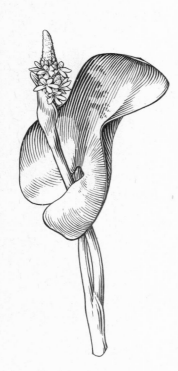

118. Pontederia cordata

some water lilies become available in May; not until June will virtually all pond plants be ready. The season continues until August, or later if water temperatures remain high.

SOIL AND METHODS Rich, heavy loam is the ideal, but any good fertile garden soil is suitable. Chopped turf should be mixed in, especially with light soil or with clay. Avoid acid, sandy soil and chalky soil. Peat is useless, compost polluting, manure unnecessary, fertilisers encourage algae.

Maximum plant growth is achieved by spreading 6in(15cm) of soil over the bottom of the pool, but the eventual result is an uncontrollable tangle of the toughest survivors. Container planting is more satisfactory. Soil will have to be replaced from time to time but much less will be needed. With no soil between containers, wandering roots find no encouragement, and plants are confined to tidy clumps. Fish have less scope for mud-stirring. When the pond needs a spring clean, containers greatly simplify the job.

Containers for marginals should be about 6in(15cm) deep. On the normal marginal shelf this leaves about 2in(5cm) of water above it which suits the great majority without adjustment. The container should be broad-based for the sake of stability. Different species or cultivars should not be mixed in the same container. One 10in by 10in by 6in(25cm by 25cm by 15cm) will take two or three plants of most marginal varieties and soon make a bold clump. The same size will suit an *Aponogeton*, *Nymphoides* or *Orontium*; or a water lily from Groups I or II.

The largest container offered commercially as a 'lily basket', 12in by 12in by 8in(30cm by 30cm by 20cm) with tapered perforated sides, holds ¼ bushel (8 quarts or 9l) of soil. From the details of the water lily groups this will be seen to be totally inadequate for the larger water lilies without annual soil changes. To avoid this, larger containers must be found for the bigger water lilies. Almost anything that will not disintegrate in water – or pollute it – will do. Wooden boxes and casks will serve, but plastic tubs and bowls are even better. Perforated sides are unnecessary when the container is wide and shallow, the ideal proportions. The wide range of plastic washing-up bowls will cater for virtually all needs. One 18in (45cm) in diameter and 6in(15cm) deep holds a generous ½ bushel(4 gal or 18l); one 21in(52.5cm) in diameter and 6in(15cm) deep contains ¾ bushel (6gal or 27l); and one 24in(60cm) in diameter and 6in(15cm) deep holds enough to nourish even a Group VII water lily. The larger the container the longer it will nourish the plant, but remember that containers have to be lifted and a bushel of soil will weigh about a hundredweight (51kg) before it is saturated.

While planting is in progress care must be taken to keep plants moist. Oxygenators in particular shrivel rapidly on exposure to sun and wind. They must not be unwrapped until needed and their immersion in the pool must not be delayed a moment longer than necessary.

WATERSIDE PLANTS

If the pool is a natural one the adjoining soil will contain ample moisture to support the lush summer growth of foliage plants such as *Rheum*, *Rodgersia*, *Hosta*, *Carex*, *Peltiphyllum*, and even *Gunnera*. It can enjoy a flowering succession from April to August by planting only primulas and astilbes, with *Iris kaempferi* and *I. sibirica* thrown in for good measure.

For the majority of pools nowadays these traditional waterside plants are not appropriate. A pool made of concrete or any kind of impermeable plastic is surrounded, not by permanently moist soil, but by plain garden soil in what was deliberately chosen as the sunniest spot in the garden. Plants that need summer moisture will not flourish here, but many others will, the choice being defined by the soil type and the owner's fancy. The pool will show few signs of plant life from November to late March.

Waterside planting might well be designed, not to compete with the pool's lush summer growth, but to bring some form and colour to the bleaker months by planting dwarf conifers, early bulbs and patches of winter-flowering heathers.

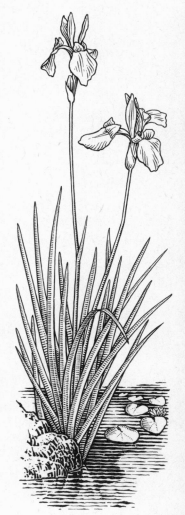

119. Iris laevigata
'Variegata'

18.

Plants for Containers
Outdoors

No garden centre of style and vitality today lacks its section displaying tubs, urns, troughs and pots – in concrete, terracotta, timber and plastic. Often these containers – unfortunately there is no more elegant umbrella term for them – are given an importance as great as the plants and the equipment have. Container gardening is no longer a vogue. Growing plants in these receptacles – another unfortunate collective term – has become part of everyday home horticulture wherever the garden is seen either as an extension of the house or a flattering setting for it.

But one must distinguish between the two kinds of container gardening. With the ambivalence of much horticultural language, the expression has two distinct meanings. It can imply raising plants in pots of some kind for instant effect when they are set in the open ground – or in the tubs, urns or troughs. But it also applies to a whole section of the gardener's craft, impinging on the designer's world, when plants are grown to make their mature effect in a receptacle that has an identity of its own which the plants in turn embellish. Then special techniques are required, and possibilities are revealed which are often closed to the open-ground gardener. It can make gardening possible to those whose only canvas is a paved patch behind a terraced house or even just a balcony. Again, every terrace is enhanced by potted plants. In the overall garden scene they can make points of focus where the only alternative might be a costly piece of sculpture, and they can make strong accents in a garden that might otherwise have a prevailing muted tone.

Why grow in containers out of doors, though, plants that can often be grown just as well in the open ground? Fashion partly. Holidays abroad have shown British home gardeners just how much urns and tubs can add architecturally to a garden scene. The smaller the site the greater their contribution. In sunny countries container gardening derives from shortage of space and the need to treasure what little soil can be found. Then a plant in its pot becomes something of special significance, softening the prevailing harshness of masonry, offering some living thing to cherish in an almost entirely man-made environment.

Translated to our more lush and fertile scene such containers can offer, first, architectural effects and variation of texture, since they usually stand out in relief from their setting; and, second, a means of displaying a range of plants that would either be inappropriate to a particular garden through their character or degree of hardiness or others which through inadequate numbers would appear lost in more expansive settings.

For instance, many plants, enticing as individuals – perhaps the selected forms of spotted laurel or the yuccas – can look artificial in a garden yet acceptable, even dramatic, when set in large pots. Or the soil might be inhospitable to them, as in the case of camellias, which make fine tub plants for areas when the soil contains lime which, of course, they dislike. Again, plants that are on the tender side when exposed to frost can often be brought safely through the winter when they are kept rather dry in winter – which container plants can be if they are given ample drainage or they are temporarily brought under cover for the worst months of the year.

In permanently planted gardens composed of shrubs, hardy perennials and bulbs for easy maintenance, often there is neither room nor a fitting setting for half-hardy bedding plants which are almost invariably the plants that yield the most striking colours. They need not be eschewed altogether. Containers can be employed as a medium for displaying such plants in small numbers, most suitably on a paved terrace where their rather theatrical appearance is most in keeping. In gardens or courtyards that are almost completely paved, because that is the most suitable treatment for the limitations of a site or of the owner's capacity for upkeep, container plants, largely of an architectural character, can restore the horticultural element.

To achieve a satisfactory effect the container must be large enough in itself to make a mark on the site and to hold a volume of soil sufficient to maintain enough moisture to see a bush safely through dry periods without the need for constant watering. Containers that seem large enough when one is close to them in a garden centre are frequently insignificant when installed in the garden itself and are seen at a distance from the windows. A sound rule is always to acquire a larger container than seems adequate. Better, though, to take measurements and make a mock-up to set in position and then form a judgement on it.

If a container is to be made a focal point in a garden scheme it needs to be to scale with its site. Often it should be of really bold proportions. This does not necessarily mean that it will be an unchangeable feature due to its great weight when filled with soil. In fact, it is not necessary to fill it at all but to set in it a large plastic pot containing the growing medium, either hung on the rim of the main container or standing on a heap of bricks within it. Then the container remains manoeuvrable and the plants can be changed through the seasons, permitting, say, an evergreen shrub in winter, bulbs in spring, followed by summer bedding plants which can themselves be changed each year. The same scheme can be adopted with troughs, partly filling them with peat and plunging in these plants grown in small pots, clay in this case so that there is an exchange of moisture through the sides.

However, really large containers can prove very expensive indeed to acquire. An alternative scheme for embellishing a terrace is to have at regular intervals round it, several smaller containers, perhaps 12 to 14in(30 to 35cm) across, that are identical and filled with the same kind of plants. An alternative for a focal point is to build up an assembly of potted plants of varying sizes into a broad cone shape, perhaps clustered round a single palm, as is frequently glimpsed in patios on holiday visits to Spain. This particularly applies when one maintains a collection of tender plants in a greenhouse over the winter and which can be stood out for the summer.

SOIL Though plants set permanently in containers will grow successfully in soil simply dug up from the garden, it is much better to use a compost of the kind mixed for greenhouse plants. For the sake of easy handling, when a terrace or patio has to be swept, one based on peat is better than a soil compost, since this type is very light in weight, though when the containers are of plastic and therefore very light themselves a soil base is better in order to avoid their being blown about in gusty weather.

Soilless composts can prove expensive when the containers to be filled are large. A satisfactory medium can be made by mixing perlite into coarse peat or composted bark at the rate of one part by volume to ten and adding a general fertiliser at the rate of about 1 to 40, again by volume. To keep the plants in good health they should be fed during the summer either at the root or through the leaves, but to what degree depends upon their nature.

Whether or not drainage should be provided at the bottom of the pot is a point for some debate. A few crocks are useless. They quickly get clogged and become impotent. But you do need to stop the soil running through what will most likely be large drainage holes, which are, of course, essential, and a handful of fallen leaves over each will do very well for this.

On the other hand, if tender plants are being used – which, on the whole, prefer being kept on the dry side, particularly in winter – then these must certainly have drainage. In this case the container might be filled to about an eighth of its depth with broken crocks or pebbles and covered with leaves before any soil is added to prevent it from washing down and destroying the effectiveness of such a drainage layer.

PROTECTION   All timber containers have to be protected against rotting by treating them on the inside with a preservative of the type declared to be harmless to plants. Never use creosote or a proprietary substance that is not known to have this property. Terracotta pots, which are inclined to break or at least craze and flake in cold weather due to the action of frost when they are charged with moisture, can be protected against this by painting them with one of the silicon preparations sold by builders' merchants for treating brick walls. Alternatively they can be sealed by painting them with an adhesive like Unibond.

To give new concrete containers the patina of weathering quickly, paint them over with cow dung mixed into water. This will discolour them at once and encourage lichen to grow on them in very short time. Nothing can be done to affect the colour or texture of plastic, so it is best always to grow some trailing plants hanging over the rims of these even though the main plants in them may be evergreen shrubs.

SUITABLE CONTAINER PLANTS

EVERGREEN SHRUBS   The first choice among shrubs should always be for those that keep their leaves through the winter, whether their flowering is of any significance or not. Their enduringly lively appearance is all the greater if they have variegated markings on the foliage. This is especially important in closely confined gardens, where they seem to give an illusion of being struck by shafts of sunshine.

Some kinds are advisedly clipped formally, even making topiary specimens of them, to enhance the architectural effect, but others which have a naturally interesting silhouette are better left to reveal this in their own way, odd shoots being pruned away occasionally, and others pinched back at the tips, in order to preserve the scale.

Box and bay are pre-eminent among evergreens for clipping, both surviving for long periods in large pots or tubs without any watering. In heat they give off a scent redolent of sun-baked holiday places. Bay can prove frost-tender in some areas in the coldest winters, but the position where these plants are likely to be grown is also usually sheltered. In very cold periods the bushes will be safe dragged into a shed or garage.

Box has several variegated forms, while bay has a golden-leaved variety, *Laurus nobilis* 'Aurea'. Both grow more slowly than their parents. The many variegated forms of holly are readily clipped, and these again grow slowly enough for this to be necessary only once a year. Like box, it adapts well to being used for topiary. So does yew, which will also endure quite long periods of dryness without being harmed.

The Portugal laurel, *Prunus lusitanica*, will suffer clipping and this is a particularly valuable shrub for making small ball-headed standard trees, which resemble bay but are much cheaper. They resemble still more the citrus trees seen as pot plants in Italian gardens yet, unlike them, Portugal laurel is robustly hardy.

Due to the high polish on their foliage camellias are some of the finest shrubs which can be allowed to form their natural outline as tub plants, particularly the *C. japonica* varieties, among which the greatest variation exists and whose leaves are the most opulent. Among rhododendrons, similarly lime-hating, it is better to choose some of the compact growers with some distinction of foliage, like 'Bow Bells', *Rhododendron* × *cilpinense* and 'Bric-a-Brac' – all of which are early flowerers and suitable for enclosed areas – rather than the lush hardy hybrids. Both *Kalmia latifolia* and any of the forms of pieris, also lime haters, look well in tubs, the one because of the intricacy of its "wedding-cake decoration" flowers, the other for its bunches of tiny urn-shaped flowers.

For flowers in the late winter combined with a decorative outline, *Garrya elliptica*, which, in its male form produces long greenish catkins, and all the hybrid mahonias, like 'Charity', 'Underway' and 'Winter Sun', are satisfactory, particularly in places where they are shaded most of the day. The sarcococcas make neat small bushes with scented white flowers in winter. The skimmias will carry large scarlet berries all through the year if both a

120. *The tender mimosa,* Acacia dealbata, *which makes an attractive container plant.*

male and a female plant are put in the same pot together. The same conjunction can be employed to get a crop of turquoise berries on *Viburnum davidii* without the need for having male and female in different pots, the one lacking berries altogether. The Mexican orange, *Choisya ternata*, in spite of its name and its origin, is a particularly valuable pot shrub, often producing a crop of its perfumed white flowers in autumn as well as in late spring and having aromatic leaves that are always a bright apple green.

Supreme among the variegated evergreens which can be allowed to reveal their natural silhouette are the selected forms of spotted laurel, *Aucuba japonica*, in which the golden markings are markedly pronounced. They put up with spells of dryness as good-naturedly as do the variegated forms of elaeagnus which look well as container shrubs provided the tips of the shoots are pinched frequently to encourage a good overall shape.

Among tender evergreen shrubs suitable for the purpose but which have to be given some protection in a light place in winter, such as an unheated greenhouse, a garage or shed with windows or even a veranda where a sheet of close-mesh netting can enclose it during the worst weather, are the myrtles, which have scented white flowers in summer and aromatic leaves, and plants like mimosa, *Acacia dealbata*, with its fern-like leaves and yellow flowers. By growing mimosa in a container its chances of flowering are enhanced and its embarrassing size will be restricted.

Tender plants all need the ripening influence of summer sun, and this at once suggests the employment of the Australasian daisy bushes, species and varieties of *Olearia*, with white, blue or mauve flowers; the silver-leaved *Convolvulus cneorum*, which has the white flowers of the common weed but which are to be treasured in this role; *Daphne odora* 'Aureomarginata', with gold-margined leaves and white and pink flowers which some declare to be the most highly scented of all shrub flowers; all the cistus, but particularly those with large flowers like the white, maroon-centred *C. aguilari* 'Maculatus', *C.×cyprius* and the particularly tender *C. ladanifer*; pittosporums,

121. *The golden-leaved bay*, Laurus nobilis *'Aurea' (left) makes a handsome clipped specimen plant for growing in a container. Also shown is an ivy* (Hedera) *which has been allowed to scramble attractively over a framework of canes.*

122. *The spotted laurel*, Aucuba japonica *'Variegata', which makes an admirable tub plant able, if the need arises, to put up with a spell of dryness.*

123. *Impatiens in their various bright colours make showy container plants for summer display.*

especially those with interesting leaf markings like the *P. tenuifolium* 'Warnham Gold' and 'Garnettii', with both silver and pink on the foliage; and *Griselinia littoralis*, whose large leaves are perennially a refreshing light green and which has several golden-variegated forms of lively appearance.

With these must be grouped the variegated leaved New Zealand flax, or phormiums, which have crimson, pink, bronze and golden stripes on their leaves and which make dramatic incidents when ingeniously sited. Also the spiky yuccas, in particular those with bands of silver or gold on their foliage; though due to the sharp points which the leaves have these should not be used in areas where children are likely to play.

FLOWERING BULBS Following the premise that the most appropriate plants for growing in containers are those with a somewhat theatrical style, then the bulbs used should be those that would mostly be found grown in bowls in the house rather than in a wild garden. Thus the big Dutch crocuses would be more at home than the more retiring species; and bold trumpet daffodils or those with highly coloured cups and particularly the double daffodils rather than the kinds naturalised in grass. On the other hand, the bulbs must have stocky rather than willow stems, which makes the early tulips, especially the doubles, more suitable than, say, the parrots which are indeed sophisticated looking flowers to be admired individually at close quarters. Perhaps only in containers can the flamboyant, massive-flowered *Tulipa fosteriana* cultivars find a suitable setting.

Hyacinths are the finest of all spring bulbs for container growing. In the open ground, it is only when they are planted on a huge scale that they do not look out of place, but a few in a large pot – better still, a few in several large pots arranged on a terrace – particularly on a warm, late spring day, when the perfume is most strong, can make a dramatic impact.

Similarly, the summer lilies make excellent container plants, provided the stems can be unobtrusively staked with thick canes to prevent them from assuming the lolling or arching stance that would be appropriate to a wild garden. Both lilies and hyacinths, crocuses and daffodils can be left in their containers year after year, summer bedding plants being set among them for when their day is over. This means that the bulbs have to be put well down in the compost to avoid damaging them with the tip of the trowel when the bedding plants are inserted. This is an easy way of making the containers yield a two-season effect.

Indeed, if hardy fuchsias of the more showy, flamboyant type are used for making the summer effect, the containers could be planted up permanently with these and the bulbs, avoiding the need for any later spring changeover.

SUMMER BEDDERS Next in supremacy to fuchsias as summer bedders are the petunias, and here the best types are the handsome doubles which rarely have an appropriate place in the open garden. Similarly, the massive-flowered marigolds of what have been dubbed the Afro-French types, make stylish pot plants when otherwise they would bring a municipal look to a garden. Impatiens also make showy plants for containers.

In the main, though, the longest flowering summer bedders are perennials grown as one-season plants, notably gazanias, zonal and ivy-leaved pelargoniums, heliotrope, marguerites and the trailing *Helichrysum petiolatum*.

While the climbers which are raised afresh from seed every season and grown as annual plants – morning glory, canary creeper, eccremocarpus and thunbergia – will flourish as pot plants out of doors, the most desirable of climbers, roses and clematis, are not really adaptable. They need a large volume of soil – at least the equivalent of an old bushel apple crate.

However, all the ivy (*Hedera*) cultivars grown as house plants will do well in this role, particularly if they are allowed to scramble over four or five canes put round the rim of the container and tied together at the top to make a wigwam. Since they endure close spur pruning, even the honeysuckles can be made to serve as tub plants, while the rampant passion flower, *Passiflora caerulea*, is likely to remain biddable and flower well when

124. *Apple trees (and pears as well) can be both decorative and productive grown as container specimens.*

grown in this fashion. Although not a natural climber but a scrambler, the winter jasmine, *Jasminum nudiflorum*, can be used as a trailing plant in tall urns, the plants being kept in pots on a standing ground in the summer, pinched frequently and brought out for making their winter effect.

OTHER POSSIBILITIES Water plants need not be eschewed for some of the more adventurous gardeners have found that water lilies that will flourish in a foot of water will make good container plants. Even concrete or terracotta bowls can be used as a home for the cultivars of the tiny *Nymphaea tetragona*.

Nor need fruit trees be passed over. The fig has a long history of being grown as a pot plant out of doors, while both apple and pear trees, close spurred and trained as small pyramids, can be both fruitful and decorative as terrace plants in tubs or large pots, provided they are fed frequently during the growing season.

Thus the scope of container gardening widens and in turn widens the scope of small garden owners and lead them to grow plants which they might otherwise admire only in the larger gardens of others.

125. *Fuchsias and the trailing* Helichrysum petiolatum *are combined to achieve a planting which has much of the artistry of a flower arrangement.*

Part III

ENTHUSIASTS' PLANTS

19.

Roses

For sheer versatility there is no family of plants which can match the rose. What else is there that can be used in its multitudinous forms for bedding, for specimen planting, in a mixed shrubbery or to form a shrub planting on its own, for hedging, for edging, for growing in stone sinks and other containers or on rock gardens, for ground-cover, for covering walls, arches, pergolas and pillars or, at the extreme end of the upward scale, for scrambling to an altitude of 40ft(12m) or more into the branches of a tree to decorate it with great swags of scented bloom? In addition to this, roses can and should be in flower in every garden from May until October or November, in all colours of the spectrum, always excepting, despite the optimistic naming of some cultivars, that of blue. The flower size and form, and the habits of growth of the complete range, are seemingly almost limitless. A large number of both the old and the new kinds are perfumed, and a well-grown and well-tended rose bush should live at the very least for 20 years. Some will double or treble this.

In all, quite a catalogue of virtues, but what of the other side? In the nature of things there must be some faults, and indeed there are. However, if you make sure of seeing the roses you are considering buying growing in garden conditions, preferably over a whole summer, and then buy from a reliable supplier, you can eliminate a number of the faults before you even make out your order. You can, for instance, pick only those roses the flowers of which will stand up well to rain, which hold their shape and their colour well in strong sunlight, and which shed their petals cleanly as they age. You can pick those that are sturdy, bushy growers and which carry a profusion of bloom in the exact tones you want right through the season. You can pick those which seem least affected by the two most common and

126. *The striking cluster-flowered rose 'Priscilla Burton' which has carmine-red blooms with a silvery-white eye.*

Note: The new rose classification now coming into general use has been followed in this chapter. The idea behind it is to dispense where possible with botanical and semi-botanical terms such as floribunda, grandiflora and hybrid tea, and others such as hybrid musk, which are really meaningless (except through use) to the average gardener, and to substitute names based on the use of the roses in the garden or purely descriptive ones. Much does, in fact, remain the same.

Species roses now become wild roses, subdivided into climbing and non-climbing. Cultivars introduced before the first hybrid tea (the 1860s) are old garden roses, subdivided into climbing and non-climbing. Group names such as gallica, damask, bourbon, noisette, Ayrshire, etc, remain the same. Anything else is a modern garden rose, subdivided into climbing and non-climbing, and recurrent and non-recurrent types. Ramblers are still ramblers, and climbers still climbers, the main changes coming in the non-climbing modern garden roses. The hitherto rather vague term shrub rose now applies only in this modern group, and the other two main subdivisions are into bush roses and miniatures, the latter, and also polyanthas, remaining unchanged. Floribundas and grandifloras become cluster-flowered bush roses and hybrid teas are large-flowered bush roses. Like anything new, it will all take a little getting used to.

persistent rose ills, powdery mildew and black spot, and the fortunately less common rose rust. There are a number of varieties which are markedly healthier than others, but even with the rest, modern sprays will deal effectively with fungus diseases with the exception of black spot, which as yet can only be to some extent controlled. One spraying will nowadays eliminate over a long period the multitude of insects that nibble flowers and leaves, or suck sap so relentlessly if given half a chance.

That, then, is the balance between the good and the bad, with the scales dipping heavily towards the former. And as a number of generalizations and assertions have been made, now is the time to set out to prove them by more detailed comment.

ROSES FOR BEDDING This is an extremely effective use for roses, both colourful and permanent. Either large-flowered bush roses such as 'Silver Jubilee' and 'Just Joey' or cluster-flowered varieties like 'Priscilla Burton' and 'Iceberg' can be used, the latter type repeating much more quickly and best for a sheer mass of colour, rather than for quality in individual blooms. In either case, use those that make compact, bushy plants, not too tall, and space them so that the outer leaves of each just overlap. This means that little soil will show, allows for proper air circulation (important for health), and gives room for spraying and the application of mulches.

One cultivar can be grown in a bed or they can be mixed; if the latter is the choice, it is best to plant cultivars in groups of three or four of the same cultivar. Each cultivar will reach its peak of blooming at a slightly different time, and in this way there will always be substantial clumps of colour, rather than a rather spotty effect at certain times if the varieties are dotted about at random. Give considerable thought to the blending of colours, avoiding, for instance, putting a strong cerise next to a brilliant scarlet. White roses and those in the soft pastel shades can be used to separate those which otherwise might clash.

Generally speaking, the smaller the bed, the smaller the roses in it should be. A tiny bed with roses 3ft(1m) or more tall will look top-heavy, but there is an ever-increasing number of low-growing cluster-flowered bush roses on the market. In addition, many of the China roses will be found suitable as well. Cultivars like 'Hermosa' come into flower very early, bloom well into the autumn, and have an elegance of carriage many other roses lack. However, for a garden extensive enough to need "You Are Here" signs and where very large beds can be accommodated, the Pemberton group of shrub roses (hitherto hybrid musks) can be used. As most of them spread outwards far and wide, they make an economical planting, and they can be pruned quite hard if they intrude on surrounding paths.

Tall roses can have their place in a bedding scheme, at the back of a bed against a wall, or possibly for forming a clump at one end of it. A change in level – providing variety for the eye – is always important, and another way of achieving it is to plant standard roses at intervals of 5ft(1.5m) or so down the centre of a long rose bed, or one as a solitary specimen in the centre of a round one. Either that or a pillar rose, though the latter, having more than the standard's single stem, will need greater space allowed for it at ground level.

Blue violas and some other plants are frequently recommended for underplanting bedding roses. They can certainly look attractive and do provide early colour and one not found in the rose family, but as they make mulching, weeding, spraying and dead-heading much more difficult if the bed is of any width at all, they can be of more trouble than they are worth. An edging of the bed with something else is another matter, and without doubt the best of all for this is dwarf lavender, both its grey foliage and the flowers setting off the roses remarkably well.

ROSES WITH OTHER PLANTS The belief that roses should not be mixed with other plants dies hard. Probably it dates from Victorian times when flowers for cutting were confined to a special part of the garden and tucked well out of sight, but nevertheless it is undoubtedly true – though difficult to be precise about the reason – that large-flowered bush roses and most

127. 'Silver Jubilee', one of the finest and most significant large-flowered bush roses of recent introduction. The beautifully moulded pink flowers are suffused with peach and cream colouring.

cluster-flowered ones, do show to greater advantage in isolation. Their guardsman stance may have something to do with it, and, on the practical side, if they are growing in close association with other plants in a mixed border, their cultivation will be much more difficult. Sprays which the roses need may cause havoc elsewhere, for instance, but there are kinds of roses which need little if any protection from disease, that have a less formal habit of growth, will not get too large, and which will mix very happily in any border. Pre-eminent among these are the China roses, practically all of them recurrent, and the polyantha types like 'Yesterday', 'Cécile Brunner' and 'Perle d'Or', the soft colours of which will blend with practically anything. As was the case with bedding roses, a large and bushy old garden rose such as the soft pink damask 'Ispahan' at one end of a bed of other plants will look well and form a point of special interest.

Mixing shrub roses and old garden roses with other shrubs can, particularly in the case of the latter, be of distinct advantage to the roses. Some, like the enormously vigorous 'Complicata' or 'Scarlet Fire', welcome the support of an evergreen such as holly and will weave their way into its branches. Others like the large alba cultivars will stand on their own, and their attractive grey-green leaves will add distinction when the flowering of the other shrubs is over. However, many of the old garden roses do look rather untidy towards the end of the summer and not all their foliage ages well. Something else close by will help to divert the eye, though an exception must be made of those wild and old garden roses that bear orange or scarlet hips and which can light up a shrub border and give it a second life late in the year.

SHRUB AND OLD GARDEN ROSES ON THEIR OWN A planting such as this needs considerable care in its planning and patience over several years before its full glory will be achieved. Concentration on the less rampant growers like the gallicas and most of the damasks will allow for relatively close planting and there will be quicker maturity, but with the larger roses it is very difficult to picture in the mind the ultimate spread and, in fact, the sheer bulk (if one can use so inelegant a term for a rose) that will eventually be reached and to make adequate allowance for it. A wild rose such as *R. soulieana*, to take only one example, will build up year after year into a 7ft(2.25m) mound covering many feet of ground, but on the other hand *R. moyesii* and its variants may reach 8 to 10ft(2.5 to 3m) but will be comparatively open in growth, so that the sun can filter through it to other roses planted not too far away.

If you cannot bear the large spaces which are necessary between the young rose plants, these can be temporarily filled with spring bulbs, violas, herbaceous geraniums such as 'Johnson's Blue' and some of the less profligate campanulas, or else, for the longer term, with lilies or foxgloves. Pushing straight up through the canes of the roses when they are fully grown, their spikes and the formal flowers of the lilies (provided the hot orange colours are avoided) will complement the rather undisciplined rose growth very well.

Use lax, spreading roses like the gallicas 'Empress Josephine' or 'Cardinal de Richelieu' for foreground planting, where they will do a reasonable job of suppressing weeds. In general, build up height towards the back – or the centre if a bed is of the island type – though pockets of lower-growing cultivar which can form bays here or there in a big bed will make a change. So, too, will the mixing in of a bush or two of *Senecio* (Dunedin Hybrid) 'Sunshine' (which we knew in the past as *S. greyi*), rosemary, *Potentilla davurica* var. *veitchii* or *P.* × *vilmoriniana*, grey-green and silvery-foliaged respectively, to add contrast in colour and leaf form.

Bear in mind when deciding what to grow that there are some roses – many of the centifolias and the modern shrub 'Magenta' being examples – that not only benefit from but positively need support if their blooms are not to trail in the mud. A stake or two is generally sufficient for them and will be quite quickly hidden by the leaves. Some of the more exuberant bourbons may not actually need support, but their wandering canes can be disciplined by using 5 to 6ft(1.5 to 2m) tripods formed from rustic poles to tie them in to. As an alternative, both these and the often lanky hybrid perpetuals can be made to cover a lot of ground with the minimum of cost and maximum attraction by tipping the long canes in winter, arching them over, and tying the ends to pegs driven into the ground at suitable intervals. Flowering side shoots will break into life, forming a low carpet of bloom.

Finally, it should not be forgotten that gallicas, if on their own roots, spread freely by suckers. Albas do it more slowly, but the suckers of certain wild roses, of which *R. pimpinellifolia (R. spinosissima)* is a prime example, seem to move through the soil with the speed and facility of eels through water. A close watch must be kept or things may get out of control.

CLIMBING AND RAMBLING ROSES Climbers grown on pillars have already been touched on briefly (see p.177). In what other ways can they be used?

All climbers are suitable for walls, but a problem may be faced if there are only narrow spaces between tall windows in a house wall, as this makes the proper fanning out of the canes impossible. For such situations, pick one of the less vigorous semi-shrub cultivars such as 'Golden Showers', which will not go much over 8ft(2.5m) and flower quite low down, even without much training. Use a pillar rose, in fact, but never grow ramblers on walls or close-boarded fences, as the lack of proper air circulation will encourage their natural tendency to suffer from mildew.

Either climbers or ramblers are suitable for arches or pergolas. The lax canes of the ramblers (in contrast to the rather stiff ones of many climbers) make training and tying-in easier, but they will only flower once a year, albeit over many weeks, and pruning them properly will be a task not to be undertaken lightly if the structure is large.

An excellent and colourful hedge of a height greater than would be possible using old garden or shrub roses can be made by training climbers or ramblers on wires between strong wooden uprights, although there will almost inevitably be gaps which somehow never get filled. This sort of screen should, therefore, be avoided if complete privacy is needed.

The most exciting way of all of growing these roses is up trees. For this, the really important thing is to make a careful choice of cultivar according to the size and state of preservation of the tree or trees to be used. Many of the incredibly robust ramblers allied to the Far Eastern musk rose group, such as *R. filipes* 'Kiftsgate', will in time completely overwhelm a tree of moderate size or bring crashing to the ground a half-decayed one. To help in the provision of moisture for the roots, plant climbers or ramblers well away from the tree trunk on the windward side. Train on bamboo canes in towards the tree and the prevailing wind will give you a hand.

Many of the less vigorous climbers make excellent, informal, free-standing shrubs, most of the modern ones being fully recurrent. Remember that climbers, however they are used, tend to be slow starters, and they should be given their head without any attention from the secateurs for two or three years until they are well away. Ramblers on the other hand develop with considerable speed and can be dealt with accordingly.

ROSES FOR HEDGES Roses make just about the most colourful hedging plants there are. With many of the best of them, such as the Pemberton shrubs and the rugosas, allow for a width of 4 to 5ft(1.25 to 1.5m) and a height of 5 to 6ft(1.5 to 2m). Both can be controlled to some extent by light pruning, and the rugosas can be clipped over gently in winter to neaten them, though without distorting too much their natural shape. It is, in fact, possible to train the Pemberton roses on horizontal wires, but their canes do like going their own way, which is not always the way one expects, so they are best avoided alongside narrow paths. Rugosas give a very dense and practically disease-proof leaf coverage from very early in the year, and not even a cat will venture through their prickly stems. Almost continuously in flower, they provide, in the single and semi-double varieties, a fine display of huge scarlet hips with the later blooms, and in autumn the leaves turn yellow before they fall.

The two big white alba roses, *R.* 'Alba Maxima' and *R.* 'Alba Semiplena', are both upright and well branched enough to make substantial screens or boundary hedges, once-flowering only, of course, but with a dense covering of leaves afterwards of considerable attraction. The same cannot really be said for gallicas such as 'Rosa Mundi', often recommended for hedges. Spectacular in bloom, yes, and more than worth while in a large garden where their often disease-ridden foliage in late summer may not be so easily noticed. If space is limited, better by far for a low hedge or one of medium height, to pick one of the more bushy, cluster-flowering bush roses such as 'Chinatown', 'Red Gold', 'Iceberg', 'Pink Parfait' or 'Southampton', or else a large-flowered bush rose such as 'Alexander'. The immensely tall 'Queen Elizabeth' will be particularly economical of space, and the pruning of the canes of each bush to varying lengths will encourage flowering shoots low down and make this beautiful but sometimes rather awkward customer bush out reasonably well. Staggered planting will always give a more substantial hedge than a single line, but in general hedging roses may be planted more closely than usual as air circulation and access for cultivation will not be impeded by anything else. Roots can spread out sideways with little competition for food and water. Also, see the advantages of single-line planting detailed in Chapter 8 (pp. 93–94).

SPECIMEN PLANTINGS In a small garden, if a specimen rose is to be the focal point of the garden's only path or is to grace a pocket-handkerchief lawn, it should, naturally, produce the maximum number of flowers over as long a period as possible. A moderately vigorous and really recurrent pillar rose such as 'Aloha', 'Compassion' or 'Pink Perpètue' is one answer. Another is to use one of the taller cluster-flowering bush roses mentioned for hedging (see above) which, if lightly pruned, will reach 4 to 5ft(1.25 to 1.5m), or 'Fred Loads', which will give an extra 2ft(60cm) or so. A clump of three 'Queen Elizabeth' roses is effective, too.

If allowance can be made for a spread of at least 5 to 6ft(1.5 to 2m), a big shrub rose like 'Nevada' (or its pink sport 'Marguerite Hilling') will be truly breathtaking at the end of May and on through June, rather less so later. The great, globular, scented blooms of the bourbon 'Mme. Isaac Pereire' reverse this pattern, the second flowering being even more voluptuous than the first, while 'Golden Wings' really will keep going all the time. If you do not mind once-flowering beauty (combined with elegance of carriage), the great 8ft(2.5m) tall, arching, flower-laden branches of 'Frühlingsgold' in May, and those of many of the wild roses like 'Canary Bird' are hard to match.

Extend the bed of a rose grown in a lawn far enough to keep your mower more or less clear of the outer branches, particularly if there are thorny canes which will whip about in the wind. Mulch it well to keep down weeds.

The best weeping standards, which should be on 6ft(2m) stems, come from once-flowering ramblers as these alone have canes flexible enough to hang down to the ground all round as they should do. The best way to use these is for specimen planting.

PATIO ROSES Although their size or habit of growth makes some cultivars obvious discards, examples of practically all rose groups – even climbers – can be grown in wooden troughs, stone sinks, or tubs for the larger ones, which should allow for a root depth of not less than 18in(45cm) and have a diameter of 24in(60cm) or so. Stone sinks, usually quite shallow, are for the less vigorous polyantha types and for miniatures.

In all cases special attention must be given to providing a good planting mixture to start with, and then to subsequent watering and feeding, for the roots cannot spread beyond the confines of their containers. They must live on what is there or is added in the way of fertilisers, and any container, which should always be provided with good drainage holes, will quickly dry out if neglected – especially as they should always be placed where the sun can shine on the roses.

A patio surrounded by walls may tend to draw the roses upwards towards the light, so naturally short and bushy growers are to be preferred, though climbers can be used on the walls themselves. Avoid using ramblers because of likely mildew.

ROSES FOR GROUND-COVER Plants which suppress weeds are a boon. So, too, are those which will cover a difficult area such as a steep bank which otherwise might become a tangle of weeds or uncut grass. There are two groups of roses which will perform both these functions.

First, and really most effective as weed-smotherers, are the low-growing but wide-spreading types of which R. × *paulii* and its pink sport R. × *paulii* 'Rosea', and 'Raubritter' are examples. The first two will, after a few years, cover 15ft(4.5m) or so of ground in a dense mound of very thorny canes with rugosa-type leaves (they are rugosa hybrids) but will not exceed 4ft(1.25m) in height. 'Raubritter' will be rather smaller all round.

The second group of roses is largely based on the rambler R. *wichuraiana* which, if left to itself and not given artificial support, will send its long, lax shoots creeping over the ground, rooting where they touch it. They could thus, in theory, spread indefinitely, but can safely be cut back after flowering. Quite a lot of training will be needed if the canes are to achieve an even, dense coverage, and weeding between them, which can be painful, must continue until this has been achieved. Pink-flowered 'Max Graf', strangely enough also a rugosa hybrid (this time with R. *wichuraiana* itself) is the best-known of this kind.

For comparatively small areas there are other creeping roses such as 'Nozomi' and 'Snow Carpet', the latter an early example of a new race with clusters of small flowers which are recurrent. All the others mentioned only flower once, though they are of great beauty over many weeks. (See also Chapter 12, 'Ground-Cover Plants', p. 134.)

ROSES FOR EDGING Miniature roses can be used for edging a bed of other roses and have the advantage of being earlier into bloom than most bedding roses. However, the very small ones tend to be overwhelmed, and if they are on the north side of a bed may be almost permanently in shade. So, for maximum effect, choose cultivars like the cream 'Easter Morning' or the orange-vermilion 'Starina', which will reach 15in(38cm) or so in height and have large flowers for the type. Even with these, allow a strip of soil about 18in(45cm) wide for planting, particularly if the bedding roses are spreading or lax cultivars. Lavender and plants like anaphalis really do a better job.

Cultivation

Site Almost any position where the sun shines for most of the day will do. However, avoid overhanging trees, which will take nourishment from the roses and make them spindly. Roses can tolerate wind in moderation, but do not like draughty places such as may be found between two houses.

Soil Roses do best in a slightly acid loam (pH about 6.5) which is well-drained but retains some moisture. Really heavy clay soils will need double digging with humus-forming material being added to improve the structure and drainage. Only a few roses (in particular the hybrid perpetuals) will survive in chalk with a thin layer of soil over it. For other types of rose substantial planting holes must be dug in the chalk and refilled with soil containing plenty of peat to increase the acidity.

Planting Prepare the beds at least three months before planting to allow the soil to settle again. Dig in planty of organic matter. Well-rotted stable manure or compost is preferable. Both peat and leafmould can be used, but they will increase the acidity of an already acid soil. Plant firmly in holes about 18in by 18in(45 by 45cm) so that the roots can be well spread out with the budding union just below soil level. Allow 18 to 24in(45 to 60cm) as an average planting distance between cluster-flowered and large-flowered bush roses unless you know from observation that they require less or more because of size or habit. Firm the soil well and re-firm it after winter frosts.

To avoid soil dryness near walls, plant climbers about 18in(45cm) away from the base, fanning the roots of the plants outwards. Do not plant standards too deeply, especially those on rugosa stock, as this will encourage suckers.

Feeding   Mix a small handful per rose of bonemeal or a ready-prepared rose fertiliser into the soil when planting. Add a further small handful after pruning and again in late June each year. A later application would encourage soft autumn growth, which frost is likely to kill. Mulch rose beds with well-rotted manure or compost in April, when the soil has warmed up a little.

Training   Always fan out the canes of ramblers and climbers, tying them in as near to the horizontal as possible. This encourages flowering shoots low down. For pillars and tripods, weave the canes round in a spiral instead of taking them straight up, as this has the same effect.

Dead-heading   Carry this out regularly on all bush roses and other recurrent kinds to encourage a second flush of bloom. Do not simply pull the blooms off. Cutting above the third or fourth leaf down the stem will produce a really strong new flowering shoot. It is not necessary to dead-head non-recurrent roses, and foolish to do it with those from which a display of hips is expected.

Suckers   In leaf type, colour and thorn formation, suckers differ markedly from cultivated rose shoots. If in doubt, gently scrape the soil away to trace a suspected sucker's source. If this is below the budding union, pull the sucker away. Cutting it will only make for more vigorous growth.

Taking cuttings   Experience seems to show that the nearer a rose is to its wild ancestors the more ready cuttings from it are to take. Thus, the form most highly developed by man, the large-flowered bush rose, is the most difficult to root and ramblers perhaps the easiest, along with the species themselves. However, there will be few problems in rooting in the open 9in(23cm) cuttings taken in late August, September and October in the south of the country, or in the latter month under cover in the north. With many roses less vigorous plants may result, but with some, such as the miniatures, this is a distinct advantage as they will keep more in scale with their flower and leaf size.

Pruning   See Chapter 36 "Mastering the Craft of Pruning", pp.316 and 317.

COMMON INSECT PESTS   Control as suggested below:

Aphids (greenfly)   Tiny green or sometimes light brown insects clustering on buds, flower stalks, new shoots and leaves, sucking the sap and distorting growth. Spray, as directed, with derris, or a systemic insecticide such as malathion.

Caterpillars   The signs are holes eaten in leaves or smaller holes bored into flower buds. Pick off caterpillars by hand or, in a bad attack, use a trichlorphon or fenitrothion-based spray.

Froghoppers   Blobs of white foam (cuckoo spit) in leaf and shoot axils conceal these greenish-yellow, sap-sucking insects. Wash away this foam with a jet of water and use a dimethoate, formothion or menazon-based spray.

Leaf-rolling sawfly   Winged insects, rather like flying ants, which lay eggs in the leaf margins. At the same time a toxic injection causes the leaves to curl up longitudinally to protect the grub. Only preventive sprays in early May-June with a fenitrothion, pirimiphos-methyl or trichlorphon-based spray is effective, but if this is missed and only a few leaves are affected, they may be picked off and burned.

128. *'Ballerina', the recurrent flowering hybrid musk shrub rose with apple-blossom pink, white-eyed flowers. Introduced in 1937, it is now more popular than it has ever been. It is ideal for patio garden settings and will also make a low hedge.*

Thrips Nibbled flower buds, particularly in a hot summer, are a sign of these minute, brownish-yellow insects. Use a dimethoate, formothion, fenitrothion or gamma HCH spray.

Chafers Nibbled petals and anthers indicate attack by these large brown flying beetles. Use a trichlorphon or fenitrothion spray.

COMMON ROSE DISEASES   Control as suggested below:

Black spot Round black spots with fringed edges, usually first seen from July onwards on the lower leaves, spreading rapidly upwards and to other roses by air-borne spores. The spots grow in size and the leaves gradually yellow and drop off, so that the plant may be defoliated and seriously weakened. Incidence of black spot varies from place to place, but in a bad area preventive spraying every 10 days may be needed. Otherwise, spray as soon as spots are seen, removing and burning leaves already infected. A benomyl, triforine, thiophanate-methyl, or best of all a bupirimate-triforine-based spray will give some control. Remove dead leaves from beds in autumn and give the bushes one or two winter sprays with Jeyes fluid or Bordeaux mixture, applying according to the manufacturer's recommendations.

Powdery mildew First seen as grey, powdery-looking spots on leaves and flower stalks, but spreading rapidly over the whole plant and to others by wind-blown spores. It is very unsightly and will stunt and distort growth. Spraying straight away with any of the sprays mentioned under black spot will give good control.

Rose rust Fortunately not prevalent everywhere or on all kinds of rose, but it can be a serious menace where it does occur. Small, orange pustules under the leaves are the first sign. Plantvax 75, with an oxycarboxion base, gives complete control, but at present is only available in quantities more suitable for the commercial grower.

RECOMMENDED ROSES FOR DIFFERENT PURPOSES

For bedding Any of the cluster-flowered and large-flowered bush roses. 'Hermosa' and other China roses. 'Cécile Brunner', 'Perle d'Or' (tea-polyanthas), 'Ballerina', 'Marjory Fair'. *For small beds*: 'Stargazer', 'Topsi', 'Tip Top', 'Esther's Baby'.

For specimen planting Tall-growing cluster-flowered roses. On a larger scale, 'Frühlingsgold', 'Frühlingsmorgen', 'Nevada', 'Marguerite Hilling', 'Canary Bird', 'Golden Wings', *R. moyesii* and most other wild roses. Also the larger old garden roses like *R.* 'Alba Maxima' and the damask 'Mme. Hardy'.

Shrubbery background roses The larger albas, 'Complicata' (will scramble into others), *R. rubrifolia* and most other species, 'Roseraie de l'Hay', 'Pink Grootendorst', 'Nevada', 'Nymphenburg'.

Shrubbery foreground roses 'Natalie Nypels', 'Empress Josephine' and other gallicas; 'St Nicholas' and most other damasks; 'Fru Dagmar Hastrup', 'Ballerina', China roses; 'Königin von Danemarck' and 'Felicité Parmentier'; among the albas; the centifolia 'Chapeau de Napoléon'; the shrub roses 'Lavender Lassie' and 'Angelina'.

Tall hedges 'Roseraie de l'Hay', 'Scabrosa', 'Blanc Double de Coubert' and other rugosa hybrids, 'Penelope', 'Vanity', 'Buff Beauty' and other Pemberton shrub roses, *R.* 'Alba Maxima', 'Queen Elizabeth'.

Medium hedges 'Iceberg', 'Pink Parfait', 'Southampton', 'Alexander', 'Eye Paint', and 'Angelina', 'Ispahan' (damask).

129. *The centifolia rose 'Chapeau de Napoléon' which has beautifully moulded pink blooms and makes an excellent foreground rose in a mixed planting of shrubs.*

130. 'Fru Dagmar
Hastrup', rose-pink and
some 4ft (1.5m) tall, is a
rugosa rose of real
attraction. The crinkly
foliage is of dark green
colouring (see p.183)

Low hedges 'Ballerina', 'The Fairy', 'Danaë', 'Mutabilis', 'Rosa Mundi' and
'Officinalis' (gallicas, so remember possible mildew), 'Yesterday'.

Sinks and troughs Miniature roses, 'The Fairy', 'Yesterday', and low-
growing cluster-flowering bush roses.

Ground-cover 'Max Graf' and other rambler hybrids like 'Temple Bells',
R. × paulii and *R. × paulii* 'Rosea', 'Raubritter', 'Snow Carpet'.

Pillar roses 'Golden Showers', 'Pink Perpêtue', 'Royal Gold', 'Joseph's
Coat', 'Morning Jewel', 'Aloha', 'Dortmund' and the more vigorous old
roses like 'Mme Isaac Pereire' (Bourbon) and 'William Lobb' (moss rose).

More vigorous climbers and ramblers 'Handel', 'Danse du Feu', 'Maigold',
'Parkdirektor Riggers', 'Altissimo', 'Galway Bay', 'Swan Lake', 'Mermaid',
'Gloire de Dijon', 'Mme Grégoire Staechelin', 'Albéric Barbier', 'Albertine'.

Tree climbers *R. longicuspis*, 'Wedding Day', 'Seagull', 'Silver Moon', 'The
Garland', *R. filipes* 'Kiftsgate'.

SPECIALIST SOCIETY: The Royal National Rose Society.

17.   *Water, and especially running water, adds a new dimension to any garden. The beauty of this streamside planting in the garden at Froyle Mill, Bentley, Hampshire stems directly from its simplicity – the restrained and artistic use of* Mimulus *'Whitecroft Scarlet' and colour variants of* Viola tricolor.

18. *The polyantha-type rose 'The Fairy' gives this pool-side scene at The Royal National Rose Society's gardens at St. Albans, Hertfordshire a special quality of lightness and grace.*

19. Nymphaea *'Marliacea Chromatella', a beautiful water lily which is "tough, robust, reliable and free-flowering" (see p.165).*

20. Fuchsia *'Lady Thumb'*, a cultivar suitable for permanent planting in the garden (see p.188).

20.

Fuchsias

Fuchsias are natives of Peru, Venezuela, Bolivia, Brazil, Columbia, Mexico, Chile and the Falkland Islands as well as Tahiti and New Zealand on the other side of the Pacific. Those in cultivation and their derivatives are easy to grow in pots or in the open, flowering continuously for long periods with a modest amount of attention. The colours range from pure white to extremes of violet in the most vivid tones; creams, pinks of every hue and shade, from a barely perceptible tinge of deep rose and coral; reds, through scarlet to richest carmines; crimsons of great intensity; delicate orange shades to deep turkey red, underlaid with orange; and, in many newly opened flowers, mauves, lavender, the richest of purples, and even green. The flowers include single, semi-double, double and petaloid forms while in the species *Fuchsia triphylla* the long-tubed, orange-red flowers are borne in terminal racemes, as they are also, for example, in the hybrid 'Thalia' (see Fig.133 overleaf).

In habit they vary greatly, and they can be trained to grow to almost any shape. As they do not flower very profusely during the short days of winter, most gardeners allow them to be dormant then. With the most modest equipment fuchsias will flower under glass for four to eight months continuously, and outdoors for four to five months.

Suitable composts The most commonly available loam-based composts are those made up to the John Innes Institute formulae, known as John Innes (or J.I.) No. 1, No. 2 and No. 3. The alternative is to use a loamless compost with a peat base (see Chapter 32, Potting Composts, pp. 286 to 289). Fuchsias will grow as well in these as in loam-based composts, but two important factors must be taken into account. First, nutrition. Loamless composts generally have a lower nutrient content than loam-based ones, particularly in respect of minor elements. The supply of nitrogen needs to be watched and it is necessary to start feeding earlier than with loam-based composts to ensure that vegetative growth (for which nitrogen is needed) does not slow down. Secondly, the watering technique. It is very important that peat-based composts should never be allowed to dry out because of the difficulty of re-wetting them properly. Overwatering is just as bad because the composts become compacted and sodden, and without oxygen the roots soon rot.

Rooting cuttings Cuttings need to be inserted in an open-textured medium to encourage root growth. A good mixture consists of 1 part sphagnum peat and 1 part sharp silver sand; little or no extra nutrients are needed at this stage. Cuttings may be taken at any time but, for preference, do this in June, July or August, depending on the temperature which can be maintained during the winter. If the minimum winter temperatures maintained are 45°F to 47°F(7.5°C to 8.5°C) take the cuttings in June or early July; if 47°F to 50°F(8.5°C to 10°C) then take the cuttings in July or August. Select young growing shoots about 3in(8cm) long, with two or three pairs of leaves. Cut the shoots just below the point where the lowest pair of leaves joins the stem, and then remove this pair of leaves. Insert the prepared cuttings in 3in(8cm) pots, four to a pot in the rooting mixture. Place the cuttings in a closed propagating case in the greenhouse and water and shade as

131. *Potting a young plant. The technique varies depending on whether clay or plastic pots are used, as explained in the text, above right.*

required. (A propagating case can be made from a fairly deep, open-topped wooden box over which can be placed a sheet of glass or plastic film.) The cuttings will root in two to three weeks. Gradually ventilate the propagating case to harden-off the rooted cuttings. Aim to make the final potting at the end of January or early February. The plants will then flower from May to September under glass.

The next stage is to pot on the rooted cuttings into 3in(8cm) pots. If using a loam-based compost and clay pots, place a few pieces of crock (broken pot) over the drainage hole (see Fig.131), then a little coarse peat over these; fill the pot about half-full with compost and firm slightly. Sit the base of the rooted cutting on the compost and fill with more compost, firming down lightly but leaving ½ to ¾in(1 to 2cm) space between the compost surface and the rim of the pot for watering.

The same technique is used with loamless compost, except that the bottom layer of coarse peat is not necessary, nor, as plastic pots generally have several drainage holes, do they need to be crocked. The chief advantage of using clay pots is that they absorb moisture and so the chance of damaging the plant by overwatering is less.

The next stage is to transfer the plants to pots of 5in(13cm) size, using the same John Innes No. 1 potting compost or loamless compost used previously. Grow on the plants until they have made plenty of fresh roots and then transfer them to their final pots of 7 or 8in(18 or 20cm). Use John Innes No. 3 potting compost for this potting and leave 1½in(4cm) of space between the surface of the compost and the rim for watering purposes.

Watering   How often should fuchsias be watered? That is one of the most difficult questions to answer. There is no short answer; it all depends on the prevailing weather conditions, and whether the plants are being grown in plastic or clay pots. When plants are in active growth they should be checked at least once, and preferably twice, a day if the weather is hot and sunny. When water is given, fill the pot to the rim, and if it does not soak through the pot pour off the surplus, knock out the soil ball and check to see if a worm could possibly have clogged the drainage hole. If a worm is present a tap on one side of the root ball will probably make it emerge.

Feeding   The primary need of the fuchsia is for a feed containing the three main nutrients, nitrogen, phosphorus and potassium (for shoot growth, root growth and flowering respectively) in balanced proportions. These are incorporated in the compost before potting but they are gradually used up and regular feeding is needed. Plants in loamless composts are likely to need feeding while they are still in small pots. Those grown in loam-based compost will not usually need feeding until they are in flower in their final pots. Feed with diluted liquid fertiliser at the rate recommended by the manufacturer; once a week when growing plants in loamless composts, once a fortnight in the case of loam-based mixtures.

Training

Bush Specimens   When the plants are growing away well in 3in(8cm) pots, remove the tips of the shoots at three sets of leaves and allow side shoots to produce two or three sets of leaves before removing their tips. The procedure – known as stopping – is carried out as many times as the size of plant demands. The plants will flower about seven weeks after the final stopping. Always stake and tie all plants securely.

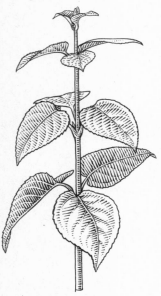

132. *When selecting fuchsia plants to grow as standards, look for those with three leaves at a joint instead of the more usual two.*

Hanging baskets   Choose a cultivar with a cascading habit of growth, i.e. 'Trail Blazer', 'Eden Beauty', 'Cascade', 'President Margaret Slater'. The training is the same as for bush specimens except that after planting in the basket allow all growths to produce six or seven sets of leaves before stopping. The growths will then cover the sides of the basket, and the resulting side shoots may be stopped at two sets of leaves before flowering.

Standard specimens   When selecting plants to be grown as standards, it is worth looking for those plants which have three leaves at a joint instead of the more usual two (see Fig.132). This characteristic is sometimes varietal in origin and sometimes a result of climatic conditions. In a group of 20 cultivars it would be reasonable to hope to find three or four plants with this characteristic. With such a plant three shoots will break after each stopping instead of two, so making a bushier head. When calculating the total height of a mature standard specimen remember that the head, when complete, will add 1 to 2ft(30 to 60cm) to the stem from the position of the first stopping. Remove all side shoots while the stem is still growing, except for the last three or four sets of leaves. Do not remove leaves when taking away side shoots because these help the development of the plant by drawing up nutrients from the pot.

All growths which result from the final stopping of the stem should then be treated as in bush-specimen pruning to form the head. Cultivars for growing in this way include: 'Avocet', 'Mission Bells', 'Sleigh Bells', 'Snowcap', 'Party Frock' and 'Olive Jackson'.

Pyramid specimens   An upright, single-stem plant is selected and grown to a height of 2½ft(75cm). Remove the tip and allow side-shoots to develop. These are stopped at two or three sets·of leaves, but allow the topmost shoot to continue to grow upwards for a further 12 to 15in(30 to 38cm). Stop again, allowing more side-shoots to grow. This process is repeated until the required height is reached. It will often take two years to produce a well-shaped plant. Suitable cultivars for this form of training are: 'Moles-worth', 'Television', 'Rose of Castile' and 'Southgate'.

Fan specimens   Select a strong-growing cultivar such as 'Jack Acland' or 'Swingtime'. Allow the plant to produce four or five sets of leaves before making the first stopping. When the side shoots have made good growth train to the fan shape. Stop these shoots when they have produced six or seven sets of leaves. Any resulting side shoots are stopped at two or three sets of leaves except for the topmost one which is grown on to a further six sets of leaves. This procedure may continue until the required size is reached.

Over-wintering plants   Plants may be stored in a frost-free shed during the winter. Make sure the growth is well ripened before storing. To induce this, gradually reduce the amount of water given from late September onwards until growth stops. At the same time place the plants outside in the sun during the day to help harden the bark on the shoots. Inspect the plants regularly because if the conditions become too warm they will start into growth. If this happens move them to cooler conditions.

Early in spring prune the plants back to one or two buds per shoot. Remove all weak and crossing shoots so that plant has a reasonably open habit. Remove the plant from the pot and take away as much of the old soil as possible. Then re-pot the plant in John Innes No. 1 potting compost using

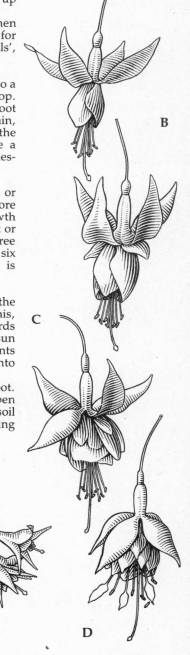

133. *Flower shapes in fuchsias;* **A**, *single;* **B**, *semi-double;* **C**, *double;* **D**, *petaloid; and with the flowers borne in terminal racemes as in* Fuchsia *'Thalia'* **E**.

a pot just large enough to accommodate the root ball. Place the plant in a greenhouse or other warm place and syringe it once or twice each day. The plant should not be watered until it starts into growth for it is easy to kill fuchsias by overwatering. Once growth starts, water sparingly until the shoots are growing vigorously. Then the shoots can be stopped to increase the size of the plant's head. When the pots are full of roots re-pot into 7 or 8in(18 or 20cm) pots using John Innes No. 3 potting compost.

GROWING FUCHSIAS OUTDOORS There are several hardy fuchsias such as *F. magellanica*, its cultivars 'Riccartonii', 'Gracilis Variegata' and others which will survive our winters outdoors.

There is increasing interest in growing fuchsias outdoors and many of the indoor cultivars are quite happy outside if one or two basic rules are observed. First, when planting from pots make sure that the lower part of the stem (at least 4in[10cm]) is buried below ground level. This ensures that several growth buds are protected from frosts during the winter. These buds then produce flowering shoots the following summer. Some protection should be given with bracken, straw or the like. Secondly, do not cut down the stems until spring for if this is done earlier water from winter rains may collect on the cut surfaces and cause rotting which, in turn, helps frost to penetrate the base of the plant. A few cultivars suitable for such cultivation are: 'Brilliant', 'Dr. Foster', 'Lena', 'Mrs. Popple', 'Sealand Prince', 'Lady Thumb', 'Madame Cornelissen', 'Trase' and 'Thompsonii'.

PEST AND DISEASE CONTROL The key to the successful control of pests and diseases is to keep a close watch and, at the first indication of trouble, spray or fumigate to eliminate before they become established. Pests which may be a trouble are aphids, whitefly, red spider mite, capsid bugs and caterpillars, and the diseases rust, grey mould and black root rot.

SPECIALIST SOCIETY: The British Fuchsia Society.

21.

Dahlias

Although dahlias will grow and flower to a reasonable standard in any soil and in any position, to obtain good results, the careful preparation of the soil must be considered the most important aspect of the cultivation of these beautiful plants.

Each type of soil requires a different approach. Always, however, the beds should be bastard trenched or double dug in the first season. Manure, compost, or other humus-forming materials such as peat should be worked into the top spit, at the rate of 1cuft to each 5 square yards (.0283m^3 to each 4.18m^2) of soil. The dahlia will only thrive on well-drained soil, and it relies on humus being present as a store for moisture. Heavy soils need to be prepared in the autumn to get the full benefit of the frost; lighter soils, on the other hand, are best dug after the turn of the year. Lighter soils are generally acid and require a dressing of hydrated lime at about 4oz per square yard (110g per m^2), which should be applied some six weeks after digging, and the addition of manure, otherwise ammonia is liberated and much nitrogen lost.

Propagation

Advice on the propagation of dahlias differs from expert to expert, but all would agree that the earliest blooms are obtained from old tubers (these generally flower in August).

Where tubers have been stored from the previous season, propagation can be effected by cuttings, division or, alternatively, by planting the old tubers directly into the flowering positions. If cuttings are required, the tubers should be taken from the store in January or February, and brought into a heated greenhouse to start into growth. All signs of damage, rot and so on must be removed, and the cut surfaces dusted with dry Bordeaux powder or flowers of sulphur, to prevent bleeding and any further spread of disease.

Starting tubers into growth Tubers may be started into growth in beds of prepared soil on a greenhouse bench, or in boxes which should not be less than 4in(10cm) deep. The compost used will depend upon the length of time that the tubers are to be plunged, and how many cuttings from each tuber are required. If the propagation period is a lengthy one, the compost needs to be rich in plant foods, as in the case of the John Innes No. 1 potting compost. If only a few cuttings are required, and the propagation time therefore reduced, a mixture of equal parts sharp sand and finely granulated peat will suffice.

Place a layer of moist peat in the bottom of the box or bench, and cover with 2in(5cm) of compost. Place the tubers close together on the peat and press lightly. Cover the tubers with compost, leaving the crowns or collars exposed. It is from this area that new growth will arise, not from the tuber as is often thought, because, like the potato, the dahlia is a stem tuber. Watering must be carried out with great care, so as not to wet and fill the crowns with standing water, as collar rot may develop and prevent the formation of growths from which cuttings can be made. A daily syringe with tepid water is advantageous; and bottom heat of 60 to 65°F(16 to

18.5°C) should be maintained, with an air temperature of not less than 48°F(9°C). At this stage, aphids and slugs should be controlled, particularly the former, which are vectors of virus diseases, to which dahlias are prone.

Taking and rooting cuttings Material from which cuttings can be made will appear in 14 to 21 days depending on cultivar, and should be removed when about 3in(8cm) in length. They may be struck in John Innes No. 1 potting compost or a sand and peat mixture. Remove the cuttings from close to the tuber with a razor blade or thin-bladed knife. Trim to the required length by cutting just below the leaf joint. Should cuttings be found to be hollow, reject them as they will be almost impossible to root. To stimulate and increase the production of roots, a proprietary hormone rooting powder preparation for softwood cuttings may be used. With a small dibber, make a hole 1in(2.5cm) deep in the box or pot. Insert the cuttings 1in(2.5cm) apart in the box, or four around the outside of a 3½in(9cm) pot. Press firm and label immediately.

Water in with tepid water using a sprayer or watering-can with a fine rose attached. Place in the warmest part of the greenhouse, with bottom heat, if possible, out of draughts and shaded from direct sunlight. Rooting will take place in two to three weeks. Avoid propagating cases as they tend to encourage damping off.

Division Division is the most simple method of propagation, the tubers being started into growth in March on a bench or in boxes just as when increase is by means of cuttings. However, in this case, less heat is required and a temperature of 45°F(7.5°C) is adequate. By the middle to the end of April sprouting will have started and the tubers ready for dividing. Take a sharp knife and cut the clump of tubers into as many pieces as possible, each piece consisting of a tuber and portion of old stem with new shoot attached. Tubers without a portion of the old stem and new shoots attached will not produce new growth, because bud initials will be absent.

Growing on Once rooted, cuttings take on a different appearance. The tip starts to lengthen and the leaves enlarge. Remove the cuttings carefully from the compost and pot into 3½in(9cm) pots using John Innes No. 1 potting compost; label, and water to settle the soil around the roots. After potting, return the pots to the greenhouse bench, preferably with bottom heat, for a few days, and spray with tepid water at least once a day. Move into cold frames about mid-April in the south of the country, two weeks later in the north. Set the plants 6in(15cm) apart with each plant having a supporting cane. Keep the frame closed for 10 days or so, then allow a little air in during good weather; gradually increase the ventilation until the frame light can be dispensed with altogether.

Planting and Aftercare

Conditions are usually suitable for setting the plants out in their flowering positions by the end of May in the south, and 10 days later in the north. A week or so before planting the beds should finally be broken down and a general fertiliser, such as Growmore, raked into the top few inches of the soil at the rate of 4oz(110g) per square yard (m²). Planting distances depend, of course, on the type and ultimate height of the dahlia to be planted; supporting stakes should be driven into the ground at the chosen planting positions. Allow a spacing of 3ft(1m) for Large Decorative and Cactus cultivars; 2½ft(75cm) for smaller cultivars; and 18in(45cm) for bedding dahlias. Check each plant and discard any that are stunted or show any signs of disease. When the plants are fully turgid (having been well-watered some hours previously), make a hole with a spade or trowel large enough to take the entire root ball. Gently tap the plant from the pot and place it carefully in the hole against the stake. Firm well, leaving a shallow depression around each plant to act as a reservoir for water, and tie a name label to the stake. Tie the plant in with soft twine to the main stake, leaving enough room for the stem to expand.

Stopping To obtain a bushy plant the growing tip must be removed. This is best done a few days before planting, or 10 days after this takes place, by pinching out the growing tip when the plant has formed four good pairs of leaves. This will ensure that under good growing conditions each plant will produce up to eight flowering branches.

General cultivation Extra supports will be needed by the end of July. Provided that a stout stake was used at the time of planting, bamboo canes pushed into the soil around the plants will suffice. They are best placed at an angle, sloping outwards, and using four canes to form a square. Space them about 20in(50cm) apart at the top. Loop a strong, soft twine at 12in(30cm) intervals up the canes as the plants increase in height, so confining the growths within the area of the canes and ties. The roots of dahlias tend to be close to the surface, so it is important to avoid unnecessary treading on the growing area or hoeing too close to the plants. Further applications of nitrogenous fertilisers should be avoided, as with most cultivars this tends to promote excessive leaf growth which hides the blooms. However, a dressing of sulphate of potash applied at the rate of 1oz(25g) per square yard(m^2) would, perhaps, be an advantage on most soils.

Regular spraying against insect pests needs to be carried out in an endeavour to keep the plants clean, bearing in mind that aphids can carry virus from one plant to another with disastrous results. Keep a watch for slugs and treat as necessary, especially just after planting. The growing areas benefit from mulching at the beginning of August to conserve moisture and smother weeds. This also makes it easier to walk around the plants without damaging the plant roots. Materials such as peat litter, spent mushroom compost, and straw are suitable, and can, with benefit, be worked into the soil after the tubers have been lifted at the end of the season.

Disbudding and thinning For garden or house decoration, disbudding and thinning need not be too drastic. The removal of thin or weak growth will divert the sap flow to the remaining, more robust laterals. At the end of each lateral growth three buds will form, the central bud being larger than the two side buds. Remove the latter, leaving the central bud to develop and flower. Remove also the side shoots which form in the leaf axils, to allow for a sufficient length of stem when growing for cut flowers. This will also encourage the production of stronger breaks lower down the plant.

Lifting and storing During the growing season, make notes on the cultivars you are growing so that you can later form an opinion on which to keep for the following season. Before lifting, make sure that labels marked with the name of each plant are securely fastened to the main stem with wire. Dahlia tubers take up a lot of storage space, so do not increase the problem by retaining inferior material, or too many examples of a single cultivar.

Tubers usually form when the days shorten, around the end of September, and the plants should be left in the ground as long as possible, weather permitting, and providing that soil conditions allow. Frost generally terminates the flowering season and blackens the top of the plants. Before lifting the tubers, remove canes and stakes and store them away. Next, use secateurs to cut the stems of the plants to within about 6in(15cm) of the ground. If possible, leave the plants in the ground for a few more days to allow the tubers to mature. Then lift them with a garden fork on light soils or a spade on heavier soils (the tubers are likely to be larger on soils of this type). Shake as much soil as possible from the tubers, removing that which remains with a blunt-pointed stick. Do not wash it off with water as this tends to encourge moulds. Reduce the stems to 1in(2.5cm) above the collar, and dust with flowers of sulphur to discourage store mould. Store in boxes in a frost-free but cool, airy place – a garage, shed or spare room. Alternatively, clamp as for potatoes, by placing a layer of clean straw on a well-drained part of the garden. Cover this with a layer of tubers laid close together; cover with another layer of straw and, with more tubers on top to

A

B

C

D

E

F

form a pyramid; finish with a 6in(15cm) covering of straw, followed by a good layer of soil to keep out frost and heavy rain.

Exhibiting This can be fun, but it is demanding of time and considerable skill is required. The art of exhibiting lies in the timing; getting blooms into tip-top form on the day of the show. There are so many imponderables, such as the vigour of the particular cultivar, and, of course, the weather, that it is difficult to advise. Plants from old tubers will, without doubt, flower earlier than those from cuttings as pointed out earlier, and the time of stopping will largely determine the flowering time. In the main, the Large Decorative and Cactus groups are the most difficult to time; and the novice exhibitor would be well advised to leave these groups alone until experience has been gained with other groups. The general principle is to select a number of growths, and disbud to leave one bloom to mature. The time taken to achieve this varies with the group, and the cultivar within the group.

It is, therefore, wise to concentrate on one group, growing large numbers of each cultivar and stopping them at different times. This results in having blooms in show perfection over a longer period of time, so as to have some in just the right condition on the day of the show.

It may be necessary to shade some cultivars to avoid fading. Purples, pinks and lavenders are vulnerable; and shading may be done with polythene tents. Cutting for show is important. First, decide on the classes that you are going to enter, and read the show schedule to find the number of blooms required. Select blooms which are of the same size and colour tone, so far as this is possible. Cut early in the evening and place the stems immediately in deep water to avoid air locks forming in the stem cells. Stand in a cool shed for several hours.

Transporting blooms to shows is not without its problems. Whether they are stood in water or packed in boxes, the ultimate aim is to arrive with undamaged material, and so blooms must be packed in such a way that they do not rub together on the journey. It is very necessary to obtain a copy of "The Classified Directory and Judging Rules", published by the National Dahlia Society, before exhibiting. This is free to all members, and available for a small charge to non-members. A copy can usually be borrowed from the show secretary. In it will be found details of the best cultivars in commerce, and their groups, rules for judging, ideals, faults and many other useful tips for the new exhibitor. Arrive at the show with plenty of time to stage your exhibit. Unpack your blooms immediately, and place them in deep water, first cutting an inch(2.5cm) off the stems while these are held in water to avoid an air lock. Always take along a few spare blooms – accidents can, and often do, happen.

Staging the blooms in vases is quite an art in itself, and needs to be practised at home before the show. Check that you have the correct number of blooms, top up the vase with water and take it to the area allotted for that particular class; then forget about it until the final check-up, which should include: making out the class card; re-checking on bloom numbers and the water; re-checking that you have put your exhibit in the correct class; and, finally, making sure that you have labelled your exhibit. Above all, when judging is over, try to be satisfied with the results, even if you have lost, when you perhaps thought you should have won. Judges are experienced people and have far greater knowledge. Their job is to judge what they see before them at the time; whereas you may be assessing the competition some hours later. After all, in a marquee or small village hall on a hot summer's day, there can be a considerable change in the condition of the blooms in quite a short space of time.

Dahlia classification

"The Classified Directory and Judging Rules", published by the National Dahlia Society, should be consulted if you wish to know which group a particular cultivar belongs to. There are 10 groups in all, and some of these are further divided into sub-sections, the cultivars contained therein depending on the size of the flowers of the cultivar in question. Many dahlia cultivars are superseded by others at quite short intervals. Those listed below are excellent examples of their groups and some have been with us for many years. The newer ones, too, can be expected to be available from specialist nurseries for some years to come.

Group I Single-flowered cultivars, e.g. 'Coltness Gem', 'Princess Marie José' and 'Yellow Hammer'.

Group II Anemone-flowered. These have more than one outer ray of florets surrounding a dense group of tubular florets which resemble a pincushion, e.g. 'Comet' and 'Bridesmaid'.

Group III Collerette. Blooms similar to Group I, with the addition of a ray of florets – the collar, e.g. 'Clair de Lune', 'Grand Duc' and 'Ruwensori'.

Group IV Peony-flowered. There is a limited number of cultivars in this group, which is best represented by 'Bishop of Llandaff' and 'Fascination'.

Group V Decorative. Possibly the largest group. Fully double flowers showing no disc, with the ray florets broad and bluntly pointed. Sub-divided five times to accommodate various maximum flower sizes from over 10in(25cm) diameter, to not exceeding 4in(10cm), e.g. 'David Howard', 'Gay Princess' and 'Hamari Girl'.

Group VI Ball. Fully double blooms which are ball-shaped or slightly flattened. Florets blunt tipped and spirally arranged, e.g. 'Vaguely Noble', 'Worton Joy' and 'Betty Armstrong'.

Group VII Pompon. Blooms similar to Group VI, but more globular, and of miniature size, not exceeding 2in(5cm), e.g. 'Don's Diana', 'Willo's Violet' and 'Little Con'.

Group VIII Cactus. The second largest group, sub-divided five times, dependent on the size of the bloom, e.g. 'Perran Moonlight', 'Doris Day' and 'White Rays'.

Group IX Semi-Cactus. Fully double florets, generally narrower than in Group V, but broader than those in Group VIII, e.g. 'Quel Diable', 'Highgate Torch' and 'Symbol'.

Group X Miscellaneous. This group covers any type which does not fall into one of the foregoing groups, such as the Water-Lily or the Orchid-flowering types, which are very popular with flower arrangers, e.g. 'Giraffe', 'Jescott's Julie' and 'White Orchid'.

The Wisley trials For those who can travel to Wisley Garden conveniently in late summer and early autumn the trials of dahlias are, like the shows of the National Dahlia Society, an education for any gardener keenly interested in this flower. These trials are conducted by the Royal Horticultural Society and judged by a joint committee of the National Dahlia Society and the R.H.S. Most of the cultivars on trial will already have been named (rather than still under number) so very useful notes can be made for the future.

SPECIALIST SOCIETY: The National Dahlia Society.

134. *The different groups of dahlia:* **A**, *Single-flowered (Group I);* **B**, *Anemone-flowered (Group II);* **C**, *Collerette (Group III);* **D**, *Peony-flowered (Group IV);* **E**, *Decorative (Group V);* **F**, *Ball (Group VI);* **G**, *Pompon (Group VII);* **H**, *Cactus (Group VIII);* **I**, *Semi-cactus (Group IX); and* **J**, *Miscellaneous (Group X), depicting, in this case, an Orchid-flowered cultivar.*

G

H

I

J

22.

Chrysanthemums

Many gardeners wrongly believe that producing quality chrysanthemums means embarking upon a complicated cultural and feeding programme. While it may be true that chrysanthemums require a little more care and attention than many other flowers, they do not demand that you become a slave to them. Any keen gardener is capable of obtaining excellent results.

FLORAL STYLES AND USES The attraction of modern chrysanthemums as plants for the enthusiast is their varied forms and their long season of flowering; from August to the end of October for outdoor flowering types, and continuing on into November, December and early January for pot-grown cultivars flowered in conservatory or greenhouse. To choose the most suitable types for your purpose it will be helpful to know their characteristics. They are described on pp.197 and 198.

Cultivation of Outdoor Cultivars

PREPARATION OF GROWING SITE Dig heavy ground, if possible, before Christmas to allow the frosts to assist in the breaking down process. Light soils are best left until February or early March. Final ground preparation is required during April before planting out in May. It is imperative, however, that no attempt should be made to tread on very wet ground as this compacts the soil and excludes the air so vital to good root development. Carefully fork over the soil to a depth of 6 to 9in(15 to 23cm) incorporating a handful each of general fertiliser and commercial Epsom salts per square yard (m²). If chrysanthemums are being grown in borders, there are obviously limitations to the degree of preparation possible as consideration must be given to the permanent residents, namely perennials and shrubs. In mixed borders, areas large enough to take blocks of six to nine plants are the most effective.

TREATMENT OF PLANTS RECEIVED FROM NURSERY In the first instance, plants will be obtained from a nursery. Whenever possible it is better to collect these personally but many of us, of course, have to rely on the postal services for delivery. Carefully unpack the plants on arrival and, if they seem dry, stand them in water for a few hours to recharge the compost with moisture before planting into containers. Whether you use boxes or pots for this purpose is a matter of personal preference, but when planting is completed and if you have a greenhouse keep them on the floor for several days before placing them on staging in full light. Transfer the plants to a cold frame as soon as possible. Should you not have a greenhouse they will have to go straight into the cold frame. Keep the light closed for a few days and the plants shaded; then gradually reduce the shading and open the light to give more air, only closing it down if frost threatens. If you do not have greenhouse or cold frame, make sure that plants are not despatched to you until mid-May when they can be placed in a sheltered spot in the garden for about a week before planting out.

PLANTING OUT Immediately before planting out, the plants should be hardened-off. Short canes are inserted at each planting position, where the plants are to be grown and, if in a special bed, a spacing of 15in(38cm) between the plants will be sufficient, allowing a greater width for pathways. In borders, the best effect will be obtained, particularly with sprays, if these are planted closer together; a spacing of 9 to 12in(23 to 30cm) is suggested. At a later stage, longer canes can be inserted where necessary, their size depending on the height that plants are expected to attain. Planting can start when weather conditions allow, usually about mid-May. Water the plants well a few hours beforehand, then make a hole as near to the cane as possible; carefully remove the plant from its box or pot, place it in the hole and, after drawing surrounding soil around it, firm with the fingers and knuckles. Water the plants in and tie them loosely to their canes, label them and sprinkle a few slug pellets closely around each plant. One final important task is to wind black cotton around the canes just above the growing tips of the plants, otherwise birds will quickly nip these tips out.

STOPPING AND TIMING If left to their own devices, chrysanthemums develop into bush-like plants which bear small flowers in spray form – in other words, you end up with spray chrysanthemums. To obtain larger specimen blooms suitable for use as cut flowers or for other purposes, this natural tendency must be controlled. Some cultivars will grow with single stems until a break bud is produced; then side shoots develop giving branches which are gradually reduced to the number required. The break bud is then removed. If this process has not taken place by early June then artificial stopping must be resorted to. This is accomplished by pinching out the growing tip of the main stem back to the nearest pair of fully developed leaves. Branches (known as breaks) will then develop in the same way as a natural break. During June and July, the remaining breaks will form side shoots from their own leaf axils. Remove these when they are about 1in(2.5cm) long and easy to handle. By late July or early August a bud forms at the tip of each break, surrounded by many small buds or shoots. The latter are all removed gradually when they are large enough to handle easily until finally the main large central bud is left to provide a specimen bloom.

FEEDING After proper ground preparation, some supplementary feeding helps to give better blooms. The use of dry or liquid fertilisers is a matter of choice, but which is used will depend largely on the prevailing weather. It will be found most convenient to give a liquid feed when watering during dry spells and to scatter a dry feed on the surface at other times to be washed into the soil by rain. There are many well-balanced proprietary fertilisers, all excellent products if used according to the manufacturer's directions. As a guide, it is better to use a fertiliser with a higher nitrogen content during dry periods while one with a higher potash content will help ripen the plants in wet, dull weather. In between, during changeable weather, use an evenly balanced fertiliser. Feed at intervals of 10 to 14 days from the latter part of June until the buds begin to show colour. While exhibitors continue to feed beyond this point to obtain super-sized blooms there is a risk that this will cause damping of the florets. In any case, this extra size is not usually required.

PESTS The following are the most common troubles you are likely to come against:

Leaf Miner One of the most common pests of chrysanthemums, the leaf miner's presence is made evident by the white wavy lines on the foliage as the grub of the fly tunnels its way along the leaf. Once established in the leaf it is difficult to eradicate so spraying regularly with an insecticide containing pirimiphos-methyl, HCH (formerly BHC) or malathion when this fly is active – usually during the months of May and June – is the ideal control.

Aphids Aphids, including greenfly and blackfly, are too well-known to require additional identification. Control with the sprays suggested for leaf miner, with the addition of pirimicarb.

Capsid Bugs and Froghoppers These are green or brown in colour, easily recognized by the way they jump like grasshoppers. Froghoppers in the young stage are better known as cuckoo-spit and cause damage by piercing the stem just below the buds. As the wound heals, the skin tightens and then buds keel over at right-angles to the stem. At a later stage the bud itself is attacked and a complete segment of florets will be missing when the bloom develops. Spray with any of the insecticides recommended for leaf miner, and fenitrothion.

DISEASES The identification of disease is often very difficult and allowance must always be made for the fact that in cold spells foliage discoloration will occur. This will not have any ill effect. Generally, wilting plants, stunted growth, mottled foliage or distorted flowers will indicate that either verticillium wilt or a virus of some description is present. In all of these cases the best and surest remedy is to pull up and dispose of the suspect plant, preferably by burning. Powdery mildew on foliage can be controlled with benomyl. Damping off of blooms can arise in various ways; the only control is to spray the buds as soon as they begin to show colour with benomyl, mancozeb or captan.

WINTER CARE Outdoor chrysanthemums cannot be relied upon to survive the winter if they are left in their growing positions as, apart from frosts, losses also occur from excessive damp and the ravages of slugs. It is, therefore, advisable to lift and store the plants in shallow boxes inside a cold frame or cool greenhouse. As soon as the plants have finished flowering cut down the main stems to about 9in(23cm) from the ground and lift the plants between mid-October and mid-November. Before lifting them, trim all the basal growths to soil level and, after digging up the plants, cut back any thick roots and remove the top thin layer of soil as this tends to become scummy. Place the plants in boxes (tomato trays are ideal for this purpose) and fill the spaces between the plants with an equal proportion of fresh peat and John Innes No. 1 potting compost. Give the plants a light watering to settle them in, dust with Gamma-HCH powder and sprinkle a few slug pellets on the surface. The boxes are best kept on the dry side until after the end of the year, as the plants survive much better if they are kept dry in cold weather. A cold frame is the best place in which to stand the boxes, and if a layer of weathered ash or shingle covers its base this will help to deter slugs. Keep the boxes as cool as possible, only completely closing the lights and covering them with sacking if frost is expected.

TAKING CUTTINGS Early in the new year, the boxes are taken into the greenhouse where, after watering, slight heat is given. This encourages the plants to produce a crop of new shoots from which cuttings can be prepared in February. The ideal cutting is from 2½ to 3in(6.5 to 8cm) long and about ⅛in(2.5mm) thick. Make a square cut immediately below the bottom joint of the shoot with a sharp razor blade, which will give a clean, thin cut. This prepared cutting will now be 1½ to 2in(4 to 5cm) long. Immerse the cutting completely in a jar of weak insecticide and, after dipping the bottom ¼in (5mm) of stem into a combined hormone and fungicide rooting powder, insert it into a pot or box of a suitable rooting medium and firm lightly.

There are many suitable rooting media; soil-less seed compost, John Innes seed compost, and an equal mixture of John Innes, peat and sharp sand all give equally good results. After insertion give the cuttings a light watering. They will root in about 14 days and once rooted should be transplanted without delay into pots or boxes. Water sparingly as the greatest danger during this period is over-watering, particularly when cuttings flag in the initial stages. The treatment now follows the same pattern as that recommended for new plants once they have been transferred to a cold frame.

If you have no greenhouse there are two alternative methods of propagation. The plants can either be divided in the same manner as many other perennials – using single growths with a few roots attached taken from points as far away from the main stem as possible – or the cold frame can be used as a propagator with the cuttings being started into growth later in the season. Cuttings rooted in this way will obviously provide plants which bloom later, but this should not matter for garden decoration.

Cultivation of greenhouse cultivars

By growing greenhouse cultivars, the period during which mature blooms are available is greatly extended, but there are some fundamental differences in cultivation compared with outdoor flowering types. Cuttings are generally taken about a month earlier (in January) and while the pots in which the plants are growing are standing outdoors during the summer months, feeding is carried out once every seven to 14 days from approximately one month after the final potting until the buds begin to show colour. Most late cultivars are given two stoppings, the first in late April and the second at the end of June. The buds are then produced during late August and September.

Late sprays are grown three plants to a 9in(23cm) pot and if the cuttings are not taken until mid-June, the resulting plants can be allowed to break naturally or they can be stopped in late July or early August. If three or four breaks are then retained on each plant, a dozen nice stems should be available in November from each pot.

Chrysanthemum Classification and Cultivars

As such a large number of cultivars are registered each year, any list of recommendations would soon be out of date. It is, therefore, more useful to comment on how to choose the cultivars you wish to grow. Each year outdoor trials are conducted at Wisley by the Royal Horticultural Society in conjunction with the National Chrysanthemum Society, while a further trial is carried out at Peel Park, Bradford by the Bradford Metropolitan Council, which is also an official R.H.S./N.C.S. trial. Some 100 disbudded and 50 spray cultivars are grown at each venue for garden purposes. These trials are visited by the Joint Chrysanthemum Committee with awards being given to cultivars of sufficient merit. If you can visit either of these trials during September this will greatly help you in making a selection. An additional indoor trial of late sprays is carried out at Wisley in November. Chrysanthemum shows held during September and November also provide an opportunity to see a range of first-class cultivars suitable for garden or greenhouse decoration. Finally, the catalogues of specialist chrysanthemum nurseries invariably list cultivars under their various headings and give details of the National Chrysanthemum Society's classifications from which form and time of flowering can be ascertained. The classification table given below will help you to interpret such catalogues when making a selection. I have deliberately left out the large and medium late exhibition sections as these are purely exhibitors' flowers.

SECTIONS   Late-flowering Indoor Chrysanthemums   Sections: 3, Incurved. 4, Reflexed. 5, Intermediate. 6, Anemone centred. 7, Singles. 8, Pompons and Semi-pompons. 9, Sprays. 10, Spiders, Quills and Spoons. 12, Charms.

October-flowering Chrysanthemums   Sections: 13, Incurved. 14, Reflexed. 15, Intermediate. 17, Singles. 18, Pompons and Semi-pompons. 19, Sprays.

Early-flowering   Outdoor   Chrysanthemums   Sections: 23,   Incurved.   24, Reflexed. 25, Intermediate. 26, Anemone-centred. 27, Singles. 28, Pompons and Semi-pompons. 29, Sprays.

In all sections except those for Sprays, Pompons and Charms, a letter following the number indicates the size of bloom obtained when the plant is disbudded, i.e. (a) large, (b) medium, (c) small.

Incurved   These are looked upon by many as the chrysanthemum aristocrats. The florets curve tightly inwards to give the flower a completely globular appearance. This form is found in both outdoor and late greenhouse cultivars.

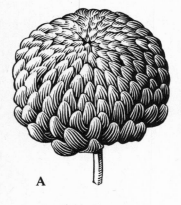

A

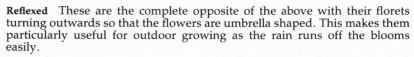

Reflexed These are the complete opposite of the above with their florets turning outwards so that the flowers are umbrella shaped. This makes them particularly useful for outdoor growing as the rain runs off the blooms easily.

Intermediate As the name implies, neither fully incurved nor reflexed.

Sprays Grown naturally, these carry many small flowers on a branched stem rather than one large bloom per stem when disbudded. No garden should be without these chrysanthemums in its borders. Equally good cultivars are available for late, pot cultivation.

Pompons and Semi-pompons These are bushy plants with small spherical or half spherical flowers. They are suitable for border decoration and window-boxes as the heights vary from 1 to 2ft(30 to 60cm).

Anemone-centred These are similar in appearance to the annual scabious with a central "pincushion" of tubular florets. They are mainly late flowering cultivars with a few in the early-flowering sprays. The latter are not disbudded as are the late-flowering cultivars.

Spidery These have long, quilled florets. 'Rayonnante' is the best-known example.

Charms These decorative pot plants are usually grown from cuttings taken in February to make plants which will flower in November. Wonderful specimen plants can be raised which will bear 2,000 to 3,000 small blooms similar in form to those of the Michaelmas daisy. 'Golden Chalice' is probably the most reliable cultivar.

SPECIALIST SOCIETY: The National Chrysanthemum Society.

B

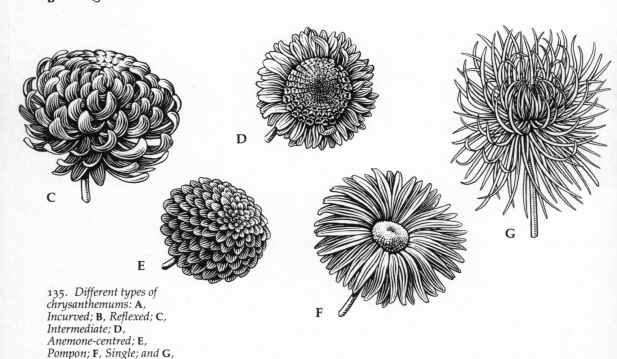

C

D

E

F

G

135. *Different types of chrysanthemums:* **A**, *Incurved;* **B**, *Reflexed;* **C**, *Intermediate;* **D**, *Anemone-centred;* **E**, *Pompon;* **F**, *Single; and* **G**, *Spidery.*

23.

Irises

When considering "enthusiasts' plants" it would be impossible to leave out the genus *Iris*. Within this genus there is considerable variation, most of its members are completely hardy, generally easy to grow and hybridise and with a colour range in the flowers wider than that of almost any other flowering plant – hence the descriptive name, "rainbow flower".

Irises can be grown in all gardens except those on pure chalk. Moreover, it is possible to have irises of one kind or another in flower during every month of the year. What more could an enthusiast want?

As the genus is so large, this chapter is concerned only with those kinds which can be categorised as "garden irises"; rare, more difficult and less interesting species are omitted.

BULBOUS IRISES

The bulbous irises include the so-called florists' irises – Dutch, Spanish and English – and various other species and hybrids from other sections of the genus.

DUTCH AND SPANISH IRISES The Dutch and Spanish hybrids are derivatives of *Iris xiphium* and are the irises usually seen in florists' shops. They require a sunny, well-drained position where they can dry out after flowering. Given such conditions the bulbs can be left in the ground to form clumps which should increase in size. Plant the bulbs in September at a depth of 4in(10cm); growth will usually be showing by the end of the year. The Dutch irises will flower from early June, the Spanish irises from late June. Their average height is 1½ to 2ft(45 to 60cm) and the Dutch are of somewhat more robust appearance than the Spanish. The colour range of the Spanish irises is from purple and blue to yellow and white, while that of the Dutch irises includes purple and bronze, smoky violet and yellow to numerous shades of blue, yellow and white. Examples of the latter type are the cultivars 'Professor Blaauw', ultramarine violet-blue; 'Princess Irene', white, with deep orange falls; and 'Purple Sensation'. The Spanish irises include the deep blue, yellow blotched 'King of the Blues', 'Canary Bird', rich yellow; and 'King of the Whites' (syn. 'L'Innocence'), white.

ENGLISH IRISES The English irises, forms and hybrids of *I. latifolia* (syn. *I. xiphioides*), did not originate in England but were introduced from the Pyrenees long ago. With a height of about 2ft(60cm) they flower in July, usually opening their blooms just after the bearded irises have finished their display. Unlike the Dutch and Spanish irises they like cool, moist soil conditions during their period of growth. Plant the bulbs of these, too, in September at a depth of 5in(13cm) and expect growth to be showing after the turn of the year. No named cultivars are offered, only mixtures, and the flower colours include shades from white, through shades of blue and violet to purple. There are no yellow shades. Plants often become infected with virus which gives the flowers a mottled appearance which is attractive. In spite of this, however, the infected bulbs should be burnt as soon as the symptoms are seen to avoid spreading the virus. This is not seed-borne, however, and seedlings are virus-free.

IRIS BUCHARICA This species from Turkestan, height 1 to 1½ft(30 to 45cm), belongs to the Juno group of bulbous irises, unlike other members of the genus in that they have thick storage roots and untypical foliage. The flowers, with white standards and golden-yellow falls, are carried in the axils of the leaves. This very hardy species likes a well-drained soil and a sunny position and can be left in position to continue its display each April.

THE RETICULATA GROUP The Reticulata group of small, early-flowering bulbous irises includes species of great attraction. They are quite hardy and may be left in the ground to reappear year after year without attention. They do, however, need lifting and dividing every five years or so when they become overcrowded. Do this in late summer when the foliage has died down.

The first to flower is *I. histrioides* which is in bloom by early January. These flowers have falls of blue-violet and standards of a paler shade of blue. Its height is about 7in(18cm). *I. danfordiae*, only 4in(10cm) tall, has pale yellow flowers with an attractive hint of green in them. This makes its display in the latter part of January and February. It is followed in flowering by *I. reticulata* itself, which gives its name to the group. This has numerous named cultivars of which 'Joyce' is perhaps currently the best, although new named ones have appeared in Holland which are not yet available here. 'Katharine Hodgkin' is an unusual hybrid with soft grey-blue markings over a pale yellow ground. All have a height of about 6in(15cm).

RHIZOMATOUS IRISES

The bearded irises of the rhizomatous irises, the members of the bearded section are without doubt the best known and most popular. They also include far more cultivars than other sections of the genus.

Bearded irises are hardy and easy to grow, and with more dwarfs and intermediate kinds now coming onto the scene they provide colour and interest between them from around the end of April until early July, with the occasional remontants making a display in late summer. The season starts with the dwarf species and cultivars, is followed by the intermediates (in May) and concludes with the tall bearded cultivars.

Two basic requirements of the bearded irises are sunshine and good drainage. All other aids, such as soil of good quality and provision of fertilisers, are, as it were, "icing on the cake". They can be planted at almost any time of year, but the best time is a few weeks after flowering has finished. Planted then, they will soon establish themselves and have a long period of growth before entering their winter dormancy. These irises are shallow rooted and should be planted with their rhizomes level with the surface of the soil to enable the sun to bake them in summer and with their roots set at an angle of 45 degrees. To maximise the effect of this exposure to sunshine plant so that the leaf fans face north. Within three years good clumps will have formed. Tall irises in particular are heavy feeders and clumps of dwarf and intermediate kinds will need lifting and dividing every three years, tall bearded kinds every four years, a task to do after flowering or in late summer, discarding the worn-out centres and re-planting the newer rhizomes from the outside of the clumps. Plant as suggested above. One watering should suffice to get them started into growth.

THE DWARF BEARDED IRISES These have a height range of 5 to 10in(13 to 25cm) and usually carry one flower on each stem. Making good clumps which become covered with bloom, they are excellent for the rock garden or the front of borders. Most of the modern hybrids are derived from *I. pumila* and many carry the typical *pumila* spot pattern on the falls. The colour range is wide and recommended cultivars are 'Marhaba', violet with a white beard; 'Buttercup Charm', yellow; 'Dunlin', white with blue dots; and 'Scribe', white, with blue stripes on the falls.

THE INTERMEDIATE BEARDED IRISES These have a height range of 10 to 28in(25 to 70cm) and have three to five flowers to a stem. These result from

136. Parts of a bearded iris:
1. *standard;* 2. *fall;* 3. *crest;* 4. *beard;* 5. *haft of fall;* 6. *anther;* and 7. *stigma.*

crosses between miniature dwarf and tall bearded irises and have been developed in the past 30 years. They are ideal for windy gardens. Many new cultivars have been registered and tried and trusted award winners are 'Curlew', pale yellow with a white mark on the falls; 'Sea Fret', white, with a green fret on the falls; 'Double Lament', two shades of violet with an orange beard; 'Golden Fair', golden-yellow; 'Cotsgold', a yellow self; 'Arctic Fancy', violet stitching on a white ground; 'Whiteladies', a white self; and 'Eyebright', yellow, with brown lines on the falls.

THE TALL BEARDED IRISES

These are the queens of the iris world, hardy and free-flowering and with heights of from 28in to 4ft(70cm to 1.25m). Modern cultivars bear from eight to 15 or even more buds, all of which will open up. Given sunshine and good drainage, the tall bearded irises are easy to grow and will reward one with a wealth of flowers. The optimum planting time is from late July to September, when the plants are starting to make new growth. Bearded irises are dormant in winter and the plants will die down to small green points by November with growth starting up again in March. They flower for about six weeks from late May to July with the flowering time depending on the cultivar in question.

The plants should be lifted and divided once every four years, as recommended earlier (see p. 200). Seed is the other method of increase, this being sown in the open, about ½in(1cm) deep in October. By February germination should have started to take place. Do not sow seed of these plants under glass as the seeds need chilling before they will germinate well. Also, of course, they will not come true from seed.

The tall bearded irises have a very wide colour range and many new cultivars (some say too many) are registered each year. Selection standards can, therefore, be strict and the following are tried and tested modern cultivars: 'Stepping Out', violet stitching on white; 'Winter Olympics', a white self; 'Prince Indigo', large-flowered deep violet; 'Marshlander', a chocolate and brown bi-colour; 'Tracy', a bright tan self; 'Chesterton', with white standards and mid-blue falls; 'Jane Phillips', an old pale blue variety but still good; 'Annabel Jane', lilac shades; 'Blue-Eyed Brunette', brown, with a blue spot below beard; 'One Desire', pink; 'Jewel Tone', ruby-red; and 'Sarah Louise', a brick-red self. There are, of course, a great many other cultivars from which to make a choice.

THE BEARDLESS IRISES

Foremost among these are *I. sibirica* – which actually comes from central Europe and southern Russia, where it grows in moist fields – and its hybrids. These grow up to 3ft(1m) tall, have graceful narrow leaves and flowering stems bearing one or two branches in addition to the terminal bloom. The flowers, which are borne in late June-early July, are generally in proportion to the height of the plant with the falls about 1½in(4cm) across, although larger than this in some of the newest cultivars. The colour range is from white through shades of violet to purple; it even includes wine-red. They are among the best irises for general garden planting, being hardy and deciduous, and they will grow happily in the border year after year without feeding, although a dressing of general garden fertiliser in spring will encourage them to flower better. Having derived from a species which appreciates moist soil, they are quite at home in moist places but in the British climate they like a certain amount of sunshine to go with it. They seem to be remarkably free from disease.

There are many cultivars which can be relied upon to give a good show in late June-early July. The following can be recommended; 'Anniversary', white; 'Dreaming Spires', dark blue-violet; 'Cambridge', pale blue; and 'Limeheart', white, with green suffusions. Two other species within this same Sibiricae section of the Apogon group, or beardless iris, are *I. forrestii* and *I. chrysographes*, both shorter than the last, with a height in the region of 2ft(60cm) and also good garden plants. *I. forrestii* has yellow flowers and *I. chrysographes* deep velvety-red-violet blooms with golden lines and dots on the falls, hence its name. It has a shorter form named *rubella* which has the same red-violet flowers but without the markings. All are good growers and trouble-free. They are short enough to make good rock garden plants.

137. *A stem of a tall bearded iris*

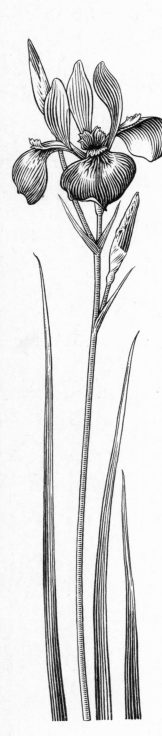

Another interesting section of beardless irises is that known as Spuria from the species of that name. They are not so well known as they should be, probably because most of the good garden cultivars like a good baking after they have flowered, which they seldom get here. They are June-July flowering. The flowers resemble those of the Dutch bulbous irises but the spikes are generally taller. There are several species which grow well in the milder parts of this country but north of the Midlands they might prove difficult to grow. The writer grows and flowers some of them regularly in the Cotswolds. Of the taller species the following can be recommended;

I. orientalis (usually grown as *I. ochroleuca*). This has white flowers with a prominent yellow signal area on the falls. With a height of 4ft(1.25m) it is one of the tallest irises and is good for the back of a border.

I. crocea. This has deep yellow flowers and can grow to 5ft(1.5m) tall. It has long, sword-like leaves. In this same group are several low-growing species, usually only 1 to 2ft(30 to 60cm) high. They are dormant in winter and require a reasonably warm soil, plenty of water in spring and in times of summer drought. Of these the following can be recommended:

I. graminea. Some 12in(30cm) tall this has flowers coloured purple on a white ground. It has a greengage scent.

I. sintenisii. This is roughly the same height as *I. graminea* and has charming little violet or purple flowers.

I. kernerana. This is 15in(38cm) high with narrow, twisted leaves and yellow flowers. It is an elegant little iris which the writer has grown for years without any attention. It does, however, like a sunny spot. Useful relatives are *I. × monnieri* (a natural hybrid of lemon-yellow colouring); 'Wadi Zem Zem', yellow; 'Driftwood', brown; and 'Ila Crawford', white.

PACIFIC COAST IRISES   The Pacific Coast irises should not be missed for they offer a full range of colours except for real red and black and they are a flower arranger's dream. There are approximately a dozen species emanating from the Pacific coast and foothills of the U.S.A., and, through intercrossing and breeding, many fine cultivars are now appearing. These grow well in Britain. Height ranges from 9 to 30in(23 to 75cm) in height and they usually carry three buds on each flexuous stem. Flowering in this country is in May. Except for the hybrids of *I. munzii*, which are a bit tender, they are quite hardy and although they are supposed to prefer an acid soil they grow well for the writer on limestone in full sun or partial shade. They produce few roots and, once established, should be moved as little as possible. They will make large clumps sometimes nearly 3ft(1m) across.

The foliage is not deciduous. Reliable varieties are 'Amiguita', pale lavender with a violet splash; 'Banbury Welcome', burgundy; and 'No Name', pale yellow and short. The flowers should be cut in bud. Pacific Coast irises can easily be raised from seed to flower after three years and they are among the most worthwhile of beardless irises.

MOISTURE-LOVING IRISES

I. pseudacorus, the British yellow flag iris. Very hardy, it will grow well in wet ground or shallow water, and it is quite hardy in the border. It spreads rapidly and is trouble free. The usual height is 4ft(1.25m) but there are several forms and some of these reach a height of 6ft(2m). An attractive hybrid is 'Holden Clough' which resulted from a cross between this species and *I. chrysographes* (see p. 201). It is about 3ft(1m) tall, has flowers of a pleasant brown colour and is quite unusual.

I. laevigata. This species grows well in shallow water or boglands. It is about 2ft(60cm) tall and has flower colours from light to deep violet; there is also a white-flowered form and one with a reddish tinge. The flowering time is June. Hybrids are difficult to obtain in this country, but such breeding is being carried out in the plant's native Japan, where it and its derivatives have been grown for over a thousand years.

Another relative of *I. laevigata* is *I. versicolor*, the so-called American flag iris. This species, which flowers in late May and early June, has blue-purple colouring in various shades and can also be wine-red. Its height is up to

138. *The beardless* Iris sibirica *(see p.201)*

3ft(1m). Although it likes moist soil, it will grow very well in ordinary garden soil and will make a clump 3ft(1m) across. It is hardy, very floriferous and a fine garden iris.

I. kaempferi, the Japanese iris. This grows in shallow water or in a border but it should be allowed to dry out after flowering. The flowering time is July when the large, flat flowers each several inches across come in many colours from reddish-purple to blue, pink and white. There are many cultivars but these are difficult to obtain up to the time of writing, except from Japan.

THE HEXAGONAE OR LOUISIANA IRISES These irises originated in the swamplands of the southern United States and the Mississippi Valley and they like damp places although they grow quite well in borders. They like sunshine and a reasonably warm climate and are unlikely to do well in this country outside the south of England. They grow well in Melbourne, Australia, where there is occasional frost. Their height is about 3ft(1m) and as they are robust plants they should be given plenty of room. The flowers – borne in the latter part of June and July – are large and flat and in the new hybrids showy.

In this country *I. × fulvala*, an old brick-red hybrid, seems hardy but its size is small compared with that of modern hybrids. To any garden owner with a warm enough climate to grow them the new cultivars 'Charlie's Michelle', 'Ila Nunn' and 'Clyde Redmond' can be recommended. These could probably be obtained from the United States.

THE EVANSIA OR CRESTED IRISES This is a very variable group which includes irises with heights from 3in(8cm) to 3ft(1m). All are stoloniferous and have crests on the falls of their flowers instead of beards. They include four small species which are all hardy and make good garden plants; all like some shade and a well-drained soil. Acid woodland conditions are very suitable. All are spring or early summer flowering. The four are:

I. lacustris. Only 3in(8cm) high, this species has slate-grey flowers. Its natural habitat is sandy woods around Lake Superior in Canada.

I. cristata. This is slightly larger and brighter than *I. lacustris* and is happy in well-drained soil which contains plenty of humus. It is ideal for the rock garden flowering in May.

I. tenuis. With a height of about 7in(18cm) this is taller again than *I. cristata*. It has white flowers. It likes moist, cool, shady places and for this reason alone is a distinct asset in the garden.

I. gracilipes. This species bears tiny lilac flowers on wiry, branching 8in(20cm) stems in May. It likes shady situations where the soil is acid and should not be disturbed more than is necessary. There is a white form but the lilac form is the stronger grower. It is a lovely little iris with an untypical flower.

Taller than the above four midgets is *I. japonica* which carries a multi-branched stalk of up to 2ft(60cm) with many prettily fringed flowers in pale lavender with an orange crest on the falls. It grows best outdoors, in part sunshine, in cool, frost-free conditions in well-drained slightly acid soil which is full of humus. Mulching is a help in winter where frost may be a problem. A form called 'Ledger's Variety' is generally hardy.

THE WINTER-FLOWERING IRIS

I. unguicularis. The winter-flowering *I. unguicularis* is a native of Algeria and the eastern Mediterranean through the Greek islands to Turkey. Used to hot, dry summers, it likes a sheltered position in our gardens, preferably against a south-facing wall. The flower colours range from dark violet to white through lavender, which is the most common colour. It can start to flower as early as October and go through to April.

This iris should be planted when flowering finishes and it should be watered well for a few weeks after planting until it is evident that it is making growth. Then desist. The foliage can be trimmed back in summer to let the sun ripen the rhizomes. The various cultivars vary in height from 9in(23cm) as in 'Mary Barnard', to 15in(38cm). The so-called stems are really

139. *The Pacific Coast irises, of which this is an example, are "a flower arranger's dream".*

long perianth tubes which are brittle so picking should be done gently. Another cultivar is 'Walter Butt', a good grower with pale lavender flowers. It is best when buying plants to see them at the nursery for there are considerable variations in performance with this iris.

DISEASES AND PESTS   Few diseases or pests trouble irises. Rhizome rot is the most common trouble, this causing the rhizomes to become soft and slimy and give off a bad smell. It is encouraged by over-warm and over-moist conditions. Affected rhizomes should have the affected parts cut away with a sharp knife and the cut surfaces dressed with a fungicide before replanting.

Scorch, in which the leaves take on reddish suffusions, sometimes affects plants and is not curable. The leaves look as if they have been scorched by fire and die. Dig up and burn the affected plant. Scorch is usually experienced after a long, dry period and is uncommon and not infectious. Botrytis occasionally occurs in winter and the affected parts should be cut away and the cut surfaces dressed with fungicide.

Viruses affect the leaves of some plants and the flowers of I. *latifolia* (syn. I. *xiphioides*) and affected plants should be burnt. Iris rust – which shows as rusty looking spots on the leaves – is rare, not contagious and can generally be ignored.

The pests of irises are few. Slugs are the worst trouble, eating into the base of the rhizome and letting in the bacteria which cause rhizome rot. The usual slug controls can be used and watering with a weak solution of alum will often drive them away without killing them. Aphids are occasionally a nuisance in flower sockets, but nothing more than that. The iris borer, a moth grub which bores into the rhizomes, is a nuisance in the United States but has fortunately not reached here yet.

HYBRIDISING   Space does not allow detailed information to be given on iris hybridising, but this can be a rewarding hobby. Iris flowers pollinate freely, seed can be harvested in September and plants can be flowered in two years or so from seed sowing. The complicated genetic make-up of bearded irises ensures that some startling results can be obtained by intelligent breeding. Advice on this can be obtained from the British Iris Society. Information on species and cultivars which are difficult to obtain can also be obtained from the same source.

SPECIALIST SOCIETY: The British Iris Society.

24.

Rhododendrons and Azaleas

The gardener blessed with an acid soil will find few shrubs more rewarding to grow than rhododendrons. Comprising nearly a thousand different species (natural forms) and countless hybrids, the diversity within this single genus is enormous.

Although rhododendrons have been grown in Britain for around 200 years, the genus is one of the oldest in the plant world, going back millions of years and tracing its origins from that vast area of Asia centred around Nepal and along the great Himalayan mountain range, through Burma to the northern Chinese provinces of Yunnan and Szechwan. Southward the genus spread through Thailand to Indonesia, and north-eastwards across China and Korea to Japan, and finally over the Bering Strait to America, the natural home of so many azalea species. Westwards rhododendrons have spread from Asia into Europe by way of the Caucasus and the Balkans, from whence came the now common *R. ponticum* which has naturalised itself in so many parts of the British Isles.

It stands to reason, evolving as they have over such a wide area and under very different climatic conditions, rhododendrons have undergone considerable changes in their structure in order to establish themselves in their far-flung habitat. Hence, on one hand we find the primitive, large-leaved, towering trees from the warmer, wetter regions, and at the other extreme the hardy, often prostrate growing, small-leaved species which survive on the high moorlands exposed to the full fury of the elements, often covered by snow or lashed by icy winds. The flowers too vary greatly, from the massive, waxy-looking trusses of the large-leaved species to the tiny nodding bells and small, neat flowers of the alpines. These variations add greatly to the interest in growing rhododendrons. The gardener with time to develop his interest should endeavour to create as much variety among his plants as the size of his garden permits. With such a wealth to choose from, even the patio gardener can make a fascinating collection of rhododendrons. Nevertheless, when planning to plant in a given area, natural habitat should always be borne in mind. Within the British Isles, the milder, wetter areas have always produced the best of the large-leaved species, while the dryer, colder districts are well suited to many others.

Selected species

No rhododendron garden is complete without a selection of species and the following are recommended to give the necessary variety in habit, foliage and flower. All are hardy, or reasonably so throughout Britain, and their cultivation is not difficult.

A key indicates size and suitability for different gardens: **W** = woodland; **L** = large garden; **A** = average or small garden; **R** = rock or patio garden.
Rhododendron aberconwayi (A). A neat shrub with small, dark green leaves and pretty contrasting pale pink, or white, saucer-shaped flowers. May.
R. augustinii (WLA). Tall, but slender growing with masses of clear lavender-blue flowers with prominent stamens. The best forms have a lovely green eye. Allied species having similar habit and flower formation are *R. davidsonianum*, shades of pink, and *R. yunnanense*, palest lilac or white with crimson spotting. April.

140. Rhododendron fulvum, *with light pink, crimson-blotched flowers and dark green leaves.*

R. barbatum (WL). A fine tree with beautiful bark, dark green leaves and superb rounded trusses of blood red flowers. March.

R. calophytum (WL). A large shrub or tree with long, narrow, bright green leaves and large trusses of campanulate white or pale pink flowers with a crimson blotch. March.

R. calostrotum (R). A charming little plant with small grey leaves and bright magenta saucer-shaped flowers. The form 'Gigha' has very pretty rosy-red flowers. May-June.

R. cinnabarinum (WLA). Fairly tall but slender growing with distinctive aromatic foliage, very pungent after a shower of rain. Two particularly attractive forms are 'Nepal' with narrow, tubular, orange-yellow flowers rimmed scarlet, and var. *roylei* with larger plum-red flowers. April-May.

R. fulvum (WLA). A shapely small tree, slow growing, with fine shiny, dark green leaves, thickly felted on the undersides with rich cinnamon-coloured indumentum, contrasting with neat trusses of light pink flowers blotched crimson. April.

R. impeditum (R). The ideal patio rhododendron with a 'pin-cushion' habit, grey-green leaves and tiny, compact lavender-blue flowers. April.

R. macabeanum (WL). A very attractive species with large, dark green leaves and fawn indumentum. The flowers are borne in large trusses – up to 20 in a truss – and are greenish-yellow with a purple blotch.

R. orbiculare (A). A most attractive and distinctive species forming a rounded bush with beautiful almost circular light green leaves and dainty trusses of rose-pink bells. May.

R. racemosum (WLA). Another very distinctive species. The form 'Rock Rose' has especially bright pink flowers often carried in racemes along red branchlets, and small leathery, dark green leaves very glaucous on the undersides. April.

R. rex (WL). The easiest of the large-leaved species to grow, with the advantage of flowering at a young age. Fine, shiny, dark green leaves with fawn indumentum and large trusses of pale pink or white flowers blotched crimson. April-May.

R. wardii (WLA). One of the most attractive yellow-flowered species. Neat in habit with smooth, rounded leaves and saucer-shaped flowers, often with a crimson blotch. May-June.

R. yakushimanum (AR). A most important and distinctive Japanese species regarded by many as the perfect rhododendron. Very slow growing with recurved, small, dark green leaves with thick creamy-buff indumentum. The clear pink flower buds open into neat rounded trusses the colour of apple blossom, these turning to white as they mature. In recent years *R. yakushimanum* has produced some of our finest small garden hybrids (see p.208). June.

Hybrid Rhododendrons

There is no doubt that many fine old garden hybrids still rate very highly among growers, but most of them are far too big for our small modern gardens. They are now being replaced by a new generation of much smaller growing hybrids, many of which have been bred from *R. yakushimanum* and *R. williamsianum*. Where space is not a problem there are no finer plants than the cultivars grouped under *R.* Loderi, with slender bright green and massive, scented flowers in early May, varying from white, through shades of pink to a lovely pale yellow, and certain of the old "hardy hybrids" such as 'Pink Pearl', 'Mrs. G.W. Leak', 'Cynthia', 'Britannia' and 'Purple Splendour' (all May-June flowering) will continue to retain their high popularity.

As with the species, the hybrids should be selected to give the widest possible diversity and interest with a flowering period which can be extended over nine months of the year. These are some of the better new rhododendron hybrids which are currently appearing in the catalogues of specialist growers, and to simplify matters these are grouped by colour:

141. Rhododendron macabeanum, *with greenish-yellow flowers marked with a purple blotch*

RED GROUP 'Royal Windsor' (A), rich crimson (June) and 'Hope Findlay' (A) with large scarlet trumpets in May, are strong challengers to 'Elizabeth'

(A) (April), long regarded as the best red for the small garden. 'Earl of Donoughmore' (WL) with very large crimson flowers of fine texture (June), and 'Red Glow' (WL), strong-growing with large, fleshy, crimson flowers in May, both need plenty of room, but 'Spring Dream' (R), with its spreading habit and vivid scarlet flowers (May), is ideal for the smallest of gardens; likewise 'Arkle' (R) with waxy, deep scarlet bells (April-May). Also recommended is the larger 'Lady Chamberlain', red, shading to orange.

PINK GROUP Early in the flowering season there are two extremely pretty and valuable hybrids which are not exactly new but as yet they have no worthy substitutes. They are 'Tessa Roza' (WA) with charming lilac-pink flowers in March and very attractive bronze new foliage, and 'Seta' (WA) with very distinctive tubular, bright pink and white-striped flowers also in March. As they flower so early they are best grown where there is some protection from trees which often help to prevent frost damage to blooms.

An attractive and free-flowering new hybrid is 'Phalarope' (AR), close in habit with pale lilac-pink flowers (April) and another very useful little plant. 'The Master' (WL), strong growing with exceptionally large pale pink flowers in May, and 'The Queen Mother' (A), more compact with dainty silvery-pink trusses early in May, are both very beautiful plants.

Especially good for the smaller garden are two hybrids of *R. williamsianum*, 'Moerheim's Pink' (A), with large, clear pink bells (early May) and 'April Glow' (syn. 'April Shower') (A), with pretty, frilly, rose-pink flowers in April-May. At the end of the season 'Veldtstar' (WL) makes a spectacular tree with very large, rich pink, well scented flowers, in June-July, and 'Amor' (WA), a somewhat older but little-known plant which should be much more widely grown. Coming towards the end of the season (late June) its rich pink flowers with a dark centre, contrast well with narrow, dark green leaves covered with thick creamy-fawn indumentum.

WHITE GROUP 'Caroline de Zoete' (WLA), with purest white flowers of superb shape and texture (April-May) which contrast perfectly with bright, glossy green leaves; these, combined with a good habit, make this an excellent garden shrub. 'Olympic Lady' (A), a pretty *R. williamsianum* hybrid, is a most pleasing recent introduction from America with pale pink buds opening into dainty white bells in May, and 'Ptarmigan' (R), with tiny leaves and small starry flowers (April), is an ideal plant for the patio gardener. Superb woodland shrubs flowering late in the season are 'Polar Bear' (WL), a handsome tree with light green leaves and massive, scented flowers in late July or August (one of the latest-flowering of all rhododendrons), and 'Northern Star' (WL), also very strong growing with large, scented flowers (July).

YELLOW GROUP It is only within very recent years that true yellow-flowered hybrids have been available in sufficient numbers to satisfy the

142. Rhododendron *'Veldstar', which has rich pink flowers.*

very large demand, and some are still very difficult to obtain. 'Crest' (formerly 'Hawk Crest') (WL), although rather an untidy grower, has superb clear golden-yellow flowers (April-May) to make it one of the most sought after of rhododendron hybrids. Another very beautiful plant is 'John Barr Stevenson' (WL), strong growing with large trusses of clear lemon-yellow flowers (early May). A hybrid of *R. lacteum*, it is difficult to propagate and, therefore, hard to track down.

'Queen Elizabeth II' (WL) is a hybrid of 'Crest', retaining flowers of a good colour (May) and vigorous growth but altogether a better habit. 'Golden Orfe' (WLA) is a slender-growing shrub and its fine waxy, pendulous, orange-yellow flowers (May) make it an interesting variety. 'Hotei' (A), with rich golden-yellow flowers in May-June, is a promising new introduction from America. A delightful small rock garden plant is 'Princess Anne' (R) with a neat, rounded habit, excellent foliage which takes on bronze-red tints throughout the winter and dainty lemon-yellow flowers in April. Without doubt, it is one of the most attractive dwarf rhododendrons and the perfect foil for the many dwarf blues. 'Curlew' (R), with large bright yellow trumpets in May, is another excellent patio plant.

SALMON-ORANGE GROUP   There is not a wide choice in this colour range, but 'Tortoiseshell Wonder' (LA), with fine clear orange trumpets and good foliage, is a superb variety, contrasting well with 'Champagne' (LA) which is very aptly named with its delicate coloured flowers (both May-June). 'Hydon Salmon' (A) has fine-textured flowers in a very distinctive shade of salmon-orange (mid June), and 'Anne George' (WL), strong-growing with slightly loose trusses of salmon-pink flowers flushed crimson, has remarkable substance for a plant flowering late in the season (mid June).

BLUE-PURPLE GROUP   'Blue Diamond' (A), which is an excellent garden plant, now has considerable competition from one or two newer hybrids. 'Saint Breward' (WLA) and 'Saint Tudy' (WLA) are both neat-growing shrubs with compact trusses of clear violet-blue flowers (April-May), but 'Blue Chip' (WA), with intense blue flowers borne at the same time, is possibly a better choice for colder gardens. More compact and with small flowers of the deepest blue in April is 'Saint Merryn' (R), the perfect foil for the yellow 'Princess Anne'. 'Amethyst' (A) is a lovely rich shade of purple (April-May) and 'P.J. Mezzitt' (A) from America has most attractive bright rosy-lilac flowers (April) and striking bronze foliage. 'Olive' (WA), with flowers of a similar shade, brings much needed colour to the garden in February-March.

Yakushimanum Hybrids

The following represent some of the best of their type to date, combining all the admirable features of their illustrious parent: compact habit, slow growth rate, good foliage and the ability to flower freely with fine, large compact flower trusses. Their introduction has revolutionised the growing of the traditional type of rhododendron in the average small modern garden. Unless otherwise stated, the flowering period for *R. yakushimanum* hybrids is late May to early June. 'Dopey' is the only true red in this class, with shapely firm trusses of rich crimson – a magnificent plant by any standard. 'Hydon Dawn' is also especially beautiful with frilly, warm pink flowers, distinctive 'woolly' new growth and good foliage. 'Starshine', with some Loderi blood, has very fine pale pink dome-shaped trusses flushed deeper pink, and 'Marion Street' is another delightful large-flowered, soft pink. 'Hydon Hunter', which is somewhat stronger growing, has spectacular bright strawberry-pink flowers, red-rimmed, paling at the centre with orange spotting, and 'Morning Magic' has been called the "Super Yakushimanum" having all its parent's characteristics amply magnified – pale pink buds opening into large, white, rounded flower trusses of considerable substance.

'Caroline Allbrook', a cross with 'Purple Splendour' has produced a superb lavender-flowered cultivar with charming frilly-rimmed flowers

143. Rhododendron
'Lady Bowes Lyon', a
yakushimanum *hybrid*
with apple-blossom-pink
flowers.

spotted olive-brown. Coming much earlier in the season is 'Georgette' (April-May), with lovely large blush pink trusses.

Two other *R. yakushimanum* hybrids of great quality and beauty, although much larger growing, are the magnificent 'Lady Bowes Lyon' (WL), with large rounded trusses of apple blossom pink flowers, and 'Seven Stars' (WL), a hybrid with 'Loderi Sir Joseph Hooker', which has lovely rose-pink flowers.

A number of *R. yakushimanum* hybrids have recently been introduced from America but to date these have not been fully tested in the United Kingdom.

Tender Rhododendrons

These form a big group of rhododendron species and hybrids which are far too tender for garden cultivation except in very sheltered gardens or in the mild areas of Cornwall and western Scotland. They do, however, make excellent cool greenhouse or conservatory plants, often with the added attraction of a lovely spicy fragrance. Two species of particular merit are *R. edgeworthii* (syn. *R. bullatum*), with large, sweetly scented white flowers (April) and dark green leaves with thick creamy-fawn indumentum, and *R. burmanicum*, with dainty greenish-yellow campanulate flowers and a good scent (April-May). Two excellent hybrids are 'Actress', with large white flowers, crimson on the outside (April-May), and 'White Wings', pure white flowers with a greenish blotch (April-May). With the exception of one or two yellow-flowered varieties, most of the tender rhododendrons have either white or very pale pink blooms.

Azaleas

These form a large botanical group within the rhododendron family. They fall into two sub groups, the deciduous and the evergreen. Those which drop their leaves usually colour brilliantly beforehand, and the evergreens are much smaller shrubs originating from Japan.

The best-known deciduous species is *Rhododendron luteum* (WLA) (syn. *Azalea pontica*) from eastern Europe and now naturalised in the British Isles. The bright yellow, scented flowers in late May and richly coloured foliage in autumn make it an excellent garden plant.

Lesser known kinds in the deciduous group but which should be much more widely grown are *R. albrechtii* (WLA), with a good compact habit and dainty "butterfly"-shaped, bright pink flowers in April-May, these appearing before the leaves; *R. reticulatum* (WL), taller growing with bright rosy-lilac "butterfly" flowers (April) which come before the leaves (these leaves turn purple in autumn); and *R. schlippenbachii* (WLA), a particularly pretty Korean species with soft pink flowers (April-May) and good autumn foliage colour. This last easily adapts to the smaller garden. *R. vaseyi* (WLA), from North America, also has dainty pink flowers (May) which appear before the leaves, and *R. viscosum* (WLA), the swamp honeysuckle, is a bushy shrub of medium height which will thrive in a moist situation; the small white tubular flowers, borne in July, have a strong spicy scent.

Among the evergreen azalea species two are of particular garden merit. First, *R. obtusum* (WLA), the parent of so many of the lovely Japanese Kurume hybrids. This forms a dense, spreading shrub with glowing rich magenta flowers (May), and which is equally effective in a woodland or a shady corner of the garden. Secondly, the tiny, creeping *R. nakaharai* (R) and the cultivar 'Mariko' with exceptionally large funnel-shaped, bright orange flowers (late June) and hairy, dark green leaves. These are ideal azaleas for the patio gardener.

Azalea Hybrids

Like rhododendrons, azalea hybrids now exist in very considerable numbers. The old, but ever-popular Ghent and Mollis hybrids from Belgium, and the Knaphill and Exbury strains raised early this century by Anthony Waterer and Lionel Rothschild, have been further improved by some superb new hybrids of the Knaphill type developed at the Royal Horticultural Society's Garden, Wisley. These, named after English rivers, have very large flowers which are mostly in brilliant shades of orange and yellow. Among the best are: 'Frome', with frilly, rich yellow flowers flushed red in the throat; 'Medway', large pink flowers with an orange flare; 'Stour', vivid red with an orange blotch; 'Tay', superb, very large yellow with an orange flare; 'Tamar', rich yellow flushed coral; 'Thames', deep pink with an apricot blotch; 'Trent', rich, waxy yellow tinged salmon; and 'Wye', large, frilled apricot-yellow with an orange flare. All are fairly large growing and therefore ideal plants for the woodland or larger garden and the flowering period is early June.

The evergreen hybrids are equally numerous in variety and are most effective when planted in blocks of the same colour or carefully shaded to give a rippled effect. The smaller-flowered Kurume azaleas, which are usually more compact in habit, are best grown together and not mixed with the larger-flowered Kaempferi, Malvatica, Glen Dale and Vuykiana hybrids. The original "Wilson Fifty" Kurume hybrids, brought into England early this century, still rank as some of the most beautiful of their type, along with the ever popular pink 'Hino-Mayo' and the compact-growing, rosy-lilac 'Hatsugiri'. More recently the Eira group, produced at that fine old rhododendron garden Tower Court, near Ascot, has given some very pretty new and very hardy hybrids of the Kurume type. To name a few: 'Princess Ida', glowing rosy-lilac; 'Peep-Bo', delicate pale pink; 'Tit Willow', pale silvery-mauve; and 'Nanki Poo', rich claret-pink. In turn, these have now produced some attractive taller-growing varieties in 'Kakiemon', unfading salmon-orange; 'Violet Longhurst', rich purple; 'Mary Meredith', vivid cyclamen; and 'Pamela Miles', clear pink. Outstanding among the newer larger-flowered evergreen hybrids are: 'Blue Danube', a distinctive shade of violet-blue; 'Greenway', large, pure white; 'Mother's Day', low-growing, with striking double, large, crimson flowers; 'Mahler', rich purple; 'Mini', very compact, lilac pink; 'Rosebud', double rose-pink, spreading habit; 'Snow Hill' compact habit, large white flowers with a green eye; and 'Vuyk's Scarlet', low growing, bright scarlet.

Generally speaking, all azaleas are best grown in dappled shade. Although most are perfectly hardy and will stand full exposure, the flowers will last much longer if they are given some protection from the heat of the sun. Evergreen azalea hybrids are especially versatile and may be grown effectively in large or small gardens.

Cultivation

When it has been established that soil conditions are right for growing rhododendrons (which means that the pH has to be 7.00 or less) then the ground should be prepared for planting. First, the area should be well dug over and if the ground is noticeably heavy, peat, and/or leafmould, plus some sharp sand, should be worked in to lighten it. This is most important for good drainage is essential if rhododendrons and azaleas are going to thrive. Likewise, if the soil is very light and sandy then peat and leafmould should be added to give body and help retain the moisture.

The planting holes should not be too deep. Rhododendrons are surface rooting and so it is important to see when the plant is removed from its container or sacking and is placed in the hole that the new soil level is no higher above the stem than it was previously; nevertheless the plant must be firm in the ground. It should then be given a good top mulch of peat and pine needles (if available) which should be spread around the plant about a foot (30cm) from the stem and then well watered. Planting may take place at any time between October and the end of April, provided the ground is not too dry or frosted.

Pruning is not generally required but plants may be lightly shaped when they are coming into flower and the cut growth is always welcome for floral decorations. In the case of old plants, any dead wood should be cut out; likewise straggly lower branches are best removed in order to allow plenty of light and air to get to the stem, but live branches must be painted with a wound preservative such as Arbrex to prevent loss of sap and rotting.

If grafted plants have been purchased, regular inspections must be carried out to ensure that any new growth from below the graft (a join usually at the base of the stem) is quickly removed, otherwise the stock on to which your hybrid or species has been grafted (usually the purple *R. ponticum*) will very quickly take over. In older gardens evidence of this is frequently seen – just a few branches of the old original hybrid are left among a mass of *R. ponticum*.

Where possible, plants should be dead-headed after flowering; this will help the plant to set flower again the following season, but care must be taken not to remove any new growth in the process.

Feeding of young plants is not vital but the use of a good slow-acting general fertiliser in the early spring is always beneficial. Here it is best to follow the manufacturer's instructions. Where it is noticed that a plant is showing signs of yellowing of the foliage this is usually caused by chlorosis due to lack of magnesium in the soil and is best treated with applications of Epsom salts or magnesium lime watered into the soil around the plant. Alternatively, but at greater cost, a chelated compound or fritted trace elements may be used.

Diseases and Pests   Rhododendrons and azaleas suffer remarkably little from pests and disease. Leaves are sometimes attacked by a weevil which makes notches in the leaf margins. Spraying or dusting with HCH on the foliage and soil surface at dusk when damage is occurring around the base of the stem will usually cure. Buds sometimes fail to open and turn brown; more often than not this is due to frost burn, but occasionally it is due to a disease known as "bud blast", in which case it is essential to remove and burn all unopened, unsightly brown buds. Control rhododendron leafhopper, the disease vector, by spraying with fenitrothion or HCH in late summer.

In all soils rhododendrons are very susceptible to infection by honey fungus. The plant dies from the top and it is always fatal. Dead or dying plants must be dug out and burnt and the soil treated before replanting can take place. Specialist advice should be obtained.

Evergreen azaleas are sometimes attacked by an unsightly blight known as azalea leaf gall, a wind-borne disease which forms a pale green fungus type of growth on the leaves. Affected leaves and flowers become swollen and distorted; at first they are pale green, then white. Again, this must be completely removed and burnt and the plant then sprayed with mancozeb.

After periods of severe frost or drought, plants will sometimes die. The cause is usually bark-split. If this is noticed in time, then the dying wood may be cut out and the splits painted with a wound paint, which will arrest any further splitting.

25.

Lilies

Many of those just coming into gardening are rather uncertain what a lily really is. This is not surprising, because so many other plants, some quite dissimilar, take the name "lily" in common parlance but have no connection with the genus *Lilium*. It soon becomes apparent what is, and what is not, a true lily. This may be because lilies have a way of turning up in all sorts of gardens. We meet them in the lowliest as well as in the largest and most significant. At their best they are magnificent, and it is from these encounters we begin to learn why we are drawn to cultivate them.

The cultivation of members of the genus *Lilium* should follow the sound gardening principles common to most plants. The soil should be well worked and be very well drained. Even those lilies which inhabit wet places should never be planted in stagnant conditions; moisture should be in a state of flow and the bulbs planted above. Given excellent drainage most lilies will take all the water they can get during the spring. Many live on snow melt in their natural habitats and are awash with water early on, but are in dryish, stony loam with a dry atmosphere above ground when flowering time arrives.

Lilies require feeding with a balanced fertiliser, preferably yielding a slow release of nitrates. This should be applied in early spring. Loam should contain much humus and this should be plentiful towards the surface for stem-rooting lilies. If conditions are rather unsuitable and cannot be sufficiently improved then deep planting should be avoided and instead the soil level built up with humus-rich compost. It is vitally important to treat any lily bulb with great care. Being composed of scales and not enclosed in a protective membrane, the bulb is easily damaged. Not only does wounding weaken the resulting growth, it is an invitation to disease. Bulbs should only be taken from the soil when it is essential and returned to their new abode with least delay. A few lilies will accept full sun, but most appreciate some shade, like that provided among shrubs where the base is shaded but the heads are in the open. Although not accepting anything severe, lilies will often withstand wind. Staking, where necessary, should be done neatly and carefully with slender bamboo canes. An open site may prove far better than a sheltered frost pocket, where stems will be damaged in spring and leaves will wither with botrytis in later months.

Like other plants lilies suffer from diseases and pests. Much has been said on this subject, but no exaggerated view should be accepted. Many failures have been due to the poor condition of bulbs received at a time too late for planting. Basal rot is not usually evident where good drainage and soil conditions exist. When this trouble is suspected from browning on scales or poor, bronzed growth with poor or non-existent root action, the bulbs should be given a dip treatment using a systemic fungicide. This may be followed by scaling to obtain young fresh bulbs.

Botrytis and similar disorders affecting the foliage are often dependent on environmental conditions. Spraying with a copper fungicide is the best treatment. Unfortunately, few lilies like their leaves wetted following spring growth, so garden watering by sprayer or hose can cause trouble.

Virus diseases are the *bête noire* of lily growers and destruction of affected plants is the best form of hygiene. Identification, however, of virus-ridden plants is often difficult. The commonest distinguishing factor is pale streaked, mottled or curling foliage. Before burning precious bulbs remember radiation frosts can have a similar crippling effect on plants. Some lilies have a tolerance to viruses and appear to continue to grow strongly, as does *L. lancifolium (L. tigrinum)*; other species will curl up and die within a few months, like *L. auratum* and the quickly grown *L. formosanum*, which is a good indicator to keep in the greenhouse. Complete control will prove difficult, but aphids are the main vector and so lilies must be kept clean of these pests. Groups of lilies should be kept separate from each other. Growing lilies in fresh soil is good practice, so resist the temptation of planting new bulbs where others have languished. Keep tulips away from lilies, rogue out bad specimens and especially those with broken colour.

From what has already been said it is obvious that aphids are the most important pests to eradicate, so work out a spraying programme to keep the insects completely at bay. Another major pest is the slug. It treats the lily as good food both above and below ground, so the usual controls regularly applied must be maintained. In spring one must keep a very close watch indeed, as even a few slugs can do much damage to tender shoots. Remember that when a stem is badly damaged the lily has no chance of growing again that year, and without stem growth bulbs are severely weakened taking long to recover. Mice are a great problem in places and have to be controlled, as do such underground pests as millipedes, leatherjackets and wireworms.

PROPAGATION There may be a natural reluctance among us to grow bulbs from seed, but with lilies this most natural way is the best way. This has been advocated now for many years and those who have tried it have never regretted it. Good quality bulbs in any reasonable cultivar are hard to come by, and, even given some success are normally received far too late in the season for planting outdoors (October is the best month). Of course clonal hybrids have to be reproduced by vegetative means, so bulbs are the only suitable form for distribution. Lily seed may be obtained in many different ways, traditionally from seedsmen and nurserymen, from lily groups and societies at home and abroad; from other specialist societies, such as the Alpine Garden Society, and by carefully cultivating correspondence with like-minded people throughout the world. Most lily enthusiasts are willing and able to exchange seed, whereas bulbs are a more difficult proposition, especially if the recipient is in another country. The seed is large and easy to handle individually. Although some seed, such as that of *L. regale*, may be sown outdoors on a prepared bed in rows like onions, it is usually sown in half-pots not too closely spaced, so that the seedlings may be allowed to grow on for a couple of seasons undisturbed, before being moved on to larger pots, prepared beds or their permanent positions outside.

Scaling A fairly easy means of multiplying lilies is by scaling. Scales should be detached carefully from the base of the bulb. If they are then cleaned and placed in a warm, moist and preferably sterile compost they will shortly start to grow bulblets on the edge of the scales. These may be detached when easily handled and grown on. If the numbers required are not large polythene bags can be used as the initial container and the task performed over-winter, so that the small bulbs can be brought into growth quite naturally in the spring. Some lilies readily produce bulblets on the stem just below ground level. This increase can be helped by mulching with leaf-mould or peat and sharp sand with this layer being kept moist. A few lilies will produce bulbils on the stem in the leaf axils. These should be removed in early autumn and either potted, if the numbers are small, treating them like scale bulblets, or setting them in rows outside with a covering of 1in(2.5cm) of leafmould.

Hybridizing Those who become keen on growing lilies from seed will doubtless wish to produce their own hybrids. This is a most exciting pastime for those that can bear the initial period of waiting. Once this is over there is the joy every summer of watching new, never-seen-before lilies

144. *Flower shapes in lilies:* **A**, Lilium martagon *(turkscap);* **B**, L. bulbiferum *(upright);* **C**, L. auratum *(bowl-shaped);* **D**, L. speciosum *(recoiled and papillose); and* **E**, L. regale *(trumpet).*

unfolding. The sexual parts of the lily are so obvious that few can fail to see how the plentiful pollen can be placed on the stigma. It is better to try the quicker-maturing and good seed-bearing lilies first to save disenchantment. Keep a record of all crosses and write down the results both good and bad. Some hybrids are sterile; a few are triploids and are unlikely to produce viable seed with the majority, which are diploids. Haphazard crosses made between lilies exhibiting great differences have rarely shown results, so it is better not to waste time on them. A careful study of "The International Lily Register" (published by the R.H.S.) will give an idea of what has been achieved.

LILIUM SPECIES TO GROW

Short notes follow on those lilies which are more easily obtainable, although still difficult to find at times. They give an impression of the broad spectrum covered by the genus.

LILIUM ALEXANDRAE (Ukishima, Southern Japan). A fine white trumpet lily best grown under glass when it is not difficult to please. It is closely allied if not conspecific with *L. nobilissimum* which differs only in its more erect trumpet.

L. AMABILE (Korea). A grenadine red turkscap, which, although not very exciting itself, has been very important as a parent, especially in its yellow form, var. *luteum.*

L. AURATUM (Japan). This may be the most splendid of all lilies commonly grown, but its reputation is marred by its susceptibility to virus diseases. Its great beauty has been passed on to a race of hybrids with *L. speciosum*, referred to generally as Oriental hybrids, but also as Parkmannii hybrids, recalling the original cross.

L. BOLANDERI (Western U.S.A.). This is of great interest for its distinctive deep wine-red, heavily spotted, slightly recurved flowers and semi-glaucous foliage, so making it a useful parent.

L. BROWNII (China). Little seen today and requires reintroduction. Its place in gardens is often taken by such hybrids as *L*. 'Black Dragon'.

L. BULBIFERUM (Europe). With or without bulbils in its leaf axils, this is the common orange or "crocus"-flowering lily of the alps.

L. CALLOSUM (eastern Asia). Although covering a greater range in nature than any other asiatic lily, this red turkscap has become uncommon in gardens.

L. CANADENSE (Eastern North America). Either in yellow or red form this is, perhaps, the most elegant of all lilies. Liking wet conditions, it should be attempted by all gardeners. *L. michiganense* is closely allied to it but not quite in the same class.

L. CANDIDUM (Europe). The Madonna lily is best known in its sterile forms, often growing luxuriantly in cottage gardens, but it should also be tried from seed of recent introductions, which should produce bulbs free from disease.

L. CARNIOLICUM (the Balkans). This also includes *LL. albanicum, bosniacum* and *jankae*. They are turkscaps, red or yellow, spotted or unspotted. Although slow to mature, the bulbs are long-lived and should be attempted more frequently.

L. CERNUUM (Eastern Asia). This is a lovely pink turkscap which has improved the colour range of Asiatic hybrids. However, its true grace is often lost, so this species should always be tried. It is most suitably placed in the rock garden.

L. CHALCEDONICUM. This species, including *L. heldreichii* (Greece), is a gorgeous tomato-red turkscap which, although growing on limestone in nature, will succeed on acid soil too. It brought the unique pale yellow colouring into the first lily hybrid, *L. × testaceum*, the cross being with *L. candidum.*

L. CILIATUM (Turkey). An ivory-white turkscap belonging to the Balkan group, as does *L. ponticum* which is yellow with a reddish-brown centre.

145. *Flower shapes in lilies (contd.):* **F**, L. szovitsianum *(recurved, not true turkscap);* **G**, L. canadense *(bell-shaped);* **H**, L. candidum *(broad funnel-shaped);* **I**, L. mackliniae *(deep bowl-shaped); and* **J**, L. formosanum *(narrow-tubed or long trumpet).*

F **G** **H**

I **J**

L. COLUMBIANUM (Western North America). This lily has been somewhat maligned in the past, but it is a long-lived yellow turkscap which has proved itself well in British gardens.

L. CONCOLOR (Eastern Asia). A relatively small upright flowering scarlet lily useful in the rock garden when suitably placed. The yellow form is called var. *coridion*.

L. DAURICUM (Eastern Asia). This species must have its genes in most Asiatic hybrids, but possibly is little grown itself. It is particularly hardy and it would be more than a curiosity to grow the various forms, especially those from the highest latitudes.

L. DAVIDII (China). An important red turkscap, which may now tend to be confused with hybrid strains it has helped to produce. A fully grown specimen of its var. *willmottiae* is very beautiful.

L. DUCHARTREI (China). A dainty and charming turkscap with white flowers suffused with purple spotting. It has a taller and more stately cousin, *L. taliense*, which is just as beautiful.

L. FORMOSANUM (Taiwan). Both this and *L. philippinense* (N. Luzon) are easily and quickly grown from seed and bear fine white trumpets. The dwarf variety of the former called *pricei* is considered to be the hardiest type.

L. GRAYI (Eastern U.S.A.). This species is close to *L. canadense* and almost as lovely, but not so easily obtained. The flowers are crimson-red.

L. HANSONII (Takeshima, Korea). This species belongs to the *martagon* group, with which lilies it has produced some excellent hybrids. Its flowers are orange-yellow with the petals reminding one of orange peel. Easily cultivated.

L. HENRYI (Central China). A tall lily with orange-yellow, recoiled flowers. It is usually easily grown. In 1928 Debras, using *L. sargentiae* as the other parent, created a breakthrough in hybridisation, producing *L. × aurelianense*.

L. HUMBOLDTII (California). A sturdy, handsome golden-orange, heavily-spotted lily not sufficiently grown today, having been surpassed in gardens by the Bellingham Hybrids. *L. pardalinum* was the other parent and the outstanding clone is L. 'Shuksan'.

L. JAPONICUM (Japan) A most graceful trumpet of pale pink or white. Although rarely very vigorous it is a most worthy plant to cultivate.

L. KELLEYANUM (California). This group name covers a selection of variable yellow turkscap lilies, which may also be found under the following names: *LL. fresnense, inyoense, nevadense* and *shastense*. They all deserve to be grown.

L. KELLOGGII (Western U.S.A.). A beautiful pink turkscap, but a challenge and difficult to please.

L. LANCIFOLIUM (syn. *L. tigrinum*) (Far East). Usually seen in its sterile triploid form. It has been a good parent of many hybrids, but it is treated with suspicion by many, because it carries virus disease which is so easily transmitted to other lilies less tolerant.

L. LANKONGENSE (Western China). Another fine pink turkscap, which has been used to great effect in Dr. North's new hybrids from Scotland.

L. LEICHTLINII (Japan). A pretty yellow turkscap but difficult to cultivate while the red form, *L. maximowiczii*, is less interesting and easy.

L. LEUCANTHUM (Central China). An excellent tall-growing trumpet, usually grown in the variety *centifolium*. Unfortunately, many hybrids of little distinction may be found under this name today.

L. LONGIFLORUM (Ryukyu Islands). The florists' white trumpet known under many varietal names and once very fashionable. It requires greenhouse conditions and must be kept free of disease.

L. MACKLINIAE (Manipur). A lovely bowl-shaped lily of white touched with pinkish-purple. It was found at the end of the Second World War, since when many plantsmen have sought to grow it to perfection, but it sulks if caught by virus disease.

L. MACULATUM (Japan). This name covers the upright flowering lilies of Japan other than *L. dauricum*. They may be confused with various hybrids and forms which have been cultivated in the East for hundreds of years.

L. MARITIMUM (California). This lily has orange-red, spotted flowers and in its dwarfest form is only a few inches high; otherwise 2ft(60cm) or more.

21. *Winter aconites (*Eranthis hyemalis*) naturalise freely, particularly on alkaline soils, and are happy in the open or in partial shade. Nothing is more cheerful to observe than this richly coloured bulbous flower in late winter.*

22. *Garden cultivars of crocus paint the sward bright at Wisley in March.*

23. *From as early as January the garden is enriched by the flowering of the snowdrops. Here* Galanthus nivalis, *the common snowdrop, photographed at Boughton House, near Kettering, Northamptonshire, has a backdrop of those colourful willows,* Salix alba *'Chermesina' (syn. 'Britzensis') and 'Vitellina', respectively red and yellow-stemmed.*

24. *The handsome ornamental onion,* Allium giganteum, *4 to 5ft (1.25 to 1.5m) tall (see p.110).*

L. MARTAGON (Europe and Asia). The familiar turkscap is an easy and excellent garden plant in most soils. It is best to grow the named colour forms unless they can be cultivated *en masse*.

L. NANUM, L. OXYPETALUM (Himalayas). These are purplish-white or yellow, dwarf, single-flowered lilies that have been grown more successfully in Scotland than in the south.

L. NEILGHERRENSE (Southern India). A lovely white trumpet, but not being truly hardy and having a stoloniform habit make it a little difficult.

L. NEPALENSE (Himalayas). This again is of doubtful hardiness. It is a striking yellowish-green and purple trumpet lily considered better for the greenhouse, although in recent years it has been over-wintered outside in Britain.

L. PARDALINUM (California). Perhaps the commonest, but also the most important, lily from this region. It is available in many forms and has played a vital part in producing many good hybrids.

L. PARRYI (California and Arizona). Like *L. pardalinum* this yellow scented lily has played an important part in hybridisation, but it is a fastidious plant in cultivation.

L. PARVUM (California). This species comes yellow from lower regions and red from higher altitudes. There is also a pink form called *hallidayi*, and none of them are too demanding.

L. PHILADELPHICUM (Eastern and mid-west North America). This lily has orange-red upright blooms. In cultivation it can be grown to maturity, but it has proved persistently hard to maintain thereafter.

L. POLY.PHYLLUM (Himalayas). An ivory-white lily, sometimes spotted and sweetly scented and would seem to require careful attention.

L. POMPONIUM (Southern Europe). A striking sealing-wax red turkscap accepting both acid and limestone soils, but enjoying an open, warm situation.

L. PUMILUM (Eastern Asia). A charming red turkscap of fairly dwarf stature needing an open situation. Not long-lived, but easily raised from seed.

L. PYRENAICUM (Europe). Usually with yellow turkscap flowers, it has, with *L. martagon*, the reputation of being one of the easiest lilies to grow in Britain, having become naturalised in some western counties.

L. REGALE (China). The most common trumpet lily found in gardens. It is accommodating in most soils, can be easily and quickly raised from seed, even in the open ground, and can hold its own against many fancy hybrids.

L. RUBELLUM (Japan). A pink trumpet lily which is long-lived and a beautiful addition to the woodland garden.

L. SARGENTIAE (China). A fine long trumpet of excellent form and coloration on a white ground.

L. SPECIOSUM (Japan). This is our most important late-flowering lily, continuing the season through September. It has a strong constitution. The flowers are reflexed, white or suffused carmine in varying degrees.

L. SUPERBUM (Eastern U.S.A.). It lives up to its name, being a tall and majestic orange turkscap. It comes from wet areas and usually blooms in August.

L. SZOVITSIANUM (Caucasus). The most widely grown species of a yellow-flowered group, including *L. monadelphum, L. kesselringianum, L. ledebourii* and *L. kossii*. The flowers are recurved, but not turkscap, and strongly scented. A successful cross between *L. monadelphum* and *L. candidum*, producing L. 'June Fragrance' was a great achievement a few years ago.

L. TSINGTAUENSE (Korea). Although a member of the *martagon* group, this lily has upright red flowers. It is a good grower and a useful parent.

L. VOLLMERI (Western U.S.A.). This looks like a lesser form of *L. pardalinum* but is far better than that suggests. Within its range a similar yellow lily exists called *L. wigginsii*.

L. WALLICHIANUM (Himalayas). A distinctive white trumpet with narrow foliage. It is not really hardy and seemingly rather difficult.

L. WARDII (China). A lovely pink turkscap, which is doubly useful for being later flowering than others.

L. WASHINGTONIANUM (Western U.S.A.). This white fading into purple, funnel-shaped lily is both marvellous and difficult.
CARDIOCRINUM GIGANTEUM (Himalayas). A magnificent woodlander bearing white trumpets stained wine-purple within. It should be said, perhaps, that it takes a long time to flower from seed. Its variety *yunnanense* is just as beautiful, if never so tall (the species is 6 to 12ft[2 to 3.75m] in height), but the bronzed stems and leaves are an extra distinction.

There are a number of other lily species for which space cannot be found here. Many are difficult to obtain or are not in cultivation. It is hoped this will not always be the case. Allied to *Lilium* are *Nomocharis* and *Notholirion*, which are also very beautiful plants. They are worthy of all the care and attention the plantsman can give them.

Hybrid lilies have come much to the fore in recent years and a broad selection, among the thousands which have been named, can provide an important basis in the lily grower's garden. Many will consider that the range of colour and floral display these can give will be sufficient for their needs. For the early part of the season crosses between *L. martagon* and *L. hansonii* under such general names as Backhouse Hybrids and Paisley Hybrids are essential, to be followed by those containing, often additionally, *L. tsingtauense*. One such is 'Hantsing' and there are others similarly named.

In early mid-season the Asiatics appear as the strongest group and cover a vast field of upright, outward-facing and pendant flowers. Jan de Graaff's Mid-Century Hybrids created a great stir after the Second World War, and succeeding generations with more complex parentage have provided the strong backbone to the lily grower's world. A little later the trumpet lilies command attention, and, once again, Jan de Graaff's efforts produced strains like *L.* Golden Clarion and *L.* Black Magic, which, incidentally, gave us all the opportunity to raise our own races of coloured trumpet lilies. At the same time, in the less formal woodland or "wild" garden, the tall, spectacular western American hybrids, like Bellingham Hybrids and Bullwood Hybrids, will be in full bloom. Nowadays there are many cultivars covering a wide colour spectrum, including pure yellows and delicate pale pinks.

At the latter part of the season the Orientals will be opening those enormous but still exceptionally beautiful flowers that stem from *L. auratum*. However, the range in shape and style of these hybrids is now very broad and for this we thank particularly the enthusiastic band of hybridisers from Australia and New Zealand.

26.

Cacti and Other Succulents

A vast subject has to be spanned in this chapter! Only a cross-section of the 25,000 or more succulent species can be considered, these involving nearly 60 plant families and classified within numerous genera. Succulents are distributed world-wide. Members of The *Cactaceae* are primarily New World plants; the so-called "other" succulents monopolise almost every corner of the world – certainly every continent.

A total repeat of habitat conditions is not, in the main, necessary in cultivation. An elementary knowledge of their peculiarities and require-ments is important, and the results can more than justify any understand-ing and attention given. Most species are from more arid places and are able to withstand adverse conditions, but they do not totally change their way of life when brought into cultivation – hence the importance of trying to understand them. It is possible for man to help nature to improve itself – a specimen grown from seed in cultivation is invariably superior to a wild "collected" plant! The days of trying to grow them in brick-dust, mortar-rubble and the like have passed. More rewarding results are available by making life easier for both plant and collector.

Very similar requirements apply whether the plants are cultivated in home or greenhouse, but in view of the fact that good light plays an important role in the production of good growth, there are many species unsuited for home cultivation, even on a window-ledge, and this will be referred to later.

Compost This is of prime importance! Many proprietary brands are available, and undoubtedly each has its merits. The essential factor is that the mixture should be porous – any tendency for the soil to remain wet for any length of time will prove injurious to succulents. It is, perhaps, better to make up your own mixture, especially if loam of good quality is obtainable. A suggested formula is: 1 part sterilised loam; 1 part well-sifted, thoroughly decomposed leafmould; and 1 part sharp, gritty, washed sand or fine gravel. These ingredients should be mixed together thoroughly, plus a sprinkling of slow-release fertiliser. The inclusion of charcoal chippings will help safeguard against souring of the compost.

Potting This can be done at almost any time of the year, but preferably in March when the growing season approaches. The type of pot is immaterial – clay or plastic, it is a matter of choice. Remember, however, that clay pots tend to dry out quicker than plastic ones, and may therefore require more attention. Whichever is used, always allow for good drainage. Use the size of pot most suited to the plant – overpotting is just as bad as underpotting. Do not repot for the sake of repotting; if the plant is content and looks right leave it alone.

Watering You cannot have a pre-determined time-table! It may be neces-sary each week, during alternate weeks or at longer intervals, or it might conceivably be daily, for it depends entirely on its weather conditions. Generally speaking, water is withheld during dormancy, from late October or early November to March. This is not due only to the unpredictable weather changes which prevail during these months in Britain, it also

ensures that the plants have the opportunity of depending upon their in-built store of nourishment. All succulents have this reserve, in stem, leaf or root, and they must be allowed to use it. After the resting season, water moderately at first; then, as the weather gets warmer, the hours of daylight increase and the containers tend to dry out more quickly, water thoroughly. Then wait until the soil is dry before watering again and repeating this programme throughout the whole growing season. If you are in doubt about the need for watering, it is better to leave it another day or so. Do not give "spoonfuls" repeatedly; it could prove most damaging. Never leave plants standing in water. Incorrect watering can cause rotting from the roots up.

Feeding This is important if the best results are to be achieved. Very few fertiliser formulas have been prepared especially for succulents and most lack the required trace elements. The inclusion of nitrogen and potash is necessary and just as important is the need for the presence of the elements iron, magnesium, boron, copper, manganese and molybdenum. Only feed – and feed regularly – when the plants are in vigorous growth, *never* when they are dormant or looking sick.

Position By far the greatest number of species, cacti and otherwise, prefer a truly bright position; this will encourage strong growth and flowering. Keep the plants out of draughts, which are harmful. With certain epiphytic plants, a semi-shady situation is desirable, this primarily to offset any tendency to dehydration and loss of vigour.

PEST AND DISEASE CONTROL The majority of pests can be dealt with satisfactorily by prevention rather than cure. Mealy bug, root mealy bug, scale insects, greenfly and sciarid fly can be kept at bay by periodical applications of a systemic insecticide which includes malathion (not itself, of course, systemic). White fly can prove more difficult, and these usually attack *Euphorbia* and certain other leaf succulents. Systemics will do much to keep the plants immune, but if an infestation develops, HCH or smokes can be used in a greenhouse to quickly eradicate the pest. Red spider mite appears to flourish in a dry atmosphere, when plants are left dry too long in warm weather. The use of systemic insecticides as a preventive together with good ventilation and high humidity will jointly reduce the possibility of attack. Woodlice, ants, slugs and snails are easily exterminated with freely available proprietary pesticides.

If a strict cultural regime is adhered to, very few, if any, diseases are likely to beset succulents. Incorrect ventilation is one of the main causes of disease, coupled with incorrect watering. Damping-off is usually a disease of seedlings, and fungicides such as captan, zineb or Cheshunt compound are antidotes. Black-rot is liable to attack certain species of *Asclepiadaceae* and *Epiphyllum*. This may be due to too high a nitrogen content in the soil, or, even more likely, to bacteria entering the plant and causing it to turn black and rot. The use of a copper-based fungicide will probably help to confine it, but if the disease has taken too great a hold it is best to cut away completely the affected part and to stand the plant in a shady place to allow the cut to callus over.

The only other possible difficulty is "rust" (a physiological problem) which can be prevented by ensuring that water is not permitted to remain on the surface of a plant for too long, or in full sun.

PROPAGATION Basically there are three methods of increasing cacti and succulents – by seed, vegetative propagation and grafting. We will consider these in turn.

Increase from seed Seed propagation has several advantages, and while seemingly a longer process, no other method is so rewarding. Always strive to sow fresh seeds which will give better germination, and use a specially prepared compost such as the John Innes seed compost or a similar mixture. Good drainage is of paramount importance, particularly at the base of the

146. *A flat graft. A clean cut is made across the base of the scion and the top of the stock with the edges of the stock being carefully bevelled. Stock and scion are secured firmly with a rubber band (see opposite page and p.222).*

container where there should be a layer of fine gravel and charcoal chippings to prevent water-logging and keep the compost "sweet". Then fill the container with compost to within ½in((1cm) of the rim and firm well to produce a completely level surface which will not allow water to drain into one place. Large seeds should be covered to a depth equal to their own diameter, the cover preferably being of fine sandy gravel. With very small or dust-like seeds, it is best to first sprinkle a thin layer of sharp, gritty sand over the whole surface, then very carefully scatter the seeds evenly and water them in. The seeds then become lodged between the particles of sand, and are held securely throughout the period of germination. The presence of moisture – not at all the same thing as wetness – is essential throughout the time from sowing to germination, and for the three months following. The containers should be placed in a shady position out of direct sunlight; a covering with glass or paper will help to provide the required shade and humidity. If condensation develops on the inner surface of the glass, wipe it off, as drips can be injurious to the seedlings. January to March is the ideal time for sowing in a temperature of 70°F(21°C) which must be kept constant. Germination takes place in a matter of weeks with most species, but some may germinate within a few days, others may take months. When the seedlings appear, give more ventilation and light – but not direct sunshine.

Do not be hasty in pricking-out the seedlings. They can remain safely in the original container for many months or even a year. When they have taken on the semblance of the parent plant (with cacti it is when the little spines are in evidence), and they can be handled easily, then they can be potted on satisfactorily.

Vegetative propagation This is an equally interesting method of increase, requiring the removal of offsets (as with *Mammillaria*, *Rebutia* etc.), pads (as with *Opuntia*) or severing a section of the parent plant and allowing a few days for callusing to take place before setting it in a very sandy compost, preferably with bottom heat, to root. Such material should be kept out of full sun until the roots are established.

Many species of *Crassulaceae* can be grown from leaf-cuttings, these being set in sharp sand and placed in a shady place until roots appear. They can then be potted without hesitation. There are only few exceptions to this method of propagation – members of the *Mesembryanthemaceae* offer no problem – but certain of the *Euphorbiaceae* and *Asclepiadaceae* exude a milky sap when cut, which can be staunched by placing the cut section in water for a few minutes. The essential factors in successful vegetative increase can be summarized as follows: Always use a really sharp, clean knife; use mature growth – cuttings made from new growth are more likely to rot than root; only "set" cuttings which have callused over; use a sandy compost – good drainage is important – and keep this just moist for succulents, but drier for cacti; keep the temperature at 70°F(21°C), or bottom heat at that if air temperature cannot be maintained; provide good light, but not direct sunshine; and take cuttings in the growing season, never in cold, damp weather.

Grafting This has limited usefulness in the propagation of cacti and succulents. The technique has specific applications, and notably the speeding-up of growth in those species which are exceedingly slow to increase in size when on their own roots (for example, *Blossfeldia*, *Ariocarpus* and *Obregonia*). Cristations and other abnormalities which occur with certain cacti can be preserved by means of grafting, when attractive "crests" can be developed. Grafted plants with coloured tops – red, orange or yellow – again prove the value of this process. These seedlings, which germinated without chlorophyll and would surely die immediately their cotyledons withered, can be established by grafting on to suitable stock.

The process simply consists of uniting one plant with another. The seedling or cutting, called the "scion", needs to be carefully severed and united to the stem of another plant, the "stock". Different methods are used, dependent on the type of plant being grafted. A very sharp knife is an

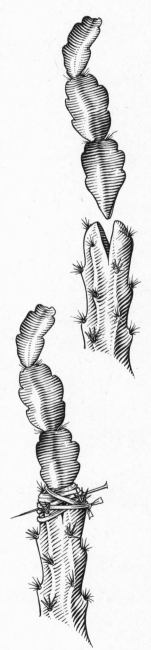

147. *A cleft graft held in place with a cactus spine and raffia (see p.222).*

essential requirement, preferably one with a razor-blade edge.

With the flat graft a clean cut is made across the base of the scion and the top of the stock, the cut surfaces being compatible. The edges of the stock needs to be carefully bevelled to avoid any subsequent drying-out detaching the scion. Then, before either surface dries, place the two together, securing them firmly with a rubber band until the union is complete.

The cleft graft is suited to slender or thin-segmented plants like *Zygocactus* and *Epiphyllum*. A V-shaped cut is made in the stock and an inverted V in the scion so that they fit neatly together; insert the scion while the cuts are still fresh, securing one to the other with a fine cactus spine. Bind the join around with raffia if this is considered necessary. It is most important that the two parts should be held very firmly together or disappointment will follow.

With the side graft the cuts are made diagonally, thus providing a larger area of contact between stock and scion. The two cut surfaces must match up and be fixed together with a spine. Then bind raffia around the join and support with a thin cane.

Many cactus species make excellent grafting stock, these including *Trichocereus pachanoi, T. spachianus, Hylocereus* spp., *Pereskia* spp., *Pereskiopsis* ssp. and *Selenicereus* spp. You must use cactus for both stock and scion, just as *Euphorbia* stock for *Euphorbia* grafts and so on. Graft in early summer, when the plants are in full growth. After the grafting operation, keep the plants in an airy, fairly shady position until the union is established. Never graft for grafting's sake – only if there is a real purpose in doing so.

SELECTED PLANTS

Abbreviations: GL (good light). RS (rest season). GH (greenhouse). IC (indoor culture). Fl. (flower). PS (partial shade). FW (free watering). SP (sunny position). Temperatures stated are the minimum required.

Cactaceae

MAMMILLARIA (Mexico, U.S.A.). Caespitose or solitary plants, quick growing, not temperamental. Require GL. Many Fl. within 18 months from seed. GH or IC. RS November – March. 45°F(7.5°C). FW in growing season. *M. bocasana* (white), *M. candida* (pink), *M. elongata* (cream), *M. glassii* (pink), *M. longimamma* (yellow), *M. marksiana* (greenish-yellow), *M. matudae* (pale purple), *M. mazatlanensis* (carmine), *M. rhodantha* (purplish-pink), *M. spinosissima* (pink to purple), *M. zeilmanniana* (reddish-purple). About 300 species and varieties. Among the best in terms of attraction and easy cultivation.
NOTOCACTUS (South America). Caespitose or solitary plants, mainly easy and fast growing. Not temperamental. Fl. 1–3 years from seed. GL. GH. IC. RS November–March. 50°F(10°C). FW in growing season. *N. allosiphon* (pale yellow), *N. crassigibbus* (sulphur-yellow), *N. haselbergii* (red), *N. herteri* (purplish), *N. mammulosus* (bright yellow), *N. ottonis* (golden-yellow), *N. rutilans* (pale purple), *N. scopus* (yellow, red centre), *N. tabularis* (yellow). About 50 species and varieties. Mainly large flowers around crown.
REBUTIA (South America). Generally caespitose plants, fast growing; not difficult but careful watering essential. Fl. about two years from seed, forming around the plant. GH. PS. RS November–April. 50°F(10°C) for safety. *R. albiflora* (white), *R. grandiflora* (carmine), *R. kesselringiana* (yellow), *R. kariusiana* (deep pink), *R. marsoneri* (deep yellow), *R. minuscula* (red), *R. violaciflora* (violet-red). About 90 species and varieties, many very uncommon.
SULCOREBUTIA (Bolivia, Chile). Among the most colourful, mainly caespitose, slow-growing, often grafted. GH. SP. RS November–April. Moderate watering. Not readily available, but extremely rewarding. *S. candiae* (yellow), *S. glomerispina* (purple), *S. kruegeri* (orange-yellow), *S. mizquensis* (magenta), *S. steinbachii* (scarlet), *S. tiraquensis* (purple), *S. tunariensis* (orange, red, purple). About 50 spp. and varieties. Not difficult if basic rules are kept. 50°F(10°C) essential.
GYMNOCALYCIUM (South America). Mostly solitary plants except in

maturity. Fl. after 1–2 years from seed. PS in growing season. FW. GH. IC.
RS November–March in SP. 50°F(10°C) for safety. *G. andreae* (yellow), *G.
anisitsii* (white), *G. bruchii* (pink), *G. gibbosum* (whitish), *G. horstii* (pinkish-
orange), *G. mihanovitchii* (yellowish), *G. quehlianum* (whitish), *G. saglione*
(pinkish-white). About 150 species and varieties, some rare, others mainly
available.
LOBIVIA (Central Peru – North Argentina). Solitary or caespitose plants.
Easy cultivation. Fl. 1–2 years from seed. GL in growing season. FW. GH.
RS November–March in SP. 45°F(7.5°C). Rich soil advised. *L. amblayensis*
(orange and red), *L. backebergii* (carmine), *L. culpinensis* (yellow or red), *L.
haematantha* (purple), *L. muhriae* (reddish-orange), *L. pentlandii* (pink, red or
yellow). Over 150 species and varieties, some uncommon, many available.
ECHINOPSIS (South America). Solitary or grouping plants with long,
trumpet-like Fl., sweetly scented. Rich compost. GL. GH. IC. FW. RS
November–March. 45°F(7.5°C). Mostly of easy cultivation. *E. aurea* (yellow),
E. eyriesii (white), *E. kermesina* (red), *E. mammillosa* (pinkish-white), *E.
multiplex* (pink), *E. oxygona* (pale red), *E. polyancistra* (white), *E. rhodantha*
(white). Over 70 species and varieties, many common but many very rare.

FEROCACTUS (Mexico, U.S.A.). Solitary, globular plants, some becoming
large cylindrical, a few offsetting. Fl. only on mature plants, with some after
four years from seed. GH. GL. FW in growing season. RS November
–March. 45°F(7.5°C). *F. acanthodes* (yellow), *F. echidne* (lemon-yellow), *F.
herrerae* (yellow, edged red), *F. latispinus* (pink-purple), *F. macrodiscus*
(purplish-red), *F. setispinus* (orange and red), *F. stainesii* (orange), *F.
wislizenii* (yellow to reddish), *F. uncinatus* (brownish-purple). Over 50
species and varieties, many readily available, a few uncommon.

148. Ferocactus, *typical of
the globular-shaped cacti
which are so attractive to
the eye.*

ECHINOCACTUS (Mexico, U.S.A.). Small genus of mainly large plants,
barrel-shaped. Fl. only in maturity. FW. GH. SP. Easy from seeds. RS
November–March. 45°F(7.5°C). *E. grusonii* (yellow), *E. horizonthalonius*
(pinkish-red), *E. ingens* (yellow), *E. platyacanthus* (yellow). Only 10 spp., a
few exceedingly rare.
ECHINOCEREUS (Mexico, U.S.A.). Mostly offsetting or branching, few
remain solitary. Fl. 3–4 years from seed. Rich soil, some require lime added.
SP. GH. Careful watering. RS November–March. 45°F(7.5°C). *E. baileyi*
(purple), *E. blanckii* and var. (violet-red, deep pink and so on), *E. coccineus*
(scarlet), *E. conglomeratus* (purple), *E. engelmannii* (red), *E. gentryi* (pink), *E.
papillosus* (yellow and red), *E. pentalophus* (lilac to carmine), *E. perbellus*

149. Echinocactus, *an
example of cacti of the
barrel-shaped type*

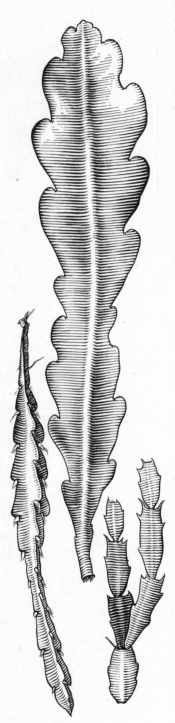

150. *Three different*
Epiphyllum, *illustrating*
the leaf-like type of cactus.

(purple), *E. websterianus* (pink). About 112 species and varieties all with colourful, large flowers. Many easily available, some rare.

CLEISTOCACTUS (South America). Columnar plants of up to 5ft(1.5m), mostly erect, some semi-prostrate, usually branching from base. Fl. often zygomorphic, tubular, slightly hairy. Easy from seed. Fl. on maturity, about five years. FW. GH. GL. RS late October–late March. 50°F(10°C). *C. baumannii* (orange-red), *C. candelilla* (purple and whitish-yellow), *C. hyalacanthus* (pale red), *C. rojoi* (red, yellow), *C. straussii* (wine-red), *C. tarijensis* (red, yellow tipped). Over 60 species and varieties, many very uncommon, others readily available.

CEREUS (South and North America). At one time a large genus, the majority now transferred to other genera. All columnar plants, and, together with *Carnegia gigantea*, *Pachycereus pringlei* and *P. pecten-aboriginum*, *Lemaireocereus* spp. and others, include some of the tallest members of the Cactaceae. Easy to raise from seeds, but few Fl. until 3ft(1m) or more tall. All night-flowering. GL position in GH. FW. RS November–March. (Stem colours given – all white Fl.) *C. azureus* (blue-green), *C. forbesii* (grey-green), *C. jamacaru* (mid-green), *C. peruvianus* (light-grey-green), *C. validus* (bluish-green). Mostly available. Others, as *C. roseiflorus* (pink Fl.) and *C. huntingtonianus* (pink Fl.), are difficult to obtain. The genus includes about 60 species and varieties.

OPUNTIA (North and South America). Plants with rounded or flattened pads, some cylindrical, tall growing, some bush-like, many dwarf and spreading. Mostly heavily spined and areoles armed with glochids (a mass of fine bristles). Easy cultivation. Fl. on mature plants. SP mostly (few exceptions). GH. FW. RS November–March. Mainly 45°F(7.5°C). *O. aciculata* (reddish or yellow), *O. articulata* (white), *O. crassa* (yellow), *O. erectoclada* (carmine), *O. macdougaliana* (orange), *O. microdasys* (white, yellow, reddish or brown glochids), *O. subulata* (red), *O. vestita* (scarlet), *O. versicolor* (yellow or reddish). These are only representative of approximately 600 species and varieties. A great number are readily available, many are unknown in cultivation.

EPIPHYLLUM (Central and South America). Including *Schlumbergera*, *Disocactus*. Epiphytic plants with flattened leaf-like stems or flat-segmented. Acid compost. Never completely dry. PS. GH. IC. Easily propagated from cuttings. Fl. November–July, dependent upon sp. FW in growing season. 50°F(10°C). *E. crenatum* (cream-white, scented), *E. oxypetalum* (whitish), *E. pumilum* (small, white), *Schlumbergera truncatus* (carmine-red) and *S. gaertneri* (scarlet) with their many variously coloured cultivars; *Disocactus biformis* (red), *D. eichlamii* (deep red). There are about 30 species and varieties within the genera listed here as well as nearly 3000 cultivars of the genus *Epiphyllum*.

HYLOCEREUS (Central and South America). Including *Selenicereus*, *Werckleocereus*. Clambering, climbing, mainly epiphytic spp. with angular, notched, flattened or rounded stems to 10ft(3m) or more long. Included here are some of the largest cactus Fl. Acid compost. PS. GH. Easily propagated from cuttings. FW. RS November–March. 50°F(10°C). *Hylocereus purpusii* (yellow tipped red), *H. triangularis* (white), *H. undatus* (whitish-yellow), *Selenicereus grandiflorus* (creamy-white), *S. wercklei* (pink), *Werckleocereus tonduzii* (creamy-white). Nearly 60 species and varieties involved, many very uncommon, others readily available.

RHIPSALIS (Mexico, South America, Madagascar). Including *Lepismium*, *Erythrorhipsalis*, *Acanthorhipsalis*. Primarily epiphytic, some saxicolous (rock-dwelling), easily propagated from seeds or cuttings. All of pendent or semi-pendent growth. Stems slender, round, angled, whorled, flattened, pubescent, segmented. Acid compost. FW. GH. IC. PS. Never allow to be completely dry. 50°F(10°C). *Rhipsalis cereoides* (three-angled stems), *R. crispata* (leaf-like segmented), *R. heteroclada* (cylindrical), *R. houlletiana* (flattened, leaf-like), *R. roseana* (flattened, notched) all with whitish Fl. *Lepismium cruciforme* (three-angled, often reddish), *L. trigonum* (three-angled, chain-like) with pinkish Fl. *Erythrorhipsalis pilocarpa* (slender rounded, greyish-green, pubescent – Fl. yellowish), *Acanthorhipsalis monacantha* (flat or three-angled, orange Fl.), *A. paranganiensis* (elongated two- or three-angled – white Fl.). All suited for hanging-basket culture. The three genera include about 100 species and varieties.

Agavaceae

AGAVE (Mexico, U.S.A., West Indies). Mainly large-growing plants, some hardy in southern England. Leaves "unwrap" from central "cone". Propagation from seeds or offsets. SP. GH. RS November–March. FW. 45°F(7.5°C) or lower if kept completely dry. *A. americana*, *A. franzosinii* have blue-green leaves, large growing. *A. filifera*, *A. parviflora*, *A. univittata* have variegated leaves, with margins often leaving white threads. *A. echinoides*, *A. striata*, *A. stricta* have dagger-like, tapering, green leaves. Particularly attractive spp. include *A. utahensis*, *A. victoria-reginae* and varieties. Over 250 species and varieties, many available, some unknown in cultivation.

Liliaceae

ALOE (Africa, Arabia). Small- and large-growing plants, mostly group quickly. Easy from seeds or offsets. SP. GH. IC. Moderate watering at all times. 45°F(7.5°C) or more in Fl. season. Fl. lily-like from centre or stem of rosette. *A. aristata* (reddish – dwarf), *A. bakeri* (orange-red and yellow – dwarf), *A. brevifolia* (red – dwarf), *A. ciliaris* (scarlet – climber), *A. cryptopoda* (scarlet – medium), *A. ferox* (scarlet-orange – large), *A. kedongensis* (scarlet – tall), *A. variegata* (pinkish-red – variegated leaves – medium). There are several hundred species and varieties and numerous cultivars; a vast number readily available, some rare.

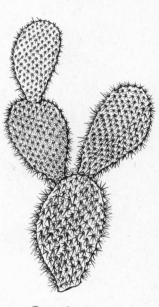

151. Opuntia, *representative of cacti with padded segments.*

GASTERIA (South Africa, Namibia). Small- to medium-sized plants, mainly very firm leaves arranged distichously (in two opposite rows). Easy cultivation, propagated from seeds or offsets. SP. GH. IC. Moderate watering. 45°F(7.5°C). Fl. swollen at base, several borne on elongated stem. *G. angulata* (spotted, angular leaves), *G. armstrongii* (thick, tuberculate leaves [covered in small projections]), *G. batesiana* (olive-green leaves, spotted and banded white), *G. liliputana* (short glossy-green, white marked and spotted leaves). Over 100 species and varieties in this somewhat confused genus.

HAWORTHIA (South Africa, Namibia). Mainly small-growing, freely offsetting plants with attractive foliage but insignificant Fl. GL. GH. IC. FW. Just moist in winter. Propagation from seeds or offsets. 45°F(7.5°C). *H. attenuata*, *H. coarctata*, *H. glabrata*, *H. limifolia*, *H. margaritifera*, *H. maughanii*, *H. planifolia*, *H. retusa* are only representative of possibly 300 or more species and varieties.

152. Agave (*left*) *and* Aloe *both illustrate the rosette shape.*

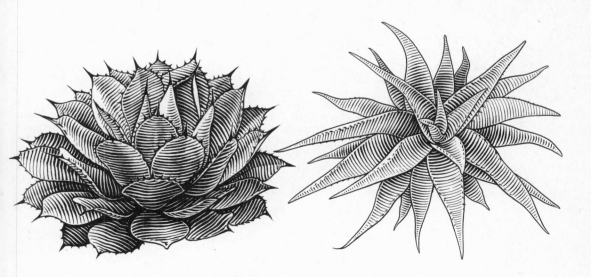

153. *Conophytums,*
mimicking plants which
have a fascination for many
gardeners making
succulents a speciality.

154. *Lithops, other*
mimicking plants which
amply repay the interest
taken in them.

Crassulaceae

CRASSULA (South Africa), Plants tree-like, rosette-forming, clambering and spreading, their habit and form being their chief attraction. Fl. usually white. SP. GH. IC. Fairly dry in winter. FW in growing season. 45°F(7.5°C) or slightly higher for some. Propagation from seeds or cuttings – of easy cultivation. C. argentea (tree-like), C. lycopodioides (like club-moss), C. perforata (leaves chain-like), C. teres (leaves in close-set miniature columns). Over 200 species and varieties.

ECHEVERIA (Mexico, U.S.A.). Rosette plants of foliage attraction, interesting, unusual and often colourful Fl. Easy cultivation. Propagated by stem or leaf cuttings. GH. IC. SP. FW – restrict in winter. 45°C(7.5°C). E. agavoides, E. nodulosa, E. potosina are representative of well over 100 species and varieties.

Other easily grown, fascinating genera within this family include Kalanchoe, Sedum, Aeonium, Monanthes, representing several hundreds of species.

Euphorbiaceae

EUPHORBIA (including Africa, Arabia). A vast family of cactus-like, shrubby, globular or other peculiarly-shaped plants. Propagation from seeds or cuttings. GH. IC (few). SP. Extreme care with watering. 50°F(10°C) or more. E. abyssinica (cactus-like), E. bupleurifolia (caudex with apical leaves), E. oncoclada (spineless, slender cylindrical stem, shrubby), E. milii (leafy-shrub, crown of thorns), E. xylophylloides (grey-green, flattened stems). One of the largest plant families, many hundreds of species.

Asclepiadaceae

Includes hundreds of species within the genera Stapelia, Duvalia, Huernia, Hoya, Stultitia and 30 others. Many species such as Stapelia variegata, Hoya carnosa and Ceropegia woodii are well-known in collections. The majority may be grown readily from seeds or cuttings. GL. GH. IC (few). Careful watering at all times. Open compost. In general, not beginners' plants.

Mesembryanthemaceae

Plants native to arid areas of Africa, Arabia, America and elsewhere, and includes about 120 genera and thousands of species. Many shrubby plants are included in genera such as Lampranthus, Ruschia and Delosperma. Most fascinating are the mimicry plants Lithops, Conophytum, Gibbaeum, Nananthus, Pleiospilos and kindred genera. These, as a group, are "specialist" plants and reference should be made to authoritative works on the subject. Most species can be grown successfully from seeds or offsets. Flowers are colourful and are readily produced in a bright sunny position. GH. IC (few). RS varies according to species, but mainly in the months from November to April – then keep completely dry. Moderate watering in growing season. 50°F(10°C) generally.

While the principal succulent plant families have been mentioned, many have, of necessity, been omitted. A great deal of information can be gathered by reference to authoritative books. Books of reference include Cactus Lexicon, by Curt Backeberg, published by Blandford, a comprehensive record of the Cactaceae, and Lexicon of Succulent Plants, by Hermann Jacobsen, published by Blandford, a complete reference book on other succulents. Practical handbooks include Cacti and Succulents, by Walther Haage, published by Studio Vista; Complete Handbook of Cacti and Succulents, by Clive Innes, published by Ward Lock; and The Illustrated Encyclopaedia of Succulents, by Gordon Rowley, published by Salamander.

27.

Other
Flower Specialities

In addition to the specialists' plants which have been given fuller treatment in preceding chapters there are, of course, countless others which provide entertaining hobbies for those who would specialize. The possibilities are endless. Almost any garden plant may be collected, hybridized and selected to provide a new range of colour or form for other gardeners. One has only to think of how lupins were transformed in shape, size and colour by a lone Yorkshire railwayman. Daffodils have become increasingly varied in size, shape and colour as a result of a long period of breeding by Cornish, Irish, Scottish and Dutch gardeners and nurserymen. Many new pinks and border carnations came for a Surrey nurseryman, and the range of colour and form in the camellia is being extended by breeders in America, Australia, New Zealand and Britain.

Wisley is full of plants raised or found there or in other gardens. We have by no means come to the end of new plants or the need for them. Even without breeding to increase the variety of plants the maintenance of a collection of a single group of garden plants is a worthwhile hobby for the gardener and for the benefit of others. Some genera and groups of plants which you may find include plants which arouse your special interest are as follows:

AURICULA Derived from two species of *Primula*; almost the whole colour range may be found with many striking patterns in the flowers. Mainly spring flowering. Quite hardy but one group, the show auriculas, need protection, but not heat, to preserve the fine bloom or meal on flowers and foliage. Best grown in small- to medium-sized pots with annual repotting. The alpine group succeed on rock gardens and in similar conditions. The auriculas have a long history and many old kinds survive. Specialist society: National Auricula and Primula Societies, with Midland, Northern and Southern sections.

BEGONIA Wide range of some 350 species, mostly from tropical countries with humid climates. There are two main groups and innumerable cultivars. One of the groups consists of garden forms used for summer bedding and grown from "corms", tubers or rhizomes and from seed. This group is also suitable for growing in pots indoors. Bright displays of red, pink, yellow and white flowers. Careful storage of resting roots gives little work during the winter. The other group includes the numerous species and their forms with similar flower colours but mainly attractive through the varied colours, sizes and textures of the typical lop-sided leaves. Best suited to warm, damp greenhouses, when they are of interest throughout the year. Many can be brought into the house for short or longer periods. They need continuous attention but automatic watering can be successful. Pests and diseases must be watched for and dealt with throughout the year. Specialist society: The National Begonia Society.

BROMELIADS A large family of plants from tropical America. The pineapple is probably the best-known member of this group of plants. Most have short stems with striking, brightly coloured flowers in almost every colour. These are often surrounded by rosettes of pointed and sometimes prickly leaves, some with long, arching stems. A few, such as *Bilbergia, Fascicularia* and *Bromelia*, will survive in cool greenhouses but most need considerable warmth. All need regular attention for trimming, splitting and re-potting. Specialist society: The British Bromeliad Society.

CAMELLIA Some 80 species from south-east Asia, mostly half-hardy shrubs, including those from which all our tea is produced. Half-a-dozen species are hardy or nearly so and have provided us with numerous cultivars that flower from mid-winter to June. Camellias need acid soil, ample moisture but no waterlogging. Most prefer light shade from tall trees. Very suitable for large pots or tubs on a patio or for growing in cool greenhouse. Many single, double and other shapely forms. New cultivars are introduced annually. Specialist society: The International Camellia Society.

CARNATIONS AND PINKS All derive from a few species of *Dianthus*. Perpetual-flowering kinds are suitable for cold greenhouse cultivation in pots or borders in well-drained alkaline soil. Border and other perennial carnations are quite hardy. Grow in open sunny beds and borders in similar soils. They were once very popular, with old names redolent of the quiet gardens of the past. All are easily propagated by cuttings and layers. There are also some interesting annuals. Specialist society: The British National Carnation Society.

CYCLAMEN A dozen or more species of perennial plants with tuberous roots. There are two main groups. First, the well-known winter pot plants bred over many generations from *C. persicum*, not hardy and needing a frost-free greenhouse in which to grow. These are best grown from seed each year, but plants can be maintained and made to flower over a number of years. The remainder of the species and forms with mauve, red, pink and white flowers are generally hardy and are the main interest of collectors. One or more can be found in flower almost throughout the year. They are grown outdoors in semi-shade with ample leafmould or peat or in pots or pans in cold greenhouses where the smaller kinds are seen to best advantage. They need attention but are undemanding and a small greenhouse can hold a large collection. Specialist society: The Cyclamen Society.

DELPHINIUM There are numerous species from many countries, and they include the annual larkspur, *Delphinium ajacis*. The stately border perennials derive from two European and Asian species and one American wildling, to which have recently been added two Californian species to produce the red and pink colours of the newer kinds. The soil in which they are grown must be well drained in the winter and protection must be provided from slugs. Wind protection is essential. Delphiniums are a major feature of the English summer flower border. Propagation is by cuttings or division; seed produces wide variety of new forms. Specialist society: The Delphinium Society.

FERNS (hardy and tender). Many but not all thrive in shaded gardens and greenhouses. Mostly need ample moisture and organic soils. They can add great variety to dark corners of the garden and over-shaded greenhouses. Interesting propagating methods. Specialist society: The British Pteridological (Fern) Society.

GLADIOLUS Mostly half-hardy corms from Southern Africa. More than 150 species, many rare in cultivation but worthy of attention. There are numerous continually changing cultivars in three or four main groups beloved by show exhibitors with mauve, red, pink, yellow and white flowers, mostly borne from June to September. Plant in succession from March to May to provide a long flowering season. They need detailed attention to weeding, staking and pest control for success on the show benches. Lift soon after flowering, dry, clean and store until following year. It is better to avoid using the same ground for subsequent plantings.

Specialist society: The British Gladiolus Society. Useful publications issued by The National Botanical Garden of South Africa.

NARCISSUS (daffodils) Some 50 species and thousands of cultivars are available. Almost all are hardy bulbs from Europe, North Africa and Asia. Yellow blooms predominate but white, orange and red ones are increasingly available. Flowers can be had from November to June. The smallest are best grown in pots or pans in a cold greenhouse, the rest almost anywhere in the garden. Two-year-old plants produce the best flowers. Short spurts of work: planting August to October; weeding or herbicide sprays December to March; pollinating and recording, if breeding, January to June; lifting and cleaning bulbs June and July. Replant on new ground – a well-manured vegetable soil suits very well. Specialist society: The Daffodil Society. *The Daffodil Year Book* is published annually by The Royal Horticultural Society.

NERINE A dozen or so half-hardy and almost hardy species of bulbs from South Africa, with an increasing number of cultivars. Clusters of red, pink and white flowers on single stems from August to October. Best grown in a cool greenhouse. Pot in July-August before flowering, but not every year. Water from then until the leaves die. Then keep dry until near the time for the flowers to appear. Specialist society: The Nerine Society.

ORCHIDS A vast range of species, hybrids and cultivars, many with long-lasting flowers in a wide variety of shapes and colours. There are very few hardy kinds (the British natives should not on any account be moved into cultivation, their needs are far too specialized and they are disappearing fast enough without any disturbance by collectors). The needs of the others vary from a frost-free greenhouse to those with quite high temperatures. Start with a few plants from a single genus or group needing the same temperature. A range of special pots, moss, peat, shredded bark, sand, sticks and tying material is needed. Meticulously careful and interesting seed-raising methods. Some greenhouse pests can be troublesome and need regular attention. There are at least four specialist societies, including The Orchid Society of Great Britain and The North of England Orchid Society.

PELARGONIUM (the geranium of home and garden) There are some 230 species of *Pelargonium* but few are in general cultivation. Numerous cultivars are grouped in the Decorative, Fancy, Regal and Show forms which were once popular. The present summer bedding and pot plants are mostly of the Zonal and Ivy-leaved groups. White, pink, red and mauve flowers are produced the year round if the light provided is adequate. Attractive foliage, sometimes scented. Valuable pot plants for the window-sill. Withstand neglect but thrive with attention. Raised from cuttings at almost any time of the year. Several new strains raised from seed. Specialist societies: The British Pelargonium and Geranium Society and the British and European Geranium Society.

SWEET PEAS All derive from the scented wild plant of southern Italy. They have been grown in English gardens for at least 200 years and are still being developed. The latest introductions are the dwarf kinds which are useful as border plants. They are annuals sown in pots from late autumn to early spring and planted in rows or clumps for summer flowering. The earlier the sowing the better and more abundant the flowers. They are trained up tall canes to produce unblemished straight stemmed flowers, or on pea boughs for garden decoration and cutting for flower arranging. A popular feature of summer flower shows. Specialist society: The National Sweet Pea Society.

TULIP Numerous species and many old and new cultivars. Wide range of colour, size and shape, in flower from March to June. Similar pattern of work to the daffodils (see *Narcissus* above) but most need regular annual lifting in June-July. Drying, cleaning and grading is necessary before replanting in October-December. The numerous small bulbs, grown separately in reserve, can greatly increase stocks of many kinds. The tulip

155. *Three narcissi which are of great interest to the enthusiast: top to bottom,* Narcissus *'Empress of Ireland',* N. *'Soleil d'Or' and* N. poeticus recurvus.

became a mania and was the cause of financial gambling in the 17th and 18th centuries.

FRUIT AND VEGETABLES Gardeners who grow their own vegetables and fruit now have the National Vegetable Society and the Fruit Group of the Royal Horticultural Society to encourage their efforts and arrange exhibits of their produce.

Specialist societies The addresses of the specialist societies referred to in this chapter have been omitted as normally these are the home addresses of honorary secretaries and are liable to change. Up-to-date advice can be obtained on this matter by writing to The Secretary, The Royal Horticultural Society, Vincent Square, Westminster, London SW1P 2PE, preferably enclosing a stamped, addressed envelope.

28.

Space-Effective Fruit Growing

All the hardy fruits, except strawberries, occupy the ground for long periods and good planning is essential. Where possible a composite fruit plot (see Fig.157) greatly facilitates operations such as feeding, spraying and netting against bird damage both to ripening fruits and to the buds in winter. Strawberries can more conveniently be accommodated in the vegetable garden to allow regular planting on fresh ground.

The Site   The range of fruits available is exciting although space and the potential of the site usually restricts the final choice. Adequate direct sunshine and reasonable shelter are essential to obtain the best quality and flavour. It is advisable to grow only early-ripening apples, pears and plums where some shading is unavoidable or where the aspect is cold and northerly. By the same token, the further north in the country one gardens the less successful will be later ripening cultivars.

Frost   Winter frosts seldom cause damage to fruit in this country, but the radiation frosts of spring are a fruit grower's nightmare – just one frost and all may be lost for a whole year. Fortunately, in the garden it is possible to cover at least some of the trees or bushes with old coats or curtains, and newspaper will protect strawberries successfully. Other useful aids are to keep any grass around trees cut short, and cultivated ground weed-free and firm; moist ground is preferable to dry. Such conditions ensure maximum

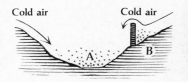

156.   *Areas of greatest frost risk. Cold air flowing down to a valley bottom* (**A**) *means that this low point carries the greatest frost risk. Hedges, walls and other obstructions across a slope which impede the passage of cold air in such motion* (**B**) *will create frost pockets.*

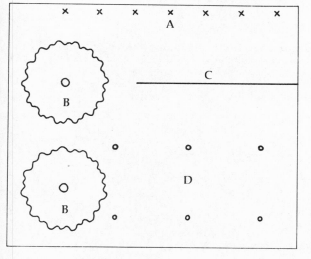

Scale: Ft

1 2 3 4 5

157.   *A basic layout for a fruit garden:* **A**, *seven cordon-trained apples and/or pears;* **B**, *two pyramid-trained pears;* **C**, *a row of raspberries and/or loganberries;* **D**, *six black currants, red currants or gooseberries.*

help from the reservoir of soil warmth, as it escapes into the night air.

Soil   A basically suitable soil is essential. Most soils are capable of growing some fruit successfully, but avoid badly drained soils. Calcareous or over-limed ground is difficult because it may cause lime-induced chlorosis (i.e., prevent the uptake of iron and manganese). This can be eased by heavy mulching to build up a more amenable top soil but expert advice may be necessary. Heavier soils will give the highest yields if well-drained; the lightest, sandy soils will give the earliest crops but need much more attention to feeding and watering.

The Soft Fruits   Strawberries, raspberries, loganberries and blackberries, red, white and black currants and gooseberries are suitable for almost any reasonable location in the British Isles. They require comparatively little space, should be both precocious and heavy cropping and together can cover a long season of fruiting from May until October. They do, however, require reasonable attention for consistent success to be achieved. Plenty of rotted farmyard manure or compost needs to be dug in before planting, and good aftercare, particularly with regard to feeding, essential pest and disease control and, where appropriate, pruning. Furthermore, because of the risk of certain serious virus diseases, it is important to obtain Ministry-certified plants and bushes as advertised.

Tree Fruits   These require more space, but dwarfing rootstocks for apples and pears and cordon training make these fruits a possibility for small gardens. Where available, EMLA status trees (denoting the healthiest material available) should be ordered but normally no manure should be used when planting as this causes excessive growth and delays fruiting. Trees growing in grass will require more nitrogen with regular mowing minus the grass box. The mowings then assist in nutrition.
   Most fruit trees need to be raised by budding or grafting onto a rootstock since they cannot easily be propagated by other vegetative means, neither will they breed true from seed. A few plums, however, are occasionally grown on their own roots (e.g., 'Pershore').

Spraying   The sensible use of pesticides will be necessary at times, and small trees will assist good coverage. Always follow the maker's instructions and avoid spraying during flowering to protect bees.

Herbicides   Simazine and paraquat can be used for weed control on larger areas but the utmost care is needed in timing and correct choice of herbicide for the crop. Expert advice should always be obtained first if in doubt and a separate can or sprayer kept specifically for herbicides.

APPLES

The apple is the most popular tree fruit and most areas of the British Isles are capable of growing one cultivar or another. Dwarfing rootstocks (see Fig.158) now make the small, quick-cropping, easily-managed tree pre-eminent and only a special requirement should dictate the growing of the large trees still common in older orchards and gardens.

158. *The effect of rootstocks on apple tree size.*

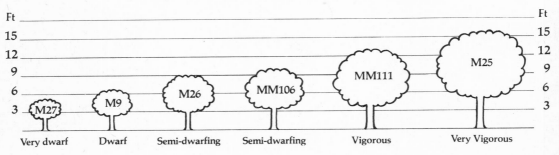

Site and Soil Reasonably sheltered, sunny sites offer the widest possibilities whereas colder, less sunny ones may necessitate the choice being restricted to cooking apples and, at best, early ripening dessert kinds. The adaptability of apples to most soil types is fortunate and only the very alkaline and badly drained ones are likely to cause persistent trouble. Deficiencies of iron and manganese often occur on soils overlying limestone and severe cases may call for remedial treatment (see p.297).

Source of Trees The source of planting material is important. Specialist fruit nurseries will offer healthy, correctly named material on a specified rootstock suitable for the purpose required. Some will include certain cultivars marked as of EMLA status, denoting that they have been raised from material derived from East Malling and Long Ashton, the two main fruit research stations in England, indicating the highest degree of health and cropping potential available.

Rootstocks As fig.158 shows M27 produces very dwarf trees of only some 5ft(1.5m) in height when fully grown. Progressing upwards in vigour are M9 dwarfing, M26 and MM106 semi-dwarfing, MM111 vigorous and M25 very vigorous. The best choice for garden trees lies between M9, M26 and MM106, with possibly MM111 for poor soil conditions. The dwarfing M27, M9 and M26 will need adequate support throughout the tree's life – they are dwarfing by virtue of possessing a fibrous root system, with no tap roots as anchors, and it is this which induces early cropping. Trees on M27 will need good cultivation to succeed.

Tree Forms The most useful tree forms for apples in the garden are shown in fig.159, viz:
CORDON   A single-stemmed tree planted at an angle of 45 degrees to the ground. Plant 2½ft(75cm) apart with post and wire supports. Height 5 to 6ft.(1.5 to 2m). Ideal for small areas.
ESPALIER   Useful for walls and fences but balanced growth is not easy to maintain without correct, regular pruning. Space 10 to 14ft(3 to 4.25m) apart.
PYRAMID   Branches radiate around a central stem; summer pruning encourages fruiting spurs. Plant 4ft(1.25m) apart; height 6 to 7ft(2 to 2.25m).
SPINDLEBUSH   Many variations exist, all with a basic pyramid shape. Plant 6 to 8ft(2 to 2.5m) apart.
BUSH   Probably the easiest form to maintain given sufficient space. Some six to seven branches radiate from a short 2½ft(75cm) stem. Plant 9 to 12ft(2.75 to 3.75m) apart on dwarfing rootstock; otherwise 12 to 18ft(3.75 to 5.5m), depending on the vigour of the cultivar.
FAN   Most apples (except the most vigorous and tip bearers) make excellent fans on walls and fences but must be correctly trained from the outset *without* a central stem (see Fig.160). Some 6ft(2m) of height and 10ft(3m) of spread is necessary.

Pollination and Fruit Thinning No apple is satisfactorily self-fertile and suitable combinations must be planted together to ensure cross-pollination, fertilization and therefore regular cropping. Not only must flowering

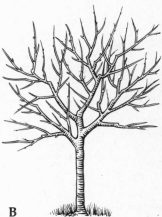

*159. Types of training: **A**, pyramid; **B**, bush; **C**, spindle; **D**, espalier; and **E**, cordon.*

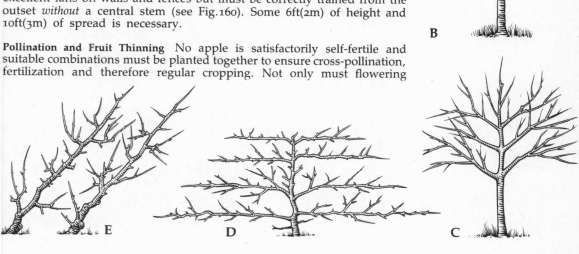

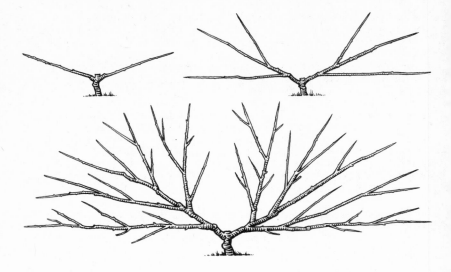

160. *The stages in the training of a fan-trained tree. With the exception of the most vigorous and tip-bearing cultivars most apples make excellent fans on walls and fences.*

coincide but in the case of triploids *two* other acceptable cultivars must be included since triploids are themselves useless as pollinators. Expert advice should be sought on the selection of cultivars to cover pollination requirements, and some specialist fruit books contain full pollination lists for all tree fruits. The catalogues of some specialist nurseries also give such advice.

Fruit thinning may be necessary in some seasons, final spacing after the natural June drop being 4 to 6in(10 to 15cm), the larger fruited cultivars requiring the greater distance. Branches need carefully supporting where necessary to prevent breakage.

Recommended Cultivars   A few of the cultivars listed below are tip bearers – much of the fruit is borne on branch tips and less on spurs – and these are best avoided for trained trees like cordons or espaliers. So are very vigorous cultivars like 'Blenheim Orange' and 'Bramley's Seedling.'

	Dessert		**Culinary**
	'George Cave' (8)		'Emneth Early' (Early Victoria)
	'Discovery' (8–9)		(7–9)
	'Laxton's Epicure' (8–9)		'George Neal' (8–9)
	'Laxton's Fortune' (9–10)		'Grenadier' (8–9)
°	'St. Edmund's Pippin' (9–10)		'Lord Suffield' (8–9)
°	'Tydeman's Early' (9)		'Rev. W. Wilks' (9–11)
	'Worcester Pearmain' (9–10)		'Golden Noble' (9–12)
	'Merton Charm' (9–11)	X	'Warner's King' (9–12)
	'Lord Lambourne' (9–11)	X+	'Blenheim Orange' (10–12)
	'Ellison's Orange' (9–10)	X°+	'Bramley's Seedling' (10–3)
X	'Ribston Pippin' (10–12)		'Newton Wonder' (11–3)
	'Sunset' (10–12)		'Lane's Prince Albert' (11–3)
	'Cox's Orange Pippin' (10–12)		'Monarch' (12–3)
	'Kidd's Orange Red' (11–1)		'Edward VII' (12–4)
	'Orleans Reinette' (11–1)	+	'Encore' (12–4)
*	'Gala' (11–1)		'Annie Elizabeth' (12–6)
	'Golden Delicious' (11–1)		
	'Laxton's Superb' (11–2)		**Key:**
	'Ashmead's Kernel' (12–2)	°	Markedly tip bearing
	'Spartan' (11–2)	X	Triploid
	'Tydeman's Late Orange' (12–4)	*	Denotes recent introduction
	'Sturmer Pippin' (1–4)	+	Freezes well
X	'Crispin' (12–3)		
*	'Pixie' (1–3)		Figures in brackets denote months of ripening

Nutrition Apple trees are not particularly demanding but on sandy soils they require adequate potash and nitrogen. If growth is good little or no nitrogen should be necessary, otherwise, and especially for trees in grass (which should be cut without the box), use sulphate of ammonia for alkaline soils or nitro-chalk for acid ones at the rate of 1oz per sq yd(25g per m^2) in March. Potash should be given as sulphate of potash at the same rate in alternate winters. Every few years give superphosphate at 3oz per sq yd(85g per m^2). Compound fertilizers can be used but tend to be wasteful since some of their content frequently is not necessary. Occasional dressings of well-rotted farmyard manure or compost are most beneficial on poorer soils. Magnesium deficiency, causing an interveinal browning in the older leaves, which then fall prematurely, can be serious and is aggravated by potash levels being too high. Spray the foliage with magnesium sulphate at 1lb to 5gal(450g to 22.5l) of water plus a little spreading agent, firstly at petal fall and two or three times thereafter at 14-day intervals.

Deficiencies of iron and manganese (lime-induced chlorosis) sometimes occur on alkaline soils and may cause recurring problems (see p.297)

Planting and Supporting This is done between late autumn and March, but earlier plantings always establish more quickly. The soil must be friable and firm; planting in a hole wide enough to spread the tree's root system is important. A little rotted manure or compost on poor soils *only* is advised. Too wet or frozen ground must be left until conditions improve, and the trees heeled-in in damp peat under shelter with protection being provided from rabbits and vermin. A supporting and preferably round stake is best driven into the base of the hole before planting, the tree stem then being positioned some 3in(8cm) away from it; make sure all the roots are spread out and not bunched. A suitable soft plastic or rubber tie must be fixed in position immediately and checked and renewed regularly thereafter (see Fig.161). Trained trees such as cordons, espaliers and fans should be tied to bamboo canes which have first been fixed securely to supporting wires.

Pruning An art in itself, pruning can only be mastered by study, by watching someone accomplished actually doing it and then putting the knowledge gained into practice. The tree will indicate whether or not any pruning treatment suits it by its growth and the regularity of its cropping.

Pruning falls into two distinct phases – training and, later, pruning the established cropping tree.

The Training Period This covers the first year or two of the tree's life, mainly in the nurseryman's hands, when the desired shape is built up. Thus, while a cordon needs a minimum of effort to develop fruiting spurs along the length of its single stem, the espalier or fan need several years of exact training – selection and tying in of the best placed shoots and the elimination or pinching back of the remainder – before the tree is fully and finally shaped. In between these two extremes are the bush, pyramid and spindle methods of training requiring selection of the approximate number of shoots in the first one or two years to produce the required number of branches. No pruning leads to a shapeless tree destined to break down under too early and too heavy crops; over-pruning causes excessive growth and delayed fruiting (see Figs.162 and 163).

The Cropping Period This means maintaining the right balance between the amount of growth made and the amount of fruit produced. The ideal situation is moderate, healthy growth coupled with moderately good, regular crops. Too severe pruning leads to excessive growth and little or no fruit; insufficient pruning encourages over-cropping, biennial bearing and loss of shape, the deterioration being most rapid on the more dwarfing rootstocks where any new growth becomes negligible. Pruning also assists spraying by maintaining an open tree.

There is a variation in routine pruning treatment for *trained* trees from that for larger free-growing trees like the bush or standard, as described overleaf.

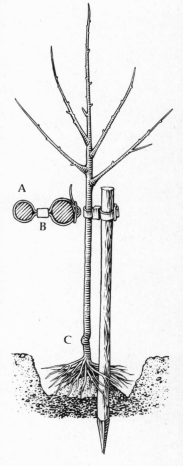

161. The importance of providing adequate support for fruit trees cannot be over-emphasised. Stakes used to support standard trees should be positioned before planting and they should be secured, as shown, with soft plastic or rubber ties. The cross-section of a tie shows **(A)** *the strap encircling the stem and the stake with the cushion* **(B)** *in between to act as a buffer between the stem and stake. Note also the position of the union between rootstock and scion* **(C)** *with the tree ready for planting and the way the roots are spread out evenly before the soil is returned and firmed.*

162. *Over-pruning* **(A)** *leads to excessive growth being made* **(B)** *and the production of a few fruit buds and, consequently, poor cropping* **(C).**

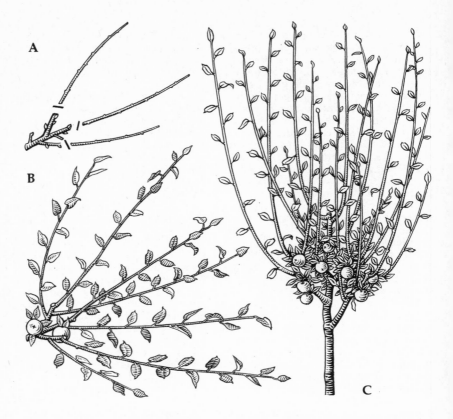

Trained Trees Regular summer pruning is practised which maintains the trained shape and, by pruning away live foliage, both helps to control vigour and encourage fruitfulness. It is done once the base of new shoots begins to ripen, usually early-mid August, cutting back to some 4 to 5in(10 to 13cm) above the base of new growth.

Trees growing poorly should not be summer pruned, neither should the leading shoot of a cordon or a pyramid. Occasional thinning out of fruiting spurs is done in winter.

Free-growing Trees Winter pruning is the rule, summer pruning being less important because the tree, i.e., bush, spindle or standard, has much more space available than a trained specimen. A few of the oldest shoots per year are either removed completely or shortened to encourage regrowth; also any branches that are too low, crowded, crossing, diseased or broken are also removed. Large wounds should be painted with an approved wound dressing. Upright shoots, particularly towards the top of the tree, are best cut back to a weaker side shoot to encourage fruiting (horizontal growth is always more fruitful and the tying down of vigorous shoots is good practice). This is particularly necessary on the spindlebush if the pyramid shape is to be maintained with regular cropping. The occasional spur thinning described under trained trees will also be necessary. Winter pruning may be done at any time between leaf fall and bud burst.

Pruning Neglected Trees Where such trees are worth keeping renovate them gradually and avoid excessive pruning. First, remove unwanted branches and paint all wounds. In subsequent years thin out growths – mainly overcrowded spurs – and remove any "water-shoots" in the summer from around old branch cuts while these still are soft and green – rub them off with the hand. Very tall branches may be shortened, or "dehorned", in winter, but only a few at a time to avoid excessive regrowth.

Deblossoming and Biennial-bearing De-blossoming prevents too heavy crop-ping and is a positive way of easing biennial bearing. Up to 90 per cent of the blossom should be removed with scissors leaving the basal rosette of leaves intact. Repeat the treatment as the biennial tendency begins to recur.

Picking and Storing First-early cultivars have a very short season of use. Later maturing apples (from September onwards) should only be picked when, gently lifted, they part readily from the tree.

Storage conditions need to be constantly cool, slightly moist and vermin-proof. Cellars and cool outhouses are ideal for the purpose, stacking the fruit in open boxes. The use of 150 gauge polythene bags, with the mouth of the bag loosely folded over, proves very successful and prevents shrivell-ing, about 5lb(2.25kg) of apples being sufficient per bag. Necessarily, only sound fruit, preferably already cool when placed in store, should be kept and regular checks must be made to remove rotting fruits.

Pests The following should be searched for and the appropriate action taken:
APHIDS: These include the rosy apple aphid, the worst of many kinds, which curls the leaves in late spring and induces small bumpy fruits. Spray with tar oil in winter or with dimethoate or malathion immediately seen.
BIRDS: Bullfinches often feed on over-wintering buds. Control this, and damage to ripening fruit, by netting.
CATERPILLARS: Damage in spring on leaves and fruit, mainly from the tortrix and winter moth caterpillars, can be controlled by spraying with permethrin or trichlorphon at bud burst. Bands of vegetable grease on the trunk in October-March will help by trapping the wingless female moths.
CODLING MOTH: Caterpillars feeding inside near-ripe fruits result from eggs laid in the eye of the young fruit in mid-late June. Control by sacking or corrugated paper bands tied around the trunk in July to attract the fully-fed caterpillars where they will develop into an over-wintering chrysalis. In

163. No pruning or insufficient pruning (A) results in over-cropping (B) which, in turn, frequently causes the tree to break and/or lose shape (C).

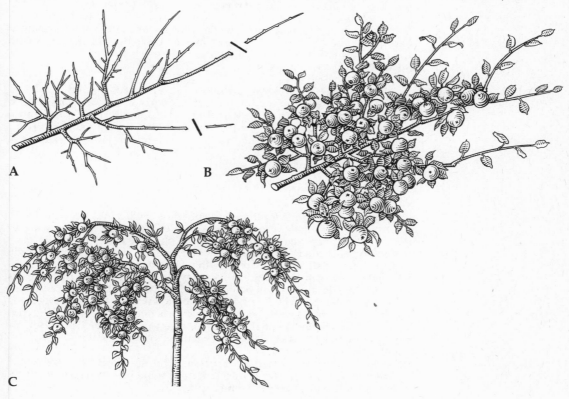

A

B

C

early winter they are removed with the banding material and burnt. Alternatively, spray with permethrin or fenitrothion in mid-June and early July.
FRUIT TREE RED SPIDER MITE: May cause bronzed leaves in warmer, drier summers. Dinocap spray for mildew will usually keep this pest in check but if it becomes a problem use dimethoate or malathion immediately after flowering.
WOOLLY APHID: The appearance is of cotton-wool (the pest's protective covering) and this particular aphid develops on spurs and particularly around the folding callus of pruning wounds. Control as soon as noticed by brushing vigorously with methylated spirit or spray with an insecticide such as dimethoate or malathion.

Diseases   The principal troubles are as follows:
BROWN ROT   This gains entry through damage caused by birds and wasps. Remove rotting fruit as soon as seen, protect fruit from birds and destroy wasps' nests.
CANKER   Apple canker is serious in some cultivars, e.g., 'Cox's Orange Pippin', and is worst under wet, poorly drained conditions. Uncontrolled scab infection leads to canker. Scrape diseased portions of stems and branches clean and treat with proprietary canker paint. Cut out diseased wood when pruning.
HONEY FUNGUS   This is a soil-borne disease often rampant where old tree roots remain. It can attack most species including all fruit trees. There is no guaranteed cure but dead trees should be removed complete with roots and burnt. It is inadvisable to replant on the same site unless the soil is treated with a proprietary phenolic emulsion or sterilised with a 2 per cent solution of formaldehyde.
POWDERY MILDEW   This is seldom a problem on trained trees where summer pruning removes infected shoots. All silvered, infected wood should be cut out when winter pruning, and any infected shoots and flowers seen at blossom time. Spray with dinocap or use a systemic fungicide at pink bud stage and repeat at 10 to 14-day intervals.
SCAB   This affects leaves, shoots and fruit and will lead to canker if left unchecked. Spray with captan or benomyl or thiophanate-methyl starting at bud burst and then every 14 days in bad cases and in humid, damp weather. Regular pruning to maintain an open tree helps.
SILVER LEAF   See plums (p.242)

Another Disorder   The following trouble needs to be kept in mind:
BITTER PIT   This is the condition which results in brown spots forming in the flesh just under the skin. It is caused by a shortage of water and a deficiency of calcium within the fruits and is worse on some cultivars (e.g., trees. Mulching and watering *before* dry conditions are experienced is advised.

CHERRIES (SWEET)
Large trees, self-sterility (with the exception of 'Stella') and bird damage to the ripening crop make the sweet cherry quite unsuitable for growing in most gardens. Fan-trained trees (see Fig.160) trained on large walls are a possibility, and good, deep soil is always essential. However, each fan will require at least 15ft(4.5m) of space with 9 to 10ft(2.75 to 3m) of head room, and unless the self-fertile 'Stella' is being grown, space for two trees is essential to allow for cross-pollination. The new and considerably less vigorous rootstock Colt is advised in preference to the very vigorous Malling F12/1. Little feeding except mulching is necessary. Netting the crop against birds will be essential. The worst insect pest is cherry black fly, for which spray as soon as noticed, with malathion or dimethoate.

Diseases   The disease bacterial canker can seriously affect trees (see p.242) and brown rot affect the fruit. Infected fruit should be removed immediately. For silver leaf disease see "Plums" (p.242).

Recommended Cultivars 'Stella' (self-fertile, late July). Good pairings for cross-pollination otherwise are 'Waterloo' (late June) with 'Van' (mid-July) or 'Early Rivers' (mid-late June) with 'Bigarreau Schrecken' (late June).

CHERRIES (SOUR)

The sour 'Morello' cherry is more compact in habit and self-fertile and makes an ideal bush (see Peaches, below) or a fan. Cultivation is as for sweet cherries except for pruning. Here the Morello's habit of fruiting only on the previous year's growth necessitates the cutting back of a few shoots each spring to a growth bud on older wood. All wounds must be painted.

NECTARINES

The nectarine is merely a smooth-skinned form of the peach but it requires warmer conditions than can normally be provided in the open garden. Only if a really warm, sheltered wall can be used should their cultivation be attempted, in which case their needs are precisely as for fan-trained peaches (see below).

Recommended Cultivars 'John Rivers' (mid-July), 'Lord Napier' (early August) both white-fleshed, 'Humboldt' (late August), 'Pineapple' (early September), yellow-fleshed.

164. *Pruning fan-trained peaches. Prune as shown* **(A)** *after fruiting or in early March.* **(B)** *indicates the replacement shoot,* **(C)** *where a surplus shoot has been pinched out.*

PEACHES

A warm wall or greenhouse is essential for consistent success, but 'Rochester' (yellow-fleshed, fair quality) is often reliable when grown as a bush in sheltered southern gardens. Others seldom are. The flowers open early and may need protecting from frost and dusting with a soft camel hair brush on sunny days to assist pollination. Peaches are generally self-fertile and the moderately vigorous trees produced by the St. Julien 'A' rootstock are preferred to those on more vigorous Brompton. Most soils are suitable if well drained but calcareous ones often cause iron and manganese deficiencies (see p.297) and are not ideal. Generous mulching is advised otherwise apply sulphate of ammonia in spring at 1oz per sq yd(25g per m²) and occasionally sulphate of potash at the same rate.

A bush tree with six or seven branches is the easiest to maintain. Any pruning is done in the summer removing older, crowded, crossing or broken shoots. Occasional heavy sets of fruit may require thinning to 9in(23cm) when the fruits are walnut-sized.

For walls a fan-trained tree is advised, but this calls for considerable time and expertise in training and reference to detailed instructions on pruning, disbudding and deshooting would be essential (see Figs. 160 and 164). 'Peregrine' (white fleshed, ripening in mid August, is a very reliable cultivar of high quality when trained as a fan. So also are 'Duke of York' (mid-July), 'Hale's Early' (late July) and 'Royal George' (early September), all white fleshed. Ripening under glass would be advanced by three weeks or so.

Diseases PEACH LEAF CURL A serious disease for trees in the open and requires a *regular* spray programme of a copper fungicide applied as soon as buds show movement (this can be late January-early February in some localities) and repeated two weeks later.
BROWN ROT Can affect fruit badly on trees in the open and all diseased specimens should be removed and burnt.

A disorder SPLIT STONE As the name implies, a disorder that fractures the stone on the ripening fruit. The cause of this is not known although dryness at the roots is possibly a contributory factor.

PEARS

Warm gardens are necessary for real success with pears which flower in April and require rather higher temperatures than apples. Nevertheless, certain cultivars like 'Conference' and 'Emile d'Heyst' can often succeed in cooler areas. Apart from the need for extra warmth, the requirements of site and soil are much as for apples (see p.233). The use of warm walls for training choice cultivars should be considered. Too alkaline soils should be avoided, and windy sites will quickly result in blackening and dessication of the tender young foliage.

Rootstocks Quince A produces good cropping trees of moderate size, while Quince C gives rather smaller trees that are quick to crop. In propagation the problem of incompatability of some cultivars, e.g., 'Marie Louise', 'Packham's Triumph' and 'Williams' Bon Chrétien', with quince can be overcome by introducing a small piece of wood from a compatible cultivar like 'Beurré Hardy' between the two (double-working as it is known).

Tree Forms The cordon, dwarf pyramid, bush and fan are ideal for pears and the espalier can also be successful. For details and planting distances see Apples p.233.

Pollination Like apples, all pears should be treated as being self-sterile so the careful selection of combinations of cultivars for planting together is very important. Expert advice should be sought. Fruit thinning is seldom necessary.

Recommended Cultivars The fruit of the two culinary cultivars needs to be sliced and cooked slowly for seven to eight hours when it will make a very pleasing, and different dish. Neither cultivar can be used as a dessert pear.

	Dessert	
+	'Williams' Bon Chretien' (9)	'Marie Louise' (10–11)
	'Fondante d'Automne' (9)	'Emile d'Heyst' (10–11)
*	'Onward' (9–10)	'Doyenné du Comice' (11–12)
	'Gorham' (9–10)	'Josephine de Malines' (12–1)
	'Bristol Cross' (10)	**Culinary**
	'Conference' (10)	'Bellissime d'Hiver' (12–3)
		'Catillac' (12–3)

Key:
+ Freezes well   The figures in brackets denote
* New introduction   months of ripening

Nutrition Basically this is as for apples (p.235) but with rather more nitrogen being given, especially in grass. Lime-induced chlorosis can also be a problem (see p.232).

Planting and Support See Apples (p.235).

Pruning Again, this is generally as for apples. Do not over-prune before cropping commences on vigorous trees like 'Doyenné du Comice'. Cropping trees produce many spurs which require thinning.

Picking and Storing First-early cultivars need picking just before they become ripe and while still green. Otherwise, pick when the fruits part readily from the spur and store individually as for apples (see p.237). Pears (not first-early ones) need several days in a normal living room temperature to ripen with maximum flavour.

Pests APHIDS Can infest the young growth. Spray with malathion or dimethoate.
BIRDS Can cause serious losses both to over-wintering buds and the fruit (see p.237).
PEAR LEAF BLISTER MITE Causes many tiny, rusty-yellow pustules on the leaves. Pick off leaves as soon as noticed; no chemical controls currently available for amateur gardeners.
PEAR MIDGE Frequently builds up on isolated trees, young fruits turning black and containing many small larvae. Collect and burn all such fruits

before, or as soon, as they drop. Spray with fenitrothion or HCH when blossom is at the white bud stage.

Diseases BROWN ROT, CANKER, HONEY FUNGUS and SCAB These can all affect pears, particularly scab on some cultivars, e.g., 'Williams' Bon Chrétien'. Treat as for Apple (p.238).
FIREBLIGHT A notifiable disease that causes blackening and withering of flowers and subsequent extension of infection in the spur and then the whole branch. If suspected consult the nearest Ministry of Agriculture official for advice.

PLUMS AND DAMSONS

Plums cover a wide and exciting range of cultivars some mainly of culinary value, others of the highest dessert quality. A number of the former, together with damsons, can be grown in many areas but the high-quality greengages and gage-type plums succeed only in the warmer south or on a sunny wall. Flowering is very early causing irregular cropping, and damage by bullfinches to overwintering buds is often severe.

Site and Soil Warm, frost-free sites and netting against birds will greatly improve regularity of cropping. The pyramid tree is eminently suited to the garden and is easy to protect against frost and birds.
    Plums succeed on most soils but they may be short-lived on sands and they suffer from iron and manganese deficiencies where conditions are too alkaline (see p.297).

Rootstocks The best rootstock for a moderate-sized tree is St. Julian 'A'. A new, dwarfing stock called Pixy is being tested but trees will require greater care in cultivation. The vigorous Brompton and Myrobalan rootstocks are best avoided.

Tree Forms The bush, pyramid and fan-trained specimens are best. Half-standards and standards are space demanding and difficult to manage.
BUSH Developed much as for the apple (p.233) but with a rather longer leg and less pruning in its formation. Space at 12 to 14ft(3.75 to 4.25m) apart.
PYRAMID Quite the best form for gardens. Most side shoots are retained and, with summer pruning in early August to leave 6in(15cm) of new growth, a compact, regular-cropping tree can easily be maintained. Space at 9 to 10ft(2.75 to 3m) apart.
FAN Best choice for gages on walls.

Pollination Some cultivars are self-fertile. Pollinators must be in close proximity for self-sterile kinds, e.g., 'Cambridge Gage', 'Jefferson', 'Kirke's'. A few combinations are incompatible.

Recommended Cultivars

Dessert		Culinary
		* 'Early Laxton' (late 7 – early 8)
sf	'Oullins Golden Gage' (mid 8)	sf 'Pershore' (syn Yellow Egg)
sf	'Early Transparent Gage' (mid-late 8)	(mid 8)
	'Count Althann's Gage' (late 8)	sf * 'Victoria' (late 8 – early 9)
sf	'Denniston's Superb' (late 8)	sf * 'Czar' (early 8)
sf	'Victoria' (late 8 – early 9)	sf 'Purple Pershore' (mid – late 8)
+	'Cambridge Gage' (late 8 – early 9)	sf * 'Marjorie's Seedling' (late 9 – early 10)
+	'Jefferson' (late 8 – early 9)	
+	'Kirke's' (late 8 – early 9)	**Key:**
	'Anna Späth' (mid – late 9)	* Also very acceptable as dessert when fully ripe
+	'Coe's Golden Drop' (late 9)	sf self-fertile
		+ Highest dessert quality
		The figures in brackets denote the month of ripening

Nutrition Similar to that for apple (see p.235) but with a greater need for nitrogen to encourage new growth, especially in grass. Mulching on light and calcareous soils is very beneficial.

Planting and support As for apples (see p.235). Avoid injury from stakes as this can encourage bacterial canker and silver leaf disease.

Pruning Early training is best done in late March, otherwise all pruning is completed in summer to reduce the risk of silver leaf infection. Wounds must be painted immediately and thoroughly. Bush and standard trees only need the occasional removal of broken, crowded, crossing or too low branches. Pyramid trees must be summer-pruned in early August shortening leading new shoots of each branch to 8in(20cm) and new side shoots to 6in(13cm). The central leader is cut back by two-thirds in March and stopped at 8ft 6in(2.65m).
  In the case of fan-trained specimens, following the period of initial training, side shoots are either tied in to fill the space available or pinched at six or seven leaves and shortened to three or four leaves after cropping.

Fruit Thinning and Branch Support This reduces the risk of broken branches and improves fruit size and quality. In June, after the natural drop of unstoned fruit, space the fruit to 3 to 4in(8 to 10cm), using pointed scissors for this task. Carefully support heavily laden branches but cushion these against rubbing.

Picking Pick the fruits complete with stalk, at the firm stage for culinary purposes but fully ripe for dessert. Splitting of the skin is common on choicer cultivars in rainy seasons and earlier picking is sensible then. Remove broken branches and paint the wounds immediately with an approved wound dressing.

Pests The following need to be watched for and the appropriate action taken:
APHIDS   The leaf curling aphid in spring and the mealy plum aphid in June-July can be very damaging. Spray with tar-oil in winter to kill overwintering eggs or with malathion when the first aphids are seen.
BIRDS   These can seriously denude the tree of buds in winter.

Diseases BACTERIAL CANKER   This is a common trouble causing flattened, dead areas on the trunk or branches and preventing leaf development. There is no cure unless branches can be cut off well behind the infection. Avoid wounding trees and thoroughly paint all pruning cuts with an approved wound dressing.
BROWN ROT   See Apples (p.238). Split fruits will encourage the disease.
SHARKA (PLUM POX)   This is a virus disease causing vague greenish-yellow mottling of the foliage and mottled brownish-yellow sunken areas on the fruit surface. It is spread by aphids, and control of these pests is important. *This disease is notifiable and the nearest Ministry of Agriculture official must be contacted.*
SILVER LEAF   This disease gains entry through wounds and broken branches. All except small pruning cuts must be painted immediately with an approved wound dressing. An isolated branch can be removed back to clean wood but a severely diseased tree should be dug up and burnt. If in doubt seek expert advice.

BLACKBERRIES
See p.245.

CURRANTS, BLACK
High in vitamin C, the black currant is one of the most valuable fruits with many culinary uses, including freezing. However, good cultivation is vital

for successful cropping to be maintained.

Site and Soil Reasonable shelter and freedom from frost is essential as flowering is early. The flowers, though self-fertile, and fruitlets, will drop or 'run-off' following too cold and windy conditions.

Most soils are suitable but sandy and calcareous ones will need regular dressings of organic material.

Source of Planting Material Obtain Ministry of Agriculture-certified bushes to ensure health standards.

Planting This is best done by January-February, if the soil conditions are suitable. Plant slightly deeper than the nursery soil mark since cultivation is on the stool system with shoots from near or below ground being encouraged. Space the plants 5ft(1.5m) apart.

Recommended Cultivars
EARLY 'Boskoop Giant', 'Laxton's Giant', 'Tor Cross'.
MID-SEASON 'Blacksmith', 'Raven', 'Wellington XXX'.
LATE 'Amos Black', 'Baldwin'.
NEW INTRODUCTIONS 'Ben Lomond', frost-resistant and some mildew resistance. 'Blackdown', mildew-resistant.

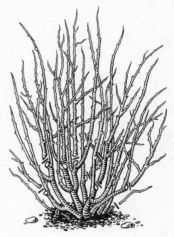

Nutrition Prepare the ground by digging in plenty of rotted farmyard manure or compost. Subsequently, mulch regularly with manure to feed, smother weeds and conserve soil moisture. Failing this apply nitrogen and potash as necessary – sulphate of ammonia (or nitro-chalk on acid soils) at 1oz per sq yd(25g per m^2) annually in late February and a similar dressing of sulphate of potash in alternate years. Superphosphate at 3 to 4oz per sq yd(85 to 110g per m^2) every few years is also advisable.

Pruning Newly planted bushes are cut to a bud just above ground level. Subsequently, retain strong young shoots (they carry the best crop) and cut out the older ones low down; in the process some young wood must inevitably be sacrificed (see illustration). Young wood must be encouraged from the base and pruning may be done at any time from after picking to early February. Shoots are *not* tip pruned.

Picking Gather firm, ripe and dry. Early cultivars will soon drop their fruit. For exhibition pick strigs intact.

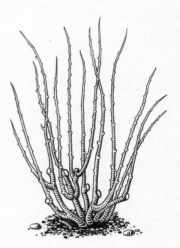

Pests APHIDS Control by tar-oil in winter or malathion or dimethoate as soon as noticed in spring.
GALL MITE (BIG BUD) It is important to spray annually against this pest which spreads reversion virus. Application of benomyl at grape bud stage is advised. Pick off and burn big buds during the winter. Discard infested bushes which crop badly.

165. *A black currant plant before and after pruning. Note the pruning points in the top illustration, marked by bold lines.*

Diseases AMERICAN GOOSEBERRY MILDEW See Gooseberries (p.245).
LEAF SPOT This causes many small, dark grey-brown spots on the leaves resulting in bad cases in early leaf-fall. Fallen leaves should be cleared and burnt. Spray directly after flowering with mancozeb or a systemic fungicide and repeat after 14 days, twice if necessary. Then follow, after picking, with a copper spray.
REVERSION VIRUS This is spread by the blackcurrant gall mite. There is no cure. Leaves and flowers become abnormal imperceptibly and cropping falls off. Seek expert advice for diagnosis of the trouble. Infected bushes must be burnt.

Propagation This is simply done by inserting in the open ground, in October, 8 to 10in(20 to 25cm) lengths of young ripe shoots with all the buds intact and with the second highest bud at ground level. Remove the leaves from the shoots.

CURRANTS, RED AND WHITE

The red currant is valued for its unique flavour, particularly in preserves. Bushes are heavy croppers and long-lived. There are also pink and white cultivars. Fruit is produced on spurs on a permanent branch framework. Plant 5ft(1.5m) apart. Cordons and fans are also easily trained on walls and fences.

Shelter and fertility   Young shoots are easily broken by wind and for this reason and to assist in fruit set adequate shelter is advised.

Recommended Cultivars   RED: 'Jonkheer Van Tets', very early; 'Red Lake', mid-season; 'Rivers Late Red', late. WHITE: 'White Grape'.

Nutrition   The presence of adequate potash (sulphate of potash) is essential; otherwise as for black currants (see p.243).

Pruning   Young bushes with a short, clean stem require the shortening of shoots by half their length to produce branches in the first two or three years. Side shoots are shortened to one or two buds each winter. Summer-prune cordons and fans shortening shoots to five leaves but not the branch leaders. Shorten further in winter to two buds.

Picking   Gather on the strig, particularly for exhibition.

Pests   APHIDS   When seen, spray with malathion or dimethoate.
BIRDS   These attack fruit and buds; summer and winter protection with netting is advisable.

Diseases   CORAL SPOT   This disease is aptly named and it can cause die-back and even the death of whole bushes. Cut out and burn infected shoots and paint all wounds with an approved dressing.

Propagation   Insert 12 to 14in(30 to 35cm) lengths of ripe young wood in open ground in October. Only the top three to four buds should be retained.

GOOSEBERRIES

Similar in its requirements to currants, the gooseberry easily suffers potash deficiency and American gooseberry mildew disease. Some shade can be tolerated but not for the best quality. Very early flowers may require protection from frost. Bushes, fans and cordons are easily trained.

Recommended Cultivars   GREEN: 'Keepsake,' 'Lancer', 'Careless'. WHITE: 'Whitesmith', 'White Lion'. RED: 'Whinham's Industry'. YELLOW: 'Leveller', the best to ripen for dessert berries. Colour stated is for *ripe* fruit. Most are picked green.

Nutrition   Potash is an important requirement, otherwise see black currants (p.243).

Planting   Plant as soon as possible after the beginning of November because growth starts in late February-March.

Pruning   As for red currants, grown as a bush, but spreading growths require cutting to upward-pointing buds. Subsequently, thinning of branches is sufficient but spur pruning to three to four buds (done in June if preferred) will produce bigger fruits and greatly reduce American gooseberry mildew infection.

Picking   Some early picking thins the crop and improves fruit size.

Pests   APHIDS   Spray with malathion or dimethoate when seen.

BIRDS   See Red Currants (p.244). Winter bud damage from bullfinches can be serious.
GOOSEBERRY SAWFLY   Green, black-spotted caterpillars occasionally cause devastation in summer. Spray with derris or malathion at the first sign of attack.

Diseases   AMERICAN GOOSEBERRY MILDEW   Spray with $\frac{1}{2}$lb(225g) of washing soda in $2\frac{1}{2}$gal(11.25l) of water plus a spreader, or with a systemic fungicide or dinocap *before* flowering and twice afterwards. Summer pruning will remove infected tips.
GREY MOULD   Remove any dead shoots back to clean wood and paint all wounds. Open, well-fed bushes are less prone to attack. Losses can be considerable, whole bushes gradually dying.
LEAF SPOT   See Black Currants (p.243).

Propagation   Insert 12 to 15in(30 to 38cm) lengths of young, ripe wood in the open ground in autumn. Only the top three buds are retained to avoid suckering. Results, however, are often poor.

LOGANBERRIES, BLACKBERRIES (AND OTHER HYBRID BERRIES)

These fruits require similar cultivation to raspberries. From time to time hybrids (hybrid berries) are selected and the loganberry and its thornless form are by far the most important. The 'Boysenberry' and the new 'Tayberry' are also worth a trial. Plant rooted tips or buds by February and mulch to avoid drying out. Support wires are necessary on which to train growths about 1ft(30cm) apart.

Pruning   Cut out old canes after fruiting and replace them with the best young ones.

Recommended Cultivars   BLACKBERRIES: 'Ashton Cross', July; 'Bedford Giant', late July-August; 'Oregon Thornless', good flavour, August-September. LOGANBERRIES: Loganberry LY59 Selection, July-August; Thornless Loganberry, a valuable thornless form. OTHER HYBRID BERRIES: Boysenberry, large dark red fruits; Tayberry, new, like small loganberry.

Pests and Disease   RASPBERRY BEETLE   Spray with derris at dusk towards end of flowering.
VIRUS DISEASES   Common and cause stunting. Burn diseased plants.

Propagation   By shoot tips inserted into friable soil in July.

RASPBERRIES

Raspberries require a cool root run, adequate moisture and good drainage. Several good autumn-fruiting cultivars greatly extend the season and the raspberry succeeds in practically all areas. Watering helps greatly.

Site and Soil   Reasonable shelter and a well-drained soil are essential. Lime-induced chlorosis (iron and manganese deficiencies) can be serious on calcareous soils but can be alleviated by copious mulching.

Source of Material   Ministry of Agriculture certified canes should be obtained to ensure freedom from virus diseases.

Planting   Autumn or early winter is best. Canes should be planted firmly in well-manured ground at 18in(45cm) apart and 2 to 3in(5 to 8cm) deep and then shortened to 10in(25cm). Rows 6ft(2m) apart. Support of some kind is essential. Posts and nylon string are an effective, inexpensive solution. Wire is longer lasting but more expensive.

Recommended Cultivars SUMMER FRUITING: 'Malling Promise' (early), 'Lloyd George'* (second-early), 'Malling Jewel'*+ (mid-season), 'Glen Clova'+ (mid-season), best grown on its own to reduce the risk of it contacting virus, 'Malling Admiral'*+ (late), 'Norfolk Giant' (late) and 'Leo' (very late). AUTUMN FRUITING: 'September', 'Zeva' and 'Heritage'.
*Best flavoured   +Good for freezing.

Nutrition Mulch as for black currants (see p.243) with rotted farmyard manure and/or compost. Otherwise, use the fertilisers quoted.

Pruning In the case of summer fruiting cultivars cut out old fruited canes at ground level in August; also surplus and small new canes. The best new canes are then trained between the parallel nylon strings or tied in at 3 to 4in(8 to 10cm) apart and their tips are removed in late February. Autumn fruiting cultivars fruit on the tips of the young canes. Cut these to ground level in late February, an important difference from the pruning of summer cultivars.

Picking Fruit must be dry and carefully pulled off the calyx, but for exhibition pick complete with stalk.

Pests APHIDS Spray with tar oil in winter and with malathion in summer if necessary. Control is important since aphids spread certain virus diseases.
RASPBERRY BEETLE To prevent the grubs of this pest infesting ripening fruit, spray with derris or malathion as the first fruits start to colour.

Diseases CANE SPOT This disease causes small purple-grey blotches on canes, foliage and fruit. Spray with benomyl when growth starts and then at 14-day intervals to the end of flowering. Thiram is an alternative on fruit *not* to be processed.
GREY MOULD This can seriously affect the crop in wet seasons. Spray with benomyl as the first flowers open and 14 days later; dichlofluanid is an alternative control.
SPUR BLIGHT This disease causes grey-purple areas to develop around buds, killing them on the cane. Cut out and burn the worst affected canes and spray with Bordeaux mixture or benomyl soon after growth commences; repeat two or three times at 14-day intervals.
VIRUS DISEASES These cause irregular mottling and puckering of the foliage and stunting. Aphid control is important as these pests are virus vectors. There is no cure; burn infected canes, their roots and suckers.

Propagation This is easy; just dig up surplus canes adjacent to the row. Ensure, however, that such material is healthy. Lift canes in winter.

STRAWBERRIES

The strawberry lends itself to cultivation in the smallest garden. Protection with polythene or glass will give ripe fruit in May and outdoor crops soon follow, continuing well into the autumn if some perpetual-fruiting cultivars are grown as well.

Site and Soil The soil must be sufficiently fertile and freely drained. The sunnier and more sheltered the site and the lighter the soil, the earlier fruit will ripen. Flowers may need protecting with newspaper against frost.

Source of Material Only use runners that are Ministry of Agriculture certified or known to be virus free.

Planting This must be done – together with adequate watering – during August or early September to achieve maximum cropping the following year. October and spring plantings should be deblossomed to enable better establishment. Spring planting is preferred for perpetual-fruiting kinds which should also be deblossomed initially.

Adequate spacing reduces fruit loss from grey mould disease. The plants are spaced 18in(45cm) apart in the rows, with the rows 2ft 6in(75cm) apart. The in-row spacing can be halved if early protection with cloches or polythene is planned, to yield the maximum crop, but alternate plants must be pulled out after the first crop (see also Chapter 30 p.263). Plant firmly with the crown base at soil level. The ground must be free of perennial weeds like couch and convolvulus and have rotted farmyard manure or compost dug in, preferably for the previous crop.

The vegetable garden is an ideal part of the garden in which to grow strawberries, but it is preferable that they should not follow potatoes because of the risk of infection from verticillium disease. Firm all plants carefully following heavy frost.

Recommended Cultivars SUMMER-FRUITING: *Early:* 'Gorella', 'Cambridge Rival'*, 'Cambridge Vigour'* (one-year-old plants only – older plants are very leafy which delays ripening), 'Royal Sovereign'*. MID-SEASON TO LATE: 'Cambridge Favourite', 'Cambridge Vigour'* (early in first year), 'Hapil', 'Talisman'*, 'Cambridge Late Pine'*, 'Tamella'.
PERPETUAL-FRUITING: 'Aromel'*, 'Gento', 'La Sans Rivale', 'St. Claude', 'Ostara'
*Best flavoured.

Nutrition Good soil preparation, by digging in manure and compost, is the key to success since it aids nutrition, in the broadest sense, and conserves moisture. Potash is important and a dressing of 1oz per sq yd(25g per m^2) of sulphate of potash raked in before planting is advisable, especially on light soils. Sulphate of ammonia may be applied at a similar rate after cleaning the bed following fruiting; alternatively, apply a mulch.

Weeds Starting off with clean ground is all-important. If in doubt, it is better to delay planting. On a small scale, hoeing is sensible; larger plantings may call for the careful use of the herbicides simazine and paraquat.

Strawing down Use dry, clean straw or black polythene but do not lay it until the fruits begin to weigh down. Applied earlier it increases the risk of frost (see p.231). The practice protects the fruit from the soil, smothers weeds and conserves soil moisture.

Watering This is most important following planting; also sometimes from late May onwards *before* the plants begin to suffer and while the fruit is still green.

Picking Garden strawberries should be allowed to ripen fully to enjoy the full flavour and be picked with the stalk, Pick every two or three days; also remove and burn diseased or damaged fruits. Fruit for jam must be firm ripe and can be pulled away from the calyx if required.

Post-fruiting Treatment Clear all straw and weeds and cut off old foliage. Allow runners to root along but not between rows (and dispense with the remainder). This increases the crop greatly but strawing down becomes difficult and grey mould disease more serious unless controlled.

Pests APHIDS Spray forcefully into plants with malathion or dimethoate in early spring and again on regrowth after fruiting. This treatment is important since aphids spread virus diseases.
BIRDS Netting is essential to protect ripening fruit.
SLUGS may require the use of slug pellets on heavier soils as fruit approaches maturity.

Diseases GREY MOULD This is serious in wetter seasons. Clean ground and wide spacing will help considerably. Spray with dichlofluanid as first flowers open (do not use under polythene or glass) and repeat two to three

166. A healthy strawberry plant (top) and one infected with virus.

times every 10 days. Benomyl and captan can also be used but not the latter on fruit for canning, freezing or preserves. Any infected fruit bearing the fluffy grey growth must be removed and burnt.

MILDEW   This can infect foliage and possibly fruit in drier seasons. Growing in good soil and watering in dry weather help; if attack is serious spray with dinocap or benomyl just as the first flowers are opening and repeat every 14 days until the first fruits colour.

RED CORE   This causes the death of plants in patches; the roots will be found to be brown-red at the centre. There is no garden remedy available and infected areas must be used for other crops.

VIRUS DISEASES   Generally viruses have a debilitating, dwarfing effect (see illustration). Control aphids, which spread virus, eliminate weeds and burn all stunted plants. Every effort should also be made to encourage the same approach in adjacent gardens. There is no known cure for infected plants and expert advice is advised where necessary.

Protected cropping   The use of polythene tunnels advances cropping by up to two weeks, and glass cloches by three to four weeks but these are expensive. Plants should be covered during February with adequate ventilation as temperatures increase and the protection should be removed after fruiting. Such covering is also invaluable for perpetual-fruiting cultivars in the autumn.

Propagation   Increase by runners is very easy but the plants must be free of virus and other diseases. It is preferable to raise runners away from the fruiting bed on de-blossomed plants.

GRAPES

Warm walls in the open are very suitable for some dessert cultivars, even more so for wine grapes.

Site and Soil   Sunny walls are essential; most well-drained soils are suitable. Avoid too rich soils.

Cultivars   The following produce acceptable dessert grapes, particularly on sunny walls. WHITE: 'Siegerrebe' (late August-early September), 'Precoce de Malingre' (late September) and 'Chasselas' (late October; on walls only). BLACK: 'Noir Hatif de Marseilles' (late September; on walls only) and 'Brandt' (mid-October; also has good autumn foliage).

Training   Planted some 9in(23cm) away from the wall, a single cordon or multiple armed "espalier" can be developed on support wires.

Pruning   During training shorten side shoots to 3ft(1m) during the summer; in winter cut them back to one bud and the leading shoot right back to hard, ripened wood. After three years of this treatment the vine will have fully established and the first bunches may be cropped. Side shoots are now stopped at 1ft(30cm) or two leaves beyond any bunch being retained. Any sub-laterals that develop later are pinched at one leaf. If growth is poor remove all bunches. Winter pruning involves cutting side shoots back to one or, at most, two buds.

Deshooting   At each spur remove surplus ones, once the cropping shoot has been safely established. Shoots at the extremities of branches for which no further room is available are broken or rubbed out completely.

Fruiting   Avoid overcropping, one bunch per foot (30cm) of rod being the maximum, less on newly cropping rods. Small fruits in the centre of the bunch can be thinned out with scissors if large fruits are required.

Nutrition   Little is necessary although an occasional mulch can help. Over-feeding is inadvisable but watering may be necessary.

Pests WASPS Nests should be destroyed.
BIRDS Netting may be necessary.

Diseases Botrytis causes fruit rot, even in the early stages in wetter seasons. Spray with benomyl or dichlofluanid commencing immediately before flowering and repeating during bunch development, if necessary. Powdery mildew is also controlled by benomyl or dinocap, the first application of the spray being made when the shoots are 2in(5cm) long; repeat every two to three weeks. The application of 6 per cent tar-oil winter wash in early January is invaluable, particularly against botrytis.
N.B. Open-ground cultivation of grapes for wine is possible on favourable sites but not for dessert grapes.

SOME UNUSUAL FRUITS

ALMONDS Occasionally trees grown for their flower produce heavy crops which must be stored dry and clean. Any almonds with a bitter taste *must* be boiled before use. Peach leaf curl disease requires regular control, see Peaches (p.239).

APRICOTS The trees flower too early (March-April) to succeed in the open but sunny walls may be used for fan-trained trees. Train as for the peach (p.239) but without the rigorous need for replacement shoots since apricots fruit on both old and new wood. It will be necessary to remove surplus shoots by pinching or rubbing out when young. Winter pruning should be avoided. A slightly alkaline soil is to be prefered.
The dying back of branches is common and occasionally whole trees die back. All dead or dying wood must be removed back to healthy tissue and the wound painted with an approved wound dressing.

BLUEBERRIES The American cultivars are large fruited and well worth trying but an acid, moist soil with plenty of peat is essential. Little or no pruning is necessary apart from the occasional removal in winter of old, worn-out wood.

Recommended Cultivars 'Berkeley', 'Coville', 'Ivanhoe' and 'Blue Crop'. It is advisable to plant at least two cultivars to assist pollination.

FIGS The cultivar 'Brown Turkey' is often successful given correct treatment on a warm, south-facing wall. Root restriction is essential to curb excessive growth and a stone or concrete-lined bed approximately 3ft(1m) long and 2ft by 2ft 6in(60cm by 75cm) deep is advisable. A fan-shaped framework of branches is developed, side shoots from which should produce the crop following timely pinching and pruning. The young shoots require pinching at the fifth leaf by the end of June; fresh shoots then develop and ripen by the autumn with embryo figs in the leaf axils. If the figs are any larger than a pea they are unlikely to overwinter for successful growth and ripening the following season.
Winter pruning is best delayed until March in case frost damages the shoots. These, together with weak and overcrowded growth, should be removed. If severe weather threatens, some winter protection may be necessary, if practicable. Feeding is not normally required and neither pests nor disease are usually a problem.

MEDLARS The medlar is a decorative, spreading tree which produces regular crops of unusual fruits that must be collected when ripe and stored and "bletted" until over-ripe and soft. It is only suitable for cultivation where space is unlimited.

MULBERRIES The black mulberry is a very attractive, slow-growing and long-lived tree. Its ripe fruit is excellent for jam. It is best grown on a lawn where the cut grass makes the collection of ripe fruit, shaken or fallen from the tree, easy. Hardwood cuttings should root readily in the open ground.

QUINCE The quince is highly prized by many gardeners but seldom grown. It is excellent for preserves, but although considered to be self-fertile cropping is often disappointing. However, cultivars such as the following should prove reliable:

Recommended Cultivars   'Vranja', a good cropper, and 'Pear-shaped'.

Any reasonable soil is suitable for the quince and a bush-type tree is usually developed. Growth is slow, and little or no pruning will be necessary. The aroma from the ripe fruit is strong, hence storage away from apples and pears is advisable.

29.
A Reasoned Approach to Vegetable Growing

There are many different reasons for having a vegetable garden; it may be no more than to provide a few salads throughout the season, or no less than a desire for complete self-sufficiency in vegetables. Whatever the objective the keen gardener naturally wants to produce the highest quality crops as efficiently as possible, and although previous experience may help to achieve this goal the full potential of new growing methods and varieties is often not appreciated.

The evolution of vegetable growing from an art to something approaching a scientific practice has gathered pace in recent years. No longer is the growing of vegetables solely dependent on experience, laboriously and often painfully obtained over many seasons. Today, with accumulating scientific evidence from research institutes such as the National Vegetable Research Station, Wellesbourne, and from the experimental centres of the Ministry of Agriculture, there is a much sounder knowledge of the various cultural and environmental factors that influence the yield and quality of vegetable crops. Although all of this work is directed towards improving the efficiency and reliability of commercial vegetable production, many of the findings are equally applicable on a small scale, and receptive gardeners, old-hands and newcomers alike, can benefit enormously from the results of these studies. The aim of this chapter is to summarise recent developments which are applicable to many crops in general terms, and then to indicate the ways in which the growing of each of the most important vegetables may be improved as a result of these recent developments.

CULTIVARS   In recent years many new cultivars of vegetables have become available to gardeners, each one contributing some significant improvement over the older cultivars. The problem is to decide whether these new introductions should be grown in preference to older, established cultivars. The answer will depend to a large extent on the crop, individual preferences and requirements, and any problems associated with growing certain crops in particular situations. Outstanding new cultivars will be mentioned later for each crop but improvements shown by the newer introductions are relevant to a number of vegetables.

The most significant development over the last 10 years has been the introduction of hybrid cultivars. The advantages of F_1 hybrids over older cultivars are generally higher yields and more uniform plants, particularly in such crops as Brussels sprouts and cabbage. However, because seeds of hybrids are much more expensive than those of normal, open-pollinated cultivars it may only be worthwhile to buy hybrid cultivars when the advantages are clear, as with Brussels sprouts: growing hybrid cultivars of carrots and onions is not justified, at present.

Examples of improved characteristics incorporated into recent cultivars include resistance to pests (lettuce root aphid), diseases (parsnip canker, downy mildew of lettuce) and bolting (in beetroot and spring cabbage), much earlier maturity (in Brussels sprouts and onions), the ability to "stand" for several weeks without becoming over-mature (cabbages), better storage characteristics (onions) and better quality (stringless French beans, improved colour of beetroot and carrots).

In addition to catalogue descriptions the gardener should study impartial information from the trials of the Royal Horticultural Society at Wisley and from the National Institute of Agricultural Botany, which lists suitable vegetable cultivars for the gardener. Then, depending on his personal requirements, a number of apparently suitable cultivars can be chosen for growing alongside old favourites so that their performance can be compared under his own conditions. In this way objective assessments can be made and decisions taken on the choice of cultivars for the future.

SEEDS AND HOW TO STORE THEM Seeds of the chosen cultivars should be stored with care, especially if they are to be kept for later sowings and subsequent years. Seeds start to deteriorate from the time they mature on the seeding plant and, in general, the longer they are stored before sowing the lower is their vigour and the percentage of seeds which germinate. The rate at which seeds deteriorate depends on the conditions under which they are kept and on the species. As a general guide, for each 9°F rise in temperature above 32°F(o°C) the storage life is halved, and for each 1 per cent increase in seed moisture content from 5 per cent to 14 per cent, the seed life is again halved. Therefore, all seeds should be stored in cool, dry conditions and even if they are in moisture-proof packets they should not be kept in a warm room; the temperature requirements to maintain vitality of seeds and human beings are not the same!

With seeds of some species the rate of deterioration can be very rapid. For example, the percentage germination of lettuce seeds which have been kept under warm, damp conditions can be progressively lower with later sowings throughout a single season. Leek, onion and parsnip seeds are also sensitive to such storage conditions whereas tomato and radish seeds may remain viable for up to 10 years or more.

Seeds store best in unopened tin-foil vacuum-packs in a cool, dry place. The packs should not be opened until sowing. Seeds in paper packets or opened vacuum packs can be stored satisfactorily in an air-tight glass jar with a small amount of cobalt-chloride-treated silica gel (a teaspoonful per ounce of seed). The silica gel takes up water from the atmosphere and the seed moisture content can be reduced and controlled in this way. Seeds stored by this method will remain in good condition for several years.

NEW SOWING METHODS Gardeners are well aware that many controllable and uncontrollable factors affect when, and how many of the seeds that they sow germinate, and produce seedlings. In recent years several new and promising sowing methods have been introduced to help overcome the problems by achieving earlier, more regularly-spaced and more predictable numbers of seedlings.

Pelleting of many vegetable seeds is now commonplace. The main purpose of pelleting is to make awkwardly-shaped seeds more uniform, and small seeds larger in size, to enable them to be handled individually and spaced accurately. They perform this role admirably and permit every seed to be used effectively. It is also possible to incorporate some fungicides and insecticides into the pelleting material but in this country only a small proportion of pellets contain such chemicals. On the debit side pelleting is not specifically intended to aid germination and may, under some dry conditions, have an adverse effect on germination and emergence.

The most recent and radical of the newer techniques is the fluid sowing of pre-germinated seeds. With this method seeds are provided with ideal conditions for germination by sowing them on wet absorbent paper in a sandwich box in a warm place indoors. The germinated seeds can then be sown outside without damage after mixing them into a protective carrier jelly which can be squeezed out of a polythene bag into the prepared seed-bed. Because the adverse effects of poor soil conditions on germination are eliminated, sowing pre-germinated seeds results in more rapid seedling emergence of most vegetables, including the very slow germinating ones like parsley and parsnip, and improved establishment of plants from the more difficult seeds such as celery. In addition, fluid sowing makes it easier to distribute very small seeds. Fluid sowing of pre-germinated seed is a simple and fascinating technique which can be practised by any gardener.

167. *Pre-germinating seeds for fluid sowing. The seeds are sown on wet absorbent paper* (**A**) *and germinated in a warm place indoors. The germinated seeds are then mixed with a protective carrier jelly which can be squeezed out of a polythene bag into the prepared seed-bed* (**B**).

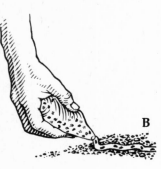

Whatever method is used to sow seeds the seed bed conditions should be made as favourable as possible for the seedlings to emerge. The soil structure should be friable and under dry conditions water should be applied to the bottom of the seed drill before sowing. Watering should not normally be done after sowing otherwise there is a risk of a hard soil cap forming on the surface which would prevent the seedlings from emerging. On poorly-structured soils it has been demonstrated that covering the seeds with compost, peat or vermiculite rather than soil, after sowing, results in much better emergence of the seedlings and this practice should be tried on soils which give emergence problems.

PLANT RAISING The introduction of small propagators, peat pots and blocks, and expanded polystyrene pro-forma's for raising containerless plants have increased reliability of establishment and given a great impetus to the use of vegetable transplants in the garden. For many crops trans-planting has several advantages over sowing *in situ*. It gives earlier crops, a more intensive use of a small area by shortening the time the ground is occupied, and enables cold-sensitive plants such as tomatoes to crop reliably in our short season.

With a greenhouse, cold-frame, cloches, or even a small propagator on a windowsill, it is worthwhile to raise one's own plants. The aim should be to produce good, sturdy plants by giving as much light as possible. For early work the plants should be grown in containers or peat or soil blocks, whereas later in the season plants can be raised in an outside seed bed. To reduce the risk of empty blocks yet avoid the need to thin seedlings, seeds can be pre-germinated and a single, pre-germinated seed carefully transfer-red to each block. For certain crops such as beetroot and onion recent experiments indicate that there are advantages in raising several plants in each block and transplanting them as a group since this economises on the number of blocks and on space.

In order to minimise the inevitable check to growth which will occur at the time of transplanting, plants should be watered well both before and after they are planted.

PLANT SPACING Gardeners are usually far too generous in the space that they give to their vegetables and if the aim is to grow as much as possible on a small area then much closer spacing can be tried with advantage. As a general rule the more plants that are grown per unit area, the higher is the total yield but the individual plants become smaller. Spacing can, in fact, be used to control size, quite precisely.

Another important general rule is that by arranging plants as evenly as possible the yield from a given area can be increased considerably over that from the same number of plants grown in widely-spaced rows. It is not always possible to consider growing broadcast crops in a completely even arrangement because of problems in gaining access to the plants for weeding and other jobs. However, it is practical to grow crops in close rows on beds about 5ft(1.5m) wide which allow plants in all the rows to be tended from the pathways. Such a bed system enables more plants to be grown per unit area by using the ground more effectively. Furthermore, because the plants are more evenly arranged they tend to be more uniform in size.

Another important advantage of growing on a bed system is that the soil need not be walked on after digging and therefore a good, uniform seed bed can be obtained over the whole bed. This should result in better and more uniform seedling establishment and growth. It also permits the ground to be used more intensively because it is easier to practise intercropping. For example fast-growing salads can be grown in between slower-growing root crops or brassicas.

It has been shown that spacing is such a powerful means of affecting plant growth and development that at extremely close spacings new crop types are produced such as mini-cauliflowers and leaf lettuce (both referred to on p. 258). Suitable spacings for the most important vegetables are discussed later crop by crop. However, because the appropriate spacing needed to produce the desired size of vegetable will also depend on such

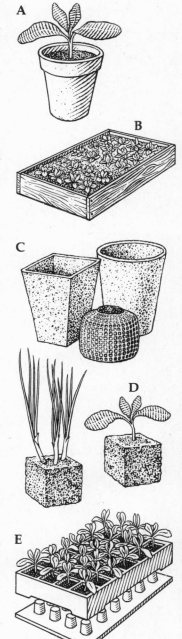

168. *Transplants can be raised in various ways other than in traditional pots* (**A**) *and seed boxes* (**B**). *For example, in peat containers* (**C**) *of various types; in soil or peat blocks singly or in groups* (**D**) *or pro-forma* (**E**).

169. **A.** *If uniform-sized sprouts are wanted on Brussel sprouts for freezing then the plants should be close-spaced in the rows (see p.257).*
B. *Leeks and carrots can be left in the ground until required, the first being earthed up and the carrots given a covering of soil, straw or polythene (see "Vegetable Storage", p.255).*

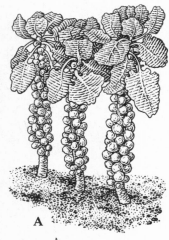

A

B

factors as the soil fertility and micro-climate of each garden, keen gardeners should experiment with different spacings under their conditions as a guide for the future. They may well be surprised with the results which they obtain.

WATERING Contrary to popular belief, watering of vegetable crops is not always beneficial because it may encourage only the growth of the non-edible part of the plant, discourage root growth and may reduce the flavour of vegetables. Apart from these reasons watering is time-consuming and water supplies may be limited. It is, therefore, worth planning with some care the most effective watering policy to adopt in your garden.

Top priority must obviously go to establishing crops. If it is essential to sow seeds under dry conditions the bottom of the drill should be watered before sowing. Later when watering small seedlings use a fine rose to give small droplets which will do less damage to the young plants and soil structure. Transplants should be thoroughly watered before planting and afterwards small amounts of water should be given immediately around the base of the plant.

Second priority should be given to watering those crops where the leaf or the shoot is eaten; for example, cabbage, cauliflower, lettuce and celery, because rapid growth is needed to get good quality. As a general guide watering once a week at a rate of 2 to 3 gal per square yard(9 to 13.5l per m^2) will keep the plants growing well, but if regular watering is impossible, make sure that a good watering is given about two weeks before the crops are ready to cut.

For fruiting vegetables such as peas, beans, tomatoes and marrows, once crops are established they should not be watered until the plants start to flower, otherwise too much leaf will form. Then, throughout the flowering and fruiting period, water should be given every two to three days at the rate of 1 gal per square yard(4.5l per m^2).

Root crops such as carrots and parsnips should not be watered frequently otherwise lush foliage growth will be made. In general, potatoes should be watered after the tubers start to form but the timing will vary with variety and will be discussed later.

It should also be remembered that the need for watering can be reduced to some extent by spacing plants widely apart, by making the soil as retentive as possible through adding organic manures, and by mulching. Soil moisture can also be conserved for your crops by removing weeds at an early stage.

WEED CONTROL Weeds compete with vegetable plants for water and nutrients and so should be killed at the earliest opportunity. Hoeing and hand-weeding are the usual methods used in the garden but there are also effective chemical weed-killers. For example, chloropropham/diuron/propham (Herbon Garden Herbicide) can be applied to the soil after sowing a range of vegetables where it remains for some weeks selectively killing off weed seedlings as they emerge. At a later stage paraquat/diquat (Weedol) can be used to control weeds between rows of plants by applying it with a sprinkler-bar on a watering can.

Individual perennial weeds should be dug up or spot-treated with a weed-killer containing 2,4-D or glyphosate (Tumbleweed); larger infestations can be treated with glyphosate or, if couch or other grasses are the problem, with dalapon.

Mulching will help to keep down annual weeds. As all annual and many perennial weeds are spread by seeds a firm resolution should be made to prevent weeds from producing seeds for it should be remembered that "one year's seeding is seven years' weeding".

PEST AND DISEASE CONTROL A logical and commonsense approach is needed to the control of pests and diseases in the vegetable garden. The aim should be to recognise an attack at the earliest opportunity, decide whether any action is needed, and, if so, what control measure is required. Frequent inspections are needed to spot early signs of attack and to note whether the damage is increasing. However, not all damage caused by pests and diseases is important, especially if it is confined to the parts that are not eaten and it is not usually worthwhile or realistic to aim to have crops completely free of damage. If action is needed then other control methods should be considered before chemical treatments are used. Do not despise hand-picking of the pest and infested or infected leaves; and if chemical control has to be adopted follow exactly the recommendations for use.

In recent years many new chemicals have been developed for the prevention or the control of pests and diseases which have advantages over older materials. A great advance is the introduction of systemic insecticides and fungicides which, unlike the old materials, are taken up and translocated to all parts of the plant. Sap-sucking pests will be killed if they feed on any part of a plant so treated while some systemic fungicides will often check a fungus disease that has become established within the plant. A further advantage of these systemic compounds is that they are largely absorbed within a few hours and are not then washed away by rain.

In general, newer insecticides are less persistent and some have less harmful effects on beneficial insects, than those used a decade ago. The new synthetic pyrethroid insecticides are especially toxic to caterpillars but unfortunately to fish also. As an alternative to mercury compounds to control club-root disease of brassicas, benomyl or thiophanate-methyl can be used. A whole range of products are now available from garden sundriesmen and most are environmentally more acceptable than those used in the past. Provided the manufacturers' instructions are strictly followed they are safe to use in the garden.

Also in recent years chemical seed treatments have been developed for the control of certain seed-borne diseases; for example, neck rot of onions, or to give protection against soil-borne damping-off diseases. While at present it is not always possible for gardeners to buy small quantities of treated seed, it is a simple and worthwhile operation to treat your own seed at home.

Although many advances have been made in chemical control methods it is still the best policy to try to avoid attacks of pests and diseases. Strict attention to garden hygiene (removal and destruction of infected material) crop-rotations, growing varieties resistant to pests and diseases, using barriers and other pest deterrents and sowing crops out of season, should all be practised whenever possible for they will help to reduce the risk of attacks from pests and diseases.

VEGETABLE STORAGE It is not generally appreciated that vegetables deteriorate from the time of harvest and throughout any storage period. Vegetables should therefore be harvested and stored only when there are good reasons for not leaving them in the ground. Where storage is essential only undamaged produce free from pest and disease attack should be stored. The crop should be handled very carefully to avoid damage which allows fungi and bacteria to enter and increases the rate of deterioration and wastage. Wastage also results from drying-out in store.

As a general guide root crops such as carrots, parsnips and swedes should, if possible, be left in the ground protecting them from heavy frosts from mid-November by covering with soil, straw or polythene sheeting. If these crops have to be lifted they may be stored in layers of damp sand or in polythene bags folded over to restrict ventilation. Potatoes are best stored in double-thickness paper sacks away from light at a temperature of about 39°F(4°C). Leafy vegetables such as lettuce and sprouts are best stored in polythene bags in a domestic refrigerator whereas those vegetables susceptible to chilling injury such as French and runner beans, marrows and tomatoes should not be kept at a temperature lower than 41°F(5°C). Onions for storing should be thoroughly dried and hung up in cotton or plastic nets in a garden shed; alternatively, place in a refrigerator to prolong their life.

170. *Onions and potatoes should be lifted and stored in a shed or garage. Onions should be placed in cotton or plastic nets or strings, as shown; potatoes stored in double-thickness paper sacks, away from light and off the ground. Leafy vegetables such as lettuce or cauliflower can be kept for a short period in a polythene bag in a refrigerator (see "Vegetable Storage", left).*

CULTIVARS AND GROWING METHODS

The most significant recent developments in the growing of individual vegetable crops are outlined below for the benefit of those keen gardeners who may wish to try new cultivars and cultural techniques for themselves.

BEANS – BROAD, FRENCH AND RUNNER There have been considerable improvements in the pod quality of the newer dwarf French and runner beans cultivars. In particular the stringless, flesh-podded cultivars of French beans such as 'Tendergreen' and 'Pros Gitana' freeze well and 'Loch Ness' and 'Bina' are also good for slicing, while 'Glamis' and 'Glen Lyon' have been bred for Scottish conditions. Relatively stringless cultivars of runner beans such as 'Desiree', 'Red Knight' and 'Mergoles' are also now available.

Experimental work has shown that the optimum spacing of bean crops for maximum yields are as follows: broad, 18 by 4½in(45 by 11.5cm) for tall cultivars and 9 by 9in(23 by 23cm) for compact varieties; dwarf French, 18 by 2in(45 by 5cm), and for runner beans, 24 by 6in(60 by 15cm). These spacings are closer than those normally used in gardens and so higher yields should be obtained.

All of the bean crops respond well to watering around the base of the plants during the flowering and podding period by increasing pod-set and yield but they should not be watered before flowering unless the soil is very dry. Furthermore, and contrary to popular belief, it has been demonstrated conclusively that syringing around the flowers of runner beans to aid pod-set is not effective, so it is suggested that you save your time and effort for more productive jobs. (See also Chapter 32 "The Soil, Its Management and Moisture Requirements", p. 290 to 296.)

BEETROOT With the introduction of cultivars resistant to bolting such as 'Avonearly' and 'Boltardy', early sowings can be made in March under cloches and outdoors in April with little risk of the plants bolting. These varieties are almost free from white rings and can be sown at intervals until July. For early crops a plant spacing of 7 by 4in(18 by 10cm) should be used, and later for maximum yields of medium-sized roots a spacing of 12 by 1in(30 by 2.5cm).

Early crops can also be grown from plants raised in pots or blocks and transplanted when small. Several plants can be grown in each block and should be planted in a clump to produce early, small beet.

BRASSICAS These important crops which include Brussels sprouts, cabbages and cauliflowers are usually grown from transplants. Experimental work has shown that the conditions under which transplants are raised can greatly affect the yield and quality of the subsequent crop. In order to produce good, sturdy, fast-growing plants plenty of space should be allowed with not more than 10 seedlings per foot (30cm) of row. Growth should be encouraged by frequent watering and the plants should be planted out as soon as possible. Plants raised in a sterile compost in pots or blocks get a good start and establish themselves rapidly after planting provided they are kept watered and have not grown too large. Only good, healthy plants should be bought in to prevent the introduction into the garden of such soil-borne diseases as clubroot.

All brassicas suffer from the same pests and diseases, the most important of which are cabbage fly, cabbage aphid, caterpillars and clubroot disease. If clubroot becomes established the affected areas can now be treated with chemicals such as dazomet but several weeks must elapse before planting. The roots of transplants can be dipped in either thiophanate-methyl, benomyl or calomel to help control this disease.

Two of the most important pests of brassicas, caterpillars and cabbage root fly can be controlled on a small scale without the use of chemicals. Plants should be carefully examined, especially the undersides of leaves, twice weekly for evidence of caterpillars feeding which, if found, can be removed by hand. Plants can be protected from cabbage root fly by physical barriers in the form of a 6in(15cm) disc of foam carpet-underlay which, with a slit to a $\frac{1}{10}$in(.25cm) drinking hole can be fitted closely around the stem. Alternatively, plastic drinking cups with the bottom removed can be slipped over the plants shortly after transplanting and the rim pressed lightly into the soil. Carefully fitted barriers can prevent up to 70 per cent of the root damage caused by the fly maggots.

Aphids can be effectively controlled by spraying the plants with a systemic aphicide such as dimethoate or formothion.

Brussels sprouts Hybrids now available produce sprouts of excellent quality which hold on the stem in good condition over a long period of time. So it is now possible to pick sprouts from September until March by growing only two cultivars; for example, 'Peer Gynt' for picking before Christmas, and 'Valiant' for later production. Alternatively, with the widespread use of home freezers, the gardener may want to produce all of his sprouts in the autumn and freeze some for later use. Here again, the newer hybrids are ideal for this purpose because of the uniformity in size and quality of the buttons.

If small uniform-sized sprouts are wanted for freezing the plants should be closely spaced at 20 by 20in(50 by 50cm). The growing point of the stem of early cultivars should also be removed ("stopped") when the lowest sprouts are about ½in(1cm) in diameter and this will tend to make the buttons more uniform in size. They can then all be removed at a single picking. However, if larger sprouts are wanted or if they are to be picked over a long period, a wider spacing of 36 by 36in(1m) should be used to allow adequate growth and access for sequential picking.

Cabbages The newer hybrids produce very uniform, high-quality heads many of which will hold for several weeks when mature without deteriorating, so it is now much easier to provide continuity of cabbage supply throughout the year if required. Examples of the newer cultivars which should be considered for the different seasons are: 'Avon Crest' (March –May); 'Derby Day', 'Hispi' and 'Marner Allfrüh' (June–July); 'Market Topper', 'Minicole' and 'Stonehead' (August–September); 'Hisepta' (September–November); 'Hidena' and 'Jupiter' (November–December); and 'Aquarius', 'Avon Coronet', 'Celtic' and 'Ice Queen' (December–February).

If large heads are wanted plants should be spaced up to 18 by 18in(45 by 45cm) and watered regularly if conditions are dry. For high yields of smaller heads it is better to reduce the spacing of summer cabbage to 14 by 14in(35 by 35cm). Even at this spacing the heads will be large enough for most families provided the crop is regularly watered.

Chinese cabbage is becoming increasingly popular. The crop needs fairly high temperatures and shortening days to avoid bolting and so can be sown *in situ* from late June to August. Transplanting can be used to give earlier crops but the plants must be raised in pots or blocks in warm conditions otherwise they will bolt. Hybrids now available include 'Tip Top' and 'Nagaoka'.

171. *The "stopping" of early varieties of Brussels sprouts will result in earlier picking and buttons of more uniform size for freezing. Pinch out the tops when the lowermost sprouts are ½in (1cm) in size.*

Calabrese This, too, is a crop which is increasing in popularity and which matures from June to October. The best spears are usually produced on plants which have been sown *in situ* at intervals from early April until June to provide continuity. The plants should be grown at a population of one to two plants per square foot(10 to 20 per m²), and should be watered regularly, especially when the spears are developing. After the large, terminal spear has been cut smaller secondary spears will develop for later harvesting. 'Corvet,' 'Express Corona', 'Green Comet', 'Green Duke' and 'Premium Crop' are cultivars which have done well in recent trials.

Cauliflower Many new cultivars which have been introduced in recent years are more reliable in their cropping and give better quality curds than older varieties. For summer and autumn production newer cultivars include 'Mechelse-Classic' and 'Mechelse-Delta' which can be cut at the end of June and 'Dominant' in July. 'Nevada' will then produce crops maturing in July, August and September from successional sowings while 'Flora Blanca' will crop in September/October and 'Barrier Reef' is useful for the October/ November period. This crop is particularly sensitive to dry conditions and to ensure high-quality curds regular watering is essential.

Experiments have shown that curd size can be controlled by plant spacing with the largest heads being produced on plants grown at wide spacing – 30 by 30in(75 by 75cm). With cauliflowers, however, it has been shown that certain cultivars of the 'Alpha', 'Mechelse' or 'Snowball' type can be grown as close as 6 by 6in(15 by 15cm) to produce a new type of crop, "mini-cauliflower". Small curds only 1½ to 3in(4 to 8cm) in size are produced but nearly all at the same time and they are particularly suitable for freezing whole. Alternatively, by successional sowings from mid-March to the end of June, a continuous supply of small curds can be obtained fresh for the table from July to October.

CARROTS Most gardeners could improve their yields by applying some of the newer developments in cultural methods. For early crops of the 'Amsterdam Forcing' type sown into cold soil, seed should be dusted with thiram or captan as a precautionary measure against the "damping-off" disease of seedlings. There are also advantages in pre-germinating the seed and fluid-sowing to get much earlier seedling emergence. Rows should not be more than 6in(15cm) apart and the aim should be for a low population of five to seven plants per square foot(50 to 70 plants per m²) for these early crops in order to get rapid growth.

For main crops of medium-sized roots cultivars of the 'Chantenay' or 'Autumn King' types should be sown at the end of May, aiming to get 15 to 20 plants per square foot(150 to 200 plants per m²) of ground. The roots can be lifted in November for storage or, preferably, be left in the ground protected by a layer of leaves or other material, for lifting during the winter.

Carrot root fly is the main pest and to minimise attacks sow early and late to avoid the main periods of attack; do not thin the crops, and apply diazinon, chlorpyrifos or bromophos along the rows at sowing time. The willow-carrot aphid can also be troublesome but this pest can now be readily controlled by spraying with a systemic aphicide such as dimethoate.

CELERY The self-blanching cultivars such as 'Avonpearl', 'Greensnap' and 'Lathom Self-Blanching' use much less room than the trench types. Provided they are grown on very fertile soil and are watered frequently a spacing of 12 by 10in(30 by 25cm) will give good quality sticks and if only celery hearts are wanted the plants can be as close as 6 by 6in(15 by 15cm). However, these cultivars will not survive hard frosts and will tend to bolt if growth is checked. There are advantages in pre-germinating the seeds of celery and then transferring the germinated seeds to pots or blocks of compost to raise the plants under warm conditions, 55 to 65°F(13 to 18.5°C), before carefully planting outdoors on a bed system.

LEEKS On good fertile soil maximum yields of medium-sized leeks are obtained from growing the plants 6in(15cm) apart in 12in(30cm) rows. As the largest leeks at lifting time come from the largest transplants, the aim should be to raise good plants in uncrowded conditions within the seed bed. For early crops in September and October there are new cultivars such as 'Autumn Mammoth-Early Market', while for winter production 'Autumn Mammoth-Herwina' and 'Catalina' have given good results in recent trials.

LETTUCE Many gardeners experience problems in producing a succession of lettuces throughout the summer. These are often caused by failure to establish successional crops at the correct time as a result of high soil temperatures or dry conditions preventing seed germination. Experiments have shown that to ensure rapid seedling emergence the bottom of the seed drill should be watered *before* sowing and if the weather is hot the soil should be shaded and the seeds sown in the *early afternoon*. Alternatively, pre-germinated seed can be fluid sown or transferred to pots or blocks for transplanting later. Such methods should give rapid seedling emergence. In order to time the sowings correctly make each sowing when the seedlings of the previous sowing are just emerging.

Provided that hearted lettuce are not required it is easy to obtain a continuous succession of lettuce leaves by growing plants, especially of cos varieties, at very close spacings, 5 by 1in(13 by 2.5cm), so that they cannot produce hearts. The crop is ready for cutting in 40 days in mid-season and after cutting the stumps will produce a second crop of leaves. The equivalent of four normal-hearted lettuce per week from May to October can be obtained from sowing an area of less than one square yard(m^2) on each of ten dates.

Of the newer butterhead cultivars 'Avondefiance' is reliable for cropping up to October and is resistant to root aphid and some races of downy mildew, 'Hilde II' is similar in appearance and is useful for cutting until August. Of the crisphead cultivars 'Great Lakes' and 'Minetto' have done well in trials while the cos varieties 'Lobjoit's Green' and 'Little Gem' continue to give satisfaction.

Every effort should be made to control foliage aphids on lettuce not only for culinary reasons but to prevent the spread of virus diseases. Sprays of systemic insecticides such as dimethoate or formothion effectively control these aphids but near to harvest time only derris should be used. (See also Chapter 30, p. 264 on growing this salad crop under low glass or plastic.)

MARROW (Courgettes) Courgettes have become very popular in recent years, partly as a result of the many new high-yielding cultivars available. The F$_1$ hybrids are very suitable for courgette production and the following have given good results in recent trials: 'Chefini', 'Early Gem' (also known as 'Storr's Green'), 'Golden Zucchini' and 'Zucchini'.

Open-pollinated cultivars suitable for marrow production include 'Green Bush' and 'Smallpak' (bush types) and 'Long Green Trailing'. Unfortunately, marrows are very susceptible to virus infection and any stunted and distorted plants should be destroyed.

ONIONS It is now possible to grow and provide the kitchen with bulb onions throughout the year through developments in growing the over-wintered crop, better control of disease in store and new cultivars. Very early bulbs can be harvested from the end of May until July by sowing Japanese overwintered onions in mid-August. These are winter-hardy, bolting-resistant, intermediate day-length cultivars. Suitable ones in order of earliness are 'Express Yellow', 'Imai Yellow' and 'Senshyu Semi-globe Yellow'. These can withstand severe frosts but will not succeed on badly-drained soil. Crops can then be produced in August from sets of cultivars such as 'Stuttgarter Giant' or 'Sturon' planted in March or early April. The danger of bolting will be reduced if small-sized or heat-treated sets are used.

Bulbs for storing are lifted in September from crops sown in March choosing cultivars recommended for their storage qualities; for example, 'Hydro' and 'Rijnsburger-Balstora'. The bulbs should be thoroughly dried and stored in shallow layers or in nets hung up to get plenty of ventilation in a cool place. Storage life can be prolonged by keeping the bulbs in a refrigerator, and under these conditions they will keep until late spring. The scourge of long-term storage, neck rot of the bulbs caused by *Botrytis allii*, can now be easily controlled by a simple seed or set dressing with a dust of benomyl before sowing.

The highest yields per unit area are obtained from close spacing of plants but the closer the spacing the smaller are the individual bulbs. For pickling-sized onions highest yields will be given at a population of 35 plants per square foot(350 plants per m^2), but if 1½ to 2in(4 to 5cm) sized bulbs are wanted the best population is eight plants per square foot(80 plants per m^2) with the plants being grown in rows no more than 12in(30cm) apart. As bulb size and yield also depend to a large extent on the size of plant when bulbing starts it has been shown that highest yields of spring-sown crops are obtained if transplants are raised in heat and transplanted in March or April to give them a good start. Plants can be raised in boxes or blocks and planted out singly, or four or five plants can be grown in each block giving clumps of plants. As the bulbs grow they push each other apart and develop normally into medium-sized bulbs. This method economises on compost and space in the greenhouse. It is also a particularly useful technique for producing bulb onions in the north of

England and Scotland where the growing season is shorter.

If transplants cannot be raised or purchased, fluid-sowing pre-germinated seed (see p. 252) instead of normal seed will advance seedling growth by two to three weeks and gives higher yields.

PARSNIPS To produce high yields of roots with 1½ to 2in(4 to 5cm) diameter crowns this crop should be grown at a population of six or seven plants per square foot(60 to 70 plants per m²), but if larger or earlier roots are wanted more space needs to be given (two to three plants per square foot[20 to 30 plants per m²]). It is an advantage to fluid sow pre-germinated seeds of this crop in March to get earlier and better seedling emergence.

'Avonresister' and 'White Gem' have good resistance to canker and they should be grown where this is a problem.

PEAS Of the many new cultivars most have been developed for the single harvesting requirements of the freezing industry. In the garden, therefore, several sowings of these cultivars will be needed to give picking over a long period. However, these dwarf cultivars have the advantage of not requiring support and should be grown in close rows at a population of six to eight plants per square foot(60 to 80 plants per m²). Because all the pods tend to mature together only small areas should be sown at a time. Of the new cultivars 'Hurst Beagle', 'Hurst Canice', 'Victory Freezer' and 'Hurst Green Shaft' have given good results in recent trials and they are ideal for use fresh or for freezing. The yield of peas can be greatly increased by watering at flowering time and as the pods are filling. (See also Chapter 30, p. 267 regarding an early sowing under cloches.)

Especially for early sowings, seeds should be dusted with captan to control "damping-off". To reduce damage by pea moth caterpillars, sprays of permethrin or fenitrothion should be applied seven to 10 days after the first flowers appear from early June onwards.

POTATOES Although the established cultivars such as 'Sutton's Foremost' and 'King Edward' continue to be widely grown by gardeners, newer proven ones are challenging them for popularity. For example, 'Maris Bard' and 'Pentland Javelin' are good first-earlies; 'Maris Peer' is a good second-early although susceptible to drought; and maincrop cultivars such as 'Desiree', 'Maris Piper', 'Pentland Dell' and 'Pentland Squire' produce high yields of good eating-quality tubers.

Recent experimental work has shown that for really early crops large seed tubers should be obtained as early as October and stored at about 60°F(16°C) until the "eyes" break into growth. They should then be kept in cool conditions (45°F [7.5°C]) until planting time with lighting to give sturdy green sprouts. For maincrops, tubers should be stored cool until the early spring. For maximum yields the spacing within the row can range between 8 and 14in(20 and 35cm) depending on cultivar. All cultivars should be planted only when the soil temperature at a depth of 4in(10cm) exceeds 43°F(6°C) on more than three consecutive days.

Yields of early cultivars can be increased by regular waterings at 10 to 14-day intervals throughout growth. For maincrops watering should not normally be done until the tubers have formed, and for most cultivars a single heavy watering should be given when the tubers are the size of a marble.

Some recent developments in the control of the pests of this crop include the application of bromophos, chlorpyrifos, or diazinon to the soil at planting if wireworms and cutworms are troublesome, and the introduction of cultivars, such as 'Maris Piper', which are resistant to one type of potato cyst eelworm. Sprays for the control of blight include maneb, mancozeb, or the copper-based fungicides.

SWEET CORN This crop requires warm conditions and unprotected crops should not be sown until May when the soil temperature reaches 50°F(10°C). For early crops earlier sowings can be made if the soil is warmed beforehand by protecting with cloches or by using clear plastic mulches (see also Chapter 30, p. 267). This will not only speed up seedling emergence but will give earlier-maturing crops. As an alternative to sowing directly plants can be raised in pots or blocks in heat and transplanted when the risk of frost has passed. They should be planted in a compact area to assist pollination and to improve the size and quality of cobs watering should be done at "tasselling" and when the cobs are swelling. Reliable F_1 hybrids include 'Kelvedon Sweetheart' and 'Northern Belle'.

TOMATOES (OUTDOOR) Traditionally, outdoor tomato crops have been grown by raising plants of "staked" cultivars such as 'Harbinger', 'Moneymaker' and 'Alicante' and planting them when the risk of frost has passed. An alternative, cheaper system has now been developed using the newer bush or dwarf cultivars which require no thinning, pruning or staking. Of these cultivars the early 'Sub-arctic Plenty' is capable of growing and setting fruit well at low temperatures and the small, ripe fruits can be picked from mid-July; 'Sleaford Abundance' and 'Sigmabush' are mid-season hybrids and are well adapted to growing outdoors in the U.K.; and 'Alfresco' is later-maturing with much larger fruits. The fruit flavour of these bush cultivars is excellent.

Plants of these cultivars can be raised in the traditional way in pots or blocks under heat and then planted out. They can also be produced by sowing pre-germinated seeds about 2in(5cm) apart under cloches or polythene tunnels in mid-April provided that protection has been in place for a few days to warm up the soil. By the end of May the plants will be large enough to plant out. Alternatively, pre-germinated seeds can be sown directly to leave the plants to crop *in situ* without transplanting. For this latter system two or three pre-germinated seeds should be "spot" sown about 1ft(30cm) apart in a single row down the centre of a cloche; no thinning is required. With both of these systems there is some risk of frost damage by late spring frosts but growth is not severely affected provided the night temperature does not fall below 29°F(−1.5°C). Protection can be removed in June and fruit of the early varieties will be ready in July. After the crops are established watering will not be necessary unless the soil is dry during flowering and fruiting. Furthermore, provided a general fertiliser is incorporated into the soil before planting additional feeding will not be required. If control of potato blight is necessary the plants should be sprayed with maneb, mancozeb, or a copper-based fungicide. (See Chapter 30, p. 266 for details of growing tomatoes in frames or under cloches and Chapter 31, p. 277, for tomato cultivation in greenhouses.)

30.

Protected Cropping

For those who grow some of their own food the value of early crops is almost priceless. The first crops of strawberries, peas, lettuce and other salads are always most welcome. There is usually a late winter and spring gap to fill before the glut of summer salads and vegetables and the change from parsnips to peas and from tired shop lettuce to those fresh cut from the garden can be dramatic and welcome.

Such earliness can only be obtained by earlier sowing and planting and by greater warmth during growth. This warmth need not be dearly bought from coal, gas, oil or electricity but by reducing heat loss and by trapping solar heat.

We deal here with the facilities needed to get these higher temperatures, not in greenhouses that are dealt with elsewhere (pp. 269 to 285) but in frames, cloches and tunnels. The use of rigid and pliable plastics has extended the size, shape and convenience of this low cover as it is often called. Let us first define our terms.

Frames These have been in use for generations and were once more or less permanently sited. They are rigid and may be made of brick, concrete, wood or metal. Those with solid sides may be covered with multipane English or French lights, the former about 6ft by 4ft(2m by 1.25m) and the latter about 4ft(1.25m) square, or by single pane (Dutch) lights. More modern frames have glazed sides as well as tops where the glass, or rigid plastic, is fitted into the frame but made moveable for access. The dividing line between frames and the larger cloches is not now very clearly defined.

Cloches These were, of course, first of all the French bell jars once used for early crops and for striking more or less hardy cuttings. After this square or rectangular "cloches" were made with wooden, wire or other metal supports. The next step was to remove the ends and place these rectangular cloches end-to-end to make the "continuous" cloches that are now in such general use. Rigid plastic is now widely used in continuous cloches in place of glass. Continuous single sheets of pliable plastic stretched over curved wire and held down by other wire or string simulate continuous cloches and are usually known as tunnels or low tunnels. When such tunnels are stretched over curved metal pipes and are large enough to work in they become plastic structures or greenhouses and are discussed in Chapter 31.

Whatever the size or shape and whatever the material used, less heat will be lost from the soil and plants under them than from uncovered crops. This reduction of heat loss is by the direct trapping of the heat of the sun after absorption by the soil, and glass is better for this purpose than any plastic. Such cover also prevents the heat loss caused by wind (see p. 271). Cloches and frames also reduce evaporation and slow down transpiration from the plants, but they also throw off rain and prevent it reaching the soil. With

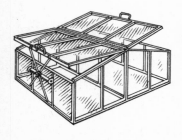

172. *A modern frame*

narrow cloches this is of no great disadvantage as the water seeps under them from the sides but with wider frames watering may be necessary, particularly for seedlings or newly planted crops. The reduction in evaporation will increase humidity under cloches and frames and thus increase the risk of some fungal diseases.

Crop needs Before discussing the most useful individual crops for this kind of cultivation let us consider the general methods used and the needs of protected crops. A well-drained fertile soil is almost essential. A waterlogged soil keeps down the temperature and delays sowing and planting and thus discounts the value of protection. A poor soil, particularly one lacking in organic matter, will produce poor growth and will soon be short of water in dry periods. Thus all the cost and time will be lost.

It almost goes without saying that all perennial weeds should be completely removed before engaging in protected cropping. They will flourish under the cover and be much more difficult to remove. The annual weed population should also be reduced as far as possible but this is a continuous struggle and the earlier flowering and seeding under cover can only make this more difficult. A rotation of the cover with open-ground crops will help to reduce these weeds by their being attacked while the ground is unencumbered with glass or plastics.

With any cover more than about 2ft(60cm) in width it is essential to have convenient means of watering readily available.

A little careful planning is desirable in the kitchen garden generally, but it can be particularly valuable when cloches or low tunnels are in use. The full use of such protection and the minimum of movements should be the objects of such planning. Many plans have been evolved and these are discussed in relation to the various crops surveyed in the following paragraphs.

Remember that various protective devices may be used to dry the soil surface and thus allow earlier sowing or planting of crops that may be uncovered when established and before their final maturity. Such protective devices may also be used to grow tender crops that would not normally mature in the open in the average British summer; or they may be used to cover established crops for the period of ripening or maturity.

THE MOST USEFUL CROPS

STRAWBERRIES This fruit can be ripened up to a month earlier under low cover, a little earlier under glass than plastics. Use early cultivars, preferably with small foliage. Plant early runners in August or early September. Cover in January–February and picking can be expected in May and June. Second- or third-year crops tend to be more leafy and later. It is, therefore, best to plant a fresh batch of runners each autumn for covering for early cropping and only to cover the older rows after uncovering the earlies. In this way the main crop can be protected from birds without the use of netting.

In soils at all short of fertiliser a dressing of 2oz(55g) per square yard of sulphate of potash is desirable before planting. It may be necessary to bait for slugs and spray with an approved fungicide against grey mould in damp seasons. (See also Chapter 28, p. 246 and 247.)

MELONS The melon is the other fruit that can be produced under cloches. 'Ogen' and other small-fruited cultivars are best for this form of cover; the larger fruited kinds are really better in greenhouses or warmer frames. Sow seed singly in 3 to 4in(8 to 10cm) pots in March and place in a warm greenhouse or living-room window. The pots must never dry out and a high temperature of 70 to 75°F(21 to 24°C) is most desirable for a week or two. Thereafter the seedlings will grow, albeit more slowly, at lower temperatures. Plant under cloches in early May, one plant to each 2ft(60cm) of continuous cloche or one per square yard(m²) of frame.

If the soil tends to be on the wet side plant with the ball of roots only half buried in the soil, thus allowing the roots to grow into the soil but enabling the base of the stem to be kept dry and escape a stem rot that can be

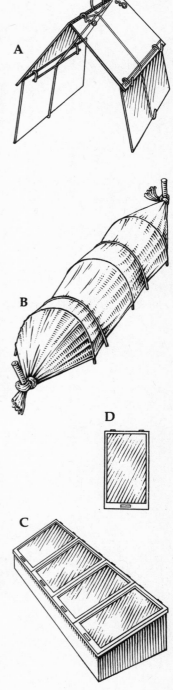

173. *A barn cloche* (**A**), *a low plastic tunnel* (**B**), *and a Dutch light frame* (**C**), *showing a Dutch light detached* (**D**).

damaging or fatal. The young plants may have to be protected from slugs by baiting. Pinch out the tip of the shoot when it begins to grow after planting in order to encourage several branches. Male flowers, without obvious young fruit below the flowers, will appear first. They will be followed by the females with easily recognized fruitlets below the petals. When three or four female flowers are open pollinate them by picking some male flowers and thrusting one each into the centre of the female and thereby transferring the pollen from one to the other. This aided pollination ensures fruit setting that is not always obtained where insects have limited access. After the fruit begins to swell the shoots may be shortened in order to reduce the foliage and encourage fruit growth and ripening.

If the number of available cloches is limited, these may be removed from early strawberries and replaced with nets which are then placed over the melons. This plan makes use of a set of cloches from February to September, only leaving them free for an autumn crop or, say, lettuce for winter use.

SALADS   These are among the most valuable crops to be obtained from low cover of all kinds. The produce is not only earlier maturing grown in this way but, being grown more quickly, is more tender and palatable.

CUCUMBERS   This almost universal salad fruit can be obtained throughout the year, but the trouble and cost of winter production is hardly worthwhile. The earliest cucumbers are obtained from heated greenhouses in which no other crop is grown. They are discussed in Chapter 31, p. 277. Quite early crops, from June onwards, can be obtained under low cover, first in frames and then under cloches. Later crops may be started under cover or entirely in the open and a late autumn crop, if wanted, may be grown in frames or cloches from July or August sowings.

Greenhouse cultivars such as 'Telegraph' or 'Butcher's Disease Resisting' may be sown in March for growing in frames. As with melons, sow one seed in each small pot and provide a high temperature until germination has taken place. If each frame can have a wheelbarrow load of farmyard manure or half-rotted compost beneath a 6in(15cm) layer of soil it will give some extra heat and encourage earlier and better growth. Cucumbers should not be pollinated; in fact some modern cultivars have only female flowers so that pollination is prevented. While greenhouse plants are carefully trimmed and tied to supporting wires, those in frames may be allowed to trail and fruit until exhausted. For the main summer crop the "ridge" or hardy cultivars are best, e.g. 'Long Green', 'Tasty Green' and 'Perfection'. They may be sown in pots, as for the earlier ones, and planted one to each 2ft(60cm) run of cloche when two or three adult leaves have expanded. Another sowing may be made in late May under cloches or in the open and, if autumn crops are desired, a final sowing can be made in July or August to be covered in September and to fruit until cold or damp defeats the plants.

Cucumbers really respond to rich soils and ample water. Dry plants produce small fruits and suffer attacks from red spider mite. This tiny pest can be controlled by chemical sprays but is best kept in check by regular and thorough spraying of both sides of the leaves with clear water.

LETTUCE   The lettuce is the basis of most salads and may be needed and grown in even small gardens throughout the year. To have them for cutting in the first three months is not easy, however, without the use of a heated greenhouse and we will start with the earliest spring crops.

The number and range of lettuce cultivars have been greatly extended in recent years and these now meet all tastes, soil conditions and seasons. The most generally grown are the butterhead type. They travel well and are therefore the most common in the shops. There are cultivars in this group to suit every season. Some gardeners prefer the more crisp types such as the tiny and very tight 'Tom Thumb' or the large 'Webb's Wonderful' or 'Great Lakes' group. Others favour the tall cos types such as the hardy 'Lobjoit's Green' or semi-cos cultivars like the summer-cropping 'Little Gem' or the more hardy 'Winter Density'.

25. *The beautiful* Iris *'Arizona Violet', a Louisiana hybrid. The origin of these irises in the southern United States makes them suitable only for growing in the southern part of this country, in warm, preferably damp places. They are as yet comparatively little known in this country (see p.203).*

26.   Lilium candidum, *the Madonna lily, has its ethereal qualities strikingly enhanced by its close association with the brilliantly coloured* Lychnis chalcedonica *(see p.215).*

27.   Rhododendron *'Lady Chamberlain', a hybrid of great beauty and of unusual flower form (see p.207).*

28. *Little space is required to grow a group of succulent plants exhibiting the diverse range of foliage shown here. It includes* Agave americana *'Variegata';* echeverias; Euphorbia meloformis, *with ball-like outline and horizontal banding;* Sedum sieboldii *'Medio-variegatum' and* S. pachyphllum; *kalanchoes and crassulas (see pp. 219 to 226).*

As a general rule, lettuce mature some two-and-a half to three months after sowing, except those sown in the autumn for spring cutting or in winter for use in late spring or early summer. A good rule is to sow a few seeds each time seedlings from the last sowing are ready for thinning or pricking off. Remember each seed can produce an edible lettuce.

The protection of low glass or plastic helps greatly to extend the season of lettuces and improve their quality. The chart below will probably give the best explanation of the timing of sowing and harvesting. Outdoor and greenhouse crops have been included for completeness.

LETTUCE – SOWING AND HARVESTING CHART

Cultivar	Jan	Feb	Mar	Apr	May	Jun	Jul	Aug	Sep	Oct	Nov	Dec
'Fortune'												
'Lobjoit's Green'												
'Little Gem'												
'Tom Thumb'												
'Webb's Wonderful'												
Any summer "butterhead", e.g. 'All the Year Round', 'Avondefiance', 'Continuity'												
'Winter Density'												
'Dandie' (heated houses or frames)												

Key:

– – – – – = sow under cover   ——————— = sow in the open

= = = = = = harvest under cover   ═══════ = harvest in the open

Much labour may be saved by sowing direct into the ground where the lettuce are to be harvested, and the time from sowing to cutting is slightly less than when seedlings are transplanted from a seed bed. On the other hand seed, and therefore cost, is saved by pricking out all the seedlings, or by thinning the seedlings to leave them 6 to 9in(15 to 23cm) apart where they are to mature and then pricking out the remainder. The method of sowing and then pricking out has to be practised when seed is sown in greenhouses, frames or cloches for open-ground production.

A fertile soil which provides ample moisture without waterlogging is necessary in order to produce high-quality heads. A thoroughly moist soil following ample rain or adequate watering at sowing or planting will see most lettuce crops to maturity, and watering during growth should not be necessary.

Slugs and snails can be devastating during damp weather. So can cutworms, leatherjackets and wireworms during most of the summer months. Trapping or baiting or searching around the plants after dusk can keep all these pests in check on a small scale.

Weeds need to be hoed off or otherwise removed while lettuce seedlings are young.

GREEN OR SALAD ONIONS These can be grown for use during most of the year without the assistance of any glass or plastic protection, but better quality may be obtained under cloches during the winter months. It is a matter of finding spare cloches in December to place over a row or two of seedlings sown at the usual time in late August or early September. Others sown at the same time can usually be harvested right through the winter and will continue to be usable until others sown in March are ready for pulling. 'White Lisbon' is the standard cultivar for this purpose. A winter-hardy strain has been developed for the autumn sowing.

RADISHES For those who would nibble a radish for most of the summer, open-ground sowing will produce a quite long season of supply but the season can be considerably extended by sowing earlier and later under cloches or in frames. A fertile soil with a fine tilth is needed for the thin shallow sowing that produces the quickly grown roots that are most welcome. A few seeds sown at weekly intervals from early spring to late summer will keep up supplies and avoid the gluts that soon become inedible when too many are sown at one time. These regular sowings can start earlier under frames or cloches when they are placed in position a week or two before sowing in order to allow the soil to dry and warm a little to produce a better seed bed. At the other end of the season crops can be obtained well into the winter by sowing the 'Black Spanish' or 'China Rose' radishes in July and August in frames or in the open and later covering them with cloches. Almost any of the several summer radishes will provide edible crops through the summer.

TOMATOES To supply a really long season of this valuable salad fruit a heated greenhouse or conservatory is a necessity. Outdoor crops are very limited in their season and often at risk from potato blight and other diseases. A cold greenhouse, frames and cloches can extend the season at the start and the end and produce fruit of rather better quality. The cultivation of outdoor tomatoes is discussed in Chapter 29 (p. 261) and of tomato cultivation in greenhouses in Chapter 31 (p. 277). Here we describe methods of cultivation for those who wish only to use their frames or cloches for this attractive fruit. Most greenhouse cultivars can be planted under cloches during May and early June, according to site and season, and then uncovered and staked to produce three to four trusses of fruit in the open. 'Outdoor Girl' or 'Gardeners' Delight' may be rather better for this method but, like the others, they need to have their sideshoots removed as they appear and then stopped above the third or fourth truss. Any fruits allowed to set on later trusses are unlikely to reach maturity and will certainly not ripen.

The bush or many-branched types such as 'The Amateur' and 'Roma' may be similarly planted and uncovered but not staked or they can be left covered under the widest and tallest cloches to grow and ripen under cover. All, whether under cover or in the open, will have green fruit left on the plants when autumn arrives. It is best then to pick them all, using them for chutney or placing them in single layers in a warm place to ripen. The use of low cover in this way can produce ripe fruit from the plants from July to September and steadily ripening fruit from those picked green well into the autumn until nearly Christmas.

The usual soil pests can be troublesome to tomatoes grown in this way, but it is the fungi that cause leaf mould, grey mould, stem rot and blight that are the most serious menaces. All are worst in moist seasons and regular fungicidal spraying must be a regular part of a tomato growing programme. There are now many reliable fungicides for this purpose. It is essential to apply them regularly and thoroughly.

OTHER VEGETABLE CROPS In addition to the fruit and salads many vegetables may be better grown with the aid of frames and cloches by producing earlier crops and by protecting them from a number of pests. Few vegetables need protection for the whole of their growth.

Earlier Brussels sprouts, cauliflower, summer cabbage, carrots, turnips, marrows and sweet corn may be obtained by starting these crops under cloches, or by growing them wholly in frames with the lights removed after they have started their growth. Ground dug in the autumn may be partially prepared during the first dry spell in the new year. If necessary, the work may be made easier and the soil surface left undamaged by standing on boards laid temporarily for the purpose. Having levelled the surface, place cloches over the intended seed bed to allow the surface to dry and warm up until it is fit for sowing or planting. Another light raking will then prepare a tilth fit to receive the seed, sown in drills or broadcast as may be preferred.

Carrots and turnips sown in February in this way may be left covered and pulled for the table from May onwards. 'Amsterdam Forcing' carrot and 'White Milan' or 'Jersey Navet' turnips are most suitable for this purpose. Brassica seedlings such as cabbage, cauliflower and sprouts sown in this way will be ready for earlier planting than those sown in the open at about the same time. There is the added advantage for both these groups of vegetables that the cloches will give greater protection against such pests as the carrot and cabbage root flies. The dressings of insect repellent chemicals that should be applied after sowing any of these crops seem to be more effective under cover than in the open. The brassica seedlings are also protected from the attention of sparrows and finches that like to pull them up as they emerge, and the cats that seem to delight in scratching any fine seed bed. (One way of deterring cats from uncovered seed beds is to water immediately after sowing but this carries with it the risk of a surface soil cap forming and inhibiting seed emergence on some soils [see p. 253].)

The earliest crops of potatoes may be obtained by planting in permanent frames and keeping the lights on until they are ready for lifting in March or April. Then an early row planted and covered in February will give an earlier and more certain crop than those planted in the open as the late spring frosts are unlikely to damage the tops just as they are making good growth.

Marrows and sweet corn plants raised indoors from seed sown one each in 3 or 4in(8 or 10cm) pots and planted in April will make earlier and better growth in their cropping positions than if put straight from a house or frame into uncovered positions. A few weeks of cover will produce much stronger and more fruitful plants.

Broad, dwarf and runner beans and peas will also make an earlier and safer start under cloches than when sown in the open. The hardiest broad beans may be sown in the open in November but if the weather is wrong for such sowings or the winter kills them off others may be sown under cloches in February to produce almost equally early crops and with greater certainty in some districts. The first peas may be sown at the same time, if necessary using the same preparation techniques as for the smaller seeds already described. In the same way dwarf and runner beans may be sown under cloches in late April or early May for uncovering at about the same time as they are being sown in the open.

All sowings of these pulse crops are susceptible to attacks by jackdaws and other birds that search for the seeds or pull up the seedlings. Cloches prevent such depredations as well as giving an earlier start. Mice are also serious pests of beans and peas and traps can more safely be set under cloches where small birds are unlikely to be trapped as they are in the open. In addition to their use in producing early fruit and salads cloches can be most useful in advancing and protecting quite a wide range of vegetable crops.

Planning

Permanent frames covered with suitable lights may be used for the various crops mentioned above. For many of them a really good supply of compost or farmyard manure dug into the soil in the autumn will do much to ensure good growth and early crops. The choice of crops will be a matter of personal preference and the succession of cropping can follow as one is finished and the other needs to be sown or planted. Movable frames and continuous cloches are different for every move entails time and energy. Thus planning to ensure the shortest possible moves each time will save both time and energy and make best use of the ground. They are all in greatest use in the spring and early summer and while uses can be found for them it may be better to plan for them to be stacked or stood on unused ground rather than press them into uses that are unrewarding and costly in time and energy. If, at first, only sufficient cloches are available for placing across one row of the vegetable plot, then start at one side of the plot and arrange to plant each succeeding crop to be covered in sequence to the first. In this way the distance the cloches have to be moved can be kept to a minimum. When two rows of cloches are available it may be better to start in the middle of the plot, covering two adjacent rows and then moving outwards to the next crops to be covered. In this way the least effort will be involved. The simple diagram below gives an indication of how this method works. Many alternative plans can be devised according to the needs of the crops and your personal preferences.

A CROPPING PLAN

	April–June Beans – beans	February–March Two rows carrot and turnip	April–June Peas–peas–peas	
		July– Cloches stacked on ground from which above-mentioned crops have been cleared		
September Winter radish	May–August 1 row Melon	February–May 1 row 1 row Strawberry Potato	May–August 1 row Cucumber	September 1 row Lettuce

31.
Making Your Greenhouse a Major Asset

A bewildering range of makes, types and materials face the gardener who wishes to buy a greenhouse. If a greenhouse is to do its job efficiently, contribute to the needs of the family by producing good-quality vegetables, fruit, cut flowers or pot plants and provide its owner with an enjoyable hobby, it must be correctly designed for the purposes for which it is required. So, first decide which crops you wish to grow; all too many people buy a greenhouse first and then decide which crops shall be grown. If the aim is to produce lettuce in winter, tomatoes and perhaps aubergines or peppers in summer, then a greenhouse with sloping sides and glass to ground level is best for the purpose; if a display of pot plants on staging is required, then sloping sides will be a disadvantage and glass to ground level results in unnecessary heat losses.

Various materials, types and makes all have their merits and their defects and it is wise to become acquainted with these, even though personal preference will play a large part in the final choice.

Many types of greenhouse can nowadays be inspected at sales centres. The following important points should be checked: The quality and strength of materials, internal bracing, which must be adequate. The draught-proofing of doors and ventilators. Freedom from air leaks, so inspect the structure carefully. Ensure that ventilation is adequate. Check the width of the door – 2ft(60cm) is the absolute minimum, a greater width is preferable. Check the door-sill for ease of access with a wheelbarrow. Does a "kick panel" replace glass in the lower part of door? (it should). Are glazing clips and overlap clips (on metal houses) strong and of stainless steel? Are the following items included in the purchase price or charged as extras: the greenhouse base; guttering and down-pipes; louvre ventilators; the automatic ventilator openers; the plant staging and shelves.

Materials Used in Framework

In Favour

ALUMINIUM
Maintenance negligible. Glass easily installed or replaced. Strength without bulk. Thin frame members and good light reflection give good internal light.

WESTERN RED CEDAR
Pleasant and unobtrusive. Shelves, insulating materials etc. easily fitted. Heat loss through frame members is small. Usually partly prefabricated, easily erected.

WHITE WOOD
Apart from appearance, the advantages are as for Cedar. Light reflection good when painted white.

Against

Projecting fin on most glazing bars conducts heat out of house. Obtrusive in garden setting but sometimes coated with acrylic paint. Air leaks can be a problem.

Regular preservative treatment essential. Admits less light than aluminium unless very large sheets of glass are used. Unless substantially made may warp with age.

Good initial preservative treatment and regular maintenance essential. May warp with age.

174. Strelitzia reginae, *the bird of paradise flower, which bears its orange and blue blooms in spring (see p.285).*

Galvanised Steel   Usually used in the construction of polythene tunnels and similar structures or to provide strength in large greenhouses. Satisfactory if galvanised after fabrication. Welding, done after galvanising, may be weak and entry is provided for rust.

Laminated Wood   Modern laminates can give strength without undue bulk or weight, are useful for double-skinned houses and may be seen more in the future.

Materials Used in Cladding

In Favour	Against
GLASS (3mm NORMAL, 4mm LARGE SHEETS)	
Long life. Transmits light, retains warmth better than most plastics.	Places heavy load on structure. Breakages expensive to replace.
CLEAR POLYTHENE SHEETING	
Initial cost relatively low. Raises temperatures in sunlight and protects from cold winds. Crops grow well under it.	Short life (two to three years). Appearance drab. Does not restrict radiation heat loss nor reduce frost intensity.
CLEAR P.V.C. SHEETING	
Similar to polythene, a little more costly and with a slightly longer life.	Small margin of protection from frost.
FIBRE-REINFORCED PLASTIC	
A plastic film excluding ultra-violet light can be bonded onto the outside surface giving a much longer life, but the cost is high.	Discoloured by sunlight. Surface wear exposes glass fibres which then collect dirt and exclude light. Useful life about seven years.
CORRUGATED SEMI-RIGID PLASTICS	
Relatively cheap. Simple to use.	Heat loss through corrugated surfaces is 50 per cent greater than through flat surfaces of the same substance.
FLAT ASBESTOS SHEET (Sometimes used around lower part of greenhouse walls)	
Possibly less likely to be broken than glass.	Light is excluded but heat loss little less than glass.

Modern Plastic Films   Greater advances have been made in longevity, and they lend themselves to use in double-skinned structures, but cost, wind noise and other drawbacks are against their use at present.

Types of Structure

Span Roof   Free standing and the most popular type. Available with glass to ground or with walls of brick, wood or asbestos all round or on one side only; with vertical sides or with sides sloping inward. Sloping sides admit more light, vertical sides give more space at bench height. Wooden infill panels to reduce heat loss from glass at a low level are available from some manufacturers.

Lean-to   For erection against a wall or building. If a suitable site exists a lean-to structure has much to commend it. Heat losses are reduced. The cost per square foot (.092m²) of ground covered is slightly higher than for a span roof structure.

Round or Near Round   Usually chosen because they look better in a flower

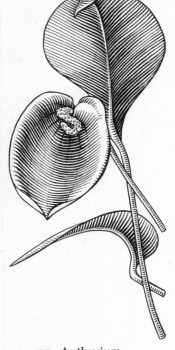

175. Anthurium scherzerianum *with scarlet spathes in summer (see p.285).*

garden than other types. They are costly and it is not easy to use their space efficiently.

Plastic "Walk Through" Tunnels   Much used commercially, in a limited way in private gardens, mainly because of aesthetic considerations.

Ventilation

Many of the greenhouses produced for sale to amateur gardeners are sadly under-ventilated in their basic form. For the majority of crops the total area of all ventilator openings should be approximately one-fifth of the total floor area of the structure and they should preferably be equally divided between roof ventilators and side ventilators. Automatic ventilator opening devices – working hydraulically by means of a substance extremely sensitive to temperature changes – are occasionally fitted as standard equipment. They can be obtained to fit either orthodox ventilators or louvres and are well worth their cost. If electricity is available, extractor fans can be used instead of normal ventilators or to boost ventilation. Standard fitments should, however, be retained in case of power failures.

Siting a Greenhouse

Good light is a major factor in the cultivation of most greenhouse plants and is of particular importance in winter. The house should, therefore, be sited where it will get the maximum possible light at all times, bearing in mind, of course, the low sun and long shadows of winter. Protection from strong winds is also important as heat losses rise alarmingly when a cold wind is moving rapidly across the surface of the glass.

Orientation of the structure should, if possible, be such that the ridge runs on an east-west line, thus presenting a broad front of glass to the sun's rays. Houses with sloping sides are so designed that they hold the glass as nearly as possible at right angles to the sun's rays to allow them to take the shortest route through the glass. The fairly steeply pitched roof of a well-designed modern greenhouse will also allow good light transmission, but these advantages are lost if the house is placed end-on to the south.

The site area must, of course, be level and well-drained and it can be helpful on a cold winter evening if it is fairly near the home. The distance from a water supply point needs to be considered and the position of the nearest electrical distribution cannot be ignored, even if there is no thought of using electricity in the immediate future.

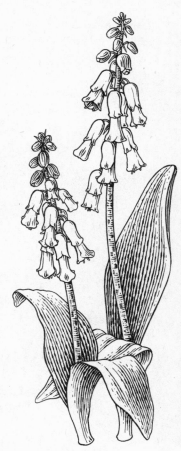

176. Lachenalia aloides *'Tricolor', with waxy, red, green and yellow flowers in February-March (see p.283).*

Heating Equipment

Choosing the type of heating system for a greenhouse is something to ponder deeply, bearing in mind fuel prices. If nothing more than frost protection is needed greenhouse heating is a relatively inexpensive matter; and maintaining a minimum temperature of 40°F(4.5°C) in a small area is within the reach of most gardeners. With every 10°F rise in temperature, however, the cost of heating will approximately treble, depending on the part of the country you live in and on local conditions.

INSULATING TO REDUCE HEAT LOSS   Most of us are very aware of the need to insulate against heat losses whether in the home or the greenhouse, and in the case of the latter more and more insulation aids are becoming available. With wooden houses it has always been a simple matter to fix some form of lining (usually polythene secured with drawing pins). With metal houses fixing insulating material has been a problem in the past, but numerous clips and fixing studs are now available and these, used in conjunction with one of the many insulating materials now offered, make it possible to line virtually any house without too many difficulties. There are thermal screens which can be used to separate any section of the house which is to remain unheated; bubble films, which have proved their worth; double skinned, box-section clear plastic (Correx insulating board) which

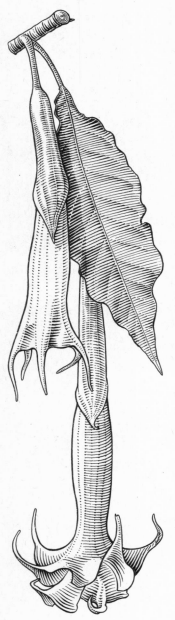

177. *Datura cornigera*
with handsome white,
scented flowers (see p.281).

has a high insulating value but will warp if not firmly fixed; and various other plastic materials from which to choose. Double-glazed and double-skinned greenhouses are now marketed on a limited scale. The problem with double-glazing has always been the extra weight of glass which the structure has to bear; the extra cost of the structure, and the doubled cost of glass, making the project uneconomical in this country. The future of double-skinned houses will depend on the quality and longevity of the plastic film used. Loss of light inevitably occurs when a house is insulated and this must be balanced against the saving effected.

Condensation, resulting in drips from the roof, will become a nuisance if a greenhouse is lined with plastic film and care must be taken to keep the air as dry as possible to reduce this trouble. Ventilators should be opened whenever the temperature and other weather conditions permit.

CALCULATING HEATING REQUIREMENTS Before buying any heating apparatus it is necessary to know the maximum load it will be asked to carry on the coldest nights of winter. These calculations are usually based on a minimum outdoor temperature of 20°F(−6.5°C) but in known cold districts a few degrees lower should be allowed for. For the precise calculation of heat losses each material involved has its own index value but, for the average small greenhouse, it is sufficient to allow a value of one for every square foot (.092m²) of surface area of glass and asbestos and one for every 2 square feet (.184m²) of surface area of wood, brick or concrete. The Electricity Council has a simple formula for anyone wishing to maintain a minimum temperature of 45°F(7.5°C); it is to add to the surface area of glass in square feet half of the surface area of wood, brick or concrete in square feet, and multiply the resulting total by 9.3 to obtain the loading in watts of the heater needed.

Those who wish to calculate their own requirements should add half of the area of brick, timber or concrete to the total surface area of glass (both in square feet), multiply the figure thus obtained by 1.4 to allow for fortuitous losses, and then multiply again by the lift required above outdoor temperatures in degrees Fahrenheit. The answer is the requirement in B.T.U.s per hour which, if divided by 3,412, will give the loading required of a heater in kWs.

Types of Heater

Solid-Fuel-Fired Boilers Small, efficient units can be obtained. They need regular stoking and cleaning but they provide a good alternative to gas or oil.

Oil-Fuelled Boilers Automatic and labour saving. The oil storage capacity should be generous to ensure that there is no risk of a shortage occurring while awaiting a delivery of fuel. With a low chimney the combustion fumes may linger near ground level.

Mains Gas-Fired Boilers The convenience of oil fuel without the disadvantages. A piped gas supply rules out the worries of when to re-order, possible delay in delivery, and so on, which can occur with oil fuel.

Dual Home-Greenhouse Heating Linking the greenhouse heating with the domestic heating system is often practicable and worth considering if the greenhouse is very close to the house.

Electrical Space Heaters Electricity is a simple, clean and convenient form of heating which can be precisely controlled. There is the risk of power failure to consider. It is still the most costly means of heating but with present trends may not remain that way.

Electrical Tubular Heaters These provide a safe, completely automatic permanent installation for the larger unit or when high temperatures are needed.

Electric Fan Heaters A popular type for small greenhouses. They can be thermostatically controlled and can keep the air moving even when the heating element is not in use, reducing disease risks which stagnant air can cause. Careful placing of the unit is necessary lest the warm, dry outflow of air scorches delicate foliage.

Immersion Heaters Used in conjunction with 4in(10cm) diameter cast iron pipes and a header tank these units are still obtainable. The hot water gives a useful short-term reserve of heat in power failures.

Flueless Air Heaters Can be fuelled by piped natural gas or bottled gas. They can have serious ill-effects on plants when used to maintain high temperatures but at temperatures of 40°F(4.5°C) and below troubles are not noticeable although growth is slowed down (see Dr A.W. Davison and Sally Wharmby, R.H.S. Journal, *The Garden*, January, 1980). When using heaters of this type it is essential that ventilation is given in accordance with the manufacturer's recommendations.

Paraffin Heaters Another form of flueless heater, but as these are seldom used for more than frost exclusion no obvious harm is done, provided that the equipment is kept scrupulously clean and the wick neatly trimmed. The modern blue-flame heaters are well designed and far more efficient than the yellow flame types. All flame heaters give off water vapour when burning and some ventilation is advisable to release this.

Flues with Heat Exchangers These are the logical answer to the problem of fumes from flame heaters. Gas air-heaters with flues are appearing on the market and suitable flues for paraffin heaters can be arranged by most gardeners with a little initiative.

Bench Heating This generates heat exactly where it is wanted, under and around the plants, and heat wastage is minimal. A soil-heating cable is needed, giving a loading of 10W to 12W per square foot (.092m²) of bench, a strong bench with 6in(15cm) high sides and some form of insulating material to prevent heat escaping downwards. For this a 1in(2.5cm) deep layer of clean, ½in(1cm) gravel, topped by a layer of domestic aluminium foil serves quite well, with a 1in(2.5cm) depth of clean horticultural sand being placed on top of that. The heating cable is then spaced out evenly over the bench area before adding another 3in(8cm) layer of sand into which pots may be plunged. A thermostatic heat control is advisable for the sake of economy, and the sensing rod or capsule should be set just below the surface of the sand.

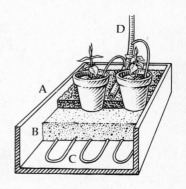

178. *A heated sand bench with soil-warming cable and trickle watering.* **A**, *layer of peat;* **B**, *layer of sand;* **C**, *electric cable;* **D**, *a small-diameter plastic tube which supplies water to each plant pot.*

Ancillary Equipment

Benches Whether these are purchased as units or built at home, priority should be given to strength even though it may be felt at the time that such strength will not be required. For most people a bench height of 2ft 4in(70cm) to 2ft 6in(75cm) is convenient, but it should be remembered that the higher the bench the more difficult it is to reach the plants at the rear. Bench width is usually governed by the width of the greenhouse less the width of the path, which needs to be a minimum of 2ft(60cm). Aluminium angle and wood are the materials most used for benches; wood should be well soaked with green (horticultural grade) wood preservative. Steel angle should be avoided because of the virtual impossibility of preventing rust under greenhouse conditions. Sheet asbestos or sheet aluminium are used as working tops for benches, but the former breaks easily and needs treating with care. Wooden battens, also used, are useful in winter for they allow good air circulation around the plants, but in summer plants on such a base miss the humidity arising from a bench covered with moist sand or gravel.

Shelves These can be quickly and simply fitted to either wooden or metal

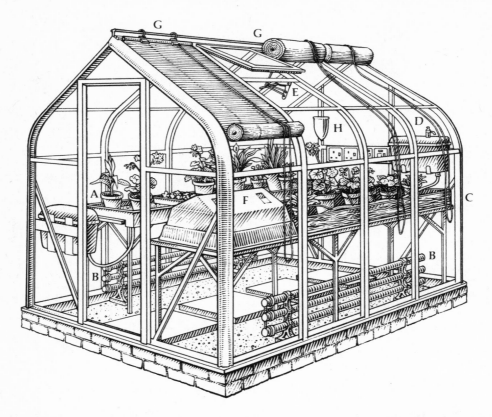

179. *A well-equipped
greenhouse.* **A**, *capillary
sand bench*; **B**, *tubular
heating*; **C**, *heated sand
bench*; **D**, *trickle watering
system*; **E**, *automatic
ventilator opener*; **F**,
propagating cabinet; **G**,
shade blinds; **H**, *electric
fumigator.*
*Inset below is a capillary
sand bench.* **A**, *layer of
sand*; **B**, *staging*; **C**,
fibre-glass wick; **D**, *water
level*; and **E**, *wick support.*

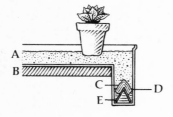

houses and provide valuable extra plant space. Although available as units,
the special bolts and brackets for fitting these oneself for metal houses are
easily obtainable.

Watering Systems   For the gardener who is away from home all day, or
perhaps for several days at a time, some form of automatic watering system
is essential if the greenhouse is not to become a worry. Although watering
equipment for the smaller greenhouse is limited, good automatic or
semi-automatic systems are available.

Capillary Watering Benches   These can be adapted to any area, large or small,
provided all the area involved is at *exactly the same level*. The slightest
deviation will result in either a dry or a wet area on the bench. The systems
work from an adjustable float chamber with feeder tubes to a bench lined
with polythene and covered with capillary matting or a ½in(1cm) deep layer
of sand. For small areas or slatted benches, special fibre-glass sand trays can
be obtained. Pots over 6in(15cm) in diameter cannot obtain all of their water
by capillarity (the upper layers of compost remain dry) but the 6in(15cm)
size or smaller are satisfactory if good contact is preserved between the
compost and the moist sand or matting.
   When plants are placed on the bench the pots must be pressed down
hard, then watered thoroughly to establish capillary contact. The process
must be repeated if plants are lifted. Pots must not be crocked; clay pots
need a fibre-glass wick inserted in the drainage hole, but plastic pots are
more suited to this form of watering. The advantages of this system are that
it can be completely automatic if supplied via the mains and a header tank; it
is unlikely to fail suddenly, is able to cope with large numbers of small pots
and it does not leach plant foods from the potting compost. The disadvantages are the formation of moss and algae on the sand; the penetration of
the sand by roots which would be better in the pots (algicides can be

obtained to deal with these); and humidity from the bench, which, while beneficial in summer, can be detrimental when low temperatures prevail in winter.

Trickle Watering System   These supply water to each pot through a small-diameter plastic tube; some systems have an adjustable nozzle at the end of the tube controlling the flow rate. This method of watering will adapt well to a display bench carrying pots of widely disparate sizes; it is not easy to manage with a multitude of small pots. The frequency of watering can be governed by a time clock; by a timing device controlled by the rate at which water drips into a header tank; or, more logically, by an electrical control which is triggered by the evaporation of water from a small reservoir. Trickle systems adapt well to use on crops planted in greenhouse beds or a perforated hose known as "Seephose" may be laid along the rows. The systems are fairly simple to instal, and can be fully automatic or semi-automatic in operation.

Overhead Spray Lines   These have limited use in a greenhouse. Flowers are sometimes damaged even by clear water and few water supplies are without lime, chlorine or some substance which can be deposited on foliage and will build up until it becomes unsightly.

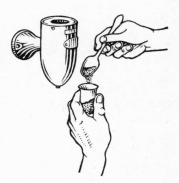

180. *An electric fumigator (used strictly in accordance with the manufacturer's instructions regarding dosages and so on) can be a significant factor in keeping plant troubles at bay.*

Roller Shades   Shading from hot sunshine is essential for most plants grown in greenhouses. If it is not given the surface tissues of leaves become too hot and burn, water fails to reach tips or edges of leaves and marginal scorching occurs. Those plants which dislike bright light will become yellow and unhealthy looking. The commonest forms of shading are the paint-on types but these have several weaknesses: they cannot be removed in dull weather; they do not prevent glass from becoming very hot and passing that heat into the greenhouse; and scrubbing the remains from the glass in autumn is a task nobody likes. Internal roller shades are easily fitted to most green-houses and can be adjusted according to weather and time of day but still allow the glass to become hot. External roller shades will keep the glass and the greenhouse cool, but because they need to be very strongly made they are the most expensive form of shading. Shade blinds can be used to assist in the exclusion of frost from a greenhouse in winter.

Garden Frames   These are invaluable in providing a handy means of hardening plants off in spring or growing plants on in summer for winter flowering in the greenhouse. Even in winter many uses can be found for them, not the least of which could be overwintering chrysanthemum stools.

Timber, or timber and brick, with glass, still produce the best unit provided the timber is rot-proofed. Sheet aluminium will not keep out much cold and insulated units of this kind have still to prove their worth.

THE ART OF GOOD GROWING

In the final analysis the good grower is the person who watches plants with a sympathetic and keenly observant eye and acts promptly whenever action is needed. If a plant needs feeding, or tying, or more, or less water, something is done about it at once, not a week later.

Potting   Potting-up seedlings from a tray or potting-on plants into larger pots needs to be done when the plants have sufficient roots to run quickly into the new compost but before they become root-bound and starved in their old containers. A 3in or 3½in(8 or 9cm) pot is usually a suitable first size, and from then on increase the size of the pot by 1½ to 2in(4 to 5cm) in diameter each time a move is made. Plants in loam-based compost should be moved on into loam-based; those in peat-based compost go on into peat-based. Peat-based composts should be only lightly firmed; if consoli-dated they become too retentive of water and the plants are not happy. The light consolidation of loam-based composts is also usual nowadays, except when potting some woody subjects, but undue harm is unlikely to follow firm potting as was both taught and practised some 30 years ago.

Watering When watering is done by hand those plants known to need less than average quantities of water can receive individual attention. With automatic systems this cannot happen; the alternatives are either to take them off the system, to reduce the flow to their jets or to put more and coarser drainage material into their compost. Frequency of watering can vary from twice a day in the heat of summer to once in two days in a cool greenhouse in winter. If a capillary bench is in use the problem does not arise. In summer when in doubt give water, in winter when in doubt withhold it; but when water is given it should be sufficient to wet all of the compost in the pot. Most plants prefer rain water if it can be collected and stored for them, and for orchids and ericaceous plants it is almost essential.

Feeding Feeding should be started as soon as plants are well rooted in their final containers. This is of particular importance when peat-based composts are used as they cannot carry a reserve of plant foods so readily as loam-based composts, although modern slow-release fertilisers help in this respect. With most plants feeding should start about six weeks after potting, and as a rough guide feeds should be given once a week in spring and summer, once a fortnight in autumn and occasionally in winter. The exceptions are those plants which grow throughout the winter to flower in spring. These should be fed while in growth; bulbs and corms also in the early stages of ripening. All plant feeds should show an analysis on the pack; in winter high potash feeds should be used while in summer feeds should be chosen to suit the plants grown.
    Foliar feeds are of special use in giving backward plants a boost or for feeding plants which may resent chemicals in the compost, as might orchids or other epiphytes.

Humidity Control This is usually associated with the frequent damping-down of floor and staging in a greenhouse on a hot day. Maintaining a moist atmosphere in summer is an important factor in keeping plants healthy and discouraging pests. In a cool greenhouse in winter atmospheric moisture can aggravate disease problems and humidity control takes a reverse role. Drips from can or lance, water spillage in any way must be avoided in the effort to maintain dry air in the greenhouse.

Light and Shade In October, or as soon thereafter as possible, the greenhouse should be thoroughly cleaned down, the glass scrubbed to remove any persistent deposits, old shading paint or algae, and the glass overlaps cleared with a forceful jet of water and the aid of a thin plastic label. The object is not just to ensure a clean start for the new season, but to give the occupants of the house the maximum possible light in winter; this helps all plants but is particularly advantageous for crops of winter lettuce.
    In summer the sun becomes too hot under glass (see comments on roller shades, p.275) and from about the end of March to the end of September some form of shading is required, either as roller blinds, open-weave plastic material erected in the greenhouse or as paint-on shading. A green colour is mostly chosen but white is marginally better for plants and lets through more light when wet.

Hygiene Good hygiene will help to keep plants disease- and pest-free. Dead leaves, flowers or plants should be removed and destroyed.

Vegetables in the Greenhouse
A greenhouse can be used in two ways to assist in vegetable production for the home. It can be used to produce crops or to provide plants intended for cloche or open garden cultivation with an early start. Early types of cauliflower can be sown in late September and over-wintered in 3in(8cm) pots in a cool greenhouse for early planting, or they can be sown in February together with early cabbages and pricked-off into trays for early

planting. At about the same time – earlier if heat is available – onions may be sown to produce giants for the show bench, and leeks to get them away to a good start. Peas sown five seeds to a 3in(8cm) peat pot and planted, when large enough, with the pots at 6in(15cm) centres under a cloche, will be ready for cropping two weeks earlier than if sown under the cloche. Runner beans, French beans and sweet corn are all worth starting off under glass to be planted out, without root disturbance, when the danger of frost has receded.

Plants for cropping in the greenhouse in summer will need warmth in the early stages; if this cannot be provided they should be purchased at planting time. The following vegetables are, for the majority of people, the most useful choice for cultivation.

AUBERGINE (*Solanum melongena*, or egg plant) Sow the seeds in late February in a temperature of 65°F(18.5°C). Moved on through successive pot sizes, aubergines can be cropped in 8 or 9in(20 or 23cm) pots, but they are much happier if planted in borders or growing bags. The plants should be pinched after the fourth true leaf and the resultant shoots trained up canes or strings. Give a high potash (tomato type) liquid feed weekly in summer.

CUCUMBER (*Cucumis sativus*) The sowing date will vary from late February to early May depending on the temperatures to be provided during the plant's life. Nothing is gained by sowing or planting in unsuitable conditions. The newer F_1 hybrids which carry only female flowers are even more sensitive to low temperatures than are the older types such as 'Telegraph'.

Cucumbers are far happier in prepared beds or growing bags than in large pots. To be kept cropping they must be kept growing; regular high nitrogen feeds help, and an occasional light top dressing of peat should be given, building it up around the base of the stem to encourage new roots to form at this point. Throughout the season all shoots produced on the lateral growths should be stopped after their second leaf; this controls cropping and prevents growth from getting out of hand.

SWEET PEPPER (*Capsicum annum*) Conditions for the propagation and growing of these and hot peppers are similar to those required by tomatoes (see below). Sow in late March, do not stop but support as required. Feed weekly with a balanced liquid feed.

TOMATO (*Lycopersicon esculentum*) A temperature of 70°F(21°C) is desirable for seed germination. Lower temperatures will be tolerated but the vigour and cropping ability of the plants will be lessened. The sowing time should be mid-March for cropping in a cold greenhouse; earlier, as required, for growing in a warm house. If grown in borders the soil should be either sterilised or changed at least every second year. The alternatives are cultivation in growing bags; in pots (including cultivation by the ring-culture method), or by grafting the fruiting plants when about 4in(10cm) tall onto a disease-resistant rootstock known as 'Rootstock K.N.V.F.'. A simple approach graft is used and the two root systems are potted into one pot after grafting. The unwanted (scion) roots can be cut away at planting time.

LETTUCE This provides an ideal crop to follow tomatoes in a cold or cool greenhouse. Good "short day" types are available. In a greenhouse with some heat the variety 'Dandie' may be sown from August to November for cutting between November and April. If the greenhouse is unheated 'Kwiek' may be sown in late August to provide lettuces in November and December, or 'Kloek', sown in October, can be cut in March and April.

OTHER POSSIBILITIES Radishes and carrots can often be sown beside the greenhouse path as catch-crops in late summer or early spring. A few parsley seeds sown in a pot or an odd corner of the house in June will keep the supply going through the winter irrespective of outside weather. Small clumps of chives can be potted, roots of mint boxed and cuttings of sage and thyme rooted for winter or early spring use.

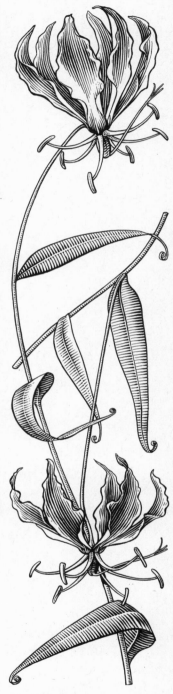

181. Gloriosa rothschildiana *is a striking plant in summer when bearing its distinctive crimson and yellow, reflexed flowers (see p.285).*

Fruits in the Greenhouse

A greenhouse can add both variety and quality to the range of dessert fruits grown. Fruits may be grown in containers or in borders and the borders may be in the house or outside with the plant (or plants) led through a hole low down in the wall to be trained up inside the house. Outside borders have much to commend them. They are easy to prepare and maintain, nature looks after much of the watering and inside borders are left free for other crops. Should greenhouse space be limited and watering no problem, growing fruits in pots or tubs might be considered for it enables a variety of these to be grown in a limited amount of space. The plants can be stood or plunged outdoors after they have fruited until the end of their winter rest.

Compost   The compost for containers or inside borders should be prepared to the John Innes No 1 potting compost formula, but to each bushel should be added ¼lb(110g) of a granular show-release fertiliser such as Enmag. Outdoor borders can be prepared to good kitchen garden soil standards.

Containers   The containers for the older and larger trees may well be in the 18 to 24in(45 to 60cm) range but they should always be the smallest into which the roots will conveniently go and the 12 to 15in(30 to 38cm) sizes will keep fruiting plants going for several years. Trees required for container growing should be obtained as maidens, if possible, to enable roots and top to be trained to this form of cultivation.

Annual Overhaul   An annual overhaul is needed at the end of the winter rest and before starting deciduous trees into growth in late February. They are removed from their pots; drainage materials are cleaned; some of the compost is teased away from the top and sides of the root-ball with a pointed stick; any long fleshy roots are pruned back to encourage the formation of fibrous feeding roots, and the trees are repotted using fresh compost to replace that removed.

Borders   Borders, both inside and out, are renovated each winter. Old mulch materials and the top inch (2.5cm) of compost or soil are raked off and taken away, fresh compost or soil is added and then, in spring, a mulch is given of well-rotted farmyard manure, peat or similar material.

POPULAR FRUITS   While many other fruits, including gages, dessert plums, apples, pears, apricots and cherries can and have been grown in greenhouses, the following are perhaps the most popular: figs, grapes, melons and peaches and nectarines.

FIG (*Ficus carica*)   This fruit must be grown in a container or a restricted area of border; a free root-run leads to excess vigour. It may be grown as a bush or be fan-trained. Grown in a cool house with a minimum temperature of 34°F(1°C), it will ripen one crop of fruit in late summer. In a warm house, with a minimum temperature of 55°F(13°C), it will ripen two crops each year. Pruning is done on a replacement system, cutting out old, fruited wood and training in new wood after the fruit has been harvested. Some pinching of tip growth is necessary to check unwanted shoots and encourage growth at a lower level.

GRAPE (*Vitis vinifera*)   Grapes are best planted in borders 4ft(1.25m) apart and grown on a single cordon, rod and spur system. When grown in containers, both length of rod and weight of crop must be restricted, i.e. use a 15in(38cm) pot, have an 8ft(2.5m) rod and secure 10lb(4.5kg) of grapes. To ensure the even breaking of buds along the rods, they should be arched over with the tips pointing toward the ground when starting into growth in spring. Afterward, they should be tied to wires mounted not less than 14in(35cm) from the roof glass. Allow only one growth from each spur, stop this at two leaves beyond a flower bunch and stop all subsequent shoots after they have made one leaf. Assist the pollination of flowers daily by briskly shaking the rods or by stroking the flowers gently through the hands. Restrict the crop to one bunch per spur; fewer if the bunches are large. Do not allow wide temperature variations and always ventilate in good time. In winter frost will do no harm; in summer allow temperatures in excess of 70°F(21°C) only when there is generous ventilation.

MELON (*Cucumis melo*) If growing melons in an unheated greenhouse, the choice is restricted to cantaloupe and modern F_1 hybrid types (see also chapter on protected cropping, pp.263 and 264). If warmth is provided, it is possible to grow the superbly flavoured, large-fruited greenhouse melons such as 'Hero of Lockinge' and 'Superlative'. These need a minimum temperature of 55°F(13°C) rising to 80°F(27°C) in the heat of summer sunshine, and abundant moisture in the air. The main stem is trained upward to be stopped at 4ft(1.25m). The laterals, trained horizontally on wires, are stopped at 1½ft(45cm). The fruits are carried on the sub-laterals and need supporting in nets as they become heavy. Only two should be carried on each plant and these should have been both hand-pollinated on the same day or one very large and one quite small fruit will result. The base of the main stem is liable to attack by a bacterial rot at ground level; for that reason the top of the root ball is left slightly "proud" when planting and no water is applied in the immediate area of the stem.

PEACHES AND NECTARINES (*Prunus persica* and *P. persica* var. *laevis* respectively) These are normally planted in beds and fan-trained, but they may be bush-trained and grown in containers. They should be pruned immediately after fruiting, the oldest of the fruited growths being cut away and younger growth retained to replace them. The greatest enemy of peaches and nectarines in a greenhouse is the red spider mite, and to avoid undue reliance on chemical controls the underside of the foliage of these plants should be forcefully sprayed with clear water early and late each day through the growing season, except at flowering time or when fruit is ripening. In winter a period of rest and low temperature is needed (40°F[4.5°C] or below), or many of the buds will fall in spring. A gradual transition in spring to 50°F(10°C) may be followed by even higher temperatures provided that ventilation is generous. Young unwanted shoots are progressively rubbed out in spring and pinched in summer to direct vigour to the growth wanted for the replacement of fruited wood in autumn. Shoots next to fruit should be allowed to make two good leaves before pinching. Fruits should be thinned after setting to about 8in(20cm) apart and again after stoning to 12in(30cm) apart. Hand pollination of the flowers with a camel-hair brush will be necessary unless bees are seen to be working over the flowers.

Decorative Plants in the Greenhouse

Some greenhouses are devoted entirely to decorative plants; many more are a mixture of the utilitarian and the ornamental, and this works quite well if the plants are chosen with care. Many late winter and early spring flowering plants can be grown on in garden frames in summer to be moved to the greenhouse after summer crops have been cleared and the house has received its annual clean-down.

Permanent plantings of shrubby, bulbous or herbaceous greenhouse plants save a great deal of work and worry over watering, but they occupy the greenhouse (or a section of it) for the whole of the year and so limit the display which can be provided. Ideally, a display house will have some space for pot plants which can be changed according to the season; it will accommodate hanging baskets to utilise the air space, and there will be climbers to fill roof and wall space.

The Unheated Greenhouse in Winter

The obvious plants for an unheated greenhouse in winter are of course alpines (see Chapter 14, "The Alpine House", pp.145 to 149) but not everyone's interest lies in that direction. An empty and neglected green-

182. *The blue-flowered* Campanula isophylla, *so much in demand for hanging basket displays (see p.281)*

183. Streptocarpus *'Constant Nymph' which bears its blue flowers throughout summer (see p.285).*

house is a depressing sight, and unnecessary, as it can be filled with colour in later winter and early spring by using pots and half-pots of small bulbs, some of the modern hybrid primroses with their bright colours and young pot-grown plants of *Erica herbacea* (syn. *E. carnea*), *Euonymus radicans* and dwarf conifers. These can be plunged in the garden for the summer when the greenhouse is filled with other plants. The secret of success with these plants in a cold house is to plunge the pots in peat, gravel, vermiculite or perlite so that the root balls are never frozen solid.

SOME DECORATIVE PLANTS FOR THE COOL GREENHOUSE (FROST EXCLUSION ONLY).

Botanical Name	Decorative Feature(s)	Cultural Needs	Method of Increase
Abutilon species and hybrids.	Pendulous flowers, mainly red, orange or yellow from May to October.	Pots or borders. Prune in March for shape or size restriction.	Stem cuttings taken from April to September. Seed in spring.
Acacia dealbata *Acacia baileyana*	Flower, late winter, panicles of yellow balls.	Prune in spring to restrict size. Stand outdoors in summer. Grow in pots.	Seed, sown in spring.
Begonia sutherlandii	Large numbers of small orange flowers in summer.	Good for hanging baskets. Dry off in autumn. Store tubers in the dry compost until March.	Growing-on tiny tubers found in leaf axils in autumn. Seed sown in spring.
Billardiera longiflora	Deep blue berries in autumn. Evergreen foliage.	A climber for a low wall or trellis. Grown in pot or border.	Seed, sown in spring. Cuttings, taken in summer.

Botanical Name	Decorative Feature(s)	Cultural Needs	Method of Increase
Callistemon speciosus	Scarlet "bottle brush" flowers in early summer.	Grow in large pots. Stand outdoors after flowering.	Cuttings, taken in late summer. Seed, sown in spring.
Camellia sasanqua varieties and cultivars.	Single, white or pink flowers in early winter.	Lime-free compost. Stand plants outside in summer.	Stem cuttings, taken in July. Leaf/bud cuttings, taken in October.
Camellia japonica cultivars and hybrids. *Camellia reticulata* cultivars and hybrids.	Flowers March and April; of various forms and colours.	Lime-free compost essential. Stand plants outside in summer.	Cultivars of *C. reticulata* must be grafted in January or late summer. Others, increase by stem cuttings in July or November. Leaf bud cuttings in April.
Campanula isophylla	Blue flowers in summer.	Good for hanging baskets.	Increase by seeds in March or cuttings taken in June-July.
Cobaea scandens	Purple-green, bell-shaped flowers. Summer-autumn.	Quick growing perennial climber. Grow in 9in(23cm) pot to reduce vigour.	Seeds, sown in March.
Cordyline indivisa	Attractive foliage plant.	Well-drained, loam-based compost.	Seeds, sown in spring.
Correa × harrisii	Pendulous, red, tubular flowers.	Peaty soil, pots or borders.	Cuttings, taken in July.
Datura cornigera	Pendulous, white, scented trumpet flowers.	For large pots or tubs.	Increase by hardwood cuttings in February, young shoots in August-September.
Jasminum polyanthum	Scented, white flowers, reddish on the outside of the petals in late spring.	Train climbing stems in slowly ascending spiral from pot.	Cuttings, taken in April-August.
Lapageria rosea	Pink, waxy bells in summer.	Climber for pot or border cultivation. Train in all shoots. Shade from hot sun.	Seed, sown fresh. Serpentine layering.
Nerine sarniensis *Nerine* hybrids	Flowers October-November. Scarlet, pink or white, shot with gold or silver.	Sun-loving bulbous plants. Dry off May-August.	Offsets potted singly, in September.
Pentapterygium (*Agapetes*) *serpens*	Pendulous, lantern-like, red flowers with darker "V" markings. June.	An ericaceous, peat-loving plant.	Cuttings, taken in June-July.
Pittosporum tobira	Creamy-white, scented flowers. Summer.	Loam-based compost. Large pot or greenhouse border.	Seeds, sown in March or cuttings taken in late summer.
Plumbago capensis	Spikes of showy, pale blue flowers in summer.	Prune all young growths back hard in winter and restrict watering.	Cuttings, taken in May-August.

Botanical Name	Decorative Feature(s)	Cultural Needs	Method of Increase
Punica granatum var. *nana* (dwarf pomegranate)	Orange-scarlet flowers in late summer. Leaves yellow in autumn.	Enjoys sunshine.	Cuttings, taken in June-August, or by seeds sown in spring.
Rhododendron cubittii	Flowers, white, flushed pink with yellow eye, scented in March.	Lime-free compost, large pot or tub. Shade in summer.	Cuttings, taken in June.
Trachelium caeruleum	Heads of numerous, small, blue flowers. Late summer.	Treat as annual. Flower in 5 or 6in(13 or 15cm) pot.	Seeds sown in early March.
Trachelospermum jasminoides 'Variegatum'	Attractive evergreen foliage. Scented, white flowers in July.	Climbing shrub for large pot or border.	Cuttings, taken in August.

SOME DECORATIVE PLANTS FOR THE COOL GREENHOUSE (40°F[4.5C] MINIMUM TEMPERATURE)

Botanical Name	Decorative Feature(s)	Cultural Needs	Method of Increase
Babiana, species and hybrids	Richly coloured flowers in spring.	Pot and start into growth in August. Dry off slowly as foliage dies after flowering.	Natural increase of corms. Seeds, sown in June.
Bougainvillea, species and hybrids	Clusters of showy bracts. Summer and autumn.	Restrict roots, train growths in slowly ascending spiral. Give high potash feeds.	Cuttings, taken in summer.
Bouvardia hybrids	Red, pink or white flowers. Summer.	Restrict water in winter. Prune hard in February and repot.	Cuttings, 2in(5cm), taken in spring.
Carnation, Perpetual-flowering	Flowers grown for cutting.	May be grown cooler, or 10°F warmer. Growth and flowering cease at about 40°F(4.5°C).	Cuttings of side-shoots 3in(8cm), long, taken in spring or autumn.
Calceolaria × *herbeohybrida*	Pouch-shaped flowers of red, yellow, orange and brown in spring.	Well-drained compost, cool, airy surroundings.	Seed, sown in June.
Cineraria (*Senecio cruentus* derivatives)	Large heads of daisy-like flowers, bright colours in spring.	Special care needed with regard to watering. Shade from hot sun.	Seed, sown in June.
Clivia miniata	Umbels of orange-scarlet, funnel-shaped flowers in late spring.	Loam-based compost. Shade in summer. Reduce water in winter.	Increase by division after flowering or seeds sown in spring.
Cytisus canariensis var. *ramosissimus* and *C.* × *spachianus*	Racemes of bright yellow, scented, pea-shaped flowers in early summer.	Loam-based compost. Shorten young growths after flowering.	Increase by seed, sown in March or by cuttings taken in June-July.
Erica canaliculata	Massed clusters of whitish flowers from March to May.	Lime-free compost. Prune, if necessary, after flowering.	Cuttings of soft tip growth, taken in summer.

Botanical Name	Decorative Feature(s)	Cultural Needs	Method of Increase
Francoa ramosa	Branched panicles of white flowers in July-August.	Of easy cultivation. Pot on in loamy compost to 7in(18cm) pot for flowering.	Seed, sown in spring.
Freesia hybrids	Scented flowers in a wide range of colours from January to March.	Well-drained compost, good light, cool airy conditions.	Seed, sown in flowering pots in April. Corms potted in August.
Fuchsia species and hybrids	Pendulous flowers in reds, pinks and purples from June to October.	Rest in winter. Repot late February. Water and feed generously in summer.	Cuttings, taken in June-August, or in March for late summer flowering.
Gerbera jamesonii hybrids	Large daisy-like flowers in bright colours throughout summer.	Rest, almost dry, in winter. Water sparingly at other times.	Seed sown in spring; by division of old plants in February-March, or cuttings of side shoots taken with a heel in July.
Haemanthus coccineus	Brush-like umbel of red flowers and bracts. Summer.	Feed rather than repot annually.	Offset bulbs in February, or seeds, sown in spring.
Hoya carnosa	Clusters of waxy-looking, pinkish flowers. Summer and autumn.	Take care not to overpot or overwater. Train in new shoots.	Cuttings, taken in summer.
Lachenalia aloides 'Tricolor'	Waxy, pendulous, red, green and yellow flowers, in February-March.	Pot corms in August. Dry off slowly after flowering.	Increase by offsets, when repotting in August.
Lantana camara	Heads of flower, colour varies with age. Summer.	Cut back old plants in February. Restrict water in winter.	Cuttings taken in spring, or seeds sown in March.
Oxypetalum (Tweedia) caerulea	Cambridge-blue flowers in summer.	Support sprawling shoots.	Seeds, sown in March.
Maurandia barclaiana	Purple, rose or white flowers for much of summer.	Low, climbing perennial, good plant for hanging baskets.	Seeds, sown in spring.
Nerium oleander	Terminal clusters of showy pink flowers in July-August.	Prune flowered growth hard in autumn.	Cuttings, taken in summer. Seeds, sown in spring.
Passiflora caerulea hybrids	Passion flowers, in shades of purple, pink and white borne throughout summer by this climber.	Grow in a large pot to restrict vigour. Spur back laterals in winter.	Cuttings, taken in summer.
Pelargonium domesticum cultivars. (Regal Pelargoniums)	Masses of showy flowers from May to July.	Prune back hard and repot in August.	Cuttings, taken in July-August.
Pharbitis learii	Broad, funnel-shaped, bright blue flowers in summer.	A strong climber for tub or border. Prune to shrubby base in winter.	Cuttings made from young growth in spring.

Botanical Name	Decorative Feature(s)	Cultural Needs	Method of Increase
Primula × *kewensis*	Tiers of fragrant, yellow flowers from January to April.	Shade from hot sun, avoid water splashing into crowns of plants, maintain dry air at low temperatures. Give high potash (tomato type) feeds when in active growth.	Seeds, sown in May-June.
Primula malacoides	Tiers of flowers, reds, pinks, whites and mauves from January to April.		
Primula obconica	Clustered heads of red, white, pink or blue flowers from January to April.		
Schizanthus × *wisetonensis* and other hybrids	Masses of zoned and patterned flowers in spring.	Well-drained compost, good light and cool, airy conditions.	Seeds, sown in August-September.
Solanum capsicastrum *Solanum pseudocapsicum*	Orange-scarlet berries from October to December.	Free ventilation, good light and manual assistance with pollination.	Seeds, sown in March.
Sprekelia formosissima	Curiously shaped bright red flowers in June.	Give good light, high potash feeds. Dry-off after flowering.	Seeds sown in March or bulb offsets taken in February.
Tibouchina d'urvilleana (syn. *T. semidecandra*)	Rich purple flowers in summer and autumn.	Prune old plants back in February and repot. Restrict water in winter.	Cuttings, taken in spring and summer.
Tritonia crocata	Flowers, colour variable, mainly orange-red in spring.	Shake out corms and repot, August. Dry off when leaves die back.	Offset corms when repotting.
Vallota speciosa	Funnel-shaped, scarlet flowers in July.	Repot in June if this becomes necessary. Do not dry-off bulbs.	Offsets taken in March or seeds sown in March.
Veltheimia bracteata	Pink and greenish-cream flowers in February.	Dry off when leaves yellow. Repot or top-dress in August.	Offset bulbs when repotting. Seed, sown in June.

SOME DECORATIVE PLANTS FOR THE INTERMEDIATE GREENHOUSE (50°F[10°C]) MINIMUM TEMPERATURE)

Botanical Name	Decorative Feature(s)	Cultural Needs	Method of Increase
Asparagus setaceus (syn. *A. plumosus*) *Asparagus densiflorus* 'Myersii (syn. *A. sprengeri* 'Myersii')	Delicate fern-like foliage. "Fox-tails" of dark green foliage.	Shade from hot sun. Water and feed generously in summer, more sparingly in winter.	Division in spring, or by seeds.
Begonia 'Lucerna'	Large pendulous clusters of pink flowers throughout summer.	Shade from hot sun. Prune out oldest growths in late winter.	Cuttings of shoots 4in(10cm) long, in summer.

Botanical Name	Decorative Feature(s)	Cultural Needs	Method of Increase
Browallia speciosa	Blue flowers in summer and autumn.	Pinch tips at 4in(10cm). Flower in 5in(13cm) pots.	Seeds, sown in February-March.
Citrus mitis	Small "oranges" set freely and carried through most of the year.	Loam-based compost. Good light. Water sparingly in winter.	Cuttings , taken in summer.
Schlumbergera cultivars	Flamboyant magenta, red or orange-scarlet flowers in winter.	Good drainage, shade and a short rest after flowering.	Cuttings made from stem segments in June, but can also be taken at other times.
Strelitzia reginae	Orange and blue bird of paradise flowers in spring.	Loam-based compost. Sunshine.	Division in April or seed sown in March-April.
Streptocarpus 'Constant Nymph'	Blue flowers throughout summer.	Shade from hot sun. High potash feeding necessary.	Increase from leaf-section cuttings at almost any time or by division in March-April.
Zantedeschia rehmannii	Pink "arum" flowers in May.	Pot in September. Dry off after flowering.	Offsets taken in August-September, or by seed sown in spring.

SOME DECORATIVE PLANTS FOR THE WARM GREENHOUSE (60°F[16°C] MINIMUM TEMPERATURE)

In addition to foliage plants such as *Begonia rex*, *Caladium hortulanum*, *Codiaeum variegatum*, *Dieffenbachia picta*, *Monstera deliciosa* and *Philodendron scandens* commonly seen in warm greenhouses the following flowering plants will enjoy the warmth and humidity provided:

Botanical Name	Decorative Feature(s)	Cultural Needs	Method of Increase
Aechmea fasciata	Patterned foliage. Imposing pink and blue inflorescence.	Open, fibrous compost.	Increase from surplus side-shoots when these are 4 to 5in(10 to 13cm) long.
Anthurium scherzianum	Scarlet spathes, summer	Moist, well aerated compost.	Division of old plants, April-May.
Episcia cupreata	Red and yellow flowers in summer, colourful foliage.	Grow in pan or basket.	Cuttings taken in May-August.
Gardenia jasminoides	White flowers in summer.	Lime-free compost and water.	Cuttings, taken in spring.
Gloriosa rothschildiana	Crimson and yellow, reflexed flowers in summer.	Pot tubers, March. Dry-off after flowering.	Seed, or natural increase of tubers.
Smithiantha hybrids	Orange-red flowers in September-October. Attractive foliage.	Loamless compost. Pot in May. Dry-off after flowering.	Seeds sown in February or small tubercles potted in May.
Stephanotis floribunda	White, scented flowers in summer.	Train in twining shoots. Pot-on or top-dress in spring.	Cuttings taken in May-July, or by seeds sown in March.

32.

Potting Composts

The environmental conditions under which pot plants are grown within greenhouses differ in two important ways from those of plants grown in garden borders. First, by being in small containers the plants have a very restricted root system; secondly, the air temperature in the greenhouse is usually higher and consequently the potential growth rate is much greater. The media or compost in which the plants are growing has, therefore, the important and difficult task of supplying, from a *smaller volume* than usual, all the water, air and nutrients required to sustain the *higher growth rates*.

It is universally accepted that an ordinary garden soil is not adequate in either its physical or chemical properties to meet these requirements. Various additives (physical soil conditioners) have been used and in some composts the mineral soil has now been entirely replaced. Before discussing the various potting compost formulations the physical and chemical requirements for good growth should be understood.

Physical Properties

There are three principal physical requirements for a compost.

Root anchorage This is provided naturally in mineral soils, but in some media having low bulk-density and large particles there is insufficient cohesion of the particles to support a seedling or young plant. Also, there may be difficulty in using plant supports in such mixtures. These problems largely disappear when the plant has produced sufficient roots to bind the particles together.

Water and aeration These are inversely related and can, therefore, be considered together. From the physical viewpoint the compost is composed of solids, either of mineral or organic matter, and inter-connecting voids known collectively as the pore space. Whereas a field soil may have about 50–60 per cent of pore space a good potting compost will have 75–95 per cent pore space, with some of the pores being much larger than those in garden soils.

The small and medium-sized pores act as water reservoirs and the large pores, which drain quickly after irrigation, allow air to reach the roots. A good potting compost will have 10–15 per cent of its total volume as air-filled pores within a few hours of watering.

Sometimes pot plants can have very high water requirements. For example, under hot, sunny conditions in mid-summer a fully grown pot chrysanthemum may require watering three times in one day. It is also equally important that there is sufficient oxygen in the compost to support the metabolic activity of the roots. If the pore space is low in terms of the total volume of the compost, or if the pores are small and filled with water, insufficient air will diffuse to the roots. Under such conditions in winter, when transpiration and evaporative losses are low, the compost can remain in a near saturated conditions for many days, this frequently resulting in the death of the plant. The traditional advice of the skilled craftsman on when to water is still applicable. "In summer, when in doubt – water; in winter, when in doubt – don't".

Container Depth and Potting   Although pots have adequate drainage holes to release free water, drainage from the compost is nevertheless impeded by the base of the pot, i.e. there is no continuity of pores through which the water can drain naturally. The water content of any soil is a function of its depth, shallow layers remain wetter than deep soils. This can easily be demonstrated by placing the flat side of a rectangular sponge on a wire tray, i.e. it resembles a wide, shallow depth of compost. Saturate it with water and when drainage has stopped turn it on to its narrow end, i.e. it now resembles a deep, narrow pot. Water will again drip from the base.

Other factors that can affect the water-air relations are firm potting and the use of "crocks". Firm potting not only reduces the total pore space, it also reduces the size of the pores, and as small pores do not drain as freely as large ones the compost remains wetter. Placing "crocks" in the bottom of the pot effectively reduces the compost depth, and as already shown this reduces the amount of water which drains from the compost.

Chemical Properties

The most important single chemical requirement of a compost is that it is free from mineral or organic substances that are toxic to plants. It is usually much easier to correct a deficiency in a compost of one or more of the mineral elements that are essential for plant growth than to remove toxic concentrations.

Other desirable chemical properties of materials for compost making are:
1   They should be slightly acid rather than alkaline in reaction. If the pH is above the neutral point certain nutritional problems can arise, for example, lime-induced iron deficiency. While the pH of acid materials can easily be raised by liming, it is much more difficult to acidify or reduce the pH.
2   If possible the material should have a "cation" or "base exchange" capacity. This allows nutrients such as calcium, magnesium, potassium and ammonium to be retained by the media and slowly released for use by the plant. Without this mechanism these nutrients are easily lost from the compost by leaching.
3   Slowly decomposing organic material which will give a steady supply of mineral nitrogen to the plants.

Neither of the last two features is essential, however. Plants can be grown quite successfully in materials that are chemically inert, provided that they receive a constant or frequent supply of minerals in the irrigation water.

Types of Compost

Composts can be divided into two groups:
1   Loam based, e.g. the John Innes compost.
2   Loamless composts which do not contain mineral soil.

John Innes Composts   These composts, developed in the 1930s at the John Innes Horticultural Institution, were the first attempt to produce standardised composts suitable for a wide range of plants. Prior to this gardeners had often made up a special compost for each species.

The most important component for producing a good quality J.I. compost is a medium-clay turf loam, having about 20 per cent clay and 2 to 7 per cent of organic matter. Using a turf rather than an arable loam ensures that it has a better physical structure, and the organic matter provides a slow release of mineral nitrogen. Alkaline soils must not be used if nutritional and post-sterilisation problems are to be avoided. Turves should be cut in the spring and made into a loam stack, sufficient chalk being added to alternate layers to raise the pH to 6.3. A 2in(5cm) layer of strawy horse manure alternating with the chalk improves the fertility. Before the loam is used to make a J.I. compost it is essential that it is steam sterilised; this destroys any weeds, pests and diseases that are present. After the loam is sterilised its physical properties are improved by adding granular peat and grit or coarse sand; the nutrient levels are also increased by adding a balanced base fertiliser.

SEED COMPOST

Bulk ingredients by volume	Fertiliser	Rate per bushel (8 gal[36l])	grams per 1ol
2 parts loam	Superphosphate	1½oz	11.7g
2 parts peat	Ground chalk	¾oz	5.8g
1 part sand			

POTTING COMPOST J.I. No. 1

Bulk ingredients by volume	Fertiliser	Rate per bushel (8 gal[36l])	grams per 1ol
7 parts loam	J.I. Base	4oz	31.2g
3 parts peat	Ground chalk	¾oz	5.8g
2 parts sand			

The J.I. base fertiliser is a mixture of 2 parts by weight hoof and horn, 2 parts superphosphate, 1 part sulphate of potash. Its analysis is N 5.1, P_2O_5 7.2, K_2O 9.7 per cent. The John Innes composts Nos 2 and 3 are made by adding double or treble the quantities of fertiliser and chalk; these composts are used for the more vigorous plants, e.g. tomatoes that are to fruit in pots and chrysanthemums.

Loamless composts Difficulties experienced in obtaining the correct type of loam in sufficient quantities have led to the formulation of composts without mineral soil. Peat is the most popular substitute, but other materials are also used, either to impart specific physical or chemical properties to the compost or simply on the grounds of availability and economics.

Materials of organic origin used in composts include peat, shredded bark, sawdust and animal wastes. Municipal wastes are not recommended, however, because of the risk of heavy metal toxicities, e.g. nickel, zinc and chromium. Inorganic materials include vermiculite, perlite and sand. Expanded plastic foams such as urea-formaldehyde, polyurethane and polystyrene flakes are also used.

These materials do not normally require pre-treatment before use; either they have been heat treated in their manufacture, e.g. perlite, or they do not usually contain any pathogens, e.g. peat. One material that does require pre-treatment, however, is bark. Softwood bark contains organic compounds known as monoterpenes which are toxic to plants. They are easily removed by allowing heaps of pulverised bark, to which nitrogen, phosphorus and iron sulphate have been added, to heat-up by natural bacterial action for about eight weeks. Practically all the bark offered for sale has been treated in this way and is safe to use.

Materials used to make loamless composts have varying nutrient contents and characteristics. For example, perlite does not contain any plant nutrients, whereas vermiculite has some magnesium and potassium. Peat has a small amount of available nitrogen, whereas sawdust decomposes quickly and locks-up mineral nitrogen, thereby creating a temporary nitrogen deficiency. In comparison with the loam in a J.I. compost, however, all these materials contain much less nitrogen, phosphorus and potassium; also they do not have sufficient amounts of the micro or trace elements that are essential for normal growth. It will be apparent that in preparing loamless composts it is essential to achieve the correct fertiliser balance.

The numerous published formulations for loamless composts have resulted from experience in growing a diverse range of crops under the environments and cultural practices pertaining to different countries. The following compost, based on work at the Glasshouse Crops Research Institute, Rustington, Littlehampton, West Sussex, is suitable for a wide range of vegetable and ornamental plants:

Bulk ingredients, by volume
3 parts sphagnum peat, 1 part fine, lime-free sand

Fertilisers

	ounces per bushel (8 gal [or 36l])	grams per 10 litres
Ammonium nitrate	½	3.9
Superphosphate	2	15.6
Potassium nitrate	1	7.8
Chalk	3	23.4
Dolomite limestone	3	23.4
Frit WM 255	½	3.9

The frit supplies the micro elements boron, iron, copper, manganese, zinc, and molybdenum in a form that gives a slow rate of release over a long period, thus avoiding problems with micro element toxicities.

If an all-peat compost is preferred the same fertiliser rates are used, apart from increasing the chalk and Dolomite limestone to 3½oz(100g) per bushel.

Slow-release Fertilisers   The nitrogen, phosphorus and potassium used in the above formulation are in an inorganic form and are, therefore, immediately available to the plant. Another group of proprietary fertilisers, known as "slow-release" fertilisers, have been specially formulated so their nutrients are in forms that are not immediately available. These fertilisers either dissolve slowly or are mineralised by bacterial action to supply nutrients over a long period. The advantage of using this type of fertiliser is that liquid feeding can either be postponed or, in the case of short-duration crops, be avoided altogether. Problems can arise, however, when composts made with these fertilisers are stored in a moist condition for a long period before being used. If the fertiliser is of the type that releases its nitrogen in the ammonium form this can build up to concentrations that are toxic to young plants. This problem is greatest in winter when the light-intensity and plant growth rates are low. It will usually be safer for the amateur gardener who prefers to make a single large amount of compost rather than the frequent preparation of small quantities, to use the inorganic fertilisers given above. Composts made with slow-release fertilisers should not be stored for more than a couple of weeks.

Liquid Fertilisers   If plants are to be grown in containers for long periods they will require feeding, either with a top-dressing or a liquid fertiliser in the irrigation water. The latter method is usually the most convenient and either proprietary or home-mixed feeds can be used.

A general-purpose feed can be prepared by first making a stock solution:

	Ounces per Imperial gallon	grams per litre
Ammonium nitrate	5.1	31.8
Mono-ammonium phosphate	2.0	12.5
Potassium nitrate	8.4	52.4

This must be diluted at 1 part in 200 parts of water to give a feed having: Nitrogen 100, Phosphorus 15, Potassium 100 parts per million.

The frequency of application must be governed by the plant's growth rate. Slow-growing plants under poor light conditions in a dwelling house would not require feeding more frequently than every 21 days whereas carnations growing in a greenhouse in summer could be fed at every watering. While the nutrient ratios in this feed are suitable for most plants, tomatoes require about twice as much potassium as nitrogen in order to produce good-quality fruit.

Part VI

PRACTICALITIES

33.

The Soil, its Management and Moisture Requirements

In this chapter, except where obviously inapplicable, the term "soil" includes growing media like sands, aggregates, artificial materials and composts. Natural soil is a mixture of different sizes of mineral particles and organic matter. The spaces between the particles may be filled with air and/or water, the latter containing dissolved substances. In the soil lives a complex flora and fauna of fungi, algae, bacteria, worms, insects and slugs, some beneficial and some harmful. Almost all of them take part in the important process of breaking down (decaying) organic matter into humus, which can be regarded as the cement which binds the particles together in porous crumbs and so improves soil structure.

The soil provides anchorage and support for the aerial parts of plants and is the essential reservoir of nutrients, water and air supply for roots. It provides protection and housing for underground organs such as tubers, bulbs, rhizomes and swollen roots. Soil must be managed with all these functions in mind.

Soil Texture This term indicates the proportion of sand, silt and clay in a given soil (see Table 1). To a limited extent texture may be improved for a particular purpose by admixture of sand or ashes to a heavy soil, or clay or marl to a light one. Normally, it is more economical to adjust the gardening activities engaged in to suit local soil than to attempt the reverse. The wise gardener concentrates on plants which he finds are suited to his particular soil.

Organic matter Soil contains constantly changing amounts of organic material which must be supplemented to maintain fertility. Peat soils are exceptional in that they consist almost entirely of organic matter derived from ancient, tightly-packed vegetation; this decomposes only slowly unless repeatedly disturbed, when it can disappear with alarming speed, lowering the land level and often exposing intractable clay.

Soil Structure The soil particles are aggregated in crumbs and blocks whose conformation can be profoundly changed by management. Judicious cultivation forms aggregates with pore-spaces adequate for the water and air needs of roots; over-cultivation destroys structure so that when wetted the soil becomes caked. A caked soil can be re-structured only by autumn forking into large clods which are then left loose to benefit from the action of frost and weathering throughout the winter.

Soil pH This borrowed mathematical term describes the acidity of soil, with pH7 representing neutral. Most crop plants thrive best on slightly acid soil, i.e. pH just below 7. Some plants must have markedly acid conditions, although lime-tolerant cultivars have been developed; tea (*Camellia sinensis*)

TABLE 1
PARTICLE COMPOSITION AND AVAILABLE WATER CAPACITY OF DIFFERENT-TEXTURED SOILS

Particle name	Approximate percentage by weight				Moisture percentage*		Inches of water available to plants in top 2ft(60cm) of soil*
	coarse sand	fine sand	silt	clay	at field capacity	at wilting point	
SIZE RANGE (International System)	2-.2 mm	.2-.02 mm	.02-.002 mm	below .002mm	FC	PWP	AWC
SOIL TYPE (i.e. texture)							
coarse sand	82	13	1	3	8	4	2
sandy loam	50	31	4	15	19	9	3
loam	2	53	24	19	30	13	4.2
clay	32	15	10	41	42	25	4.2

*This data is explained on p. 292 and shown pictorially in the diagram below

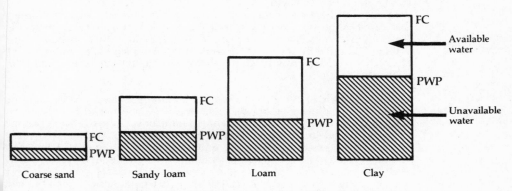

can grow in soil as acid as pH4, but this is exceptional. In contrast, plants derived from those indigenous to chalk and limestone regions do best when the pH value exceeds 7.

Soils under intensive cultivation can become sour, i.e. excessively acid, and then require liming to bring pH nearer to 7 to restore fertility. Acidity can be increased by the admixture of peat or acidic inorganic fertiliser such as sulphate of ammonia.

Adjustment of a limy soil to accommodate calcifuge (lime-intolerant) subjects is difficult; if such plants *must* be grown in a limy district it is better to line a pit with polythene sheet and import naturally-acidic soil. The lime-tolerance of many plants can be improved by application of sequestered iron.

Adjustment of soil pH must be regarded as temporary; the acidity of intensively-cropped soil should be kept under review, using a simple test kit available in garden shops.

Soil Nutrients The major nutrients, nitrogen, phosphorus and potassium, and the dozen or more minor and trace nutrients can be taken up by roots only when in solution. Slow-acting fertilisers are those which dissolve slowly and therefore need only occasional replenishment; quick-acting, readily-soluble fertilisers need annual or more frequent supplementation. As described later, good drainage is essential for good growth; this means that during heavy rainfall water drains through the soil, leaching out nutrients.

Detailed fertiliser recommendations are made in Chapter 34 (see pp.297 to 303).

Soil Water When water falls on the soil surface it enters the spaces between particles. Exceptionally, certain materials, e.g. mica, absorb water *inside* individual particles, between the flat plates of which they are composed, so that the total stored is more than would be expected from the dimensions of the spaces between the particles. Micaceous growing media such as vermiculite are used for rooting cuttings which require large quantities of readily-accessible water.

Water does not move downwards through soil until all the pores above the advancing front have been filled. Therefore, the more water which falls on the surface the deeper is the layer whose pores are filled to the exclusion of air. Reducing the volume of water applied merely reduces the depth of soil which becomes saturated; it is not possible by simple watering to raise the moisture content of soil to any level other than saturation. One cannot merely "dampen" a soil.

After precipitation ceases, gravity continues to pull water downwards while air enters the partially-emptied pores. Eventually gravity is balanced by surface tension holding the layer of water round each soil particle. Drainage ceases and the soil has reached the equilibrium state of Field Capacity (FC)*, holding its maximum amount of water against free drainage. Soil at field capacity contains air, water and nutrients and is in ideal condition for plant growth.

As roots abstract water the layer round each soil particle becomes thinner and capillary tension increases until the roots are unable to overcome it, water uptake ceases, and the plant wilts. The soil is then at Permanent Wilting Point (PWP), the moisture content below which plants are unable to abstract water for growth. Crop plants should not, of course, ever be allowed to reach this state.

Available Water Capacity (AWC) Soils of different textures have differing dimensions of pores holding different amounts of water at field capacity and wilting point and hence different amounts of water available to plants. Heavy soils have greater AWC than light soils (see Table 1). Available water is usually expressed in the same units as rainfall, 1in(2.5cm) being the volume which would inundate the land evenly to that depth (approximately 26,610gal per acre or 4½gal per square yard [20.2l per m^2]).

Thus, if there are 2in(5cm) AWC per 1ft(30cm) depth of soil, when the soil is at field capacity, the plants can draw on over 106,000gal per acre, or 18gal per square yard (81l per m^2).

Abstraction of Soil Water The energy required to evaporate water from soil and from plants (transpiration) comes from the sun and the rate of evaporation ("evapo-transpiration") is regulated by temperature, humidity and movement of the air. Evaporation from soil unsheltered by foliage proceeds as long as the surface remains wetted by water brought by capillarity from below. Up to ¾in(2cm) may be lost before surface drying halts the process; after irrigation more than ½in(1cm) of the water applied is wasted by evaporation from bare soil.

Evaporation from leaf cells sets up tension in the column of water which extends through stems and roots to the root hairs in contact with water around the soil particles. In effect, the sun sucks water out of the soil through the plant acting as a wick. (This is a gross simplification but is a reasonable picture on which to base garden practice.)

When the sun has sucked up so much water that soil moisture status approaches permanent wilting point, or when evaporation rate is so high (in hot sunshine) that the plant loses water faster than replacement can move towards the roots from surrounding soil, the plant cells begin to lose turgidity, including those cells bounding the stomata, the pores through which the water is being evaporated. The greater the plant internal water deficit, the smaller these pores become. This elegant self-regulating mechanism has a profound horticultural implication. These pores allow the ingress of atmospheric carbon dioxide needed for photosynthesis.

*Symbols in brackets are those commonly used. This applies also to other abbreviations used in this chapter.

The main reason for watering plants is to keep their stomata wide open for maximum photosynthetic use of sunlight.

Soil Moisture Deficit (SMD) As water abstraction proceeds soil moisture content falls; the difference between current soil moisture content and that at field capacity is the soil moisture deficit. Expressed in the same terms as precipitation, it represents the maximum amount of water which the soil can currently absorb without drainage. Irrigation must never exceed SMD; maintainance of low SMD avoids plant water deficit, stomatal closure and reduction in growth rate.

Evapo-transpiration Quantities In the United Kingdom on a bright summer day evaporation totals about 1/10in(2.5mm). In exceptionally hot sunshine and dry wind evaporation can reach 2/10in(5mm). In dull, cold weather it can be nil and in the special case of heavy mist it may be negative, i.e. a gain in soil moisture (mist watering is used in greenhouses, and attempts have been made to irrigate field crops with mist, to avoid damage to plants and soil by impact of thrown drops).

In hot bright summer about 1in(25mm) of water evaporates from crops every 10 days and this is the maximum water requirement (irrigation plus rainfall), i.e. 4½gal per square yard (20.25l per m^2).

SOIL MANAGEMENT

Cultivation For annual crops it is common practice in autumn to dig as deeply as practicable to bury weeds, trash and organic fertiliser, to loosen compacted soil and aid root and water penetration and to begin the process of seed-bed formation. The soil should be left in clods; winter frosts break these into a better crumb structure than can be achieved artificially. Spring cultivation should be kept to the minimum needed for the particular crop, i.e. a fine tilth for small seeds such as onions, but larger crumbs for broad beans. Over-cultivation must be avoided; repeatedly bringing damp soil to the surface denudes the potential root zone of water stored from winter rains. When winter rainfall has been insufficient to restore the profile to field capacity this should be done in spring during seed or plant bed preparation. This precaution delays and may even obviate any need for irrigation in summer.

Deep cultivation of some soils, especially those with high organic content, may result in a "fluffy" condition which causes rapid drying of a considerable depth of the profile. This can be alleviated by careful rolling or treading.

This is not the place to enter the controversy regarding no-cultivation methods of gardening, which many devotees find highly successful. Most gardeners find weed-destruction, fertiliser-incorporation and the establishment of small-seeded crops easier by traditional methods.

Once the crop is established cultivation should be confined to the minimum necessary to control weeds; the soil should never be deeply stirred for fear of losing the valuable water stored below. Repeated stirring of the surface to form a "dust mulch" is not recommended for the same reason. Certainly there is little or no evaporation from a dry soil surface, but once the surface has become dry it should be left alone.

Cutivation among perennials is likewise unnecessary; here it is usually best to control weeds with mulches or herbicides. Trash mulching under shrubs and trees inhibits weed growth, conserves moisture and supplements soil organic matter. It can, however, be unsightly and the first two of these objectives can be attained by mulching with opaque polythene sheet covered with gravel and punctured at low points for ingress of water.

Clayey soil left undisturbed for years beneath shrubs tends to cake, the hard cap interfering with water entry. The whole surface should not be cultivated; only a patch round the base of each shrub or tree stem should be loosened. Much rainfall is trapped by leaves and flows down stems, thus entering the soil at the focal point of the root system.

A few soils can tolerate cultivation when moist but the vast majority, especially clays, should not even be walked upon when wet. In a vegetable or cut-flower plot where one must walk among the plants, narrow tracks should be established from which several rows can be reached for cultivation, watering or harvesting. In autumn these tracks should be forked up and left for restoration by frost. Boards or stepping stones are useful to provide access over wet soil. Cultivation should be undertaken only for a specific purpose; at all other times the soil should be left alone.

Water Supplies   The plant's need for water is greatest in hot dry weather when water authorities often ban the use of hose-pipes. House plants and small greenhouses can be supplied from the domestic tap, but be aware that extra chlorine may have been added to the public supply by an authority hard-pressed to meet demand; chlorine has disastrous effects on delicate plants. For the garden, it is necessary both to reduce the plants' demand and to store water.

Water Storage   House roof down-pipes can be tapped to collect rainwater in tubs but provision must be made for draining away any surplus. Tanks must be strongly supported; 1gal(4.5l) of water weighs 10lb(4.5kg). The outlet must be high enough for a can to be placed beneath it, and a hose connection is useful for conveying water to the garden under low pressure. In severe drought domestic waste water should be collected. Ordinary detergents and soaps are harmless but water contaminated with chlorine from bleaches, disinfectants and some harsh washing-powders must not be used on plants, although it is harmless on bare soil.

A tank to store all the requirements of the average suburban garden would be impossibly large; 3,000 square feet(280m^2) of vegetation evaporates 1,500gal(6,750l) every 10 days. Water can and should be stored in the soil by ensuring that the profile is at field capacity during spring preparation (when hose-pipes are not usually banned) and keeping it so by minimising cultivation and protecting with mulches.

Water Conservation   In the open garden little can be done to combat high transpiration caused by high temperature and low humidity, but shading from the sun and sheltering from wind are both practicable. The provision of wind shelter is discussed fully in Chapter 8, Hedges and Screens, pp.90 to 97.

Supplementing Soil Water   In the United Kingdom adequate crops can be grown without irrigation, but in most seasons even good crops can be improved by watering at times when stress would affect the part of the plant to be harvested. Stress reduces vegetative growth so crops whose leaves are the desired produce should ideally never be allowed to be short of water. This is often impracticable, but watering such crops within a week or two of harvest improves yield. In contrast, some plants, such as peas, have well defined growth stages when watering increases yield, while watering at other times does not. Most decorative trees and shrubs have wide-ranging root systems which make them more or less impervious to the effects of temporary water shortage. Fruit trees, on the other hand, respond to watering by increased vegetative growth which will enhance next season's crop. Individual crop requirements are detailed elsewhere in these pages.

Soil Drainage   Throughout this chapter it has been assumed that the soil is freely draining. Soil drainage is of paramount importance in gardening, but on a small scale bad drainage is extremely difficult to correct. The laying of tile drains or stone-filled ditches subsequently covered with topsoil, while effective, is costly in money and labour. An alternative is to throw the soil up into raised beds, based on a layer of loosely packed stones. On a sloping site contour ditches may reduce waterlogging. All ditches and drains must have adequate outfalls or soak-aways to prevent them becoming mere stagnant canals.

It cannot be too strongly emphasised that supplementary watering (irrigation) should never be carried out on poorly drained soil.

Watering in the Open The sprinklers and rainers used in commercial horticulture to save labour at the expense of some water wastage have little application in home gardens where the water supply is limited and labour not usually a problem. Sprinklers do have a use on lawns or when raising an unsown bed to field capacity, but in small gardens the aim should be to apply water only at the stem bases, under the foliage, leaving the surrounding soil dry. All the applied water then enters the root zone, and weed seeds are not encouraged to germinate between the rows.

This kind of watering may be done with a rose-less can or a low-pressure hose; the hose should end in a 3ft(1m) long 1in(25mm) bore rigid pipe (not a nozzle) which can be held so as to dribble water accurately at the stem base. Posts at the row ends permit the hose to be dragged along without damaging the plants (Fig.184). The water applied should be measured. This presents no difficulty when using a can; the hose may be roughly calibrated in terms of gallons(litres) per minute.

Watering practice is governed by soil texture. A light soil holds less than a heavy one and needs irrigation sooner. A heavy soil can hold more available water per foot(30cm) depth than a light one and so more water can be applied at a single irrigation, enabling the next application to be postponed. Care must be taken never to apply more than the top 2ft(60cm) – the root zone – can hold or the surplus will be wasted (see Table 1).

The application methods suggested avoid problems over drop size. With sprinklers it is necessary to use the smallest water drops available; if a can is used for overall watering of bare soil it must have a fine rose, held close to the soil to reduce the size and kinetic energy of the drops. All thrown drops damage soil structure, breaking down the aggregates to form a cap which inhibits water entry and seedling emergence. The finer the soil texture, the larger the drops, and the further they travel through the air, the more severe the damage.

Practical Watering for Gardeners Crop water needs depend on soil moisture deficit and plant growth stage. Commercially, soil moisture deficit (SMD) is measured directly or estimated from meteorological observations, methods impracticable for amateur gardeners. Commercial growing aims at bringing the whole crop to maturity simultaneously for one-off harvesting; the amateur seeks a succession of vegetables or cut flowers. Thus, overall uniform watering used in commercial horticulture is unsuitable for amateur gardening. The amateur should check SMD at intervals during dry weather so as to be ready to water *some* of his plants should they reach a moisture-sensitive stage of growth. Those left un-watered will mature later.

SMD can be checked by observing, at intervals, soil at the bottom of a hole at least a spit deep in the root zone of the plants. If this soil feels noticeably damp all is probably well, but if it feels dry watering should be considered, bearing in mind the soil texture. A clay soil may feel damp even when all its available water has been used; a sand can feel dry while still retaining water available to plants. There is no substitute for getting to know one's own soil and the way it feels when plants are doing well or when they can be seen to be suffering. It is good self-education to examine such soil samples at intervals through a season, noting the feel of the soil and the condition of the plants. Wilting is obvious, but incipient water stress is often accompanied by subtle change in leaf posture and darkening of the green colour which can be recognised with practice.

Once irrigation has been decided upon the aim should be to restore the root zone to field capacity. Restoring 2ft(60cm) of a clay soil from wilting point to field capacity could use over 4in(10cm) of water (18gal per square yard [81l per m^2]); a sandy soil might need less than 3in(8cm). However, these are maxima; in practice less will be needed because the soil will not have been at PWP before watering was decided upon, and provided a substantial proportion of the root system is restored to field capacity, plant water stress will be relieved sufficiently to re-open the stomata and

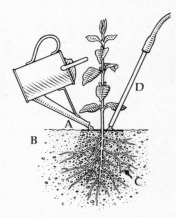

184. *When watering plants in the open garden – with a watering can or a low-pressure hose fitted with a 3ft (1m) long 1in (25mm) bore rigid pipe (**D**) – the aim should be to concentrate the applied water on the root zone and leave the surrounding soil dry to avoid encouraging weed germination between the rows.* **A**, *water dribbled on surface near plant stem;* **B**, *soil between plants is left dry;* **C**, *part of root zone thoroughly wetted (see text).*

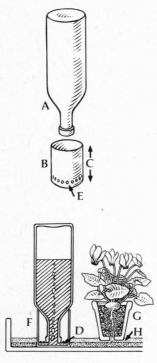

185. *An automatic,
home-made pot-watering
device. The diameter* (A) *of
the reservoir-bottle
shoulders must exceed that
of the tin* (B) *and the height
of this* (C) *must be such that
the mouth of the bottle is
just clear of the tin's bottom*
(D). *A few holes must be
punched near the tin's
bottom* (E). *When the bottle
is in position in the
sand-filled water-tight
trough* (F) *air can enter it to
release more water only
when the trough water-level
falls below the bottle mouth.
Thus, so long as there is
water in the bottle, the sand
in the trough will remain
damp and provide water for
the compost in the pot* (G)
*by capillarity. The water
level in the trough or tray is
about ½in (12.5mm) below
the surface of the sand* (H).

stimulate growth rate.

To sum up, if the soil sample feels dry, apply as much water as can be spared to the base of each plant stem, leaving the surrounding soil dry. If successional harvesting is required, do not water the whole crop at the same time.

Attempts to alleviate stress by daily sprinkling over the foliage are a waste of time and water; the water should be saved up for a single substantial irrigation as described.

Greenhouse Watering Under glass all water must be supplied artificially. There are many excellent devices available for sprinkling, misting, trickling, subsoil- and capillary-watering. Drop-size and danger of capping present no problem in greenhouses because the artificial growing media used are designed to stay "open" and well-drained under severe conditions. It is well-known that more house plants and greenhouse subjects die of over-watering than any other cause, but even over-watering can be tolerated if the medium is freely draining and the excess water can easily run to waste. Over-watering is lethal only if the growing medium becomes saturated so that air is excluded.

Drainage is especially important with continuous or automatic watering systems. Fig.185 shows a simple but effective home-made device which can be adapted for automatic watering of house-plant trays, window-boxes or even small greenhouse benches. It is in effect a capillary trough; the medium in the pots, in intimate contact with the wet sand, takes up just the amount of water the plants have used and so remains near to field capacity. This device is useful for maintaining plants when the owner is away. In regular use, especially for house plants in indifferent light, the water supply should be allowed to dry up between refillings. This ensures that air really does enter the growing medium from time to time and also provides an opportunity for leaching out accumulated salts and applying feed. Before the water container is refilled each pot should be removed and copiously watered from above in the conventional way, first with plain water and then, after draining, with dilute feed. It can then be replaced on the sand and the water-bottle refilled.

29. *Planned well in advance, a greenhouse or conservatory can be a riot of colour in April – and how welcome that can be after the long months of winter.*

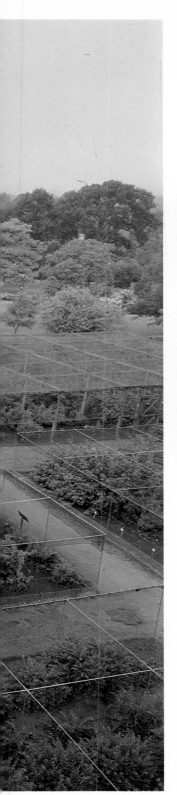

30. *An aerial view of part of Wisley Garden with the Model Fruit Gardens in the foreground. As with so much else at Wisley, the fruit gardens provide the visitor with ideas which can readily be translated into action in the small home garden.*

31. *The dessert apple 'Kidd's Orange Red', photographed at Wisley. This cultivar of good flavour is in season from November to January (see p.234).*

32. *Part of the model vegetable garden at Wisley which is especially rewarding to study during summer to see a wide range of vegetable cultivars grown in the open and protected under glass or polythene.*

34.

Manures and Fertilisers

The difference between fertilisers and manures is essentially one of bulk. Fertilisers provide nutrients in relatively highly concentrated form and are used in small quantities. Manures usually provide major nutrients in only small quantities but also supply "trace" or minor elements to the soil, together with fibre which, as it decays, forms the essential soil-binding material known as humus.

THE NEED FOR MANURES AND FERTILISERS Plants make their own food, for growth and reproduction, from nutrients they take from the soil, air and water. Carbon, oxygen and hydrogen come from the carbon dioxide in the air and from water taken up from the soil by the roots, and are needed in large amounts.

Nitrogen, phosphorus and potassium are also required in large quantities. They are to be found in all fertile soils in sufficient amounts to support plant life, being continuously replenished in the never-ending cycle of plant growth and decay, but are usually not available in quantities sufficient for the growing of short-lived, vigorous, high-yielding food crops without regular replenishment by means of fertilisers or manures.

Calcium, sulphur and magnesium are needed in smaller amounts. Calcium is readily available in alkaline soils or where a naturally acid soil is kept at a satisfactory pH level by applying lime.

Sulphur, in the form of sulphur dioxide, is released to the atmosphere when coal and oil are burned, and in industrialised regions dissolved sulphur ample for plant needs is returned to the soil when it rains. Sulphur is also supplied to the soil when fertilisers based on sulphate are used.

Magnesium is a nutrient often deficient on lighter sandy soils where crop demands and heavy use of potassium fertilisers may create a deficiency.

Sodium is needed by some members of the beet family but for most plants does not seem to be an essential element.

Some nutrients are needed in only minute quantities. These are often termed "trace" elements. On well-manured and on medium and heavier soils they are usually present and available in amounts ample for crop needs. Of the trace elements, boron, copper, iron, manganese, molybdenum and zinc may become deficient in lighter acid soils through leaching or may become unavailable to plants through rising pH reaction following excessive liming. Molybdenum becomes increasingly unavailable as soil acidity increases.

Summary: To ensure there are always adequate available nutrients for plant growth:
1. The soil pH must be maintained at a satisfactory level   2. There should be regular return of organic matter to the soil   3. Additional supplies of nutrients in the form of fertilisers should be applied to the soil to compensate for the large amounts of nutrients taken from the soil by crops.

MANURES: NUTRIENTS FROM BULKY ORGANICS Digging in annual dressings of bulky organic matter such as farmyard manure will provide a reserve of nutrients and trace elements in the soil. Fresh, rapidly decaying soft vegetable matter dug in during the winter months will contribute considerably towards crop feeding the following summer, but there will be less direct nutritional benefit from old well-rotted materials or fibrous materials such as leafmould or peat. The nitrogen value of dressings of manures dug in more than two growing seasons ago should be disregarded when assessing crop requirements.

If manure is delivered before it is to be used it should be stacked on a cement or similar hard base and given overhead protection against rain. If stored for any length of time check regularly to guard against excessive drying out.

Although providing nutrients, for the purposes of soil improvement bulky manures are best regarded as soil conditioners to be used in generous quantities whenever available; when digging in farmyard manure or composts apply at the rate of up to one good barrow-load to each three square yards of plot; when incorporating fibrous materials such as peat or leaf-litter dig in as a 1 to 2in(2.5 to 5cm) surface dressing.

Moister and more bulky materials should be dug well in. Cover with several inches of soil and allow a period of several weeks for the soil to settle before sowing or planting. Peat, well-decayed leafmould or compost can, however, be worked into the top few inches of soil just before sowing or planting where the soil is light and sandy or silty to improve retention of moisture and applied nutrients.

The nutrients in organic matter are not immediately available for use by growing plants. Plant and animal remains are chemically transformed in the soil by the action of soil organisms, principally bacteria. Some of the organic nitrogen is released, becoming available as ammonium and nitrate, the remainder accumulating in the soil as humus. Plants assimilate a little nitrogen as ammonium but most ammonium is converted to nitrate before it is taken up by plants.

Soft green vegetable matter, such as grass mowings and the remains of green vegetables, are rich in nutrients, including nitrogen. They rot rapidly in the soil releasing most of their nutrients quite rapidly. They have little fibre and do not provide either long-term reserves or give much improvement to soil texture.

Fibrous plant remains such as fallen tree leaves, straw and hedge-trimmings are largely woody or fibrous, decaying slowly and releasing few nutrients. They are excellent materials for longer-term improvement of soil texture but have little value as sources of plant nutrients. Woody tissues such as wood shavings and twiggy prunings contain lignin, which decays very slowly. It is very low in nitrogen, so that nitrogen from the soil is utilized by soil bacteria in its decomposition. A deficiency of nitrogen can occur where large quantities of woody material are dug into the soil.

As fibrous material rots in the soil it forms humus, a colloid which coats the soil particles, encouraging them to adhere together as stable crumbs. It is of particular value on lighter sandy or silty soils which, without adequate supplies of humus, have poor capacity for moisture retention. Humus also absorbs other applied nutrients and reduces excessive leaching of them into the sub-soil. Heavy soils amply supplied with humus are easier to cultivate than those lacking in humus.

BULKY ORGANIC MANURES AS MULCHES Surface mulches of bulky organic manures applied around fruit trees and bushes, woody ornamentals and climbers, promote growth in several ways; supplying nutrients, depressing the competition of weed growth, conserving soil moisture. Mulches also encourage root development in the more fertile near-surface layers. On poorer soils feeding roots are encouraged to develop into deep permanent mulches. Mulch generously where ample material is available, applying as a 2 or 3in(5 or 8cm) layer. Keep clear of plant stems, extending the mulch well beyond the perimeter of branch spread.

SOME BULKY ORGANIC MANURES: Green manures The practice is to grow a rapid-maturing leafy crop such as mustard or rape, digging it in six to eight weeks after germination to improve organic matter and nutrient levels. Sowing rate 1oz(25g) per square yard(m²). Quick nitrogen release but produces little fibre and therefore only short-term improvement. Little value when taken as an autumn crop. For appreciable improvement sow ryegrass in spring, cut regularly and dig in the following winter.

Garden Compost Requirements for good compost are fibrous vegetable material, a supply of nitrogen, lime to neutralize acidity, sufficient moisture in the heap and the generating of a suitable temperature. Straw can be used. For each 100lb(45kg) of straw add 5lb(2.25kg) of calcium carbonate and 4lb(1.8kg) of sulphate of ammonia (can be less if soft green material is included as a nitrogen source). Build to a height of 5 or 6ft.(1.5 to 2m) firming the wet straw into 6in(15cm) layers, adding lime and nitrogen to alternate layers. Allow to decompose for several months. Partially decayed outer material can be used to form a new heap.

Farmyard manure An excellent source of organic matter and trace elements, plus moderate amounts of nutrients, particularly potash.

Leafmould Essentially a source of humus as decaying leaves contain only low levels of nutrients. Leafmould from broad-leaved trees on alkaline or well-limed soils may contain too much calcium for safe use with acid-loving plants. For this purpose use only conifer litter or mould from broad-leaved trees growing on fairly acid soils.

Sewage Sludge Air-dried digested sewage sludge can be used for horticultural purposes, as a source of organic matter. Also supplies nitrogen, phosphates, magnesium, calcium and trace elements. Some sewage sludges from industrial areas contain too high concentrations of heavy metals to be suitable for horticultural uses. Salad or other crops to be eaten raw should not be sown earlier than 12 months after application to the vegetable garden.

Poultry Manure Rich in nitrogen but low in fibre, and on its own should be used moderately (at 4 to 6oz[110 to 170g] per square yard) as a nitrogen fertiliser. Often it is mixed with sawdust or wood shavings which utilize most of the nitrogen leaving it as a good organic matter source but low in nutrients.

Peat An excellent, long-lasting soil conditioner and humus source but with negligible nutrient values. Usually fairly acid, but East Anglian peats are often strongly alkaline.

Seaweed Analytically a variable material but a useful source of potash with some nitrogen. Lacks fibre and its benefits are similar to those of green manure.

Processed Bark A long-lasting soil improver and source of humus. Very stable as a mulching material.

Other Materials There are many proprietary organic materials, based on plant or animal remains, such as fish waste, seaweed, poultry and other manures, but with nutrients added to improve nutritional value. Check the levels of nutrients they contain and use according to manufacturers recommendations and crop requirements.

NITROGEN FERTILISERS Given satisfactory soil temperature and seasonal conditions, the amount of nitrogen available as ammonia and nitrate is the limiting factor in crop growth. Nitrogen encourages stem and leaf growth and to achieve high vegetative growth rate, adequate nitrogen must be available to meet plant needs. Provided that the soil is moist and warm (above 41°F[5°C]) a steady supply of nitrate from decomposing organic matter will be available for plant growth.

During the winter months there is little bacterial activity and very little release of nitrate. As the soil warms in spring nitrate becomes increasingly available, reaching a peak about mid-June – by which time crops are growing rapidly and utilizing large quantities of nitrogen. Nitrate continues to be released during the autumn, and where crops are ripening or have been harvested will not be used and will be washed from the soil by winter rains.

The most critical period of nitrogen availability is early spring, where spring crops are coming into strong growth during April and early May, when a shortage of soil-released nitrate will often result in a considerable check in growth, ultimately seriously affecting crop yield. This is the period when quick-acting nitrogenous fertilisers are needed, either as base dressings prior to sowing or planting, or as surface dressings around established plants.

It is important to remember that the application of large amounts of nitrogen will encourage lush stem and leaf growth. Although this may be desired with leafy vegetable crops, *balanced* growth is required from crops or plants grown for their flowers, fruit or edible roots.

While the application of quick-acting nitrogen fertilisers will encourage rapid growth, growth will be limited by the availability of other nutrients as in utilising larger amounts of nitrogen a plant's demands on available phosphorus or potassium will also increase. Where there is any doubt regarding levels of available phosphorous or potassium it is better to use a balanced base fertiliser dressing in spring. On heavily manured soils there is less need for nitrogen because of the larger amount of nitrogen released from the soil.

Nitrogenous fertilisers: organic:

Hoof and horn meal	(13 per cent N)
Shoddy (wool waste)	(9–12 per cent N)
Dried blood	(14 per cent N)

These are all of animal origin, rotting in the soil to produce ammonia, then nitrate. Although they are regarded as slow-acting the rate of bacterial break-down is related to soil temperature. Applied in spring outdoors there will be little soluble nitrogen available in the early part of the year and they are more useful for crops or plants which make their growth during mid to late summer.

Under glass, where soil temperatures are higher, nitrogen release is more rapid. Do not, however, use before or immediately following steam sterilizing of greenhouse soils as steaming temporarily affects the balance of soil bacteria and there can be a build-up of ammonia in the soil of sufficient concentration to damage plant roots.

Nitrogenous fertilisers: inorganic:

Sulphate of ammonia	(21 per cent N)
Ammonium nitrate	(35 per cent N)
Ammonium nitrate plus calcium carbonate (Nitrochalk)	(21 per cent N)
Nitrate of soda	(15.5 per cent N)
Urea	(46 per cent N)
Urea-formaldehyde	(38 per cent N)

These are all inorganic sources of nitrogen. Urea-formaldehyde is slow in its action; the others are quick-acting being soluble salts containing ammonia or nitrate, the latter being immediately available to plants.

PHOSPHORUS FERTILISERS Phosphorus is taken up by plant roots as dissolved phosphates. There is relatively little movement of phosphates in the soil, particularly on heavier soils and for this reason fertilisers supplying phosphates are most effectively applied by mixing thoroughly with the soil prior to sowing or planting. They can be used around established perennial plants in surface dressings but they are only leached slowly from the surface downwards without cultivation.

Phosphate is particularly concerned with the areas of rapid growth and is an important requirement of vegetable crops and of flowering annual plants. It is not stored in dead woody tissue. In trees and shrubs it is being continuously moved to younger parts and re-utilized, and with them there is likely to be little benefit gained from phosphate applications except on peat soils or poor acid sands.

Phosphorus fertilisers: organic:

Bonemeal	(16–20 per cent P_2O_5) (+4 per cent N)
Steamed bone flour	(20–29 per cent P_2O_5) (+1 per cent N)

(Both dependent on bacterial action and slow-acting; slightly alkaline reaction.)

Phosphorus fertilisers: inorganic:

Superphosphate	(18 per cent P_2O_5)
Triple superphosphate	(46 per cent P_2O_5)

(both readily available to plants)
Basic slag (variable up to 14 per cent P_2O_5)
(An agricultural fertiliser, slow-acting and alkaline)

POTASSIUM FERTILISERS In plants potassium is particularly associated with water uptake and photosynthesis, being concentrated in the sappy parts of plants. Potash fertilisers dissolve in the soil water but only move very slowly in the soil.

In heavier soils and those well enriched with organic matter potassium is soon absorbed by the clay or organic particles, from where it can be easily assimilated by extending plant roots. On sandy soils there is little capacity for retention and potassium may be readily leached out in wet conditions. Potassium is less readily available to plants on heavily limed soils.

Leafy plants such as tomatoes and potatoes use large quantities of potassium and as large quantities are removed when crops are harvested it is important to maintain good levels in the vegetable plot. Fruit crops and many woody ornamentals also benefit from high levels although uptake is less than that of soft, leafy plants.

Potassium fertilisers: inorganic:

Muriate of potash	(60 per cent K_2O)

(Mainly an agricultural fertiliser. Contains chloride which may cause leaf scorch on some horticultural crops)

Sulphate of potash	(48 per cent K_2O)

(Derived from muriate and safe for all horticultural crops)

Potassium nitrate	(45 per cent K_2O) (+13 per cent N)

(Dissolves easily in water and is used for the preparation of liquid feeds, its lower level of nitrogen being balanced with urea)

Wood ash	(variable 5–10 per cent K_2O)

(Must be ash from young sappy wood, ash from older wood having little value; alkaline in reaction)

MAGNESIUM FERTILISERS Magnesium deficiency is most likely to occur in chalky, peaty or sandy soils, and following dressings of potash applied to these soils to increase potassium availability. Heavy dressings of farmyard manure will help to correct both deficiencies. Epsom salts (10 per cent magnesium) is effective, particularly as a foliar spray, but is highly soluble. Longer-term effect can be obtained from magnesium monoammonium phosphate available as Enmag or MagAmp.

Magnesium limestone can be used on sandy soils lacking both calcium and magnesium. It contains up to 45 per cent magnesium carbonate. It has strong neutralizing values and for general purpose use can be regarded as equivalent to ground chalk or limestone, although slower-acting.

Dolomitic limestone, used widely in soil-less potting composts, contains 15 per cent or more magnesium oxide.

LIME AND SOIL CONDITIONING When considering the nutrition of plants the first step is to affirm that roots can function efficiently by checking that soil drainage is satisfactory and there is no waterlogging of the top-soil in wet weather. With established perennials check that the soil surface is not tightly packed so that air and water penetrate only with difficulty, a condition often encountered near the trunks of well-established trees.

The second step is to check that the soil is at a suitable pH level for the crop or plants being grown.

A pH of 6.5 is most suitable for vegetable and fruit crops and most ornamentals, the main exceptions being ericaceous plants and some alpines. For ornamental turf pH.6 is preferable. At the slightly acid reaction of pH 6.5 major nutrients are usually in good supply; also trace elements released by the break-down of organic matter which decomposes readily at this pH level. With increasing acidity nutrients are less freely available. There is a progressive decline in magnesium. Potassium availability begins to fall below pH6. Phosphates are most readily available between pH6 and pH7.5. The most favourable reaction range for nitrification lies between pH6 and 8 with a rapid decline below pH6.

Lime is present in the soil as calcium carbonate. It is progressively dissolved by the carbonic acid in rain water. Some is utilised by plants but most is leached out in drainage water. In shallow soils over chalk, cultivation continuously brings chalk to the surface, the soil remaining alkaline, but deeper soils over chalk may be strongly acid.

In most soils there is an annual loss per square yard of 1 to 2oz(25 to 55g) calcium carbonate, depending on rainfall, and the soil will become increasingly acidic, lower in calcium and less productive unless lime is applied.

Lime is available to the gardener as ground chalk and ground limestone, both finely crushed, quick-acting forms of calcium carbonate originating from natural rock formations. Hydrated lime is of similar origin but is reduced to a fine-particle form by first heating the rock to produce calcium oxide (quicklime) then treating with water to give calcium hydroxide (hydrated or "slaked" lime) which is quickly converted to calcium carbonate when incorporated into the soil.

Choice of liming material may be determined by cost, requirements and neutralizing value. Ground chalk and ground limestone have the weakest neutralizing effect but are the most rapid in action and are the forms usually used for potting composts.

The same neutralizing effect will be obtained from: 2 parts (by weight) quicklime, 3 parts (by weight) hydrated lime and 4 parts (by weight) ground chalk or limestone. All forms are most effectively applied by thorough incorporation into the soil before sowing or planting but can be applied as surface dressings around growing plants, with the exception of quicklime, an agricultural lime which can scorch plant foliage.

The gardener in any doubt as to his soil's pH reaction should check it (and do so regularly every three or four years) using one of the easy-to-use kits obtainable from most garden centres. The amount of lime required by soils of the same pH reaction varies, depending on soil texture, organic matter content and kinds of plant or crops being grown, necessitating both careful reference to the recommendations for liming enclosed with the kit and careful assessment of one's own soil and crop needs.

THE GARDEN USE OF FERTILISERS   See other chapters for more detailed references.

Vegetables Incorporate as a base dressing before sowing or planting out either:

1.   A compound 7.7.7 fertiliser at 3 to 4oz(85 to 110g) per square yard (m^2) for legumes and root crops; at 8 to 10oz(225 to 285g) per square yard(m^2) for main-crop potatoes and brassicas.

2.   1 to 1½oz(25 to 40g) sulphate of ammonia per square yard(m^2) or equivalent (a *higher* percentage nitrogen may depress seedling growth in dry conditions; supplement as inter-row dressings where necessary): 2oz(55g) superphosphate per square yard(m^2) or equivalent; and 1oz(25g) sulphate of potash per square yard(m^2) or equivalent. Apply nitrogen in spring to overwintering crops, e.g., cabbage, onions.

An important aspect of vegetable nutrition is to return all crop residues to the soil as compost.

Fruit Tree fruit requirements are not high on good soil but regular dressings are important in poor soil or grassed down trees. All soft fruits need regular spring feeding.

Turf Needs regular N.P.K. feeding in spring with supplementary nitrogen in late spring-early summer. Also phosphate-potash in early autumn if in poor condition.

Annual Flowers A good phosphate level essential. Promote balanced growth by incorporating a balanced compound fertiliser (see vegetable recommendations) at 2 to 3oz(55 to 85g) per square yard before sowing or planting out.

Ornamental Trees and Shrubs These have little demand for phosphate and therefore obtain little value from heavy use of bonemeal when planting. Incorporate good dressings of organic matter, supplementing nutrient levels with a compound slow release fertiliser or hoof and horn meal as a source of nitrogen.
   Established trees can be fed by means of slow-release fertilisers in cartridge form inserted at intervals within the area of feeding roots.
   Roses are an exception, producing a large amount of new growth each year. These need an annual spring dressing of a compound fertiliser (with magnesium on poorer soils) after pruning, and a supplementary dressing at each flush of bloom.

Herbaceous perennials These need a balanced level of nutrients. If replanted every third year in organic-enriched soil with pre-planting base fertiliser, there should be little need for fertilisers except for a light spring dressing of a quick-acting nitrogen fertiliser to compensate for low seasonal levels of organic-based nitrogen. On poorer soils or where not regularly moved apply in spring a light dressing of a compound 7.7.7. fertiliser at 2oz(55g) per square yard.

Some Terms Explained:
NUTRIENT CONTENT: is expressed in percentages of N (nitrogen), P_2O_5 (phosphoric acid) and K_2O (potash).
COMPOUND OR GENERAL FERTILISER: containing two or more nutrients.
STRAIGHT FERTILISER: containing only one nutrient.
BALANCED FERTILISER: containing equal amounts of nitrogen, phosphorus and potassium.
SLOW-RELEASE FERTILISER: provides a regular supply of nutrients, by means of ion exchange resins, over a period of several months.
LIQUID FERTILISER: all nutrients are immediately available to provide quick growth response. Good for supplementary feeding but as nutrients are in very dilute form repeat applications are necessary.
FOLIAR FEEDS: are a useful means of providing growth stimulus and deficient trace elements where root development is poor or root action faulty.
BASE DRESSINGS: are fertilisers in solid form incorporated into the soil before sowing or planting to provide a steady release of plant foods over an extended period as young plants develop.

35.

Background to Plant Propagation

The mention of plant propagation conjures up differing visions in different gardeners' minds. Some will think of making cuttings (and perhaps treating them with hormone powder); some will envisage budding roses or grafting apple trees; others sowing (and germinating) seeds; while still others will think of such practical matters as the use of mist, frames or propagators. All are part of the plant propagation scene, but too often these are the limits of vision, whereas, in reality, they are only components of what should be considered as a complete concept.

It is not suggested that it is necessary for any one person to be able to understand and carry out all the various techniques involved in propagation, but simply that a necessary basis for success in whatever is attempted, is that the whole process involved should be analysed, understood and implemented. This requires a knowledge of all those aspects of plant growth, and the conditions for regeneration, which affect a particular propagation technique.

The aim when propagating is to create a new generation, and, in so doing, produce a well-established young plant. In the past it has often been assumed that it is necessary to have "green fingers" to achieve successful results consistently, but nowadays much of this mysticism can be replaced by reliable information and applied techniques. The accumulation of knowledge and its wide dissemination over the last two decades has made it possible for most gardeners to succeed in propagating plants by the application of well-understood basic principles. No doubt there is still, and probably always will be, an art in applying these principles, for although success can be achieved by applying these, and knowledge, it is necessary to appreciate that plant growth and condition is an ever-changing and dynamic phenomenon, although the changes are often imperceptible. Keen observation and experience are essential ingredients of success.

When determining how to approach any particular technique of plant propagation it is necessary to be able to categorise the various techniques involved and then be able to break these down into their various stages or component parts for analysis. The intention now is not to detail the whole range of propagation techniques but to endeavour to stimulate thoughts on, and an understanding of, the processes involved.

Plant Propagation Techniques

Plant propagation embraces a wide field of activity, and because of this and the many techniques practised, it is necessary to divide the latter into their component parts. There are two major groups of propagating technique, separated by the genetic processes involved. Either propagation results in plants being produced as a result of the sexual process (i.e. flowering and seed production) or through an asexual process, when the vegetative parts of plants provide basic propagating material. This can be defined as follows:

THE BASIC SYSTEMS
i) The SEXUAL process produces a variable genetic status as a result of the flowering process.
   a) Seed

ii) ASEXUAL processes maintain a fixed genetic status as a result of vegetative methods.
   a) Division: into complete pieces to develop a new plant.
   b) Grafting: the joining of separate pieces to produce a new plant.
   c) Regeneration: the development of the missing part on a single vegetative part to produce a new plant.
   d) Tissue Culture: the production of a new plant from microscopic pieces.

THE SEXUAL PROCESS This, by definition, requires the mixing of genetic characters from two parents (sets), so that the subsequent generation has a variability (because of its reconstituted genetic status). Thus, when plants flower and produce a crop of seeds, and these seeds are used to produce a new generation, it is not surprising that the resulting population shows some variation. In nature the variation overall will be slight, with the majority of the population being "typical". Under garden conditions, however, and artificial breeding programmes, the amount of variation may increase enormously. Having said that, though, the variation in desirable characteristics can be virtually eliminated by the adoption of certain controlled crossing techniques such as are used in the breeding of flower and vegetable cultivars by the choice of parents.

THE ASEXUAL PROCESS This implies propagation from vegetative parts of a plant, and thus infers that no change in the genetic status is to be anticipated. Each succeeding generation must resemble its parent exactly in all characters. If part of a plant is used for producing a new generation then it is not possible for genetic change to occur so cultivars and clones can be perpetuated continuously, relying on the stability of their characteristics. However, genetic change does sometimes occur in such situations, despite what has just been said. These changes are relatively infrequent and occur as a result of natural forces which may alter the structure of an individual gene and so affect the expression of that character in the plant.
   Such changes occur as a result of environmental conditions altering, and to the influence of radioactivity or chemical instability; the plants that result are variously termed "bud sports" or "mutations". The best examples of this phenomenon are to be found in a glasshouse crop of carnations or chrysanthemums in which the odd flower of a different colour will suddenly appear. These occurrences have given rise to related groups of cultivars, such as the Sim cultivars which all arose from the red 'William Sim', or chrysanthemums such as the 'Shoesmith' or 'Princess Anne' groups.

Vegetative or Asexual Propagation

This involves an extraordinarily wide spectrum of techniques, and it is therefore necessary to try to break down these into basic groups so that the factors affecting their implementation can be identified and applied. The three basic functions are: *Division*, *Grafting* and the *Regeneration of separate vegetative parts*.

DIVISION The simplest form of propagation is division of a plant into a series of complete pieces, each with a root and shoot system, which then merely requires rehabilitation and re-establishment in order to form a new plant. This technique can only be practised on those plants which grow in such a way that it is possible to divide them at the crown. The immediate concern is to ensure the survival of the individual divisions while these re-establish themselves and develop balanced and integrated root/shoot systems. This "survival period" should be reduced to a minimum by carrying out the operation of division just before, or co-incidental with, a period of vegetative growth when new shoots are being developed. This usually occurs in herbaceous plants in the early spring when the basal growth buds are swelling or, less often, in plants like pyrethrum, just after flowering. In woody plants, it is associated with the spring flush of growth.

GRAFTING   This is an entirely separate concept of plant propagation. Two parts of different plants are joined together to form a new plant. The success of this operation depends on making a suitable join (a simple carpentry operation) and then ensuring that the parts make a suitable union. This is achieved by providing the right environmental conditions for a new, fully balanced and integrated plant to develop. Grafting is, therefore, one step forward from division in terms of propagating complexity.

In division, the whole of the potential new plant is present and merely needs rehabilitating, whereas in grafting, although the component parts of the potential plant are present, they are separate (as, basically, a root system and a shoot system) and success depends on joining the two parts together to produce the new plant. Sometimes, as with certain pear cultivars, things can be further complicated by the need for double working because of incompatibility between stock and scion. In this case, an intermediate cultivar, which is compatible both to the quince stock and the scion of the desired cultivar, is grafted between them.

Grafting is perhaps one of the most difficult plant propagation systems to understand. In the past, the basic concepts of the system and the treatment of the plant material concerned, have been clouded by the mysticism surrounding the many complicated forms of carpentry involved in the joining operation. Although many of these joinery techniques have a place in grafting the carpentry involved is merely a skill in matching the tissues together efficiently. The plant material used must be in such a condition that the growth patterns of both parts (stock and scion) can be synchronised, a union achieved and a common structure produced, leading to the development of a new, integrated plant. The basic process is the stimulation of tissue production by wounding the stems. At first undifferentiated cell tissue (callus) is produced and later this differentiates into the various cell types present in an unwounded stem which are capable of conducting water or nutrients between the two halves now joined as one.

In commercial horticulture simplified grafting techniques are much in evidence nowadays. The wide variety of carpentry joints used in the past for grafting have been reduced to a few basic patterns and greater attention is given to the production of rootstocks and scions with a propensity to form unions quickly and effectively.

Grafting is, nevertheless, a time-consuming and relatively expensive way of producing plants and it also requires, of course, the skills of a joiner. Consequently, it is usually only resorted to when all other techniques fail or because it is also desired to control plant growth by the use of a particular rootstock.

THE REGENERATION OF PLANTS FROM SEPARATE VEGETATIVE PARTS   This is probably the most widely practised of all systems of vegetative propagation as it involves increase from parts of stems, leaves and roots. To put the technique into practice, part of a plant is taken and an attempt made to encourage regeneration and development of the missing part, or parts, to make another complete plant. Thus it involves the production of roots on a stem cutting or a layered stem; the production of stems on a root or the development of root and shoot systems from a leaf.

Success with this type of propagation depends primarily on one factor – the ability or capacity of the chosen piece of plant material to regenerate those missing parts. More often than not the failure or the lack of real success with this type of plant propagation can be attributed to the inability of the propagating material to initiate the regenerative processes and so respond. Therefore, successful propagation will only be achieved by making sure that it has a high latent capacity to regenerate those missing parts. This is most easily achieved by bringing about the development of a highly "vegetative" condition in the plant material. The term "vegetative" in this context is not easy to define, but in reference to stems it can be seen as the opposite of "flowering", which accounts for the ease of rooting associated with cuttings taken from juvenile forms from plants that produce one type of growth when the tree or shrub is young, another when it is mature. The vegetative condition (or "rejuvenation") is most readily achieved by encouraging vigorous growth, this vegetativeness being reflected by a reduction in flowering or an inability to flower – at least in stems. The same encouragement to rapid growth in roots achieves the same latent capacity to regenerate.

This vigorous growth is best achieved by causing an imbalance in the root/shoot ratio of the plant by rigorously pruning the part needed to provide material for propagation, so that rapid growth is required to redress the root/shoot balance. However, it must be understood that this rapid growth will not necessarily eliminate flowering (witness the behaviour of fuchsias), while other plants may simply have a low genetic capacity to regenerate despite pruning.

Now that the basic systems of plant propagation have been delineated, let us analyse the process of propagation so that an understanding of the entire process is achieved. It is possible to divide the process into four sequential phases, each of which is sufficiently distinct to warrant consideration as a separate component. However, it must be appreciated that all of these phases are inter-related and cannot be considered in isolation.

a) PRELIMINARY PHASE: the selection of suitable plant material for propagation.

b) PREPARATION PHASE: the manipulation of the plant material to a condition suitable for successful propagation.

c) REGENERATION PHASE: the provision of conditions suitable for allowing the propagating processes to proceed.

d) ESTABLISHMENT PHASE: the treatment of the propagated material to a stage at which it has become an integrated and established plant.

The Preliminary Phase This concerns the basic plant material to be used for propagation. The plant to be propagated must be fully assessed to ensure that it is a satisfactory subject and is worthwhile perpetuating. It must be pest and disease free.

The first essential is that the plant from which the material is taken should have a correct and acceptable name. This becomes increasingly important the more specialist the plant under consideration – and especially when the plant's separate identity is dependent on very small differences from other cultivars etc. It is also as well, when dealing with well-established and/or widely propagated plants, to assess whether there have been any discernible variations which have developed in the population as a result of mutation or sporting, bearing in mind that such variations may occur in any character – not just flower colour or size. It is, therefore, as well to compare plants from several different sources if this is possible, so that the most typical or the most desirable form can be selected and propagated.

Variation in such stocks may, however, be due to virus infections which can alter the character of the plant and will almost certainly depress its ability to reproduce. Thus, unless the particular virus infection has some ornamental significance, it should be general policy to select material for propagation purposes from subjects which are free of disease. It is important to appreciate the existence of viruses and their widespread presence in plant material.

Preparation phase The second phase concerns the preparation and manipulation of the plant material into a condition that allows regeneration and so the production of a new plant. Aspects of this phase vary from technique to technique but the fundamental pattern remains the same.

When raising plants from seed, germination initially depends upon the passive uptake of water by the dry seed, so that it eventually contains the full complement of water. Once it reaches this fully imbibed stage, however, the chemical processes which allow the growth of the embryo and the movement of stored food materials can be triggered off by subjecting it to suitable environmental conditions (i.e. warmth, air, moisture etc.). However, in many plants this process may be prevented from occurring by some physical or physiological block. Generally, this condition is referred to as dormancy, which can take three basic forms: 1, a seed coat condition which either prevents the access of water or constrains embryo growth; 2, a chemical inhibition which prevents the growth of the embryo either by restricting the oxygen supply or by blocking a particular biochemical chain of reactions in the growth process; and 3, a condition in which the embryo is not sufficiently developed to pass into the germination stage.

This blockage of the germination process therefore requires the manipulation of the seed by treatments which will eliminate these limitations, and allow germination once it is exposed to suitable environmental conditions. This manipulation may take several forms, but can involve a reduction of the seed coat, if it is physically preventing water uptake, by acid digestion, scarification, chipping or by warm, damp storage, so causing decomposition. Chemical problems can often be resolved by leaching in running, or frequently changed, water. Many plants from temperate to arctic conditions have a dormancy control which is neutralised by exposure of the imbibed seed to a period of low temperature. Immature embryos can be brought up to size by the warm storage of seeds that have been kept in damp conditions to take up imbibed water. When manipulating seeds physiologically, and so preparing them for germination, it is always necessary to use an imbibed seed sample so that the normal growth processes affected can be activated.

Although these dormancy conditions provide difficulties for the propagator seeking to achieve seed germination, they are, of course, very necessary to the plant to ensure its survival from generation to generation. Germination may be spread, for instance, over several years or it can be prevented from occurring until environmental conditions are better suited both to germination and seedling survival.

These dormancy problems often prove difficult for the gardener to overcome, either because of the small quantities of seed to be treated or the complexities of the treatments themselves. The only feasible alternative lies in the possibility of avoiding dormancy. This will normally involve the collection of seed while it is still "green" – at a stage when embryo development and food storage have been completed but before any intractable dormancy conditions develop, usually during the drying phase before dispersal.

To propagate plants vegetatively, material must be produced in a highly vegetative condition. The normal method of survival employed by most plants is to produce seeds and a natural ability to propagate vegetatively is not, therefore, a high priority. The propagator must, therefore, attempt to determine those aspects of "vegetativeness" in the plant which might enhance asexual propagation, so providing a high capacity to regenerate, and subsequently try to encourage the development of this condition in the parent plant.

In the life of a plant there are three stages – juvenility, maturity and senility. In the juvenile stage (i.e. before sexual maturity and an ability to flower is developed) it is easy to show that the plant has a high capacity to regenerate vegetatively, as layers or cuttings can be rooted quickly. However, once a plant reaches maturity and is capable of flowering this ability declines dramatically, and continues to decline with age. It is, therefore, reasonable to suggest that the physiological conditions associated with flowering depress regenerative capacity. Thus, if the metabolism could be influenced so that the flowering process is suppressed, it could be expected that the plant would be stimulated towards an increased ability to regenerate. This is achieved by hard pruning which encourages the development of vegetative non-flowering material in stems; and as, in practice, "vegetative" growth is rapid and vigorous, the same principle can be applied to root generation.

This treatment does not, however, always work, and this may be due to the age of the cultivar being propagated. It has already been said that the latent capacity for regeneration decreases through the mature phase, and it continues to decline even if the plant is "rejuvenated" regularly by pruning and propagation to establish new generations. Thus, old cultivars often present more problems for the propagator than recent introductions.

One further consideration is significant when considering what is, after all, a physiological balance within the plant and that is the effect of seasonal influence. When considering particular techniques of propagation, it is pertinent to determine whether the regenerative capacity induced is being over-ridden by seasonal changes. This type of information is often significant as it can prevent a great deal of wasted effort. Much has been written elsewhere on "timing" as related to plant propagation, but little concrete evidence is available on its real effects. It is possible to demonstrate seasonal effects very simply by a continuous programme of propagation over the period when propagating material is available, noting any changes in regeneration. This is easily seen in subjects like root cuttings of woody plants (see Graph 1), where regeneration only occurs in the dormant season; and in hardwood cuttings where, contrary to traditional advice, the most successful periods for regeneration are the beginning and the end of the dormant season (see Graph 2).

The nutrition received by plants may also influence propagation, insofar that the indiscriminate use of fertilisers may produce conditions within the propagating material which are not conducive to regeneration. This is especially so when plants take up unnecessary quantities of nitrogen, for high levels of free nitrogen are reputed to depress regeneration.

The Regeneration Phase   This is the phase which most gardeners equate with the production of new plants. It is the stage at which seeds are germinated, cuttings rooted, grafts achieve unions and so on. The achievement of this objective depends on two factors. The first factor concerns the survival of the plant material in an ideal condition for growth and metabolic activity, thus allowing regeneration to proceed quickly. The second factor is the regenerative processes themselves, these involving the encouragement of the reactions which cause the different stages of germination, root or stem production or graft union to occur successfully. Both factors depend on the carrying out of various treatments and the maintenance of certain environmental conditions.

Leading on from this, the "survival period" should be kept to a minimum, and this can only be achieved by using propagating material with the highest capacity to regenerate. If the conditions provided are optimal – and one is usually thinking in terms of providing the correct amount of warmth, moisture and air – the period over which regeneration occurs is kept as short as possible and the chances of things going wrong reduced. If this period is extended the condition of the material will certainly change and will, in all probability, deteriorate. As a consequence of that, the rate of regeneration is slowed down, food reserves are employed solely in maintaining the status quo and the chances of external agencies interfering (e.g. disease infection) must increase and the possibility of survival decrease.

During this phase some degree of control of the environment is necessary to improve the chances of regeneration. Usually, this means increasing the temperature as, in general terms, the higher the temperature in the region of regeneration the faster will be the plant's response (within biological limits). However, these increased levels of temperature may also provide problems as they may "force" unnecessary growth and reduce the chances of survival. With increased temperatures, too, there is the need to provide adequate aeration so that respiration is not a limiting factor in the provision of energy.

There is another factor to be taken into account, in addition to the provision of the correct temperature and supply of air; this is the provision of moisture. The moisture content of the plant material can also be critical. Water loss and dehydration are detrimental, affecting the plant's metabolism and eventually, if the moisture level falls below a critical level, causing the plant's death.

In certain cases the ability to regenerate and/or survive may be a function of light: as a necessary source of energy for food production; in terms of day-length requirements; or simply in terms of its presence or absence in relation to stimulating necessary reactions, as in germination.

It is also possible to improve the chances of survival and encourage

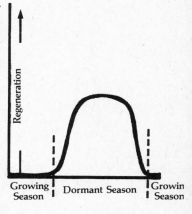

Graph 1. *The seasonal response to regeneration in root cuttings.*

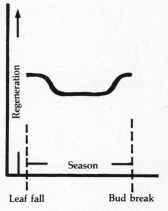

Graph 2. *The seasonal response of hardwood cuttings to rooting.*

regeneration by subjecting propagating material to certain treatments before exposing it to the required environmental conditions. These treatments include the use of fungicides, anti-transpirants, plant growth regulating substances, wounding, the maintenance of polarity – e.g. making sure that root cuttings are planted the right way up – and artificial feeding. Apropos root cuttings, it is very easy to ensure that they are planted correctly if, at the time they are severed from the parent plant the end nearest the crown of the plant (the top) is made with a right-angled cut and the cut at the other end (the bottom) is made to slope.

From what has been said it will be appreciated that the factor of overriding importance in plant propagation is the provision of propagating material with an inherently high regenerative capacity: the right material at the right season. Given this, extra aids should not be needed, at least in theory; in practice, there are many instances in which the plant material available is below the optimum, either because it has not been possible to provide the ideal, manipulated parent or because the plant is difficult to propagate, due to age, genetically low capacity, or lack of knowledge concerning its reproduction. With such material the aids referred to can be beneficial.

Many plants can be propagated readily, of course, but the more difficult a plant in this respect the greater the need for correct preparation and manipulation of the material beforehand.

The Establishment Phase   After the regeneration phase and with the development of the new plant proceeding satisfactorily, it is necessary to consider its establishment. The task is to wean it into an integrated plant which will be capable of growing on normally into a mature specimen. This phase may seem an unnecessary complication, but with many types of propagation it is an essential element in the sequence of events.

In many cases the new plant is assumed to be complete after its propagation and is often subjected to unsuitable conditions. However, just because a plant has all the expected parts, i.e. roots, stems, and leaves, does not mean that it is immediately capable of surviving as a mature specimen. It cannot be deemed to have reached this stage until the root and shoot systems are growing in unison and have developed an integrated and balanced pattern of growth. When the plant is thus physiologically established then the propagation stage can be regarded as complete.

These remarks will usually be relevant to plants which are propagated after mid-summer and which become dormant early, shown by the setting of the terminal bud and the cessation of growth. At this stage the newly regenerated material will respond to the same stimulants and it is unlikely any integrated growth will be achieved unless these particular conditions are altered artificially. Integrated growth is often an essential feature for winter survival, especially with rooted cuttings or late season divisions. The major problem is that, despite its survival thus far, the material, because it has not achieved an integrated status, does not seem capable of coming out of dormancy in the following growing season.

In conclusion, it is emphasised that successful propagation depends on using plant material in its most suitable condition, at the correct time in the most suitable environmental conditions. If all three precepts are followed much of the "magic" can be taken out of plant propagation and replaced by hard fact or intelligent supposition.

36.

Mastering the Craft
of Pruning

The pruning operation has been defined as the removal of any part of a plant, either stems, branches or roots, in order to direct the energies of growth into channels desired by the cultivator. The gardener is most often concerned with the pruning of trees and shrubs, cutting away part of these plants to achieve particular effects.

Pruning may be carried out as a regular annual operation or at intervals, as and when it becomes necessary to achieve particular objectives. Many of our loveliest specimen shrubs, magnolias, acers, hamamelis and the like, need virtually no regular pruning. It will be sufficient to remove any dead or thin, weak growths which may occur from time to time in the centre of the plant, where they have been starved of light or air, or to cut away the odd branch which may be spoiling the natural shape and outline of the shrub.

Three basic objectives must be clearly borne in mind in any pruning:

THE MAINTENANCE OF PLANT HEALTH This is a primary requirement. Cutting out dead or damaged growth removes a possible source of infection, since the spores of airborne plant diseases may alight on such tissue where they can multiply and infect healthy growth, increasing the damage and even leading to the death of the plant.

The removal of thin, weak growths from the centre of a shrub encourages a free circulation of light and air throughout the plant and thus the development of sound, well-ripened growth which resists winter cold better than soft tissue.

THE MAINTENANCE OF SHAPE AND BALANCE Pruning must enhance and not detract from the natural shape and form of the shrub. This in itself can be an attractive feature, as in the vertical line of *Viburnum × bodnantense*, the rounded hummocks of *Acer palmatum* 'Dissectum' or the tiered horizontal branching of *Viburnum plicatum* 'Mariesii'. Such qualities are of value throughout the year, even with deciduous shrubs, and not just for the week or two of the flowering period.

We must also aim at producing a well-balanced shrub which can be viewed from all sides, which is neither top-heavy nor growing out at an awkward angle, as may occur if part of the plant is in shade.

When pruning to maintain shape, it is important to appreciate that there will be a long-term as well as an immediate reaction to a pruning cut, and that by pruning in the wrong way, the result may well be the exact opposite of what was intended. Development of a shrub occurs through the growth buds placed along the branches, sometimes alternately, sometimes opposite one another, sometimes in clusters. This development growth is sustained by food passing up the stem from the root system, and the amount which reaches the bud clearly depends on the diameter of the stem. Obviously, more will be able to travel along a plump healthy branch than through a thin weak one.

In annual pruning, all cuts are made in relation to one of the growth buds, and we speak of "severe" or "light" pruning according to the amount of stem removed. The amount of food passing up the stem is the same, but in the case of severe pruning this is shared among perhaps only two or three buds, whereas in light pruning the number may be six or eight, or even more. Clearly we may expect to get much stronger growth from the former than the latter, and we therefore establish the important principle, that severe pruning promotes a vigorous growth reaction and vice versa.

If we now apply this principle to our efforts to maintain shape and balance in a shrub, we can understand why it is so important to look ahead and try to envisage the reaction of the plant to any cuts that we make. Often we find a shrub growing unevenly, with strong healthy branches on one side, and only weak, twiggy growth on the other; our natural impulse may be to cut the strong growth hard back in order to bring it down to the same height as the other side of the plant. But this would, in fact, only achieve exactly the opposite effect, since the vigorous reaction of the severely pruned healthy branches would result in the production of strong growth on the same side of the plant, thus accentuating the unbalanced state of the shrub.

The answer is to prune the weak growth severely, in the hope of obtaining one or two vigorous branches which will balance up with the lightly pruned stems on the healthy side, where the resultant growth has been comparatively short (see Fig. 186).

In carrying out what may be called remedial or compensatory pruning of this type, it may well take more than one season's growth to bring a badly neglected shrub back into proper shape and balance. But as long as we understand the principles behind what we are doing, then we shall achieve the desired effect in the end.

To avoid producing a top-heavy plant which is particularly at risk from wind damage, as well as being unsightly, it is desirable to encourage the production of a regular supply of young, vigorous growths, either from ground level or at least from low down in the shrub. Such young growth will also, in due course, provide replacement for any older, exhausted or damaged branches which may have to be removed.

PRUNING TO OBTAIN THE MAXIMUM DECORATIVE EFFECT Although we tend to think mainly of ornamental shrubs as having beautiful flowers, there are several other characteristics which can be of equal decorative value, and which may well have a considerably longer period of effect. These include leaf shape and colour (of particular importance in variegated forms), beauty of fruit, stem colour, the system of branching or the outline of the shrub, its screening value or the protection that it affords to other plants.

All of these aspects can be considerably enhanced by correct pruning, in ways which will be considered in detail later. One example which may be mentioned here is the hard pruning of forms of *Cornus alba* (dogwood) in

186. Correcting the balance of a lop-sided shrub. In illustration (A) severe pruning on the righthand side of the shrub contrasts with light pruning on the other side, where growth is adequate. The result is as shown in illustration (B) with the severe pruning stimulating growth on the righthand side of the shrub and so correcting the imbalance.

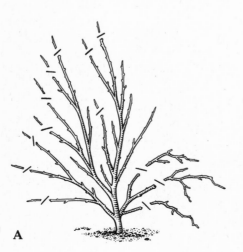

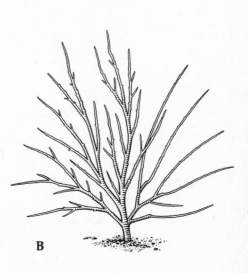

A   B

late March to encourage the production of long, unbranched, young stems, which will have more brightly coloured bark for winter effect than will the short twiggy side shoots on the older wood.

PRINCIPLES OF PRUNING

From the above remarks it will be seen that in order to apply these objectives successfully, we must understand the way shrubs grow, and their potential value in the garden. Pruning is not a haphazard operation, but entails looking ahead, anticipating what the results of a particular cut will be and pruning to enhance the natural beauty and form of a shrub rather than confining it within an artificial space or form. The only exceptions to this are topiary work or the regular clipping of formal hedges.

Wise planting will eliminate the need for much restrictive pruning, which can only spoil the natural beauty of the shrub. To site a plant in the right position we must know something of its requirements – the type of soil and the aspect that it prefers, and above all, the ultimate size that the plant will attain. If we put a large shrub such as a lilac or a forsythia in a narrow bed beneath a window, or a berberis or other prickly shrub too close to a pathway, this is obviously going to lead to trouble. We shall be forced in time to prune severely, encouraging a vigorous growth reaction and perpetuating the problem, which, with a little foresight, need never have arisen.

Shrubs are living things, and, like humans, vary in health and vigour – they also have a natural life-span. Much can be done by correct pruning to prolong their life, but the time comes when this is no longer possible. It is better to cut one's losses, to dig up an old moribund shrub or one whose shape and beauty has been irreparably spoilt, perhaps by excessively severe pruning over a number of years, and to replant with a young, vigorous specimen of the same type, or to try something different.

We tend to accept shrubs in the garden merely because they are there, and it is worthwhile, from time to time, to cast a critical eye over our shrubs to see whether they are really paying dividends for the space that they occupy.

Each shrub should be regarded as an individual, even if it is growing as one of a group. Individual specimens can vary, and before making any pruning cuts it is essential to assess the state of health and vigour of a particular specimen, its balance and general appearance. This implies some prior knowledge of, if possible, the generic and cultivar name, and particularly the species, since members of one genus can vary drastically in their pruning requirements. One has only to compare the evergreen ceanothuses, flowering on the growth made during the previous year, and pruned immediately after flowering, with the deciduous cultivars flowering in late summer on shoots of the current year's growth and pruned in early spring just as growth is starting. A similar difference occurs between the two deciduous species of buddleia, the June flowering *Buddleia alternifolia*, and *B. davidii*, the popular butterfly bush.

Making a Pruning Cut In principle, all pruning cuts should be made immediately above a growth bud and as close to it as possible. In annual pruning where we are dealing with no more than one year old wood, these buds are easily distinguished, and although they may not be immediately apparent in older specimens, the act of pruning will normally stimulate dormant buds into growth; a further cut can be made later to get rid of any surplus wood. Every pruning cut must be finished cleanly with no rough edges, torn or loosened bark, squeezing or bruising of the stem. When removing damaged, weak or unhealthy wood, it is important to cut back to healthy vigorous tissue, even if this is 6in(15cm) or more beneath the apparent extent of the damage.

An important distinction must be made between "clipping" and "pruning" a shrub. It is often better to remove a branch completely back to the point where it joins the next main stem or to where fresh growth is being produced rather than merely shortening back the stem. This is liable to

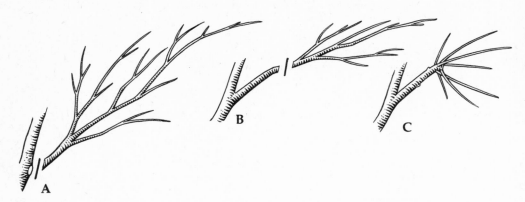

187. *With trees in particular, it is important to retain the natural branching habit and outline. Consequently, it is better to remove an entire single branch (A) cleanly back to the main branch rather than shorten it back (B) and encourage a forest of growth which would give an unattractive pollarded appearance to the tree (C).*

stimulate the development of a cluster of fresh shoots and produce an ugly tufted, "shaving brush" effect (Fig. 187).

The tools that are used for pruning must be adequate to cope with the size of branches being pruned. For normal annual pruning, secateurs of various types are most popular and provided that they are of good quality and properly maintained, they enable excellent results to be achieved. A good sharp knife is one of the basic tools that every gardener should possess. In pruning, its value, even if it is not used for making the initial cuts, lies in trimming back damaged tissue, paring smooth the rough surfaces left by a saw or pruner, or in making cuts in a confined space where a larger tool cannot be used.

When and How to Prune For those shrubs which benefit from regular, annual treatment, the best time of year for pruning is that which allows the plant as long a growing period as possible in which to produce wood of the desired type. One should always be guided by the stage of growth which the plant has reached, and never prune by the calendar. Weather conditions can vary considerably from year to year and there may be a variation of several weeks in the time when a particular shrub should be pruned.

Obviously there is less unnecessary waste of the energy of the plant if pruning is carried out at the optimum time, but this timing is not critical, and generally extends over a period of several weeks. The operation should not be undertaken in adverse weather conditions, for example when the ground is frozen or very wet, or in periods of severe drought when the plant is under considerable stress.

Having assessed the general condition of the shrub the actual operation of pruning can then begin. The first stage is to remove all unwanted material, dead or damaged wood, weak or exhausted branches, and any old flowering stems which clearly are of no further value. We are then left with sound, healthy growth which can be pruned in the appropriate manner.

While pruning, it is essential to move around the shrub, assessing it from all sides and, particularly important, getting into the best position for making the pruning cut. If we stand in one position, it is very easy to break some of the tender, young growths by leaning over to make a cut on the other side of the shrub. Also, unless one is standing properly, it is difficult to make the cut in the correct way.

Although a great diversity of ornamental shrubs can be grown in our gardens, these can broadly be classified into three main groups according to their pruning requirements:

Firstly, those deciduous shrubs flowering in spring and early summer, up to about the end of June, and producing their best flowers on growth made during the previous year. Many of our most popular garden shrubs, from forsythia to weigela, fall within this category, and they are all pruned as soon as the flowers have faded, cutting out the old flowering stems back to where fresh, young growth will already be apparent.

The second group comprises those deciduous shrubs flowering from mid- or late July to early autumn on growth made during the current year. To allow the maximum period for flowering wood to be produced, this group is pruned in the early spring just as growth is beginning, shortening back the previous year's stems to within two or three buds of their base. This fairly severe treatment encourages vigorous growth and maximum flower production.

Certain deciduous shrubs are grown for other qualities than flower, the shape or colour of their foliage or the ornamental effect of coloured bark. Any such shrubs, to whichever category they would normally belong if judged by their flowering period, are usually pruned in the early spring. This stimulates vigorous young growth, the production of fewer but much larger and more conspicuously variegated leaves, or clean, unbranched stems with brilliant winter bark colour.

Pruning Evergreen Shrubs   Evergreen shrubs occupy an important place in the garden, not merely for the ornamental effect of their often attractive shape or foliage, but particularly because they retain their leaves throughout the year and thus provide protection from wind and cold. It must be remembered that most of the evergreen shrubs in our gardens are not native to Britain but have been introduced from warmer climates, and are thus liable to damage during a severe winter.

Therefore, whether grown as single specimens, in groups, or perhaps as hedges, for all these reasons evergreen shrubs usually receive little regular pruning beyond the removal of any winter damage. This is done in late spring, April or May, just as the shrubs are coming into growth.

Pruning Freshly Planted Shrubs   Most shrubs, including those which, when established, are pruned every year, do not require any treatment during their first growing season after planting in the garden. The root system needs time to become fully established and able to provide the energy and plant foods necessary to develop and maintain fresh growth, little of which may be made during the first year, especially if weather conditions are unfavourable. The nurseryman will have provided a good bushy, well-shaped plant with a vigorous root system, and every effort should be made during the first season by watering and feeding as necessary to assist the shrub to settle down in its new position.

When moving a shrub from one part of the garden to another, however, some pruning may be advisable, thinning out up to a third of the branches to reduce the demands on the root system, and encourage the production of fresh growth which will maintain the natural shape and habit of the shrub.

Pruning Wall Shrubs and Climbers   Walls and fences provide valuable planting space in the garden with a variety of aspects, ranging from full sun to complete shade, thus greatly increasing the range of plants that can be grown. The general principles applied to pruning specimen shrubs in the open are equally relevant when considering wall plants and climbers. But it is particularly important to provide sufficient space for full development and also to ensure that adequate supports are provided for what may in time develop into a very heavy plant (see Chapter 7, p. 77).

There are two stages in the pruning of wall shrubs and climbers. For the first few years after planting, depending upon the rate of growth of the shrub, the main consideration must be to establish and tie out a basic framework or skeleton of branches which will evenly cover the space allotted to the plant. Once this has been achieved and the plant is well established, then the pruning becomes similar to that advised for open-ground specimens.

Fresh young growth will normally be produced from fairly high up in the plant, growing out away from its support, and this is often brittle, tender, and liable to damage by wind or early frosts. It is, therefore, a good practice, before the onset of autumn gales, to secure this young growth loosely back against its support to prevent any damage. This is in no sense a pruning operation, which will take place later at the appropriate time of year.

The protection afforded by the wall or fence, often encourages climbing shrubs to start into growth much earlier in the spring than their counter-parts in the open garden; the dormant season may consequently be very short, a matter of a few weeks in December and early January, and this is the most suitable time for pruning many wall shrubs.

Vigorous wall shrubs and climbers can often produce several feet of growth in the course of a single season, and if this is allowed to get up into guttering, beneath a tiled roof or behind a drainpipe, damage can often occur as the stem develops and thickens. At least once a year, therefore, attention should be paid to keeping such growth at least a foot or so beneath the eaves and well away from any pipes, windows or ventilation bricks.

Pruning Roses Our national flower, the rose, provides a great diversity of colour and beauty and there is a corresponding range in size from tall vigorous species, capable of climbing 20 or 30ft(6 to 9m) up into a tree, down to the modern miniature cultivars only a few inches high. Each type requires a particular pruning treatment, but, broadly speaking, they can be classified into two main groups: the true species and their hybrids, the old garden roses, hybrid musks and shrub roses, and what may be called the modern display roses, large-flowered bush roses (hybrid teas), cluster-flowered bush roses (floribundas) climbers and the like.

The first group are normally grown as single specimens and can be pruned as deciduous flowering shrubs which happen to be roses, differen-tiating mainly between those flowering on the current season's and those on the previous year's growth. Many of them will benefit from regular annual attention, but this is not nearly so drastic as in the second group.

Of the display roses all, with the exception of the rambler roses, flower on the current season's growth, and benefit from regular annual pruning, not only to improve the quality and production of flower, but also to keep plants well shaped and maintain a constant supply of vigorous young wood.

The best time for pruning this class of rose depends to a large extent on the location of the garden. Traditionally, and certainly in colder districts and in the open country, early March to mid-April would be the favoured time, just when the top-most buds on the stem are starting into growth. In mild districts and particularly in town gardens where the protection and warmth of the buildings provides a much more sheltered environment, roses may safely be pruned when they are fully dormant, usually in December and early January. This is a quiet time in the garden, the plants suffer no check to growth once this begins, and the first flowers appear two to three weeks earlier than from spring-pruned plants.

With spring-pruned roses it is worth noting that the cluster-flowered bush roses (floribundas), with their greater vigour, usually start into growth a week or so before the large-flowered bush roses (hybrid teas), and will therefore be pruned first. For the same reason they will receive somewhat less severe treatment.

In open situations where the plants are exposed to strong winds, it is a good practice to reduce the top growth of tall-growing cultivars by about one third in the early autumn, to minimise wind resistance which, by loosening the plant in the soil, may expose the root system to damage by frost or drought during the winter months.

With many of the older cultivars of climbing and rambling roses, pruning can be a major problem, since they are capable of reaching 15 to 20ft(4.5 to 6m) in height. In most gardens today space is limited, and for the wall of a bungalow or a garden fence, the modern pillar roses have a much more suitable habit, reaching only some 8 to 10ft(2.5 to 3m), and with a virtually continuous production of flowers of high quality throughout the summer. Flowering on the current season's growth they are pruned in the early spring, the short lateral growths being pruned back to two or three buds from the base in the normal way.

The true rambler roses have only one period of flowering and have usually finished their display by July or early August. This is the time to prune, the growths which have borne flowers being cut out down to ground level and the developing young shoots tied in to take their place.

Heathers The heathers that we grow in our gardens, cultivars and forms of *Calluna, Erica, Daboecia* and the like, are among the loveliest of broad-leaved evergreen shrubs, providing a continuity of flower and foliage effect virtually throughout the year, unequalled by any other group of plants. Most of the cultivars that we grow are native to Britain or western Europe and are generally well suited to our climate, but in the artificial conditions of garden cultivation some pruning is necessary to keep them well shaped and attractive and to improve the length and quality of the flower spike.

We are concerned with three main groups: 1. summer flowering, from June to October; 2. winter flowering from November to April; and 3. taller-growing tree heaths.

To start with Group 1, the summer-flowering heaths, for the first two or three years after planting until the individual plants have grown together to form one group, some pruning is required in order to avoid them becoming leggy, particularly in the case of the taller-growing cultivars of *Calluna* and *Erica vagans*. This must not be overdone, and all that is needed is to remove – either after flowering, or, better still, in March or early April – about two-thirds of the long central flower spike, encouraging the side growths to develop. This is best done with a knife or secateurs, but once the plants have grown together to form a group, shears or trimmers can be used, taking care to vary the angle of cut to avoid producing a flat or clipped appearance.

Although heathers may live to a considerable age their effective life in the garden, especially of the taller summer-flowering types, is limited. After seven to 10 years the flower spikes shorten, growth becomes hard and woody, and when this stage is reached, pruning has little effect in rejuvenating the plants. It is better to take cuttings and raise a fresh stock of young plants or to replace the old group with a different cultivar.

Many heathers have handsome foliage in tones of gold, yellow or grey, and in winter, after severe frost, these deepen to shades of russet and flame. The dead flower spikes of *Erica vagans* and *E. ciliaris* show up well when lit by low winter sunshine, and all these plants are best left until the end of March or early April before being trimmed.

Now to Group 2 and the many cultivars of *Erica herbacea* (syn. *E. carnea*) and *E.* × *darleyensis* which are among the finest winter-flowering shrubs, colourful from November through to March or early April. Most of them are low-growing and compact and require little or no regular pruning. Very vigorous cultivars such as *E. herbacea* 'Springwood White' having a spreading, invasive habit of growth and may well smother less vigorous cultivars unless they are kept under control by pruning immediately they have finished flowering.

Group 3 comprises the taller-growing species such as *Erica lusitanica, E. terminalis* and the beautiful but somewhat tender *E. australis*. These need no regular pruning beyond the occasional removal of old or dead wood and the maintenance of shape and balance. If heavy snow breaks the stems of tree heaths or they are split by severe frost, any such winter damage should be removed in the spring when the risk of severe weather is over, and when fresh growth will quickly hide the scars of pruning.

Tree Pruning While some pruning and shaping of young trees can be undertaken by the amateur gardener, it cannot be emphasised too strongly that treatment of mature and large specimens should always be left to the professional. While a few lower branches can probably be removed with perfect safety while standing on a stepladder, there is a very considerable risk of falling and injury if an unskilled person climbs up into a tree and attempts to prune high branches.

However, much useful work can be achieved by the gardener in the first few years after a tree is planted, the essential objective being to establish and maintain its natural form and habit of growth. It is vital to ensure that the leading shoot, the vertical continuation of the central stem, is maintained until such time as it grows out of reach. Should this be damaged,

188. *In the case of taller-growing heathers, like some cultivars of* Calluna vulgaris, *it is necessary to prune the individual flowering stems during the two or three years following planting. Remove about two-thirds of the long central flower spike in March or early April to encourage side growths to develop. Note where the cuts are made in the above illustration.*

then the side shoots will become dominant, and the natural outline of the tree be lost. If the leading shoot is broken or frosted, the shoot immediately below it should be tied in vertically, either to the dead leader or to a cane tied to the main stem, and after a year or two this will take over as the new leading shoot.

Even more than with shrubs, the natural branching habit and outline of a tree is a characteristic and important part of its value as a feature in the garden. Pruning of side branches and lateral growth therefore needs to be done most carefully to avoid destroying this quality. Thinning, or the removal of complete branches, is much better than merely shortening them back, which tends to produce an unattractive pollarded appearance, accentuated by the vigorous growth reaction consequent upon such restrictive pruning.

Trees can be pruned either when they are dormant or in full leaf, but with some, such as birch, walnuts and maples it is best to avoid the period in late winter or early spring when the great surge of growth may cause the tree to "bleed" through an open pruning cut. While this is unlikely to cause the death of a tree, it is obviously an unnecessary loss of energy and can also be unsightly and worrying.

Pruning fruit   See Chapter 28, "Space Effective Fruit Growing", pp.231 to 250 where the pruning of individual fruits is dealt with separately.

189. *If the leading shoot of a young tree is broken or frosted* (A), *the shoot immediately below it* (B) *should be tied vertically, either to the dead leader or a cane tied to the main stem* (C).

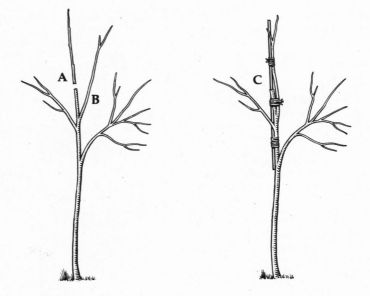

37.

Pest and Disease Control

It is impossible to keep every plant in a garden completely healthy but it is essential to carry out some measures to control pests and diseases to enable ornamentals to show their true worth and for fruit and vegetables to produce high yielding crops of good quality. The first basic principle to observe therefore is to buy good seed, bulbs or plants as pests and diseases can so easily be introduced into a garden on cheap plants bought in bulk. It is then vital to make sure that the plants are well cared for by correct feeding, mulching and watering. Control weeds (see Chapter 38) and cut grass regularly even in orchards. Irrespective of whether trees are grown in grass or under arable conditions, always maintain a clear area around the base of each tree. Prune trees and shrubs as necessary to prevent dense growth and allow a good circulation of air. Be hygienic in the garden.

In this chapter it is not possible to mention all those troubles which have been recorded on plants so only the commoner pests, diseases and disorders are included. The term pest encompasses all animals that damage plants. The definition of a disease, however, is any deviation from the normal, but here the term covers only those troubles caused by parasitic organisms. Any symptom due to unsuitable cultural conditions is described as a disorder.

Some pests are large enough to be seen, but for most diseases and microscopic pests such as eelworms and mites it is necessary to identify the pest or disease from the symptoms alone. Shortage of space does not permit full descriptions of all the troubles mentioned in this chapter and such information should be obtained elsewhere.

PESTS

Pests range in size from microscopic organisms such as eelworms and gall mites to large animals such as deer. The main groups of pests and the ways in which they damage plants are as follows:

NEMATODES Nematodes or eelworms are microscopic worm-like creatures that feed by sucking the contents of plant cells. Some, like root knot eelworms and potato cyst eelworms, attack the roots of plants. Others, like the narcissus, onion and phlox eelworm, live inside the stems and leaves of plants, while the chrysanthemum and fern eelworms are largely confined to the foliage. Most of the nematodes that damage garden plants live inside the host plant and cannot be seen unless extracted and examined with a microscope. The symptoms caused include brown leaves, distorted and stunted growth, and early death of plants. There are no chemical controls available to amateur gardeners and so control is limited to burning affected plants and adopting a policy of crop rotation. For cyst eelworms and root knot eelworms it may be necessary to rest infested ground for up to seven years but two years should be sufficient for other eelworms.

SLUGS AND SNAILS These damage seedlings and the foliage and flowers of many herbaceous plants. Keeled slugs are also a problem below soil level where they tunnel into potato tubers, root vegetables and bulbs. Damage can occur throughout the year but is most serious during spells of warm, wet weather. Slugs and snails often leave a tell-tale trail of silvery slime where they have been feeding. They can be controlled with slug pellets based on metaldehyde or methiocarb. The latter is the more effective, especially under damp conditions which is when the greatest number of slugs and snails are likely to be feeding.

WOODLICE AND MILLIPEDES These are common soil animals which sometimes damage seedlings. They rarely damage mature plants although they may enlarge holes started by slugs and other pests. Much of their food consists of rotting plant material, so good garden hygiene reduces their hiding places. If damage does occur, these animals can be controlled with HCH dust or methiocarb slug pellets.

MITES This is a large and diverse group which damages plants in a number of ways. Red spider mites, such as occur on greenhouse plants, apple and plum, conifers, lime and willow, feed by sucking sap from the undersides of the leaves. This causes a fine mottled discoloration of the upper leaf surface. Heavy infestations may be accompanied by a fine silken webbing, and damaged leaves may dry up and fall prematurely. Eriophyid mites are also known as gall mites. Some, like blackcurrant big bud mite and cytisus mite, are harmful because they prevent the normal development of the buds. Other species, like pear leaf blister mite, lime nail gall mite and acer pimple gall mite, are less damaging since, although they cause galls on the leaf surface, they do not cause any real harm to the plant. Tarsonemid mites are minute creatures that develop in the shoot tips, crowns and flower buds of plants such as strawberry, Michaelmas daisy, cyclamen, begonia, narcissus and amaryllis. Their feeding causes stunted growth and distorted or abnormal flowers.

Red spider mites can be controlled with dimethoate, formothion, malathion and derris. Several applications are necessary as these mites breed rapidly and the egg stage is not killed by these chemicals. As an alternative, biological control can be used against the glasshouse red spider mite (see p. 328). None of the chemicals currently available to amateur gardeners gives good control of tarsonemid or eriophyid mites. Plants affected by the former will never make good plants and should be burnt. Eriophyid mite infestations can often be tolerated although it is advisable to pick off and burn galled buds during the winter. The fungicide benomyl gives some protection against big bud mite if applied to black currants as the first flowers open, with two further treatments at two-week intervals.

INSECTS Insects are by far the largest group of pests the gardener has to contend with. The insect orders which contain plant pests are as follows:
1. *Dermaptera* A small order containing only earwigs. These feed at night on the flowers and foliage of many plants, especially clematis, salvia, dahlia and chrysanthemums. They can be controlled by spraying or dusting at dusk on warm evenings with HCH, carbaryl, fenitrothion or trichlorphon.
2. *Hemiptera* A large order that includes capsid bugs, froghoppers, leafhoppers, adelgids, suckers, aphids, whiteflies, scale insects and mealybugs. All feed by sucking sap, and the last five types mentioned may also soil the foliage with a sticky sugary liquid known as honeydew. This attracts ants and may become colonised by a black sooty mould. A wide range of chemical controls is available for these pests. Scale insects and mealybugs are best dealt with by malathion or nicotine; whiteflies with permethrin, bioresmethrin, pirimiphos-methyl sprays or HCH smokes; aphids with pirimicarb, malathion, HCH, pirimiphos-methyl, dimethoate, formothion or menazon; the other hemipterous pests are controlled by the chemicals listed for aphids with the exception of pirimicarb and menazon. For glasshouse whitefly and mealybugs see also biological control (p. 328).
3. *Thysanoptera* Thrips are small, narrow, yellow or black insects that suck sap from the leaves and flowers of plants such as gladiolus, pea, privet and lilac. They cause a silvery discoloration of the upper leaf surface. The chemicals mentioned above under Hemiptera, with the exception of pirimicarb and menazon, also control thrips.

4. *Lepidoptera* Moths and butterflies have caterpillar larvae that attack a wide range of plants. Most caterpillars eat holes in the foliage but some feed on roots, e.g., cutworms, swift moth larvae, while others tunnel into fruits, e.g., codling moth, pea moth. The caterpillars of tortrix moths attack a wide range of shrubs and herbaceous plants in greenhouses and the garden. They have a habit of binding leaves together with a silken webbing and feeding out of sight. Other moths, such as the buff tip moth, the hawthorn webber, small ermine moths and the lackey moth, have gregarious larvae that often cover their feeding area with a dense silken webbing. Gregarious caterpillars can be dealt with by pruning out infested branches, but insecticides may be required. Insecticides effective against caterpillars include permethrin, derris, fenitrothion, trichlorphon, HCH and carbaryl. They are best used against young caterpillars, since the later instars are more difficult to kill. Soil dwelling caterpillars such as cutworms and swift moth larvae can be controlled with chlorpyrifos or diazinon granules.

5. *Coleoptera* Some beetles have soil-dwelling larvae that feed on roots and are known as wireworms, chafer grubs and vine weevil grubs. They can be controlled with granular soil insecticides, such as diazinon, chlorpyrifos or bromophos. Other beetles, such as flea beetles, asparagus beetle and the red lily beetle, feed mainly on the foliage, and in many cases damage is caused by both the larval and adult stages. Some beetles attack fruits and these include the raspberry beetle and strawberry seed beetle. Leaf and fruit feeding beetles can be controlled with derris, malathion, fenitrothion or pirimiphos-methyl. Methiocarb slug pellets can also be used against strawberry seed beetles.

6. *Diptera* With all fly pests it is the larval stage, a legless maggot, that causes the damage. Some important examples, e.g., leatherjackets, onion fly, cabbage root fly and carrot fly, attack the roots of plants. Leatherjackets can be controlled by watering turf with HCH in October but vegetable root flies should be controlled by using diazinon, chlorpyrifos or bromophos at planting time. Some flies have larvae that feed as leaf miners and they tunnel the foliage of plants such as chrysanthemum, delphinium, holly and celery. Leafminers are controlled with insecticides such as pirimiphos-methyl, nicotine and trichlorphon. Another important group of fly pests are the gall midges. These have tiny orange-white maggots that cause distorted leaves on violets and black currant shoot tips, and cause pear fruitlets to blacken and fall a few weeks after petal fall. Gall midges can be controlled by spraying with HCH or fenitrothion. Bulbs such as narcissus and amaryllis are tunnelled by maggots of the large narcissus fly and this results in the death of the bulb. This pest is difficult to control but bulbs can be given some protection by dusting the base of the plants with HCH in May–June when the adult flies are laying their eggs.

7. *Hymenoptera* This group includes the ants, wasps, gall wasps and sawflies. The last-mentioned is the most important type of pest. Sawflies have caterpillar-like larvae that can defoliate plants such as Solomon's seal, aquilegia, *Aruncus dioicus*, willow, gooseberry and currants. Other damaging sawflies are the rose leaf-rolling sawfly and the apple sawfly. The former causes rose leaves to become tightly rolled up in late May–June, while the latter tunnels into apple fruitlets, causing them to fall from the trees in June. Sawflies can be controlled with derris, permethrin, pirimiphos-methyl, fenitrothion and HCH. Ants and wasps can be a nuisance if they are numerous and it may be necessary to control their nests by using a proprietary ant or wasp powder containing HCH, chlordane or carbaryl. Gall wasps mainly attack oaks and they cause various bizarre structures such as oak apples, marble galls, spangle galls and knopper galls on the twigs, leaves and acorns. None of these galls cause any real harm and so control measures are not necessary.

BIRDS Birds are mostly welcome in gardens but some can be serious pests. Bullfinches eat the flower buds of tree and bush fruits and some ornamentals during the winter; blackbirds eat ripening fruits; sparrows shred the flowers of crocus and polyanthus and they eat grass seed; pigeons eat brassicas. The best protection is given by fruit or vegetable cages or some other form of netting. Where this is not possible bird repellent sprays and bird-scaring devices can be used, although this type of protection is generally of a short-term nature.

MAMMALS Mammals have various ways of damaging plants. Bulbs, corms and pea seeds are eaten by mice, voles and squirrels; the stems of woody plants are gnawed by voles, rabbits and squirrels; foliage and young shoots are eaten by rabbits and deer; fruits are taken by squirrels, mice and voles; lawns and flower beds are spoiled by the soil heaps thrown up by moles. In some cases mammals can be controlled by trapping or shooting, but in most gardens plants have to be protected by netting or the use of repellent substances.

DISEASES

Various types of parasitic organisms, commonly called pathogens, can cause plant diseases. By far the largest and the most important group is the fungi. These organisms are plants but as they contain no chlorophyll (green colour) they are unable to synthesize their own carbohydrates and have to use as food those which have been manufactured by green plants. Most fungi are multicellular and are composed of microscopic threads, but large masses of threads may grow together to form structures which can be seen with the naked eye. Resting bodies of many fungi are formed in this way and they can remain viable for many months or even years under adverse conditions. Similarly the fruiting bodies by which some fungi produce their spores, are formed in the same way.

Some bacteria can also infect plants although they cannot break down the cuticle of higher plants as can most pathogenic fungi. Infection, therefore, takes place through natural openings or wounds. Although very simple in structure, being one-celled organisms, bacteria can reproduce very rapidly by division of each cell so that a chain or cluster of spores is formed. Those bacteria which are plant pathogens are mobile and can remain alive when dry as on the surface of seeds, so that they are readily transmitted on seeds, tubers, bulbs and other plant organs, and also by wind, water, insects, slugs and snails.

Although much smaller than bacteria, as they can only be seen under an electron microscope, viruses and virus-like organisms are very important plant pathogens. Virus particles are able to multiply within plant cells, but have more characteristics in common with chemicals than with living organisms. Infection of plants can occur through wounds caused when the epidermal cells are broken by handling and by physical contact between a diseased and healthy plant and a few viruses are seed-borne or pollen-borne. Most viruses, however, are introduced into plants by pest vectors particularly aphids or eelworms. Following infection nearly every cell of a virus-diseased plant becomes infected thus preventing an easy cure, so that destruction of a virus-infected plant is usually recommended.

FUNGI

1. Downy Mildews These diseases can be difficult to identify as in most cases the fungus grows only on the under surface of the leaves and is not very obvious, though it may show as a grey, white or purplish bloom of spores. Affected leaves show yellow blotches on the upper surface or may be deformed, as on severely affected wallflowers, or even collapse, as in onions. Other plants most likely to be affected are seedlings of lettuce and brassicas, particularly cauliflowers, but downy mildews are only really troublesome where the seedlings are overcrowded and aeration is poor. They can, therefore, be prevented by sowing seed thinly on a fresh site each year in well-drained soil with a good tilth. If infection occurs spray the seedlings with Bordeaux mixture or mancozeb, but use dichlofluanid on young cauliflowers. Sterilize the soil in frames with formalin before sowing the next crop to kill resting bodies of the fungi, which may have contaminated the soil.

2. Powdery Mildews Such diseases are easily identified as they show as a white powdery coating on leaves, stems and flowers of many types of plants, e.g., apples, gooseberries, roses, begonias and Michaelmas daisies. Some powdery mildews of herbaceous plants have a wide host range, including weeds, but others are specific to only one type of plant, e.g., rose mildew. These fungi flourish in humid atmospheres but plants are more susceptible to infection if dry at the roots. Prevent infection, therefore, by ventilating greenhouses well to reduce the humidity, and by mulching and watering plants, especially those against walls, to prevent the soil from drying out. At the first signs of trouble spray with benomyl, thiophanate-methyl, triforine with bupirimate or dinocap (or use the latter as a fumigant in greenhouses), but copper and sulphur fungicides can be used on herbaceous plants or shrubby plants in hedges. As most powdery mildew fungi overwinter in buds or on shoots, cut off and burn infected shoots at the end of the season.

3. Moulds Many fungi which can be classified as moulds can infect plants, the commonest and most troublesome being grey mould (*Botrytis cinerea*). This fungus shows as a greyish-brown mould on rotting tissues and is best known on strawberries. It can also be troublesome on greenhouse plants where the atmosphere is very humid, and can also cause dieback of woody shoots which have been injured. Spores of the fungus are always present in the air and infect plants through wounds and dead and damaged tissues, but infection can occur by contact between diseased and healthy tissues.

All diseased or dying parts should be removed and burned to control this disease. Ventilate greenhouses well to reduce the humidity and fumigate with tecnazene smokes. Soft fruit should be sprayed as the first flowers open with benomyl, dichlofluanid (except under glass) or thiophanate-methyl, repeating twice at 10- to 14-day intervals, or with captan or thiram except on fruit to be preserved.

4. Other Botrytis Species Several other *Botrytis* species attack plants but most are specific to one type of host, e.g., one causes lily disease and another paeony wilt. In most cases the fungi cause rotting of the tissues which may become covered with a greyish-brown mould in which develop small roundish black resting bodies of the fungus. All diseased parts should be removed, the crowns of plants dusted with dry Bordeaux powder and the developing leaves and shoots sprayed with a copper fungicide in the case of lilies or dichlofluanid for paeonies.

5. Other Moulds Blight causes brown blotches on tomato fruits, a dry rot of potato tubers and blackening and rotting of the leaves on both hosts. Prevent infection by spraying with mancozeb or a copper fungicide before potato haulms meet in the rows and from early August onwards for outdoor tomatoes. Use the same fungicides to prevent leaf mould which causes severe blotching on tomatoes under glass and grow cladosporium-resistant cultivars in a well-ventilated greenhouse.

6. Rusts A true rust is a fungus which usually affects the leaves but can also attack shoots, flowers and fruits. Brown, orange or yellow powdery masses of spores are produced on the affected tissues, occasionally arranged in concentric rings. Rust diseases can be troublesome on weak trees of plum, birch etc. causing premature defoliation, but such rusts can usually be prevented by mulching, watering and feeding the trees. Diseased leaves should be raked up or removed, and burned no matter what the host. Rose rust can be partially controlled by spraying with maneb or thiram but the best fungicide, oxycarboxin is only available in commercial packs. These fungicides can also be used to control pelargonium rust provided the greenhouse is ventilated well to reduce the humidity. Hollyhock rust is difficult to control and it is advisable to raise new plants every other year. It may be possible to prevent antirrhinum rust by growing rust-resistant cultivars but the resistance has broken down in many localities.

Leaf Spots Most leaf-spotting fungi are specific to certain hosts, thus rose black spot will affect only roses. This disease shows as roundish black blotches from around the edges of which fine fungal threads grow outwards over the leaf surface. Similarly, the spots caused by scab on apple, pear and pyracantha fruits and leaves do not have a definite margin. Some other leaf spots are small, e.g., those of anthracnose on weeping willow which causes premature defoliation, others are larger and spread outwards in concentric rings as in hellebore leaf blotch. Yet other leaf spots bear pin-head sized black fruiting bodies of the fungus, e.g., chrysanthemum leaf blotch.

Over-wintering of most leaf-spotting fungi occurs on fallen leaves so these should be raked up and burned. The following spring spray with benomyl, captan, copper, dichlofluanid, mancozeb or thiophanate-methyl as the leaves unfold and repeat as necessary through the summer. Winter treatments have not proved effective in controlling black spot at Wisley. This disease as with other similar leaf diseases is worse on weak plants so apply a foliar feed at the same time as a compatible fungicide to encourage vigour. If the trouble persists in spite of regular spraying check if the bushes were planted correctly; if necessary, lift and replant more carefully.

OTHER LEAF DISEASES Two common diseases cause distortion of leaves, namely azalea gall and peach leaf curl. In each case the leaves become very swollen and distorted, are at first pinkish in colour but later become covered with a white bloom of spores. They eventually turn brown and, in the case of peaches, fall prematurely. If possible affected leaves should be removed and burned before they turn white. Diseased indoor azaleas should be sprayed with mancozeb but on outdoor deciduous azaleas use a copper fungicide and spray as soon as the new leaves appear. Peaches should also be sprayed with copper in January or early February, repeating a fortnight later and just before leaf fall.

CANKERS AND OTHER SHOOT DISEASES Apple canker is the most troublesome disease of this type. Deep cankers develop on the branches, thus exposing the inner tissues. Dieback occurs if the stem is girdled. The fungus can enter through wounds caused by other diseases and pests, which should be controlled. All dying branches and diseased tissues should be cut out and burned and the wounds painted with a canker paint. Spray severely diseased apples with Bordeaux mixture just before leaf fall, at 50 per cent leaf fall and at bud burst when most spore release occurs.

Many small cankers are produced by willow anthracnose but remove cankered shoots on small, slightly affected trees. A copper fungicide or thiophanate-methyl applied at bud burst, repeating two or three times at fortnightly intervals, may help to control it.

Raspberries are affected by several shoot diseases including cane spot and more importantly spur blight and cane blight. Spur blight leads to death of buds or dieback of shoots whereas cane blight kills complete canes causing them to become brittle so they are easily snapped off. Remove any diseased canes preferably to below soil level. Spray with a copper fungicide, benomyl, dichlofluanid or thiophanate-methyl as new canes develop, repeating at fortnightly intervals until flowering ceases.

OTHER FRUIT DISEASES Brown rot causes a rapid decay of top fruits on trees and in store. The fungus produces cushions of white spores on the brown rotting fruits before they dry up. It then overwinters on the mummified fruits on the tree or ground and also on small shoot cankers. It can only be kept in check by destroying all rotten or withered fruits and by cutting out dead shoots.

WOUND PARASITES A typical example of a wound parasite is the silver leaf fungus which causes silvering of the foliage on an infected branch, followed by progressive dieback of the tree or shrub. Many types of woody plants are susceptible to infection and not only plums; for example, rhododendrons and roses are other plants affected. Another very common and troublesome wound parasite is the coral spot fungus. Once it has gained an entrance it causes dieback of branches or occasionally the complete death of a plant. The dead shoots bear numerous coral-red pustules of spores. Plants most susceptible to infection are acers, elaeagnus, figs and red currants.

Affected branches should be cut out to a point several inches below the apparently diseased tissues, which, in the case of silver leaf, show a stain in the wood, and all wounds should be painted with a protective paint. Destroy all woody debris on which the fungi can live as saprophytes.

SOIL-BORNE DISEASES Club root, which produces swollen distorted roots on brassicas, wallflowers, etc., occurs where susceptible plants are grown year after year in acid soils, particularly those which are poorly drained. Liming, together with the use of 4 per cent calomel dust, or preferably benomyl or thiophanate-methyl may help to prevent it but it is impossible to check it completely unless the soil is sterilized with dazomet, and crops are rotated.

Petunias, china asters, pansies, sweet peas and beans are also susceptible to infection by soil-borne fungi which attack the roots and cause the plants to wilt. Such troubles can be prevented by rotating bedding plants and also vegetables. Once the fungi causing these troubles have built up in the soil, the only good method of control is soil sterilization. Some control, however, may be achieved by watering regularly with captan, Cheshunt compound or zineb, particularly in the case of damping-off. This disease is due to several different soil and water-borne organisms. They cause the collapse of all types of seedlings at ground level. The disease is most troublesome where seedlings are overcrowded due to too thick seed sowing, or on seedlings which are over-watered or are in unsterilized compost or watered with water from a dirty tank or butt. It can be prevented, therefore, by sowing thinly in sterilized compost or soil of a good tilth, and by watering carefully with clean water.

The commonest and most troublesome root parasite is the honey fungus which causes the death, often rapidly, of woody plants. White fan-shaped growths of fungus develop beneath the bark of the roots and the main stem of the plant at and just above ground level. Brownish-black root-like structures known as rhizomorphs grow from the diseased tissues and out through the soil to spread the disease. In autumn honey-coloured toad-stools may appear at the base of the dying plant. Dead and dying plants should be dug out together with as many roots as possible and burnt. The soil should be treated with a proprietary phenolic emulsion or sterilized with a 2 per cent solution of formaldehyde, 1 pint(570ml) in 6gal(27l) water applied at the rate of 5gal(22.5l) to the square yard(m^2), or changed completely before replanting.

BULB DISEASES Bulb diseases are also frequently soil-borne. Thus tulip fire which shows as rotting of the shoots and spotting of the flowers is often due to soil infection. If any bulbous plant looks unhealthy it should be lifted and the bulb or corm examined for signs of rotting or the presence of fungal resting bodies which show as small black structures on or between the scales. Such diseased bulbs should be burned and the remainder dusted with quintozene and this dust should also be raked into the soil before replanting on a fresh site. Alternatively, dip bulbs, and in particular, gladiolus corms, in a solution of captan, benomyl or thiophanate-methyl after lifting or before replanting.

BACTERIAL DISEASES The most important bacterial diseases of plants can be grouped broadly into three main types according to the nature of the tissues affected and the effects produced. When the soft tissues alone are attacked they disintegrate and a soft rot occurs. Such bacterial soft rots are usually secondary and follow injury by such pests as slugs, by diseases such as potato blight or even frost damage. Once the fleshy tissues of carrots, potatoes, celery, rhizomes, bulbs etc. have been entered, the bacteria reduce the tissues to a foul-smelling wet rot. There is no cure for such diseases and badly affected vegetables and plants should be destroyed. It is best, therefore, to grow crops well, avoid injuries by pests, diseases and mechanical damage and to store root crops and bulbs well. In the case of irises affected by rhizome rot, however, the diseased tissues should be cut out and the cut surfaces and healthy clumps dusted with dry Bordeaux powder. This fungicide can also be used to try and save cucumbers affected by stem canker which is a similar type of disease.

When woody plants are affected by bacteria, the most common symptom produced is a canker. Bacterial canker of *Prunus* species including plums and cherries results in dieback and the affected shoots are flattened and bear exudations of gum. All dying branches should be cut out and Bordeaux mixture applied to severely diseased trees in mid-August, September and October.

A disease which looks similar to bacterial canker is fire blight but it is found only on apples, pears and related ornamentals such as *Cotoneaster*, *Sorbus* etc. This disease causes blackening of the flowers and progressive dieback of shoots on which hang brown and withered leaves. If this disease is suspected, the owner is obliged by law to notify the Ministry of Agriculture office in the locality who will give instructions as to how the plant should be treated if fire blight is confirmed.

Some bacteria affect the outermost layers of meristematic cells and stimulate them to reproduce abnormally so that tumours or galls are formed. In crown gall one large gall or a chain of smaller galls are produced on the roots of many woody plants or occasionally on the shoots of roses, blackberries and daphnes. This disease is not considered to be serious but leafy gall is much more troublesome as it affects herbaceous plants and results in the production of numerous abnormal leafy shoots at ground level. Chrysanthemums, sweet peas, pelargoniums and dahlias are affected most frequently. Any galled plant should be destroyed.

VIRUSES AND VIRAL-LIKE ORGANISMS Very many different symptoms can be caused by viruses and viral-like organisms. The main symptoms are stunting, distortion, mottling or striping of leaves, deformed flowers and breaking of the flower colour. Plants most susceptible to infection are marrows, tomatoes, sweet peas, lilies, raspberries and strawberries but almost all types of plants can become infected. Any severely diseased plant should be burned and, in the case of soft fruit, only plants certified to be free of virus infection should be planted. As aphids are frequently vectors of viruses, particularly cucumber mosaic virus which has an enormous host range, these pests should be controlled by suitable insecticides. Weeds can also harbour viruses so should be destroyed.

Chemical Control

In the previous pages of this chapter various chemicals have been mentioned for the control of pests and diseases, as for some troubles spraying is the best or only method of control. Chemicals used properly are efficient but they can be a danger to plants or user if misused. The gardener should, therefore, use chemicals only when really necessary, selecting those suitable for the type of pest or disease to be controlled and applied at the correct times and at the correct concentration, according to the manufacturer's recommendations. It is essential, therefore, to read carefully the label on the pack.

All chemicals should be handled carefully and stored safely out of reach of children and away from food. Spray equipment must be washed out carefully after use so that no traces of chemical are left, and insecticides and fungicides should not be applied with apparatus which has been used for weedkillers.

When diluting chemicals for use rubber gloves should be worn and they should be washed carefully afterwards. If possible spraying should be carried out when it is dry, calm and frost-free but if there is a breeze adjacent plants should be protected with plastic sheets if the spray is likely to damage them, e.g., when using tar oil on fruit trees. When using non-systemic chemicals try to obtain an even cover on both upper and lower leaf surfaces by applying the spray from all sides and spraying to run off. Do not spray with insecticides when plants are in flower except in unavoidable situations and then only in the evening when bees are not working. If much spraying with insecticides is to be carried out, notify local beekeepers so that hives can be kept closed. In addition, take care to prevent contamination of ponds, ditches and waterways with chemicals or used containers.

INSECTICIDES Many chemicals have been developed for the control of invertebrate pests. These can be divided between five chemical groups, and it is useful to know which grouping a chemical belongs to, since if pesticide resistance occurs it will be necessary to use a chemical of another type.

"Natural" insecticides and Related Compounds These are chemicals such as nicotine, derris, quassia and pyrethrum, which are derived from plants. Included with this group are synthetic compounds related to pyrethrum, such as resmethrin, bioresmethrin and permethrin. These are sometimes known collectively as pyrethroids. All of the chemicals in this group have a low toxicity to mammals and birds, and, with the exception of permethrin, are of short persistence. They are contact poisons which control aphids, leafhoppers, thrips, beetles and caterpillars. The pyrethroids are particularly useful against whiteflies.

Organochlorine Compounds Only two, HCH and chlordane, are currently available to amateur gardeners. They are persistent chemicals and this is why other members of this group, such as DDT, dieldrin and aldrin, are no longer sold for garden use. HCH, or gamma-BHC as it was formerly known, controls many pests, including aphids, caterpillars, whiteflies, capsids, beetles, leatherjackets, ants, woodlice, millipedes and thrips. The use of chlordane is confined to the control of earthworms in lawns and ants.

Organophosphorus Compounds This group contains the largest number of compounds and can be divided into contact and systemic types. The latter group includes dimethoate, formothion and menazon. These chemicals are absorbed into the plant tissues and will move upwards in the sap stream. They control sap feeding insects and red spider mites, including those which are feeding in concealed places, e.g., underneath curled leaves. Pests which eat the entire leaf rather than just the sap are not very susceptible to systemic compounds. Contact insecticides include bromophos, chlorpyrifos, diazinon, dichlorvos, fenitrothion, malathion, pirimiphos-methyl and trichlorphon. The first three chemicals are used principally against soil insects such as vegetable root flies, wireworms, chafer grubs, leatherjackets and cutworms. Most of the others control a wide range of pests such as caterpillars, aphids, scale insects, mealybugs, red spider mites, earwigs, beetles and sawflies. Trichlorphon is more selective and is used mainly against caterpillars, leafminers and earwigs.

Carbamate Compounds A small group consisting of carbaryl and pirimicarb. The former is a contact poison used against caterpillars, beetles, earwigs and wasp nests. The latter is of interest as it is a selective poison, controlling aphids but not harming beneficial insects such as ladybirds, bees and animals used in biological control systems.

Other Compounds This is a mixture of unrelated chemicals. It includes tar-oil wash for the control of overwintering eggs on deciduous trees and shrubs; metaldehyde and methiocarb which are used as poison baits for slugs and snails; greasebands to stop female winter moths from climbing the trunks of fruit trees; and naphthalene which is a soil fumigant used against vine weevil grubs and other soil pests.

FUNGICIDES The name fungicide is given to any chemical which will control diseases whether caused by fungi or bacteria. Most diseases can be controlled by several different fungicides. It is not always possible to determine which will be the most useful in controlling the diseases present in a garden as the effectiveness of some fungicides does depend to a certain extent on the environmental conditions. Some are available as dusts, e.g., dry Bordeaux powder, but most are either wettable powders or liquids which are mixed with a large quantity of water for spraying. Most fungicides, e.g., captan, thiram and mancozeb, used by gardeners act as protectants in that they stop the germination of fungal spores thus preventing infection. They must, therefore, be applied before any symptoms are seen or at the very first signs of trouble. However, some fungicides have systemic properties, e.g., benomyl, thiophanate-methyl and triforine. As they are taken in and translocated for short distances in plant tissues they will control some types of fungal growth inside the host plant and so control existing infections. Unfortunately, too frequent use of such fungicides can lead to the build up of tolerant strains of fungi so that in some areas grey mould, rose black spot and certain powdery mildews are no longer controlled by some systemic fungicides. There are very few contact fungicides available to amateurs which will eradicate diseases, but formaldehyde is of this type as it will kill soil-borne fungi.

Biological Control

Most pests have natural enemies which either prey on or parasitise them and so help to limit their numbers. Some well-known examples are ladybirds preying on aphids, thrushes eating snails, and ichneumon wasps parasitising the caterpillars of moths and sawflies. Although useful, these natural enemies do not usually give good enough control to prevent pest damage, since their life cycles are related to those of the pest species and they do not become numerous until the pest population is high. In some cases it is possible to manipulate the circumstances under which the predators and parasites operate and so increase their efficiency. This type of pest control is known as biological control and for some pests it can be an effective alternative to the use of chemicals. The opportunities for using biological control occur mainly in greenhouses against pests such as glasshouse whitefly, glasshouse red spider mite and mealybugs. The controls available for these pests are, respectively, a parasitic chalcid wasp, *Encarsia formosa*, a predatory mite *Phytoseiulus persimilis*, and a predatory ladybird, *Cryptolaemus montrouzieri*. For the control of lepidopterous caterpillars there is a spray containing spores of the bacterium *Bacillus thuringiensis*. This is sprayed onto plants being attacked by caterpillars and the spores are ingested as the leaves are eaten. Once inside the insect's gut the spores become active and the caterpillar soon becomes ill and dies. This bacterial disease is specific to lepidopterous larvae and so is harmless to other invertebrates and higher animals. The above-mentioned biological controls are available during the summer months from specialist suppliers who can be found through their advertisements in gardening magazines. In the future it may be possible to obtain parasites for the control of chrysanthemum leaf miner and certain aphid species.

Biological control has some advantages over the use of chemicals. The predators and parasites are very specific in their feeding habits and they will not feed on other animals or plants. Some plants are liable to be damaged by pesticides, and food plants may be spoiled by unpleasant tastes or poisonous residues if a chemical is used too close to harvesting. These problems do not occur with biological control. Pests can develop resistance to pesticides but not to predators or parasites. Once established, the biological controls will breed and control the pests without any further attention. This avoids the need for frequent spraying and biological control continues until the pest is eliminated, even while the greenhouse owner is on holiday. This system of pest control is not perfect and it has its limitations. The predators and parasites can tolerate cool conditions but, if they are to breed faster than the pests and so give control, they require daytime temperatures of 70°F(21°C) or more with a good light intensity. Their effective season is usually from late April to September, and cold weather in the winter often kills the biological controls. Predators and parasites cannot give the instant reduction in pest numbers that one gets with a pesticide. They first need to breed and increase their numbers until they are able to start reducing the pest population. If pest damage is to be avoided, the biological controls need to be introduced before the plants become heavily infested. There is no point in introducing them before the pests are present as they are unable to breed or survive for long without the pests. Most insecticides and the fungicide benomyl are harmful to predators and parasites and this can make the control of pests for which there are no biological controls difficult. One insecticide, pirimicarb (ICI Rapid Greenfly Killer), can be used safely but this does not control pests other than aphids. If it becomes necessary to spray against pests such as glasshouse leafhopper, thrips, leaf miners or scale insects, short persistence insecticides such as nicotine, derris, pyrethrum, resmethrin or bioresmethrin should be used. Before spraying, some plants with active predators or parasites on them should be removed and kept out of the greenhouse for seven days until the effects of the insecticide have gone.

Cultural Control

A gardener can do a great deal to prevent the build-up of pests and diseases by good cultural treatment. Indeed, correct gardening techniques and treatments are essential for the good growth of plants, otherwise the physiological disorders discussed later are likely to occur.

SOIL PREPARATION Thorough preparation of the soil before planting or sowing will ensure that plants get off to a good start so that they will not be subject to diseases such as damping-off and downy mildew. A good tilth aids quick germination which is of benefit against seedling pests such as flea beetle and bean seed fly.

SOWING AND PLANTING Seeds should be sown at the correct time taking into account local conditions. Germination will be poor and plants will not thrive if seed is sown prematurely or too late or too deeply. However, late sowing of carrots will help to avoid attack by the first generation of carrot fly. Too dense sowing will result in thin and weak seedlings which are susceptible to downy mildew and other diseases. When planting any type of plant a hole large enough to accommodate the roots should be prepared, the roots should be well spread out in all directions and the plant should not be inserted too deeply. A tree or shrub which is poorly planted, or a plant incorrectly potted on or planted out, will not thrive but will start to die back after a year or so.

CHOICE OF PLANTS Local advice should be sought as to which plants are likely to do well or badly under the local soil and climatic conditions. It is particularly important to check the pH (see Chapter 33, p. 290) of the soil before planting acid-loving plants such as rhododendrons and camellias as these will never flourish in an alkaline soil. Wherever possible grow cultivars of plants which are resistant to pests and diseases, e.g. 'Avoncrisp' and 'Avondefiance' lettuces resistant to lettuce root aphid and 'Avonresister' a parsnip resistant to canker. 'Maris Piper' and 'Pentland Javelin' are examples of potatoes resistant to the golden potato cyst eelworm, whereas 'Maris Peer' and 'Pentland Beauty' are less susceptible to blight.

ROTATION As mentioned earlier rotation of crops is essential to prevent the build-up of soil-borne diseases such as club root and foot and root rots. It also helps to avoid problems with less mobile soil pests such as eelworms.

HYGIENE Weeds should be destroyed as many of them harbour pests and diseases. Their presence can in some cases nullify the benefits of plant rotation. Remove and burn diseased plants and do not put diseased material on the compost heap. Dispose of pest-infested plants, but not roots, by burying them in the compost heap. Clean out hedge bottoms, collect fallen leaves and fruits, remove and burn dead wood and burn prunings to destroy overwintering eggs and fungal spores.

CARE OF PLANTS Plants are very sensitive to their environment and there is only a relatively small range of conditions where a plant will reach its maximum potential. When cultural conditions are unsuitable, plants are not only more susceptible to pests and diseases but certain well characterized disorders can occur.

Physiological Disorders

LIGHT Good light is needed for most plants. In overcrowded greenhouses which do not receive much sunlight, particularly in long, dark winters, the low light intensity will produce etiolated plants, i.e., thin, weak and colourless plants which may fail to flower. If better light conditions are provided affected plants should recover.

TEMPERATURE Most hardy plants will tolerate a wide range of temperatures but extremes of heat or cold can cause damage. Leaves can be scorched and tomatoes show greenback when hot sun strikes through glass onto moist tissues so prevent such troubles by shading and ventilating greenhouses well. Scalding of fruits can occur in hot summers, causing creamy sunken blotches on the skin. Bulbs stored at too high temperatures may be completely blind the following spring or produce withered flowers.

Cold nights can cause silvering, e.g., on tomatoes or yellowing of young soft foliage as in magnolias. Frost damage results in longitudinal splitting of stems, distortion of leaves and russeting of fruit. Do not grow tender plants in frost pockets. Protect small plants when frost is forecast but protect the crowns of half-hardy perennials throughout the winter, e.g. using a cover made by packing bracken between wire netting.

ATMOSPHERE Humid atmospheres encourage many diseases including powdery mildews, grey mould and tomato leaf mould. Too high humidity can also cause oedema which shows as raised corky patches on the undersurfaces of leaves of many types of plants. Ventilate greenhouses well and water, syringe or spray early so that plant tissues can dry off before evening. Outdoors, peach leaf curl, willow anthracnose and blight are encouraged by wet weather.

In greenhouses and dwelling houses too dry an atmosphere can cause poor growth, bud drop and leaf browning. Those plants which need humid conditions should be syringed daily in hot weather. In centrally-heated houses stand pot plants in large containers packed with moist peat or moss.

WATER SUPPLY Faulty root action will result if the soil is too wet or too dry, leading to poor growth, discoloured leaves, premature defoliation and dieback of shoots. Affected plants will also be susceptible to disease. The most obvious symptom of drought is wilting of leaves but if a plant is affected to this extent it will not recover immediately it is watered. Drought when flower buds are developing can result in bud drop of camellias etc. the following spring. Mulch all plants well with organic matter and water before the soil dries out completely.

Roots affected by waterlogging show a bluish-black discoloration. Drain heavy soils or improve the texture over a wide area and not just in planting holes, otherwise these will act as sumps into which water from the surrounding heavier soil will flow.

Plants affected by faulty root action benefit from foliar feeding during the growing season. It is better, however, to maintain an even supply of moisture in the soil for all plants. Irregular watering can cause such disorders as blossom end rot of tomatoes which shows as a brownish blotch on the fruits and cracking and distortion of vegetables and fruit.

NUTRITION Although many food materials are required by plants most of them are unlikely to become deficient except in some soil-less composts, when plants are fed incorrectly. Even deficiencies of the major nutrients, nitrogen, potassium and phosphorus are less likely to occur than general malnutrition due to neglect, in gardens. A neglected plant, particularly a tree or shrub, will grow poorly, have discoloured leaves which may fall prematurely and start to die back. Make sure that all plants, including woody ones, are fed at least once annually (see Chapter 34, pp. 297 to 303).

Magnesium deficiency however is a common trouble as magnesium is easily leached out of soils by heavy rain. It is also made unavailable by excess potassium in the soil so plants fed with high potash fertilisers e.g. tomatoes and chrysanthemums frequently show typical symptoms, i.e. an orange-yellow and/or purplish discoloration, commencing between the veins on the leaves. Correct this trouble by spraying with ½lb(225g) magnesium sulphate in 2½gal(11.25l) of water plus a spreader.

Lime-induced chlorosis causes pale yellowing between the veins but in severe cases the leaves, especially on the young growth, become almost white. These symptoms develop on certain plants growing in very alkaline soils and those most susceptible are hydrangeas, chaenomeles, ceanothus, raspberries and peaches. The pH must be low for acid-loving plants such as rhododendrons and camellias otherwise in addition to chlorosis of the leaves growth will be poor and flowering reduced. When chlorosis occurs the green colour can often be restored to the foliage by applying proprietary products containing chelated compounds or fritted trace elements. Such treatments are only worthwhile, however, if some attempt is made to reduce the alkalinity by digging in pulverised bark, peat or crushed bracken or sulphur or other chemicals.

CHEMICAL AND MECHANICAL INJURY Carelessness in the garden often results in damage to plants, thus strangling of woody plants caused by tight ties or labels leads to dieback, and wounds caused by lawnmowers, hoeing or other mechanical activities often become infected. The most frequent type of damage, however, is due to the mis-use of chemicals. Hormone weedkillers in particular frequently damage roses, vines and tomatoes causing distortion of the leaves which become narrow and twisted with the stems and leaf stalks showing a spiral twist. Plants injured by herbicides available to amateurs usually grow out of the symptoms and tomatoes produce edible but not necessarily palatable crops.

Conclusion

It is obvious that it is better to try and prevent diseases, disorders and pest infestations rather than to cure them. Make sure, therefore, that plants are well cared for so that they will be less susceptible to infection. Rotate ornamentals as well as vegetables and be hygienic in the garden. If a trouble can only be corrected by spraying with a chemical use the correct one at the right time and follow the instructions. If the trouble persists seek advice from the staff at Wisley*. Whenever possible send specimens showing typical symptoms, packed in a dry polythene bag. Give as much information as possible about the plant including its age, the type of soil in which it is growing and the cultural treatment it has received – the more information that is given, the easier it is to identify the cause of the trouble and recommend appropriate remedial measures.

*Address any correspondence to: The Director, R.H.S. Garden, Wisley, Woking, Surrey, GU23 6QB, enclosing a stamped, addressed envelope for the reply.

38.

Weed Control

For centuries gardeners have dreamed of conquering the weed problem but significant progress towards this goal has been made only during the last few decades. Gardeners now have two main ways of controlling weeds – physical and chemical.

PHYSICAL METHODS OF WEED CONTROL

Physical methods of weed control include hand pulling of weeds, soil cultivation or tillage and mulching. These methods have been used for centuries and many of our present-day garden practices, such as the spacing of vegetable crops, are dictated by the need for soil cultivation.

HAND PULLING AND HOEING Hand pulling is probably the oldest method of controlling weeds. In spite of many revolutionary discoveries and the introduction of new practices this method still survives. Hand pulling can be very effective especially against weeds such as groundsel (*Senecio vulgaris*) and sun spurge (*Euphorbia helioscopia*) that can be uprooted easily, but it is almost useless against perennials. It is often the only appropriate method for rock gardens containing a large number of valuable alpine plants. Hand pulling is not very practical as the sole method of weed control in a large area but is useful for dealing with the few resistant weeds which often survive a herbicide treatment.

Hoeing can be done more rapidly than hand pulling and is very effective against many annual and biennial weeds. It is less satisfactory against perennials unless hoeing is repeated at appropriate intervals to deplete the food reserves in their roots.

A knowledge of the growth habit of weeds can help greatly in the choice of a suitable method of control. Although cleavers (*Galium aparine*) is a very troublesome weed when its straggling shoots have become entwined with cultivated plants, it can be killed easily by hand breaking the thin stem at ground level. It is not necessary to remove the root system. In contrast the well developed tap root of many weeds such as dandelion (*Taraxacum officinale*) must be removed to achieve control. If the root is not dug out the weed will regenerate from adventitious buds on the lower part of the root. Not all weeds with tap roots will regenerate in this way. Hogweed (*Heracleum sphondylium*) is only capable of resprouting from basal buds within 3in(8cm) or so of the soil surface. If the rootstock is severed below this depth no regrowth will occur.

MULCHING Mulching is an old method of weed control that has been revitalised with the availability of more convenient materials. Mulching controls weeds by excluding light and preventing plants from photosynthesising. In the past many types of organic mulches have been used such as leaves, sawdust and peat. Such mulches control weeds that germinate near the surface, but they are ineffective against perennials with vigorous shoots such as couch grass (*Agropyron repens*). Much better control of perennial weeds can now be achieved with black polythene. This type of mulch will suppress all weeds for several years as long as the polythene remains intact. It is most useful in the fruit garden or around trees or shrubs. It is also very effective around cuttings that can be rooted in their final position. Clear polythene is unsuitable because weeds will germinate and grow vigorously under the mulch as light is not excluded. In situations where black polythene would be unsightly it can be covered with a thin layer of leaf mould or gravel. A mulch of black polythene results in increased plant vigour because of excellent weed control and improved moisture conditions.

Physical methods of weed control are very suitable in many situations but are less satisfactory on lawns and paths. Digging to bury trash and regular hoeing are still the simplest, cheapest and most convenient methods of weed control in cropped areas in small gardens. These physical methods of control have the advantage that they are relatively simple to use and carry little risk of causing severe plant injury. Nevertheless, herbicides (chemical weed-killers) can now be used as an acceptable alternative to hoeing and digging in many garden situations and are usually cheaper than mulching with polythene.

CHEMICAL METHODS

Herbicides have revolutionised commercial horticulture during the last 25 years. Their use has eliminated laborious tillage operations and has provided growers with cheaper, more reliable methods of suppressing weeds. Herbicides can also be used effectively in many parts of the larger garden but here a number of additional problems arise which are unlikely to concern the commercial grower. Stricter segregation of the different types of plants will usually be necessary because herbicides that would be safe on fruit crops are likely to damage vegetables, and herbaceous plants are generally more susceptible to damage than shrubs. With most herbicides, excluding paraquat (Weedol) and glyphosate (Tumbleweed), accurate application is essential; the dose of herbicide applied per unit area is critically important. The gardener will have to spend relatively more time than a commercial grower calibrating his sprayer because he deals with smaller areas. Further, serious difficulties and errors can arise if he has to measure out very small amounts of chemical. For example if simazine is being used at a dose of 3lb(1.6kg) of the 50 per cent product per acre(4046.9m^2), this is equivalent to only 1oz to 100 square yards(25g to 83.61m^2).

Nevertheless the gardener who is prepared to spend a little time learning the properties of the herbicides available and mastering the technique necessary for accurate application can attain great benefits from chemical methods of weed control. Conversely the gardener who applies herbicides carelessly and without sufficient knowledge of their mode of action is courting disaster. At best he will obtain unsatisfactory weed control; by overdosing he may cause considerable crop injury and may sterilise his ground for long periods.

APPLICATION OF HERBICIDES A few herbicides are normally applied as granules e.g. dichlobenil (Casoron G) but most are formulated so that they can be diluted with water and applied by means of a knapsack sprayer or, on small areas, with a watering can. The following definitions are important:

Directed application – where the herbicide is directed towards the ground or weeds to avoid contact with garden plants.

Overhead application – where the spray is applied over plants as opposed to directed applications.

Spot treatment – application of a herbicide to small patches, clumps or individual weeds.

Two important garden herbicides, paraquat and glyphosate, will damage all foliage that they contact. As they are inactivated by soil, spray that falls on the ground is unlikely to cause any damage to plants by being taken up by the roots. For this reason these herbicides can be used in most parts of the garden as carefully directed spot treatments. In contrast, simazine and some other herbicides, can be used on tolerant shrubs as an overhead spray.

CLASSIFICATION OF HERBICIDES Herbicides enter plants through roots,

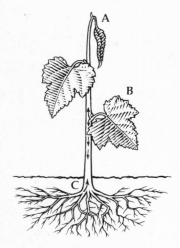

190. *Different kinds of herbicides: leaf-acting – sub-divided into contact herbicides* (A) *and translocated herbicides* (B) *– and soil-acting herbicides* (C) *which are absorbed by the roots of plants, (see text, right).*

the epidermis of stems or the surface or stomata of leaves. Although they exert their toxicity in different ways they can be divided broadly into leaf-acting and soil-acting herbicides. Leaf-acting herbicides may be further sub-divided into contact and translocated herbicides (Fig.190), according to whether they act by contact only or are absorbed and moved (translocated) within the plant. Contact herbicides, e.g. paraquat, kill only those parts of the plant that they touch. They are used mainly as directed sprays (i.e. onto the weeds) for controlling seedling or annual weeds and do not eradicate deep-rooted perennial weeds unless used repeatedly. Leaf-acting, translocated herbicides, e.g. glyphosate, move through the sap-conducting tissue (phloem) and are carried with the sap stream from the leaves to regions of active growth. Soil-acting herbicides are absorbed by roots and move through the xylem in the transpiration stream to the actively growing parts of the plant. Because leaf-acting, translocated herbicides move from the site of application to other parts of the plant, they are often effective against weeds with deep roots. Weed foliage must be present if these herbicides are to be effective and it is futile to apply glyphosate to bare soil. Full spray coverage of foliage with translocated herbicides may not be necessary. With contact herbicides full spray coverage is essential for effective control.

Although this method of classifying herbicides helps towards sensible application, many herbicides fall into more than one group and can affect plants in a number of ways. The mode of action of a number of important herbicides is shown in Table 1.

TABLE 1 – MODE OF ACTION OF HERBICIDES

Herbicide		Leaf-acting		Soil-acting
Chemical name	Proprietary product	Contact	Translocated	
Alloxydim-sodium	Clout*	-	XXX	-
Aminotriazole	Weedazol TL*	-	XXX	X
Atrazine	Numerous products	-	-	XXX
Bromacil	Hyvar X*	-	X	XXX
Chlorthiamid	Prefix*	X	-	XXX
Dalapon	Dalapon	X	XXX	X
Dichlobenil	Casoron G	X	-	XXX
Diquat	Reglone*	XXX	X	-
Diuron	Karmex*	-	-	XXX
Glyphosate	Tumbleweed Roundup*	-	XXX	-
Ioxynil	Actrilawn	XXX	X	-
Lenacil	Venzar*	X	-	XXX
MCPA	Numerous products	-	XXX	X
Mecoprop	" "	-	XXX	X
Oxadiazon	Ronstar*	XXX	X	XXX
Paraquat	Weedol Gramoxone W*	XXX	X	-
Propachlor	Covershield Ramrod*	-	X	XXX
Propyzamide	Kerb*	X	-	XXX
Simazine	Numerous products	-	-	XXX
Sodium chlorate	" "	X	X	XXX
2,4–D	" "	-	XXX	X

*available only in larger commercial packs/quantities

XXX Principal mode of action   **X Minor mode of action**

NON-SELECTIVE AND SELECTIVE HERBICIDES Herbicides may also be divided into two groups according to how they are used in the garden.
(1)   Non-selective or total herbicides are used to kill all vegetation present, e.g. on garden paths (see Table 2).
(2)   Selective herbicides are used to kill some plants without affecting others, i.e. they show selectivity between the undesirable plants (weeds) and the crop (see Table 3).

Some herbicides may be used either selectively or non selectively depending on the dose. For example, simazine at high doses can be used as a total weedkiller on paths or at low doses as a selective treatment to kill germinating weeds without harming shrubs. Selectivity is the result of a chemical reaching and disrupting a vital function (such as photosynthesis or cell division) in one plant and not in another. The selectivity of herbicides is influenced by many factors, the most important being physical and physiological.

Selectivity can be achieved physically when the growth habit of weeds and crops is sufficiently different to enable the herbicide to be applied to the weeds without touching the foliage or shoots of the crop, e.g. the use of paraquat as a directed spray on low-growing annual weeds at the base of taller growing shrubs.

Some soil-acting herbicides can be used selectively in crops because when applied to the soil they are retained close to the soil surface and are not leached downwards to any great extent. They will kill weed seedlings with shallow root systems but do not come into contact with most of the root system of the deeper rooted plants (see Fig. 191B). Selectivity due to physical factors is often dependent on conditions outside the control of the person using the herbicides. For example, heavy rain may wash a soil-acting herbicide more deeply into the soil than usual and damage may result.

Physiological selectivity is considerably more certain and reliable, as it is due mainly to fundamental differences in growth processes between weeds and cultivated plants. An effective translocated herbicide, after penetration into a plant, moves to a site of metabolic activity and then disrupts some vital function. Some of the barriers which may prevent a herbicide from reaching and disrupting some vital plant process are shown in Fig.191. For example, herbicides do not move in all plants at the same rate and this differential movement can result in selectivity (Fig.191C). A herbicide may also be non-toxic because it is absorbed by plant tissue along the path of movement and is therefore rendered unavailable for further translocation (Fig.191D). Alternatively, as a herbicide moves through the plant it may be broken down (detoxified) by plant enzymes. These may prevent a herbicide from reaching a site of toxic action by converting it into harmless compounds (Fig.191E).

In a short chapter it is not possible to describe all the herbicides that can be used in the garden. Three valuable herbicides are described here, viz., simazine, paraquat and glyphosate, representing the three important groups of herbicides – soil-acting, contact and translocated, respectively.

SIMAZINE Simazine is a soil-acting herbicide which, as already mentioned, can be used either selectively or non-selectively. At low doses simazine is generally safe to use around trees and shrubs, most woody plants being uninjured by doses which are effective against germinating weed seedlings. Simazine has a low solubility in water and moves downwards very slowly in the soil after application. Most of the simazine is retained in the top 2in(5cm) of soil even when rain falls shortly after application.

On heavy and peaty soils part of the simazine is adsorbed by the clay and organic matter and becomes non-available. Simazine is most active on light, sandy and silty soils that are lacking in clay or organic matter, giving more effective weed control at low doses than on heavy soil, but the risk of damage to ornamental plants is also greater. It is necessary, therefore, to apply lower doses of simazine to medium soils and light loams than to heavy or peaty soils. The variable results obtained from simazine on different soil types raises difficulties for the person using herbicides for the

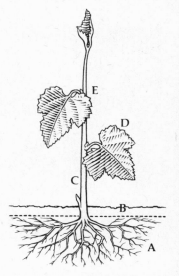

191. *Barriers which may prevent a herbicide from reaching and disrupting some vital plant process.* **A**, *slow absorption by roots;* **B**, *lack of absorption;* **C**, *slow movement in plant tissues;* **D**, *adsorption and immobilisation by plant tissues;* **E**, *breakdown of herbicides by plant enzymes.*

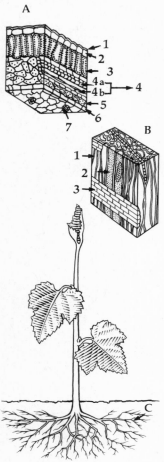

192. *Black currants have tolerance to simazine and the explanation may be that while it is absorbed by the roots of the plant and moves up the stem in the xylem it does not move freely from the conducting tissue in the leaves to the mesophyll where it would affect the process of photosynthesis (see p.335).*
A, *magnified portion of leaf:* 1, *cuticle;* 2, *upper epidermis;* 3, *palisade;* 4, *conducting tissue (*4a, *xylem, and* 4b, *phloem);* 5, *mesophyll;* 6, *lower epidermis; and* 7, *stoma.*
B, *magnified portion of stem.* 1, *wood fibre;* 2, *xylem; and* 3, *medullary ray.*
C, *simazine absorbed by roots (see text, above right).*

first time. Great care and restraint must be used in the early years until experience has been obtained on the tolerance of a range of species under local conditions.

Simazine is absorbed almost exclusively through the roots, moves up to the leaves through the xylem and, in susceptible species, acts as a powerful inhibitor of photosynthesis. As there is little or no foliage penetration simazine is unlikely to damage trees and shrubs as a result of leaf uptake. Precautions need not be taken, therefore, to avoid wetting shrub foliage when spraying. A deposit of simazine will often be retained on plant foliage but this will eventually be washed off onto the soil by rain.

Because simazine is retained in the upper soil layers the tolerance of established plants is due to the greater proportion of their root system being below the depth penetrated by the herbicide (see Fig.191A and B). This is not the complete explanation as many ornamentals are shallow rooted and large numbers of shrub and tree genera, e.g. *Cupressus* and *Cotoneaster*, can sometimes be found germinating freely in simazine-sprayed soil. Simazine is readily absorbed by plant roots and many woody species have some degree of physiological tolerance of the herbicide either because of detoxification mechanisms or limited mobility of the herbicide in the plant tissue. In black currants the herbicide does not move freely from the conducting tissue in the leaves to the mesophyll where it would affect the process of photosynthesis (Fig.192). This restriction with the partial breakdown of the herbicide in the leaves may be responsible for the good field tolerance shown by a number of woody species.

Because simazine has a low solubility and does not penetrate deeply into the soil it must be applied to clean moist soil when used selectively at low doses. When applied to dry soil it is adsorbed near the soil surface and does not reach the roots of most germinating weeds. Even when applied to moist soil most of the simazine is likely to be retained in the top 2in(5cm) and so simazine at low doses is not effective against established annual weeds or against weeds developing from perennial root systems.

PARAQUAT   Paraquat is a leaf-acting, contact herbicide which is rapidly absorbed by leaves and damages plant tissue very quickly. It kills a wide range of annual plants and also damages any green parts (leaves, buds, stems) of perennials. Paraquat is translocated only to a limited extent and does not kill perennial weeds with underground food reserves unless used repeatedly for a number of years.

Paraquat and the related herbicide diquat are very rapidly and completely inactivated as soon as the spray reaches the soil. Trees and shrubs can be planted into paraquat-sprayed ground shortly after treatment without any risk of damage. Paraquat can be used in the garden as a chemical hoe. It can be used to clean up ground infested with annual weeds before seed-sowing or planting. As a contact herbicide, only affecting those parts of the plant that it touches, it can also be used as a carefully directed spray between growing crops or plants. The use of a dribble bar is useful where small areas are being treated because it eliminates the risk of damage to plants by spray drift.

GLYPHOSATE   Glyphosate is also a leaf-acting herbicide but, in contrast to paraquat, it translocates over long distances in plants. Under suitable conditions it moves rapidly from treated foliage and stems to underground roots and rhizomes and is effective against a wide range of annual and perennial weeds, including couch grass. To be effective glyphosate must be absorbed by the weeds and it is best applied to fully emerged actively growing green foliage. Weeds that are brown or have started to die back in the autumn are unsuitable for treatment. As glyphosate is easily washed off plant foliage by rain, application should only be made in periods of settled weather, when at least six hours and preferably 24 hours without rain after spraying is expected.

Glyphosate is rapidly inactivated by microorganisms in the soil. Plants can be planted into ground that has been sprayed a few weeks beforehand provided dying foliage does not come into contact with the transplants. Like simazine it has low toxicity and presents little risk to the person applying it or to the environment.

Conclusions   Weed control in garden plants is easiest with herbicides when there are large differences between plants and weeds. Obviously when there is a close botanical relationship between weed and crop, e.g. brassica weeds in wallflowers, chemical control is very difficult, if not impossible. Only a few herbicides can be used in annuals, biennials, bedding plants and herbaceous ornamentals and these are described in the *Weed Control Handbook*, edited by J.D. Fryer and R.J. Makepeace.

Herbicides can be used effectively for weed control in vegetables but each crop requires a different programme. In general, weed control in vegetables grown on a garden scale is best achieved by physical rather than by chemical means, although glyphosate and paraquat are useful for cleaning ground before sowing or planting vegetables.

Herbicides in the garden are most valuable for use on lawns, paths and around trees and shrubs (see Tables 2, 3 and 4).

Owners of small gardens can benefit from herbicides available for lawns and paths; the techniques for using herbicides in these areas are already well established. The work load on owners of large gardens can also be reduced significantly by the use of herbicides in trees and shrubs. But gardens vary enormously in such factors as soil type, plants grown and basic design. No one herbicide is effective against all weeds or is safe in all circumstances. It is impossible, therefore, to produce a standardised plan for weed control which is suitable for all gardens. Ideally the methods used should be adapted for individual situations. This can only be achieved with experience. By beginning in a small way on part of the area, many gardeners have become familiar with the chemicals available for different weed problems and have reduced enormously the effort required to maintain their gardens in a satisfactory condition.

TABLE 2 – HERBICIDES FOR PATHS

Optimum time of application	Chemical name	lb per acre (active ingredient)	Proprietary products	Notes
Oct.-Mar.	Atrazine†	20(9kg)	Numerous products (mostly*)	Has some contact as well as residual effect. May damage trees with roots below treated area
Feb.-April	Bromacil	6.4–11(2.88–4.95kg)	Hyvar X*	May damage trees if roots below treated area
Feb.-April	Dichlobenil Chlorthiamid	15–16.5(6.75–7.425kg)	Casoron, Prefix	Warm dry weather conditions likely to reduce performance
Feb.-April	Diuron†	20(9kg)	Karmex*	May damage trees if roots below treated area
Growing season	Sodium chlorate	200–400(90–180kg)	Numerous products	Risk of damage to nearby plants
Oct.-Jan.	Simazine†	20(9kg)	" "	Effect reduced if applied in prolonged dry weather. Little risk of damage to nearby plants

†½ dose of these herbicides controls moss on hard-surfaced paths and tennis courts

*available only in larger commercial packs/quantities.

Most path weeds are controlled at doses recommended. On weed-free paths ¼ dose is generally suitable for maintenance (but ½ dose of sodium chlorate required).

Proprietary products for paths usually contain mixtures of herbicides to give a quicker kill and to reduce costs.

Proprietary products sold in small quantities for use in home gardens should be applied at rates which are strictly in accordance with the manufacturers' instructions.

TABLE 3 – HERBICIDES FOR USE AROUND ESTABLISHED SHRUBS AND TREES

Chemical name	Proprietary product	lb per acre (active ingredient)	Method of application	Notes
Simazine	Numerous products* Weedex	1.0–1.5(450–675g)	Overhead	A few woody plants are susceptible. Apply to clean moist soil to control most germinating weeds
Lenacil	Venzar*	1.6–2.4(720g–1.08kg)	"	Safer than simazine on lighter soils but control is often short term. Better than simazine on knotgrass
Propyzamide	Kerb*	0.75–1.25(340–560g)	"	Safe on a wide range of woody ornamentals. Use only in autumn or winter. Effective against couch grass and certain annuals
Dichlobenil	Casoron G4* Casoron G	6–7.6(2.70–3.420kg)	"	Safe on many ornamentals but some are susceptible. Apply late autumn or winter before bud movement. Apply when plants are dry so that granules do not lodge on them. Effective against many difficult perennial weeds
Propachlor	Ramrod* Covershield	4(1.8kg)	"	A safe herbicide which gives short term control of a number of annual weeds
Alloxydim-sodium	Clout*	1.5(675g)	"	Active only against grasses. Effective on couch but established annual meadow grass is resistant
Paraquat	Weedol Gramoxone*-†	0.5–1.0(225–450g)	Carefully directed	Use any time of year to kill annual weeds and creeping buttercup
Glyphosate	Tumbleweed Roundup*	1.5(675g)	"	Use on actively growing weeds. Effective against couch grass and many perennial weeds
Mecoprop	Numerous products	2–3(900g–1.350kg)	Carefully directed	Use low pressure. Effective against cleavers, nettles and clover. Risk of severe damage if plants wetted by spray drift
Oxadiazon	Ronstar*	2.0(900g)	Directed	Avoid wetting new young leaves and shoots. Effective against bindweeds

NOTES:
Doses of soil-acting herbicides must be varied according to soil type. These herbicides are usually unsuitable on light soils or those deficient in organic matter.

Proprietary products sold in small quantities for use in home gardens should be applied at rates which are strictly in accordance with the manufacturers' instructions.

*available only in larger commercial packs/quantities
†subject to the provisions of the Poisons Act 1972

TABLE 4 – HERBICIDES FOR LAWNS

Time of application	Weeds controlled	Chemical name	lb per acre (active ingredient)	Proprietary products	Notes
			Newly sown lawns		
Young grass at 2 leaf stage onwards	Most seedling weeds	Ioxynil	1(450g)	Actrilawn	Herbicidal effect will be supplemented by competition from grass
			Established lawns		
Growing season	Most common weeds	MCPA or 2,4-D	1.25–2.5(560g–1.13kg) 1–2(450–900g)	Several products	Clover and chickweed are not controlled
" "	Clover, trefoils, chickweed and many common weeds	Mecoprop	2–3(900g–1.35kg)	Several	Available in mixtures with 2,4-D
Early spring	*Veronica filiformis*	Ioxynil-salt + mecoprop	0.5(225g) 1.7(770g)	Iotox*	Apply before flower heads have formed
Any time; preferably early autumn	Moss	Calcined sulphate of iron	50(22.5kg)	-	Improved cultural methods also required
Growing season	"	Lawn sand	1120(504kg)	Several products	" "

*available only in larger commercial packs/quantities

Further information on the use of herbicides in ornamentals is contained in other publications: these include the *Weed Control Handbook* (edited by J.D. Fryer and R.J. Makepeace – Vol. I, Principles; Vol. II, Recommendations) issued by the British Crop Protection Council, published by Blackwell Scientific Publications, Oxford; *Weed Control in the Home Garden*, edited by A.V. Percival and published by Percival Best Publications, Milverton House, West Byfleet, Surrey; and *Lawns, Ground Cover and Weed Control*, by David Pycraft, a publication which forms part of the Royal Horticultural Society's *Encyclopaedia of Practical Gardening*, published by Mitchell Beazley, London.

Biographical Notes

John D. Bond Mr. Bond is Keeper of the Gardens, Windsor Great Park, these gardens including the superb Savill Garden which is unquestionably one of the finest gardens in Britain. He is a fine plantsman with wide interests, these embracing rhododendrons and the ornamental conifers he writes about here. Previously, he was on the staff of Hillier Nurseries and had responsibility for the early planting of the Hillier Arboretum at Ampfield, near Romsey, Hampshire. He then became Head Gardener at Leonardslee, near Horsham, Sussex before moving to Windsor. He is a member of the Royal Horticultural Society's Floral B and Rhododendron and Camellia Committees.

C. D. Brickell, B.Sc. (Hort.), V.M.H. Director of Wisley Garden since 1969 and formerly Botanist at Wisley. The special interests of this distinguished plantsman include the two subjects on which he writes here: plant nomenclature – he is Chairman of the International Commission for the Nomenclature of Cultivated Plants – and bulbous flowers. He has carried out much taxonomic work on the genera *Galanthus*, *Colchicum* and *Daphne*. Widely travelled, he has botanised extensively in the Mediterranean region and especially in Greece and Turkey. He serves on many specialist committees, including those of the International Dendrology Society, Westonbirt Arboretum, The National Council for the Conservation of Plants and Gardens and the International Society for Horticultural Science, of which he is a Council member.

Audrey Brooks, B.Sc., M.I. Biol. Miss Brooks is Plant Pathologist at Wisley with an unrivalled experience of this subject, particularly as it affects the home gardener. As a senior scientist on the Wisley staff she is also responsible for coordinating scientific and educational work at this world-famous establishment.

A.C. Bunt, N.D.H. (Hons.), M.I.Biol. Research on potting composts has been the professional concern of Mr. Bunt for over 30 years. Eleven years at the John Innes Institute have been followed by over 20 years at the Glasshouse Crops Research Institute at Rustington, Littlehampton, Sussex where he has been, and continues to be, deeply engaged in research into soilless composts and plant nutrition. He is the author of *Modern Potting Composts* (Allen and Unwin), a manual for professional horticulturists and scientists and a standard work on the subject.

John Clayton A senior member of the Wisley staff and Public Relations Officer for the Garden. The fourth generation of his family to be engaged in horticulture, he was formerly Superintendent of the Floral Department at Wisley. Prior to that he had wide nursery experience.

Geoffrey Coombs Gardens Advisor to the Royal Horticultural Society and based at Wisley, Mr. Coombs has been designing gardens for many years for members of the Society in all parts of the country. He was formerly on the staff of Jackman's of Woking, Surrey, where he was in charge of the advisory department of that well-known nursery.

Robert Corbin, F.L.S., A.H.R.H.S. A former Wisley student who had previously gained experience in various notable gardens. Mr. Corbin had a distinguished career as Horticultural Manager to the Greater London Council's Housing Department from 1947 until 1980. His territory covered 620 square miles and involved horticultural responsibilities of the most diverse kinds. He is a member of the Joint Dahlia Committee of the R.H.S. and the National Dahlia Society.

John Dyter, N.D.H. A former Wisley student and a director of Notcutt's Nurseries, Woodbridge, Suffolk, Mr. Dyter's specialities include trees and shrubs and the ground-cover plants which are of such significance in present-day gardening. He was the first recipient, in 1957, of the Bowles Memorial Scholarship (awarded by the Royal Horticultural Society) which enabled him to travel and work extensively in the United States in nurseries and botanic gardens, an experience which has proved invaluable to him in his career.

Roy Elliott, T.D., F.L.S., V.M.H. Mr. Elliott is a member of Council of the Royal Horticultural Society and a Vice-President of The Alpine Garden Society whose quarterly *Bulletin* he has edited with distinction for over 20 years. His prowess as a plantsman has brought him fame in alpine plant circles and he grows a notable collection of these plants in his Birmingham garden. He has shared this knowledge in his book, *Alpine Gardening*.

Derek Fox   Mr. Fox is a hybridiser and unusually successful grower of lilies and other bulbous plants, in his woodland garden situated at Hockley, Essex. He is a member of the R.H.S. Lily Group.

Arthur George   A rhododendron specialist with a nursery in Surrey, Mr George has won an enviable reputation as a rhododendron breeder. His introductions have included a superb range of *Rhododendron yakushimanum* hybrids, and he won the Loder Rhododendron Cup in 1974 for his achievements in connection with the genus. He is a member of the R.H.S. Rhododendron and Camellia Committee.

Michael Gibson   Mr. Gibson is a Vice-President of the Royal National Rose Society and also serves on a number of that society's specialist committees. He is the author of several books on roses, including *The Book of the Rose* (Macdonald) and *Shrub Roses for Every Garden* (Collins).

George Gilbert, N.D.H.   Mr. Gilbert is a former Wisley student who later became Fruit Officer at Wisley and has been for many years Plantations Officer at Long Ashton Research Station near Bristol, Avon, where research into fruit growing is of a quality which has won it world-wide renown. His work has, therefore, brought him into the closest possible contact with the many significant advances made in this sector of horticulture in recent times. He is a member of the R.H.S. Fruit and Vegetable Committee.

Andrew Halstead, M.Sc.   Mr. Halstead is the Entomologist at Wisley and, in consequence, is especially well-informed on the problems which confront home gardeners endeavouring to keep their plants pest-free. In the course of a year he deals with thousands of queries on insect pests and their elimination, as well as problems caused by mammals, birds, eelworms and mites.

Arthur Hellyer, M.B.E., F.L.S., V.M.H.   Doyen of horticultural journalists and authors and a notable plantsman, Mr. Hellyer was Editor of *Amateur Gardening* for many years until his retirement in 1967 and has been Gardening Correspondent of *The Financial Times* since 1959. He is the author of many works of which *The Amateur Gardener* is perhaps the best known having been in print, with revisions, since 1948. He has won an enviable reputation as an observer of the contemporary gardening scene, in all its wide diversity. He is a member of the R.H.S. Floral A Committee and a member of Council of the Royal National Rose Society.

Bill Heritage   One of the leading authorities in Britain on aquatic plants and water gardening generally, Mr. Heritage has long been engaged in this specialised area of the nursery trade in a managerial capacity. He is well known also for his writings on this subject.

Will Ingwersen, V.M.H.   As a plantsman Mr. Ingwersen is a legend in his own lifetime. He is a Vice-President of the Royal Horticultural Society and served on its Council for many years. He is Chairman of Floral A Committee and a member of many other R.H.S. committees. He has also over many years been closely associated with the floral trials carried out at Wisley. He is the President of the Alpine Garden Society and is Managing Director of the alpine plant nursery at East Grinstead, Sussex founded by his equally distinguished father. Wisley features in his life in another connection for his father was, before setting up in business on his own, in charge of the famous Wisley rock garden.

Clive Innes   A former member of Council of the Royal Horticultural Society and a member of the Wisley Advisory Committee, Mr. Innes is a specialist on cacti and succulents. He is Managing Director of Holly Gate Nurseries at Ashington, Sussex where he has an outstanding collection of these fascinating plants. His books on this subject include *The Complete Handbook of Cacti and Succulents* (Ward Lock).

F.P. Knight, F.L.S., V.M.H.   A student at both the Royal Botanic Garden, Edinburgh and the Royal Botanic Gardens, Kew, Mr. Knight was subsequently appointed Arboretum Propagator at the latter establishment. He is a leading authority on plant propagation. A plantsman of the highest calibre and an authority on trees, shrubs, rhododendrons and many other groups of ornamental garden plants, his experience has been exceptionally varied. He was Managing Director of Notcutt's Nurseries at Woodbridge, Suffolk before becoming Director of Wisley Garden in 1955, a post he held until retirement in 1969. He has been to the United States and Canada to lecture on numerous occasions and in 1968 gave the Banks Lecture in New Zealand, one of the most important annual horticultural-botanical events in that country. In the summer of 1981 he was invited to Kenya where he judged flower shows and gave talks. He is a member of the R.H.S. Floral B and Rhododendron and Camellia Committees.

Roy Lancaster, F.L.S.   A horticultural consultant and notable plantsman who has been awarded the Veitch Memorial Medal by the R.H.S., Mr. Lancaster was formerly Curator of The Hillier Arboretum at Ampfield, near Romsey, Hampshire. Widely travelled and a member of numerous plant-hunting expeditions to remote parts of the world, he has been to China on several occasions in recent years. A specialist on trees and shrubs, he is a member of the R.H.S. Floral B Committee.

John Main, N.D.H., D.H.E. Curator of Wisley Garden, Mr. Main was formerly Superintendent of the Northern Horticultural Society's garden at Harlow Car, Harrogate, Yorkshire and before that was Gardens Supervisor in charge of the famous rock garden at the Edinburgh Botanic Garden, where he had previously been a student.

P.D.A. McMillan Browse, B.Sc. Mr. McMillan Browse is a foremost authority on the science and practice of plant propagation in its broadest aspects and Head of the Department of Horticulture at Brooksby Agricultural College, Melton Mowbray, Leicestershire. He is a Past-President of The International Plant Propagators Society.

Robert Pearson A former Wisley student, he joined *The Gardeners' Chronicle* editorial staff in 1949, and was Deputy Editor of that journal from 1956 to 1964, when he was appointed Editor of Collingridge Books. When Collingridge was incorporated in the newly formed Hamlyn Publishing Group in 1967 he became the Group's Gardening Editor, was subsequently Editorial Development Manager for gardening and allied publications and is now Publisher of Collingridge Books. He has been Gardening Correspondent of the *Sunday Telegraph* since 1971. He is also a member of Council of the Royal National Rose Society.

David Pycraft A former Wisley student, Mr. Pycraft is Horticultural Officer at Wisley where he deals with a wide range of queries on many different aspects of gardening and particularly turf culture, weed control and soils.

David W. Robinson, B.Sc. (Hort.), M.S., Ph.D. Dr. Robinson studied horticulture at Reading University. He obtained a M.S. from Cornell University and a Ph.D. from Queen's University, Belfast for a thesis on "Chemical Methods of Weed Control in Fruit Crops". From 1950 to 1953 he worked as Horticultural Advisor in the Ministry of Agriculture for Northern Ireland and from 1953 to 1964 as Deputy Director of the Horticultural Centre, Loughgall, Co. Armagh. In 1964 he became Director of Kinsealy Research Centre, which forms part of the Agricultural Institute of Ireland in Dublin. He is a Past-President of the Horticultural Education Association and a Council member of the International Society for Horticultural Science.

Peter J. Salter, Ph.D., D.Sc., F.I.Biol. Dr. Salter is Head of the Plant Physiology Section and Assistant Director of the National Vegetable Research Station, Wellesbourne, Warwickshire. He has been especially closely identified with research into the irrigation of vegetable crops and new methods of growing seed crops, essentially for the commercial grower but with many applications for home gardeners, as his contribution to this book makes clear. He has written much on this subject and is a major contributor to *Know and Grow Vegetables* (Oxford University Press).

F.W. Shepherd, N.D.H. (Hons.), F.I.Biol., V.M.H. A former Wisley student, Mr. Shepherd spent ten years in local government advisory services before joining the Government advisory service (N.A.A.S.) of which he eventually became Senior Horticultural Advisor, based in Westminster. Mr. Shepherd was Director of the Rosewarne Experimental Horticulture Station at Camborne, Cornwall during its formative years, initiating work into shelter belts, the commercial production of bulbous flower crops and early vegetable and fruit production. Now retired, he is a member of the R.H.S. Narcissus and Tulip Committee and the R.H.S. Examinations Board.

J.F. Smith Mr. Smith is a member of the Joint Chrysanthemum Committee of the R.H.S. and the National Chrysanthemum Society and has been a leading amateur chrysanthemum grower and exhibitor for the past 30 years. He is also a member of the National Chrysanthemum Society Executive and an official judge. He is the author of several books on chrysanthemums.

J.D. Taylor A specialist on the genus *Iris*, Mr. Taylor is Chairman of the Joint Iris Committee of the R.H.S. and the British Iris Society. He is also a Past-President of the latter society. He grows a wide range of these beautiful plants in his garden in the Cotswolds, including all types of bearded irises from dwarf, through intermediate to tall, and a selection of species and hybrids thereof which suit his climate. Mr. Taylor is an accredited judge of the American Iris Society and has judged at the Florence iris trials, elsewhere in Europe and in Australia.

Graham Stuart Thomas, O.B.E., V.M.H., D.H.M. A plantsman of towering stature who is Gardens Consultant to the National Trust, of which he had been Gardens Advisor for many years, Mr. Thomas is internationally known for his unrivalled knowledge of the old roses, rose species and modern shrub roses and climbers. But that is only one part of his achievement for he is an acknowledged authority on hardy garden plants of many kinds, woody, herbaceous and bulbous. His books on roses, herbaceous plants, ground-cover plants and other subjects are required reading by those seeking a fuller understanding of such aspects of gardening. He is a Vice-President of the Garden History Society and a member of the R.H.S. Floral B and other committees. He also holds the Royal National Rose Society's highest award, the Dean Hole Medal, for his services to the rose, and is a Vice-President of that society.

Arthur Turner, A.H.R.H.S. Mr. Turner received a training in horticulture which it would be virtually impossible to receive today, working his way up the ladder in notable large private gardens – including Exbury, the famous rhododendron garden on the Beaulieu River in Hampshire – to become Head Gardener at Borde Hill, near Haywards Heath, Sussex, an equally famous woodland garden. He joined the staff at Wisley in 1957 to take charge of Battleston Hill with its renowned collection of rhododendrons and other woodland plants, and became Glasshouse Superintendent in 1964, a position he held until his retirement in 1980. As a horticulturist he is an all-rounder in the fullest sense of that term.

Fred Whitsey, A horticultural journalist who has been awarded the Veitch Memorial Medal by the R.H.S., Mr. Whitsey is renowned for his acute observations and gift for exposition. He began his journalistic career on the *Gardeners' Chronicle* in 1947. Two years later he moved to *Popular Gardening*, of which magazine he has been the distinguished Editor since 1967. When the *Sunday Telegraph* was founded in 1961 he was appointed its Gardening Correspondent, a position he held until he took up the same position on *The Daily Telegraph* in 1971, and for which he continues to write weekly in his inimitable way. A compulsive gardener with a deep love of plants, Mr. Whitsey has for some years been researching into the possibilities of making greater use of plants in containers outdoors, based on repeated visits to Mediterranean gardens, on which he has won a reputation as a specialist.

George Wells Mr. Wells has had a very long career in horticulture dating back to the 1920s. He trained in numerous large establishments and was subsequently Head Gardener at Swyncombe House, near Henley-on-Thames, Oxfordshire. He then started his own nursery at Alresford, Hampshire which he ran for 14 years before selling the land and joining the Wisley staff in 1961. He was Foreman of the Glasshouse Department until he retired in 1974. During that time he built up the fine collections of fuchsias so well known to visitors to the Garden.

E.J. Winter, M.C., M.Sc. As a soil scientist Mr. Winter has had vast experience, for after some years working on tea research in Assam he joined the National Vegetable Research Station, Wellesbourne, Warwickshire at its inception in 1951 and remained there until his retirement in 1973. He was in charge of the irrigation department at the N.V.R.S. where his researches into the commercial production of food crops had many applications for home gardeners. He was also latterly Scientific Liaison Officer at Wellesbourne. He is a Past-President of the Horticultural Education Association.

Dennis Woodland A former Wisley student and outstanding plantsman, Mr Woodland has for many years been Horticultural Consultant to Hillier Nurseries of Ampfield, near Romsey, Hampshire, giving garden owners in this country and abroad advice on every aspect of plant choice and plant care. He has accompanied numerous botanising tours to Europe and the Himalayan region.

Index

Colour Illustration Acknowledgements

The Editor is grateful to the following photographers who have provided colour transparencies reproduced in this book: Michael Warren (4,5,6,11,17,18,20,21 and 32); The Harry Smith Horticultural Photographic Collection (8,9,12,13,16,22,25 and 30); Pat Brindley (2,10,19,24,27,28 and 29); Valerie Finnis (1,7,14,23 and 26); Roy Lancaster (15); C. D. Brickell (31); and Roy Pembrooke (3).